Frederick Martin

Handbook of Contemporary Biography

Salzwasser

Frederick Martin

Handbook of Contemporary Biography

1. Auflage | ISBN: 978-3-84605-102-3

Erscheinungsort: Frankfurt, Deutschland

Erscheinungsjahr: 2020

Salzwasser Verlag GmbH

Reprint of the original, first published in 1870.

HANDBOOK

OF

CONTEMPORARY BIOGRAPHY.

HANDBOOK

OF

CONTEMPORARY BIOGRAPHY.

BY

FREDERICK MARTIN,

AUTHOR OF "THE STATESMAN'S YEAR-BOOK," ETC.

London:

MACMILLAN AND CO,

1870.

PREFACE.

THIS volume is an attempt to produce a book of reference, furnishing, in a condensed form, some biographical particulars of notable living men. The leading idea has been to give only facts, and those in the briefest form, and to exclude opinions. While the book went through the press, many changes occurred, which must to some extent account for errors and imperfections, as well in inserting the names of dead as omitting those of living persons. A number of omissions have been rectified in the Appendix.

F: M.

HANDBOOK

OF

CONTEMPORARY BIOGRAPHY.

AASEN, Ivar Andreas, Norwegian philologist, b. at Oersten, Aug. 5, 1813 ; elected member of the Norw. Academy of Sciences, 1850. Author of 'Det norske Folkesprog Grammatik,' Christiania, 1848 ; 'Ordbog over norske Folkesprog,' ib. 1850 ; 'Norske Ordsprog,' ib. 1856 ; and other philological works.

ABADIE, Paul, French architect, b. at Bordeaux, July 22, 1783 ; appointed diocesan architect of the sees of Angoulême and Perigueux. 1853. Designed the Palais de Justice and mansion of the prefect at Angoulême, with other edifices in the Gothic style.

ABBOTT, Jacob, American author, b. at Hallowel, Maine, in 1803 ; took the degree of doctor of theology at the college of Andover in 1827. Author of 'The Young Christian,' Boston, 1825 ; 'The Corner Stone,' ib. 1826 ; and various other volumes of 'The Young Christian Series.'

ABBOTT, John, American author, brother of the preceding, b. at Hallowel, Maine, in 1806 ; appointed minister of the Independent Congregationalist body, 1827. Author of 'Kings and Queens, or Life in a Palace,' New York, 1839 ; 'The Mother at Home,' ib. 1845 ; and 'Life of Napoleon,' 2 vols. ib. 1855.

ABD-EL-KADER, Sidi-el-Hadji-Ouled-Mahiddin, Arab chieftain, b. near Mascara, Algeria, 1807 ; besieged Oran, 1832 ; acknowledged Emir of Mascara by the French government, 1834 ; ordered a massacre of Europeans, 1839 ; driven into the territory of the Sultan of Morocco ; taken captive by the French troops, 1843 ; imprisoned in the castle of Pau, 1844–48 ; and in the castle of Amboise, 1848–52 ; released by order of Napoleon III. and retired to Damascus, Dec. 2, 1852.

ABDUL-AZIZ, Sultan of Turkey, thirty-second, in male descent, of the house of Othman ; b. at Constantinople, Feb. 9, 1830, the second son of Sultan Mahmoud II. ; succeeded to the throne at the death of his brother, Sultan Abdul-Medjid, June 25, 1861.

ABOUT, Edmond François, French author, b. at Dieuze, Meurthe, Feb. 14, 1828 ; educated at the Lycée Charlemagne, Paris, and at the École française, Athens, 1843–53. Author of 'La Grèce contemporaine,' Paris, 1855 ; 'Les Mariages de Paris,' ib. 1856 ; 'Germaine,' ib. 1857 ; 'Trente et Quarante, ib. 1858 ; 'La Question Romaine,' Brussels, 1860 ; and numerous comedies, dramas, and political pamphlets.

ABRAHAMS, Nicholas Christian, Danish archæologist, b. at Copenhagen, Sept. 6, 1798 ; appointed professor at the University of Copenhagen, 1829. Author of 'De Roberti Waci carmine quod inscribitur Brutus,' Copenhagen, 1828 ; and 'Balthasari Castilionei aulici liber tertius secundum veterem versionem gallicam,' ib. 1848.

ACHARD, Amedée, French author, b. at Marseilles, Apr. 9, 1814 ; appointed secretary of the prefect of Herault, 1835 ; secretary of the Duke de Montpensier, son of Louis Philippe, 1846. Author of 'Lettres Parisiennes,' Paris, 1845 ; 'La Chasse Royale,' 7 vols. ib. 1849–50 ; and numerous dramatic pieces and pamphlets.

ACHENBACH, Andreas, German painter, b. at Cassel, Sept. 29, 1815 ; studied at Düsseldorf under Schadow, 1834–39. Painted 'Coast of Scheveningen, Holland,' 1861 ; 'Shore of Ostend at high water,' 1864 ; and numerous other landscapes and architectural views.

ACHENBACH, Oswald, German painter, brother of the preceding, b. at Düsseldorf, Feb. 2, 1827. Painted 'Pilgrims going to Rome,' 1858 ; 'The Mole at Naples,' 1859 ; 'Monument to Cecilia Metella,' 1864 ; and many other, chiefly Italian, views.

ACHTERMANN, Wilhelm, German sculptor, b. at Münster, Aug. 15, 1799; studied at Berlin under Rauch, 1831–33. Sculptor of the 'Descent from the Cross' in the cathedral of Münster.

ACLAND, Henry Wentworth, English physician and sanitary reformer, b. 1815; studied at Christ Church, Oxford, and took the degree of M.D. 1848; appointed physician to the Radcliffe Infirmary, 1849. Author of several books and pamphlets on sanitary matters.

ADALBERT, Prince of Prussia, German admiral and author, b. at Berlin, Oct. 29, 1811; entered the Prussian army in 1827, but quitted it in 1832, setting out on a course of travels through Europe, Asia, and America; appointed high admiral of the North German navy, 1867. Author of 'Aus meinem Reisetagebuche,' Berlin, 1842; and 'Denkschrift über die Bildung einer deutschen Flotte,' ib. 1848.

ADAM, Jean Victor, French painter, b. at Paris, Feb. 29, 1801; educated at the Paris École des Beaux-arts, 1817–19. Painted 'Henry IV. after the battle of Coutras,' 1837; 'Entry of the French into Mayence,' 1838; and numerous battle-pieces exhibited at the Museum of Versailles.

ADAMS, Charles Francis, American statesman, b. at Boston, Mass., in 1807, the son of John Quincy Adams, President of the United States; studied jurisprudence, and became barrister at Boston in 1828; elected member of the Senate of Massachusetts, 1844; elected member of the Congress of the United States, 1858; appointed American envoy to Great Britain, March, 1861, resigned Feb. 1868. Author of 'Life and Works of John Adams,' Boston, 1846; and 'Letters of Mrs. Adams,' ib. 1848.

ADAMS, John Couch, English astronomer, b. at Bodmin, Cornwall, in 1817; studied at St. John's College, Cambridge, and passed Senior Wrangler, 1843; discovered, simultaneously with M. Le Verrier, the planet Neptune, 1845; appointed Lowndean professor of astronomy at the University of Cambridge, 1858. Author of 'The observed irregularities in the motion of Uranus,' Cambridge, 1847.

ADDERLEY, Rt. Hon. Charles Bowyer, English statesman, b. at Norton, Staffordshire, in 1814; studied at Christ Church, Oxford, and graduated B.A. 1838; elected M.P. for the northern division of Staffordshire, 1841; president of the Board of Health, and vice-president of the Committee of Council of Education, 1858–59. Author of 'Transportation,' and several other pamphlets.

ADELSWARD, Renauld Oscar, French author, b. at Longwy, Moselle, Dec. 18, 1811; entered the French army, 1830; retired with the rank of captain, 1844; elected deputy to the National Assembly for the department of Meurthe, 1848. Author of 'La Liberté de Conscience en Suède,' Paris, 1861; and other works.

ADHE'MAR, Alphonso Joseph, French mathematician, b. at Paris, Feb. 15, 1797. Author o 'Cours de Mathématique à l'usage de l'ingénieur civil,' 18 vols. Paris, 1832–56; and numerous elementary treatises on mathematics and civil engineering.

ADOLF, Ex-Duke of Nassau, b. July 24, 1817, the son of Duke William of Nassau; succeeded to the throne at the death of his father, Aug. 20, 1839; deprived of his crown by the Prussian government, 1866.

ADOLPHUS, Prince of Schaumburg-Lippe, born Aug. 1, 1817. the son of Prince George and of Princess Ida of Waldeck; succeeded to the throne at the death of his father, Nov. 21, 1860; married, Oct 25, 1844, to Hermina, Princess of Schaumburg-Lippe, born Sept. 29, 1827, daughter of the late Prince George of Waldeck.

ADRIAN, Johann Valentin, German author, b. at Aschaffenburg, Sept. 17, 1793; appointed professor of modern literature at the University of Giessen, 1824. Author of 'Bilder aus England,' 2 vols. Frankfort, 1827–28; 'Die Priesterinnen der Griechen,' ib. 1838; and 'Mittheilungen zür Geschichte,' ib. 1846. Editor of a German translation of the works of Lord Byron, 12 vols. Frankfort, 1837.

AGASSIZ, Louis, American naturalist, b. at Orbe, canton de Vaud, Switzerland, May 28, 1807; studied medicine at Zürich, Heidelberg, and Munich; professor of natural history at Neufchatel, Switzerland, 1836–45; professor of zoology at Charleston, South Carolina, U.S. 1846–48; appointed professor of natural history at New Cambridge, Boston, U.S. 1848. Author of 'Etudes sur les Glaciers,' Neufchatel, 1840; 'Zoological Bibliography,' 4 vols. London, 1848–50; 'Grundzüge der Zoology,' Stuttgart, 1854; and numerous other works on natural history.

AINMULLER, Maximilian Emmanuel, German artist, b. at Munich, 1807, painter on porcelain. Exhibited at Munich, 1848, 'Notre Dame' of Munich; 'The Church of St Mark at Venice;' 'The Chamber of Prelates at Strasbourg;' and drawings of the interior of the chapel at Windsor; and Westminster Abbey, 1849.

AINSWORTH, William Francis, English traveller and physician, b. at Exeter, November 9, 1807; studied medicine, and took the degree of M.D. 1827. Author of 'Researches in Assyria, Babylonia, and Chaldea,' 1838; 'Travels and Researches in Asia Minor, Mesopotamia, and Armenia.' 1842; 'Travels in the Track of the Ten Thousand Greeks,' 1844; and other books of travel.

AINSWORTH, William Harrison, English novelist and journalist, b. at Manchester, Feb. 4, 1805. Author of 'Sir John Chiverton,' London, 1825; 'Rookwood,' ib. 1834: 'The Miser's Daughter,' 1843; 'Old St. Paul's,' 1843; 'Windsor Castle,' 1843; 'The Flitch of Bacon,' 1854; 'Cardinal Pole,' 1863; and numerous other works of fiction, chiefly historical romances.

AIRD, Thomas, English poet, b. at Bowden, Roxburghshire, August 28, 1802: studied at the University of Edinburgh; editor of the 'Edinburgh Weekly Journal' for one year; editor of the 'Dumfries Herald' since 1835. Author of 'Religious Characteristics,' 1827; 'The Old Bachelor,' 1845; 'Poetical Works,' 1842. Edited 'Dr. Moir's Poems,' 1852; and other works.

AIREY, Sir Richard, English general, b. at Newcastle-on-Tyne, 1803; entered the army, 1821: served in the Ionian Islands, 1827; in Canada, 1830; deputy adjutant-general, 1838; military secretary to the commander-in-chief at the Horse Guards, 1852; quartermaster-general of the British army in the Crimea, 1854–55; created K.C.B. and major-general, 1855; colonel of the 17th regiment, 1860; lieut.-general, 1862; quartermaster general at the Horse Guards since 1857.

AIRY, George Biddell, English astronomer, b. at Alnwick, Northumberland, July 27, 1801; studied at Trinity College, Cambridge, 1819; graduated B.A. 1823; M.A. 1824; elected Lucasian professor, 1824; elected to the Plumian professorship, and entrusted with the management of Cambridge Observatory, 1828; Astronomer Royal, 1835. Author of 'Gravitation' for the 'Penny Cyclopædia,' 1837; 'Ipswich Lectures on Astronomy;' 'Treatise on the Errors of Observation,' 1861; 'The Figure of the Earth;' and other works on Astronomy.

AIVAZOOSKI, Gabriel, Armenian author, b. at Theodosia, Crimea, May 22, 1821; entered the convent of the Mekhitarists, near Vienna, 1826; appointed professor of European and Oriental languages, 1843; in the Armenian College of Samuel Moorat near Paris, 1848. Author of 'History of the Ottoman Empire;' and other works in the Armenian language.

AIVAZOOSKI, Ivan, Russian painter, brother of the preceding, b. at Theodosia, Crimea, July, 1817; admitted by a special order of the Czar Nicholas to the Imperial Academy of Fine Arts, St. Petersburg. 1833. Author of a great number of historical paintings, representing battle-fields and naval engagements.

AKERMAN, John Yonge, English writer, b. in Wiltshire, 1805. Author of 'A Descriptive Catalogue of Rare and Unedited Roman Coins, to the fall of the Empire of the East;' 'A Numismatical Manual;' and other works.

AKRELL, Charles Frederick, Swedish topographer, b. Jan. 13, 1779; instructor of fortifications in the Military School of Carlsberg, 1807 to 1827; chief of the Topographic Corps and staff-major, 1831. Published 'Chart of Sweden,' commenced 1840; 'Chart of Stockholm and its Environs,' 1805; and other topographical works.

AKROYD, Edward, English politician, b. 1810, son of the late Mr. Jonathan Akroyd; deputy lieutenant for the West Riding of Yorkshire; M.P. for Huddersfield, 1857–59; returned for Halifax, 1865.

ALARD, Jean Delphin, French violinist, b. at Bayonne, March 8, 1815; admitted to the Conservatoire, Paris, Feb. 5, 1827. Author of 'L'École du Violon;' 'Symphonie pour deux Violons,' 1855; and other works.

ALARY, Jules Abraham Eugene, called **ALARI,** French musical composer; b. at Mantua, Italy, 1814; studied at the Conservatoire of Milan, 1827 to 1831. Composed 'Rosmonda,' Florence, 1840; 'The Redemption,' Paris, 1850; 'The Human Voice,' 1861; and other works.

ALANZET, François Isidore, French political economist, b. at Alexandria, Piedmont, April 10, 1807; studied law, and called to the bar, 1840. Author of 'Essai sur les Peines et le Système Pénitentiaire.' 1842; 'Traité Général des Assurances,' 1843–44; 'De la Qualité de Français et de la Naturalisation,' 1851; and other works.

ALBACH, Joseph Stanislas, Hungarian writer, b. at Presburg, Feb. 2, 1795; studied theology at the Seminary of Pesth. Author of 'Geography of Hungary,' Pesth, 1834; 'General, Physical, Mathematical, and Political Geography,' ib. 1834.

HANDBOOK

OF

CONTEMPORARY BIOGRAPHY.

HANDBOOK

OF

CONTEMPORARY BIOGRAPHY.

BY

FREDERICK MARTIN,

AUTHOR OF "THE STATESMAN'S YEAR-BOOK," ETC.

London:

MACMILLAN AND CO.

1870.

brigade, Aug. 12, 1857; commander of the Légion d'honneur, March 14, 1860.   Author of 'Éloge du Maréchal Moncey,' 1842; 'La Colonne Napoléon et le Camp de Boulogne,' 1839; 'Soldat,' 1854; and other works.

AMELIE, Marie Fredericka Augusta, Duchess of Saxe, dramatic authoress, b. Aug. 10, 1794; pseudonym 'Amalie Heiter.'   Author of 'Der Krönung's Tag,' 1829; 'Originalbeiträge zur deutschen Schaubühne,' 1837–42; and other works.

AMET, Josephine Junot d'Abrantes, French authoress, b. Jan. 5, 1802; married to M. James Amet, 1841.   Author of 'Histoires morales et édifiantes,' 1837; 'Une Vie de jeune Fille,' 1837; 'La Duchess de Valombray,' 1838; 'Les Deux Sœurs,' 1840; 'Étienne Saulnier,' 1850.

AMMON, Frederick Wilhelm Philip von, German Protestant theologian, b. at Erlangen, Feb. 7, 1791; studied at Göttingen, Jena, and the university of his native town; minister at Buttenheim and at Merzbach; archdeacon at Erlangen, 1820; professor of theology at Erlangen.   Author of 'Letters of Rodolph Ida, on the Dogmas which distinguish the Protestant and Catholic Churches,' Dresden, 1837; and other works.

AMMON, Frederick Augustus von, German physician, brother of the preceding, b. at Göttingen, Sept. 10, 1799; graduated M.D. 1822; professor and director of the Academy of Surgery and Medicine, Dresden, 1829; physician to the King of Saxony, 1837; councillor of medicine, 1844.   Author of 'Ueber den Krankhaften Schlaf,' Göttingen, 1830; 'Die ersten Mutterpflichten und die erste Kindespflege,' Leipsic, 1857; and other medical works.

AMSBERG, Augustus Christian Theodore von, German statesman, b. at Rostock, July 17, 1789; secretary to the Grand Duke of Brunswick; director of the Brunswick College of Finances, 1832; director of the Administration of Railways and Posts of Brunswick, 1850.

ANASTASI, Augustus, French lithographic artist, b. at Paris, 1819; studied painting under MM. Delaroche and Corot, and exhibited in 1843.   Executed 'Les Bords de la Touque,' 1850; 'La Saison des Foins,' 1852; 'Les Bords de la Sprée,' 1855; 'Retour du Troupeau,' 1861; 'Aqueducs de Claude,' 1864.

ANCEL, Daniel Edouard Jules, French politician, b. at Havre, Oct. 16, 1812; president of the Chamber of Commerce of Havre; mayor of the town, and member of the General Council; member of the Legislative Assembly for Havre and of the Corps Législatif since 1852.

ANCELET, Gabriel Auguste, French architect, b. at Paris, Nov. 21, 1829; studied under MM. Lequeux and Baltard, 1845, and in the School of Fine Arts.   Exhibited 'Un Hospice dans les Alpes,' 1851; 'Restauration de la Voie Appienne,' Oct. 1856.   Appointed architect of the château of Pau, 1858.

ANCELOT, Marguerite Louise Virginie Chardon, French authoress, b. at Dijon, Côte-d'Or, Mar. 17, 1792; married M. Ancelot, 1818, who died 1854.   Author of 'Cardinal et Page,' 1832; 'Emprunts aux Salons de Paris,' 1835; 'Mariage raisonnable,' 1835; 'Le Château de ma Nièce,' 1837; 'Le Baron de Fresmoutiers,' 1861; 'Antoine Vernon, ou les jeunes Filles pauvres,' 1863; and many other novels.

ANCKARSWŒRD, Charles Henry, Count of, Swedish politician, b. at Sveaborg, 1782; entered the army, 1799; aide-de-camp to Count Armfelt in the war with Norway, 1808; colonel, and staff-major to Bernadotte, royal prince of Sweden, 1813; entered the Diet, 1817, and became leader of the opposition.   Author of 'Political Principles,' 1833.

ANDELARRE, Jules de Jaquot, Marquis of, French magistrate and politician, b. at Dijon, Côte d'Or, Oct. 25, 1803; mayor of Andelarre, 1831; member of the General Council of the Haute-Saône, 1837; deputy to the Corps Législatif from 1852 to 1863. Author of 'Forme et Réforme du Budget de l'État,' 1859; and other works.

ANDERS, Gottfried Engelbert, French writer, b. near Coblentz, 1795; employed in the Royal Bibliothèque, Paris, in the department of music, since 1833.   Author of 'Nicolo Paganini, sa Vie, sa Personne, et quelques Mots sur son Secret,' 1831; 'Détails biographiques sur Beethoven,' 1839; contributor to several musical magazines.

ANDERSEN, Hans Christian, Danish poet and novelist, b. at Odense, April 2, 1805.   Author of 'The Improvisatore,' 1834; 'O. T.' 1835; 'Only a Fiddler,' 1837; 'Tales from Jutland,' 1859; 'The Sandhills of Jutland,' 1860; 'Tales for Children,' 1861; 'The Wild Swans, a Fairy Tale,' 1863; 'The Ice Maiden,' 1863; 'From Spain,' 1866; and other works.

ANDERSON, Henry, American mathematician, b. 1798; professor of mathematics and astronomy at Columbia College, New York, 1825; resigned, 1843; travelled through Asia Minor, and, with Lieut. Lynch, explored the Dead Sea and the Jordan. Author of 'Geological Survey of part of the Holy Land,' 1848; and other works.

ANDERSON, Rev. James Stuart Murray, English divine, b. 1798: educated at Balliol College, Oxford; graduated B.A. 1820; chaplain in ordinary to her Majesty, 1836; preacher of Lincoln's Inn from 1844 to 1858; rector of Tormarton, near Chippenham, 1851; Bristish chaplain at Bonn. Author of 'History of the Church of England in the Colonies and Foreign Dependencies of the British Empire,' 1851.

ANDERSON, Robert, American general, b. in Kentucky, 1806; graduated at West Point, 1825; inspector of the Illinois volunteers during the 'Black Hawk war;' assistant instructor and inspector of West Point Military Academy from 1835 to 1857; aide-de-camp to General Scott in the Indian war and Florida; commander of Fort Sumter and Charleston at the breaking out of the civil war, 1860; brigadier-general, 1861.

ANDERSON, William, Scottish theologian, b. at Kilsyth, Stirling, 1800; studied at the University of Glasgow; minister of John Street Relief Church in that city since 1822. Published 'The Mass, Penance, Regeneration;' and other theological works.

ARDIGNE' DE LA CHASSE, Charles, Marquis of, French politician, b. at Paris, Jan. 6, 1791; member of the General Council of Ille-et-Vilaine; representative for the department d'Ille-et-Vilaine after the revolution of February, 1848.

ANDLAW, Heinrich Bernard von, German politician, b. 1802; entered the army of the Grand Duchy of Baden, 1821; resigned his commission, 1825; councillor of Friburg; deputy in the Baden Chamber, 1833. Published 'Der Aufruhr und Umsturz in Baden,' Friburg, 1850.

ANDOUILLE', Edmond, French administrator, b. at Mézières, 1804; studied law at Paris, and entered the Ministry of Finance; appointed chief deputy-governor of the Bank of France, 1858.

ANDRÆ, Charles Christopher George, Danish politician, b. Oct. 14, 1812, at Hjertebjerg; entered the army as second lieutenant, 1828; lieutenant-colonel, 1851; member of the Academy of Sciences, Copenhagen, 1853; member of the First Chamber of Parliament, 1850–51; member of the Second Chamber, 1853; minister of finance, Dec. 12, 1854; president of the Council of Ministers, 1856–58.

ANDRAL, Gabriel, French physician and author, b. at Paris, Nov. 6, 1797; studied at the College of Louis le Grand, and obtained the degree of M.D. 1821; professor of hygiène at the Academy of Medicine, Paris, 1827; professor of internal pathology, 1830, and of general pathology, 1839; member of the Academy of Sciences, 1842. Author of 'Clinique Médicale,' 1824; 'Essai d'Hématologie pathologique,' 1843; and many other works.

ANDRASY, Julius, Count of, Hungarian statesman, b. in 1825; took an active part in the Hungarian Revolution, 1848–49; ambassador of the 'Republic of Hungary' to the Sultan of Turkey, 1849; exiled 1849–60. Appointed minister of war and president of the Hungarian council of ministers by royal rescript, Feb. 24, 1867.

ANDRE', Jean François Gustave, French politician, b. Oct. 17, 1805; notary at Aigre, Charente, 1830; member of the General Council for the canton, 1841; member of the Corps Législatif, 1852–57.

ANDRE', Jules, French painter, b. at Paris, 1804; studied under M. Watelet, 1827; first exhibited, 1831. Executed and exhibited 'Entrée de Forêt, les Bords de l'Ource dans la Côte-d'Or,' 1835; 'Les Bords de la Vienne,' 1855; 'Un Chemin près de Cambes, Gironde,' 1861; 'Vue prise dans la Vallée de Streture, Vosges,' 1863; 'Marais près de Saint-Yrieux, Haute-Vienne,' 1864; and many others.

ANDRE', l'Abbe' Jean François, French priest and writer, b. at Menerbes, 1810; curé of Vancluse. Author of 'Le Cœur du Christ et le Cœur de l'Homme,' 1839; 'Vie des Saints de l'Église d'Avignon,' 1836; 'Histoire de Saint Roch,' 1854; 'Précis de l'Histoire de la Maison de Rusti chelli-Valori,' 1855; and other works.

ANDRE', l'Abbe' Michel, French priest and writer, b. at Avallon, Yonne, Apr. 29, 1803; studied in his native town, and was ordained vicar-general of Quimper, 1829. Author of 'Cours alphabétique et méthodique de Droit Canon, mis en rapport avec le Droit Civil ecclésiastique, ancien et moderne,' 2 vols. 1844–45; third edit. 1859; and other theological works.

ANDRE', Louis Jules, French architect, b. at Paris, 1819; studied under Huyot and M. H. Lebas; appointed inspector of the Louvre and inspector to the Imperial Bibliothèque, 1852; diocesan architect of the department of Corse, 1855.

ANDREA, Je'rome, Italian statesman, b. at Naples, April 12, 1802 ; archbishop *in partibus*, abbé of Subiaco, and prefect of the Congregation of the Index ; commissioner extraordinary of the Pontifical government in the revolution of 1849 ; promoted cardinal, March 15, 1852..

ANDRIES, l'Abbe' Joseph Oliver, Belgian ecclesiastic, b. at Ruddervoorde, Flanders, 1796 ; curé of Middelburg till the Revolution of 1830 ; envoy to the National Congress for the district of Eccloo ; returned, 1835, for the district of Gand ; canon of the cathedral of Bruges, 1841. Published 'Recherches sur les Voies d'Écoulement des Eaux des Flandres.'

ANDRIEU, Mathieu Maurice, French politician, b. June 22, 1813 ; mayor of Maringues, and member of the General Council for the same canton ; member of the Corps Législatif since 1863.

ANDRIEUX, E'mile, French physician, b. at Paris, March 10, 1797 ; studied medicine, and obtained the degree of M.D. 1820 ; physician to the Hospice des Quinze-Vingts, 1840. Author of 'Mémoire sur l'Application méthodique du Galvanisme au Traitement des Maladies,' 1824 ; 'Mémoire sur l'Ophthalmo-plantôme,' 1840.

ANETHAN, Jules Joseph, Baron, Belgian magistrate and politician, b. 1803 ; procureur to the king, 1831 ; advocate-general at the Court of Appeal of Brussels, 1836 ; entered the cabinet as minister of justice, 1843, and retained his portfolio until 1847 ; representative of Louvain since 1844.

ANGELIS, Pietro de, Italian writer, b. at Naples, 1798 ; secretary to King Murat ; travelled over America, and fixed his residence at Buenos Ayres. Published 'Coleccion de Obras y Documentos relativos a la Historia antiqua de las Provincias del Rio de la Plata,' Buenos Ayres, 1836.

ANGLADE, Hippolyte Cle'ment, French politician, b. at Nes, Ariége, Dec. 20, 1800 ; member of the Chamber of Deputies, 1833–34 ; deputy to the Constituent Assembly, 1848 ; member of the Legislative Assembly ; after the coup d'état of Dec. 1851, retired from political life.

ANGLEMONT, Edouard Hubert Scipion d', French writer, b. at Pont-Audemer, Eure, Dec. 28, 1798. Author of 'Berthe et Robert,' 1825 ; 'Tancrède,' 1827 ; 'Légendes françaises,' 1829 ; 'Le Duc d'Enghien,' 1832 ; 'Pèlerinages,' 1835 ; 'Amours de France,' 1841 ; and other novels.

ANGLESEY, Henry Paget, Marquis of, English politician, b. 1797 ; colonel of a cavalry regiment, 1838 ; M.P. for Anglesey, 1830–32, when he entered the House of Lords ; lord chamberlain to the Queen, 1839–41 ; privy councillor, and lord-lieutenant of the county of Anglesey, 1854.

ANICET BOURGEOIS, Auguste, French dramatic author, b. at Paris, Dec. 25, 1806. Author of 'Gustave, ou le Napolitain,' 1825 ; 'La Vénitienne,' 1834 ; 'Djengis-Khan, ou la Conquête de la Chine,' 1837 ; 'Stella,' 1843 ; 'Les Maréchaux de l'Empire,' 1856 ; with M. J. Barbier, 'La Sorcière, ou les États de Blois,' 1863.

ANNE, The'odore, French writer, b. April 7, 1797 ; entered the army, 1814 ; retired after the Revolution of July, 1830. Author of 'Éloge historique du Duc de Berri,' 1820 ; 'Le Guerillero,' 1842 ; 'Marie Stuart,' 1844 ; 'L'Enfant du Régiment,' 1854 ; 'La Chambre Rouge,' 1854 ; 'Le Comte de Chambord à Wiesbaden,' 1850 ; 'L'Homme au Masque d'acier,' 1850 ; 'La Folle de Savenay,' 1856 ; 'La Reine de Paris,' 1857–58.

ANNESLEY, Hon. Hugh, English politician, b. 1830 ; educated at Eton ; lieut.-colonel in the Scots Fusilier Guards ; served in the Kaffir war, 1852 ; and the Crimea, 1854–55 ; M.P. for the county of Cavan since 1857.

ANOT DE MAIZIE'RES, Cyprien, French writer, b. at St.-Germain, Mont Ardennes, Apr. 27, 1794 ; studied at Rheims ; entered the University, and became professor of grammar and history ; inspector of the Academy of the Seine-et-Oise, 1851. Author of 'Discours sur la Nécessité du maintien de la Charte constitutionelle," 1819 ; 'Cours gradué de Narrations françaises,' 1848 ; 'Cromwell,' 1861.

ANSDELL, Richard, English painter of animals. b. at Liverpool, Lancashire, 1818 ; exhibited at the Royal Academy since 1848 ; chosen A.R.A. 1860. Painted 'The Hunted Slave,' 1863 ; and many other works of art.

ANSON, Hon. Augustus Henry Archibald, English politician, b. 1833 ; served in the army during the Crimean war, 1854–55 ; in India, 1857–59 ; in China, 1859–60 ; M.P. for Lichfield since 1859.

ANSPACH, Philippe Le'on, French magistrate, b. 1805, of Jewish parents at Metz ; advocate in Paris, 1830 ; procureur-général, 1851 ; president of the Cour Impériale, and the first Israelite admitted to the bench in France, 1853. Author of 'De la Procédure devant les Cours d'Assises : Doctrine et Jurisprudence en cette matière,' 1856.

ANSTED, David Thomas, English geologist, b. in London, 1814; educated at a private school, London, and Jesus College, Cambridge, where he graduated M.A.; professor of geology at King's College, London, 1840; lecturer on geology at the East India Military Seminary, Addiscombe, 1844, and professor of geology at the College of Civil Engineers, Putney, 1845; vice-secretary of the Geological Society, 1844. Author of 'Geology: introductory, descriptive, and practical,' 1844; 'Scenery, Science, and Art,' 1854; 'Great Stone Book of Nature,' 1863; and many other scientific works.

ANSTEY, Thomas Chisholm, English barrister and writer, b. in London, 1816; educated at University College, London; called to the bar of the Middle Temple, 1839; professor of law and jurisprudence at Bath; M.P. for the Irish borough of Youghal, 1847–52; attorney-general at Hong-Kong, 1854–58. Author of 'British Catholics and the New Parliament,' 1841; 'Guide to the History of the Laws and Constitution of England;' and other legal works.

ANSTRUTHER, Sir Robert, English politician, b. 1834; educated at Harrow; magistrate and deputy-lieutenant for the counties of Fife and Caithness; formerly captain and lieut.-colonel in the Grenadier Guards; M.P. for Fifeshire since 1864.

ANTHOINE DE SAINT JOSEPH, François, Baron, French general, b. at Marseilles, 1787; entered as a volunteer a regiment of dragoons; passed the Military School at Fontainebleau, 1804; served in Poland as aide-de-camp to Marshal Soult, and under Marshal Suchet in the campaigns of 1811 to 1813; colonel, 1814; major-general, Oct. 11, 1832; lieut.-general, April 14, 1844; nominated grand officer of the Légion d'honneur, Aug. 15, 1851.

ANTHON, Charles, American author, b. in New York, 1797; entered the College of Columbia, 1811, and graduated, 1815; called to the bar of the Supreme Court of New York, 1819; professor of languages at Columbia College, 1820–35; rector of the College Grammar School, 1830; LL.D., 1831. Editor of a new edition of 'Lemprière's Classical Dictionary,' 1822; 'Horace,' 1830; and many other works.

ANTIER, Benjamin, French dramatic writer, b. at Paris, March 24, 1787; studied at Paris, and served in the army. Author of 'L'Habit de Cour,' 1818; 'Les Femmes, et le Mérite des Femmes,' 1824; 'La Muette des la Forêt,' 1828; 'L'Irlandais, ou l'Esprit national,' 1831; 'Les Chiens du Mont Saint-Bernard,' 1838; 'Mon Gigot et mon Gendre,' 1861; and other dramas.

ANTIGNA, Jean Pierre Alexandre, French painter, b. at Orleans, 1818; studied under M. Salmon and M. Norblin, 1836, also under M. Delaroche; exhibited paintings on religious subjects, 1841–45. Painted 'Le Coin du Feu,' 'Le Premier Joujou,' 'L'Orage,' 'Les Baigneuses,' 1846; 'Le Matin,' 'Le Soir,' 'L'Atelier,' 'Le Sommeil de Midi,' 1859; 'Bergère,' 1863; 'Fontaine à Auso,' 1864.

ANTONELLI, Giacomo, Italian statesman, b. at Sonnio, near Terracina, April 2, 1806, the son of a woodcutter; educated at Rome; bishop *in partibus*, 1840; under-secretary of state for the Roman ministry of the interior, 1841; minister of finance, 1845; cardinal-deacon, 1847; minister of state and of foreign affairs, appointed Apr. 12, 1850.

ANTROBUS, Edmund, English politician, b. 1818; educated at Eton and St. John's College, Cambridge, and graduated B.A. 1840: M.P. for East Surrey, 1841–47, and for Wilton since 1855.

APJOHN, James, Irish chemist and physician, b. at Sunville, co. Limerick, Sept. 1, 1796; studied at Trinity College, Dublin, and passed B.A. 1818, and M.B. 1821; appointed professor of chemistry at the Royal College of Surgeons in Ireland, 1828. Author of 'A New Method of investigating the Specific Heats of the Gaseous Bodies,' 1837, and articles on 'Spontaneous Combustion,' on 'Electricity,' on 'Galvanism,' &c. in the *Encyclopædia of Practical Medicine.*

APPERT, Eugene, French painter, b. at Angers, 1820; studied under M. Ingres. Painted 'Sarah et les Braconniers,' 1841; 'La Vision de Saint-Ovens,' 1844; 'Le Christ descendu de la Croix,' 1846; 'Une Armure,' 1850; 'L'Adoration des Mages,' 1853; 'Venise,' 1863; 'Le Pape Alexandre III.,' 'Pivoines,' 1864.

APPIANI, Andrew, Italian painter, b. at Milan, 1812; studied under M. François Hayez. Painted 'Petrarch at Avignon' and 'A young Italian Emigrant pressing his national colours to his heart.'

ARAGO, Emmanuel, French advocate and politician, b. at Paris, June 6, 1812; called to the bar, 1837; took part in the Revolution of 1848; renounced politics after the coup d'état of Dec. 2, 1852, but continued to practise at the French bar. Author of 'La Demande en Mariage, ou le Jésuite retourné,' 1830; 'Un grand Orateur,' 1837; and other works.

ARAGO, Etienne, French journalist, b. at Perpignan, Feb. 9, 1802; studied at the Colleges of Perpignan and Sorreze; founded the journals La Réforme and, with M. Maurice

Alhoy, *Le Figaro;* director of the Théâtre du Vaudeville, 1829; took part in the Insurrection of 1834 and in the Revolution of 1848; condemned to transportation by the High Court of Versailles, 1849; fled from France, but returned 1859. Author of 'La Vie de Molière,' 1832; 'Les Aristocraties,' 1847; 'Les Bleus et les Blancs,' 1862; and other works.

ARANY, Janos, Hungarian poet, b. at Nagy-Szalonta, 1819; studied at the College of Debreczin; professor of Latin at the Normal School of Szalonta. Author of 'Az Elvezett Alkotmany,' a prize poem; 'Toldi,' 1847; 'Murany ostroma,' Pesth, 1848; 'Katalin,' ib. 1850.

ARBOIS DE JUBAINVILLE, Marie Henri d', French archæologist, b. at Nancy, Dec. 5, 1827; studied at the college of his native town, 1848–51. Author of 'Répertoire archéologique de l'Aube,' 1861; 'Les Armoiries des Comtes de Champagne,' 1852; 'Voyage paléographique dans le Départment de l'Aube,' Troyes and Paris, 1855; 'Études sur l'État des Abbayes,' 1858; 'Histoire des Ducs et des Comtes de Champagne,' 1859–63.

ARCHAIE, E'tienne Desmier de Saint-Simon, Vicomte d', French geologist, b. at Rheims, Sept. 24, 1802; entered the Military School of St.-Cyr, 1819; became an officer of cavalry, but retired 1830; professor of palæontology at the Paris Museum, 1861. Author of 'Zizim, ou les Chevaliers de Rhodes,' 1828; 'Histoire des Progrès de la Géologie de 1834 à 1862,' 1847–62; 'Précis de l'Histoire de la Paléontologie,' 1863.

ARENALES, Jose, American geographer, b. at Buenos-Ayres, 1790; entered the army; lieut.-colonel of artillery, 1825; charged with the Topographical Department of Buenos-Ayres, 1835. Published 'Noticias históricas y descriptivas sobre el gran pais del Chaco y Rio Bermejo,' Buenos-Ayres, 1833.

ARETIN, Karl Maria, Viscount von, Bavarian diplomatist, b. at Munich, July 4, 1796; took part in the campaign of 1813–15; councillor of legation to the minister of foreign affairs, 1834; chamberlain and councillor to the king of Bavaria. Author of 'Darstellung der auswärtigen Verhältnisse Baiern's,' Passau, 1839; and other works.

ANGELANDER, Frederick William Augustus, German astronomer, b. at Memel, Prussia, March 21, 1799; educated at the University of Königsberg; studied astronomy under Bessel, and employed by him as assistant in the observatory under his charge, 1820; undertook the supervision of the Observatory of Abo, Finland, 1823–28; professor of astronomy in the University of Bonn, 1837. Published 'A Catalogue of 560 Stars, with Observations on their Motions,' 1830; and other astronomical works.

ARGYLL, George Douglas Campbell, Duke of, English statesman, b. 1823; succeeded his father, 1847; lord privy seal, 1852–55, and again 1859–66; postmaster-general, 1855–1858; lord rector of Glasgow University, 1854; chancellor of the University of St. Andrew's, 1851. Author of 'Presbytery examined,' 1848; 'The Reign of Law,' 1867.

ARISTARCHI, Nicholas, Greek ecclesiastic and head of the patriarchate of Constantinople, b. at Constantinople, 1800; keeper of the seals to Prince Alexander Soutza of Wallachia, 1818; exiled in 1821; returned to Constantinople as grand logothete; appointed *kapon kiaja* or plenipotentiary of Wallachia, 1854.

ARJUZON, Pe'lix Francois Thomas, Count d', French politician, b. 1810; gentleman in waiting to Charles X.; member of the Corps Législatif, 1852; resigned, 1863; elected deputy for the dep. of Eure, 1864. Chamberlain to the Emperor.

ARKWRIGHT, Richard, English politician, b. 1835; educated at Harrow and Trinity College, Cambridge; graduated B.A. 1855, and M.A. 1858; a deputy-lieutenant for the county of Hereford; returned M.P. for Leominster, 1866.

ARMAGH, Marcus Beresford, Archbishop of, English divine, b. 1801; educated at Richmond School and Trinity College, Cambridge; admitted to holy orders, 1824; rector of Kildallen, 1825; vicar of Drung and Lara; vicar-general of Kilmore and archdeacon of Ardagh; consecrated to the sees of Kilmore, Elphin, and Ardagh, 1854; translated to Armagh, 1863; primate of all Ireland, and lord almoner of Ireland.

ARMAND, Alfred, French architect, b. at Paris, Oct. 3, 1805; entered the School of Fine Arts under the direction of M. Achille Leclerc; designed the railway stations of Versailles, 1839; St. Cloud, 1840; Calais, 1848; St. Quentin, 1850; Douai, 1851; and other buildings.

ARMENGAUD, Jean Germain De'sire', French writer, b. at Castres, Tarn, 1797. Author of 'Histoire des Peintres de toutes les Écoles, depuis la Renaissance jusqu'à nos jours,' 1849; 'Les Galeries publiques de l'Europe,' Rome, 1856; 'Le Parthénon de l'Histoire,' 1863–64; and other works.

ARMITAGE, Edward, English painter, b. in London, May 20, 1817. Executed some of the frescoes for the new Houses of Parliament; 'Disembarkment of Julius Cæsar in England,' 1847; painted also 'The Battle of Balaclava,' 'The Battle of Inkerman,' 1856, and other works of art; elected A. R. A. 1867.

ARMSTRONG, Richard, English politician, b. 1815; educated at Trinity College, Dublin; graduated B.A. 1839; M.A. 1865; called to the Irish bar, 1839; appointed Queen's serjeant-at-law, 1861; returned M.P. for Sligo, 1865.

ARMSTRONG, Sir William, English mechanician, b. at Newcastle-on-Tyne, 1810; invented the 'Hydro-electric machine,' for which he was elected F.R.S.; the 'Hydraulic crane,' the 'Accumulator,' 1845–50; constructed the gun which bears his name, 1854; was knighted and made a C.B.; LL.D. from the University of Cambridge, 1862; president of the British Association, 1863.

ARNAL, Etienne, French actor, b. at Meulan, Seine-et-Oise, Feb. 1, 1794; took part in the defence of Paris, 1814; played at the Théâtre du Vaudeville, and the Palais-Royal, from 1817 to 1864. Author of 'Épitre à Bouffé,' 1840; Boutades en Vers,' 1861; 'Les Gendarmes,' 1826; new edition, 1859.

ARNAUD, Fanny, French authoress, b. at Arles, France, 1803; married to M. Charles Reybaud. Author of 'La dernière Bohémienne;' 'Le Cabaret de Gaubert;' 'Les deux Marguerites;' 'Le Denier Oblat;' 'Les Aventures d'un Renégat;' 'Mdlle. de Chazeuil;' 'Les Anciens Couvents de Paris.'

ARNDTS, Louis, German lawyer, b. at Arnsburg, Prussia, Aug. 19, 1805; studied at the Universities of Bonn, Heidelberg, and Berlin; and graduated LL.D. 1825; joined the Faculty of Law at Bonn, 1826; professor extraordinary, 1837; professor ordinary, 1839; professor of law at the University of Munich since 1839. Published 'Lehrbuch der Pandecten;' 'Rechtslexicon;' and other legal works.

ARNOLD, Edwin, English author, b. June 10, 1831; educated at King's School, Rochester, King's College, London, and University College, Oxford; graduated in honours, 1854; second master of the English division of King Edward the Sixth's School, Birmingham; principal of the Government Sanskrit College, Poona, Bombay Presidency, till 1960. Author of 'Poems, narrative and lyrical;' 'History of the Administration of India under the late Marquis of Dalhousie,' 1862–64; translated the classical Sanskrit work 'Hitopadesa,' under the title of 'The Book of good Counsels.'

ARNOLD, Matthew, English poet, b. at Laleham, near Staines, Dec. 24, 1822; educated at Winchester, Rugby, and Oxford; fellow of Oriel College, 1845; private secretary to Lord Lansdowne, 1847–51; lay-inspector of schools, 1851; professor of poetry at the University of Oxford, 1858. Author of 'The Strayed Reveller, and other poems;' 'Empedocles on Etna;' 'Essays in Criticism;' 'Schools and Universities on the Continent;' 'Popular Education of France;' 'Three Lectures on Translating Homer;' 'Last Words on Translating Homer;' 'Poems, First and Second Series;' and 'New Poems.'

ARNOTT, James Moncrieff, English surgeon, b. 1794; educated at the High School and University of Edinburgh; surgeon to the Middlesex Hospital; and professor of surgery in King's College, London; one of the council of Royal College of Surgeons, 1840.

ARNOTT, Neil, English physician, b. 1789; educated at the Grammar School, Aberdeen, and at the University of that town; graduated M.A. 1812; appointed surgeon in the East India Company's naval service, 1835, physician extraordinary to the Queen, and member of the senate of the London University. Author of 'Elements of Physics,' 1827–64; 'A Survey of Human Progress,' 1861.

ARNOULD, Sir Joseph, English barrister, b. 1815; educated at the Charterhouse, and Wadham College, Oxford; graduated first-class in Classics, 1836; fellow of Wadham College, 1838; called to the bar of the Middle Temple, 1841; judge at Bombay, and knighted, 1859. Author of 'Treatise on Marine Insurance;' and contributor to several periodicals and newspapers.

ARNOULD-PLESSY, Jeanne Plessy, French actress, b. at Metz, Sept. 7, 1819; made her début, March 10, 1834, at the Comédie Française; married J. F. Arnould, a dramatic writer, July, 1845, who died 1854; engaged for the French theatre of St. Petersburg, 1855.

AROUX, Eugène, French magistrate and author, b. at Rouen, Oct. 21, 1793; called to the bar of his native town, 1815; represented the town of Dieppe in the Chamber of Deputies, 1831–37. Published translations of Milton's 'Paradise Lost,' 1842; Dante's 'Divina Commedia,' 1842; 'Dante hérétique, socialiste et revolutionaire,' 1858; and other works.

ARRIVABENE, Giovanni, Belgian political economist, b. at Mantua, Italy, 1801; imprisoned at Venice, 1821; condemned to death for political offences, 1824; naturalized in Belgium, 1840. Author of 'Des Moyens les plus propres à améliorer le Sort des Ouvriers,' Lugano, 1832; 'Situation économique de la Belgique,' Brussels, 1843; translated into Italian 'Mill's Principles of Economy,' 1833; and other works.

ARSAKIS, Apostolos, Roumanian statesman, b. at Epirus, Greece, 1789; studied at the college founded by the Greek princes at Bucharest, and at Jena, in Germany; councillor of Prince Gregory Ghika, 1854; minister in the first cabinet of the Principalities, Feb. 1862. Author of 'De Piscium Cerebro et Medulla spinali,' Halle, 1813.

ARROWSMITH, John, English geographer, b. early in the present century. Author of 'An Overland Expedition to Australia;' 'Narrative of Missionary Travels in Africa,' London; 'Atlas of Universal Geography;' and other works.

ARTHUR, Thomas, American novelist, b. at Newburgh, New York, 1809. Author of 'Lights and Shadows of Real Life;' 'Tired of Housekeeping;' 'History of Kentucky,' Philadelphia, 1852; 'Tales of Married Life;' 'Ten Nights in a Bar-room;' and other works.

ARUASON, Jon, Icelandic author, b. at Hof, in Iceland, Aug. 17, 1819; educated at the College of Bessestad; appointed keeper of the library at Reykjavik, 1849; secretary to the Bishop of Iceland, 1856. Author of 'Icelandic popular Tales and Adventures,' Leipsic, 1862–64; and other works.

ASCHBACH, Joseph, German historian, b. at Höchst, Nassau, April 29, 1801; studied at Heidelberg; professor of history at Frankfort, 1823; professor at the University of Bonn, 1842. Author of 'History of Spain and Portugal during the dominion of the Almoravides and Almohades,'Frankfort, 1833–37; 'History of the West Goths,' ib. 1827; 'History of the Emperor Sigismund,' Hamburg, 1838–44; and other works.

ASHBURNHAM, Thomas, English general, b. 1808; entered the army, 1823; took part in the campaign in India, 1840–45; aide-de-camp, 1846; lieutenant-colonel; major-general, 1854; charged with the command of the English forces in China and India, 1857; colonel of the 82d, 1859.

ASSAKI, George, Roumanian poet and statesman, b. at Jassy, 1788; studied at several German universities, and in Italy; elected member of the Academy of Rome under the name of *Alviro*, 1811; represented the new Moldavian government at Vienna, 1822; chief of the Ministry of Public Instruction, 1856. Author of 'History of Russia,' 1817; 'Poems,' Jassy, 1854.

ASSOLLANT, Jean Baptiste Alfred, French writer, b. at Aubusson, Creuse, 1827. Author of 'Scènes de la Vie des États-Unis,' 1858; 'Brancas,' 1859; 'Les Aventures de Karl Brunner, docteur en Théologie,' 1861; 'D'Heure en Heure,' 1862; 'Pensées diverses, Impressions intimes, Opinions et Paradoxes de Cadet Bordiche,' 1864; and other works of fiction.

ASTON, Sir Arthur Ingram, English diplomatist, b. in London, 1798; studied at Oxford; entered the diplomatic service, and became attaché to the embassy at Vienna, 1819; envoy to Rio Janeiro, 1826; secretary of legation at Paris, 1833; minister plenipotentiary to Spain, 1840 to 1843; on his return created K.C.B.

ATHERSTONE, Edwin, English author, b. towards the end of the last century. Author of "The Sea-Kings of England;' 'The Fall of Nineveh,' published 1828; 'The Handwriting on the Wall;' 'The Last Days of Herculaneum;' and other poetical works; has a literary pension of 100*l*. per annum.

ATHLUMNEY, Rt. Hon. William Meredyth, Baron, English Statesman, b. 1802; magistrate and deputy-lieutenant for the county of Meath, and visitor of Maynooth: M.P. for Drogheda from 1837 to 1852; under-secretary for the Home Department, 1846–47; chief secretary for Ireland, 1847–52; privy councillor, 1847; elevated to the Irish peerage, 1863.

AUBER, Daniel François Esprit, French musical composer, b. at Caen. Normandy, Jan. 29, 1782. Produced 'Le Séjour Militaire,' 1813; 'La Muette de Portici,' 1828; 'Masaniello;' 'Le Cheval de Bronze,' 1835; 'Fra Diavolo,' 1836; 'Les Diamants de la Couronne;' 'Le Domino Noir,' 1837; 'Janetta,' 1840; 'La Circassienne,' 1861; 'La Fiancée du Roi de Garbe,' 1864. Author of about twenty-five great operas, and numerous smaller musical works. Appointed director of the Paris Conservatoire de Musique, 1842.

AUBER, Theophile Charles, French physician, b. 1805; studied at the University of Paris, and obtained his diploma of doctor of medicine, 1831. Author of numerous medical works: among them 'Traité de philosophie médicale,' Paris, 1839; 'Hygiène des femmes nerveuses,' ib. 1841; and 'Esprit du Vitalisme et de l'Organisme,' 1855.

AUBERT, Constance, French authoress, b. at Paris, May 12, 1803, eldest daughter of the Duchess of Abrantes. Published 'Les Abeilles Parisiennes,' 1843; 'Les Etrennes,' 1849; and 'Manuel d'économie élegante,' 1859. Married to M. Louis Aubert, retired captain of infantry.

AUBERT, Pauline, French actress, b. at Toury, Eure et Loire, 1802; appeared on the stage of the Théatre français, Paris, 1816; engaged at the Odéon, Paris, 1821; admitted as sociétaire, or partner, at the Théatre français, 1834.

AUBRY BAILLEUL, Tranquille, French naval officer, b. Jan. 8, 1798; entered the French navy, 1812; first lieutenant, 1828; captain of a corvette, 1838; captain of a frigate, 1845; rear-admiral, June 7, 1855; governor of Guadeloupe; titular member of the Council of the Admiralty; grand officer of the Légion d'honneur, 1859.

AUCKLAND, Rev. John Eden, Baron, English divine, b. 1799; studied at Eton and Cambridge; admitted to holy orders, 1822; successively rector of Eyam, Derbyshire, of Hertingfordbury, Herts, and of Battersea, Surrey; one of the chaplains to her Majesty, 1838; bishop of Sodor and Man, 1847; succeeded his brother to the title and seat in the House of Lords, 1849; translated to the see of Bath and Wells, 1854. Author of 'Life and Correspondence of the first Lord Auckland,' 1860.

AUDIFFRET, Charles Louis Gaston, Marquis d', French politician, b. at Paris, Oct. 10, 1787; entered the Administration of Finance, 1805; chief of the bureau, 1812; councillor of state, 1828; appointed president of the Council of Administration of Credit, Commerce, and Industry, 1859. Published 'Examen des Revenus Publics,' 1839; 'Système financier de la France,' 1840; third edition, 1863–64; and other works.

AUDIGANNE, Armand, French author, b. at Ancenis, 1814; studied law at Paris; entered the Ministry of Commerce, 1840; placed at the head of the Service of Industry, 1848; appointed secretary to the Commission of the Universal Exhibition of 1855. Author of 'Monsieur Guizot,' 1838; 'Les Chemins de fer aujourd'hui et dans cent ans chez tous les peuples,' 1858; and other works.

AUER, Alois, German writer, b. at Wels, Upper Austria, May 11, 1813; received his education at the University of Vienna, and became director of the Imperial Printing Office at Vienna, 1840. Published 'Paternoster in 608 languages,' Vienna, 1844; 'Die Entdeckung des Naturselbstdruckes,' ib. 1864; and other works.

AUERBACH, Berthold, German author and poet, b. of Jewish parents, at Nordstetten, Black Forest of Wurtemberg, Feb. 28, 1812; studied at Tübingen, Munich, and Heidelberg, 1832–35. Author of 'The Jewish Nation and its Literature,' Stuttgart, 1836; 'Village Tales from the Black Forest, 1843; 'Andreas Höfer,' Leipsic, 1850; and many other works of fiction.

AUERSPERG, Charles William Philip, Prince of, Austrian statesman, b. May 1, 1814; succeeded his father, Jan. 25, 1827; privy councillor and hereditary grand chamberlain to the Emperor of Austria; nominated president of the Upper Chamber of the Austrian Empire, 1861.

AUERSPERG, Vincent Charles Joseph, Prince of, Austrian statesman, cousin-german of the preceding, b. July 16, 1812; privy councillor, lord chamberlain, and hereditary grand marshal of the Tyrol.

AUGER, Hippolyte Nicolas Just, French writer, b. at Auxerre, May 25, 1797; entered the Russian service, and was officer in the Guards, 1817. Author of 'Martha,' 1818; 'La Folle,' 'Pierre le grand,' 1836; 'Le Commissionnaire,' 'Madame Brice;' and 'Le Roi des Petits-Maîtres,' 1852.

AUGIER, Guillaume Victor Emile, French poet and dramatist, b. at Valence, Sept. 17, 1820. Author of 'La Ciguë,' 1844; 'Gabrielle,' 1849; 'Les Effrontés,' 1861; 'Le Fils du Giboyer,' 1862; 'Maître Guérin,' 1864.

AUGUSTENBURG, Christian August, duke of Schleswig-Holstein-Sonderburg-Augustenburg, b. at Copenhagen, July 19, 1798; succeeded duke Frederick Christian, 1814; married Louisa Sophia, countess of Danniskjold Samsoe, 1820; had his estates confiscated by the king of Denmark, 1850; ceded his claims to the Danish crown, 1851. Author of several works on the breeding and training of horses.

AUGUSTENBURG, Frederick Christian August, duke of Schleswig-Holstein-Sonderburg-Augustenburg, son of the preceding, b. July 6, 1829; major of 1st infantry regiment of the Prussian Guards; married Adelaide Victoria, daughter of Prince Ernest of Hohenlohe-Langenburg, 1856; asserted his right to the dukedom of Schleswig-Holstein, 1863.

AUMALE, Henri Eugène Phillippe Louis d'Orle'ans. Duke d', Prince of the family of Orleans, b. at Paris, Jan. 16, 1822, fourth son of King Louis Philippe and Queen Marie Amelie; entered the army and became captain 1839, and colonel, Oct. 1842; married Marie Caroline Auguste de Bourbon, daughter of Prince Leopold of Salerno, Nov. 25, 1844; commander-in-chief of the camp of Gironde, 1845; governor-general of the French possessions in Africa, 1847–48.

AUSTEN, Sir Francis William, English admiral, b. at Steventon, Hants, 1774; entered the navy, and became lieutenant, 1792; served in the war of 1814; commander of the frigate *Canopus* in the naval expedition to St. Domingo; knighted, 1837; vice-admiral, 1862; admiral, 1863.

AUTRAN, Joseph, French poet and dramatic writer, b. at Marseille, June, 1813. Author of 'Ode to M. de Lamartine,' 1832; 'Ludibria Ventis,' Paris, 1838; 'Italie et la Semaine Sainte à Rome,' Marseille, 1841; 'Les Poëmes de la Mer,' Paris, 1852–59; 'Le Poëme des beaux Jours,' 1862; 'Le Cyclope d'après Euripide,' 1863; and other works.

AUZOUX, Theodore Louis, French anatomist, b. at St.-Aubin d'Ecroville, 1797; graduated M.D. at Paris, 1822. Author of 'Un Mémoire sur la Vipère;' 'Considérations générales sur l'Anatomie;' 'Un Mémoire sur le Cholera-Morbus, son siége, sa nature, son traitement, 1850.

AVELLANEDA, Gertrude, Spanish authoress, b. at Cuba, 1816, the daughter of a naval commander; married Don Pedro Sabator, member of Congress, 1846, and after his death, at the end of a few months, retired to a convent at Madrid. Author of 'Poesias Lyricas,' Madrid, 1841; 'La Cruz,' ib. 1846; 'Las Glorias de España,' ib. 1850–51; and numerous other poems, dramas, and works of fiction.

AVENEL, Denis Louis Martial, French journalist, b. at Orbec, Calvados, May 28, 1789; auditor to the Council of State of Westphalia, and secretary to King Jerome, 1806. Contributor to the *Temps*, the *Moniteur Universel*, and other journals; published 'State Letters and Diplomatic Instructions of Cardinal Richelieu,' 1863.

AVENEL, Paul, French novelist, b. at Chaumont, Oise, 1823; educated for a commercial career, but left it in 1850. Author of 'Antithèses Morales,' Paris, 1854; 'Le Roi de Paris,' ib. 1860; 'Le Duc des Moines,' ib. 1864; and other novels.

AVEZAC-MACAYA, Armand Pascal D', French geographer, b. at Bagnères de Bigorre, 1799; educated for the law, and admitted to the Paris bar, 1823; head of department in the Ministry of Marine, 1831; secretary-general of the Paris Geographical Society, 1834. Author of 'Esquisse generale de l'Afrique,' Paris, 1837; 'Des Découvertes faites au Moyen-Âge dans l'océan Atlantique,' ib. 1845. Contributor to the *Revue des Deux-Mondes*, and various scientific publications.

AWDRY, Sir John Wither, English administrator, b. 1795; educated at Winchester, and Christ Church, Oxford, and graduated first class in classics, 1816; called to the bar, 1822; puisne judge and commissioner of the Insolvent Debtors' Court at Bombay, 1839; chief justice of the Supreme Court of that Presidency, 1839; resigned, 1842; one of the commissioners for the Reform of the University of Oxford, 1844.

AYME, Jules Gabriel, French magistrate and politician, b. at Medouville, Vosges, June 14, 1806; studied law, and called to the bar, 1830; judge of instruction to the tribunal of Neufchâteau, 1835; member of the Corps Législatif for the department of Vosges, 1852–57, and since 1863.

AYRTON, Acton Smee, English politician, b. 1816; called to the bar of the Middle Temple, 1853; returned M.P. for the Tower Hamlets, 1857.

AYTOUN, Roger Sinclair, English politician, b. 1823; educated at Trinity College, Cambridge; graduated B.A. 1846; M.A. 1848; a magistrate, and deputy-lieut. for Fifeshire; M.P. for Kirkcaldy since 1862.

AZEGLIO, Massimo Taparelli, Marquis D', Italian statesman, b. at Turin, 1801; studied painting and sculpture at Rome, 1816–29; elected deputy to the National Assembly of Sardinia, 1848; president of the Sardinian Council of Ministers, May 11, 1849, to Oct. 30, 1852; Italian ambassador extraordinary to Great Britain, 1861. Author of 'Ettore Fieramosca,' Turin, 1833; and other works of fiction of a political tendency.

AZEGLIO, Victor Emmanuel Taparelli, Marquis D', Italian diplomatist, b. 1815, nephew of the preceding; entered the diplomatic career, 1841; minister-plenipotentiary and ambassador to Great Britain since Nov. 13, 1850.

B.

BABBAGE, Charles, English mathematician, b. Dec. 26, 1792; educated at Trinity College, Cambridge, and graduated 1812; undertook the construction of a calculating machine, or 'difference engine' for the government, 1821; professor of mathematics at Cambridge, 1828; construction of calculating machine suspended, 1833. Author of 'Economy of Manufactures,' 1821; 'Passages from the Life of a Philosopher;' 'Autobiographical Reminiscences,' 1864; and other works.

BABINET, Jacques, French astronomer, b. at Lusignan, March 5, 1794; entered the Polytechnic School, 1812; lieutenant of artillery; quitted the army, and became successively professor of mathematics at Fontenoy-le-Comte, at Poitiers, and at the College of Saint Louis; professor of meteorology at 'l'Athénée,' 1825 to 1828; at the Collége de France, 1838; and at l'Académie des Sciences, 1840; astronomer to the Bureau of Longitudes. Author of 'Memoire sur la détermination de la Masse de la planète Mercure,' 1825; 'Sur la Pluie et les Inondations,' 1855; 'De la Télégraphie Electrique : ligne de jonction des cinq parties du Monde,' 1860; and other scientific works.

BABINGTON, Charles Cardale, English botanist, b. 1808; educated at St. John's College, Cambridge, and graduated B.A. 1830; professor of botany at the University of Cambridge. Author of 'Flora Bathoniensis;' 'Flora of the Channel Islands;' 'A Manual of British Botany;' and other works.

BABINGTON, Rev. Churchill, English writer, b. 1821; graduated in honours at St. John's College. Cambridge, 1843; senior fellow, 1845; chaplain at Horningsea, Cambridge, 1848 to 1861. Edited from MSS. recently discovered, 'Oration of Hyperides against Demosthenes;' 'Funeral Oration of Hyperides,' from papyrus in the British Museum ; and many other works.

BABO, Lambert von, German chemist, b. at Meinhem, grand duchy of Baden, 1790; president of the Society of Agriculture, Baden, 1831; professor of chemistry at the University of Friburg, 1853. Author of 'Instruction for the Culture of Prairies,' 1836; 'The Vine and its Varieties,' 1843; 'The Principles of Agriculture,' 1851; and other works.

BACH, Alexander, Baron von, Austrian statesman, b. at Loosdorf, Lower Austria, Jan. 4, 1813; studied law, and was called to the bar at Vienna; deputy of the order of Advocates, and one of the Provisional Commission for administration of the city of Vienna in 1848; obtained the portfolio of Justice in the ministry of Schwartzenberg Stadion, 1848; minister of the Interior, 1849; ambassador and minister plenipotentiary to Rome, Aug. 1859, to Sept. 1865.

BACHE, Alexander Dallas, American military writer, b. in Philadelphia, July 19, 1806; educated at the Military Academy, West Point, U.S.; lieutenant of engineers, 1825; professor of mathematics at the University of Pennsylvania, 1827; president of Girard College, Philadelphia; superintendent of United States coast survey, 1843. Published 'Different Systems of Instruction,' Philadelphia, 1839; and other works.

BACHE, Franklin, American physician, brother of the preceding, b. at Philadelphia, Oct. 25, 1792; graduated B.A. at the University of Pennsylvania, 1810; M.D. 1814; entered the medical department of the U.S. army, 1813; professor of chemistry in Franklin Institute of Pennsylvania, 1826–32. Author of 'System of Chemistry for the use of Students in Medicine ;' and other medical works.

BACHELET, Jean Louis Theodore, French writer, b. at Pissy-Pôville, 1820; studied at the schools of Rouen and Versailles, and entered l'École Normale, 1840; graduated 1846; successively professor of history at the colleges of Havre, Chartres, and St. Quentin, at Clermont, Ferraud, Contances, and Rouen. Published 'The War of a Hundred Years,' 1852; 'The Catholic Kings of Spain, to Ferdinand and Isabelle,' 1853.

BACHMAN, John, American naturalist, b. in Duchess county, state of New York, 1790; pastor of the German Lutheran Church at Charleston, South Carolina, for nearly fifty years. Author of 'Quadrupeds of North America ;' 'Examination of Professor Agassiz's Sketch of the Natural Provinces of the Animal World, and their Relation to different Types of Men,' 1855; and other works.

BACK, Sir George, English navigator, b. at Stockport, 1796; entered the Royal Navy, 1808; appointed to the *Trent*, lieut-commander John Franklin, 1818; sailed with Captain Franklin on the Arctic Expedition, 1819; lieutenant, 1821; commander of the expedition to discover Sir John Ross, 1833; appointed to the *Terror*, 1836; knighted, 1839; flag rank, 1857. Author of 'Narrative of the Arctic Land Expedition to the Mouth of the Great Fish or Back River, and along the Shores of the Arctic Ocean, in 1833–35;' and other works.

BAECKER, Louis de, French archæologist, b. at St. Omer, April 16, 1814; studied law at Paris, and practised as barrister in his native town; judge at Bergnes, 1844. Author of 'Château de la Motte aux Bois,' 1843; 'Analogie de la Langue des Goths et des Franks avec le Sanscrit,' 1858; 'Langue neerlandaise,' 1863; and other archæological and historical works.

BAEHR, Johann Christian Felix, German philologist, b. at Darmstadt, June 13, 1798; studied at Heidelberg; titular professor of Classical Literature in the University of that town, 1826; chief librarian, 1833; superior inspector of the Lyceum. 1839; director of the Philological Seminary, 1845. Author of 'Herodotus,' Leipsic, 1832–34; edited the 'Annals of Heidelberg;' and numerous historical and philological works.

BAER, Charles Ernest de, Russian naturalist, b. in Esthonia, Feb. 17, 1792; studied medicine at the University of Dorpat; professor of zoology at Königsberg, 1819; appointed professor at the Academy of St. Petersburg, 1834; nominated correspondent of the French Academy of Sciences, 1858. Author of 'History of the Development of Animals,' Königsberg, 1828–37; 'Researches on the History and Development of Fishes,' Leipsic, 1835; 'Studies on the Russian Empire,' St. Petersburg, 1856.

BAGGALLAY, Richard, English politician, b. 1816; educated at Caius College, Cambridge, where he graduated B.A. 1839, and M.A. 1842; called to the bar at Lincoln's Inn, 1843; made a Q.C. 1861; returned M.P. for Hereford, 1865.

BAGGE, Sir William, English politician, b. 1810; educated at the Charterhouse, and Balliol College, Oxford; is a magistrate and deputy-lieutenant for Norfolk; made a baronet, 1867; M.P. for West Norfolk, 1837–57, and since 1865.

BAGNALL, Charles, English politician, b. 1827; educated at King's College, London; is a magistrate for Staffordshire and North Riding of Yorkshire; returned M.P. for Whitby, 1865.

BAGOT, William Bagot, Baron, English politician, b. 1811; studied at the University of Oxford; M.P. for Denbighshire from 1835 to 1852; was lord-in-waiting to the late Prince Consort; succeeded his father, second baron, 1856.

BAGWELL, John, English politician, b. 1811; educated at Winchester; is a magistrate for Waterford, and a magistrate and deputy-lieutenant for the counties of Waterford and Tipperary; was high sheriff, 1834; M.P. for Clonmel since 1857.

BAILEY, Crawshay, English politician, b. 1794; is a magistrate and deputy-lieutenant for the county of Glamorgan; has been high sheriff of Monmouth and Brecon; M.P. for Monmouth since 1852.

BAILEY, Sir Joseph Russell, English politician, b. 1840; educated at Harrow, and Christ Church, Oxford; is a magistrate for the counties of Hereford and Brecon; high sheriff, 1864; deputy-lieutenant for Brecon and Radnor; returned M.P. for Herefordshire, 1865.

BAILEY, Joseph Roosevelt, American Catholic priest, b. at New York, 1814; studied for the Protestant Episcopal Church; embraced Catholicism, 1842, and entered the Seminary of St. Sulpice, at Paris; ordained priest, and returned to the United States, 1844; consecrated to the Bishopric of Newark, 1853.

BAILEY, Philip James, English poet, b. at Nottingham, April 22, 1816; educated at various schools, and matriculated at the University of Glasgow, 1831; studied law, and admitted of Lincoln's Inn, 1835; called to the bar, 1840. Author of 'Festus,' London, 1839, seventh edition 1864; 'The Angel of the World,' 1850; 'The Mystic,' 1855; 'The Age,' 1858, and other works in verse and prose.

BAILLARGER, Jules Gabriel François, French physician, b. at Montbazon, 1806; studied medicine at Paris; assistant at the Hospital of Salpêtrière, 1840; devoted principally to the treatment of nervous and mental diseases.

BAILLIE, Henry James, English politician, b. 1804; is a magistrate and deputy-lieutenant for the county of Inverness; was joint secretary of the Board of Control, 1852 and 1858–59; M.P. for Inverness-shire since 1840.

BAIN, Alexander, English writer, b. at Aberdeen, 1818; entered Marischal College, 1836; graduated M.A. 1840; assistant secretary to the Metropolitan Sanitary Commissioners, 1847; examiner in logic and moral philosophy in the University of London, 1857 to 1862; appointed crown professor of logic in the University of Aberdeen, 1860. Author of 'Moral Philosophy,' 1852; 'The Study of Character, including an Estimate of Phrenology,' 1861; and several scholastic works.

BAINES, Edward, English politician, b. 1800; educated at the Protestant Dissenters' Grammar School, Manchester; M.P. for Leeds, in his brother's place, since 1859. Author of 'A Visit to the Vaudois of Piedmont;' 'The Woollen Manufacture of England;' and 'The Life of the late Edward Baines.'

BAIRD, Robert, American writer, b. at Fayette, county Pennsylvania, 1798. Author of 'History of Temperance Societies,' 1836; 'A View of Religion in America,' Glasgow, 1842; 'The Christian Retrospect and Register,' New York, 1851; and contributions to American periodicals.

BAIRD, Spencer, American naturalist, b. at Reading, [Pennsylvania, 1823; professor of natural science at Dickenson College, and assistant secretary of the Smithsonian Institution. Editor and translator of the 'Iconographie Encyclopædia,' 1851; and author of various papers on zoology and natural history.

BAITOR, Johan Georg, Swiss philologist, b. at Zurich, 1801; studied at Munich, Göttingen, and Königsberg; professor at the University of Zurich, 1827; resigned 1849. Published 'Des Orateurs Attiques,' Zurich, 1837–50; the collected works of Plato, in 21 vols.; and other classical works.

BAKE, John, Dutch philologist, b. at Leyden, Sept. 1, 1787; professor of Greek and Latin literature at the University of Leyden, 1815; member of the Institute of the Netherlands, 1821; and of the Academy of Sciences, 1855. Author of 'Posidonii Reliquiæ,' Leyden, 1810; 'Scholia Hypomnemata,' ib. 1837–52; and numerous books and pamphlets on political economy and Greek and Roman antiquities.

BALARD, Antoine Je'rome, French chemist, b. at Montpellier, Sept. 30, 1802; professor to the College Royal and School of Pharmacy, at Montpellier, 1826; professor of chemistry to the Faculty of Sciences; member of the Academy of Sciences, 1844; master of the conferences at the Normal School, 1849; appointed to the chair of chemistry at the College of France, 1851.

BALFE, Michael William, English composer, b. at Dublin, May 15, 1808; appeared in the Opera 'Freischütz,' 1824, at the Norwich Theatre; director of the Italian Opera in London, 1845; lessee of the English Opera House, 1839. Among his numerous operas are 'The Bohemian Girl,' 'The Daughter of St. Mark,' 'Satanella,' 'The Armourer of Nantes,' 'Blanche de Nevers,' and 'The Puritan's Daughter.'

BALFOUR, John Hutton, English botanist, b. 1802; graduated M.A. and M.D. at Edinburgh, 1831; professor of botany at the University of Glasgow; secretary to the Royal Society, Edinburgh. Author of 'Manual of Botany;' 'Phyto-Theology, or Botany and Religion;' 'The Plants of Scripture;' and other botanical works.

BALPOURIER, Adolphe Paul Emile, French painter, b. at Montmorency, August 11, 1816; studied law, and called to the bar at Paris. Exhibited, 1853–57, 'Views of Porezza;' 'Mazeppa;' 'Bois de Pins au bord de la Mer,' 1864; and many others.

BALLANTINE, William, English lawyer, b. 1808; called to the bar of the Inner Temple, 1834; made a Q.C. 1863.

BALTZER, Johan Baptist, German Catholic theologian, b. July 16, 1803, at Andernach on the Rhine; studied at the University of Bonn, under Professor Hermès, 1823 to 1827; professor of theology at Breslau, 1830–31; ecclesiastical examiner, 1844; and canon at Breslau, 1846. Author of 'Theological Letters,' 1844–53; and numerous other theological works.

BALTZER, Wilhelm Eduard, German Protestant theologian, b. at Hohenleine, Prussia, Oct. 24, 1814; studied theology at the Universities of Halle and Leipsic, 1834–38; Protestant minister of the town of Delitzch, 1840; resigned and went to Nordhausen, 1847; took part in the Parliament of Frankfort, 1848. Author of 'The New Prophets, Discourses on their Life, Character, and Importance,' Leipsic, 1853; and other theological works.

BALUFFI, Gaetano, Italian author, b. at Ancona, March 29, 1788; secretary to Pope Gregory XVI.; bishop of Imola, Sept. 21, 1846; cardinal, Dec. 1846. Published 'History of Religion in America,' Rome, 1848; 'The Divinity of the Church of Rome,' 1858.

BALZE, Jean E'tienne Paul, French painter, b. in Rome, Aug. 25, 1815; studied in Paris at the School of Fine Arts, 1831; and, under M. Ingres, executed 'The Combat between Fitz-James and Roderick Dhu, from the Lady of the Lake,' 1855; 'La Vindication de Saint Étienne,' 1861; and other paintings.

BANCROFT, George, American politician and historian, b. at Worcester, Massachusetts, Oct. 3, 1800; graduated with honours at Harvard College, 1817; studied at Göttingen and Berlin, 1818; tutor of Greek in Harvard College; collector at the Port of Boston, 1838 to 1841; democratic candidate for governor of the State of Massachusetts, 1844; administrator of the Navy Department, 1845; minister-plenipotentiary to Great Britain, 1846 to 1849. Author of 'History of the United States,' first vol. 1834, vol. viii. 1860; contributor to the *North American Review*, and other works.

BANVILLE, Theodore de, French poet, b. at Paris, 1820. Author of 'Les Nations,' an opera, 1851; 'The Cousin of the King,' 1857; 'Scenes of my Life,' 1859; and a great number of dramas in verse and prose.

BARAGUAY, D'Hilliers Achille, Comte de, French general, b. at Paris, Sept. 6, 1795; entered the army, 1807; became lieutenant, 1812; captain, 1814; captain of the Royal Guard, 1815; chief of a battalion, 1818; lieutenant-colonel, 1825; colonel, 1830; governor of the Military School of St. Cyr, 1833; maréchal de camp, Sept. 29, 1836; major-general, 1836; general of division, 1844; chief in command of troops in the third military division, 1851; vice-president of the Senate; ambassador of France to Constantinople, 1853–54; field-marshal, Aug. 28, 1854.

BARALT, Rafael Maria, American writer, b. at Maracaibo, Venezuela, at the beginning of the present century. Published 'History of Venezuela,' Paris, 1841; and other works.

BARATEAU, Emile, French writer, b. at Bordeaux, 1792; studied law at Paris; contributed to several literary journals; inspector of royal hospices in Spain; resigned and obtained a pension, 1830. Author of 'Georgine,' 1820; 'Bagatelles,' 1831; and other romances.

BARBARA, Louis Charles, French novelist, b. at Orleans, 1822; studied at the College of his native town, and at the College of Louis le Grand, Paris. Author of 'Revue de Paris,' 1854; 'Histoires émouvantes,' 1855; 'Ary Zang,' 1862; and other novels.

BARBAROUX, Charles Oze', French magistrate, b. at Marseilles, Aug. 16, 1792; studied at the Lyceum of Louis le Grand, and at l'École d'Aix; called to the bar of Nîmes, 1814; procureur-général at Pondichery, 1830; councillor of state, 1852; senator, Feb. 8, 1858. Author of 'History of the United States,' 1824; and other works.

BARBES, Armand, French politician, b. at Pointe à Pitre, Guadeloupe, Sept. 18, 1809; studied law at Paris; arrested for conspiring against the life of Louis Philippe, Aug. 1835; governor of the Luxembourg at the Revolution of 1848; represented the department of Aude at the Constituent Assembly, 1848; arrested and sentenced to imprisonment for life, 1849; liberated by order of the Emperor, 1854.

BARBEY D'AUREVILLY, Jules, French journalist and novelist, b. at St. Sauveur le Vicomtes, 1811. Author of 'L'Amour impossible,' 1841; 'Dix-neuvième Siècle, les Hommes et les Œuvres,' 1861–63; 'Le Chevalier Destouches,' 1864; and numerous works of fiction.

BARBIER, Henri Auguste, French writer, b. at Paris, April 28, 1805. Author of 'Les Mauvais Garçons,' 1830; 'Il Pianto et Lazare,' 1837; 'Rimes Héroiques,' 1843. Translated Shakespeare's 'Julius Ceasar' into French; and is the author of numerous satires.

BARBIER, Paul Jules, French dramatic writer, b. at Paris, 1822. Author of 'Le Poët,' 1847; 'Voyage autour d'une jolie femme,' 1852; 'La Reine de Saba,' 1862; 'La Fille d'Egypte,' 1862; 'Peines d'Amour perdues,' 1863; and numerous dramas.

BARCLAY, Alexander Charles, English politician, b. 1823; educated at Harrow, and Trinity College, Cambridge; returned M.P. for Taunton, 1865.

BARDELEBEN, Kurt Von, German politician, b. in Prussia, April 24, 1796; entered the army, 1813; married the daughter of President Anerswald, at Königsberg, 1819; deputy of the nobles to the provincial Diet, 1834; signed the petition addressed to the King Frederick William IV. 1840; envoy to the National Assembly at Frankfort, 1848.

BARDSLEY, Sir James Lomax, English physician, b. at Nottingham, 1801; graduated M.D. at Edinburgh, 1823; consulting physician to the Manchester Infirmary; fellow of the Royal College of Physicians, London; deputy-lieutenant and magistrate for the county of Lancaster. Author of articles in the *Cyclopædia of Practical Medicine*, and 'Hospital Facts and Observations,' 1837. Knighted, 1853.

BARGES, l'Abbe' Jean Joseph Le'andro, French philologist, b. at Auriol, Bouches du Rhône, Feb. 27, 1810; studied Arabic and Hebrew at Marseilles; ordained priest, 1834; professor of Arabic at Marseilles, 1837; and of Oriental languages at Paris,

1842; honorary canon of Notre-Dame, 1850. Author of 'Temple de Baal à Marseilles, Grand Phœnician Inscription,' 1847; and other works.

BARING, Hon. Alexander Hugh, English politician, b. 1835; educated at Harrow, and Christ Church, Oxford; graduated B.A. 1857; M.P. for Thetford since 1857.

BARING, Henry Bingham, English politician, b. 1804; educated at Christ Church, Oxford; graduated B.A. 1825; M.P. for Callington, 1831–32; lord of the Treasury, 1841–6; M.P. for Marlborough since 1832.

BARING, Hon. Thomas George, English politician, b. 1826; educated at Christ Church, Oxford; was a lord of the Admiralty, 1857–58; appointed under-secretary for India, 1859; under-secretary for war, Jan. 1861; re-appointed to India Office, July, 1861; M.P. for Penrhyn and Falmouth since 1857.

BARING, Thomas, English politician, b. 1800; educated at Winchester; M.P. for Yarmouth from 1835 to 1837; and for Huntingdon since 1844; offered the post of Chancellor of the Exchequer, which he declined, 1852 and 1858; one of the commissioners of the International Exhibition, 1862.

BARKLY, Sir Henry, English administrator, b. in London, 1815; studied law; M.P. for Leominster, 1845 to 1849; governor and commander-in-chief of British Guiana, 1849; governor of Jamaica, 1853–56; governor of Victoria, 1856; governor of the Mauritius, 1863; K.C.B. civil division, 1853.

BARNABO, Alexandro, Italian cardinal, b. at Foligno, March 2, 1801; held several offices in the Papal States, and elevated to the dignity of a cardinal priest, under the title of St. Susanna, 1856; prefect of the Sacred Congregation of the Propaganda.

BARNARD, Henry, American scholastic writer, b. at Hartford, Connecticut, United States, 1811; graduated at Yale College, 1830. Author of 'School Architecture;' 'Normal Schools in the United States, and in Europe;' 'Reports on Common Schools in Connecticut,' 1838–54; and other publications on the system of public schools.

BARNES, Rev. Albert, American theological writer, b. at Rome, State of New York, Dec. 1, 1798; studied theology at Princetown Seminary, and appointed minister of the first Presbyterian church in Philadelphia, 1830. Author of 'Commentaries on the New Testament, and on the Books of Job, Isaiah, and Daniel.'

BARNES, Thomas, English politician, b. 1813; is a magistrate and deputy-lieutenant for the county of Lancaster; M.P. for Bolton, 1852–57, and since 1861.

BARNES, Rev. William, English poet and philologist, b. at Rushhay, Bagber, Dorset, 1810; kept a school at Dorchester; curate of Whitcombe, Dorset, 1847; rector of Winterbourne Carne, 1862. Author of 'Poems of Rural Life in the Dorset Dialect;' 'A Philological Grammar:' 'Views of Labour and Gold;' 'A School-book of Geography and Ethnology;' and numerous philological and scholastic works.

BARNETT, Henry, English politician, b. 1815; is a magistrate and deputy-lieutenant for Oxon, and major of Oxfordshire yeomanry cavalry; M.P. for Woodstock, 1865.

BARNI, Jules Romain, French writer, b. at Lille, Nord, June 1, 1818; studied at the Royal College of Amiens; entered the École Normal, 1837; professor of philosophy at Rouen, 1851; professor of history and philosophy at the Academy of Geneva, 1861. Author of 'Observations on the Sentiment of the Beautiful and the Sublime,' 1846; 'Philosophy of Kant,' 1850; 'The Martyrs of Liberty of Thought,' 1862; and numerous metaphysical and critical works.

BAROCHE, Pierre Jules, French statesman, b. at Paris, Nov. 8, 1802, the son of a merchant; studied jurisprudence, and became advocate in 1823; nominated bâtonnier of the bar of Paris, 1846; elected deputy for Rochefort, 1847; deputy to the Constituent Assembly for the department of Charente-inférieure, 1848; appointed procureur-général of the Republic, 1849; minister of the Interior, 1850–51; minister of Foreign Affairs, April 10 to Oct. 14, 1851; appointed president of the Council of State and minister, 1861; nominated minister of Justice and keeper of the Great Seal—Garde des Sceaux—June 24, 1863.

BARON, Vincent Alfred, French actor and sculptor, b. at Trévoux, June 11, 1820; went to Paris, 1835; entered the School of Design and studied at the School of Fine Arts, 1837; as a sculptor, he exhibited in 1848 several medals and portraits, 'Samson,' 'Bauvalelt,' and many others; as an actor, he played in 'Le Courrier de Lyon,' 'Benvenuto Cellini,' and other pieces.

BARRAULT, Emile, French writer, b. at Paris, 1802; called to the bar, 1830; representative of Algeria in the Legislative Assembly, 1850. Author of ' Aux Artistes, du

Passé et de l'avenir des Beaux Arts,' 1830; 'History of the War of Mehemet-Ali in Syria and Asia Minor,' 1836; 'Le Christ,' 1864; and numerous religious, historical, and political works.

BARRIERE, Theodore, French dramatic writer, b. at Paris, 1823; assistant in the Ministry of War and Marine, 1834–43; devoted himself to dramatic literature; first piece, 'Rosière et Norrice,' played at the theatre of Beaumarchais and at the Palais Royal, 1842; 'Filles de Marbre,' 1853; 'Un Ménage en Ville,' 1864; and many other dramas.

BARRON, Sir Henry Winston, English politician, b. 1795; educated at Trinity College, Dublin; magistrate and deputy-lieutenant for the county of Waterford; was high sheriff, 1857; M.P. for Waterford, 1832 to 1852, and 1865.

BARROT, Camille Hyacinthe Odillon, French statesman, b. at Villefort, Lozère, July 19, 1791; studied law, called to the bar, and practised at the Court of Cassation from 1814 to 1831; entered the Chamber of Deputies, 1830; was prefect of the Seine, 1830-31. Published 'Centralization and its Effects,' 1861. Took part in the conferences held in Paris in favour of Poland, 1864.

BARROT, Ferdinand, French statesman, b. at Paris, Jan. 10, 1806; studied law, and called to the bar; member of the Chamber of Deputies, 1845; represented Algeria in the Constituent Assembly, 1848; secretary to Louis Napoleon when president, and acted as minister from Oct. 1849 to March, 1850; ambassador to Turin, 1850-51; senator and municipal councillor of Paris, 1864.

BARROT, Adolphe, French diplomatist, b. 1808, brother of the two preceding; envoy to Haïti; consul-general in Egypt, and minister of the Republic to Lisbon, 1830 to 1849; envoy to Naples, 1851-53; envoy extraordinary and minister plenipotentiary to Belgium, 1853, and ambassador to Madrid, 1858; senator, Oct. 5, 1864.

BARRY, Rev. Alfred, English theological writer, b. 1826; studied at King's College, London, and Trinity College, Cambridge; graduated B. A. 1848, and fellow, 1848; ordained, 1850; head master of the Grammar School at Leeds for eight years; principal of Cheltenham College, 1862. Author of 'Introduction to the Old Testament,' 'Notes on the Gospels.'

BARRY, Charles Robert, English politician, b. 1824; educated at Trinity College, Dublin; graduated B. A. 1845, M. A. 1863; called to the Irish bar, 1847; appointed law adviser to the Irish government, 1865; M.P. for Dungarvan, 1865.

BARRY, Edward, English architect, brother of preceding, b. 1830; standing architect to the Houses of Parliament; erected the New Grammar School at Leeds, and numerous other public buildings.

BARRY, François Bernard, French painter, b. at Marseilles, 1815; studied at Paris under M. T. Gudin. Exhibited 'Effet de brouillard,' 1840; 'Arrivée des eaux de la Méditerranée au lac Timsah,' 'Ceremony of Nov. 18, 1862,' 'Thebes,' 'Ruins of Karnac,' 'Chonna,' 'First Cataract of the Nile;' 1864, and numerous landscapes and marine paintings.

BARRY, George Richard, English politician, b. 1825; educated at the Royal College of Mauritius; a magistrate for the county of Cork; returned M.P. for county of Cork, 1865.

BARRY, Michael, English lawyer, b. 1810; educated in France, and at the Queen's University, Ireland, where he graduated D.L. 1860; called to the bar of Lincoln's Inn, 1859; appointed Queen's advocate at the Gold Coast, 1864.

BARRY, Sir Redmond, English administrator, b. 1813; educated at Trinity College, Dublin; called to the Irish bar, 1838; solicitor-general for the colony of Victoria, 1850; judge in the Supreme Court there, 1851; knighted, 1860; chancellor of the New University at Melbourne. Published a volume of essays and inaugural addresses.

BARTHELEMY, Auguste Marseille, French poet, b. at Marseilles, 1796; studied at the College of Juilly. Author of 'Les Adieux à Sidi-Mahmoud,' 1825; 'Napoléon en Egypte,' 1828; 'Constantine,' 1837; 'Nouvelle Némesis,' 1844–45; 'Les deux Marseilles,' 1858; and many other poems and political satires.

BARTHELEMY, SAINT HILAIRE, Jules, French author, b. in Paris, Aug. 19, 1805; member of the Institute; attached to the Ministry of Finance; appointed professor of Greek and Latin philosophy at the College of France, 1838; after the coup d'état of Dec. 2 refused to take the oath, and voluntarily quitted his chair in the College of France. Author of 'Politique d'Aristote,' 1838; 'La Logique d'Aristote,' 1839–44; 'Des Vedas,' 1854; 'Le Boudha et sa Religion, &c.' 1859; new edition, 1862; and many other philosophical works.

BARTLETT, John Russell, American ethnologist, b. at Providence, Rhode Island, Oct. 23, 1805; educated at New York and in different schools in Canada; founded the American Ethnological Society with A. Gallatine; secretary of state of Rhode Island. Author of 'Progress of Ethnology, &c.' 1847; 'Personal Narrative of Explorations and Incidents in Texas, New Mexico, California, in the years 1850–53–54.'

BARTTELOT, Walter Barttelot, English politician, b. 1820; educated at Rugby; magistrate and deputy-lieutenant for Sussex, and lieutenant-colonel of Sussex rifle volunteers; M.P. for West Sussex since 1860.

BASCLE DE LAGREZE, Gustave, French magistrate and archæologist, b. at Pau, Aug. 23, 1811; studied law at Paris, and called to the French bar, 1835; procureur-général at Pau, 1837; councillor at the Imperial Court in the same town, 1852. Author of 'Le Droit Criminal à l'usage des Jurés,' 1854; 'Antiquities of Béarn,' 1846; 'Histoire Religieuse de la Bigorre,' 1863; and other archæological works.

BASS, Michael Arthur, English politician, b. 1837; educated at Harrow and Trinity College, Cambridge; graduated B.A. 1860, M.A. 1863; is a magistrate for Stafford; M.P. for Stafford, 1865.

BASS, Michael Thomas, English politician, b. 1799; educated at Burton Grammar School; deputy-lieutenant for the counties of Stafford and Derby; M.P. for Derby since 1848.

BASSANO, Napoleon-Joseph-Hugues Maret, Duke of, French diplomatist, b. at Paris, July 3, 1803; entered the diplomatic service after the Revolution of July, 1830, as secretary to the ambassador at Brussels; accredited minister in the Grand Duchy of Baden, 1849, and in Belgium, 1851; senator, Dec. 31, 1852; grand chamberlain to the imperial palace.

BASSANVILLE, Anaïs Lebrun, Comtesse de, French authoress, b. 1806; founded *Le Moniteur des Dames et des Demoiselles* and *Le Dimanche des Familles.* Author of 'Aventures d'une Epingle,' 1845; 'Les Deux Familles,' 1859; 'La Chambre Rouge,' 1863; and other works.

BASTARD D'ESTANG, Henri-Bruno, Vicomte de, French magistrate, b. at Paris, Nov. 14, 1797; studied law and was called to the bar; procureur-général at Alençon, 1820; at Puy, 1822; at Nîmes, 1825; councillor of the Royal Court at Paris, 1833. Author of 'Recherches sur l'ancien duché pairie de Randan,' 1830; 'Parliament de Toulouse,' 1854; 'Les Parlements de France, Essai historique sur leur Usages, leur Organisation, &c.' 1858.

BASTIDE, Jules, French writer and politician, b. at Paris, Nov. 21, 1800; studied at Paris, and became editor of the *National* and the *Révue Nationale,* 1836 to 1847; secretary-general to the minister for foreign affairs, 1848; minister for foreign affairs, 1848. Author of 'Public Religion in France,' 1847; 'War of Religion in France,' 1859; and other works.

BASTIDE, Jenny Dufourquet, French authoress, b. at Rouen, July 8, 1792; has written under the double name of Jenny Bastide and Camille Bodin. Author of "La Belle Mère,' 1828; 'Les Mémoires d'un Confesseur,' 1845; 'Francine de Plainville,' 1850; and several dramas and works of fiction.

BATBIE, Anselme Polycarpe, French lawyer, b. at Seissan, May 31, 1828; auditor to the Council of State, 1849; LL.D. at Paris, 1850; charged with the reorganization of the Council of State, 1851; professor and examiner-in-law to the Faculty of Paris, 1862. Author of 'Treatise on the Theory and Practice of the Public Administration of Law,' 1863; and other legal works.

BATEMAN, Kate Josephine, American actress, b. at Baltimore, United States, 1842; first appeared as one of the 'Bateman Children' in London, 1851; studied for the stage, and re-appeared 1859; played at the leading American theatres, and in England the part of 'Leah,' and other tragedies.

BATES, Edward, American lawyer, b. at Goochland, Virginia, 1793; studied law at St. Louis, 1814; called to the bar, 1817; attorney-general in President Lincoln's Cabinet, 1861.

BATESON, Sir Thomas, English politician, b. 1819; is a deputy-lieutenant for the county of Londonderry; M.P. for Londonderry, 1844 to 1857; was a lord of the Treasury in 1852; M.P. for Devizes since 1864.

BATHURST, Allen Alexander, English politician, b. 1832; educated at Eton, and Trinity College, Cambridge; M.P. for Cirencester since 1857.

BATTAILLE, Charles Amable, French musical writer, b. at Nantes, Sept. 30, 1822; studied medicine at Caen, and obtained the diploma of M.D.; professor of singing at the Conservatoire, 1851. Author of 'Nouvelles Recherches sur la Phonation,' 1861; 'De la Physiologie appliquée à l'Étude du Mécanisme Vocal,' 1863.

BAUCHART, Alexander-Quentin, French politician, b. at Villiers-le-Sec, Aisne, Feb. 7, 1809; studied law, and was called to the bar at Laon; member of the Council-General at Aisne; member of the Constituent Assembly, 1848; after the coup d'état, Dec. 2, 1852, was made councillor of state.

BAUDRILLART, Henri-Joseph Le'on, French political economist, b. at Paris, Nov. 28, 1821; studied at the College of Bourbon. Author of 'Discours sur Voltaire,' 1844; 'Manual of Political Economy,' 1857; 'Publicistes Modernes,' 1862–63; and other works on political economy.

BAUER, Bruno, German Biblical critic, b. at Eisenburg, Saxe-Altenburg, Sept. 6, 1809; studied at the Schools and University of Berlin; doctor of theology, 1834; professor at Bonn, 1839. Author of 'Review of the Life of Jesus, by Strauss,' 1835; 'Review of Gospel History of John,' 1840; 'Review of Gospels, and History of their Origin,' 1850; and many other theological and critical works.

BAUER, Reinhard Edwin, German writer, b. at Walda, Saxony, July 7, 1816; studied theology at the University of Leipsic. Published 'Primitive Christianity,' 1846; 'Christianity of the Apostles,' 1847; 'Christianity of the Church,' 1848.

BAUERLE, Adolphe, German dramatic author, b. at Vienna, April 9, 1786; founded, 1808, the *Theatrical Journal of Vienna.* Author of 'Theresa Krones,' 1854–55; 'Ferdinand Raymond,' 1855; 'Director Karl,' 5 vols. 1856.

BAUERNFELD, Eduard, German poet and dramatic author, b. at Vienna, 1804; studied law; employed in the administration of the Austrian government, 1826. Author of 'Lustpiele,' 1833; 'Saemtliche Gedichte von Shakespeare,' 1827; 'Baron Ringelstern,' 1829; 'Ein Deutscher Krieger,' 1848; and other poems and dramas.

BAUMGARTNER, Karl Heinrich, German physician, b. at Pforzheim, Baden, Oct. 21, 1798; studied at the Universities of Tübingen and Heidelberg; graduated M.D. 1818; surgeon, 1820 to 1824; professor of medicine, University of Friburg; privy councillor of the Grand Duke of Baden. Published 'Elements of Physiology, Pathology, &c.' 1837, second edition 1842; 'New Treatment of Pneumonia,' 1850; and many other medical works.

BAUMGARTNER, Andre, Baron von, Austrian statesman, b. at Friedberg, Bohemia, Nov. 23, 1793; studied at the School of Linz, 1810, and at the University of Vienna; professor of medicine at Ollmütz, 1817; professor at University of Vienna, 1823; founded *Journal of Physics and Mathematics,* 1826; minister of public mines, 1848; minister of finances, and commissioner of the government, 1851; minister of commerce, 1855; member for life of the Upper Chamber of Austria.

BAUMGARTNER, Gallus Jacques, Swiss politician, b. at St. Gall, Oct. 18, 1797; studied law at the School of Fribourg; member of the Council of the Canton of St. Gall, 1825; contributed to the adoption of the Constitution of 1831; member of the Executive, 1832; retired, 1841; founded the *New Swiss Gazette,* 1843. Published 'Events on the Political Battle Field,' 1844.

BAUMSTARK, Eduard, German political economist, b. at Sinzheim, March 10, 1807; studied at the University of Heidelberg; professor at the University of Greifswald, 1838; professor and one of the directors of the Academy of Sciences, Eldena, 1840; head master, 1843; deputy to National Assembly of Prussia, 1848; nominated member of the First Chamber, 1849. Published 'On Taxes upon Income,' 1849; 'History of the Working Classes,' 1863.

BAUR, Ferdinand Christian, German Protestant theologian, b. June 21, 1792; professor at the Seminary of Blaubeuren, 1817; at the University of Tübingen, 1826. Published 'Symbolical, Mythological, and Natural Religion of Antiquity,' 1825; 'The Evangel of St. Mark, its Origin and Character,' 1851; and other theological works.

BAUTAIN, l'Abbe' Louis Eugenie Marie, French author, b. at Paris, Feb. 17, 1796; entered the École Normale, 1813; professor of theology at the College of Strasbourg, 1816; entered holy orders, and appointed professor of philosophy, and canon of Strasbourg cathedral, 1828. Author of 'Moral Philosophy,' 1842; 'Christians of our Time,' 1859; 'The Art of Public Speaking,' 1863.

BAVA, Jean Baptiste Euse'be, Baron de, Italian general, b. at Verceil, Aug. 1790; studied at the Military School of St. Cyr, and became lieutenant, 1814; captain and major, 1840; governor of the province of Alexandria, 1847; commanded a corps d'armée on the declaration of war with Austria, 1848; general, 1848; minister of war, 1849; inspector-general of infantry, 1852; organized the army for the expedition to Crimea, 1855.

BAXTER, William Edward, English politician, b. at Dundee, 1825; studied at Dundee, and at the University of Edinburgh; travelled in Europe and America; M.P. for Montrose since 1855. Author of 'Tagus and the Tiber,' 1848; 'America and the Americans,' 1850.

BAZA'INE, François Achille, French general, b. Feb. 13, 1811; studied in the École Polytechnique; entered the army, 1831; served in Africa, 1832; captain, 1839; lieutenant-colonel, 1848; commanded brigade of infantry in the East, 1853; general of division in the Crimea; inspector-general of infantry, 1856; commander of the French expedition to Mexico, 1862; marshal of France, Sept. 5, 1864.

BAZALGETTE, Joseph William, English civil engineer, b. 1819; engineer to the Metropolitan Commission of Sewers; engineer-in-chief to the Metropolitan Board of Works; designer of the Thames embankment from Westminster to Blackfriars Bridge, and of the new street from Blackfriars to the Mansion House.

BAZLEY, Thomas, English politician, b. at Hilton, near Bolton, 1797; educated at Bolton Grammar School; opened the free trade campaign at Liverpool with Cobden and Brooks, 1837; president of Manchester Chamber of Commerce from 1845 to 1859; one of the Royal Commissioners of Great Exhibition of 1851; M.P. for Manchester since 1858.

BEACH, Sir Michael Edward Hicks, English politician, b. 1837; educated at Eton, and Christ Church, Oxford; graduated B.A. 1858, and M.A. 1861; is a magistrate and deputy-lieutenant for Gloucestershire; retrned M.P. for East Gloucestershire, 1864.

BEACH, William Wither Bramston, English politician, b. 1826; educated at Eton, and Christ Church, Oxford; graduated B.A. 1849, and M.A. 1852; is a magistrate for Hants; M.P. for Hants since 1857.

BEAL, Rev. William, English author, b. 1815; educated at King's College, London, and Trinity College, Cambridge, where he graduated B.A.; vicar of Brooke, Norfolk, since 1847; LL.D. from the University of Aberdeen. Author of 'The Nineveh Monuments and the Old Testament;' 'A Letter to the Earl of Albemarle on Harvest Homes;' editor of *West of England Magazine.*

BEALE, Lionel, English physician, b. 1820; graduated M.B. at the University of London, 1851. Author of "The Microscope in its Application to Practical Medicine;' 'Anatomy of the Liver;' and other medical works.

BEAUCHAMP, Henry Lygon, Earl of, English politician, b. 1829; entered the army, 1843; M.P. for Worcestershire, 1853–63; deputy-lieutenant of Worcestershire, 1859; succeeded his father, fourth earl, 1863.

BEAUCHESNE, Alcide Hyacinthe Du Bois de, French writer, b. at Lorient, March 31, 1804; studied at Noyou and at Douai. Author of 'Poetical Souvenirs,' 1830; 'Louis XVII., his Life, Agony, and Death,' 1852, third edition 1861.

BEAUFORT-D'HAUTPOUL, Charles Marie Napoleon, French general, b. at Naples, 1804; studied at the Military School of St. Cyr, 1820–24; went with the expedition to Algeria, 1830; staff-major to Ibrahim Pasha, 1834–37; attaché of the embassy to Persia; served in Algeria, 1848; lieutenant-colonel and staff-major to General Pelissier, 1849; colonel, 1850; general of brigade, 1854; commander of the expedition to Syria, 1860.

BEAUMONT, Gustave Auguste de la Bonniniere de, French writer and politician, b. at Beaumont-le-Chartre, Feb. 16, 1802; called to the bar, 1824. Author of 'Traité du Système Pénitentiaire aux États-Unis, et de son Application à la France,' 1833; 'Ireland, its Social, Religious, and Political Condition,' two vols. 1839, seventh edition 1863.

BEAUMONT, Henry Frederick, English politician, b. 1833; educated at Eton, and Trinity College, Cambridge; a magistrate for the North Riding, and deputy-lieutenant for the West Riding, of Yorkshire; M.P. for South-west Riding of Yorkshire, 1865.

BEAUMONT, Joseph, English colonial judge, b. 1832; called to the bar at the Inner Temple, June, 1852; appointed chief justice of British Guiana, and judge of the Vice-Admiralty Court, April, 1863.

BEAUMONT, Wentworth Blackett, English politician, b. 1829; educated at Harrow, and Trinity College, Cambridge; deputy-lieutenant for Northumberland; M.P. for South Northumberland since 1852.

BEAUREGARD, Peter Gustav Toussaint, American general, b. at New Orleans, 1817; entered the Military Academy of West Point, 1833, and graduated, 1835; captain of engineers, 1853; superintendent of the Academy of West Point, 1854; resigned his commission in U.S. army, 1861, and joined the Confederate States; commanded the southern army at the battle of Bull Run, July, 1861; second in command at the battle of Shiloh, April 6, 1862; defended Charleston, 1863; surrendered with General Lee at the end of the civil war, 1865.

BEAUVAU, Charles Juste François Victurnien, Prince of Craon, French senator, b. at Haroué Meurthe, March 7, 1793; entered the army, 1810; officer of carabiniers in the campaign against Russia, 1812; nominated senator, and elected councillor-general of the Meurthe, 1852.

BEAVAN, Rev. James, English author, b. 1800; educated at St. Edmund's Hall, Oxford, and graduated B.A. 1824; successively curate of Leigh, Staffordshire, and vicar of Welford, Northamptonshire; professor of divinity at the University of Toronto, 1842. Author of 'An Account of the Life and Writings of St. Irenæus,' 1841.

BECHSTEIN, Ludwig, German writer, b. in the duchy of Saxe-Meiningen, Nov. 28, 1801. Author of 'Der Fürstentag,' 1834; 'Grumbach,' 1839; 'Philidor,' 1842; 'Wollen und Werden,' 1850; and other works of fiction.

BECK, Karl, German poet, b. at Baja, Hungary, 1817; studied medicine at the Universities of Vienna and Leipsic. Author of 'Night,' 1838; 'Songs of a Poor Man,' 1846; 'Saul,' a tragedy; and other works.

BECKER, Johan Philipp, German writer and politician, b. at Frankenthal, Bavaria, March 19, 1809. Author of 'History of the Revolution of May, 1849;' and several political works.

BECQUEREL, Antoine Ce'sar, French physician, b. at Chatillon sur Loing, Loiret, March 7, 1788; quitted the Polytechnic School as officer of engineers, 1808; served in Spain under General Suchet; inspector of the Polytechnic School, 1813; quitted the army, 1815; member of the Academy of Sciences, and professor of physics in the Museum of Natural History, Paris. Author of 'Treatise on Electricity and Magnetism,' 1834–40; 'Treatise on Electro-Chemistry;' and other works.

BECTIVE, Thomas, Earl of, English politician, b. 1822, eldest son of second Marquis of Headfort, in the peerage of Ireland; state-steward to Lord Eglinton when lord-lieutenant of Ireland, in 1852; high sheriff of Meath; M.P. for Westmoreland since 1854.

BEDFORD, Paul, English comedian, b. at Bath, 1798; first appearance in London, at Drury Lane, Nov. 2, 1824. Author of 'Recollections and Wanderings,' 1864.

BEECHER, Catherine Esther, American authoress, b. at East Hampton, Lower Illinois, 1800; educated at Lichfield, U.S.; principal of a school at Cincinnati. Author of 'Duty of American Women to their Country;' 'The True Remedy for the Wrongs of Women,' 1851; 'Common Sense applied to Religion,' 1857.

BEECHER, Rev. Charles, American theological writer, b. 1810; pastor of a church at Newark, New Jersey. Author of 'The Incarnation; or, Pictures of the Virgin and her Son,' 1849; 'Review of Spiritual Manifestations,' 1853; 'Pen Pictures of the Bible,' 1855; &c.

BEECHER, Rev. Edward, American writer, b. 1804; educated at Yale College, where he graduated, 1822; studied divinity at Andover, and New Haven; tutor in Yale College, 1825; pastor at Park Street Chapel, Boston, 1826 to 1831; president of Illinois College, Jacksonville, 1831 to 1844; pastor at Salem Street Church, Boston, 1846 to 1856; pastor of a church at Galesburg, Illinois. Author of 'Baptism; its Import and Modes;' 'The Conflict of Ages;' and other works.

BEECHER, Rev. Henry Ward, American writer and orator, b. at Lichfield, Connecticut, United States, 1813; graduated at Amherst College, 1834; studied theology at Lane Seminary; presbyterian minister at Laurenceburg, Indiana, 1837; removed to Indianapolis, 1839; pastor of Plymouth Church, Brooklyn, New York, 1847. Author of 'The Star Papers,' 1858; 'Life Thoughts,' 1858; and other works.

BEECROFT, George Skirrow, English politician, b. 1809; a magistrate and deputy, lieutenant for West Riding of Yorkshire; M.P. for Leeds since 1857.

BEGBIE, Matthew, English colonial judge, b. 1825; educated at St. Peter's College, Cambridge; called to the bar of Lincoln's Inn, Nov. 1844; appointed judge in British Columbia, Sept. 1858.

BEISLER, Hermann von, German politician, b. at Bensheim, 1790; served in the war of independence, 1813–15; minister of Justice of Bavaria, 1847, and minister of Public Instruction, 1848; member of the National Assembly at Frankfort, 1848; minister of the Interior, 1849; Bavarian councillor of state, and president of the Supreme Court.

BEKE, Charles Tilstone, English traveller, b. in London, Oct. 10, 1800; studied law at Lincoln's Inn; acting British Consul in Saxony, 1836 to 1838; secretary of the National Association for Protection of British Industry and Capital in London, 1849 to

1853. Author of 'An Essay on the Nile and its Tributaries,' 1847 ; 'On the Geographical Distribution of Languages in Abyssinia,' 1849 ; 'Sources of the Nile, with History of Nilotic Discovery,' 1860.

BEKKER, Emmanuel, German philologist, b. at Berlin, 1785 ; finished his studies at Halle ; professor of Greek literature at Berlin since 1807 ; member of the Berlin Academy of Sciences. Author of 'Attic Orators,' 1823 ; 'Sextus Empiricus,' 1842.

BELBEUF, Antoine Louis Pierre Joseph Godard, Marquis de, French statesman, b. at Rouen, Oct. 20, 1791 ; councillor-auditor to the Court at Paris, 1814 ; first president to the Court at Lyons, 1829 ; member of the Chamber of Peers, 1837 ; appointed senator, 1852.

BELCHER, Sir Edward, English navigator, b. 1799 ; entered the navy, 1812 ; present at the battle of Algiers ; assistant-surveyor to Captain Beechy in the *Blossom*, 1824 ; commander, 1829 ; in command of the *Etna*, 1830 ; commander of the *Terror* and *Erebus* for Arctic service, 1833 ; commander of the *Sulphur* from 1836 to 1842 ; knighted, 1843 ; captain of the *Samarang* in the East Indies, 1843-49 ; commanded the expedition in search of Sir John Franklin, 1852 to 1854 ; obtained flag rank, 1861. Author of several 'Narratives' descriptive of his voyages, of various nautical works, and of a sea romance entitled 'Horace Edward Brenton.'

BELCREDI, Count Richard, Austrian statesman, b. Feb. 12, 1823 ; president of the civil administration of Silesia, 1862-63 ; vice-president of the Bohemian government, 1863-64 ; governor of Bohemia, May 27, 1864, to July 27, 1865 ; appointed minister of state and president of the Council of Ministers, July 27, 1865.

BELGIOJOSO, Christine Trivulzio, Princess of, Italian authoress, b. at Milan, June 28, 1808 ; daughter of the Marquis of Trivulzio ; married to Prince Emile di Barbian e Belgiojoso, 1824. Author of 'Asia Minor and Syria,' 1858 ; 'Scenes in the Life of a Turk ;' and other works.

BELHAVEN and STENTON, Robert Montgomery Hamilton, Baron, Scottish statesman, b. at Wishaw-house, Lanark, 1793 ; commissioner of the General Assembly of the Church of Scotland ; obtained the title of Baron Hamilton and seat in the House of Lords, 1831 ; lord-lieutenant of the county of Lanark, 1863.

BELL, John, American politician, b. at Nashville, Tennessee, 1791 ; elected to the House of Congress, 1827 to 1841 ; senator, 1847 to 1859 ; candidate for the presidency of the United States, 1860.

BELL, Sir John, English general, b. at Bonytoun, Fife, 1782 ; entered the army, 1805 ; major-general and governor of Guernsey, 1848 to 1854 ; colonel, 1853 ; general, 1860 ; Knight of the Bath, 1860.

BELL, John, English sculptor, b. in Norfolk, 1812. Exhibited at the Royal Academy, 1832, 'Girl at a Brook ;' executed the 'Eagle Slayer,' 1837 ; 'The Child's own Attitude,' 1845 ; 'The Guards' Memorial,' 1860 ; and numerous other statues and works of sculpture.

BELL, Thomas, English naturalist, b. at Poole, Dorset, Oct. 11, 1792 ; entered Guy's Hospital, 1814 ; fellow of Linnæan Society, 1815 ; president of the Ray Society, 1859 ; professor of zoology at King's College, London, 1832 ; lecturer at Guy's Hospital from 1816 to 1880. Author of 'The Anatomy and Diseases of the Teeth ;' 'Natural History of British Reptiles ;' and other works on natural history.

BELLANGE, Joseph Louis Hippolyte, French historical painter, b. at Paris, Jan. 17, 1800. Exhibited 'The Battle of the Alma,' 1855 ; 'Two Friends,' 'Sebastopol,' 1855 ; and other paintings.

BELLET, Benjamin Louis, French writer, b. at Paris, Nov. 7, 1805. Author of 'Queen of France,' 1839 ; 'Le Timbre et l'Exposition Universel,' 1855 ; and other works.

BELLOWS, Rev. Henry Whitney, American author, b. at Boston, U.S. June 10, 1814 ; graduated at Harvard College, 1832 ; and at the University School of Cambridge, U.S. 1834 ; pastor of First Congregational Society, New York, 1838. Author of 'Defence of the Drama,' 1857 ; and other works.

BELMONTET, Louis, French poet and politician, b. at Montauban, March 26, 1799. Author of 'Les Tristes,' 1824 ; 'Le Souper d'Auguste,' 1828 ; 'Les Nombres d'or,' 1855 ; 'Le Luxe des Femmes et la Jeunesse de l'Epoque,' 1858 ; and other poems and political works.

BELMORE, Somerset Richard Lowry Corry, Earl of, English statesman, b. 1835 ; eldest son of the third Earl of Belmore, in the peerage of Ireland ; educated at Eton and Trinity College, Cambridge, and graduated M.A. 1856 ; elected representative peer of Ireland, 1857; under-secretary of state for the Home Department, July, 1866, to August, 1867; appointed governor of New South Wales, Australasia, Aug. 22, 1867.

BELPER, Right Hon. Edward Strutt, Lord, English statesman, b. 1801; educated at Trinity College, Cambridge, and graduated, 1823; M.P. for Derby, 1830; privy councillor, 1845; chief commissioner of railways, 1846 to 1848; M.P. for Arundel, 1851; M.P. for Nottingham, 1852; chancellor of the Duchy of Lancaster, 1852 to 1854; raised to the peerage, 1856.

BENDEMANN, Eduard, German painter, b. in Berlin, Dec. 3, 1811; professor at the Academy of Arts at Dresden, 1840; director of the Academy at Dusseldorf, 1860; executed 'The Grief of the Jews;' 'Jeremiah amidst the Ruins of Jerusalem,' 1837; fresco of 'Poetry and the Arts;' and many others.

BENEDEK, Louis, Austrian general; b. at Oldenburg, Hungary, 1804; entered the Austrian army as a cornet, 1822; colonel, 1843; brigadier-general, 1849; governor of Hungary, 1860; commander-in-chief of the Austrian army in Italy, 1864; commander-in-chief in the war against Prussia, 1866.

BENEDICT, Jules, English composer, b. at Stuttgart, Würtemberg, Nov. 27, 1804; produced his first English opera, 'The Gipsy's Warning,' 1838; accompanied Jenny Lind to America, 1850; composed 'The Lily of Killarney,' 1862; 'Richard Cœur de Lion,' 1863; 'St. Peter,' for the Norwich Festival, 1866.

BENFEY, Theodore, German philologist, b. at Nörthen, near Göttingen, Jan. 28, 1809; educated at Göttingen and Munich; professor of Sanscrit and comparative grammar at Göttingen, 1834. Author of 'The Names of the Months in use among Ancient Nations,' 1836; 'The Cruciform Inscriptions of Persia,' 1847; 'Handbook of the Sanscrit Tongue,' 1852–54; and other philological works.

BENNETT, William Sterndale, English composer, b. at Sheffield, 1816; studied at the Royal Academy of Music; professor of music at Cambridge, 1856. Composed 'Naiades;' 'The Merry Wives of Windsor;' 'Paradise and the Peri;' and many others.

BENNETT, Rev. William James Early, English theological writer, b. 1805; studied at Christ Church, Oxford, and graduated B.A. 1827; incumbent of Portman Chapel, and St. Paul's, Knightsbridge, till 1851; vicar of Frome. Author of 'Principles of the Book of Common Prayer;' 'Errors of Romanism;' 'Lives of the Fathers of the Church of the Fourth Century;' and other works.

BENNETT, William Cox, English poetical writer, b. at Greenwich, 1820. Author of 'War Songs,' 1855; 'Queen Eleanor's Vengeance, and other Poems,' 1857; 'The Worn Wedding Ring,' 1861; and other works.

BENSON, Sir John, English civil engineer, b in Sligo, 1812: architect of the Great Industrial Exhibition of Dublin, 1852. Knighted at the opening of the Exhibition.

BENTINCK, George Augustus Frederick Cavendish, English politician, b. 1821; educated at Westminster; called to the bar at Lincoln's Inn, 1846; M.P. for Taunton, 1859 to 1865; M.P. for Whitehaven, 1865.

BENTLEY, Robert, English botanist, b. 1820; member of the Royal College of Surgeons, 1847; professor of botany at King's College, London, and professor of materia medica and botany in the Pharmaceutical Society of Great Britain. Author of 'A Manual of Botany;' contributor to the *Pharmaceutical Journal.*

BENTON, Thomas Hart, American politician, b. in Orange county, North Carolina, 1783; advocate at Nashville, 1811; member of Congress, 1820 to 1851. Author of 'Thirty Years' Views, or a History of the Working of the American Government,' 1853; and other works.

BENYON, Richard, English politician, b. 1811; educated at Charterhouse, and St. John's College, Cambridge; graduated B.A. 1833, and M.A. 1835; called to the bar at Lincoln's Inn, 1837; is a magistrate and deputy-lieutenant for Berks; high sheriff, 1857; M.P. for Berkshire since 1860.

BERENGER, Alphonse Marie Marcellin Thomas, French magistrate, b. at Valence, May 31, 1785: president of the Court of Cassation, 1849; retired 1860. Author of 'De la Répression Pénale, ses Formes et ses Effets,' 1855.

BERESFORD, Dennis William Pack, English politician, b. 1818; educated at the Royal Military Academy, Woolwich; appointed second lieutenant, R.A. 1836; captain, 1846: retired, 1854; magistrate and deputy-lieutenant for the county of Carlow; high sheriff, 1856; M.P. for county of Carlow since 1862.

BERESFORD-HOPE, Alexander James, English politician, b. 1820; educated at Harrow, and Trinity College, Cambridge; graduated B.A. 1841, M.A. 1844; is a magistrate for Kent; M.P. for Maidstone, 1841–52 and 1857–59, and for Stoke-on-Trent, 1865–68; returned M.P. for Cambridge University, 1868.

BERESFORD, Right Hon. William, English politician, b. 1794; educated at Oxford, and graduated, 1819; served in the army, and attained the rank of major; M.P. for Harwich, 1841; M.P. for North Essex, 1847 to 1865; secretary of the War Department, 1852.

BERGHAUS, Heinrich, German geographer, b. at Cleves, May 3, 1797; studied engineering, and served as volunteer in the army of 1815; professor of mathematics at the Berlin School of Civil Engineering, 1824. Author of 'The Indians of North America,' 1848; and other geographical works.

BERGK, Theodore, German author, b. at Leipsic, May 22, 1812; professor of Latin at Halle, 1835; professor at Berlin, 1839, and at Cassel, 1840; professor of philosophy at Marbourg, 1842 to 1847; professor at Friebourg, 1852. Author of 'Anacreon,' 1834; 'Fragments of Aristophanes,' 1840; and several other works on classical literature.

BERIOT, Charles August de, Belgian violinist, b. at Louvain, Belgium, Feb. 20, 1802; studied at Paris; married Madame Malibran, 1836. Composed 'The Siege of Corinth,' and other concert pieces.

BERKELEY, Francis Henry Fitz-Hardinge, English politician, b. 1794, younger son of the fifth Earl of Berkeley; educated at Christ Church, Oxford; M.P. for Bristol since 1837.

BERKELEY, Hon. George Charles Grantly Fitz-Hardinge, English author, b. 1800; entered the Coldstream Guards, 1816, but retired from the service in 1821; M.P. for the Western Division of Gloucestershire, 1832 to 1847. Author of 'Berkeley Castle,' 1836; 'Love at the Lion;' and other works of fiction and miscellaneous writings.

BERKELEY, George, English colonial administrator, b. 1815; appointed colonial secretary and comptroller of customs, Honduras, 1845; lieutenant-governor of St. Vincent, April, 1864.

BERKELEY, Rev. Miles Joseph, English botanist, b. at Biggin, 1803; educated at Rugby, and Christ's College, Cambridge; graduated, 1825; incumbent of two parishes near Wansford, Northamptonshire, and rural dean for Oundle and Weldon, 1833. Author of 'English Flora,' 1836; 'Antarctic and New Zealand Flora,' 1860.

BERNARD, Aristide Martin, French politician, b. at Montbrison, Loire, Sept. 17, 1808; fought at the barricades, and condemned to deportation, May, 1839; liberated, 1848; refugee in Switzerland after 1849. Author of 'Dix Ans de Prison au Mont St. Michel, et à la Citadelle de Doullens,' 1854.

BERNARD, Claude, French physician, b. at St. Julien, near Villefranche, July 12, 1813; studied in Paris; M.D. 1843; elected to the Academy of Sciences, 1855; professor of experimental physiology at the Paris University, 1856. Author of 'Lessons on Physiology, experimental and applicable to Medicine,' 1855; and other medical works.

BERNARD, Hon. Henry Boyle, English politician, b. 1812; magistrate and deputy-lieutenant for county of Cork, and colonel of South Cork light infantry; M.P. for Bandon since 1863.

BERNARD, William Bayle, American dramatist, b. at Boston, United States, 1808. Author of 'The Nervous Man and the Man of Nerve;' 'His Last Legs;' and other dramas.

BERNERS, Right Hon. Henry William Wilson, Baron, English agriculturist, b. 1797; educated at Eton, and Emmanuel College, Cambridge; succeeded to the title, 1851; magistrate and deputy-lieutenant for Leicestershire; president of the Royal Agricultural Society of England, 1859, and of Smithfield Club, 1860, 1861.

BERNHARD, Karl Saint Aubin, Danish novelist, b. early in the present century. Author of 'The Chronicles of the Times of King Eric of Pomerania,' 1850; 'Christian VII. and his Court,' 1847; and other works of fiction.

BERNSTORFF, Arthur, Count von, Prussian diplomatist, b. at Berlin, Feb. 21, 1808; entered the diplomatic service, 1831; took part in the conference of London on Dano-German question, 1864; ambassador from the court of Prussia to Great Britain.

BERRYER, Pierre Antoine, French lawyer and politician, b. at Paris, Jan. 4, 1790; studied for the bar; deputy for the department of Haute Loire, 1830: member of the French Academy, 1855; defended Count Montalembert, 1858; elected to the Corps Législatif, 1863.

BERTHOUD, Samuel Henri, French writer, b. Jan. 19, 1804. Author of 'Contes Misanthropiques,' 1831 ; 'La Mare du Diable,' 1847 ; 'Zéphyr d' El-Arouch,' 1850 ; and other works.

BERTRAND, Joseph Louis François, French mathematician, b. at Paris, 1822 ; studied at the College of St. Louis and the Polytechnic School ; professor at the Lycée, St. Louis, 1850 ; professor of physics and mathematics at the College of France, 1862. Author of 'Treatise on Algebra,' and other works.

BERWICK, William Noel, Baron, English officer, b. 1802 ; entered the army, 1817, and served chiefly in India ; retired from service with the grade of colonel, 1855 ; succeeded his brother, fifth baron, in the title and seat in House of Lords, 1861 ; deputy-lieutenant of Shropshire, 1852.

BESSBOROUGH, John George Brabazon Ponsonby, Earl, English diplomatist, b. in London, 1809 ; studied at Trinity College, Cambridge ; entered House of Commons, 1831 ; ambassador at St. Petersburg, 1833 ; succeeded his father, fourth earl, in the title and seat in the House of Lords, 1847 ; lord-lieutenant of Carlow, 1838 ; master of the buckhounds to the Queen, 1859.

BEUST, Friederich Ferdinand, Baron von, Austrian statesman, b. at Dresden, Jan. 13, 1809 ; educated for the diplomatic career ; secretary of Legation for Saxony in England, 1836–38 ; in France, 1838–41 ; in Bavaria, 1848 ; minister of Foreign Affairs of the kingdom of Saxony, Feb. 1849 till Sept. 1866 ; appointed minister of Foreign Affairs of the Austrian monarchy, Oct. 30, 1866 ; president of the Council of Ministers, Feb. 24, 1867 ; invested, by decree of the Emperor, with the title of Reichskanzler, or chancellor of the empire, July 1, 1867.

BIARD, François Auguste, French painter, b. at Lyons, June 27, 1800 ; studied in the Academy of Fine Arts ; exhibited 'Arabian overtaken by the Simoon in the Desert,' 1833 ; 'The Sequel of a Masquerade ;' 'Slave Market on the Gold Coast ;' 'Combat of the Polar Bears ;' and other paintings.

BIBER, Rev. George Edward, English author, b. 1801 ; educated in Germany ; Ph.D. of Tübingen, and LL.D. of Göttingen ; naturalized in England, 1839, and admitted to holy orders in the Church of England. Author of 'Memoir of Henry Pestalozzi, and his Plan of Education ;' 'Bishop Blomfield and his Times ;' and other works.

BIBESCO, George Demetrius, Roumanian statesman, b. at Craïova, 1804 ; educated at Bucharest and Paris, 1817 to 1824 ; under-secretary of state in Wallachia, 1830 ; secretary of General Assembly, 1841 ; hospodar of Wallachia, 1843 ; resigned and retired to Vienna, 1848.

BICKERSTETH, Ven. Edward, English theological writer, b. at Acton, Suffolk, 1814 ; studied at Cambridge, and graduated B.A. 1832 ; studied theology at Durham University, and ordained 1839 ; vicar of Aylesbury, and archdeacon of Buckingham, 1853. Author of 'God's Judgments in India ; a Warning to England ;' and other works.

BIDDER, George Parkes, English civil engineer, b. 1800 ; one of the engineers of the Blackwall Railway, and the Electric Telegraph Company ; president of the Institution of Civil Engineers, 1860–61.

BIDDULPH, Michael, English politician, b. 1834 ; educated at Harrow ; magistrate and deputy-lieutenant for the county of Hereford ; M.P. for Herefordshire, 1865.

BIDDULPH, Robert Myddleton, English politician, b. 1805 ; educated at Eton, and Christ Church, Oxford ; lord lieutenant of Denbigh, and colonel of Denbigh militia ; M.P. for Denbigh, 1830–32 ; M.P. for Denbighshire, 1832–34, and since 1852.

BIEDERMANN, Friederich Karl, German philosopher and politician, b. Sept. 25, 1812 ; professor of philosophy at the University of Leipsic, 1838. Author of 'Fundamental Philosophy,' 1837 ; 'The German Parliament,' 1848 ; and several political and philosophical works.

BIGSBY, Robert, English writer, b. at Nottingham, 1806. Author of 'Visions of the Times of Old, or the Antiquarian Enthusiast,' 1848 ; 'Ombo,' 1853. Has a literary pension of 100l. a year.

BILLING, Archibald, English physician, b. in Ireland, 1791 ; educated at Trinity College, Dublin, and Oxford ; fellow of the Royal College of Physicians, London, 1818 ; physician of London Hospital from 1817 to 1836 ; member of the senate of London University, and examiner for degrees in medicine. Author of 'First Principles of Medicine,' and other medical works.

BINGHAM, Lord George, English politician, b. 1830 ; educated at Rugby ; appointed captain and lieutenant-colonel of Coldstream Guards, 1859 ; retired, 1860 ; was aide-de-camp to his father in the Eastern expedition, 1854 ; returned M.P. for the county of Mayo, 1865.

BINNEY, Rev. Thomas, English theological writer, b. at Newcastle-on-Tyne, 1799; educated at Wymondley College; minister of Independent Chapel at Newport, Isle of Wight, 1825; pastor of Weigh House Chapel, Fish Street Hill, London, 1829. Author of 'Dissent not Schism;' 'The Closet and the Church;' and other writings.

BIRCH, Rev. Henry Mildred, English clergyman, b. 1820; educated at Eton. and King's College, Cambridge, and graduated B.A. 1843; assistant-master at Eton, 1845 to 1851; took holy orders, and became rector of Prestwich, near Manchester, 1852; chaplain to the Queen and to the Prince of Wales.

BIRCH, Samuel, English author, b. in London, Nov. 3, 1813; educated at Greenwich, Blackheath, and Merchant Taylors' School, 1831; commissioner of Public Records, 1834; keeper of Oriental, Mediæval, and British Antiquities in the British Museum, 1861. Author of 'History of Ancient Pottery,' 1857; 'Papyrus of Naskhem,' 1863; and other antiquarian works.

BIRKS, Rev. Thomas Rawson, English author, b. Sept. 1810; graduated at Trinity College, Cambridge; rector of Kelshall, Herts, 1844. Author of 'First Elements of Prophecy;' 'Modern Astronomy;' 'Treasures of Wisdom;' and other works.

BISCHOFF, Theodore Louis Wilhelm, German anatomist, b. at Hanover, Oct. 28, 1807; studied at Dusseldorf, Bonn, and Heidelberg; graduated Ph.D. 1829, and M.D. 1832; professor of anatomy at Munich, 1854.

BISMARCK-SCHONHAUSEN, Count Otto von, German statesman, b. 1813, the son of a landowner in Saxony; studied jurisprudence at Berlin and Göttingen; elected member of the German Constituent Assembly, 1848; Prussian minister pleni-potentiary at the Diet of Frankfort, 1851–59; ambassador to the Court of St. Peters-burg, 1859–62; ambassador to the Emperor of the French, May, 1862; Prussian minister of Foreign Affairs, and chief of the Cabinet, Sept. 28, 1862; chancellor of the North German Confederation, July 14, 1867.

BLAAUW, William Henry, English antiquarian, b. 1793; educated at Eton, and Christ Church, Oxford, and graduated, 1813; magistrate and deputy-lieutenant for Sussex. Author of 'The Baron's War,' 1844; and other works.

BLACKALL, Samuel Wensley, English colonial administrator, b. 1820; M.P. for the county of Longford, 1847 to 1851; lieutenant-governor of Dominica, 1851 to 1857; governor of Sierra Leone, 1862.

BLACKBURN, Sir Colin, English judge, b. 1813; educated at Eton, and Trinity College, Cambridge, and graduated B.A. 1835; called to the bar of the Middle Temple; puisne judge of Queen's Bench, 1859.

BLACKIE, John Stuart, English author, b. at Glasgow, July, 1809; educated at Aberdeen and Edinburgh, Göttingen, Berlin, and Rome; professor of Greek in the University of Oxford. Author of translation of 'Faust,' 1834; 'Poems in English and Latin,' 1860; and other poetical works.

BLACKLEY Rev. William, English writer, b. 1813; educated at St. John's College, Cambridge, and graduated B.A. 1835; vicar of Stanton-on-Hine, Heath, Shropshire, 1855. Editor of 'Diplomatic Correspondence of the Right Hon. Richard Hill,' 1845.

BLAIR, Montgomery, American statesman, b. 1812; educated at West Point, New York; studied law at St. Louis; secretary of the navy, 1861; postmaster-general, 1863–64.

BLAKE, John Aloysius, English politician, b. 1826; educated at Waterford and at Pau, France; formerly a merchant in Waterford; mayor, 1855–6–7, and president of the Chamber of Commerce, 1858–59; M.P. for Waterford since 1857.

BLANC, Louis, French author and politician, b. at Madrid, Oct. 28, 1813; founded the *Revue du Progrès*, 1838; member of the Provisional Government of France, 1848; one of the representatives of Paris to the National Assembly, 1848; went into exile to England, 1849. Author of 'Histoire des Dix Ans, 1830–40,' 4 vols. Paris, 1841; 'Histoire de la Révolution française,' 10 vols. ib. 1852–62; 'Lettres sur l'Angleterre,' 2 vols. 1866–67; and numerous other historical and political works.

BLAND, Rev. Miles, English writer, b. 1786; educated at St. John's College, Cam-bridge, and graduated B.A. 1808; rector of Lilley, Herts, 1823; prebend of Wells cathe-dral, 1826. Author of 'Algebra;' 'The Elements of Hydrostatics;' 'Mechanical and Philosophical Problems;' and other elementary works.

BLAND, William, English writer, b. Jan. 21, 1788; educated at Caius College, Cambridge, and at the University of Edinburgh. Author of 'Principles of Agriculture,' 1827; 'Ex-perimental Essays on the Principles of Construction in Arches, Piers, and Buttresses,' 1862.

BLENNERHASSET, Sir Rowland, English politician, b. 1839; educated at Stonyhurst, and Christ Church, Oxford; a magistrate for the county of Kerry; M.P. for Galway since 1865.

BLIGH, Hon. Sir John Duncan, English diplomatist, b. 1798; educated at Eton, and Christ Church, Oxford, and graduated B.A. 1818; entered the diplomatic service as attaché at Vienna, 1820; envoy extraordinary and minister plenipotentiary to Stockholm, 1835; minister plenipotentiary to Hanover, 1838–56.

BLOOMFIELD, Right Hon. John Arthur Douglas, Lord, English diplomatist, b. 1802; entered the diplomatic service, 1818; envoy extraordinary and minister plenipotentiary to St. Petersburg, 1844; to Berlin, 1851; ambassador at Vienna, 1860.

BLUHME, Christian Albert, Danish statesman, b. at Copenhagen, Dec. 27, 1794; judge of the Court of Appeal, 1822; minister for the Colonies, 1823 to 1825; director-general of Customs, 1843; minister of the Interior, 1851; president of the Council of Ministers, 1852–53; minister of Foreign Affairs, and president of the Council of Ministers, July, 1864, to Sept. 1865.

BODE, Rev. John Ernest, English writer, b. 1816; educated at Eton, Charterhouse, and Christ Church, Oxford; graduated B.A. 1837; rector of Castle Camps, Cambridgeshire. Author of 'Ballads from Herodotus,' and other works.

BOETTCHER, Adolf, German writer, b. at Leipsic, May 21, 1815. Author of 'On the Watch Tower,' 1847; 'The Pilgrimage of the Flower Spirits,' 1851. Translated the poems of Shakespeare, Byron, Pope, 1842; Milton, 1846; Ossian, 1847; and many others, into German.

BOETTIGER, Karl Wilhelm, German historian, b. at Bautzen, Aug. 15, 1790; studied at Weimar, Gotha, Leipsic, and Göttingen; professor at the University of Leipsic, 1819; professor of literature and history at the University of Erlangen. Author of 'Universal History,' 1849; 'History of Germany and the Germans,' 1845; and many other historical works.

BOGARDUS, James, American inventor, b. at Catskill, New York, March 14, 1800; apprenticed to a watchmaker, 1814; invented the 'King Flyer,' for cotton-spinning, 1828; a 'Dry Gas-meter,' 1832; an 'Engraving Machine,' 1836; a 'Machine for Pressing Glass,' about 1840; and made many other mechanical improvements.

BONAPARTE, Prince Louis Lucien, English philologist, b. in Worcestershire, Jan. 4, 1813; second son of Lucien, brother of Napoleon I.; entered France after the Revolution of 1848; returned deputy to the Constituent Assembly for Corsica, 1849; French senator, Dec. 1852. Published, at his own press, in Bayswater, London, several works in the Basque language; the 'Parable of the Sower,' in seventy-two European languages and dialects; and numerous other philological works.

BOND, William Cranch, American astronomer, b. at Portland, Maine, 1789; one of the earliest American discoverers of the comet of 1811; astronomical observer to Harvard College, 1840. Author of parts of 'Annals of the Observatory of Harvard College,' for 1855–66.

BONHAM, Sir Samuel George, English colonial administrator, b. 1803; was governor of Prince of Wales Island, Singapore, and Malacca, 1837–47; governor and commander-in-chief of Hong Kong and its dependencies, and plenipotentiary and chief superintendent of British trade in China, from March, 1848, to April, 1854; created a baronet, Nov. 22, 1852.

BONHEUR, Rosa, French animal painter, b. at Bordeaux, March 22, 1822; painted 'Chèvres et Moutons,' 1839; 'Labourage Nivernais,' 1849; 'Horse Fair,' at the French Exhibition of pictures in London, 1855; 'Haymaking Season in Auvergne,' 1855; and numerous other pictures of the same class.

BONHEUR, Auguste, French painter, b. at Bordeaux, Nov. 4, 1824, brother of the preceding; painted 'Les Enfants aux Hannetons,' 1845; 'Souvenir de la basse Bretagne,' 1857; 'Le Combat, la Mer, le Ruisseau,' 1863; and other paintings.

BONHEUR, Jules, Isidore, French sculptor, b. at Bordeaux, May 15, 1827; brother of the preceding; executed 'Le Combat d'une Lionese et d'un Cavalier Africain;' 'Hercule et les Chevaux de Diomède,' 1855; 'Zèbre et la Panthère,' 1853; 'Enfants et Chiens;' 'Un Jockey,' 1864.

BONJEAN, Louis Bernard, French politician, b. at Valence, Drôme, Dec. 4, 1804; called to the bar; LL.D. 1830; advocate-general to the Court of Cassation, 1850; senator, 1855; member of the Council of Education.

BONNECHOSE, François Paul Emile-Boisnormand de, French writer, b. at Leyerdorp, in Holland, Aug. 18, 1801; librarian at the Palace of St. Cloud, 1829. Author of 'Rosemonde,' 1826;' 'Histoire de France,' tenth edition 1855; and other works.

BONOMI, Joseph, English traveller and writer, b. in London, 1796 ; studied anatomy and sculpture at the Royal Academy. Author of 'Nineveh and its Palaces,' third edition 1857 ; 'Egypt, Nubia, and Ethiopia,' 1862 ; and other works.

BOOTH, George Sclater, English politician, b. 1826 ; educated at Winchester, and Balliol College, Oxford ; graduated B.A. 1847, M.A. 1849 ; called to the bar of the Inner Temple, 1851 ; magistrate for Hants, and lieutenant of Hants yeomanry ; M.P. for Hants since 1857.

BOOTH, James, American chemist, b. 1810 ; professor of applied chemistry in Franklin Institute ; melter and refiner in the United States mint, Philadelphia. Published 'Encyclopædia of Chemistry, Practical, Theoretical, &c.' 1850 ; 'Recent Improvements in the Chemical Arts,' 1851.

BOOTH Rev. James, English writer, b. 1814 ; graduated in honours at Trinity College, Dublin ; rector of Stone, near Aylesbury, 1859 ; magistrate for the county of Bucks. Author of 'New Method of Tangential Co-ordinates ;' 'Examination of the Province of the State,' 1846.

BOOTH, Sir Robert Gore, Bart. English politician, b. 1805 ; educated at Westminster, and at Queen's College, Cambridge ; graduated M.A. 1826 ; M.P. for Sligo since 1850.

BORGES DE CASTRO, Jose Ferreira, Portuguese diplomatist, b. at Porto, Oct. 3, 1825 ; attaché in Russia 1841, at Berlin 1844, at Rome 1847 ; secretary at Madrid, 1851 ; chargé d'affaires at Turin, 1860. Published 'Colleccao dos Tradados, Convenços, &c.' 1856.

BORROW, George, English writer, b. at East Dereham, Norfolk, 1803 ; articled to a solicitor, 1818 ; entered the service of the British and Foreign Bible Society, 1833. Edited at St. Petersburg the New Testament in Mandchu, or Chinese-Tartar ; twice imprisoned in Spain for circulating the Scriptures. Published 'Zincali,' 1841 ; 'The Bible in Spain,' 1842 ; 'Lavengro,' 1851 ; 'The Romany Rye,' 1857 ; and numerous other works.

BORSINI, Lorenzo, Italian poet, b. at Sienne, 1800 ; D.D. 1819 ; studied law ; advocate at Rome, 1823. Author of 'Sentimental Voyage,' 1842 ; 'Le mie Prigioni in Sicilia,' 1841 ; 'L'Asino,' 1844 ; 'Novissimo Galateo,' 1851 ; and other poems.

BOSWORTH, Rev. Joseph, English philologist, b. in Derbyshire, 1790 ; graduated at Aberdeen ; M.A. LL.D. and Ph.D. at Leyden, 1831 ; D.D. 1839 ; professor of Anglo-Saxon at Oxford ; rector of Water-Stratford, near Buckingham, 1858. Author of 'Elements of Anglo-Saxon Grammar,' 1823 ; 'Anglo-Saxon Dictionary,' 1848 ; and other philological works.

BOTTA, Paul Emile, French archæologist and traveller, b. 1805 ; French consul at Alexandria and Mosul. Author of 'Excavations at Khorsabad,' 1843 ; 'Inscriptions discovered at Khorsabad,' 1848.

BOUCHER DE CREVECOUR DE PERTHES, Jacques, French writer, b. at Rethel, Sept. 10, 1788. Author of 'Voyage to Constantinople and Greece,' 1856 ; 'Voyage to Russia,' 1859 ; 'Les Maussades, Complaintes,' 1862 ; 'Sous dix Rois, Souvenirs de 1791 à 1860,' 1864 ; and other miscellaneous works ; also published accounts of his archæological discoveries at Abbeville.

BOUCICAULT, Dion, English actor and dramatic author, b. in Dublin, Dec. 26, 1820. Author of 'London Assurance ;' 'Colleen Bawn ;' 'The Octoroon ;' 'The Vampire ;' and many other dramas.

BOUDET, Paul, French statesman, b. at Laval, Mayence, Nov. 13, 1800 ; called to the bar at Paris, 1821 ; represented the College of Laval at the Chamber of Deputies, 1834 to 1848 ; minister of the interior, June 28, 1863 ; senator, March 31, 1865 ; secretary of the Senate ; member of the Council General of Mayence.

BOUET-WILLAUMEZ, Count Louis Edouard, French naval commander, b. April 24, 1808 ; admitted to the naval service, 1823 ; ensign, 1829 ; lieutenant, 1835 ; captain, Sept. 17, 1844 ; rear-admiral, Aug. 12, 1854 ; took part in the Crimean expedition under Admiral Hamelin ; prefect-maritime of Cherbourg ; prefect-maritime of Toulon, March 4, 1861 ; vice-admiral, July 9, 1860.

BOUGENEL, Jean François, French military commander, b. at Paris, May 16, 1786 ; attaché to the Prince of Neufchâtel, 1806 ; officer of ordnance in campaigns, 1813, and prisoner in Russia ; took part in the battle of Waterloo ; lieutenant-colonel, 1827 ; colonel of 6th Lancers, 1830 ; field-marshal, 1838 ; lieutenant-general, Dec. 28, 1846 ; staff-major-general of reserve, 1851.

BOUILLIER, Francisque, French philosopher, b. at Lyons, July 12, 1813 ; studied at Paris and Lyons, 1834–37 ; professor of philosophy at Orleans ; president of the

Imperial Academy of Lyons, 1856. Author of 'Histoire et Critique du Cartesianisme,' Paris, 1842; 'Du Principe vital et de l'Ame pensante, ou Examen des diverses Doctrines spéciales et psychologiques, &c.' 1862; and several translations from the German of Kant and Fichte.

BOUISSON, François, French physician, b. at Manguis, Hérault, 1813; studied medicine at Montpellier and Delpech; professor of surgery to the Faculty of Strasbourg, 1837; professor of pathology and surgery at Montpellier, 1840; professor of surgery to the Faculty of Medicine at Paris, 1851; chief surgeon at the civil and military hospital of Saint Eloi de Montpellier, 1845. Published 'De la Bile, de ses Variations physiologiques, de ses Alterations morbides,' Montpellier, 1843; and many other medical works

BOULANGER, Gustave Rodolphe Clarence, French painter, b. in Paris, April 25, 1824; studied under P. Delaroche, in the School of Fine Arts. Painted 'Jules César arrivé au Rubicon,' 'La Maison du Poet tragique à Pompeii,' 1857; an 'Arab,' 1861; 'Jules César à la tête de la dixième Légion,' 'Cavaliers Sahariens,' 1864; and many other historical pictures.

BOULANGER, Henri Alexandre Ernest, French composer, b. at Paris, Dec. 16, 1815; educated at the Conservatoire of Paris under Lesneur and Halévy. Composed 'Le Diable à l'Ecole,' 1842; 'Les Sabots de la Marquise,' 1854; and other comic operas.

BOULANGER, Louis, French painter, b. at Verceil, Piedmont, March 11, 1806; studied under Guillon, Lethière, and Ach; appointed director of the Imperial School of Fine Arts at Dijon, 1860. Exhibited 'Mazeppe, le Depart,' 1828; 'Le Triomphe de Petrarque,' 1836; 'Les Georgiques de Virgile,' 'Le Marchand de Lacets,' 1863; and numerous portraits.

BOULATIGNIER, Sebastien Joseph, French politician, b. at Valognes, Manche, Jan. 11, 1805; studied law at Paris; chief of the bureau to the ministry of the interior, 1837; elected representative of the department of the Manche, councillor of state, 1849.

BOULAY, De La Meurthe, François Joseph, French statesman, b. in Paris, 1800; councillor of state, 1837; vice-president of the Republic, 1848; president of the Committee of the Interior for Public Instruction, 1855; entered the Senate, June 9, 1857.

BOULE, Louis Auguste De'sire', French dramatic writer, b. Sept. 1, 1799. Author of 'Les 20,000 Francs,' 1832; 'L'Honneur de Mamère,' 1837; 'Les Ruines de Vaudemont,' 1845; 'Les Œuvres du Démon,' 1854; and other dramas.

BOULET, Jean Baptiste Etienne, French lawyer, b. at Metz, Feb. 4, 1804; studied law and was called to the bar of the Royal Court of Paris. Published 'Ferrière moderne, ou nouveau Dictionnaire des Termes de Droit et de Pratique,' 1824; 'Sur l'Affranchissement des Colleges communaux,' 1852.

BOULLE'E, Anne Auguste, French historian, b. at Bourg, Ain, Nov. 4, 1795; studied law, and became a magistrate in his native town, 1821; procureur du roi at Bergerac, 1823, and at Mâcon, 1826; resigned, 1830. Published 'Histoire de France pendant la dernière Année de la Restauration,' 1839; 'Histoire complète des États Généraux et autres Assemblées Représentatives de la France depuis 1802 jusqu'en 1826,' Paris, 1845; and other historical works.

BOUQUET, Charles Jean Claude, French mathematician, b. Dec. 7, 1819; admitted to the École Polytechnique, 1839; appointed professor of mathematics at the Royal College of Marseilles, 1841; to the Faculty of Sciences at Lyons, from 1845 to 1852; professor in Paris at the Lycée Bonaparte, and at the Lycée Louis le Grand. Author of 'Sur le Calcul des Variations,' 1841, and of numerous essays and contributions to the *Journal de Mathématiques.*

BOURASSE, l'Abbe' Jean Jacques, French author, b. at St. Maure, Dec. 22, 1813; studied at the Seminary of Tours; professor at Tours, and appointed titular canon of the cathedral of that town in 1843. Author of 'Histoire Naturelle des Oiseaux, des Reptiles et des Poissons,' Tours, 1840; 'Histoire de notre Seigneur Jésus-Christ,' 1861; and numerous archæological and theological works.

BOURBAKY, Charles Denis Santer, French military commander, b. at Paris, April 22, 1816; lieutenant of the Zouaves, 1836; captain, June, 1842; chief of a battalion, 1846; lieutenant-colonel, Jan. 1850; colonel, Dec. 1851; general of brigade, Oct. 14, 1854; general of division, Aug. 12, 1857; took part in the Crimean campaign, and the expedition to Italy in 1859.

BOURBEAU, Louis Oliver, French lawyer, b. at Poitiers, March 2, 1811; studied law, and was called to the bar at Poitiers; elected mayor of Poitiers, 1847; represented

Vienne at the Assemblée Constituante, 1848 ; professor to the Faculty of Law at Poitiers, 1841. Author of 'Théorie de la Procédure Civile,' Paris, 1837–45.

BOURBON, Pierre Henri Dieudonne', French politician, b. at Port au Prince, June 22, 1801 ; member of the General Council for the canton of Charroux, and manager of the Orleans Railway Company ; deputy to the Corps Législatif for Vienne.

BOURBOUSSON, The'ophile Euge'ne, French politician, b. at Vaucluse, July 6, 1811 ; studied medicine, and graduated M.D. ; elected to the Constituent Assembly, 1848 ; returned to the Legislative Assembly, 1861.

BOURCIER DE VILLIERS, Charles Jean Baptiste, Comte de, French politician, b. Dec. 8, 1798 ; entered the army, and retired as captain of cavalry. Member of the Council General for the canton of Épinal ; representative at the Corps Législatif of the department of the Vosges since 1852.

BOURDON, Jean Baptiste Isidore, French physician, b. at Merry, Orne, Aug. 26, 1796 ; studied medicine at Montpellier and Paris ; graduated M.D. 1823; member of the Academy of Medicine, 1825. Author of 'Lettres à Camille sur la Physiologie,' Paris, 1829 ; 'Cours complet d'Education des Filles,' ' Précis d'Hydrologie médicale, ou les Eaux minérales de France,' 1860 ; and numerous other medical works.

BOURGADE, l'Abbe' François, French philologist and missionary, b. at Ganjou, July 7, 1806; studied theology at the Seminary of Auch ; ordained a priest, 1832 ; sent as missionary to Africa, 1838, and founded at Tunis a hospital and college. Author of 'Soirées de Carthage,' 1847 ; and other historical and philological works.

BOURNE, James, English politician, b. 1812 ; educated at Shrewsbury ; is a deputy-lieutenant for the county of Lancaster, and lieutenant-colonel of the Royal Lancashire Artillery Militia ; M.P. for Evesham, 1865.

BOURQUELOT, Louis Felix, French writer, b. at Provins, Seine et Marne, Aug. 19, 1815; studied law, and was called to the bar of the Royal Court of Paris ; president of the Society of Antiquaries of France, 1856. Author of 'Histoire de Provins,' Provins, 1839–40; 'Inscriptions antiques de Nice, de Cimez, et de quelques lieux environnants,' Paris, 1850 ; 'Littérature français contemporaine ;' and numerous memoirs, articles, and pamphlets.

BOURQUENEY, François Adolphe, Baron de, French diplomatist, b. at Paris, Jan. 7, 1800 ; entered the diplomatic service as third secretary to the embassy at Rome ; secretary to the embassy in London, 1840 ; ambassador to Constantinople, 1844 ; ambassador at Vienna, 1853 ; senator, March 31, 1856.

BOUSQUET, Jean Baptiste Edouard, French physician, b. 1794 ; studied medicine at the Faculty of Montpellier, and received the diploma of M.D. May, 1815 ; practised in Paris, and was appointed chief of the bureaux of the Academy of Medicine, 1820 ; titular member, 1824 ; secretary of the Council of Administration, 1830. Author of 'Traité de la Maladie scrofuleuse,' 1821, and numerous other medical works.

BOUSSINGAULT, Jean Baptiste Joseph Dieudonne', French chemist, b. at Paris, Feb. 2, 1802 ; educated at the Mining School of St. Etienne ; professor of chemistry at Lyons, 1839; professor of agriculture in the Conservatory of Arts and Trades, Paris. Author of 'Mémoires de Chimie agricole et de Physiologie,' Paris, 1854 ; and other works on chemistry and agriculture.

BOUTARIE, Edgar, French historian, b. at Châteauxdun, July 1, 1830 ; studied at the Bourbon College, and at the Paris School of Administration. Author of 'La France sous Philippe le Bel,' 1862 ; 'Les Institutions militaires de la France,' 1863 ; and edited, with M. Delisle, 'Les Acts du Parlement de Paris.'

BOUTHORS, Jean Louis Alexandre, French antiquarian, b. at Beauquesne, Somme, June 27, 1797 ; studied law at Paris, and was an advocate at the Royal Court of Amiens. Author of 'Voyage du Roi au Camp de Saint Omer,' Amiens, 1828 ; 'Cryptes de Picardie, etc.' ib. 1838 ; 'Les Proverbes, Dictions, et Maximes du Droit rural traditionnel,' ib. 1859 ; and other antiquarian works.

BOUTOWSKI, Alexander, Russian political economist, b. at St. Petersburg, 1814 ; entered the government service, and received the title of councillor of state ; member of the Imperial Society of Agriculture of Moscow. Author of 'Essay on National Wealth, and the Principles of Political Economy,' St. Petersburg, 1847.

BOUVERIE, Rt. Hon. Edward Pleydell, English statesman, b. 1818 ; educated at Harrow, and Trinity College, Cambridge, where he graduated M.A. 1838 ; M.P. for Kilmarnock since 1844 ; under-secretary of state for the Home Department from 1850 to 1852 ; chairman of committees of the House of Commons, 1853 to 1855 ; vice-president of the Board of Trade and paymaster-general, March, 1855 ; president of the Poor

Law Board, 1858; second church estates commissioner, 1859; member of the Privy Council, 1855.

BOUVET, François Joseph Francisque, French writer, b. at Vieux-d'Izenave, Ain, April 25, 1799. Author of 'Loisirs de la Solitude de Poésies et Novelles,' Paris, 1828; 'De la Confession et du Célibat des Prêtres,' 1845; and numerous political and theological works.

BOUVIER, Sauveur-Henri Victor, French physician, b. at Paris, Jan. 22, 1799; studied medicine in Paris, and obtained the diploma of M.D. 1823; professor of the Academy of Medicine, and chief physician of the Infant Hospital. Author of 'Recherches sur quelques Points d'Anatomie et de Physiologie, etc.' 1823; 'La Surdi Mutité,' 1852; and numerous other medical works.

BOUZIQUE, Etienne Ursin, French writer, b. at Châteauneuf-sur-Cher, Jan. 7, 1801; educated at the College of Bourges; studied law in Paris, and was called to the bar at Bourges; member of the General Council, 1833; mayor of Bourges, 1848. Author of 'Théatres et Souvenirs,' Paris, 1857; 'Servius Tullius,' a tragedy, 1826.

BOVILL, Sir William, English judge, b. 1814; called to the bar, 1841; M.P. for Guildford, 1857–65; chief justice of the Common Pleas, 1866.

BOWEN, Francis, American writer, b. at Charleston, 1814; studied at the University of Cambridge; contributed to the *North American Review* from 1843 to 1853; professor of moral philosophy and political economy at Harvard College. Author of 'Critical Essays on the History and Present Condition of Speculative Philosophy,' Boston, 1842; and several lectures on metaphysics.

BOWEN, Sir George Ferguson, English colonial administrator, b. in Ireland in 1822; educated at the Charterhouse, and at Trinity College, Oxford; elected fellow of Brasenose College, Oxford, 1844; admitted a member of Lincoln's Inn, 1844; appointed president of the University of Corfu, 1847; resigned, 1851; chief secretary to the Government of the Ionian Islands, 1854; C.M.G. 1855; K.C.M.G. 1856; and promoted to G.C.M.G. 1860; first governor of Queensland, 1859–67; governor of New Zealand, 1867. Author of 'Ithaca,' 1850; 'Mount Athos, Thessaly, and Epirus.'

BOWERS, Very Rev. George Hull, English theological writer, b. 1794; studied at the Grammar School, Pembroke, and Clare College, Cambridge, where he graduated B.D. 1829; D.D. 1849; rector of St. Paul's, Covent Garden, London, 1831; dean of Manchester, 1847. Author of numerous sermons.

BOWMAN, William, English medical writer, b. at Nantwich, 1816; studied at King's College, London. Author of 'Lectures on the Parts concerned in the Operations of the Eye;' 'Observations on Artificial Pupils;' and many others.

BOWRING, Edgar Alfred, English writer, b. 1826, younger son of Sir John Bowring; educated at the London University; entered the Civil Service in the Board of Trade, 1841; successively private secretary to the Earl of Clarendon, Earl Granville, and Lord Stanley of Alderley; secretary to the Royal Commission for the Great Exhibition of 1851. Author of 'The Book of Psalms,' and English versions of the poetical works of Schiller, Goethe, and Heine.

BOWRING, Sir John, English politician and author, b. in Exeter, Oct. 17, 1792; editor of the *Westminster Review*, 1825 to 1830; M.P. for the Clyde boroughs, 1835 to 1837; M.P. for Bolton, 1841 to 1849; appointed British consul at Canton, 1849; plenipotentiary in China, governor of Hong-Kong, and received the honour of knighthood, 1854; concluded a treaty of commerce with Siam, 1855; retired on a pension, 1859. Author of a great number of geographical, historical, and poetical works, and of translations from the Russian, Danish, German, Spanish, Portuguese, and other languages.

BOWYER, Sir George, Bart. English politician, b. in Berkshire, 1811; studied at Oxford; was called to the bar of the Middle Temple, 1839; convert to the Roman Catholic faith in 1850, having previously been created an honorary D.C.L. of Oxford; M.P. for Dundalk since 1852. Author of 'Commentaries on the Constitutional Law of England,' several legal works, and a pamphlet on the Roman Catholic question.

BOXALL, William, English painter, b. at Oxford, 1800; entered the Royal Academy as a student in 1819; exhibited at the R.A. 'Milton's Reconciliation with his Wife,' 1829; 'Cordelia,' 1830; and 'Hope' in 1838; elected A.R.A. in 1851, and R.A. in 1863.

BOYD, Rev. Andrew Kennedy Hutchinson, English writer, b. at Auchinleck, Ayrshire, Nov. 1825; educated at the University of Glasgow; ordained, 1851; incumbent of St. Bernard's, Edinburgh. Author of numerous articles in *Fraser's Magazine* under the signature of A. K. H. B.; republished in separate volumes under the title of 'Recreations of a Country Parson.'

BOYD, Rev. James R. American writer, b. in New York in 1804; professor of moral philosophy and college preacher at Hamilton College. Author of 'Eclectic Moral Philosophy,' and numerous scientific and philosophical works.

BOYE, Caspard Johann, Danish poet, b. at Kongsberg, Norway, in 1791; studied in Denmark, and was appointed professor in the Seminary of Instrup in 1818; became pastor at Sölleröd in 1826, and at Helsingford in 1835. Author of 'Conrad;' 'Kong Sigurd;' and several dramas and religious poems.

BOYER, Philoxe'ne, French writer, b. at Grenoble in 1827; studied at the College of Stanislas. Author of 'Sapho,' Odéon, 1850; 'Le Cousin du Roi,' *ib.* 1857; 'Les Chercheurs d'Amour,' 1855; 'Délaissées,' 1856; and numerous dramatic pieces.

BRADDON, Mary Elizabeth, English novelist, b. in London, 1837. Author of 'Loves of Arcadia,' London, 1860; 'Lady Audley's Secret;' 'Aurora Floyd;' 'Eleanor's Victory;' 'John Marchmont's Legacy;' 'Only a Clod;' 'The Lady's Mile;' and numerous other novels and works of fiction.

BRADLEY, Rev. Edward, English writer, b. in 1827; educated at Durham University; graduated at Durham; was ordained 1850, and appointed incumbent of Bobbington, Staffordshire, 1857, and rector of Denton, Hunts, 1859. Author of 'Verdant Green;' 'Glencreggan,' 1861; 'The Curate of Cranston, with other Prose and Verse,' 1862; 'A Tour in Tartan Land,' 1863; 'Wild Cantire,' 1864; and numerous other works; also contributor to *Punch*, the *Illustrated London News*, and other periodicals, under the pseudonym of 'Cuthbert Bede.'

BRADLEY, Rev. George Granville, English clergyman, b. in 1821; educated at Rugby, and University College, Oxford, where he graduated B.A. 1844, and was elected a fellow; assistant-master in Rugby School for several years, and was appointed head-master of Marlborough College, 1858.

BRADY, John, English politician, b. 1812; is a member of the Royal College of Physicians, and of the College of Surgeons; a magistrate for the county of Leitrim, and M.P. for the same since 1852.

BRADY, Right Hon. Maziere, English magistrate, b. in 1796; educated at Trinity College, Dublin; called to the Irish bar, 1819; solicitor-general for Ireland, 1837, and attorney-general, 1839; chief baron of the Irish Exchequer, 1840, and advanced to the Irish Chancellorship, 1846; vice-chancellor of the Queen's University in Ireland.

BRADY, Sir Francis, English colonial judge, b. 1810; called to the Irish bar, 1836; appointed chief justice of Newfoundland, and judge of the vice-admiralty, 1847; knighted, 1860.

BRAGG, Braxton, American military commander, b. in Warren County, North Carolina, in 1815; admitted into the Academy at West Point, 1833, where he graduated, 1837; served in the Mexican war under General Taylor, and at the commencement of the civil war became brigadier-general in the Confederate army; general of division, 1862.

BRAME, Jules Louis Joseph, French politician, b. at Lille, Jan. 9, 1808; member of the General Council for the canton of Cysoing; elected to the Corps Législatif for the Département du Nord, 1857, and re-elected, 1863. Author of 'L'Emigration des Campagnes.'

BRAMWELL, Sir George William Wiltshire, English judge, b. in London in 1808; called to the bar in 1838; became a Q.C. 1851; member of the Common Law Procedure Commission, 1852; elevated to the bench as baron of the Exchequer in 1856.

BRAND, Henry Bouverie William, English politician, b. 1814; secretary to Sir G. Grey; M.P. for the borough of Lewes since 1852; lord of the Treasury under the ministry of Lord Palmerston, 1855 to 1858.

BRANDE, William Thomas, English chemist, b. in London, 1788; studied at St. George's Hospital; professor of chemistry at the Royal Institution, 1813; fellow of the University of London, 1836; D.C.L. at Oxford, 1853. Author of 'Outlines of Geology;' 'Manual of Chemistry;' and other scientific works.

BRANDIS, Christian Augustus, German author, b. at Hildesheim, Hanover, Feb. 15, 1790; studied at the Universities of Kiel, Göttingen, and Copenhagen; secretary of the Prussian Legation at Rome; appointed professor at Bonn, 1821; in 1837 he went to Greece, and was member of the cabinet and councillor to King Otho for several years. Author of a work 'On Greece,' Leipsic, 1842, and numerous volumes on classics, history, and philosophy.

BRANDON, Robert, English architect, b. 1810. Published, with his brother, 'An Analysis of Gothic Architecture;' 'The Open Timber Roofs of the Middle Ages,' 1842; 'Parish Churches,' 1854.

BRANDT, Heinrich von, German military writer, b. in Westphalia in 1789; studied law at Königsberg, and entered the Prussian army; took part in the campaign of 1813–14; chief of staff, 1830; colonel, 1842; and major-general, 1848. Author of 'Ueber Spanien,' 1823; 'Handbuch für den ersten Unterricht in der höhern Kriegskunst,' 1829; and other works.

BRANISS, Christlieb Julian, German author, b. at Breslau, Sept. 18, 1792; studied at Berlin and Breslau; graduated Ph.D. at the University of Göttingen, 1823; professor to the School of Philosophy at Breslau, 1825. Author of 'Geschichte der Philosophie seit Kant,' Breslau, 1842; and numerous other philosophical works.

BRASCASSAT, Jacques Raymond, French painter, b. at Bordeaux, Aug. 30, 1805; studied under Richard and M. Hersent. Exhibited 'Mercure et Argus,' 1827; 'Étude de Chiens,' 1831; 'Le Golfe de Naples,' 1845; and numerous other paintings.

BRASSEY, Thomas, Engish civil engineer, b. at Buerton in 1805; educated at Chester; constructed the Grand Junction, Severn Valley, Lancaster and Carlisle, Caledonian, North Stafford, Buckinghamshire, South-Western, Eastern Union, Western of France, and Mediterranean railways, and several lines in Spain.

BRATIANO, Demetrius, Roumanian politician, b. at Bucharest in 1818; educated at the National College of Bucharest, and studied law in Paris, where, from 1836 to 1848 he published numerous political articles in the *National* and the *Revue Indépendante*, under the pseudonym of 'Regnault;' deputy to the Parliament of Roumania.

BRATIANO, John, b. at Bucharest, 1822, brother of the preceding; entered the army, 1838; studied in Paris, at the Polytechnic School and the College of France, 1841; deputy to the Parliament of Roumania. Author of 'Mémoire sur l'Empire d'Autriche dans la Question d'Orient,' 1855; 'Mémoire sur la Situation de la Moldo Valachie depuis le Traité de Paris,' 1857.

BRAUN, Alexander Carl Hermann, German politician, b. at Planen, Saxony, May 10, 1807; studied law at the University of Leipsic; member of the Second Chamber of State, 1839 to 1842; member of the Diet of Saxony, 1845; president of the Second Chamber, 1848. Author of 'Rechenschafts-bericht,' Leipsic, 1846; and several legal works.

BRAUN, Johann Wilhelm Joseph, German theological writer, b. at Gronan, Prussia, April 27, 1801; studied at Cologne and at Bonn; ordained at Vienna, 1825, and finished his theological studies at Rome; member of the First Chamber of Prussia in 1850. Author of 'Deutschland und die National-Versammlung,' Aix-la-Chapelle, 1849; 'Die Lehren des sogenannten Hermesianismus, über das Verhältniss der Vernunft zur Offenbarung,' Bonn, 1835; and other theological works.

BRAVO-MURILLO, Don Juan, Spanish politician, b. at Frejenal de la Sierra, Badajoz, June, 1803; entered the College of Advocates at Seville in 1825; secretary to the Department of Justice, 1836; elected to the Cortes by the province of Seville, 1837; re-elected for the province Avila, 1839; minister of justice in 1847; minister of trade and public instruction, November of the same year; minister of finance in 1849 to 1850; president of the Council of Ministers, 1851.

BRAY, Anna Eliza, English authoress, b. in Surrey, near the end of the last century; married to Mr. Charles Stothard, 1818, who died in 1821: married again in 1825 to the Rev. Edward Atkyns Bray, vicar of Tavistock, who died 1857. Author of 'Memoirs of Charles Stothard,' 1823; 'The White Hoods,' a novel, 1828; 'The Borders of the Tamar and the Tavy,' 1836; and numerous novels and biographical sketches.

BRAY, Othon Camille Hugo von, German diplomatist, b. at Berlin, May 17, 1807; entered the diplomatic service of Bavaria, and charged with several missions to Vienna, Paris, and St. Petersburg, 1831–43; minister of foreign affairs of Bavaria, 1846; envoy of Bavaria at St. Petersburg, 1849.

BRAZIL, Dom Pedro II. Emperor of, b. Dec. 2, 1825; son of the Emperor Pedro I. and of Leopoldina, archduchess of Austria; succeeded to the throne on the abdication of his father, April 7, 1831; declared of age, July 23, 1840; crowned July 18, 1841; married, Sept. 4, 1843, to Theresa, empress of Brazil, b. March 14, 1822, the daughter of the late King Francis I. of the Two Sicilies.

BRECKENRIDGE, John, American politician, b. at Lexington, Kentucky, Jan. 21, 1821; educated at Danville, and studied law at the Transylvania Institute; entered the army as a volunteer in the Mexican war, 1847; returned to Congress, 1851 and 1853; vice-president of the United States, 1857–61; general in the Confederate service, 1861–65.

BREEN, Henry Hegart, English writer, b. 1808; deputy-registrar of the Court of St. Lucia, 1832; provost-marshal of St. Vincent, 1862. Author of 'St. Lucia, Historical, Statistical, and Descriptive;' 'The Diamond Rock;' and other works.

BREHM, Christian Ludwig, German naturalist, b. at Schöcran, Gotha, Jan. 24, 1787; studied theology at Jena, and ordained minister in 1813. Author of 'Lehrbuch der Naturgeschichte aller Europ. Vögel,' Jena, 1824–27; 'Die Kunst Vögel als Bälge zu bereiten, &c.' Weimar, 1842; and other works on ornithology.

BREHMER, Heinrich, German politician, b. at Lübeck in 1800; studied law at Jena and Göttingen, and practised as an advocate in his native town; member of the senate of Lübeck, 1836; represented Lübeck at the Conferences of Dresden, 1850, and at the Diet of the North German Confederation, 1866.

BREITHAUPT, John August Friederich, German mineralogist, b. at Probotzella, near Saalfeld, May 18, 1791; studied at the University of Jena, and the Academy of Friborg; appointed professor and inspector of precious stones in the latter town. Author of 'Ueber die Echtheit der Kristalle,' Friborg, 1816; 'Die Charaktere der Klassen und Ordnungen des Mineral Systems,' ib. second edition, 1854; and numerous other works on mineralogy.

BREMOND, Jean François, French painter, b. in Paris in 1807; studied under MM. Ingres and Conder. Executed a great number of paintings on religious subjects: 'Le Christ descendu de la Croix,' 1852; 'Le Christ Consolateur,' 'Le Christ et les Enfants,' for the church of St. Lambert de Vangirard, 1863.

BRENIER, Baron Anatole, French diplomatist, b. in 1806; was successively secretary of legation at Lisbon and in London, 1831; minister of foreign affairs from Jan. 24 to April 10, 1851; minister plenipotentiary to Naples, 1855; created senator, March 24, 1861.

BRENIL, Guillaume Joseph Auguste, French writer, b. at Amiens, March 2, 1811; barrister and justice of the peace in his native town. Editor of 'Lettres inédites de Mlle. Philipon's adressées aux Demoiselles Canet,' 1840: author of 'La Confrérie de Notre-Dame du Puy,' 1854; and other antiquarian works.

BREQUET, Louis, French horologist and electrician, b. in Paris, Dec. 22, 1808; studied at Geneva, and made several discoveries in the science of horology and the use of electric telegraphs; member of the Bureau of Longitudes, 1862.

BRESSANT, Jean Baptiste Prosper, French actor, b. at Châlons-sur-Saône, Oct. 24, 1815; made his début in Paris, 1835; played in 'Clarisse Harlowe;' 'Diane de Lys;' 'Le Verre d'Eau;' 'Le Misanthrope;' and many other dramas.

BRETON, François Pierre Hippolyte Ernest, French archæologist, b. at Paris, Oct. 21, 1812; studied drawing under Regnier, Watelet, and Champin. Published 'Introduction à l'Histoire de France, ou description physique et monumentale de la Gaule jusqu'à l'établissement de la Monarchie,' 1838; 'Pompeia,' 1855; and other archæological works.

BRETON, Jules Adolphe, French painter, b. at Courrières, Pas de Calais; studied under Drolling and M. F. Devigne. Painted 'Les Glaneuses;' 'Le Lendemain de la St. Sébastien' and 'Petites Paysannes consultant les Épis,' 1857; and numerous other landscapes.

BREWSTER, Right Hon. Abraham, English lawyer, b. in 1796; studied at Trinity College, Dublin; called to the Irish bar, 1819; solicitor-general for Ireland from Feb. to June, 1846; appointed attorney-general and sworn member of the Privy Council, 1853; retired, 1855.

BRIALMONT, Alexis, Belgian military writer, b. at Venlo, May 25, 1821; studied in the Military School of Brussels; secretary to General Chezal, minister of war, 1847 to 1850; staff-major, 1855; captain, 1857. Author of 'History of the Duke of Wellington,' 1856–57; and several works on military science; also founded the *Belgian Army Journal* in 1850.

BRIALMONT, Laurent Mathieu, Belgian statesman, b. at Seraing, near Liège, in 1789; took part as a military officer in the French campaigns in Germany, Spain, and Russia, 1806–15; contributed to the revolutionary movement in Belgium, 1830; aide-de-camp to King Leopold I., and commander of Antwerp, 1837, and of Mons, 1840; minister of war, 1850.

BRICHETEAU, Isidore, French physician, b. at St. Christophe Ande, Feb. 3, 1789; studied at the Lyceum of Poitiers; physician to the Salpétrière Hospital for Children, and the Hôtel Dieu, at Paris. Author of 'Traité analytique sur le Croup, 1826; 'Traité sur les Maladies chroniques qui ont leur siége dans les Organes respiratoires,' 1852; and numerous other medical works.

BRIDGES, Sir Brook William, Bart. English politician, b. 1801; educated at Winchester, and Oriel College, Oxford; deputy-lieutenant for Kent; M.P. for East Kent, Feb. to July 1852, and since 1857.

BRIERRE DE BOISMONT, Alexander Jacques François, French physician, b. at Rouen, Oct. 18, 1797; physician to the Hospital of Bonshommes, at Paris. Author of 'Relation historique et médicale du Choléra Morbus de Cologne,' 1832; 'Des Hallucinations, ou Histoire raisonnée des Apparitions, des Visions, des Songes, de l'Extase, du Somnambulisme, et du Magnétisme,' 1845, second edition 1852; and other medical and scientific works.

BRIEY CAMILLE, Count de, Belgian statesman, b. 1799; member of the Senate, 1839; minister of finance, 1841; minister of foreign affairs, from 1841 to 1843.

BRIGHT, John, English politician, b. at Rochdale, 1811; partner in the firm of John Bright and Brothers, cotton spinners and manufacturers, Rochdale; M.P. for Durham 1843; M.P. for Manchester, 1847; for Birmingham since 1857.

BRIGHT, Sir Charles Tilston, English civil engineer, b. in 1832; engineer to the English and Irish Magnetic Telegraph Company, 1853; and one of the original projectors of the Atlantic Telegraph Company, 1856; M.P. for Greenwich, 1865.

BRION, Gustave, French painter, b. at Rothan, Vosges, in 1824; studied painting at Strasbourg under Gabriel Guérin, from 1841 to 1844. Painted 'Le Chemin de Halage,' 1852; 'Batterie de Machines de Guerre,' 1861; 'Jésus et Pierre sur les Croix,' 1863; and a number of historical paintings.

BRIOT, Charles Auguste Albert, French mathematician, b. at St. Hippolyte, Doubs, July 19, 1817; studied at the College of St. Louis; admitted to the Normal School in 1838; professor of mathematics at the Royal College of Orleans 1841, to the Faculty of Lyons 1845, and at the Lyceums Buonaparte, St. Louis, and the Polytechnic School, Paris, 1848. Author of 'Leçons nouvelles de Trigonometrie,' 1850; and several works on mathematics.

BRIQUES, Paul, French physician, b. at Chalons-sur-Marne, in 1798; member of the French Academy, 1860. Author of 'De l'Eclairage artificiel, considéré sous le point de vue de l'Hygiène publique et privée,' 1837; 'Recherches sur l'Etiologie des Tubercules,' 1842; 'Traité clinique et therapeutique de l'Hysterie,' 1859; and other medical works.

BRISCOE, John Ivatt, English politician, b. 1792; educated at University College, Oxford; graduated B.A. 1812; M.A. 1815; magistrate for Surrey and Middlesex, and a deputy-lieutenant for Surrey; M.P. for Surrey, 1830–32; for East Surrey, 1833–34; for Westbury, 1837–41; and for West Surrey since 1857.

BRISEBARRE, Edouard Louis Alexandre, French dramatic writer, b. at Paris, Feb. 12, 1818; studied at the College of Charlemagne. Author of 'La Fiole de Cagliostro,' 1835; 'Le Garçon de Ferme,' 1861; 'Léonard,' 1863; and numerous other dramas.

BRISSET, Pierre Nicolas, French painter, b. in Paris, Aug. 18, 1810; studied at the Paris School of Fine Arts. Painted 'The Death of Priam,' 1840; and other historical and ecclesiastical works.

BRISTED, Charles Astor, American writer, b. at New York in 1820; studied in England, and at the University of Cambridge; returned to America in 1847. Author of 'The Upper Ten Thousand;' 'Sketches of American Society;' 'Five Years in an English University;' and other miscellaneous works.

BRISTOW, Henry William, English geologist, b. in 1817; educated at King's College, London; appointed assistant geologist in the Ordnance Geological Survey, 1842; geologist on the Geological Survey of Great Britain, 1847. Author of 'Memoirs on the Geology of the Isle of Wight;' and other geological works.

BRIVES, Jacques, French politician, b. at Montpellier, Aug. 9, 1800; elected deputy to the Constituent Assembly, 1848; member of the Legislative Assembly, 1850; imprisoned and exiled, 1851.

BROCKHAUS, Hermann, German philologist, b. at Amsterdam, Jan. 28, 1806; studied Oriental literature at the Universities of Leipsic, Bonn, and Oxford; professor at the University of Jena 1839, at Leipsic 1841, and in 1848; titular professor of Oriental literature and languages at Leipsic, 1848. Author of 'Kathâ sarit ságara,' Leipsic, 1839; and several translations from the Sanscrit and other Oriental languages.

BRODHEAD, John Romeyn, American writer, b. in New York, Jan. 2, 1814; studied law, and was admitted to the bar of New York, 1835. Author of 'History of the State of New York,' 1853.

BROFFERIO, Angelo, Italian author and politician, b. at Castelnuovo, province of Asti, Dec. 6, 1802; studied law at Turin, and called to the bar, 1830. Founded the *Turin Messenger*. Author of 'Vitiges, King of the Goths;' 'History of Piedmont from 1814 to the present time,' 1849–52; and numerous satires, dramas, tragedies, and poems.

BROGLIE, Albert, Prince de, French author, b. June 13, 1821; became a contributor to the *Revue des Deux Mondes,* 1848. Author of 'Études morales et littéraires,' 1853; 'L'Église et l'Empire Romain au Quatrième Siècle,' 1856; 'Une Réforme Administrative en Algérie,' 1860. Member of the French Academy, 1862.

BROHAN, Augustine, French actress and dramatic authoress, b. at Paris, Dec. 2, 1824; studied music at the Conservatoire, 1817–22; appeared at the Théâtre français, Paris, 1823; admitted sociétaire, or partner, at the Théatre français, 1830. Author of 'Les Métamorphoses de l'Amour;' 'Quitte ou Double;' 'Qui femme a, guerre a;' and other comedies.

BROMLEY, William Davenport, English politician, b. 1821; educated at Harrow, and Christ Church, Oxford; deputy-lieutenant for the county of Stafford, and lieutenant-colonel of Staffordshire yeomanry cavalry; M.P. for North Warwickshire since 1864.

BRONGNIART, Adolphe Theodore, French botanist, b. in Paris, Jan. 14, 1801; member of the Academy of Sciences, 1834; professor of botany at the Museum of Natural History, 1833; inspector of the University of Paris, 1852. Author of 'Énumeration des Genres de Plantes cultiveés au Muséum d'Histoire Naturelle,' 1843.

BRONN, Heinrich Georg, German naturalist, b. at Griegelheim, near Heidelberg, March 3, 1800; studied at Heidelberg; tutor at the University, 1822; professor of natural sciences at Heidelberg, 1828; professor and director of the geological collections of the University, 1835. Author of 'System der urweltlichen Conchylien,' Heidelberg, 1827; and other works on Natural History.

BROOKS, Charles, American writer, b. at Salem, Massachusetts, June 20, 1813; studied theology; was minister in several parishes, and settled at Newport, Rhodes Island, 1837. Author of 'Poems;' 'Journey to India;' 'German Lyrics;' and various other works in prose and verse.

BROOKS, Charles Shirley, English novelist and dramatic author, b. 1816; studied for the bar, but relinquished law for literature. Author of numerous dramas and novels: among them, 'Our New Governess;' 'The Creole;' 'Aspen Court;' 'The Gordian Knot;' 'The Silver Cord;' and many others: also contributor and special correspondent to several daily and weekly papers.

BROSBOELL, Charles, Danish novelist, b. in Jutland, April 7, 1820; studied painting at the Academy of Fine Arts, Copenhagen. Author of 'De to Studenter,' Copenhagen, 1838; 'Eiags Soenner,' 1845; 'Livets Conflicter,' 1844; 'Herregaards Fortællinger,' 1853; and other dramas and novels.

BROSSARD, Ame'de'e Hippolyte, Marquis de, French military commander, b. at Follény, March 8, 1784; entered the army, 1801, and took part in the campaigns of the Empire; lieutenant-colonel, 1818; staff-major in the expedition to Algeria, 1830; field-marshal, 1833; officer of the Légion d'honneur, 1822. Author of 'Mélanges sur l'Afrique,' 1838.

BROSSET, Marie Felicite', French writer, b. at Paris, Feb. 5, 1802; studied in the College of Jesuits; professor of Armenian and Georgian literature in the Imperial Academy of Sciences of St. Petersburg, 1840; conservateur of the collection of Oriental coins in the Imperial Palace of the Hermitage, St. Petersburg, 1851. Author of 'Chronique Géorgienne,' 1830; 'Histoire de la Géorgie,' 1849–50; and other works.

BROT, Charles Alphonse, French novelist and dramatic writer, b. at Paris, April 12, 1809. Author of 'Priez pour elle,' 1833; 'Jane Grey,' 1835; 'La Comtesse aux trois Galants,' 1839; 'Deux Coups de Tonnerre,' 1853; 'La Tour de Londres,' 1855; and other dramas and novels.

BROUCKERE, Henri Marie Joseph Ghislain de, Belgian politician, b. at Bruges in 1801; magistrate and king's counsel at Maestricht and at Ruremonde till the Revolution of 1830; member of the National Congress, and one of the commissioners who offered the crown of Belgium to Prince Leopold, 1831; civil governor of Antwerp, 1833; minister of state, 1847.

BROUGHTON, John Cam Hobhouse, Lord, English politician and author, b. near Bristol in 1786; educated at Westminster, and Trinity College, Cambridge, where he graduated in 1808; M.P. for Westminster, 1820 to 1833; for Nottingham, 1834 to 1847; M.P. for Harwich; raised to the peerage as Lord Broughton in 1851; chief commissioner of woods and forests, 1846–52. Author of 'Journey through Albania and other Provinces of Turkey with Lord Byron,' 1812; and other works.

BROWN, Ford Madox, English painter, b. at Calais in 1821; studied in Belgium and Paris. Painted 'Wiclif reading his Translation of the Scriptures,' 1848; 'King Lear,' 1849; 'Chaucer reciting his Poetry at the Court of Edward III.' 1851; 'Christ washing Peter's Feet,' 1852; and many other historical pictures.

BROWN, Henry Kirke, American sculptor, b. at Leyden, Massachusetts, in 1814; studied portrait painting at Boston, 1832. Executed in bronze a statue of 'De Witt Clinton;' 'The Angel of Retribution;' in marble, 'Hope;' bas-reliefs of the 'Hyades' and 'Pleiades;' the 'Four Seasons;' and other works of art.

BROWN, John, English physician, b. at Biggar, Lanarkshire, Sept. 1810; educated at the High School and University of Edinburgh; M.D. of Edinburgh, and assessor to the rector of the University Court. Author of 'Rab and his Friends;' 'Our Dogs;' contributor to the *North British Review, Good Words,* and the *Scotsman.*

BROWN, Rev. Thomas Richard, English philologist, b. 1791; educated at St. John's College, Cambridge, where he graduated B.A. 1814; vicar of Southwick, Northamptonshire, 1834. Author of 'An Analysis of the Chaldee Text of Daniel,' 1838; 'Hebrew Hieroglyphic Dictionary,' 1858; and other philological works.

BROWN, Rev. William Haig, English divine, b. at Bromley, Middlesex, 1823; studied at Pembroke College, Cambridge, where he graduated in high honours, 1846; M.A. 1849, and LL.D. 1864; fellow and tutor of Pembroke College; assistant master at Harrow; head master of the Grammar School, Kensington, in connexion with King's College, London, 1857; head master of Charterhouse School, London, 1863.

BROWNE, Charles Thomas, English author, b. at Wellington, Somerset, in 1825; graduated at Trinity College, Dublin. Author of 'The Tower of London,' 1844; 'Irene;' 'Astrello, or the Prophet's Vision,' 1850; 'Life of Southey,' 1854; 'The United States; its Constitution and Powers,' 1856.

BROWNE, Colonel Gore, English colonial administrator, b. 1807; entered the army, 1814; commander of the 41st regiment during the Affghanistan campaign, 1842; governor of St. Helena, 1851–54; governor of New Zealand, 1854–61; appointed governor of Tasmania, March, 1862.

BROWNE, Frances, English authoress, b. at Stranorlor, Donegal, Jan. 16, 1816; lost her sight in infancy. Published 'Songs of our Land,' 1840; 'Legends of Ulster;' 'The Ericksons;' and 'My Share of the World,' 1861. Literary pension of 20l. per annum.

BROWNE, Hablot Knight, English artist, b. in 1812. Designed the illustrations to part of 'Pickwick,' 1839, 'Nicholas Nickleby,' and most of Mr. Charles Dickens' works of fiction; also to the Abbotsford edition of the 'Waverley Novels,' 'The Adventures of Sir Guy de Guy,' and numerous other works, under the pseudonym of 'Phiz.'

BROWNE, James Ross, American traveller, b. in 1817. Author of 'Etchings of a Whaling Cruise,' New York, 1846; a series of articles in *Harper's Magazine;* and 'Youself, or the Journey of the Frangi,' ib. 1854.

BROWNE, Lord John Thomas, English politician, b. 1821; lieutenant in the royal navy, 1846; magistrate and deputy-lieutenant for the county of Mayo; M.P. for the same since 1857.

BROWNE, Rev. Henry, English author, b. 1804; educated at Corpus Christi College, Cambridge, and graduated B.A. 1826; principal of the Theological College at Chichester, 1842–47; prebendary of the cathedral; examining chaplain to the bishop of the diocese, and vicar of Pevensey, 1854. Author of 'Ordo Sæclorum,' 1844; articles in Kitto's 'Cyclopædia of Biblical Literature;' and several volumes of Greek and Latin classics.

BROWNE, Ven. Robert William, English divine, b. Nov. 12, 1809; educated at Merchant Taylors' School; elected scholar and fellow of St. John's College, Oxford, and graduated B.A. 1831; professor of classical literature in King's College, London, 1835; chaplain to the bishop of Lichfield, 1843; prebendary of St. Paul's, 1845; examining chaplain to the bishop of Bath and Wells, 1854; archdeacon of Bath, and rector of Weston-super-Mare, 1860; canon of Wells, 1863. Author of 'Histories of Greece and Rome;' 'Histories of Greek and Roman Literature.'

BROWNING, Robert, English poet, b. at Camberwell in 1812; educated at the London University. Author of 'Paracelsus,' 1836; 'Pippa Passes;' 'Strafford;' 'Sordello;' 'Men and Women,' 1856; 'Return of the Druses;' 'The Soul's Tragedy;' 'Dramatis Personæ,' 1864; and numerous other dramas and poems.

BROWNSON, Orestes, American writer, b. in New Hampshire, 1802; educated as Presbyterian, and successively 'Universalist' preacher, Unitarian, and Roman Catholic. Author of 'Charles Elwood,' a novel; 'The Spirit Rapper;' 'The Convert;' and several other works. Founded the *Boston Quarterly Review,* subsequently changed to *Brownson's Quarterly.*

BRUCE, Charles Lennox Cumming, English politician, b. 1790; educated at *Winchester,* and at Corpus Christi College, Oxford; deputy-lieutenant for Elgin and

Stirling; joint secretary of the Board of Control, 1852 and 1858–59; M.P. for Inverness, 1831–32 and 1833–37, and for Elgin and Nairn since 1840.

BRUCE, John, English antiquarian, b. in London, 1802; educated for the law, but ceased to practise in 1840. Editor of 'The Restoration of Edward IV.' 1838; 'Verney's Notes on the Long Parliament,' 1844; and a great number of works for learned societies; also contributor to the *Edinburgh Review* and *Gentleman's Magazine.*

BRUCE, Lord Charles William Brudenell, English politician, b. 1834; captain in the 1st Life Guards, and captain of the Royal Wilts Yeomanry Cavalry; M.P. for North Wiltshire, 1865.

BRUCE, Lord Ernest Augustus Charles Brudenell, English politician, b. 1811; educated at Eton, and Trinity College, Cambridge; graduated M.A. 1831; vice-chamberlain to the Queen, 1841–46 and 1852–58; deputy-lieutenant for Wilts; M.P. for Marlborough since 1832.

BRUCE, Rev. John Collingwood, English historical writer, b. at Newcastle-upon-Tyne, 1805; educated at the University of Glasgow, and graduated M.A. 1826, and LL.D. 1853. Author of 'A Handbook of English History;' 'The Bayeux Tapestry elucidated,' 1856; 'A Handbook to Newcastle;' and other historical works.

BRUCE, Right Hon. Henry Austin, English politician, b. 1815; called to the bar, 1837; appointed under-secretary for the Home Department, 1862; vice-president of the Committee of Council on Education, 1864; deputy-lieutenant of Glamorgan; M.P. for Merthyr-Tydvil since 1852.

BRUCE, Sir Henry Hervey, Bart. English politician, b. 1820; deputy-lieutenant for the county of Londonderry; high sheriff, 1845; late lieutenant 1st Life Guards; M.P. for Coleraine since 1862.

BRUCKER, Raymond, French novelist, b. at Compiègne in 1805. Wrote under several pseudonyms. Author of 'Le Maçon,' 1828; 'Les Intimes,' 1831; 'Les sept Péchés capitaux,' 1853; 'Au milieu des Douleurs,' 1842; and numerous other works of fiction.

BRUCKNER, François Auguste, French politician, b. at Strasbourg, Feb. 8, 1814; entered the Polytechnic School, 1834; captain of artillery and member of the Constituent Assembly, 1848; member of the Legislative Assembly, 1851; exiled, 1852.

BRUEN, Henry, English politician, b. 1828; magistrate and deputy-lieutenant for the county of Carlow; M.P. for county of Carlow since 1857.

BRUGGEMANN, Carl Heinrich, German political writer; b. at Hopsten, Prussia, Aug. 29, 1810; studied at the University of Bonn. Author of 'Der Deutsche Zollverein und das Schutzsystem,' Berlin; editor of the *Cologne Gazette,* 1845–48.

BRUGGEMANN, Johann Heinrich Theodor, Prussian statesman, b. at Soest, Westphalia, in 1795; studied at the University of Munster; appointed professor of the Lyceum of Dusseldorf, 1815, and director of the establishment, 1817; councillor of public instruction at Coblentz, 1832; minister of public instruction, 1849; vice-president of the second Prussian Chamber, 1850–51.

BRULOW, Alexander, Russian architect, b. at St. Petersburg early in the present century; studied at the Imperial Academy of Fine Arts. Designed the theatre of Michaïloff and the observatory of the Academy of Sciences; superintended the restoration of the Imperial winter-palace.

BRUN-LAVAINNE, Elie Benjamin Joseph, French antiquarian writer, b. at Lille, July 22, 1791; appointed archivist of Lille, 1826. Author of 'Atlas topographique et historique de Lille,' 1830–36; 'Les Sept Sièges de Lille,' 1839; and other antiquarian and historical works.

BRUNET, Jean Baptiste, French military writer, b. at Limoges, Nov. 3, 1814; studied at the Polytechnic School, and captain in 1832; member of the Constituent Assembly for Haut-Vienne, 1851. Author of 'Histoire générale de l'Artillerie,' Paris, 1842; 'La Question Algerienne,' 1847.

BRUNET, de Presle, Charles Marie Vladimir, French antiquarian writer, b. at Paris, Nov. 10, 1809; member of the Academy of Inscriptions, 1852; professor of modern Greek at the School of Oriental Languages, 1864. Published 'Récherches sur les Établissements des Grecs en Sicile,' 1845; 'L'Examen critique de la Succession des Dynasties Égyptiennes,' 1850.

BRUNIUS, Carl Georg, Swedish archæologist, b. at Tanum, March 23, 1792; *obtained the degree of Ph.D. 1814;* tutor at the University of Lund, 1815; professor of. Greek, 1824.   Author of 'Life of Tyrtæus,' in Greek, Lund, 1816; 'Konstanteck-ningar under en Resa till Fahlun, etc.' 1851; and several Swedish poems, and historical and antiquarian works.

BRUNNOW, Ernst Philipp, Baron de, Russian diplomatist, b, at Dresden, Aug. 31, 1797; studied at the University of Leipsic, and received into the Russian diplomatic service at the Congress of Aix-la-Chapelle, 1818; secretary to the embassy in London, 1820–23; secretary to Count Woronzow, governor of Odessa, 1827; senior councillor to the Foreign Office, 1830; envoy extraordinary and minister plenipotentiary to the Court of Wurtemberg, 1839; envoy extraordinary and minister plenipotentiary to Great Britain, 1840 to 1854; minister plenipotentiary at the Court of Prussia, 1854–57; ambassador to Great Britain since 1858.

BRUNO, Edouard Hubert Joseph, French military commander, b. Jan. 16, 1802; general of brigade, 1859; governor and commander-in-chief of the military school of Saumur.

BRUYS, Amé'dé'e, French politician, b. at Cluny, Oct. 29, 1817; studied law at Paris, and admitted to the bar; deputy to the Constituent Assembly for Saône-et-Loire, 1849; elected member of the Legislative Assembly, 1850; exiled, 1851.

BRYAN, George Leopold, English politician, b. 1821; educated at Oscott College; justice of the peace, and deputy-lieutenant for the county of Kilkenny; returned M.P. for same county, 1865.

BRYANT, William Cullen, American poet, b. at Cummington, Massachusetts, Nov. 3, 1797; studied at William's College from 1810–12; admitted to the bar, and practised at Great Barrington.   Author of 'The Ages,' 1821; 'Indian at the Burying-place of his Fathers;' 'Hymn of the City;' 'Battle Field;' and numerous other poetical works.   Established the *New York Review* and *Athenæum Magazine;* editor of the *New York Evening Post.*

BUBE, Adolph, German author, b. at Gotha, Sept. 23, 1802; studied at the college of his native town, and at the University of Jena, 1821; secretary of the archives of Gotha, 1834; director of the Ducal Museum, of Kunstcabinet, of Gotha, 1842.   Author of 'Deutsche Sagen und sagenhafte Anklänge,' Jena, 1842; 'Neue Gedichte,' ib. 1840; and other works in poetry and prose.

BUCCLEUCH, Walter Francis Montagu Douglas Scott, Duke of, English statesman, b. 1806; studied at St. John's College, Cambridge, and graduated M.A. 1827; succeeded his father, 1819; high-steward of Westminster; governor of the Charterhouse; lord-lieutenant of Midlothian and Roxburghshire, and captain of the Queen's body-guard in Scotland; lord privy seal and lord president of the council, 1842–46.

BUCHANAN, Isaac, Canadian politician, b. at Glasgow, Scotland, in 1810; entered a mercantile house at Glasgow as partner, 1830; took an active part in the suppression of the Canadian revolution of 1837; elected deputy for Toronto, 1841; member of the executive council of the province of Quebec, and president of the Board of Trade in the city of Hamilton.

BUCHANAN, Right Hon. Sir Andrew, English diplomatist, b. 1807; entered the diplomatic service, 1825; chargé d'affaires at Florence, 1842, and at St. Petersburg, 1844; minister plenipotentiary at Switzerland, 1852; envoy extraordinary at Copenhagen 1853, at Madrid 1858, and at the Hague 1860; ambassador to the Court of Prussia 1862–66.

BUCHEZ, Philippe Joseph Benjamin, French author, b. at Matagne-la-Petite, March 31, 1796; obtained diploma of M.D. 1825; representative of the department of the Seine at the Constituent Assembly, 1848.   Author of 'L'Essai d'un Traité complet de Philosophie au point de vue du Catholicisme et du Progrès,' Paris, 1839; 'Histoire de la Formation de la Nationalité Français,' 1859; and other philosophical works.

BUCKINGHAM, Joseph, American journalist and politican, b. Dec. 21, 1779; member of the Legislature and of the Senate of Massachusetts.   Author of 'Specimens of Newspaper Literature,' Boston; 'Personal Memoirs and Recollections of Editorial Life;' and other works.

BUCKINGHAM AND CHANDOS, Richard Plantagenet Campbell, Duke of, English statesman, b. 1823, only son of the second Duke of Buckingham; educated at Eton, and Christ Church, Oxford; sat as M.P. for Buckingham, 1846–57; keeper of the privy seal to the Prince of Wales, 1852; chairman of the London and North-Western Railway Company, 1853–61; succeeded to the dukedom, July, 1861; lord president of the council, July 6, 1866, to March 6, 1867; appointed secretary of state for the colonies, March 6, 1867.

BUCKLAND, Francis Trevelyan, English naturalist, b. in 1826; educated at Winchester School, and Christ Church, Oxford, where he graduated B.A. 1848; studied medicine, and was assistant-surgeon to the 2d Life Guards, 1854 to 1863. Author of 'Curiosities of Natural History;' and editor of his father's. Dean Buckland's, 'Bridgewater Treatise on Geology and Mineralogy.'

BUCKLEY, Edmund, English politician, b. 1834; justice of the peace and deputy-lieutenant for the county of Merioneth; assumed the surname of Buckley in lieu of his patronymic, Peck, by royal licence, 1864; M.P. for Newcastle-under-Lyne, 1865.

BUCKMAN, James, English writer, b. at Cheltenham, 1816; curator and resident professor at the Birmingham Philosophical Institution, 1846; professor of geology and botany at the Royal Agricultural College of Cirencester, 1848 to 1863. Author of 'Our Triangle; Letters on the Geology, Botany, and Archæology of the neighbourhood of Cheltenham,' 1842; 'The Remains of Roman Art,' 1850; 'Science and Practice in Farm Cultivation,' 1863; and numerous other scientific works.

BUCKSTONE, John Baldwin, English actor and dramatic author, b. near London in 1802; made his début at Wokingham, Berks, 1821; first appearance in London at the Surrey Theatre, 1824; performed at the Haymarket Theatre since 1837, and became lessee and manager of the same, 1866. Author of more than one hundred and fifty comedies, dramas, and farces.

BUCKWALD, Joseph Heinrich von, Danish writer, b. at Vienna, Oct. 2, 1787; entered the military school of Copenhagen; served in the French navy, and took part in the campaigns of Austria, Spain, and Portugal; returned to Denmark in 1822, and published in French and Danish a great number of works: among them, 'L'Age poétique d'un Scandinave,' Paris, 1823; 'Tankelege og Digterforsåg,' 1851.

BUDBERG, Andrew, Baron, Russian diplomatist, b. in 1820; entered the diplomatic service, 1842; secretary of the Russian Legation at Frankfort, 1846; chargé d'affaires in the same city, 1849; envoy extraordinary and minister plenipotentiary to Berlin, 1851; and to Hanover and Mecklenburg, 1852; the same at Vienna, 1856; returned to Berlin, March 19, 1858; ambassador to France, 1862–68.

BUDDEUS, Aurelio, German writer, b. at Altenburg in 1817; studied medicine at Leipsic, and received the diploma of M.D. 1842. Author of 'Petersburg im kranken Leben,' Stuttgard, 1846; 'Halbrussisches,' Leipsic, 1847; 'Das Schweizerland,' 1853.

BUELL, Don Carlos, American general, b. in the state of Ohio in 1819; admitted as a cadet at West Point, 1837; entered the army as second-lieutenant of infantry, 1841; first lieutenant, and engaged in the war in Mexico, 1845; captain, 1846; major, 1847; assistant adjutant-general, 1848; lieutenant-colonel, 1861; major-general, 1862; retired from the army, 1865.

BUFFET, Louis Joseph, French politician, b. at Mirecourt, Vosges, Oct. 26, 1818; studied law, and practised at the Paris bar; elected to the French Constituent Assembly by the department of the Vosges, 1848; minister of commerce and agriculture, 1848–49; member of the Legislative Assembly, 1850–51; member of the general council for the canton of Thillot; deputy to the Corps Législatif, 1864–67.

BUGUET, Jean Joseph, French writer, b. at Leviers, Doubs, in 1793; studied law at Dijon, and obtained the degree of LL.D. 1821; member of the general council of Doubs, 1858. Author of 'Œuvres de Pothier, annotées et mises en corrélation avec le Code Civil et la Législation actuelle,' 1845–48; and several 'Memoirs.'

BULGARIS, Demetrius, Greek politician, b. at Hydra, 1801; entered the government service, and became senator, 1833; president of the provisional government of Athens, 1862; president of the council, and minister of the interior, 1863–64.

BULKELEY, Sir Richard Bulkeley Williams, English politician, b. 1801; lord-lieutenant of the county of Carnarvon; M.P. for Beaumaris, 1830–33; for Anglesey, 1833–37; for Flintshire, 1841–47; and again for Anglesey since 1847.

BULLER, Sir Arthur William, English politician, b. at Calcutta, Bengal, 1808; educated at Edinburgh and Trinity College, Cambridge; called to the bar of Lincoln's Inn, 1834; Queen's advocate in Ceylon, 1840; judge of the Supreme Court of Calcutta, 1848–58; M.P. for Devonport, 1859 to 1865; and for Liskard since 1865.

BULLER, Sir Edward Manningham, Bart. English politician, b. 1800; educated at Oriel College, Oxford; graduated B.A. 1821, and M.A. 1824; deputy-lieutenant for the county of Stafford, and high-sheriff, 1853; M.P. for North Staffordshire, 1833–42; for Stafford, 1842–47; for North Staffordshire, 1865.

BULLER, Sir George, English general, b. in 1804; entered the army, 1820; lieutenant-colonel in the infantry, 1841; took part in the Kaffir war, and was present at Boom

Plats, 1848; staff-major, 1852; fought at Alma and Inkerman; major-general and K.C.B. 1855; lieutenant-general, 1862.

BULOW, Friederich Kubech Heinrich von, Danish statesman, b. at Neustrup, Schleswig, Feb. 4, 1791; entered the army, and present at the siege of Copenhagen in 1807; commander of the fortress of Fredericia, 1848; governor of the duchy of Schleswig, 1851–54; minister plenipotentiary of Denmark to Great Britain, 1855.

BULOZ, François, French writer, b. at Valbens, Geneva, in 1803; studied at Paris, and founded the *Revue des Deux Mondes*, 1831, and *L'Annuaire des Deux Mondes*, 1850; royal commissioner for the Comédie Française, 1838 to 1848.

BULWER, Right Hon. Sir Henry Lytton Earle, English diplomatist, b. 1805; entered the diplomatic service in 1829, and successively attached to the British embassies at Berlin, Brussels, and the Hague; M.P. for Wilton, 1830; for Coventry, 1831–32; for Marylebone, 1834 to 1837; secretary of embassy at Constantinople, 1837; secretary of embassy at Paris, 1839; minister plenipotentiary at the Court of Madrid, 1843–48; ambassador at Washington, U.S. 1849; envoy extraordinary to Tuscany, 1852–55; ambassador at Constantinople, 1857–66. Author of 'An Autumn in Greece;' 'France, Social and Military;' 'The Monarchy of the Middle Classes;' 'Life of Lord Byron.'

BUNGE, Alexander, Russian botanist, b. at Kiew, Sept. 24, 1803; studied at the University of Dorpat, and obtained the diploma of M.D. 1825; professor of botany at Kasan, and professor and director of the Botanical Gardens at Dorpat, 1836. Author of 'Enumeratio Plantarum quas in China boreali collegit,' St. Petersburg, 1831; 'Beitrag zur Kenntniss der Flora Russlands in den Steppen Central Asiens,' St. Petersburg and Leipsic, 1851; and numerous other works.

BUNGE, Frederick George, Russian author, b. at Kiew, March 1, 1802, brother of the preceding; studied law at the University of Dorpat, and professor of jurisprudence there, 1823. Author of 'Ueber den Sachsenspiegel, als Quelle des mittleren und umgearbeiteten livländischen Ritterrechts,' Riga, 1827; 'Liv.-Esth. und Kurländisches Urkundenbuch nebst Regesten,' Reval, 1852–53; and many other legal works.

BUNSEN, Robert Wilhelm Eberhard, German chemist, b. at Göttingen, March 13, 1811; studied at Göttingen University, and at Paris, Berlin, and Vienna; professor at the Polytechnic Institute of Cassel, 1836, and at the University of Marburg, 1838; titular professor at the University of Breslau, 1851. Author of 'Eisenoxydhydrat, das Gegengift, &c.' 1837; and other works on chemistry.

BUOL-SCHAUENSTEIN, Karl Ferdinand, Count, German statesman and diplomatist, b. in the canton of Grisons, Switzerland, May 17, 1797; entered the Austrian diplomatic service, 1816; secretary to the embassy at Paris 1822, at London 1824, at Carlsruhe 1828; envoy extraordinary to the Court of Darmstadt 1831, at Stuttgard 1838; plenipotentiary at Turin, 1848; ambassador at London, 1851–52; minister of foreign affairs of Austria, 1852–59; privy councillor and chamberlain of the Emperor of Austria.

BUONCOMPAGNI, Baltassarre, Italian author, b. at Rome, May 10, 1821; appointed member of the pontifical academy, De Nuovi Lincei, 1847, of which he afterwards became librarian and treasurer. Author of 'The Life and Works of Guido Bonatti, Astrologer and Astronomer of the Thirteenth Century,' Rome, 1851; the 'Life and Works of Leonardo Pisano;' and several other historical publications.

BUQUET, Henri Alfred Leopold, Baron, French politician, b. at Paris, July 15, 1809; mayor of Nancy, and member of the General Council for the canton of that town; entered the Corps Législatif for the second department of the Meurthe in 1852; re-elected, 1863.

BURBURE WEZEMBEEK, Leon Philippe Marie, Chevalier de, Belgian writer and musical composer, b. at Termonde in 1812; studied law and received the degree of LL.D. from the University of Gand, 1832; librarian of the archives of the church of Notre-Dame of Termonde, 1842, and of the cathedral of Antwerp, 1846. Published 'Inscriptions de la Province d'Anvers,' 1852.

BURCHAM, Thomas Borrow, English lawyer, b. in 1809; studied at Trinity College, Cambridge, and graduated B.A. 1830; elected fellow of Trinity College, 1832; called to the bar of the Inner Temple, 1843; recorder of Bedford, 1848; police-magistrate in London, 1850.

BURDACH, Ernst, German anatomist, b. at Leipsic, 1801; professor of anatomy at *the University of Königsberg.* Published 'Beitrag zur mikroskopischen Anatomie der Nerven,' *Königsberg, 1837;* and an edition of his father's works on anthropology in *1847.*

BURGESS, Rev. George, American divine, b. at Providence, Rhode Island, U.S. Oct. 31, 1809; educated at the Universities of Göttingen and Bonn, Germany; rector of Christ Church, Hartford, 1840–47; bishop of Maine, 1847. Published 'The Book of Psalms in English Verse;' and 'Pages from the Ecclesiastical History of England.'

BURGESS, Rev. Richard, English author, b. 1796; educated at St. John's College, Cambridge, and graduated B.A. 1820; British chaplain at Rome, 1831; rector of Upper Chelsea, Middlesex, 1836. Author of 'Ludi Circenses,' 1827; 'The Topography and Antiquities of Rome,' 1831; 'Greece and the Levant,' 1835; and various pamphlets on education.

BURGHLEY, Lord William Alleyne, English politician, b. 1825; educated at Eton, and St. John's College, Cambridge, and graduated M.A. 1846; magistrate and deputy-lieutenant for Northamptonshire and Lincolnshire; M.P. for Lincolnshire, 1847–57; for Northamptonshire since 1857.

BURGON, Rev. John William, English author, b. 1819; educated at Worcester College, Oxford, and graduated 1848; fellow of Oriel College, 1848. Author of a translation of Chevalier Brönsted's 'Memoir of the Panathenaic Vases,' 1833; 'Oxford Reformers,' 1854; 'Historical Notices of the Colleges of Oxford,' 1857; Portrait of a Christian Gentleman,' 1861; and other works.

BURKE, Peter, English author, b. in 1813; educated at Caen College; called to the bar of the Inner Temple, 1839; parliamentary counsel in the House of Lords; Q.C. of the county palatine of Lancaster, 1858, and sergeant-at-law, 1859. Author of 'The Romance of the Forum;' 'Celebrated Trials connected with the Aristocracy and the Upper Classes;' and of several legal works.

BURKE, Sir John Bernard, English genealogical writer, b. in London in 1815; educated at the College of Caen, Normandy, and called to the bar of the Middle Temple, 1839; Ulster king-at-arms, and knight attendant of the order of St. Patrick, 1853; knighted, 1854; degree of LL.D. from the University of Dublin, 1862. Editor of 'Burke's Peerage,' and author of several books on genealogical, historical, and antiquarian subjects.

BURKEL, Heinrich, German painter, b. at Pirmasentz, Bavaria, Sept. 9, 1802; studied painting at the Academy of Munich; painted numerous landscapes and battle scenes: among them, 'Fêtes on the Alps;' 'Scenes in the Tyrol.'

BURMEISTER, Hermann, German naturalist, b. at Stralsund, Prussia, in 1807; studied medicine at the Universities of Greifswald and Halle, and obtained the diploma of M.D. in 1829; professor of zoology at the University of Halle, 1842; deputy to the National Assembly for the city of Halle, 1848, and to the first Prussian Chamber for the town of Liegnitz. Author of 'History of the Creation,' Leipsic, 1843, fourth edition 1851; 'Uebersicht der Thiere Braziliens, 1854–56; and numerous scientific works.

BURNAP, George, American theologian, b. at Merrimack, New Hampshire, 1802; studied theology, and became minister of the church of Baltimore, 1827. Author of 'Lectures on the Doctrines of Controversy,' Baltimore, 1835; 'Lectures on the Sphere and Duties of Women,' ib. 1840; 'Christianity, its Essence and Evidence,' Boston, 1855; and other theological works.

BURNET, Pierre Gustave, French writer, b. at Bordeaux, Nov. 18, 1807; member of the Academy of Belles-Lettres, and mayor of Bordeaux. Author of 'Recueil d'Opuscules et de Fragments en Vers patois,' 1839; 'Curiosités théologiques,' 1861;' and other works of general literature.

BURNOUF, Emile Louis, French writer, b. at Valogues, Manche, Aug. 25, 1821; studied at the Lyceum of St. Louis; professor of literature to the Faculty of Nancy. Published 'Extraits du Novum Organum de Bacon,' 1854; 'Essai sur le Véda, ou Introduction à la Connaissance de l'Inde,' 1863; 'Dictionnaire classique Sanscrit-Français,' 1863–64.

BURNS, Rev. Jabez, English theological writer, b. at Oldham, Manchester, in 1805; educated at Chester and Oldham Grammar School; minister of the United Christian Church at Perth, 1830–35; minister of the Baptist Church of Marylebone since 1835. Author of 'The Christian Sketch-Book,' 1828; 'Sketches and Skeletons of Sermons.' Editor of the *Temperance Journal*, 1839, and founder of the *Preachers' Magazine.*

BURNSIDE, Ambrose Everitt, American military commander, b. at Liberty, Union County, Indiana, May 23, 1824; educated at West Point Academy, 1843; second lieutenant, Sept. 8, 1847; first lieutenant, Dec. 1851; resigned, Oct. 2, 1853; colonel and brigadier-general, Aug. 1861; commander of a corps of reserve in General Grant's army, 1864; governor of Rhode Island, 1865.

BURRELL, Sir Percy, Bart. English politician, b. 1812; deputy-lieutenant for Sussex; M.P. for Shoreham since 1862.

BURRITT, Alexander, American writer, b. at New York, 1807; studied at Columbia College, and graduated, 1824; called to the bar of New York, 1828. Published 'Practice of the Supreme Court of the State of New York,' 1840;' 'A Law Dictionary and Glossary,' 1850; 'Treatise on Circumstantial Evidence,' 1856.

BURRITT, Elihu, American author and lecturer, b. in Connecticut, 1811; apprenticed to a blacksmith; studied. while working at his trade, mathematics, Latin, French, Spanish, Greek, Hebrew, Italian, German, and Russian. Author of 'Sparks from the Anvil,' London, 1848; and 'Olive Leaves,' ib. 1853.

BURROWS, George, English physician and medical writer, b. in 1802; studied at Cambridge, and graduated M.D. 1829; fellow of the Royal College of Physicians, 1832; physician to St. Bartholomew's Hospital, 1834; physician to Christ's Hospital. Author of 'The Disorders of the Cerebral Circulation, and the Connexion of Diseases of the Heart and Brain.'

BURT, Archibald Paull, English colonial judge, b. 1818; called to the bar of the Middle Temple, Nov. 1845; attorney-general of St. Christopher from 1849 to 1860; civil commissioner and chairman of quarter sessions in Western Australia, July, 1860; chief justice, 1861.

BURTON, John Hill, English author, b. at Aberdeen, Aug. 22, 1809; studied at Marischal College, where he graduated A.M.; advocate at the Scottish bar, 1831; secretary to the Prison Board of Scotland, 1854. Author of 'Life and Correspondence of David Hume,' Edinburgh, 1846; 'History of Scotland from the Revolution to the Extinction of the last Jacobite Insurrection,' London, 1853; 'The Scot Abroad,' 1864; and numerous others, chiefly historical works.

BURTON, Richard Francis, African traveller, b. 1821; entered the Indian army, 1842; became captain, 1857; military secretary under General Beatson, 1855; counsel at Fernando Po, 1861. Author of 'The Lake Regions of Central Africa; 'Abeokuta, and the Cameroon Mountains,' 1863; 'Mission to Gelele, King of Dahomey,' 1864; and several other narratives, travels, and adventures.

BURTON, Sir William Westbrooke, English colonial judge, b. in 1794; served in the navy for some years; was called to the bar of the Inner Temple, 1824; recorder of Daventry, 1826; and appointed judge at the Cape of Good Hope, 1827; transferred to New South Wales, 1833, and to Madras, 1844; president of the Council or Upper House of Representatives at Sydney, 1856. Author of 'Treatise on the Laws affecting Insolvents in New South Wales,' and 'State of Religion and Education in Australia.'

BURY, Right Hon. William Coutts Keppel, Viscount, English politician, b. in 1832; educated at Eton; entered the Scots Fusilier Guards, 1849; private secretary to Lord John Russell, 1850–51; civil secretary and superintendent-general of Indian affairs for the province of Canada, 1854; treasurer of the royal household, 1859; M.P. for Wick district of Burghs, 1860; sworn privy councillor, 1859. Author of several political and historical papers in *Fraser's Magazine* and other periodicals.

BUS, Alberic du, Belgian politician, b. at Tournai, May 10, 1810, brother of the preceding; commissioner of the district of Mons; elected to the Chamber of Representatives for the district of Turnhout, 1840; representative of Brussels, 1854.

BUS, François Louis Joseph du, Belgian politician, b. at Tournai in 1791; deputy to the National Congress, 1830; member of the Chamber of Representatives for the district of Tournai, 1834–40; and for Turnhout since 1844.

BUS DE GHISIGNIES, Bernard Ame Leonard, Vicomte du, Belgian naturalist, b. at Tournai in 1808; sent to the Chamber of Representatives for the district of Soignies, 1835–47; director of the Natural History Museum of Brussels; member of the Entomological Society of France and the Royal Academy of Belgium.

BUSH, George, American writer, b. at Norwich, Vermont, June 12, 1796; studied at the Seminary of Princeton, and was for several years missionary for the Presbyterian church to Indiana; professor of Hebrew literature at the University of New York, 1831. Author of 'Life of Mahomed,' 1832; 'Notes on Genesis, Exodus, Leviticus, etc.' New York, 1840; 'The Soul, an Inquiry into Scriptural Psychology;' and a great number of theological works.

BUSK, Hans, English writer, b. in 1815; educated at King's College, London, and Trinity College, Cambridge, where he graduated B.A. 1841, and M.A. 1844; called to the bar of the Middle Temple, 1841. Author of 'The Rifle, and How to Use it;' 'Volunteers, and How to Drill them.' Founder, and for some years editor, of the *New Quarterly Review.*

BUSONI, Philippe, French writer, b. May 15, 1806. Author of 'L'Egmont, ou Paris et Saint Cloud au 18 Brumaire,' 1831; 'Anselme,' 1835; 'Chefs-d'œuvre poetiques des Dames françaises,' 1841; 'Les Etrusques,' 1843; 'Mémoires de la Princesse Palatine Duchesse d'Orléans,' 1832; and numerous contributions to the periodical press.

BUSQUET, Alfred, French writer, b. in 1820; studied at Rouen and Paris. Editor of *La Silhouette*, 1840 to 1850; contributor to the *Pays, L'Artiste, La Liberté, Revue française.*

BUSS, Franz Joseph, German writer, b. at Zelle, in 1803; studied philosophy, medicine, and law, at Offenburg and at Friburg; professor of Public Law, 1833; member of the Second Chamber of the Grand Duchy of Baden, 1837-46; deputy to the National Assembly of Frankfort, 1848. Author of 'Geschichte und System der Staatswissenschaft,' 1839; 'Urkundliche Geschichte des national und territorial Kirchenthums,' Schaffhausen, 1851; and numerous legal and theological works.

BUSSIERE, Alfred Renouard, Baron de, French politician, b. June 14, 1804; president of the Tribunal of Commerce, Strasbourg; member of the Corps Législatif for the department of Bas-Rhin, 1852; re-elected, 1863; manager of the company of the Crédit Mobilier.

BUSSON, Julien Henri, French politician, b. at Joigny, Yonne, July 24, 1823; called to the bar, 1845; LL.D. Aug. 1848; deputy to the Corps Législatif for the department of the Ariege, 1854; member of the General Council of the department for the canton of Castillon.

BUSSY, Antoine Alexander Brutus, French physician, b. at Marseilles, 1794; admitted M.D. at Paris, 1832; director of the 'École de Pharmacie,' 1840; member of the Academy of Sciences, 1850. Author of 'Clinical Researches on the Soap-wort of Egypt,' Paris, 1833; and numerous other medical works.

BUSTAMANTE, Don Carlos Maria de, Mexican archæologist, b. in Mexico near the end of the last century. Author of 'Statistical Memoir on the Oaxacu Country,' 1821; 'Texcoco in the last Days of its ancient Kings,' Mexico, 1826; 'Descripcion Historica y Cronologica de las dos Piedras, etc.' Mexico, 1832. Editor of 'A Complete History of the Events which have taken place in New Spain,' ib. 1839.

BUTLER, Benjamin Franklin, American military commander, b. at Deerfield, New Hampshire, Nov. 5, 1818; educated at Lowell High School and Waterville College; admitted to the bar, 1840; member of the Massachusetts State Legislature, 1853; brigadier-general of militia, 1857; commanded the Federal Forces in Virginia, 1861; organized an expedition against New Orleans, which surrendered April 28, 1862; major-general, Dec. 1862.

BUTLER, Charles Salisbury, English politician, b. 1812; magistrate for Middlesex, City of Westminster, and Liberties of the Tower, and commissioner of Land, Property, and Income Taxes; M.P. for the Tower Hamlets since 1852.

BUTLER, William Allen, American writer, b. at Albany, in 1825; studied at the University of New York, and was admitted to the bar. Author of 'The Cities of Art and the Early Artists;' 'Out-of-the-way Places in Europe;' 'The Colonel's Club;' 'Barnum's Parnassus,' 1850; 'The Queen of Song;' 'Miseries of Crinoline,' 1859.

BUTT, Isaac, English politician, b. in 1813; studied at Trinity College, Dublin, and graduated, 1835; Whately professor of political economy, 1836; called to the Irish bar, 1838; M.P. for Harwich, 1852; M.P. for Youghal, Ireland, since 1852. Author of 'History of the Kingdom of Italy,' 1860; 'A Letter to Lord Morpeth,' 1837; 'Lectures on Political Economy.' For some time editor and contributor to the *Dublin University Magazine.*

BUTTERFIELD, William, English architect, b. Sept. 7, 1814. Designed St. Augustine's College, Canterbury; All Saints' church, Margaret-street, London; Baldersby church, Yorkshire; Yealmpton church, Devon; the new chapel at Balliol College, Oxford; and St. Alban's church, Baldwin's Gardens, Gray's Inn Road, and other public buildings.

BUXTON, Charles, English politician, b. 1822; educated at Trinity College, Cambridge; graduated in honours, 1843; M.P. for Newport, Isle of Wight, from 1857 to 1859; M.P. for Maidstone, 1859-65; and for East Surrey, 1865. Author of a Life of his father, Sir Thomas Fowell Buxton, and of many articles in the Reviews of the day.

BUXTON, Sir Thomas Fowell, Bart. English politician, b. 1837; educated at Harrow, and Trinity College, Cambridge; graduated M.A. 1859; deputy-lieutenant for Essex and Norfolk; M.P. for Lyme Regis, 1865.

BYLES, Sir John Barnard, English judge, b. in 1801; called to the bar of the Inner Temple, 1831; recorder of Buckingham, 1840; serjeant-at-law, 1843; Queen's serjeant, 1857; judge of the Court of Common Pleas, and knighted, 1858. Author of several legal works: among them, 'On the Usury Laws;' 'On Bills of Exchange;' and 'The Sophism of Free Trade.'

BYRON, Henry James, English dramatic writer. b. at Manchester, 1835; educated at St. Peter's School, London; called to the bar of the Middle Temple. Author of 'Fra Diavolo;' 'Esmeralda;' 'Ill-treated Il Trovatore;' 'Dundreary married and done for;' 'War to the Knife,' 1865; and numerous comedies, farces, burlesques, and pantomimes.

BYSTROM, Johan Niklas, Swedish sculptor, b. at Phillippsden, Wermeland, Dec. 18, 1783; studied art at Stockholm. Executed several colossal statues of the Swedish kings in marble, and other works. Published, in the Swedish language, 'Bystrom's Sculpture Gallery,' 1849–66.

C.

CABALLERO, Firmin Agosto, Spanish statesman, b. at Barajas del Melo, July 17, 1800; studied law and called to the bar of Madrid; took part in the Revolution of 1820; retired to Estramadura, 1823: elected to the Cortes for Madrid and Cuença, 1836. Author of 'El Gobierno y los Cortes del Estatuto, materiales para su Historia,' Madrid, 1837; 'Manual Geografico-Administrativo de la Monarquia Espanola,' ib. 1844.

CABANEL, Alexandre, French painter, b. at Montpellier, Sept. 28, 1823; studied under M. Picot, and executed 'Agonie du Christ du Jardin des Oliviers,' 1844; 'St. Jean,' 1850; 'Le Martyr chrétien,' 1855; 'Portrait de l'Empereur,' 1865; and numerous other paintings, chiefly historical.

CABAT, Nicolas Louis, French painter, b. at Paris, Dec. 24, 1812; studied under M. Camille Flers, and painted 'Le Soir au lever de la Lune,' 1855; 'Une Source dans les Bois,' 1864; and other landscapes.

CABEL, Marie Joseph Dreullette, French actress, b. at Liege, Jan. 31, 1827; studied music under M. Louis Joseph Cabel, whom she married, and at the Conservatoire, 1848–49; engaged at the Théatre de l'Opera Comique, Paris, 1850–62, and at the Théatre Lyrique,' 1863.

CABRERA, Don Ramon, Count of Morella, Spanish military commander, b. at Tortosa in Catalonia, Aug. 31, 1810; joined the cause of Don Carlos, 1833, and was made captain; lieutenant-general, 1838, and created Count of Morella; took refuge in France, 1840; resided in Lyons, 1841; landed in Spain, June 1848; fought the battle of Pasteral, Jan. 27, 1849; was wounded, and returned to France; has lived in retirement since 1854.

CADELL, Francis, English navigator, b. 1822; educated at Edinburgh and in Germany; midshipman in an East Indiaman; took part in the Chinese war as a volunteer; present at the siege of Canton, the capture of Amoy and Ningpoo; commander of a vessel, 1844; navigated the river Murray, Australia, 1851.

CADIZ, Fitzwilliams, English colonial judge, b. 1825; studied at Pembroke College, Oxford, and graduated B.A.; called to the bar of Lincoln's Inn, 1855; acting clerk of council of the island of Trinidad in 1858; member of Privy Council of the island of Tobago; appointed stipendiary magistrate in the same island, April 1862, and coroner and visiting justice of the gaol; member of the executive committee, 1860.

CADOGAN, Henry Charles, Earl of, English diplomatist, b. in London, 1812; educated at Oriel College, Oxford, where he graduated B.A. 1832; was attaché at St. Petersburg from June 1834 to July 1835; secretary of embassy at Paris from March 1858 to July 1859; M.P. for Reading from 1841 to 1847; for Dover from July 1852 to April 1857; colonel of the Westminster Middlesex Militia; succeeded his father, 1864.

CADOGAN, Hon. George, English general, b. 1814; entered the Guards as ensign and lieutenant, Feb. 22, 1823; lieutenant and captain, 1838; lieutenant-colonel, 1847; colonel, 1854; created C.B. Dec. 29, 1856; major-general, June 23, 1862; cross of commander of the order of St. Maurice, 1856, and the imperial order of Medjidie, 1858.

CADORE, Louis de Champagny, Duke de, French politician, b. Jan. 12, 1796; succeeded at the death of his father to the ducal title, 1834, and took his seat in the *House of Peers, Sept. 11, 1835*; after the Revolution of 1848 was counsel-general of the *Loire; charged to temporarily replace the Duke de Grammont at Rome, May 1861.*

CADOUDAL, Louis George de, French writer, b. at Auzon, Haute Loire, Feb. 10, 1823. Author of 'Faits et Récits contemporaines, et Recueil anecdotique,' 1860; 'Les Signes du Temps, Critiques littéraires et morales,' 1861; 'Les Serviteurs des Hommes,' 1864; and other works of general literature.

CAFFARELLI, Eugene Auguste, Comte de, French politician, b. at Milan, Dec. 31, 1806; auditor to the Council of State, July 1832; préfet of Ille-et-Vilaine, Jan. 24, 1849; resigned, March 9, 1851; member of the General Council of Aisne; member of the Corps Législatif for the second circonscription of Ille-et-Vilaine, 1852.

CAFFE, Paul Louis Balthazar, French physician, b. at Chambery, Savoy, 1803; diploma of M.D. at Paris, 1833; professor at the Hôtel Dieu. Published 'Rapport sur l'Opthalmie regnante en Belgique,' 1840; and author of several medical works.

CAHEN, Samuel, French writer, b. at Metz, Aug. 4, 1796; studied at the Jewish College at Mayence; director of the Jewish School at Paris. Author of a French translation of the Bible, in 18 vols., commenced 1831, completed 1853; 'A Course of Hebrew Reading;' and other elementary works.

CAHILL, Rev. Daniel William, English writer, b. in Queen's County, Ireland, 1802; studied at Carlow College, and at Maynooth, where he was ordained; professor of Natural History in Carlow College. Author of several pamphlets, and former editor of the *Dublin Telegraph*.

CAILLIAUD, Frederic, French traveller, b. at Nantes, March 17, 1797; studied at Paris; conservator of the Museum of Natural History at Nantes, 1827. Author of 'Recherches sur les Oases, sur les Mines d'Emeraudes, et sur l'ancienne Route du Commerce entre le Nil et la Mer Rouge,' 1822; 'Voyage à Méroé et au Fleuve Blanc, etc.' 1827; and other works of travels.

CAIN, Auguste, French sculptor, b. at Paris, Nov. 1822; studied under Reede. Exhibited 'The Dormouse and Tomtit,' 1846; 'The Frogs wishing for a King,' 1850; 'The Eagle defending his Prey,' 1852; 'An Eagle chasing a Vulture,' 1857; and numerous other works.

CAIRD, James, English politician, b. at Stranraer, 1816; educated at Edinburgh; M.P. for Dartmouth, 1857; for Stirling, 1859; member of the Fishery Board, 1860; chairman of the Royal Commission on the Sea Fisheries of the United Kingdom, 1863. Author of several works on farming.

CAIRD, Rev. John, Scottish minister, b. at Greenock, 1823; studied at the University of Glasgow, and licensed as a preacher, 1844; ordained minister of Newton-on-Ayre, 1845; minister at Errol, in Perthshire, 1850, and at Glasgow, 1858.

CAIRNS, Hugh MacCalmont, Lord, English statesman, b. 1819; educated at Trinity College, Dublin; called to the bar of the Middle Temple, Jan. 1844; appointed Queen's counsel and bencher of Lincoln's Inn, 1856; solicitor-general, March 1858, and knighted at that date; LL.D. of Cambridge, 1862; D.C.L. of Oxford, 1863; lord high chancellor, 1868.

CAITHNESS, James Sinclair, Earl of, English statesman, b. 1821; appointed deputy-lieutenant of Caithness, 1848; lord-lieutenant, 1856; succeeded his father, 1855; lord-in-waiting to the Queen from April 1856 to Feb. 1858; re-appointed, 1859; elected a representative peer for Scotland, June 1858; is the inventor of the 'Road Locomotive Steam Engine.'

CALDERON, Philippe Hermogenes, French painter, b. at Poitiers in 1833; studied at Paris under M. Picot. Exhibited at the Royal Academy 'The Gaoler's Daughter.' 1858; 'Man goeth forth to his Labour,' 1859; 'Drink to me only with thine Eyes,' 1863; 'Women of Arles,' 1864; and numerous others.

CALDERON, Don Serafin Estevan, Spanish poet, b. at Malaga about the beginning of the present century; studied at the University of Granada; professor of poetry and rhetoric there; auditor-general of the Army of the North, 1834. Author of 'Poesias del Solitario,' 1833; 'The Christians and Moors,' 1838; 'Andalusian Scenes,' 1847; and several others.

CALFA, Ambrose Yousouf-bey, Armenian writer, b. at Constantinople, March 2, 1830; studied at the College of Mekhitaristes, Venice; professor at the College of Moorat, Paris, 1848; préfet of studies in same college, 1854. Author of 'Universal History,' Venice, 1851; 'Armenian and French Dictionary,' Paris, 1860; and numerous other works.

CALLAGHAN, Jeremiah Thomas Fitzgerald, English colonial administrator, b. 1813; educated at Trinity College, Dublin; took honours in classics; held the appointment of Barrington lecturer on political economy to the Dublin Statistical Society; was counsel to the attorney-general for Ireland ; appointed chief magistrate for Hong-Kong, 1860 ; called to the Irish bar, 1854 ; appointed governor of Labuan, April 10, 1862 ; acting consul-general, 1866.

CALMELS, Anatole Celestin, French sculptor, b. in Paris, March 26, 1825 ; studied under Karl Elshoëet, Bosio, and Pradier, and at the School of Fine Arts, 1840. Executed 'La Guerre,' 1840 ; 'La Naissance de la Vierge, 'La Présentation au Temple' (bas-reliefs for the church of St. Maurice at Lille), 1850–52 ; and numerous statues and groups.

CALONNE, Alponse Bernard, Vicomte de, French politician, b. at Béthune, 1818 ; studied law in Paris, 1840 to 1842. Author of 'Bérangère,' 1852 ; 'Les Frais de la Guerre,' 1856 ; 'De la Défense des Côtes en Angleterre,' 1851 ; and numerous political works.

CALTHORPE, Frederick Gough, Baron, English politician, b. in London, 1790 ; educated at Christ Church, Oxford ; assumed the name of Gough, 1845 ; M.P. for Hindon from 1818 to 1826 ; and for Bramber from 1826 to 1830 ; deputy-lieutenant and high sheriff of Staffordshire, 1848 ; succeeded his brother in 1851.

CALTHORPE, Hon. Frederick William Henry Gough, English politician, eldest son of the preceding, b. 1826 ; magistrate and deputy-lieutenant for Warwickshire ; M.P. for Worcestershire, 1855.

CALVERT, George Henry, American writer, b. at Baltimore, 1803 ; studied at Harvard College, and at the German University of Göttingen. Author of 'Illustrations of Phrenology,' 1832 ; 'Count Julian,' 1840 ; 'Scenes and Thoughts in Europe,' New York, 1848 ; and numerous translations of German works.

CALVERT, Rev. William, English clergyman, b. in 1819 ; educated at Pembroke College, Cambridge, where he graduated B.A. 1842 ; appointed minor canon of St. Paul's, 1848 ; rector of St. Antholin and St. John the Baptist, Walbrook, 1849 ; incumbent of Kentish Town, 1858. Author of 'The Wife's Manual,' 1854 ; 'Pneuma, or the Wandering Soul,' 1856.

CAMBACE'RES, Marie Jean Pierre Hubert, Duc de, French senator, b. at Montpellier, Sept. 20, 1798 ; studied law and called to the bar at Paris, 1823 ; senator, 1851 ; grand master of ceremonies in the Emperor's household.

CAMBRIDGE, George William Frederick Charles, Duke of, English prince, b. 1819, cousin to her Majesty ; president of Christ's Hospital ; colonel in the Grenadier Guards ; ranger of St. James's and Hyde parks ; appointed colonel in the army, 1837 ; lieutenant-general, 1854 ; general commander-in-chief, 1856 ; field-marshal, 1862 ; served in the Crimea, 1854–55 ; has been inspector-general of cavalry.

CAMDEN, John Charles, Marquis, b. 1840 ; educated at Eton and Cambridge ; deputy-lieutenant of Kent ; M.P. for Brecknock, 1866 ; succeeded his father, second marquis, Aug. 1866.

CAMERON, Sir Duncan Alexander, English general, b. 1808 ; entered the army, 1825 ; became captain, 1833 ; major, 1839 ; colonel, 1854 ; major-general, 1859 ; served in the Crimean campaign of 1854–55 ; lieutenant-general commanding the troops in New Zealand, 1863 ; created K.C.B. and knighted, 1864.

CAMERON, Simon, American statesman, b. in Lancaster County, Pennsylvania, 1792 ; appointed visitor at West Point, 1832 ; senator of the U. S. for Pennsylvania, 1845 ; secretary of war to President Lincoln, 1861.

CAMOU, Jacques, French general, b. May 1, 1792 ; entered the army, 1818 ; captain, 1823 ; chief of battalion, 1837 ; lieutenant-colonel, 1841 ; colonel, 1844 ; general of brigade, April 1848 ; general of division, Feb. 6, 1852 ; commanded a division in the Crimea and in the war in Italy ; grand cross of the Légion d'honneur, 1857 ; senator, Dec. 30, 1863.

CAMOYS, Thomas Stonor, Baron, English politician, b. in London, 1797 ; lord-in-waiting to the Queen from 1846 to Feb. 1852 ; and from Jan. 1853 to Feb. 1858 ; re-appointed, June 1859 ; returned M.P. for Oxford city, 1832, but was unseated on petition ; contested Oxford in 1835, and Oxfordshire in 1837, unsuccessfully ; summoned to the House of Lords in 1839.

CAMPBELL, Sir Alexander, Bart. English colonial administrator, b. 1819 ; succeeded his father, 1842 ; appointed superintendent of police in West Australia, Sept. 1857 ; resident magistrate of Albany in that colony, 1861.

CAMPBELL, Alexander Henry, English politician, b. 1822 ; educated at Edinburgh and Paris ; partner in the firm of Finlay, Campbell, & Co. East India merchants,

London: director of the London and St. Katharine's Docks; elected M.P. for Launceston, 1865.

CAMPBELL, Sir Alexander Thomas Cockburn, Bart. English politician, b. at Madras, 1804; succeeded his maternal grandfather in 1824; assumed the name of Campbell, 1825.

CAMPBELL, Sir Archibald Islay, Bart. English politician, b. at Garscube, Dumbartonshire, in 1825; educated at Eton and Christ Church, Oxford; where he was second in classics, 1847; appointed captain of the Glasgow Yeomanry in 1849; resigned, 1857; lieutenant-colonel-commandant of 1st Lanarkshire rifle volunteers, 1860; deputy-lieutenant of Argyleshire, 1859; M.P. for Argyleshire from 1851 to 1857.

CAMPBELL, Sir Edward Fitz-Gerald, Bart. English officer, b. in London, 1822; succeeded his father, 1849; lieutenant of 60th Rifles, 1844; captain, 1850; major in the army, 1858; lieutenant-colonel, 1860; appointed aide-de-camp to the commander-in-chief in India, 1849; military secretary to the governor-general, 1859; assistant-inspector of volunteers, 1864.

CAMPBELL, Sir Hugh Hume, Bart. English politician, b. in Edinburgh in 1812; educated at Eton, and Trinity College, Cambridge; succeeded his father in 1833; J.P. and deputy-lieutenant for the county of Berwick; M.P. for Berwickshire from 1834 to 1847.

CAMPBELL, William Frederick Campbell, Lord, English politician, b. in 1824; educated at Eton, Balliol College, Oxford, and Trinity College, Cambridge; M.A. 1846; M.P. for Cambridge, 1847–52; for Harwich, 1859–60; succeeded his father, 1861.

CAMPERDOWN, Adam Duncan Haldane, Earl, English statesman, b. at Edinburgh, 1812; educated at Eton, and Trinity College, Cambridge, where he graduated M.A. 1834; was a lord of the Treasury from March 1855 to March 1858; M.P. for Southampton from 1837 to 1841; for Bath, 1841 to 1852; and for Forfarshire, 1854 to 1859; is deputy-lieutenant of Perthshire; appointed deputy-lieutenant of Forfarshire, 1850.

CAMPHAUSEN, Ludolf, German statesman, b. at Künshoven, Aix-la-Chapelle, Jan. 4, 1803; banker at Cologne, 1825; president of the Chamber of Commerce, Cologne, 1839 to 1848; member of the provincial diet of the Rhine, 1842, and of the first general states diet convened at Berlin, 1847; president of the Prussian Council of Ministers, 1848; minister of state, 1849.

CAMPHAUSEN, Wilhelm, German painter, b. at Düsseldorf, Feb. 8, 1810; studied at the Academy of Düsseldorf. Painted 'The Puritans watching the Enemy;' 'Godfrey de Bouillon at Ascalon;' and numerous battle scenes.

CANNON, Robert, English general, b. 1797; entered the military service of the East India Company; lieutenant-colonel, 1835; colonel, 1837; retired, 1847; took part in the Russian war, 1853; commanded a Turkish division in Eupatoria, 1855; lieutenant-general, 1856.

CANROBERT, François Certain, French military commander, b. at Gers, June 17, 1809; studied at the military school of St. Cyr, 1826; entered the army as a private soldier, 1828; lieutenant, 1832; captain, April 1837; lieutenant-colonel, 1846; colonel, 1847; general of brigade, Jan. 13, 1850; general of division, Jan. 14, 1853; commander-in-chief of the French army in the Crimea, 1854–55; marshal of France, March 18, 1856; commanded in the Italian campaign of 1859.

CANTERBURY, Most Rev. Charles Thomas Longley, English divine, b. near Rochester, 1794; educated at Westminster, and elected to Christ Church, Oxford, 1812; obtained first-class classical honours, and graduated B.A. 1815; M.A. 1834; public tutor of Christ Church, Oxford, from 1818 to 1828; rector of West Tytherley, Hants, from 1827 to 1829; head-master of Harrow School from 1829 to 1836; bishop of Ripon, 1836; translated to Durham, 1856; to York, 1860; consecrated 91st archbishop of Canterbury, 1862.

CANTU, Cesare, Italian historian, b. at Brisio, near Milan, Sept. 5, 1805; professor of literature in the College of Sondrio, 1823. Author of 'Universal History,' 1843–49; 'History of the last hundred Years,' 1852; 'History of the Italians,' 1859; and numerous historical and poetical works.

CAP, Paul Antoine Gratcap, French naturalist, b. at Mâcon, April 2, 1788. Author of 'De la Classification methodique des Médicaments,' 1823; 'Études biographiques pour servir à l'Histoire des Sciences,' 1857; and many medical works.

CAPEFIGUE, Jean Baptiste Honore Raymond, French historical writer, b. at Marseilles, 1802; studied law at Aix and Paris. Author of 'Essai sur les Invasions des Normands,' 1828 ; 'Histoire des grandes Opérations financières,' 1855–57 ; ' L'Église pendant les quatre derniers Siècles,' 1858 ; and other historical works.

CAPETOWN, Right Rev. Robert Gray, English colonial bishop, b. at Bishopwearmouth Rectory, 1809 ; educated at Eton, and University College, Oxford, where he graduated B.A. 1831 ; M.A. 1834 ; ordained, 1833 ; appointed perpetual curate of Stockton-on-Tees, 1845 ; honorary canon of Durham cathedral, 1846 ; and first bishop of Capetown 1847.

CAPON, Sir David, English general, b. at Bombay, 1793 ; entered the service of the East India Company at Bombay, 1809 ; lieutenant-general, 1862.

CARAGUEL, Clement, French journalist, b. at Mazamet, Tarn, 1819. Author of 'Quatre Mois en Mer,' 1840 ; ' Souvenirs et Aventures d'un volontaire Garibaldien,' 1861 ; and numerous other works. Contributor to the *Charivari*, 1848 ; the *Journal des Débats*, 1865.

CARAYON LATOUR, Edmond, Baron de, French politician, b. at Paris, July 15, 1811 ; member of the Chamber of Deputies for the Electoral College of Castres, 1846 ; member of the Corps Législatif after 1852 for the circonscription of Castres ; re-elected, 1857.

CARDEN, Sir Robert Walter, Bart. English magistrate, b. 1801 ; alderman of the city of London, 1849 ; lord-mayor, 1857–58 ; founded the City Bank ; unsuccessfully contested the borough of St. Alban's, 1850, Gloucester, 1859, and Marylebone, 1861 ; magistrate for Middlesex and Surrey ; deputy-lieutenant for London.

CARDWELL, Right Hon. Edward, English statesman, b. in 1813 ; educated at Winchester ; elected to a fellowship at Balliol College, Oxford, 1832, and graduated 1835 ; called to the bar of the Inner Temple, 1838 ; M.P. for Clitheroe, 1842 ; for Liverpool, 1847 to 1852 ; for Oxford, 1853 and 1865 ; secretary to the Treasury from Feb. 1845 to July 1846 ; president of the Board of Trade from Dec. 1852 to Feb. 1855 ; chief secretary for Ireland from June 1859 to July 1861 ; chancellor of the Duchy of Lancaster, 1861–64 ; secretary of state for the colonies, 1864–66.

CAREL, Philibert Flore, French general, born at Troyes, May 7, 1789 ; entered the army, 1807 ; colonel, 1832 ; field-marshal, April 22, 1846 ; retired with the grade of staff major-general.

CARETTE, Antoine Ernest Hippolyte, French officer and military writer, b. May 23, 1808 ; entered the Polytechnic School, 1828 ; chief of battalion, Dec. 21, 1852 ; lieutenant-colonel, Dec. 24, 1858. Author of ' Études sur la Kabylie proprement dite,' 1848–49 ; and works on Algeria.

CAREW, John Edward, English sculptor, b. 1785 ; studied under Sir A. Westmacott. Executed the sculptures on the base of Nelson's column ; the statue of ' Whittington listening to the London Bells ;' and other works of art.

CAREW, Robert Shapland, Baron, Irish magistrate, b. at Dublin, 1818 ; educated at Eton, and Christ Church, Oxford ; M.P. for Waterford, 1840 to 1847 ; succeeded his father, 1856 ; lord lieutenant of Wexford ; magistrate and deputy-lieutenant for Waterford ; colonel of the Wexford militia.

CAREY, Alice, American authoress, b. at Mount Healthy, Cincinnati, Ohio ; wrote under the signature of *Patty Lee*. Author of ' Hualeo,' 1851 ; ' The Children of Clovernook,' 1855 ; and of some volumes of poems.

CAREY, Henry, American writer, b. in Philadelphia in 1793. Author of ' On the Rate of Wages,' 1836 ; ' The Past, the Present, the Future,' 1848 ; ' Principles of Social Science,' vols. i. and ii. 1858 ; and other works on political economy.

CAREY, Sir Peter Safford, English lawyer, b. in Guernsey, 1803 ; educated at St. John's College, Oxford ; graduated B.A. 1825, M.A. 1830 ; called to the bar of the Middle Temple, 1830 ; recorder of Dartmouth, 1836 ; judge of the Court of Record in the city of Wells, 1838 ; professor of English law in University College, London, 1838 ; bailiff of Guernsey, and knighted, 1863.

CARGILL, John, English colonial judge, b. 1815 ; called to the bar of the Middle Temple, June 1841 ; appointed revising barrister at Jamaica, 1848 ; acting chairman of quarter sessions, 1855 ; appointed assistant judge of the Supreme Court of Jamaica, 1856.

CARLEN, Emilia Flygare, Swedish novelist, b. at Stockholm, 1810. Author of 'Waldemar Klein,' 1838 ; ' Rose of Thistleton,' 1842 ; ' The Maiden's Tower,' 1848 ; and many other works of fiction.

CARLETON, William, Irish novelist, b. at Clogher, Tyrone, 1798. Author of ' Traits *and Stories of the Irish Peasantry,'* 1830 ; ' Valentine M'Clutchy,' 1845 ; ' The Black *Prophet,' 1847 ; ' Willie Reilly,'* 1855. Has a literary pension of 200l. a year.

CARLISLE, Hon. and Right Rev. Samuel Waldegrave, bishop of, English divine, b. 1817; educated at Balliol College, Oxford; graduated B.A. and double first-class, 1839; elected fellow of All Souls, 1839; M.A. 1842; canon of Salisbury cathedral, 1857; consecrated 57th bishop of Carlisle, 1860. Author of 'New Testament Millenarianism,' and a volume of sermons.

CARLYLE, Thomas, English author, b. at Ecclefechan, Annandale, Dumfriesshire, Dec. 4, 1795; studied at the University of Edinburgh. Author of 'Sartor Resartus,' 1833; 'The French Revolution,' 1837; 'Lectures on Hero Worship,' 1840; 'Oliver Cromwell's Letters and Speeches,' 1845; 'Life of Frederick the Great,' 1860–64; and numerous essays and translations from the German. Elected lord rector of the University of Edinburgh, 1866.

CARMOLY, Elliacin, French philologist, b. at Soultz, Haute-Rhin, 1805. Author of 'Biography of Ancient and Modern Israelites,' in Hebrew, Metz, 1829; and a great number of Hebrew works. Founded the French periodical, *La France Israëlite*, 1855. Grand Rabbi at Brussels, 1834 to 1839.

CARMOUCHE, Pierre François Adolphe, French dramatic author, b. at Lyons, April 9, 1797. Author of 'Le Vampire,' 1820; 'Les Envies de Mme. Godard,' 1848; 'Le Bague de Thérèse,' 1861; 'La Cornette jaune,' 1864; and numerous other dramas.

CARNARVON, Henry Howard Molyneux Herbert, Earl of, English statesman, b. in London, 1831; educated at Eton, and Christ Church, Oxford, where he graduated first-class in classics, 1852; succeeded his father, 1849; appointed deputy-lieutenant of Hants, and captain of Hants Yeomanry, 1853; constable of Carnarvon Castle, 1854; high steward of the University of Oxford, 1859; secretary of state for the colonies, 1866–67. Author of 'The Druses of Mount Lebanon,' 1860.

CARNE', Louis Marcein, Comte de, French statesman and author, b. at Quimper, Feb. 17, 1804; secretary of embassy, 1825; member of the Chamber of Deputies, 1839; minister of foreign affairs, 1847; member of the French Academy, April 23, 1863. Author of 'Vues sur l'Histoire contemporaine,' 1833; 'Études sur l'Histoire du Government représentative en France de 1789 à 1848,' 1855; also contributor to the leading French periodicals.

CARNEGIE, Hon. Charles, English politician, b. 1833; deputy-lieutenant for Forfarshire; M.P. for Forfarshire, 1860–66.

CARNOT, Lazare Hyppolyte, French politician, b. at St. Omer, April 6, 1801; studied law, and became an advocate; member of the Corps Législatif for the first circonscription of Paris, 1863. Author of 'Mémoires de Henri Grégoire Evêque de Blois,' 1837; 'Mémoires de Carnot, par son Fils,' 1861.

CARO, Elme Marie, French writer, b. at Poitiers, March 4, 1826; studied at the College of Stanislas and the École Normale; master of the conferences at the École Normale, 1858; inspector of the Academy of Paris, 1861; professor to the Faculty of Letters, July 1864. Author of 'L'Idée de Dieu et ses Nouveaux Critiques,' 1864; and several other philosophical works.

CARPENTER, Mary, English authoress, b. 1820. Author of 'Reformatory Schools for Children,' 1851; 'Reformatory Schools, and their present Position,' 1855; and other works on the treatment of youthful criminals.

CARPENTER, William Bird, English physician, b. 1813; educated in Bristol, at University College, London, and at the University of Edinburgh, where he graduated M.D. 1839; appointed registrar to the University of London, 1856. Author of 'Principles of General and Comparative Physiology;' and other medical works.

CARR, John, English judge, b. 1815; educated at University College, London; graduated B.L. 1839; called to the bar at Gray's Inn, May 1840; appointed Queen's advocate at Sierra Leone, May 1840; acting governor from April to Sept. 1841; chief justice, 1841; judge of the Vice-Admiralty Court, and president of the Council of the colony.

CARRE', Michel, French dramatic author, b. 1819; studied at the College of Charlemagne. Author of 'La Jeunesse de Luther,' 1843; 'La Reine de Saba,' 1862; 'Henriette Deschamps,' 1863; and many other works.

CARRE', Narcisse Epaminondas, French magistrate, b. at Paris, March 1, 1794; studied law; called to the bar, 1815; president of the tribunal of Rochelle, 1831; of Tours, 1834; councillor of the Imperial Court of Paris, 1848. Author of 'Code des Femmes,' 1828; 'La Taxe en Matière civile,' 1839.

CARRELET, Gilbert Alexandre, French general, b. at St. Pourcain, Sept. 14, 1789; studied at the military school of Fontainebleau, 1809–11; captain, 1822; chief of a squadron, 1830; *colonel*, 1838; maréchal de camp, 1842; general of division, 1848; *appointed senator, 1852.*

CARREY, Emile, French writer, b. at Paris, Sept. 1820 ; studied at the College of St. Louis, and called to the bar at Paris. Author of 'Recueil complet des Actes du Government provisoire,' 1848 ; 'Recits de Kabylie,' 1858.

CARRIERE, Moritz, German writer, b. at Grindel, Duchy of Hesse, March 5, 1817 ; studied at Giessen, Göttingen, and Berlin. Author of 'Kölner Dom als freie deutsche Kirche,' Stuttgart, 1843 ; 'Das Wesen und die Form der Poesie,' Leipsic, 1854 ; and numerous other works.

CARRINGTON, Hon. Charles Robert, English politician, b. 1843 ; educated at Eton, and Trinity College, Cambridge ; graduated M.A. 1868 ; cornet in the Guards, 1865 ; M.P. for Wycombe, 1865.

CARRINGTON, Robert John, Baron, English administrator, b. 1796 ; studied at Christ Church, Cambridge ; succeeded his father, 1838 ; lord-lieutenant of Buckinghamshire ; colonel of the Bucks militia.

CARTER, John Bonham, English politician, b. 1817 ; educated at Trinity College, Cambridge ; is a magistrate and deputy-lieutenant for Hants ; M.P. for Winchester since 1847.

CARTER, Sir John, English colonial judge, b. 1810 ; appointed chief justice of New Brunswick, Jan. 1857 ; knighted, 1859.

CARTWRIGHT, Henry, English politician, b. 1814 ; captain and lieutenant-colonel in the Guards, 1846 ; M.P. for Northamptonshire since 1858.

CARUS, Karl Gustav, German physiologist, b. at Leipsic, Jan. 8, 1789. Author of 'Versuch einer Darstellung des Nervensystems und ins Besondere des Gehirns,' Leipsic, 1814 ; 'Letters on Landscape Painting,' ib. 1831 ; and numerous works on science and art.

CARVER, William, English colonial magistrate, b. 1819 ; graduated at Magdalen College, Cambridge ; called to the bar of the Inner Temple, 1856 ; appointed acting deputy Queen's advocate for southern circuit, Ceylon, Oct. 1858 ; acting police magistrate, Damboul, Jan. 1861 ; acting commissioner of requests, Harrispatoo, Ceylon, 1862 ; registrar of the Supreme Court, Feb. 1864.

CARYSFORT, Granville Leveson Proby, Earl, Irish magistrate, b. 1781 ; entered the British navy, 1798 ; vice-admiral, 1851 ; admiral, 1857 ; succeeded to the title, 1857 ; deputy-lieutenant of the county of Wicklow.

CASABIANCA, François Xavier, Comte de, French statesman, b. at Nice, June 27, 1797 ; studied in the Lycée Napoléon, and called to the French bar at Bastia, 1820 ; held the portfolio of Agriculture and Finance, 1851 ; senator, July 28, 1852.

CASHEL, Right Rev. Robert Daly, Irish divine, and 50th bishop of Cashel, b. 1783 ; educated at Trinity College, Dublin ; dean of St. Patrick's, Dublin, 1842 ; consecrated bishop of Cashel, 1843.

CASPARI, Karl Paul, German theological writer, b. at Dessau, Feb. 14, 1814 : studied at the Universities of Leipsic, Berlin, and Königsberg. Author of 'Biblische, theologische und apologetisch kritische Studien,' Leipsic, 1842 ; 'Ueber Michaund,' ib. 1851 ; and numerous theological works.

CASTELBAJAC, Barthelemy Dominique Jacques Armand, Marquis de, French general, b. at Ricaud, June 12, 1787 ; lieutenant in the army, 1807 ; chief of squadron, 1814 ; colonel, 1815 ; maréchal de camp, 1826 ; lieutenant-general, 1840 ; entered the Senate, June 12, 1856.

CASTILLE, Charles Hippolyte, French writer, b. at Montreuil-sur-Mer, Nov. 8, 1820 ; studied at Douai and Cambrai. Author of 'Histoire de la Seconde République française,' 1854–55 ; 'Parallèle entre César, Charlemagne, et Napoléon,' 1858 ; and other works.

CASTLEMAINE, Richard Handcock, Baron, Irish administrator, b. 1791 : educated at Trinity College, Dublin, where he graduated M.A. 1812 ; deputy-lieutenant for Westmeath, Roscommon, and King's county.

CASTLEROSSE, Valentine Augustus Browne, Viscount, English politician, b. 1825 ; magistrate and deputy-lieutenant for County Kerry ; was comptroller of her Majesty's household, 1857–58 ; re-appointed, 1859 ; M.P. for Kerry County since 1852.

CASTREN, Matthias Alexander, Russian traveller and philologist, b. in Finland, *in 1813 ; professor of Finnish literature at Helsingfors. Published a Syrian grammar, and several works on Finland.*

CASWALL, Rev. Henry, English divine, b. at Yateley, Hants, 1810; took his degrees of B.A. and M.A. at Keynon College, Ohio, U.S. 1833–34; honorary degrees of M.A. from Oxford, and D.D. from Trinity College, Hartford, U.S. 1854. Author of 'America and the American Church,' and other works.

CATHCART, Alan Frederick, Earl, English magistrate, b. at Hythe, Nov. 14. 1828; deputy-lieutenant; magistrate and chairman of quarter sessions for North Riding of Yorkshire; succeeded his father, 1859.

CATOR, Sir William, English general, b. 1785; educated at Westminster and at the Military Academy, Woolwich; entered the Royal Artillery, 1803; colonel, 1846; lieutenant-general, 1859; C.B. 1855; knighted, 1865.

CATTERMOLE, George, English painter, b. in Norfolk, 1800; R.A. 1848. Exhibited at the Water Colour Society and the Royal Academy since 1830, chiefly battle-fields and similar subjects.

CAULAINCOURT, Olivier Joseph, Marquis de, French officer, b. at Paris, 1818; entered the military school of St. Cyr, 1837; officer, 1843; member of the Legislative Assembly for Calvados, 1849 to 1851; member of the Corps Législatif for same, 1852; commander of the Légion d'honneur, July 3, 1861.

CAUMONT, Aldrick Isidore Ferdinand, French lawyer, b. at St. Vincent, Cramisuil, May 15, 1825. Author of 'Dictionnaire universel de Droit commercial maritime, ou Répertoire methodique alphabétique de Législation, Doctrine et Jurisprudence nautique,' 1855–58; and other legal works.

CAUMONT, Arcisse de, French antiquarian, b. at Bayeux, Aug. 28, 1802. Author of 'Cours d'Antiquités monumentales,' 1830; 'Abécédaire, ou Rudiment d'Archéologie,' 1850; and other works.

CAUSSIN DE PERCEVAL, Amand Pierre, French philologist, b. at Paris, Jan. 13, 1795; professor of Arabic at the College of France, 1833; member of the Institute. Author of 'Précis historique de la Guerre des Turcs contre les Russes, 1769–1774, &c.' 1822.

CAUTLEY, Sir Proby Thomas, English engineer, b. at Roydon, 1802; educated at the Charterhouse and at Addiscombe; projector and designer of the Ganges Canal, opened 1854; K.C.B. 1854; member of her Majesty's Indian Council, 1858; chairman of Indian Public Works Committee, 1859. Author of various papers on physical science.

CAVE, Stephen, English politician, b. 1820; educated at Harrow, and Balliol College, Oxford; graduated B.A. 1843; M.A. 1846; called to the bar of the Inner Temple, 1846; is J.P. and deputy-lieutenant for Gloucestershire; J.P. for Sussex; M.P. for Shoreham since 1859.

CAVE, Thomas, English politician, b. 1825; is a merchant in London; sheriff of London and Middlesex, 1864; M.P. for Barnstaple, 1865.

CAVELIER, Pierre Jules, French sculptor, b. at Paris, Aug. 30, 1814. Executed 'Pénélope endormie,' 1849; bust of 'Ary Scheffer,' 1859; 'Napoléon 1er Legislateur,' 1861; and numerous statues and groups.

CAVENDISH, Lord Edward, English politician, b. 1838; educated at Eton, and Trinity College, Cambridge; lieutenant in the rifle brigade; and instructor of musketry, 1861–64; M.P. for Sussex, 1865.

CAVENDISH, Lord Frederick Charles, English politician, b. 1839; deputy-lieutenant for county of Lancaster; M.P. for North-west Riding of Yorkshire, 1865.

CAVENDISH, Lord George Henry, English politician, b. 1810; is a magistrate and deputy-lieutenant for Derbyshire; M.P. for Derbyshire since 1834.

CAWDOR, John Frederick Vaughan Campbell, Earl, b. in London, 1817; educated at Eton, and Christ Church, Oxford; graduated B.A. 1838, M.A. 1840; M.P. for Pembrokeshire, 1841 to 1860; succeeded his father, 1860; lord lieutenant of Carmarthenshire; trustee of the British Museum.

CAYLE, Jean Mamert, French writer, b. at Vigan Lot, 1812; studied at the Royal College of Cahors. Author of 'Pape et Empereur,' 1860; 'Les Congrés de Malines,' 1864; and many other (chiefly historical) works.

CAYLEY, Arthur, English mathematician, b. at Richmond, 1821; educated at King's College, London, and Trinity College, Cambridge, where he graduated B.A. 1842; called to the bar of Lincoln's Inn, 1849; corresponding member of the French Institute, 1863.

CECIL, Lord Eustace Henry Brownlow Gascoigne, English politician, b. 1834; educated at Harrow, and Royal Military College, Sandhurst; is a magistrate for Middlesex; lieutenant-colonel in the Guards; M.P. for Essex, 1865.

CECILLE, Jean Baptiste Thomas Medee, French naval officer, b. at Rouen, Oct. 16, 1787; entered the navy, 1804; lieutenant in the navy, July 31, 1816; captain of a frigate, Oct. 30, 1829; rear-admiral, June 2, 1844; vice-admiral, Dec. 23, 1847; appointed senator, Dec. 31, 1853.

CERFBERE DE MEDELSHEIM, Maximilian Charles Alphonse, French writer, b. at Epinal, Vosges, July 20, 1817. Author of 'Voyage de la Duchesse d'Orléans d'Allemagne en France,' 1837; 'État actuel de la Metallurgie en Europe,' 1858; and other works.

CERISE, Laurent Alexander Philibert, French physician, b. at Aoste, Piedmont, 1809; took the degree of M.D. at Turin, 1828. Author of 'Exposé et Examén critique du Système phrénologique,' Paris, 1836; and several medical works.

CESENA, Amedee Gayet de, French writer, b. at Cestri, Levant, 1810. Author of 'La Conquête d'Alger,' Dijon, 1830; 'L'Angleterre et la Russie,' 1858; 'L'Italie confédérée,' 1859–60; and several other works.

CEY, François Arsene, CHAISE DE CAHAGNE, French writer, b. at Thiers, March 2, 1806. Author of 'La Fille du Curé, 1832; 'La Fiancée du Prince,' 1848; 'Quand on n'a pas le Sou,' 1854; and other romances.

CHABANNE, LA PALICE, Alfred Jean Eginnard, Comte de, French general; b. near London, Jan. 13, 1799; entered the French army, 1814; captain, 1824; chief of a squadron, 1831; colonel, 1837; general of brigade, 1840.

CHABANNE, CURTON LA PALICE, French naval officer, b. at Paris, May 6, 1803, brother of the preceding; entered the navy, 1823; captain of a frigate, 1851; rear-admiral, Dec.|1854; commander of the maritime forces in the Mediterranean, 1855; vice-admiral, Dec. 24, 1861; maritime prefect at Toulon, April 19, 1864.

CHABAUD LATOUR, François Ernest Henri, Baron de, French general, b. at Nimes, Jan. 25, 1805; entered the army; captain, 1827; chief of battalion, 1837; colonel, 1845; general of brigade, April 30, 1853; general of division, Aug. 12, 1857; member of the Imperial Council for Public Instruction, 1864.

CHACATON, Jean Nicolas Henri de, French painter, b. at Chézy, July 30, 1813; studied in the École des Beaux Arts, and under MM. Hersent, Ingres, and Marilhat. Exhibited 'The Prisoner of Chillon,' 1835; 'Christ in the Garden of Olives,' 1844; 'Convent of the Capuchins at Syracuse,' 1857; and several other works, principally landscapes.

CHADWICK, Edwin, English social economist, b. 1801; called to the bar, 1830; commissioner of the General Board of Health, 1848; C.B. 1848. Author of several papers on sanitary matters and public education.

CHAILLU, Paul du, French traveller, b. 1820; travelled in Western Africa, and brought several gorillas to Europe, 1855. Author of 'Explorations and Adventures,' London, 1861.

CHAIX D'EST ANGE, Victor Charles, French advocate, b. at Rheims, April 11, 1800; bâtonnier or chief of the Paris bar, 1842; procurator-general of the Imperial Court of Paris, 1857; senator, Nov. 2, 1862; vice-president of the Council of State, Oct. 18, 1863. Author of 'Annals of the French Bar.'

CHALLAMEL, Jean Baptiste Marie Augustin, French writer, b. at Paris, March 18, 1818; studied at the College of Henry IV.; called to the bar, 1838. Author of 'St. Vincent de Paul,' 1841; 'De la Révolution de Napoléon,' 1851.

CHALLENGER, Richard, English colonial magistrate, b. 1805; appointed notary at St. Kitt's, 1830; justice of the peace, 1838; stipendiary magistrate, Anguilla, 1842; coroner, 1846 to present time; member of Administrative Committee, Dec. 1858; member of the Executive Council, 1858.

CHALLIS, Rev. James, English astronomer, b. 1803; educated at Trinity College, Cambridge; graduated M.A. 1825; ordained, 1830; Plumian professor of astronomy, 1836. Author of 'Creation in Plan and Progress,' 1861; and numerous astronomical works.

CHALYBÆUS, Heinrich Moritz, German philosophical writer, b. at Pfaffroda, Saxony, July 3, 1796; studied at the University of Leipsic; degree of Ph.D. 1820; *professor of philosophy* at Kiel, 1839. Author of 'History of the Development of the *Speculative Philosophy* of Kant and Hegel,' Dresden, 1836; and other philosophical *works.*

CHAMBARD, Louis Leopold, French sculptor, b. at St. Amour, 1812; studied under M. Ingres. Executed 'Marius à Carthage,' 1837; 'L'Amour offrant son Cœur à une jeune Fille,' 1864; and several busts, statues, and groups.

CHAMBERLAIN, Sir Neville Bowles, English general, b. at Rio, Jan. 18, 1820; appointed to the Indian army, 1836; deputy-assistant quartermaster-general, 1843; aide-de-camp to Lord Dalhousie, 1848; C.B. 1857, and A.D.C. to her Majesty.

CHAMBERS, Thomas, English barrister, b. 1814; educated at Clare Hall, Cambridge, and graduated B.A. 1840; LL.B. 1846; called to the bar of the Middle Temple, 1840; M.P. for Hertford, 1852–57; returned for Marylebone, 1862.

CHAMBERS, Robert, English author and publisher, b. at Peebles, 1802. Author of 'Illustrations of the Author of Waverley,' 1823; 'Biographical Dictionary of Eminent Scotchmen,' 1835; and a great number of scientific and miscellaneous works.

CHAMBERS, William, author and publisher, brother of the preceding, b. at Peebles, 1800. Author of the 'Book of Scotland,' 1830; 'Sketches in America;' and other works. Founder of 'Chambers' Edinburgh Journal,' 1832.

CHAMBRUN, Aldebert Dominique Joseph, Comte de, French politician, b. at Paris, Nov. 21, 1821; prefect of Toulon, 1850; of St. Etienne, March 1851; member of the General Council for the canton of Villefort, and of the Corps Législatif, 1857.

CHAMIER, Frederick, English author, b. in London, 1796; entered the navy, 1809; retired, 1833. Author of 'The Life of a Sailor,' 1834; 'Passion and Principle,' 1843; and other sea stories.

CHAMPAGNY, François Joseph Marie Therese Nompere, Comte de, French writer, b. at Vienna, Sept. 10, 1804. Author of 'Un Mot d'une Catholique,' 1844; 'L'Histoire des Césars,' 1841–43; 'De la Critique contemporaine,' 1864; and other works.

CHAMPAGNY, Napoleon Marie Nompere, Comte de, French writer, b. at Paris, Oct. 29, 1806. Author of 'Traité de la Police municipale, ou de l'Autorité des Maires de l'Administration et du Gouvernement en Matières réglementaires,' Paris, 1844–47.

CHAMPFLEURY, Jules Fleury, French writer, b. at Laon, Sept. 10, 1821. Author of 'Chien Caillon,' 1847; 'Les Aventures de Mariette,' 1853; 'Histoire de la Caricature antique,' 1865; and many other works of general literature.

CHAMPNEYS, Rev. William Weldon, English divine, b. in London, 1807; educated at Brasenose College, Oxford, and graduated B.A.; rector of St. Mary's, Whitechapel, 1837; canon of St. Paul's, 1851; vicar of St. Pancras.

CHAMPOLLION FIGEAC, Jean Jacques, French archæologist, b. at Figeac, 1778. Author of 'Annales des Lagides, ou Chronologie des Rois grecs d'Egypt,' 1819; 'Fourier et Napoléon,' 1844; 'Monographie du Palais de Fontainebleau,' 1864; and a great number of archæological works.

CHANGARNIER, Nicolas Anne Theodule, French general, b. at Anton, April 26, 1793; lieutenant, 1815; captain, Oct. 9, 1825; chief of a battalion, Dec. 31, 1835; lieutenant-colonel, Jan. 25, 1837; general, Aug. 3, 1843; governor-general of Algiers, 1847. Imprisoned after Dec. 2, 1851; exiled from France, 1852.

CHANNELL, Sir William Fry, English judge, b. 1804; called to the bar, 1827; became a serjeant, 1840; baron of the Exchequer and knighted, 1857.

CHANNING, Walter, American physician, b. at Newport, Rhode Island, 1786; educated at Harvard College, and at the University of Pennsylvania, and graduated M.D.; professor at the University of Cambridge, U.S. Author of 'Professional Reminiscences of Foreign Travel,' 1851; and numerous medical works.

CHANNING, Rev. William Henry, American writer, b. in Massachusetts, 1810; entered Harvard College, 1829; took the degree of D.D. at Cambridge, U.S. 1833. Author of 'Memoirs of William Ellery Channing, with Extracts from his Correspondence and Manuscripts,' Boston, 1848.

CHAPIN, Rev. Edward, American writer, b. at Union Village, New York County, Dec. 29, 1814; minister of a church at Richmond, Virginia, 1838. Author of 'Moral Aspects of City Life,' New York, 1853; 'Humanity in the City;' 'True Manliness,' ib. 1854.

CHAPMAN, Henry Samuel, English colonial judge, b. 1818; appointed judge of the Supreme Court of New Zealand, June 1843, colonial secretary of Van Diemen's

Land, 1852 ; member of the Legislative Council of Melbourne, 1855; attorney-general at St. Kilda, 1858 to 1859 ; equity judge of the Supreme Court, 1862–63; law lecturer at the Melbourne University.

CHAPMAN, Right Rev. James, English divine, b. 1799; educated at Eton, and King's College, Cambridge, where he graduated M.A. 1826; rector of Dunton Waylett, Essex, 1834 ; consecrated bishop of Colombo and received the degree of D.D. 1845; resigned his see, 1862.

CHAPNY, Nicolas Marie Joseph, French architect and lithographer, b. at Paris, 1790. Published ' Monuments of France,' ' Antiquities of Athens,' and ' Monuments of Pera,' 1820 to 1850.

CHAPNYS MONTLAVILLE, Benoist Marie Louis Alceste, Baron de, French writer, b. at Tournus, Sept. 19, 1800. Author of ' Lettres sur la Suisse et le Pays des Grisons,' Paris, 1826 ; ' Étude sur Simon,' ib. 1838 ; ' Lamartine, Vie publique et privée,' ib. 1843.

CHAPUS, Eugene, French writer, b. at Paris, 1800. Author of ' Essai critique sur le Théâtre français, publié d'après des Notes anglaises,' Paris, 1827; ' Le Roman des Duchesses,' 1844 ; ' Le Turf, ou les Courses de Chevaux en France et en Angleterre,' Paris, 1853 ; and many other works.

CHARLES, King of Wurtemberg, b. March 6, 1823 ; ascended the throne at the death of his father, King William I. June 25, 1864. Married, July 13, 1846, to Grand-duchess Olga of Russia, daughter of Czar Nicholas I.

CHARLES XV., King of Sweden and Norway, b. May 3, 1826, the son of King Oscar I. Ascended the throne at the death of his father, July 8, 1859 ; married, June 19, 1850, to Louise, eldest daughter of Prince Frederick of the Netherlands.

CHARLES, Frederick Augustus William, ex-duke of Brunswick, b. Oct. 30, 1804 ; succeeded his father, June 16, 1815 ; fled the duchy, Sept. 8, 1830 ; declared unfit to govern by a resolution of the German Diet, Dec. 2, 1830.

CHARLES ALEXANDER, Grand-duke of Saxe-Weimar, b. June 24, 1818, the son of Grand-duke Charles Frederick ; succeeded his father, July 8, 1853 ; married, Oct. 8, 1842, to Sophie, daughter of the late King William II. of the Netherlands.

CHARLEMONT, James Molyneux Caulfield, Earl, Irish magistrate, b. 1820 ; M P. for Armagh, 1847 to 1857 ; succeeded his uncle, Dec. 1863 ; lord-lieutenant of County Armagh ; lieutenant-colonel of Armagh militia.

CHARLESWORTH, Maria Louisa, English authoress, b. 1830. Published ' Ministering Children ;' ' The Sabbath Given ; the Sabbath Lost,' 1856 ; ' The Ministry of Life,' 1858 ; ' The Sailor's Choice,' 1863 ; and other works for the young.

CHARMA, Antoine, French philosophical writer, b. at Charité-sur-Loire, Jan. 15, 1801 ; licentiate of the École Normale, 1822 ; Ph.D. 1830. Author of ' Leçons de Philosophie sociale et de Logique,' 1838–40 ; ' Du Sommeil,' 1851 ; and other philosophical works.

CHARNER, Leonard Victor Joseph, French naval officer, b. at St. Briene, Feb. 13, 1797 ; ensign, 1820 ; lieutenant, 1828 ; captain of a corvette, 1837 ; of a frigate, 1841 ; rear-admiral, Feb. 3, 1852 ; vice-admiral, June 7, 1855 ; admiral, Nov. 15, 1864.

CHARON, Viala, French general, b. at Paris, July 29, 1794 ; entered the army, 1813 ; captain, 1821 ; colonel, 1842 ; general and governor-general of Algiers, 1848 ; senator, Dec. 31, 1852 ; president of the Council of Algiers.

CHARPENTIER, Jean Pierre, French writer, b. at St. Priest, June 20, 1797. Author of ' Études morales et historiques sur la Littérature romaine,' 1829 ; ' Études sur les Pères de l'Eglise,' 1853 ; and other works.

CHARTON, Edward Thomas, French writer, b. at Sens, May 11, 1807; advocate at Paris, 1829. Author of ' Lettres sur Paris,' 1830 ; ' History of Paris,' 1863. Founded L'Illustration, 1843 ; and Le Tour du Monde, 1860.

CHASE, Salmon Portland, American statesman, b. in Corinth, New Hampshire, U.S. Jan. 13, 1808 ; graduated at Dartmouth College, 1826 ; admitted to the bar, 1830 ; governor of the state of Ohio, 1856 to 1860 ; secretary to the Treasury, 1861 to 1864 ; chief justice of the Supreme Court, 1864. Author of ' Statutes of Ohio,' 1832–35.

CHASSELOUP-LAUBAT, Justin Napoleon Samuel Prosper, Comte de, French statesman, b. at Alessandria, Piedmont, March 29, 1805 ; councillor of state, and member of the Legislative Assembly, 1849 ; member of the Corps Législatif, 1857 ; minister of Algiers, 1858 ; senator, May 25, 1862.

CHASSIN, Charles Louis, French writer, b. at Nantes, Feb. 11, 1831. Author of 'La Légende du petit Manteau bleu,' 1852; 'Le Génie de la Révolution française,' 1863; and many other works.

CHASTEAUNEUF, John Augustus, English colonial magistrate, b. 1805; appointed clerk in the Registration Office at Mauritius, Aug. 1840; examiner and comptroller of Revenue and Audit Office, July 1847; chief clerk, June 1854; officer in charge of Audit Office, May 1861; acting collector of Internal Revenue Office, Oct. 1861.

CHATELAIN, Anatole Julien, French geographer, b. at Paris, July 4, 1817; minister of agriculture and commerce, 1846. Published 'Les Portes d'Or,' 1853; 'Chronological Atlas of the Railways of France,' 1855.

CHAUVEAU, Adolphe, French barrister, b. May 29, 1802; professor of law, 1838. Author of 'Théorie du Code pénal,' 1834-43; 'Formulaire général et complet,' 1852-53.

CHAUVENET, William, American astronomer, b. in Pennsylvania, 1810; graduated at Yale College, 1838; professor of mathematics in the naval college of Anapolis, 1841. Author of a treatise on 'Plane and Spherical Trigonometry,' 1853.

CHAUVIN, Victor, French writer, b. at Argenton, Orne, Aug. 22, 1829. Author of 'Les Romanciers grecs et latins,' 1861; 'La Brochure d'un Paysan du Danube,' 1861; 'Traité de Rhétorique,' 1865.

CHEETHAM, John, English politician, b. 1802; magistrate for county of Chester, and J.P. and D.L. for county Lancaster; M.P. for South Lancashire, 1852-59; and for Salford, 1865.

CHEEVER, George Barrett, American author, b. at Hallowell, Maine, 1807; graduated at Bowdoin College, 1825, and at Andover, 1830; ordained, 1832. Author of 'Commonplace Books,' 1828-29; 'Windings of the River of the Water of Life,' 1849; 'God against Slavery,' 1857.

CHELMSFORD, Frederick Thesiger, Baron, English statesman, b. July 14, 1794; entered the royal navy, as midshipman, 1807; called to the bar of Gray's Inn, 1818; King's counsel, and leader of the Inner Temple, 1834; solicitor-general, April 1844 to July 1845; attorney-general, July 1845 to July 1846, and again March 1852 to December 1852; sat as M.P. for Woodstock, 1840-44; M.P. for Abingdon, 1844-52; M.P. for Stamford, 1852-58; appointed lord chancellor, with the title of Lord Chelmsford, February 26, 1858, and resigned June 18, 1859; appointed for the second time lord chancellor, July 6, 1866; resigned, Nov. 1867.

CHENU, Jean Charles, French naturalist, b. at Metz, Aug. 30, 1808. Author of 'Rapport sur le Choléra Morbus,' 1835; 'Leçons élementaires d'Histoire naturelle, 1846'; 'Manuel conchyliologique et de Paléontologie,' 1806.

CHERBONNEAUX, Jacques Auguste, French writer, b. at La Chapelle Blanche, Aug. 28, 1813. Author of 'Fables de Lokman,' 1846; 'Anecdotes musulmanes,' 1847; 'Fourberies de Delilah,' 1856.

CHERBULIEZ, Antoine Elisee, Swiss political economist, b. at Geneva, 1797; professor of political economy at Geneva, 1837. Author of 'Théorie des Garanties constitutionnelles,' 1838; 'Étude sur les Causes de la Misère tant morale que physique, et sur les Moyens d'y porter Remède,' Paris, 1853.

CHESNEY, Francis Rawdon, English general, b. at Ballyrea, N. Ireland, 1787; second captain in the Royal Artillery, 1815; brigadier-general, 1843; major-general, 1855; honorary D.C.L. of Oxford, 1851. Author of 'Survey of the Euphrates and Tigris,' 1850.

CHEVALIER, Michel, French political economist, b. at Limoges, Jan. 13, 1806; professor of political economy at the College of France, 1840; senator, 1861. Author of 'Cours d'Economie politique,' 1842-50; 'Mexico, Ancient and Modern,' 1864; and numerous works on political economy.

CHEVALLIER, Jean Baptiste Alphonse, French chemist, b. at Langres, July 19, 1793; member of the Academy of Medicine, Paris, 1824. Author of 'Dictionnaire des Substances, medicamenteuses et commerciales,' 1850-52; and other works.

CHEVALLIER, Rev. Temple, English divine, b. 1794; educated at Pembroke College, Cambridge, and graduated, 1817; professor of mathematics and astronomy at the University of Durham, 1835. Author of 'Translations of the Epistles of Clement of Rome, Polycarp, and Ignatius,' and a volume of sermons.

CHEVREUL, Michel Eugene, French chemist, b. at Angers, Aug, 31, 1786. Author of 'Recherches chimiques sur les Corps gras d'Origine animale,' 1823; 'Des Couleurs et de leurs *Applications aux Arts* industriels, à l'aide des Cercles chromatiques,' 1864; *and other chemical works.*

CHEZY, Wilhelm von, German writer, b. at Heidelberg, March 21, 1806. Author of 'Der fahrende Schüler,' Zurich, 1835; 'Der Ehrenherold,' Stuttgart, 1848; and other works.

CHICHESTER, Henry Thomas Pelham, Earl, English administrator, b. 1804: lieutenant in the army, 1820; succeeded his father, 1826; major, 1844; lord-lieutenant of the county of Sussex, 1860.

CHILD, Lydia Maria, American authoress, b. in Massachusetts, 1802; married Mr. David Lee Child, 1825. Author of 'Hobomok,' 1824; 'Fact and Fiction,' 1846; 'The Progress of Religious Ideas through Successive Ages,' 1855.

CHILDERS, Hugh Culling Eardley, English politician, b. 1827; educated at Trinity College, Cambridge; graduated B.A. 1850, M.A. 1857; magistrate for West Riding of Yorkshire; lord of the Admiralty, 1864; financial secretary of the Treasury, 1865; M.P. for Pontefract since 1860.

CHISHOLM, Caroline, English authoress, b. at Hooton, Northamptonshire, 1810; married Capt. Alexander Chisholm, 1830. Established the 'Female' Colonization Loan Society.' Published 'Voluntary Information of the People of New South Wales.'

CHODZKO, Jacob Leonard, Polish historian, b. at Oberek, Wilna, Nov. 6, 1800. Author of 'Memoirs of Oginski,' Paris, 1826; 'Histoire de la Pologne,' ib. 1855; 'Histoire de la Turquie,' 1855; and other historical works.

CHOLMELEY, Sir Montague John, Bart. English politician, b. 1802; deputy-lieutenant for Lincolnshire; M.P. for N. Lincolnshire, 1847 to 1851, and from 1857 to 1866.

CHOPART, Louis Narcisse, French naval officer, b. May 6, 1806; entered the navy, 1825; ensign, Feb. 10, 1830; lieutenant, Jan. 6, 1834; captain of a frigate, Nov. 1, 1843; captain of a ship of the line, Dec. 18, 1848; rear-admiral, Aug. 9, 1858; vice-admiral, Jan. 27, 1864.

CHOPPIN, James Clement, English colonial administrator, b. 1817; called to the bar of the Middle Temple, 1843; appointed acting police and stipendiary magistrate at St. Vincent, 1845; solicitor-general, 1853; attorney-general of St. Vincent, 1863; appointed to the Legislative Council, 1863.

CHOULANT, Louis, German physician, b. at Dresden, 1791; diploma of M.D. at Leipsic, 1817. Author of 'Tafeln zur Geschichte der Medicin,' Leipsic, 1822; 'Geschichte und Bibliographie der anatomischen Abbildungen,' ib. 1852; and other medical works.

CHOUSKI, Henry de, Russian political economist, b. at Kremenetz, Poland, 1801. Author of 'Des Institutions de Crédit foncier et agricole dans les divers États de l'Europe,' 1851; and other works on political economy.

CHRISTIE, William, English colonial administrator, b. 1800; educated at Eton, at the Royal Military Academy, Woolwich, and at the Royal Military Academy, Sandhurst; ensign, 1825; lieutenant, 1827; captain, 1833: major, 1839; secretary to Board of Education, 1848; postmaster-general of New South Wales, 1852.

CHRISTIAN IX., King of Denmark, b. April 8, 1818; fourth son of the late Duke Wilhelm of Schleswig-Holstein-Sonderburg-Glücksburg; succeeded to the throne on the death of King Frederick VII., November 15, 1863; married, May 26, 1842, to Louise, daughter of the Landgrave William of Hesse-Cassel.

CHRISTISON, Robert, Scotch physician, b. July 18, 1797; studied at the University of Edinburgh; graduated M.D. 1819; professor of medical jurisprudence at University of Edinburgh, 1822: of materia medica, 1832; twice president of the Royal College of Physicians, Edinburgh; ordinary physician to the Queen for Scotland. Author of 'Treatise on Poisons,' and other medical works.

CHURCHILL, Francis George Spencer, Baron, English administrator, b. at Blenheim, Oxford, 1802; attaché at Vienna, 1823; at Lisbon, 1828; succeeded his father, 1845; deputy-lieutenant of Oxfordshire.

CHURSTON, John Yarde Buller, Baron, English magistrate, b. at Dilhorne, 1799; graduated at Oriel College, Oxford, 1819; M.P. for South Devon from 1835 to 1858; magistrate and deputy-lieutenant of Devon; lieut.-colonel of the South Devon militia.

CHURTON, Ven. Edward, English divine, b. 1800; educated at Charterhouse and Christ Church, Oxford, where he graduated B.A. 1821; M.A. 1824; rector of Crayke, 1835; archdeacon of Cleveland, 1846. Author of 'Early English Church,' 1840; 'Vindiciae Ignatii,' Oxford, 1852; and other works.

CIALDINI, Enrico, Italian general, b. at Modena, 1813; served under General Zucchi at Bologna, 1831; lieut.-colonel in the Spanish service, 1848; general in the Sardinian army in the Crimea, 1855; fought in Italy, 1859; took Gaeta, 1861; viceroy of Naples, 1861; senator of Italy, 1864.

CIBOT, François Barthélemy Michel Edouard, French painter, b. at Paris, Feb. 11, 1799; studied at the School of Fine Arts and under M. Guérin and M. Picot. Exhibited 'Une Mère blessée allaitant son Enfant,' 1827; 'Bords de la Sarthe,' 1863; and many other works, principally landscape paintings.

CIBRARIO, Jean Antoine Louis Chevalier, Italian historian and politician, b. at Turin, Feb. 23, 1802; LL.D. 1824; minister of foreign affairs, 1855; senator of Italy. Author of 'Notizie sulla Istoria dei Principi di Savoia,' Turin, 1825; 'Libro di Novelle,' ib. 1834; and other works.

CIRCOURT, Anne Marie Joseph Albert, Comte de, French writer, b. June 25, 1809. Author of 'La Bataille de Hastings,' 1858; and several novels in French periodicals.

CLAIRVILLE, Louis François Nicolaie, French dramatic writer, b. at Lyons, Jan. 28, 1811. Author of 'Quatorze Ans, ou la Vie de Napoléon,' 1830; 'Margot,' 1837; 'Un Troupier qui suit les Bonnes,' 1860; 'Une Semaine à Londres,' 1862; with a great number of dramas, and a volume of poems.

CLANCARTY, William Thomas le Poer Trench, Earl of, English administrator, b. at Castletown, Kildare, 1803; studied at St. John's College, Cambridge; lieut.-colonel of the Galway militia; succeeded his father, 1837.

CLANRICARDE, Ulick John de Burgh, Marquis of, English statesman, b. at Belmont, Hants, 1802, son of the 13th Earl; obtained a marquisate formerly in the family, 1825; created a British peer by the title of Baron Somerhill in 1826; under-secretary of state for foreign affairs, 1825 to 1827; ambassador at St. Petersburg, 1838 to 1841; postmaster-general, privy seal, 1857–58; lord-lieutenant of county Galway.

CLANWILLIAM, Richard Meade, Earl of, English diplomatist, b. 1795; studied at the University of Oxford, and took the degree of LL.D. 1834; succeeded his father, 1805; under-secretary of state for foreign affairs, 1822; envoy extraordinary and minister plenipotentiary to the Court of Berlin, 1823 to 1827.

CLAPISSON, Antonie Louis, French musical composer, b. at Naples, Sept. 15, 1808; member of the Institute, and of the Academy of Fine Arts, 1854; composed 'La Symphonie,' 1839; 'Dans les Vignes,' 1855; 'Madame Gregoire,' 1861; and many others.

CLARENDON, George William Frederick Villiers, Earl of, English statesman, b. Jan. 26, 1800; succeeded to the title, 1838; British minister plenipotentiary to the court of Madrid, 1833 to 1839; sworn in the privy council, 1840; lord privy seal and chancellor of the Duchy of Lancaster, 1840–41; president of the Board of Trade, 1846; lord-lieutenant of Ireland, 1847 to 1852; secretary of state for foreign affairs, Feb. 1853–55, and again 1865–66; chancellor of the Duchy of Lancaster, 1864–65; chancellor the Queen's University in Ireland.

CLARK, Sir James, English physician, b. 1788; studied at King's College, Aberdeen, and the University of Edinburgh, where he took the degree of M.D.; physician to the Queen; member of the senate of the University of London. Author of several works on climate and on consumption.

CLARKE, Rev. John Erskine, English divine, b. 1828; educated at Wadham College, Oxford, where he graduated B.A. 1850; M.A. 1853; ordained, 1851; vicar of St. Michael's, Derby, 1856. Author of 'Plain Papers on the Social Economy of the People.' Editor of the *Parish Magazine.*

CLARKE, Mary Cowden, English authoress, b. June 1809; married to Mr. C. Cowden Clarke, 1828. Author of 'The Adventures of Kit Bam, Mariner,' 1848; 'Iron Cousin,' 1854; 'The Complete Concordance of Shakespeare,' 1845; and other works.

CLARKE, Robert, colonial magistrate, b. 1801; appointed assistant colonial surgeon, Sierra Leone, 1837; surgeon on the Gold Coast, Oct. 1854; sub-collector of Customs, April 1856; acting judicial assessor, July 1857 to May 1858; member of executive and legislative councils of the Gold Coast. Author of 'Manners and Customs of Liberated Africans,' and several papers on the Gold Coast.

CLARKE, Sir Robert Bowcher, English colonial judge, b. 1800; educated at Trinity College, Cambridge, where he graduated LL.B. 1827; called to the bar of the Inner Temple, 1827; solicitor-general of Barbadoes, 1837 to 1842; chief justice of Barbadoes, 1842; chief judge of St. Lucia, 1848 to 1859; knighted, 1840.

CLARY, Edmund Moritz, Prince of, Austrian statesman, b. Feb. 3, 1813; succeeded his father in the signories of Treplitz, Granpen, and of Binsdorf in Bohemia, 1831; appointed hereditary councillor of the empire, April 1861.

CLARY, Justinien Nicolas, Vicomte, French politician, b. at Paris, June 8, 1816 ; educated at the military school of St. Cyr ; studied law and called to the bar at Paris, 1840 ; member of the Corps Législatif for the department of Loire et Cher, 1852.

CLAUSEN, Hendrick Nicolas, Danish theologian and politician, b. at Maribo, on the isle of Laland, April 22, 1793 ; studied at the University of Copenhagen ; professor of theology at the University of Copenhagen, 1825 ; dean of the faculty of theology, 1834 ; rector of the University, 1837. Author of "The Confession of Augsburg explained historically and dogmatically,' 1851 ; and numerous theological works.

CLAVAUD, André' Paul, French naval officer, b. Jan. 25, 1803 ; ensign, May 22, 1825 ; lieutenant, Oct. 2, 1830 ; captain of a frigate, Aug. 21, 1839 ; rear-admiral, Dec. 2, 1854 ; vice-admiral, March 2, 1864.

CLAY, Cassius Marcellus, American statesman, b. in Madison County, Kentucky, Oct. 2, 1810 ; graduated at Yale College, 1832 ; American ambassador at St. Petersburg, 1861. Author of some articles on the abolition of slavery, published 1848.

CLAY, James, English politician, b. 1805 ; educated at Winchester, and Balliol College, Oxford, where he graduated B.A. 1827 ; M.P. for Hull, 1847 to 1852, and from 1857 to 1866.

CLAY, Rev. William Keating, English author, b. 1797 ; graduated at Jesus College, Cambridge ; ordained deacon, 1823 ; minor canon of Ely cathedral, 1837 ; perpetual curate of Holy Trinity in Ely. Author of 'History of the Scotch, Irish, and American Prayer-books,' 1846 ; and numerous works on the English liturgy.

CLAY, Sir William, English political economist, b. in London, 1797 ; M.P. for the Tower Hamlets, 1832 ; secretary to the Board of Control, and created a baronet, 1841. Author of several works on currency questions, and joint-stock banks.

CLEMENT, Jean Pierre, French historian, b. at Draguignan, Var, June 2, 1809 ; member of the French Institute. Author of 'Jacques Cœur et Charles VII., ou la France au XV. Siècle,' 1853 ; 'Lettres, Instructions et Mémoires de Colbert,' 1863 ; and several works on history and political economy.

CLEMENT, Kunt Jungbohn, Danish historian and linguist, b. in the isle of Amram, Dec. 4, 1803 ; studied at the Universities of Kiel and Heidelberg ; Ph.D. 1855. Author of 'Ueber den Ursprung der Theudisken,' Altona, 1836 ; 'Das wahre Verhältniss der süderjütischen Nationalität und Sprache,' Hamburg, 1849 ; and other historical works.

CLEMENT, William James, English politician, b. 1804 ; educated at Shrewsbury and at Edinburgh University ; J.P. and D.L. for county Merioneth ; a magistrate for Shrewsbury, and mayor of that borough, 1863 ; M.P. for Shrewsbury, 1865.

CLERK, Sir George Russell, English colonial administrator, b. 1801 ; educated at Haileybury College, and entered the civil service of the East India Company, 1818 ; political agent on the Bengal frontier, 1830 ; governor of Bombay, 1840 ; resigned, 1847 ; created K.C.B. 1848 ; under-secretary to the Indian Board, 1856 ; under-secretary of state for India, 1858 ; member of H.M. Indian Council.

CLE'SINGER, Jean Baptiste Auguste, French sculptor, b. at Besancon, 1820. Executed ' La Mélancolie,' 1847 ; 'Diane au Repos,' 1863 ; 'Bords du Tibre,' 1864 ; and a great number of busts, statues, and groups.

CLEVELAND, Charles Dexter, American writer, b. at Salem, Massachusetts, Dec. 3, 1802 ; studied at Dartmouth College. Author of 'An Epitome of Grecian Antiquities,' 1827 ; 'A Compendium of English Literature,' 1848 ; and other miscellaneous works.

CLIFDEN, Henry Agar Ellis, Viscount, English administrator, b. 1825 ; succeeded his grandfather in the peerage of Ireland, 1836 ; was lord of the bedchamber to the late Prince Consort.

CLIFTON, Sir Robert Juckes, Bart. English politician, b. 1826 ; a magistrate for Notts ; M.P. for Nottingham, 1861-65.

CLINTON, Lord Arthur Pelham, English politician, b. 1840 ; educated at Eton ; a lieutenant R.N. ; returned M.P. for Newark, 1865.

CLINTON, Charles Rodolph Trefusis, Baron, English administrator, b. 1791 ; studied at the University of Oxford ; succeeded his brother, 1832 ; deputy-lieutenant for Devon.

CLINTON, Rev. Charles John Fynes, English divine, b. 1799 ; educated at *Westminster,* and Oriel College, Oxford, where he graduated B.A. 1821 ; rector of Cromwell, *Notts, 1828.* Author of 'Fasti Hellenici,' and other works.

CLINTON, Lord Edward William Pelham, English politician, b. 1836; educated at Eton; entered the army as lieutenant of rifle brigade, 1854; captain, 1857; served in the Crimea, 1855–56; M.P. for Nottinghamshire, 1865.

CLISSOLD, Rev. Augustus, English writer, b. 1797; educated at Exeter College, Oxford, where he graduated B.A. 1819, and M.A.; ordained deacon and priest, 1821. Author of 'Swedenborg's Writings and Catholic Teaching,' and numerous theological works.

CLIVE, Caroline, English authoress, b. 1801; married to the Rev. Archer Clive, 1840. Published 'Paul Ferrol;' and a volume of poems under the signature 'V.'

CLIVE, George, English politician, b. 1806; educated at Harrow, and Brasenose College, Oxford; called to the bar of Lincoln's Inn, 1830; police magistrate in London, and judge of the Southwark county court; under-secretary for the Home Department, 1859–62; M.P. for Hereford since 1857.

CLIVE, Hon. George Herbert Windsor, English politician, b. 1835; educated at Eton; entered the army, 1852; lieutenant, 1854; captain, 1859; M.P. for Ludlow, 1860.

CLODT, Jurgensbourg Pierre, Baron de, Russian sculptor, b. May 29, 1805; studied at the School of Fine Arts of St. Petersburg; member of the Academy of Arts, Berlin, 1835; professor at the Academy of St. Petersburg, 1848. Executed several colossal groups for the public places at St. Petersburg.

CLOETE, Sir Abraham Josias, English general, b. 1794; entered the army, 1809; created K.C.B. 1836; C.B. 1848; knight-bachelor, 1854; major-general, 1855; commander of forces in the Windward and Leeward Islands with rank of lieutenant-general, 1855.

CLONCURRY, Edward Lawless, Baron, English administrator, b. at Lyons Castle, Kildare, 1816; succeeded his father, 1853; deputy-lieutenant of the counties of Kildare and Dublin.

CLOQUET, Germain Jules, French physician, b. at Paris, Dec. 18, 1790; took the degree of M.D. at Paris, 1817. Author of 'De l'Influence des Efforts sur les Organes renfermés dans la Cavité thoracique,' 1820; and numerous medical works. Member of the Academy of Medicine, 1851; and of the Academy of Sciences, 1855.

CLOSE, Very Rev. Francis, English divine, b. 1797; entered St. John's College, Cambridge, 1816, and graduated B.A. 1820; rector of Cheltenham, 1826; dean of Carlisle, 1856. Published several sermons, and pamphlets on religious subjects.

CLOT, Antoine, French physician, b. at Marseilles, April 1795; studied medicine, and took the degree of M.D. at Montpellier, 1820; physician in the Turkish army, and raised to the rank of general, 1836. Author of 'Coup d'œil sur la peste et les Quarantaines,' 1851; and several works on Egypt.

COBB, Howell, American politician, b. at Cherry Hill, Georgia, U.S., Sept. 7, 1815; studied law and admitted to the bar, 1836; solicitor-general, 1837; minister of finance, 1857. Took part with the South in the civil war of 1861.

COBBOLD, John Chevallier, English politician, b. 1797; educated at Bury St. Edmund's: banker at Ipswich and Harwich; magistrate and deputy-lieutenant of Suffolk; M.P. for Ipswich since 1847.

COBBOLD, Rev. Richard, English author, b. 1797; educated at Caius College, Cambridge, where he graduated B.A. 1820; rector of Wortham, Suffolk, 1826. Author of 'Margaret Catchpole,' 1845; 'The Young Man's Home,' 1849; and other works.

COCHET, l'Abbé Jean Benoit De'sire', French archæologist, b. at Sauvie, near Havre, March 7, 1812; studied at the College of Havre, the Seminary of Rouen, and entered holy orders, 1836. Author of 'Normandie souterraine, ou Notices sur des Cimetiéres romains et franks explorés en Normandie,' 1854; and other archæological works.

COCHIN, Pierre Suzamee Augustin, French politician, b. at Paris, Dec. 12, 1823; member of the Academy of Moral and Political Science, 1864. Author of 'Rome;' 'Les Martyrs du Japon,' 1862; and several political and religious works.

COCHRANE, Sir James, English colonial judge, b. 1794; admitted to the Inner Temple, 1818; called to the bar there, 1829; chief justice of Gibraltar, 1843; created knight-bachelor, 1845.

COCHRANE, Sir Thomas John, English naval officer, b. at Edinburgh, 1789; knight-bachelor, 1825; governor of Newfoundland from 1825 to 1834; M.P. for Ipswich from 1837 to 1841; commander-in-chief on the East India station from 1842 to 1848; K.C.B. 1847; admiral of the white, 1857; vice-admiral, 1863.

COCHRANE, Alexander Dundas Ross Wishart Baillie, English politician, b. 1814, son of the preceding; M.P. for Bridport, 1841 to 1846, and for Honiton, 1847 to 1852. Author of 'The Morea;' 'Young Italy,' 1850: and several novels.

COCKBURN, Right Hon. Sir Alexander James Edmund, Bart., English judge, b. 1802; educated at Trinity Hall, Cambridge, where he graduated LL.B. 1829; called to the bar of the Middle Temple, 1829; Q.C. 1841; M.P. for Southampton, 1847; attorney-general, March 1851; recorder of Bristol, 1854; succeeded his uncle in the baronetcy, 1858; chief justice of the Common Pleas, 1856; lord chief justice, 1859.

COCKBURN, Sir Francis, English general, b. 1788; governor and commander-in-chief of the Bahama Islands, 1837; served in Canada, and was governor of Honduras; created knight-bachelor by patent, 1841; colonel in the army, 1853; general, 1860.

COCKBURN, Samuel, English colonial magistrate, b. 1810; interpreter-general in Grenada, 1844; inspector of prisons, 1845; inspector-general of schools, 1853; provost marshal, 1854; stipendiary magistrate, 1855; immigration agent, 1856; president of Montserrat, 1860–62; police magistrate, British Honduras, June 1862.

CODAZZI, Agustino, Italian engineer, b. at Lugo, near Ferrara, 1792; entered the military service of France in an Italian regiment, 1813; colonel, 1838. Published 'Resumen de la Geografia de Venezuela,' 1841.

CODRINGTON, Sir William John, English general, b. 1800; entered the army, 1821; lieut.-colonel, 1836; major-general, 1854; commander-in-chief of British forces in the East with local rank of general, 1855; lieut.-general, 1856; made a K.C.B. 1855; grand cross of the Sardinian order of Savoy and commander of the Legion of Honour, 1856; M.P. for Greenwich, from Feb. 1857 to May 1859; appointed governor and commander-in-chief at Gibraltar, May 1859; general, 1863.

COETLOGON, Louis Charles Emmanuel, Comte de, French writer, b. at Paris, Aug. 10, 1814; studied at the Military School of St. Cyr, and entered the army, as second lieutenant, 1834; retired, 1840. Author of 'Voyage en Algérie,' 1848.

COGAN, William Henry Ford, English politician, b. 1823; educated at Trinity College, Dublin; graduated B.A.'1843; called to the Irish bar, 1845; high sheriff of County Wicklow, 1863; M.P. for Kildare since 1852.

COGHETTI, François, Italian painter, b. at Bergame, Lombardy, Oct. 4, 1804; studied under MM. Diotti and Camuccini. Executed 'The Battle of the Amazons,' 'The Fable of Prometheus,' and a great number of paintings, frescoes, and cartoons.

COGNIET, Leon, French painter, b. at Paris, Aug. 29, 1794. Executed 'Marius sur les Ruines de Carthage,' 1824; 'Tintoret peignant sa Fille morte,' 1845; and many others. Member of the superior council of the School of Fine Arts, 1863.

COHEN, Henri, French numismatist, b. 1810. Author of 'Médailles consulaires,' Paris, 1857; 'Médailles impériales,' ib. 1859–62.

COKE, Hon. Henry John, English writer, b. 1827; educated at the Royal Naval College, Portsmouth; entered the navy, 1841; lieutenant, 1847; retired from the navy and became private secretary to the Right Hon. E. Horsman, M.P., while chief secretary for Ireland. Author of 'Vienna in 1848;' 'A Will and a Way,' 1858.

COLANI, Timothe'e, French Protestant theologian, b. at Lemé, Aisne, 1824; studied at Strasbourg. Author of 'Examen de la Vie de Jésus de M. Renan,' 1864; and various sermons translated into English, German, and Dutch.

COLCHESTER, Right Hon. Charles Abbot, Baron, English statesman, b. 1798; educated at Westminster, and at the Royal Naval College; entered the navy, 1811; admiral on the reserved list, 1864; vice-president of the Board of Trade, and paymaster-general, 1852; postmaster-general, 1858–59.

COLE, Henry, English author, b. at Bath, July 19, 1808; educated at Christ's Hospital; assistant keeper of Public Records, 1824; one of the executive committee of the International Exhibition of 1851; created C.B. 1851. Published 'Henry VIII.'s Scheme of Bishoprics;' and other works.

COLE, Hon. Henry Arthur, English politician, b. 1809; magistrate for Fermanagh; high sheriff, 1854; M.P. for Enniskillen, 1844–51, and for Fermanagh, 1855.

COLE, Hon. John Lowry, English politician, b. 1813; educated at Winchester; magistrate for County Fermanagh; M.P. for Enniskillen, 1859.

COLEBROOKE, Sir Thomas Edward, English politician, b. 1813; deputy-lieutenant for County Lanark; M.P. for Taunton, 1842–52; for Lanarkshire since 1857.

COLEBROOKE, Sir William Macbean George, English general, b. 1787; lieutenant in the army, 1807; retired from service, 1856; lieut.-general, 1859.

COLERIDGE, Rev. Derwent, English author, b. at Keswick, Sept. 14, 1800; studied at St. John's College, Cambridge; principal of St. Mark's College, Chelsea, 1841 to 1864; prebendary of St. Paul's cathedral, and rector of Hanwell, Middlesex. Author of 'Scriptural Character of the English Church,' 1839; and other works.

COLERIDGE, John Duke, English politician, b. 1820; educated at Eton, and Balliol and Exeter Colleges, Oxford; graduated B.A. 1842, M.A. 1846; called to the bar of the Middle Temple, 1846; recorder of Portsmouth, 1855; Q.C. and a bencher of the Middle Temple, 1861; M.P. for Exeter, 1865.

COLERIDGE, Right Hon. Sir John Taylor, English judge, b. at Tiverton, Devon, 1790; educated at Corpus Christi, Oxford; called to the bar of the Middle Temple, 1819; serjeant-at-law, 1832; appointed one of the judges of the King's Bench, and knighted, 1835; sworn in the privy council, 1858; D.C.L. of Oxford, 1852. Published an edition of 'Blackstone's Commentaries,' 1825.

COLES, Cowper Phipps, English naval officer, b. 1819; entered the navy, 1831; took an active part in the assault on Sebastopol, Oct. 1854; designed the principle of the shield iron-clad ships, and superintended the construction of the Royal Sovereign.

COLET, Louise Re'voil, French authoress, b. at Aix, Sept. 15, 1810; married M. Hippolyte Colet, 1835, who died 1851. Author of 'Le Musée de Versailles,' 1839; 'La Religieuse,' 1856; 'L'Italie des Italiens,' 1862–64; and many other works.

COLLIER, John Payne, English author, b. in London, 1789; called to the bar of the Middle Temple. Author of 'Poet's Pilgrimage,' 1822; 'History of Dramatic Poetry:' 'Memoirs of the principal Actors in the Plays of Shakespeare,' 1846; and other works. Pension of 100l. per annum from the civil list.

COLLIER, Sir Robert Porrett, English politician, b. 1817; educated at Trinity College, Cambridge; called to the bar of the Inner Temple, 1843, and went on the western circuit; recorder of Penzance; M.P. for Plymouth since 1852; solicitor-general, Feb. 1864. Author of 'Law of Railways,' 1850.

COLLIN DE PLANCY, Jacques Albin Simon Collin, French author, b. at Plancy, Jan. 28, 1793. Author of 'The Infernal Dictionary;' 'The Devil painted by Himself;' 'Legends of the Commandments of God;' and numerous other works.

COLLINS, Wilkie, English novelist, b. in London, 1824. Author of 'Antonina,' 1851; 'The Dead Secret,' 1858; 'The Woman in White,' 1861; 'No Name,' 1863; 'Armadale,' 1866; and numerous other works of fiction.

COLLOREDO MANSFELD, Joseph Francis Jerome, Prince of, Austrian statesman, b. Feb. 26, 1813; chamberlain, privy councillor, and hereditary councillor of the empire; succeeded his cousin Prince Francis Gundacar, May 28, 1852.

COLOMBO, Right Rev. Piers Claveley Claughton, English divine, and second bishop of Colombo, b. 1814; educated at Brasenose College, Oxford, where he graduated B.A. 1835; rector of Elton, Hunts; bishop of St. Helena, 1859 to 1862; translated to Colombo, 1862.

COLONNA DE CASTIGLIONE, Adele d'Affry, Duchess of, Italian sculptor, b. July 6, 1837; married Duke Charles Colonna de Castiglione Aldoorandi, April 5, 1856. Executed a bust of Bianca Capella, Grand-duchess of Tuscany, 1863; and 'The Gorgon,' 1865.

COLQUHOUN, Sir Patrick MacChombaich, English colonial judge, b. 1815; educated at Westminster, and St. John's College, Cambridge, where he graduated B.A. 1837, M.A. 1844; called to the bar of the Inner Temple, 1838; chief justice of the Ionian Islands, and knighted, 1851; member of the Supreme Council of Justice at Corfu, Dec. 1858. Author of 'A Summary of the Roman Civil Law,' 1849–60.

COLTHURST, Sir George Conway, English politician, b. 1824; educated at Harrow; magistrate for Counties Cork and Kerry, and deputy-lieutenant for County Cork; high sheriff, 1850; M.P. for Kinsale since 1863.

COLVILE, Charles Robert, English politician, b. 1815; educated at Eton, and Christ Church, Oxford; deputy-lieutenant for Derbyshire; magistrate for Derby, Leicester, and Stafford; M.P. for South Derbyshire, 1841–59, and 1865.

COLVILE, Right Hon. Sir James William, English colonial judge, b. 1810; educated at Eton and Trinity College, Cambridge, where he graduated; called to the bar of the Inner Temple; advocate-general of the East India Company at Calcutta, 1845; puisne judge there, and knighted, 1848; chief justice from 1855 to 1858.

COLVILLE OF CULROSS, Charles John Colville, Baron, English officer, b. 1818; *captain in the army*; chief equerry and clerk marshal to the Queen, 1852, and *from Feb. 1858 to June 1859*; lieutenant-colonel Hon. Artillery Company, London.

COMBERMERE, Wellington Henry, Viscount, English administrator, b. 1819 ; entered the army ; colonel,'1862 ; M.P. for Carrickfergus, 1847 to 1857 ; deputy-lieutenant of Cheshire, 1852 ; succeeded his father, Feb. 1865.

COMBES, Charles Pierre Matthieu, French engineer, b. Dec. 26, 1801 ; engineer of mines, 1820 ; member of the Institute and of the Academy of Sciences, 1847. Author of 'Sur la Théorie du Ventilateur,' 1838 ; and numerous works on mining.

COMBES, Edmond, French traveller. b. at Castelnandarg, Aude, June 8, 1812. Author of 'Voyage en Abyssinie,' 1837–38.

COMTE, Achille Joseph, French naturalist, b. at Grenoble, Sept. 29, 1802. Author of 'Le Règne animal de Cuvier,' 1832–1841 ; 'Musée d'Histoire naturelle,' 1864.

CONCHA, Don Manuel, Marquis del Duero, Spanish general, b. at Madrid, 1794 ; entered the army, 1816 ; brigadier and field-marshal, 1824 ; captain-general of Catalonia, 1849 ; retired, 1856.

CONCHA, Don José', Marquis de la Habana, Spanish statesman, b. at Buenos-Ayres, 1800, brother of the preceding ; lieutenant-general, 1839 ; captain-general, 1842 ; commander-in-chief of Spanish cavalry, 1846 ; captain-general of the isle of Cuba, 1849 to 1852 ; re-appointed, 1854 ; ambassador to France, July 1862 ; minister of war, 1863 ; president of the Spanish senate, 1864.

CONGREVE, Richard, English writer, b. Sept. 4, 1818 ; educated at Rugby, and Wadham College, Oxford, where he graduated B.A. 1840, and M.A. Translator of 'Aristotle's Politics,' 1855 ; and author of a small history of Rome.

CONINGTON, John, English author, b. at Boston, Lincolnshire, Aug. 10, 1825 ; educated at Rugby and Oxford ; professor at the University of Oxford. Translator of the 'Agamemnon' of Æschylus, 1848 ; 'The Works of Virgil,' 1863 ; and numerous classical works.

CONOLLY, Thomas, English politician, b. 1823 ; educated at Harrow, and Christ Church, Oxford ; is deputy-lieutenant for County Donegal ; M.P. for Donegal, 1849.

CONRAD, Timothy Abbot, American conchologist, b. in New Jersey, 1803. Author of 'Fossil Shells of the Tertiary Formations of the United States,' 1832 ; 'Palæontology of the Mexican Boundary Survey,' 1854 ; and other works.

CONSCIENCE, Hendrick, Flemish novelist, b. at Antwerp, Dec. 3, 1812. Author of 'The Year of Miracles,' 1837 ; 'Aurelian,' 1859 ; and many other works of fiction.

CONSIDERANT, Victor Prosper, French political economist, b. at Salins Jura, Oct. 12, 1808. Author of 'Destinée sociale,' 1834–44 ; 'Principes du Socialisme,' 1847 ; 'La dernière Guerre et la Paix definitive de l'Europe,' Brussels, 1850.

CONSTANTINE, Nicholaewitch, Grand-duke of Russia, b. Sept. 21, 1827, brother of the Emperor of Russia ; high admiral of the imperial fleet ; married Princess Alexandra of Saxe Altenburg, 1848.

CONYNGHAM, Francis Nathaniel Conyngham, Marquis and Earl, English statesman, b. at Dublin, 1797 ; under-secretary of state for foreign affairs, 1823–26 ; succeeded his father, 1832 ; postmaster-general, 1834–35 ; lord chamberlain to the Queen ; member of the privy council.

COOK, Eliza, English verse writer, b. 1818. Conducted the 'Journal' bearing her name from 1849 to 1854 ; published 'New Echoes, and other Poems,' 1864 ; obtained a literary pension of 100l. per annum in 1864.

COOKE, Edward William, English painter, b. in London, 1811 ; studied architecture under Pugin. Executed a great number of paintings, principally of the sea-coast, and some scenes in Spain and Morocco. Elected A.R.A. 1850 ; R.A. 1863.

COOKE, George Wingrove, English author, b. 1814 ; studied at London University, and Jesus College, Oxford, and graduated B.A. ; called to the bar of the Middle Temple. Author of 'History of Party,' 1837 ; 'Inside Sebastopol,' 1855 ; 'China and Lower Bengal,' 1858 ; and other works.

COOKE, John Esten, American novelist, b. at Winchester, Virginia, Nov. 3, 1830. Author of 'Leather Stocking and Silk,' New York, 1854 ; 'The Virginia Comedians,' ib. 1855 ; and other works of fiction.

COOKESLEY, Rev. William Gifford, English author, b. at Brasted, Kent, Dec. 19, 1802 ; educated at Eton, and King's College, Cambridge, where he graduated B.A. 1825, and M.A. ; incumbent of St. Peter's, Hammersmith, 1860. Author of 'Account of the ancient City of Rome,' 1850 ; and other works.

COOPER, Sir Charles, English colonial judge, b. 1801 ; senior judge of the supreme *court of Australia ; created* chief justice by the governor and legislative council there, *June 1856; knighted in 1857.*

COOPER, Sir Daniel, English colonial administrator, b. 1807; elected to the Legislative Council of New South Wales, 1849; chosen first speaker of the Legislative Assembly under the new constitution, 1856; member of the senate of Sydney University; president of the bank of New South Wales; knighted by patent, 1857; baronet, 1863.

COOPER, Edward Henry, English politician, b. 1827; educated at Eton; magistrate for County Sligo; lieutenant-colonel in the Grenadier Guards; M.P. for Sligo, 1865.

COOPER, Susan Fennimore, American authoress, b. in the county of New York, 1815. Author of 'Rural Hours, by a Lady,' New York, 1850; 'Rhyme and Reason of Country Life,' 1854; and other works.

COOPER, Thomas, English writer, b. at Leicester, March 20, 1805. Author of 'The Purgatory of Suicides,' 1845; 'Baron's Yule Feast,' 1846; 'The Family Feud,' 1854.

COOPER, Thomas Sidney, English painter, b. at Canterbury, Sept. 26, 1803. Executed 'Going to Pasture;' 'Reposing;' and a great number of paintings. Elected A.R.A. 1845.

COPE, Charles West, English painter, b. at Leeds, 1811; studied at the Royal Academy. Exhibited 'Hagar and Ishmael,' 1836; 'The Flemish Mother,' 1839; 'Edward the Black Prince receiving the Order of the Garter in Westminster Hall,' 'Scholar's Mate,' 1862; and a great number of other works. Elected A.R.A. 1844; R.A. 1848.

COPLAND, James, English physician, b. in the Orkney Isles, 1793; studied at the University of Edinburgh, where he graduated M.D. 1815. Author of 'Dictionary of Practical Medicine and Pathology.'

COPPING, Edward, English writer, b. in London, 1828. Author of 'Alfieri and Goldoni, their Lives and Adventures,' 1856; 'Aspects of Paris,' 1858; 'The Home at Rosefield,' 1861; and other works of general literature.

COQUEREL, Athanase Laurent Charles, French Protestant theologian, b. at Paris, Aug. 27, 1795; Protestant minister, 1816. Author of 'Méditations sur des Textes choisis de l'Ancien et du Nouveau Testament,' 1859; and several theological works.

CORBALLY, Matthew Elias, English politician, b. 1797; educated at Oscott; magistrate and vice-lieutenant of Meath; high sheriff, 1838; M.P. for Meath, 1840–41, and since 1842.

CORBAUX, Fanny, English artist, b. 1812; member of the Society of British Artists, 1830. Exhibited 'Rachel,' at the Paris Exhibition, 1855. Author of several papers on the geography of the Exodus.

CORBOULD, Edward Henry, English painter, b. in London, Dec. 5, 1815. Executed 'The Fall of Phaeton from the Chariot of the Sun,' 1834; 'Scene from the Prophète,' painted for the Queen; 'The Destruction of the Idols of Basle;' and various others. Appointed instructor of historical painting to the royal family, 1851.

CORDIER, Henri Joseph Charles, French sculptor, b. at Cambrai, Oct. 19, 1827; studied in the School of Fine Arts, and under M. Fauginet. Exhibited 'Types nègres et mongols,' 1853; 'Le Maréchal Randon,' 1864; and several busts and groups in marble, bronze, onyx, and porphyry.

CORDOUAN, Vincent Joseph François, French painter, b. at Toulon, 1816; studied under Paulin Guérin. Executed and exhibited 'L'Embarquement des Zouaves partant d'Alger pour la Crimée,' 1855; 'Environs de Nersi,' 1864.

CORDOVA, Don Fernando Fernandez de, Spanish general, b. at Madrid, 1792; entered the army, 1810; captain-general of New Castile, March 8, 1850; captain-general of Cuba, 1853; minister of war, 1864.

CORK and ORRERY, Richard Edmund Sir Lawrence Boyle, Earl of, English magistrate, b. at Dublin, April 19, 1822; educated at Eton; graduated B.A. at Christ Church, Oxford; a magistrate and deputy-lieutenant of Somersetshire; succeeded his grandfather, 1856.

CORMON, Pierre Etienne Piestre, French dramatic writer, b. at Lyons, May 5. 1811. Author of 'Les Faussaires anglais,' 1833; 'Don Pédre,' 1857; 'Le Docteur Magnus,' 1864; 'Lara,' 1864; and numerous other dramas.

CORNE, Hyacinthe Marie Augustin, French writer, b. at Arras, Oct. 28, 1802. Author of 'Du Courage civil, et de l'Education propre à inspirer les Vertus publiques,' 1828; 'Lettres à Adrien,' 1856.

CORNELIUS, Peter von, German painter, b. at Düsseldorf, Sept. 27, 1787; director of the Academy at Munich, 1825. Executed 'The Last Judgment,' 62 feet high by 88 feet wide; 'The Four Horsemen,' from the Apocalypse; and a great number of other, chiefly historical, works.

CORNER, Julia, English authoress, b. 1815. Author of 'The Baronet,' 1835; 'Girls in their Teens;' 'Pictorial History of China and India;' and several books for children.

CORNEY, Bolton, English writer, b. at Greenwich, 1784. Edited 'The Seasons' by Thomson; 'Goldsmith's Poetical Works, with a Memoir,' 1846; 'Of the Conduct of the Understanding,' by J. Locke, 1859. Contributor to *Notes and Queries.*

CORNU, Sebastien Melchior, French painter, b. at Lyons, 1804; studied under MM. Richard, Bonnefond, and Ingres. Executed 'Louis IX. faisant ses Adieux à sa Mère,' 1838.

CORONINI-CRONBERG, John Baptist Alexander, Count of, Austrian military commander, b. at Gaeta, Nov. 16, 1794; entered the army, 1813; lieutenant, 1814; major, 1837; commander-in-chief of the Austrian army on the Danube, 1854; ban of Croatia, July 28, 1859; general commander-in-chief in Hungary, 1865.

CORREARD, Frederic, French general, b. at Poyols, Drôme, Sept. 9, 1789; lieutenant in the French army, 1813; captain, 1815; lieut.-colonel, 1830; colonel, 1835; staff major-general in the reserve list, 1852.

CORRY, Right Hon. Henry Thomas Lowry, English statesman, b. 1803, son of the second Earl of Belmore; educated at Eton, and Christ Church, Oxford; junior lord of the Admiralty, 1841–45; secretary to the Admiralty, 1845–46, and 1858–59; appointed first lord of the Admiralty, March 7, 1867.

CORWIN, Thomas, American statesman, b. in Kentucky, July 1794; called to the bar, 1818; member of Congress, 1830; elected to the Senate, 1845; secretary to the Treasury, 1848.

COSTA, Michael, English musical composer, b. in Naples, Feb. 1810; conductor at her Majesty's theatre, 1831; of the Philharmonic Concerts, 1846; and of the Italian Opera, 1847. Composer of 'Don Carlos,' 1844; 'Eli,' 1855; 'Naaman,' 1864; and other operas, oratorios, and smaller musical works.

COSTA-CABRAL, Antonio Bernardo Da, Count of Thomar, Portuguese statesman, b. at Fornos, Algodres, May 9, 1803; member of the Chamber of Deputies, 1835–50; prime minister of Portugal, 1839–46, and 1848–51.

COSTE, Jean Jacques Marie Cyprien Victor, French naturalist, b. at Castres, May 10, 1807. Author of 'Cours d'Embryogénie comparée,' 1837; 'Instructions pratiques sur la Pisciculture,' 1853; and other works on natural history.

COSTELLO, Louisa Stuart, English authoress, b. 1815. Author of 'Specimens of the Early Poetry of France,' 1835; 'The Queen's Prisoner,' 1841; 'The Rose Garden of Persia,' 1845; 'Clara Fane,' 1848; 'The Lay of the Stork,' 1856; and other works of fiction.

COTTA, Bernhard, German geologist, b. at Little Gillbach, Oct. 24, 1808; studied at the Academy of Mining at Freiberg, 1827 to 1831, where he was appointed professor, 1842. Author of 'The Dendroliths,' 1832; 'Geognostic Wanderings,' 1836–38; 'Letters on Humboldt's Kosmos,' 1848–51.

COTTON, Sir Arthur, English officer, b. 1803; educated at Addiscombe; entered the Madras army, 1819; colonel of engineers, 1854; knighted, 1861.

COTTON, Very Rev. Henry, English divine, b. 1790; educated at Christ Church, Oxford, where he graduated B.A. 1811; dean of Lismore; archdeacon of Cashel. Author of 'Fasti Ecclesiae Hibernicae,' 1845–62; 'Rheims and Douay,' 1855.

COTTON, Sir Sidney, English general, b. 1792; entered the army, 1810; colonel, 1854; served with the rank of major-general in India during the mutiny of 1857–58; K.C.B. 1858.

COUAILHAC, Jean Joseph Louis, French writer, b. at Lille, Nov. 28, 1810. Author of 'Les sept Contes en l'Air,' 1832; 'Les Mères d'Actrices,' 1843; and contributor to *Le Temps, Le Charivari,* and other journals.

COUDER, Louis Charles Auguste, French painter, b. at Paris, 1790; studied under Regnault and David. Executed 'La Mort du Peintre Massaccio,' 1817; 'Bataille de Lanfeld,' 1836. Member of the Institute and of the Academy of Fine Arts, 1839.

COUEDIC DE KERGOALER, Louis, Comte du, French politician, b. at Quimperlé, Dec. 12, 1810; member of the Legislative Assembly for the canton of Quimperlé; member of the Corps Législatif, 1852; for the department of Finistère since 1852.

COURBET, Gustave, French painter, b. at Ornans, Doubs, June 10, 1819. Executed 'L'Après-dinée à Ornans,' 1849; 'Les Demoiselles de Village,' 1852; 'Petit Pêcheur en Franche Comté,' 1863; and other paintings.

COURCELLE SENEUIL, Jean Gustave, French political economist, b. at Seneuil, Dordogne, Dec. 22, 1813. Author of 'Lettres à Edouard sur les Revolutions,' 1833; 'Études sur la Science sociale,' 1862; 'Leçons elémentaires d'Economie politique,' 1864.

COURNOT, Antoine Augustin, French mathematician, b. at Gray, Aug. 28, 1801; professor of mathematics to the Faculty of Sciences at Lyons, 1834; rector of the Academy of Grenoble, 1835. Author of 'Des Institutions d'Instruction publique,' 1864; and several other works, principally on mathematics.

COURSON, Aurelien de, French historian, b. at Port Louis, Isle of France, Dec. 25, 1811; studied at the College of St. Louis. Author of 'Essai sur l'Histoire de la Langue et des Institutions de la Bretagne armoricaine,' 1840; 'Prolégomènes,' 1863; and other historical works.

COURTENAY, Edward Baldwin, Lord, English politician, b. 1836; educated at Westminster, and Christ Church, Oxford; J.P. and D.L. of Devon, and captain of South Devon yeomanry cavalry; M.P. for Exeter, 1864.

COURTOWN, James George Henry Stopford, Earl of, Irish magistrate, b. in London, 1823; educated at Eton; captain in the Guards, 1840 to 1846; deputy-lieutenant and J.P. for County Wexford; high sheriff of Wexford, 1848; succeeded his father, 1858.

COUSIN-MONTAUBAN, Charles Guillaume Marie Apollinaire, Comte de Palikao, French general, b. June 24, 1796; chief of a squadron, 1836; lieut.-colonel, May 7, 1843; colonel, Aug. 2, 1845; general of brigade, Sept. 21, 1851; general of division, Dec. 28, 1855; senator, March 4, 1860; title of Count de Palikao, Jan. 22, 1862.

COUSINS, Samuel, English engraver, b. May 1801; studied under Mr. Samuel Reynolds. Executed 'Master Lambton,' after Sir T. Lawrence; 'Beauty's Bath,' after Landseer; and many others. Elected A.R.A. 1838; R.A. 1855.

COWEN, Joseph, English politician, b. 1800; magistrate for Durham; alderman of Newcastle, and M.P. for Newcastle-on-Tyne, 1865.

COWIE, Rev. Benjamin Morgan, English mathematician, b. 1817; educated at St. John's College, Cambridge, where he graduated B.A. 1839; principal of the College of Civil Engineers at Putney, 1844, and lecturer on geometry at Gresham College, 1854; minor canon of St. Paul's, 1858; government inspector of Training Schools, 1859.

COWLEY, Right Hon. Henry Richard Charles Wellesley, Earl, English diplomatist, b. 1804; educated at Eton; entered the diplomatic service, and secretary of legation, 1838; ambassador to the Ottoman Porte, 1845; minister plenipotentiary to the Swiss Cantons, 1848; at Frankfort, 1851; ambassador at Paris 1852 to 1867; succeeded his father as Baron Cowley, 1847; raised to the earldom, 1857.

COWPER, Charles, English colonial administrator, b. 1825; secretary of state of New South Wales, Aug. to Oct. 1856; and again from Sept. 1857 to Oct. 1859; colonial secretary, and represented the government in the Legislative Council in the ministry of March 9, 1860; premier, Jan. 10, 1861.

COWPER, Francis Thomas De Grey Cowper, Earl, English administrator, b. 1834; lord-lieutenant of Bedfordshire, and deputy-lieutenant of Kent; succeeded his father, sixth earl, April 1856.

COWPER, Hon. Henry Frederick, English politician; educated at Harrow, and Christ Church, Oxford; deputy-lieutenant of Kent and Herts; M.P. for Hertfordshire, 1865.

COWPER, Right Hon. William Francis, English statesman, b. 1811; president of the Board of Health, Aug. 1855; vice-president of the Committee of Council on Education, Feb. 1857; first commissioner of Public Works, 1860; M.P. for Hertford since 1835.

COX, Edward William, English barrister and legal writer, b. 1809; called to the bar of the Middle Temple, 1843; recorder of Falmouth and Helston, 1857; magistrate and deputy-lieutenant of Middlesex. Editor and proprietor of the *Law Times.*

COX, Rev. George William, English writer, b. 1828; educated at Trinity College, Oxford, where he graduated S.C.L. in 1849; entered holy orders, 1850; curate of St. Paul's, Exeter, 1854 to 1859; assistant-master in Cheltenham College, 1859 to 1863. Author of 'Tales of Thebes and Argos,' 1863.

COX, Rev. John Edmund, English theological writer, b. at Norwich, 1812; studied at All Souls, Oxford, where he graduated M.A.; perpetual curate of Adeby, 1837; vicar of St. Helen's, *Bishopsgate,* 1849. Author of 'Principles of the Reformation;' and numerous theological works.

COX, Rev. William Hayward, English divine, b. 1808; educated at Rugby, and at Pembroke College, Oxford, where he graduated B.A. 1825; examining chaplain to the bishop of Hereford, 1848; rector of Eaton Bishop, 1854; prebendary of Hereford, and rural dean. Author of 'Concio ad Clerum;' and other pamphlets.

COX, William Sands, English surgeon, b. 1802; educated at Guy's and St. Thomas's, London, and in Paris; member of the Royal College of Surgeons, 1824; founded Queen's College, 1830, and Queen's Hospital, 1841; magistrate and deputy-lieutenant of Warwickshire. Author of 'A Synopsis of the Bones;' and several anatomical works.

COX, William Thomas, English politician, b. 1808; magistrate for the borough and county of Derby; high sheriff, 1861; mayor of Derby, 1860; M.P. for Derby, 1865.

COXE, Rev. Arthur Cleveland, American author, b. at Mendham, New Jersey, U.S., 1818, and graduated at the University of New York; rector of Grace Church, Baltimore, U.S. Author of 'Advent, a Mystery,' a dramatic poem, 1837; and other works.

COXE, Rev. Henry Octavius, English antiquarian, b. 1811: educated at Westminster School, and Worcester College, Oxford, where he graduated B.A. 1833, and M.A.; chief librarian of the Bodleian, 1860. Edited the 'Chronicles of Roger of Wendover,' 1841–44. Author of the 'Catalogue of the MSS. belonging to the Colleges and Halls at Oxford,' 1852; and other works.

COXE, Very Rev. Richard Charles, English divine, b. 1799; educated at Worcester College, Oxford, where he graduated B.A. 1821, and M.A.; archdeacon of Lindisfarne, and canon residentiary of Durham. Author of 'The Symmetry of Revelation,' and several theological works and sacred poems.

COYNE, Joseph Stirling, English dramatic writer, b. at Birc, King's County, Ireland, 1805. Author of 'The Phrenologist,' 1835; 'The Tipperary Legacy,' 1847; 'The Woman in Red;' and a great number of dramas and works of fiction. Secretary to the Dramatic Authors' Society since 1856.

CRAIG, Isa, English authoress, b. in Edinburgh, 1830. Author of 'Poems' by 'Isa,' 1856; and an 'Ode,' which won the first prize at the Burns centenary festival, 1859.

CRAIG, Right Hon. Sir William Gibson, English statesman, b. 1797; educated at Edinburgh, where he was called to the bar, 1820; M.P. for Midlothian, 1837 to 1841; for the city of Edinburgh, 1841 to 1852; one of the lords of the Treasury from 1846 to 1852; lord clerk of her Majesty's Rolls and Registers in Scotland, 1862; member of the privy council, 1863.

CRAIK, Mrs. George Lillie, English authoress, b. at Stoke-upon-Trent, 1826, daughter of Thomas Muloch, Esq.; married to G. L. Craik, Esq., publisher. Author of 'The Ogilvies,' London, 1849; 'Olive,' ib. 1850; 'The Head of the Family,' ib. 1851; 'John Halifax, Gentleman,' ib. 1852; and numerous other works of fiction, poems, and essays.

CRAMAGEL, Rene' Elenthe're Fontaine, Marquis de, French officer and politician; b. at Moissy, Cramagel, July 24, 1789; lieutenant in the army, 1806; captain, 1813; colonel, 1831; staff-major, 1832; general, 1849; appointed senator, June 1854.

CRAUFURD, Edward Henry John, English politician. b. 1816; educated at Trinity College, Cambridge; graduated B.A. 1841; M.A. 1844; magistrate for Ayrshire and Bute; deputy-lieutenant of Bute; called to the bar of the Inner Temple, 1845; M.P. for Ayr since 1852.

CRAVEN, William Craven, Earl, English administrator, b. in London, 1809; studied at the University of Oxford; succeeded his father, 1825; high steward of Newbury; recorder of Coventry; lord-lieutenant of the county of Warwick, 1854.

CRAWFORD, Robert Wigram, English politician, b. 1813; partner in the firm of Crawford, Colvin, and Co.; director of the Bank of England, and chairman of East India Railway Company; M.P. for Harwich, May to July 1851; and for London since 1857.

CREASE, Henry Pellew, English colonial administrator, b. 1821; graduated at Clare College, Cambridge, B.A. 1847; called to the the bar of the Middle Temple, June 1849; appointed attorney-general of British Columbia, July 1861.

CREASY, Sir Edward Shepherd, English judge and author, b. at Bexley, in Kent, 1812; educated at Queen's College, Cambridge, where he graduated B.A. 1835, M.A. 1838; called to the bar of Lincoln's Inn, 1837; deputy assistant judge at the Middlesex sessions; appointed chief justice of Ceylon, and knighted, 1860. Author of 'The Fifteen Decisive Battles of the World,' 1851; and other historical works.

CREDNER, Karl August, German theologian, b. at Walterhausen, near Gotha, Jan. 10, 1797; studied at the Universities of Jena, Breslau, Halle, and Göttingen; D.D. at Jena, 1828. Author of 'History of the New Testament,' Frankfort, 1852; and numerous theological works.

CRE'MIEUX, Isaac Adolphe, French lawyer and author, b. at Nimes, of Jewish parents, April 30, 1796; studied at the College of Louis-le-Grand; called to the bar, 1817; minister of justice, and member of the Provisional Government of the French Republic, 1848. Author of 'Codes des Codes,' 1835.

CRESPIGNY, Claude, English colonial administrator, b. 1827; entered the royal navy as cadet, 1844; commanded the gun-boat 'Snap' in the Baltic, during the Russian war; appointed registrar of shipping in the colony of Labuan, Aug. 1862.

CRESWICK, Thomas, English painter, b. at Sheffield, 1811; exhibited, at the Royal Academy, 'Views in North Wales and Derbyshire,' 1828; 'Home by the Sands;' and many other paintings, principally landscapes. Elected A.R.A. 1842, and R.A. 1851.

CRETINEAU-JOLY, Jacques, French writer, b. at Fontenay, Vendée, Sept. 23, 1803. Author of 'Un Fils de Pair de France,' 1839; 'Cardinal Gonsalvi,' 1864; and various other works.

CROFTON, Edward Crofton, Baron, Irish magistrate, b. 1806; lord in waiting to the Queen from March to Dec. 1852, and from Feb. 1858 to June 1859; deputy-lieutenant of Roscommon.

CROFTON, Sir Walter Frederick, English magistrate, b. 1815; educated at Woolwich Academy; entered the army, 1833; captain, 1845; superintendent of convict prisons in Ireland, 1854 to 1862; knighted, 1862; magistrate for Wiltshire.

CROIX D'HENCHIN, Ernest Charles Euge'ne Marie, Marquis de, French politician, b. at Paris, Aug. 27, 1803; studied at the Military School of St. Cyr; lieutenant, 1823; captain and retired, 1832; senator, Jan. 1852.

CRONHOLM, Abraham, Swedish historian, b. at Landskrona, Oct. 22, 1809; studied at the University of Lund, 1825 to 1829, where he became professor of history, 1832. Author of 'Waringarne,' Lund, 1832; 'History of Sweden under the Reign of Gustavus Adolphus II.' 1857; and other historical works.

CROSBY, James, English colonial administrator, b. 1810; educated at Trinity College, Cambridge; called to the bar of the Middle Temple; police magistrate at Kingstown, St. Vincent, West Indies, March 1844 to 1857; stipendiary justice of the peace for the colony of British Guiana, 1857; immigration agent-general for the colony, 1864.

CROSLAND, Mrs. Camilla, English authoress, b. in London, June 9, 1812, the daughter of William Toulmin, Esq., solicitor. Author of 'Memorable Women;' 'Light in the Valley: my Experiences of Spiritualism,' 1857; 'Mrs. Blake,' a novel, 1862; and other works of fiction.

CROSLAND, Thomas Pearson, English politician, b. 1800; magistrate for the West Riding of Yorkshire; lieut.-colonel of the 6th West Riding volunteers; M.P. for Huddersfield, 1865.

CROSSLEY, Sir Francis, English politician, b. 1817; presented a park and pleasure-grounds to the town of Halifax, 1857; M.P. for Halifax, 1852 to 1859; returned M.P. for the North-West Riding of Yorkshire, 1859; created a baronet, Jan. 1863.

CROWE, Catherine, English authoress, b. at Borough Green, Kent, 1800, the daughter of S. Stevens, Esq.; married Lieut.-colonel Crowe, 1822. Author of 'Aristodemus,' 1838; 'Lily Dawson,' 1847; 'The Night Side of Nature,' 1848; 'Light and Darkness,' 1852; and numerous other works of fiction.

CRUIKSHANK, George, English artist, b. in London, Sept. 27, 1792. Executed 'The Queen's Matrimonial Ladder;' 'The Man in the Moon;' 'Tam O'Shanter;' 'Disturbing a Congregation;' 'The Worship of Bacchus,' 1863; and a great number of oil paintings, and of drawings and illustrations for books and periodical publications.

CRUVEILHIER, Jean, French physician, b. at Limoges, Feb. 9, 1791; studied medicine at Paris, and took the degree of M.D. 1816; member of the Academy of Medicine, 1835. Author of 'Traité d'Anatomie descriptive,' 1851; and other medical works.

CSASZAR, François, Hungarian poet, b. at Zalangersseg, near Pesth, 1807; professor of languages at the University of Fiume. Author of 'Magyar Valtojog,' Pesth, 1840–46; and other works. Founded the *Journal of Pesth,* 1850.

CSORICH DE MONTE CRETO, Antonio, Baron von, Austrian general and statesman, b. at Machichno, in Croatia, 1795; entered the army, 1809; major-general, 1842; lieutenant field-marshal, 1848; minister of foreign affairs, 1850 to 1853.

CUBITT, George, English politician, b. 1828 ; educated at Trinity College, Cambridge ; graduated B.A. 1851, M.A. 1854 ; magistrate for Surrey ; M.P. for Surrey since 1860.

CUCHEVAL CLARIGNY, Athanase, French political writer, b. at Calais, Feb. 1, 1821. Author of 'Le P. Loriquet, sa Vie et ses Écrits,' 1847 ; 'Considérations sur les Banques d'emission,' 1864 ; and a contributor to the *Moniteur* and other French journals.

CUGIA, Effinio, Italian general and administrator, b. 1820 ; major, 1859 ; major-general, 1861 ; under-secretary of war after the death of Count Cavour ; prefect of Palermo, 1862.

CULLEN, Right Rev. Paul, Irish divine, and Roman Catholic archbishop of Dublin, b. in Ireland, 1800 ; consecrated archbishop of Armagh, and Roman Catholic primate of all Ireland, 1850 ; transferred to Dublin, 1851 ; elevated to the dignity of cardinal, Jan. 22, 1866.

CUMMING, Rev. John, Scottish theologian, b. in Aberdeenshire, Nov. 10, 1810 ; minister of the Scotch Church, Crown Court, Covent Garden. Author of 'Apocalyptic Sketches : Lectures on the Book of Revelation ;' 'Voices of the Night ;' 'Redemption draweth nigh,' 1861 ; and numerous theological works.

CUMMING, Rev. Joseph George, English archæological writer, b. at Matlock, Derbyshire, 1812 ; educated at Emmanuel College, Cambridge, where he graduated B.A. 1834, and M.A. ; warden of Queen's College, Birmingham, 1858. Author of 'The Runic and other Remains of the Isle of Man ;' and several archæological works and papers.

CUMMINS, Thomas, English colonial administrator, b. 1811 ; appointed receiver of Barbadoes, June 1886 ; member of the Executive and Legislative Council, 1840 to 1849 ; commissioner of probates, March 1847 ; police magistrate for the city of Bridgetown, April 1849.

CUNNINGHAM, William, Scottish theologian, b. at Hamilton, Oct. 2, 1805 ; licentiate in theology of the University of Edinburgh, 1830 ; pastor of Greenock, 1833 ; joined the Independents, 1843 ; president of the New College at Edinburgh, 1847. Author of several theological works.

CURRIE, Sir Frederick, English diplomatist, b. 1799 ; educated at the Charter-house and Haileybury ; entered the Bengal service, 1817 ; successively British resident at Lahore, secretary to the government of India, and member of the Supreme Council ; raised to the baronetcy, 1848 ; director of the East India Company, 1854 ; vice-president of her Majesty's Indian Council, 1858.

CURTIS, George Ticknor, American author, b. at Watertown, Massachusetts, 1812 ; graduated at Harvard College, 1832 ; admitted to the bar, 1836. Author of 'Duties of Merchant Seamen,' 1844 ; 'History of the Origin, Formation, and Adoption of the Constitution of the United States,' 1855–58.

CURTIS, George William, American writer, b. at Providence, Rhode Island, Feb. 24, 1824. Author of 'Nile Notes of a Howadji,' 1850 ; 'Howadji in Syria,' 1852 : Is a constant contributor to American periodical literature.

CURTIUS, Ernst, German philologist, b. at Lübeck, Sept. 2, 1814 ; studied at the Universities of Bonn, Göttingen, and Berlin ; professor at Göttingen, 1856. Author of 'Zur Geschichte des Wegbaus bei den Griechen,' Berlin, 1855 ; and other works.

CURTIUS, Georg, German philologist, b. at Lübeck, April 16, 1820, brother of the preceding ; Ph.D. 1842 ; professor and director of the Philological Seminary at Prague, 1851. Author of 'A Greek Grammar' for the use of colleges ; and several philological works.

CURZON, George Augustus Frederick Louis, Viscount, English politician, b. 1821 ; educated at Eton, and Christ Church, Oxford ; graduated B.A. 1841 ; captain of the Leicestershire Yeomanry ; M.P. for Leicestershire since 1857.

CURZON, Paul Alfred de, French painter, b. at Moulinet, near Poitiers, Sept 7, 1820. Exhibited 'Petit Paysage,' 1843 ; 'L'Acropole d'Athens,' 1855 ; 'Le Vésuve,' 1863 ; 'Ruines d'un Pont romain sous les Murs de Nami,' 1864 ; and other works.

CURZON, Hon. Robert, English diplomatist, b. 1810 ; educated at the Charterhouse, and Christ Church, Oxford ; entered the diplomatic service ; attaché at the Ottoman Porte ; joint commissioner on the part of Great Britain at the conference of Erzeroum. Author of 'A Visit to the Monasteries of the Levant,' 1848.

CUSHING, Caleb, American statesman, b. at Salisbury, Essex County, Massachusetts, 1800 ; graduated at Harvard, 1817 ; member of Congress for Massachusetts, 1835 ; judge of the Superior Court of Massachusetts, 1852 ; attorney-general, 1853. Author of 'Reminiscences of Spain ;' 'Review of the Revolution of Three Days in France,' 1833.

CUSHMAN, Charlotte Saunders, American actress, b. at Boston, U.S., 1818; made her début, April 1835; retired from the stage, 1849.

CUST, Hon. Charles Henry, English politician, b. 1813; educated at Christ Church, Oxford; graduated B.A. 1836, and M.A. 1865; a magistrate of Leicestershire and Northamptonshire; high sheriff, 1859; M.P. for North Shropshire, 1865.

CUST, Hon. Sir Edward, English general and military writer, b. 1794; lieutenant-general in the army, and colonel of the 16th Dragoons. Author of 'Annals of the Wars of the Eighteenth Century;' and other works.

CUVILLIER FLEURY, Alfred August, French writer, b. 1802; studied at the College of Louis-le-Grand. Author of 'Portraits politiques et révolutionaires,' 1851; 'Historiens, Poètes, et Romanciers,' 1863.

CYBULSKI, Adalbert, German philologist, b. at Conin, Posen, Prussia, April 10, 1812; Ph.D. at Berlin, 1838; professor of Slavonic literature and language at Berlin, 1841; and at Prague, 1850.

CZUCZOR, George, Hungarian author, b. at Andod, Neutra, Dec. 17, 1800. Author of 'The Battle of Augsbourg.' 1824; 'John Huniade,' Pesth, second edition 1843; 'Life of Washington,' ib. 1845; and other historical works.

D.

DAA, Ludvig Kristensen, Norwegian politician, b. at Saltdalen, Norway, Aug. 19, 1809; studied at the University of Christiana, 1834. Author of 'Svensk norsk Haand-ordborg,' Christiana, 1841; 'Udsigt over Ethnologien,' 1845; and several political memoirs.

DACRE, Thomas Brand Trevor, Baron, English politician, b. 1808; educated at Christ Church, Oxford; M.P. for Herts, 1847 to 1852; a deputy-lieutenant of Herts; succeeded his father, 1853.

DAGHUILHON PUGOL, Pierre Jean Marie Gustave, French politician, b. Jan. 11, 1792; president of the chamber of the Imperial Court of Toulouse, and member of the General Council for the canton of St. Paul; member of the Corps Législatif for the department of Tarn, 1863.

DAGNAN, Isidore, French painter, b. at Marseilles, 1794. Painted 'Jeunes Filles romaines écoutant un Berger,' 1819; 'Marine à Marseille,' 1833; 'Route de Paris à Fontainebleau,' 1864; and numerous other landscapes.

DAHL, Wladimir Irvanowitsch, Russian writer, b. at St. Petersburg, at the beginning of the present century; studied in the naval school. Author, under the pseudonym of *Kosak Luganski*, of 'Chmœl,' and numerous works in Russian provincial dialects.

DAHLGREN, John, American naval commander, b. in Pennsylvania, 1810; entered the navy, 1826; admiral, and commanded the fleet before Charleston and Fort Sumter, 1863; inventor of the Dahlgren shell gun.

DAHLGREN, Karl Johan, Swedish poet, b. at Guillinge, Ostrogothie, June 28, 1791; studied at the University of Upsal; minister of a parish at Stockholm, 1824–44. Author of 'Samlade Arbeten,' six volumes, Stockholm, 1847–49.

DAHLMANN, Friederich Christoph, German politician and historian, b. at Wismar, May 17, 1785; studied at Copenhagen and Halle; professor at Kiel, 1813; and at the University of Bonn since 1850. Author of 'History of Denmark,' 1840–43; 'History of the French Revolution,' 1845; and many other historical works.

DALBAN, Pierre Jean Baptiste, French writer, b. at Grenoble, Dec. 14, 1784. Author of 'Les Fugitives,' 1807; 'Hercule au Mont Œta,' 1852; 'Cyrus,' 1856; 'Ariarate,' 1859; and other romances, poems, and dramas.

D'ALBERT, Charles, French musical composer, b. near Hamburg, 1815; studied under Kalkbrenner, and at the Académie Royale at Paris. Composed 'The Peri;' 'Queen of the Ball;' and a vast number of smaller pieces of music.

DALE, Rev. Thomas, English theological and verse writer, b. at Pentonville, London, Aug. 22, 1797; studied at Corpus Christi College, Cambridge, 1817; ordained, 1822; canon of St. Paul's cathedral, 1843; vicar of St. Pancras, 1846; rector of Therfield, Herts, 1860. Author of 'Widow of Nain,' 1818; 'The Golden Psalm,' 1847; and numerous other works.

DALGLISH, Robert, English politician, b. 1808 ; educated at Glasgow ; partner in the house of Dalglish, Falconer, and Co., Glasgow ; M.P. for Glasgow since 1857.

DALHOUSIE, Right Hon. Fox Maule, Earl of, English statesman, b. 1801 ; educated at the Charterhouse ; entered the army ; resigned with the rank of captain, 1831 ; M.P. for Perthshire, 1835 to 1837 ; for the Elgin burghs, 1838, and for Perth, 1841 ; secretary of state for war, Feb. 1855 to Feb. 1858 ; lord-lieutenant of Forfarshire ; succeeded his cousin in the earldom of Dalhousie, Dec. 1860.

DALKEITH, William Henry Walter, Earl of, English politician, b. 1831 ; educated at Eton, and Christ Church, Oxford ; deputy-lieutenant of Midlothian and county of Selkirk ; M.P. for Edinburghshire since 1853.

DALLAS, Rev. Alexander Robert Charles, English writer, b. towards the close of the last century ; entered the army, and fought at the battle of Waterloo ; ordained, 1844. Author of 'Lent Lectures on Christ's Temptation ;' and other theological and religious works.

DALLOZ, Victor Alexis De'sire', French advocate, b. at Septmoncel, Jura, Aug. 12, 1795 ; called to the bar at Paris, 1816. Author of 'Jurisprudence ; ou Repertoire méthodique et alphabétique de Jurisprudence générale,' 1824–30 ; and numerous legal works.

DALMAS, Albert de, French politician, b. 1823 ; chief of the cabinet of the Emperor, and member of the General Council of Morbihan for the canton of Baud ; member of the Corps Législatif for the 3rd circonscription d'Ille et Vilaine since 1859.

DALTON, Alexander, Count, French general, b. at Brives, Corrèze, April 20, 1776 ; entered the army, and lieutenant, 1791 ; chief of a battalion, 1800 ; general of brigade, 1809 ; lieutenant-general, 1821 ; entered the section of reserve, 1841.

D'ALTON, John, Irish genealogist and antiquary, b. at Bessville, Westmeath, 1792 ; educated at Trinity College, Dublin ; called to the Irish bar, 1813 ; commissioner of the Loan Fund Board, Dublin, 1835. Author of 'Dermid ; or Erin in the Days of Boroimhe,' 1814 ; 'History of the County of Dublin ;' and numerous genealogical works.

DALY, Ce'sar, French architect, b. at Verdun, 1800 ; studied under M. Felix Duban ; founded the *Revue de l'Architecture et des Travaux publics,* 1840 ; diocesan architect of Tarn.

DALY, Sir Dominic, English colonial magistrate, b. 1798 ; appointed governor of the island of Tobago, 1851 ; transferred to the government of Prince Edward's Island, 1854 to 1859 ; appointed governor and commander-in-chief of South Australia, Nov. 1861.

DAMAS-HINARD, Jean Joseph, French writer, b. at Madrid, Dec. 11, 1805 ; studied law at Paris, and called to the bar. Author of 'Chants sur Lord Byron,' 1824 ; 'Poème du Cid,' 1858 ; 'Buffon Ecrivain,' 1864 ; and other works.

DAMBRY, Pierre Charles Andre', French politician, b. Dec. 20, 1796 ; mayor of the Isle-Adam, and member of the General Council for the same canton ; member of the Corps Législatif since 1859.

DAMINOIS, Angelique Adele Huvey, French authoress, b. at Clermont, Oise, Dec. 21, 1793. Author of 'La Chasse au Renard,' 1823 ; and a great number of romances.

DANA, Richard Henry, American writer, b. at Cambridge, Massachusetts, Nov. 15, 1787 ; studied at Harvard College ; admitted to the bar of Baltimore, 1811. Author of 'The Idle Man,' 1821 ; 'The Husband's and Wife's Grave ;' 'The Buccaneer,' 1827 ; and other works.

DANA, Richard Henry, American barrister, b. at Cambridge, Massachusetts, Aug. 1, 1815, son of the preceding ; entered Harvard College. 1832 ; graduated, 1837 ; admitted to the Boston bar, 1840. Author of 'The Seaman's Friend,' 1841 ; 'To Cuba and Back : a Vacation Voyage,' London, 1859 ; and several biographical sketches.

DANIEL, Henry Joseph, French sculptor, b. at Nantes, April 1804 ; studied under Bosio and Cortot. Executed 'Le Comte Siméon,' 1842 ; 'Cléopâtre' in marble, 1847, in bronze, 1855 ; and numerous statues and busts.

DANIE'LO, Julien, French writer, b. in the department of Morbihan, 1800. Author of 'L'Histoire de la Province de Champagne,' 1833 ; 'Du Panthéisme, du Mosaïsme, et du Christianisme,' 1848 ; 'Les Conversations de M. de Châteaubriand,' 1864 ; and other works.

DANJOU, Louis Felix, French writer and musician, b. at Paris, 1812. Author of '*Archives curieuses de l'Histoire de* France, ou Collection de Pièces rares,' 1834–40 ; '*Du Paganisme dans l'Education :* quatre Lettres,' 1851–52 ; published several musical compositions.

DANTAN, Antoine Laurent, French sculptor, b. at St. Cloud, Dec. 8, 1798; studied under Bosio, and at the School of Fine Arts. Executed 'The Death of Hercules,' 1828; 'Young Bather playing with his Dog,' 1836; and a great number of busts and statues.

DANTAN, Jean Pierre, French sculptor, b. in Paris, Dec. 28, 1800, brother of the preceding; studied in Paris and Italy. Executed busts of Talleyrand, Wellington, D'Orsay, Costa, Lady Maria Hamilton, Nélaton, Aubert, and numerous other works of art.

DANTIER, Henri Alphonse, French writer, b. at Noyon, 1810. Author of 'Histoire du Moyen Age,' 1852; 'Etudes sur les Bénédictins,' 1864; and contributor to the *Moniteur* and other French periodicals.

DANTON, Joseph Arsène, French writer, b. at Plancy, Aube, Jan. 1, 1814; studied at the College of Charlemagne; secretary to the minister of public instruction, 1840; member of the Imperial Council of Education, July 2, 1864. Editor of 'Œuvres philosophiques de Fénelon,' 1843; and other works.

DARBOY, Rev. George, French divine, and archbishop of Paris, b. at Fayl-Billot, Haute, Marne, Jan. 16, 1813; studied at the Seminary of Langres; ordained, 1836; bishop of Nancy, 1859, and archbishop of Paris, Jan. 1863. Author of 'Les Femmes de la Bible,' 1859; and other theological and religious works.

D'ARCY, Colonel George, English colonial governor, b. 1816; entered the army, 1836, and became colonel, July 7, 1857; appointed governor of the Gambia, June 1859. Author of a work on light infantry drill.

DAREMBURG, Charles Victor, French physician and writer, b. at Dijon, April 14, 1817. Translated 'Œuvres choisies d'Hippocrate,' 1843; 'Œuvres complètes d'Oribase,' 1853–60. Author of 'L'Histoire de la Syphilis de l'Antiquité,' 1846.

DARESTE DE LA CHAVANNE, Antoine Cleophas, French political economist, b. at Paris, Oct. 25, 1820; professor to the Faculty of Letters at Grenoble, 1847. Author of 'Eloge de Turgot,' 1846; 'Histoire des Classes agricoles en France, depuis Saint Louis jusqu'à Louis XVI.' 1853.

DARESTE DE LA CHAVANNE, Rodolphe Cleophas, French legal writer, b. at Paris, Oct. 26, 1824; obtained the degree of LL.D. 1847; advocate at the Court of Cassation, 1851. Published 'Essai sur François Hotman,' 1850; 'Code des Pensions civiles,' 1854; and other legal works.

DARGAND, Jean Marie, French writer, b. at Paray-le-Monial, Saône et Loire, Feb. 22, 1800; studied at the Lycées Charlemagne and Bonaparte, in Paris. Author of 'La Solitude,' 1833; 'Histoire de Marie Stuart,' 1850; 'Histoire de Jane Grey,' 1862; and other historical works.

DARIMON, Alfred, French politician and journalist, b. at Lille, Dec. 17, 1819. Contributor to the *Peuple,* 1848; to the *Presse,* 1854; and other French journals. Author of 'Réforme banquière,' 1857. Member of the Corps Législatif for the 7th circonscription of Paris since 1857.

DARISTE, Jean Baptiste Auguste, French politician, b. at Martinique, June 19, 1807; member of the Council of State for War, Jan. 25, 1852; created senator, March 4, 1853.

DARLEY, Felix, American artist, b. at Philadelphia, June 23, 1822; illustrated 'Rip Van Winkle;' 'Legend of Sleepy Hollow;' Longfellow's 'Miles Standish;' and numerous other works.

DARLING, Sir Charles Henry, English colonial administrator, b. 1808; entered the army as ensign, Dec. 7, 1826; retired, 1841; appointed lieutenant-governor of the island of St. Lucia, 1847; lieutenant-governor of the Cape of Good Hope, 1851; received the order of K.C.B. and knighted, 1862; governor of Victoria, 1863–66.

DARNAUD, Firmin, French magistrate, b. at Roquefixade, Ariége, March 12, 1796; was King's counsel, 1830; councillor at the Royal Court of Toulouse, Feb. 2, 1835; president of the chamber of the Imperial Court of Toulouse.

DARNLEY, John Stuart Bligh, Earl and Viscount of, English administrator, b. 1827; educated at Eton; graduated at Oxford; deputy-lieutenant of Kent and Meath; hereditary high steward of Gravesend and Milton.

DARRELL, John, English colonial judge, b. 1794; studied at Trinity College, Cambridge, and called to the bar of Lincoln's Inn; in the colonial service since 1819; attorney-*general at Bermuda,* 1834 to 1856; chief justice of Bermuda, 1856. Published an edition of the laws of Bermuda, 1861.

DARRICAU, Daniel Charles Auguste, Baron, French statesman, b. at St. Denis, Seine, Sept. 24, 1808 ; entered the army, 1825 ; captain, 1836 ; titular councillor of state, 1852 ; minister of war, 1862–63.

DARRICAU, Rodolphe Augustin, Baron, French naval commander, brother of the preceding, b. March 7, 1807 ; entered the naval school, 1827 ; captain, 1853 ; governor of the isle of Réunion, 1858 ; rear-admiral, Jan. 17, 1864.

DARTMOUTH, William Walter Legge, Earl of, English administrator, b. at Sandwell Park, Birmingham, Aug. 12, 1823 ; educated at Eton, and Christ Church, Oxford, where he graduated M.A. 1847 ; deputy-lieutenant of Staffordshire.

DARTOIS, François Victor Armand, French dramatic writer, b. at Beauvains, near Noyon, Oise, Oct. 3, 1788. Author of 'Les Femmes Soldats,' 1809 ; 'Paris et Londres,' 1827 ; 'Reculer pour mieux sauter,' 1854 ; and many others.

DARU, Napoleon, Count, French politician, b. at Paris, June 11, 1807 ; studied at the Lycée of Louis-le-Grand, and at the Polytechnic School, 1825 ; entered the army, but retired as a captain, 1847 ; member of the Academy of Sciences, 1860.

DARWIN, Charles, English naturalist, b. at Shrewsbury, Feb. 12, 1809 ; educated at the Grammar School, Shrewsbury, at the University of Edinburgh, and Christ's College, Cambridge, where he graduated in 1831. Author of 'The Structure and Distribution of Coral Reefs,' 1842 ; 'Geological Observations on Volcanic Islands,' 1844 ; 'Origin of Species by means of Natural Selection,' 1859 ; and other scientific works.

DASENT, George Webbe, English author, b. 1818 ; educated at King's College, London, and Magdalen Hall, Oxford, where he graduated B.A. 1840 ; called to the bar of the Middle Temple, 1852. Author and translator of 'The Prose, or Younger, Edda,' 1842 ; 'Popular Tales from the Norse, with an Introductory Essay,' 1859 ; and other works.

DAUBIGNY, Charles François, French painter b. in Paris, Feb. 15, 1817 ; studied under MM. Paul Delaroche and Daubigny. Executed 'Vue de la Vallée d'Oisans,' 1840 ; 'Soleil couché,' 1851 ; 'Les Bords de la Cure,' 1864 ; and numerous other landscapes.

DAUBRE'E, Gabriel Auguste, French geologist, b. at Metz, June 25, 1814 ; studied at the Polytechnic School, 1834 ; professor of mineralogy and geology at the Academy of Strasbourg, 1839 ; professor of geology at the Natural History Museum of Paris, 1861. Author of 'Description geologique du Bas-Rhin,' 1852 ; and other scientific works.

DAUMAS, Melchior Joseph Eugene, French general and author, b. Sept. 4, 1803 ; entered the army, 1822 ; lieutenant, 1827 ; general, 1849 ; general of division, 1853 ; senator, Aug. 12, 1857. Author of 'Le Sahara algérien,' Paris, 1845 ; 'La Kabylie,' 1857 ; and other works on Algeria.

DAUMER, Georg Friederich, German author, b. at Nuremberg, March 5, 1800 ; studied at the University of Erlangen. Author of 'Die Glorie der heiligen Jungfrau Maria,' Nuremberg, 1841 ; 'Die Religion des neuen Weltalters,' Hamburg, 1850 ; and numerous philosophical and poetical works.

DAURIAC, Philippe Eugene Jean Marie, French writer, b. at Toulouse, Oct. 17, 1815. Published 'Louis Philippe, Prince et Roi,' 1843 ; 'Essai historique sur la Boucherie de Paris,' 1861 ; 'Nouveau Guide du Voyageur en Belgique et en Hollande,' 1864 ; and other miscellaneous works.

DAUTHEVILLE, François, French general, b. at Chalennon, Ardéche, May 8, 1792 ; entered the Polytechnic School, 1811 ; entered the army, 1813 ; general of brigade, Feb. 13, 1852 ; member of the Corps Législatif for the department of Ardéche since 1854.

DAUZATS, Adrien, French painter, b. at Bordeaux, 1808 ; studied under Julien Michel Gué. Executed 'Une Mosquée sur les Bords du Nil,' 1835 ; 'Cathedrale de Tolède,' 1855 ; 'Vue prise à Chateldon,' 1863 ; and numerous other landscapes.

DAVELUY, Ame'de'e, French philologist, b. 1799 ; studied at Amiens ; professor at the Royal College of Dijon, 1830 ; appointed professor at School of Athens, 1846 ; inspector-general of schools, 1862.

DAVENNE, Henri Jean Baptiste, French writer, b. at Paris, Jan. 12, 1789. Author of 'Régime administratif et financier des Communes,' 1840 ; 'Traité pratique de Voirie urbaine,' 1858 ; and other works.

DAVEY, Richard, English politican, b. 1799 ; educated at Tiverton School and Edinburgh University ; magistrate and deputy-lieutenant for Cornwall ; M.P. of West Cornwall since 1857.

DAVID, Christian George Nathan, Danish politician, b. at Copenhagen, Jan. 16, 1796 ; studied at the University of Copenhagen ; professor at the same university, 1834 ; member of the Diet, 1848 ; represented Denmark at the International Congress in France, 1856.

DAVID, Felicien Ce'sar, French musical composer, b. at Cadenes, Vaucluse, April 3, 1810 ; studied in Paris at the Conservatoire, under Réber. Published 'Mélodies orientales,' 1835 ; 'The Desert,' played first at the Conservatoire, Dec. 1844 ; 'La Perle du, Brésil,' 1851 ; 'Lalla Rookh,' 1862 ; and numerous other compositions.

DAVID, Ferdinand, German musical composer, b. at Hamburg, Jan. 19, 1810 ; studied under Spohr ; played under Mendelssohn at Leipsic, 1836. Composed 'Concertos for the Violin ;' and several romances and symphonies.

DAVID, Jerome, Baron, French politician, b. in Rome, June 30, 1822 ; was captain in the army ; mayor of Langon, and member of the General Council for the canton of St. Symphorien ; member of the Corps Législatif for the department of the Gironde since 1859.

DAVID, Maxime, French miniature painter, b. at Châlons-sur-Marne, Aug. 24, 1798 ; studied at the Lycée of Rheims. Painted the portraits of Queen Amélie, King Louis Philippe, Prince Napoleon, and of a great number of other distinguished persons.

DAVID DESCHAMPS, Louis Charles, French politician, b. in Paris, Oct. 16, 1802 ; advocate at the Imperial Court of Paris ; member of the General Council for the canton of Écouché ; member of the Corps Législatif for the 2nd circonscription of Orne since 1860.

DAVIE, Sir Henry Robert Ferguson, English politician, b. 1798 ; magistrate and deputy-lieutenant of Devon ; lieutenant-general unattached, and colonel of the 73rd Foot ; M.P. for Haddington since 1847.

DAVIS, Charles Henry, American naval officer, b. in Boston, Massachusetts, Jan. 16, 1807 ; entered the U.S. navy, 1823 ; appointed commander and stationed in the Pacific, 1856 ; had charge of the 'American Ephemeris and Nautical Almanack,' 1849. Published a translation of Gauss's 'Theoria Motûs Corporum Cœlestium,' 1856.

DAVIS, Edward Hamilton, American archæologist, b. in Ross County, Ohio, Jan. 22, 1811 ; graduated M.D. at Cincinnati, 1837 ; professor of materia medica and therapeutics at the New York Medical College, 1850. Author of 'Monuments of the Mississippi Valley.'

DAVIS, Gateward Coleridge, English colonial administrator, b. 1831 ; called to the bar of the Inner Temple, 1860 ; secretary of the executive and administrative committee in Antigua, 1861 ; attorney-general of Antigua, and crown law officer, Montserrat, 1862.

DAVIS, Jefferson, American politician, b. in Kentucky, June 3, 1808 ; educated at Transylvania College, and at West Point Military Academy, where he graduated in 1828 ; member of Congress for Mississippi, 1845 ; senator for the same state, 1847 ; secretary of war, 1853 ; re-elected to the Senate, 1857 ; president of the so-called Confederate States of North America, 1861–66.

DAVIS, Sir John Francis, English diplomatist, b. in London, 1795 ; attaché to Lord Amherst's embassy to Pekin, 1816 ; was British plenipotentiary and chief superintendent of British trade in China ; governor and commander-in-chief of the colony of Hong Kong, 1843 to 1848 ; created a baronet for services in China, 1845 ; and K.C.B. 1854. Author of 'A Description of China and its Inhabitants ;' and other works on China.

DAVIS, Nathan, English traveller and writer, b. 1812 ; for some time editor of the *Hebrew Christian Magazine.* Author of 'Tunis ; or Selections from a Journal kept in that Regency,' 1841 ; 'Carthage and her Remains,' 1861 ; and other works.

DAWSON, George, English lecturer, b. in London, 1821 ; studied at the University of Glasgow, and graduated M.A. ; minister of Mount Zion Chapel, Birmingham, 1844 ; and of the church of the Saviour, 1847.

DAWSON, Robert Peel, English politician, b. 1818 ; educated at Harrow, and Christ Church, Oxford ; magistrate and deputy-lieutenant of the county of Londonderry ; high sheriff, 1850 ; M.P. for the county of Londonderry since 1859.

DAWSON, Hon. Vesey, English politician, b. 1842 ; educated at Eton ; magistrate of the county of Monaghan ; captain in the Coldstream Guards ; M.P. for county of Monaghan, 1865.

DAY, George Edward, English physician, b. 1815 ; educated at Cambridge, where he graduated B.A. 1837, M.A. 1840 ; licentiate in medicine, 1842 ; M.D. of the University of *Giessen, and Fellow of* the Royal College of Physicians. Author of 'A Practical

Treatise on the Diseases of Advanced Life,' 1849 ; 'Physiology and Medicine,' 1860 ; and other medical works.

DE'ADDE', Edouard, French dramatic writer, b. 1810. Author of 'Odette,' 1832 ; 'Les Femmes et le Secret,' 1843 ; 'Le Fils du Diable,' 1860 ; and numerous other works. For some time director of the theatre of Porte St. Antoine.

DEAK, Francis, Hungarian statesman, b. at Kehida Zala, 1803 ; deputy to the Diet at Presburg, 1832, and has since taken an active part in the leadership of the Liberal party in Hungary.

DEAN, Sir Thomas, Irish architect, b. at Cork, 1792 ; designed the Old and New Bank Buildings and Court House at Cork ; the City Gaol, Anglesey Bridge in that city, and several other buildings ; knighted by the Lord-lieutenant of Ireland, 1830.

DEASY, Right Hon. Richard, Irish politician, b. 1812 ; educated at Trinity College, Dublin, where he graduated, and was called to the Irish bar ; made Q.C. 1849 ; third serjeant-at-law, 1858 ; solicitor-general for Ireland, 1859 ; attorney-general, 1860 ; judge, 1861 ; M.P. for Cork, 1855 to 1861.

DEBAY, Jean Baptiste Joseph, French sculptor, b. at Malines, Oct. 16, 1779. Executed 'Leonidas,' 1827 ; 'Charles Martel,' 1836 ; 'Le Choix difficile,' in marble, 1861 ; 'Faustulus,' a group in bronze, 1863 ; and numerous other statues and groups.

DEBON, Hippolyte, French painter, b. at Paris, 1816 ; studied under Gros and M. Abel de Pujol. Exhibited 'Bataille d'Hastings,' 1845 ; 'Fête de l'Agriculture du temps des Gaulois, 1850 ; 'Entrée de Guillaume le Conquérant à Londres,' 1855 ; 'Le Siége de la Rochelle,' 1863 ; and numerous other, principally historical, paintings.

DE BOW, James Dunwoody Brownson, American journalist, b. at Charleston, South Carolina, July 10, 1820 ; studied at Charleston College. and graduated in 1843 ; called to the bar in the same town, 1844. Established *De Bow's Commercial Review*, 1845 ; compiled 'Industrial Resources of the South West,' 1858 ; and other statistical works.

DEBREYNE, Pierre Jean Corneille, French physician, b. at Quædypre, near Dunkerque, Nov. 7, 1786 ; studied medicine at Paris ; degree of M.D. 1824. Author of 'Précis sur la Physiologie humaine,' 1851 ; and a great number of medical works.

DECAISNE, Joseph, French botanist, b. at Brussels, March 18, 1807. Author of 'Annales des Sciences naturelles,' 1834 ; 'Essais sur une Classification des Algues et des Polypiers calcifères, suivis d'un Mémoire sur les Corallines,' 1843 ; 'Le Jardin fruitier du Muséum,' 1859–65 ; and other botanical works.

DECAISNE, Pierre, Belgian physician, b. at Brussels, May 11, 1809 ; studied medicine and graduated M.D. at the University of Louvain ; entered the Belgian army as surgeon, 1830 ; professor to the Faculty of Medicine at Gand. Author of 'Choix d'Observations chirurgicales,' 1838 ; 'Des Plaies des Articulations et des Tendons,' 1851 ; and numerous medical works.

DECANDOLLE, Alphonse Louis Pierre Pyramus, Swiss botanist, b. at Paris, Oct. 27, 1806 ; studied at Geneva, and graduated LL.D. 1829. Author of 'Monographie des Campanulées,' 1830 ; 'Prodromus Systematis naturalis Regni vegetabilis,' 1858–64 ; and other botanical works.

DECHAMPS, Adolphe, Belgian statesman, b. at Melle, East Flanders, June 17, 1807 ; studied at the Museum of Brussels ; appointed governor of Luxembourg, 1841 ; minister of foreign affairs, 1845. Published 'Le second Empire : Dialogues politiques,' Brussels, 1859 ; 'L'Empire et l'Angleterre,' 1860.

DECHAMPS, Victor, Belgian writer, b. at Melle, 1811, brother of the preceding. Author of 'Le Christ et les Antechrists dans les Écritures, l'Histoire et la Conscience,' Tournai, 1858 ; 'Pie IX. et les Erreurs contemporaines,' 1864 ; and other theological works.

DE CHARMS, Richard, American divine, b. Oct. 17, 1796 ; graduated at Yale College, 1826 ; was pastor of the Swedenborgian Churches in Cincinnati, Philadelphia, and Baltimore. Established the *New Jerusalem Magazine*, in Boston. Author of the 'New Churchman.'

DECHASTELUS, Claude Marie Jean Antoine, French politician, b. March 28, 1798 ; judge, and member of the General Council of the Loire for the canton of St. Symphorien de Lay ; member of he Corps Législatif, 1863.

DECKER, Pierre Pacques François de, Belgian writer and politician, b. at Zèle, Flanders, Jan. 25, 1812 ; studied at the College of Fribourg ; member of the *Chamber of Representatives* for Termonde, 1839. Author of 'Religion et Amour,' 1835 ; 'De l'Influence du Clergé en Belgique,' 1843 ; and other works.

DECOURCELLE, Adrien, French dramatic writer, b. at Paris, 1824 ; studied at the College of Charlemagne. Author of ' Une Soirée à la Bastille,' 1845 ; ' Les Dragons de la Reine,' 1841 ; and a great number of other dramas.

DEFAÇOZ, Eugene, Belgian lawyer and politician, b. at Ath, 1797 ; was an advocate, and took part in the Revolution of 1830 ; councillor at the Court of Cassation ; president of the Congress, 1847. Author of ' Ancien Droit Belgique : Précis de Lois et Coutumes observées en Belgique avant le Code Civil,' Brussels, 1846.

DEFAUCONPRET, Charles Auguste, French writer, b. at St. Denis, Seine, Dec. 19, 1797 ; studied at the Lycée Napoleon ; translated Washington Irving's ' Travels of Christopher Columbus.'

DEFFES, Pierre Louis, French musical composer, b. at Toulouse, July 24, 1819 ; admitted to the Conservatoire, and studied under MM. Berton and Halévy. Composed ' Broskovano,' 1858 : ' Le Café du Roi,' 1861 ; and other comic operas.

DEFORGES, Philippe Auguste Pittand, French dramatic writer, b. at Paris, April 5, 1805 ; studied at the Bourbon College ; appointed chief secretary to the minister of war, 1830. Author of ' Henri IV. en Famille,' 1828 ; ' Les Fables de La Fontaine,' 1842 ; ' Bijou Perdu,' 1855 ; and numerous other dramas.

DEFREMERY, Charles, French philologist, b. at Cambrai, Dec. 8, 1822 ; studied at the College of France. Translated from the Persian of Mirkhond ' L'Histoire des Sultans du Kharezm,' 1842 ; from the same author ' Histoire des Seldjoukides et des Ismaeliens, ou Assassins de l'Iran,' 1849 ; and numerous other translations.

DE FREYNE, Charles French, Baron, Irish magistrate, b. 1792 ; magistrate for Roscommon, Sligo, and Mayo ; succeeded to the title Sept. 1863.

DE GREY AND RIPON, George Frederick Samuel Robinson, Earl, English statesman, b. in London, Oct. 24, 1827 ; eldest son of the first earl ; M.P. for Huddersfield, 1853 to 1857 ; for the West Riding of Yorkshire, 1857 to 1859 ; under-secretary of state for war, June 1859 ; under-secretary of state for India, Jan. to Aug. 1861 ; secretary of state for war, 1863–66 ; succeeded his father as 2d Earl Ripon, Jan. 1859 ; lord president of the council, Dec. 1868.

DEGUERRY, l'Abbe' Gaspard, French author, b. at Lyons, 1797 ; studied at the College of Villefranche ; ordained to the priesthood, 1820 ; canon of Notre Dame, 1844 ; archbishop of Marseilles, 1861. Author of ' Eloge de Jeanne d'Arc,' 1828 ; ' Notice sur le Comte de Clocheville,' 1853 ; and other biographical works.

DEHEQUE, Felix De'sire', French writer, b. in Paris, Oct. 9, 1794 ; studied at the Paris École Normale, 1813 ; elected member of the Academy of Inscriptions and Belles Lettres, Nov. 1859. Author of ' La Charte constitutionnelle traduite en Grec moderne,' 1822 ; translator of the Ludwig ' Poésies Cypriques d'Andreadis,' 1837 ; and other works.

DEINHARDSTEIN, Johann, German dramatic writer, b. at Vienna, June 21, 1794 ; professor of classic literature at the University of Vienna, 1827. Author of ' Dramatische Dichtungen,' Vienna, 1816 ; ' Künstlerdramen,' Leipsic, 1845 ; and numerous other works. Edited the *Jahrbücher der Literatur* from 1830 to 1851.

DELABARRE DUPARCQ, Nicolas Edouard, French military writer, b. at St. Cloud, April 1, 1819 ; studied at the Ecole Polytechnique, 1836–39 ; lieutenant, 1841 ; captain, Jan. 1844 ; professor of history at the School of St. Cyr. Author of ' Biographie et Maximes de Maurice de Saxe,' 1851 ; ' L'Art militaire pendant les Guerres de Religion,' 1864 ; and other works.

DELACOUR, Alfred Charlemagne Lartigue, French physician and writer, b. 1815 ; graduated M.D. at Paris, 1841. Author of ' L'Hospitalité d'une Grisette,' 1847 ; ' Le Premier Pas,' 1862 ; ' Célimare le bien-aimé,' 1863 ; and numerous other dramas.

DELACOUR, Edmond, French diplomatist, b. at Paris, near 1805 ; secretary of embassy at Vienna, 1833 to 1836 ; and at Stockholm, 1839–47 ; envoy extraordinary and minister-plenipotentiary to Vienna, 1848 ; ambassador to Constantinople, 1853 ; ambassador to Naples, 1854–56.

DELAFOSSE, Gabriel, French mineralogist, b. 1795 ; studied at the Paris École Normale ; professor of mineralogy to the Faculty of Sciences at Paris, and at the École Normale, 1813. Author of ' Précis élémentaire d'Histoire naturelle.' 1857 ; and numerous other scientific works.

DELAGE, Marie Henri, French writer, b. at Paris, 1825. Author of ' Le Sang du Christ,' 1849 ; ' L'Eternité Dévoilée,' 1854 ; ' Le Monde Occulte,' 1859 ; and several *religious works.*

DELAHUNTY, James, English politician, b. 1808 ; a merchant in Waterford ; elected M.P. for that town, 1868.

DELALLE, Louis Auguste, French theological writer, b. at Revin, Ardennes, Oct. 9, 1800 ; appointed vicar-general of Nancy, Aug. 30, 1855. Author of 'Cours de Controverse Catholique ;' and other theological works.

DELAMARRE, Edouard François De'sire', French politician, b. at Guerbaville, Dec. 16, 1797 ; member of the Corps Législatif for Guéret since 1852.

DELAMARRE, Guillaume, French political economist, b. 1799 ; elected member of the Corps Législatif for the Somme, 1852. Author of 'La Vie à bon Marché,' 1854–56 ; 'Les Eaux de Paris,' 1861.

DELAMERE, Hugh Cholmondeley, Baron, English politician, b. 1812 ; M.P. for Derbyshire, 1840–41 ; succeeded his father, 1855.

DELANE, John Thaddeus, English journalist, b. Oct. 1817 ; educated at Magdalen Hall, Oxford, where he graduated B.A. 1839 ; called to the bar of the Middle Temple, 1847 ; assistant editor of the *Times*, 1839–41 ; editor of the *Times* since 1841.

DELANGLE, Claude Alphonse, French statesman, b. at Varzy, Nièvre, April 6, 1797 ; called to the bar of Paris, 1818 ; advocate-general at the Court of Cassation, 1840 ; first president of the Imperial Court of Paris, 1852 ; minister of the interior, 1858–59 ; vice-president of the Senate, 1859–61 ; member of the Academy of Sciences.

DELAPALME, Emile, French magistrate, b. at Paris, Nov. 14, 1793 ; magistrate at the Royal Court of Paris, 1815 ; advocate-general, 1831 ; advocate-general at the Court of Cassation, 1841 ; counsellor in the same court, 1847. Author of 'Premier Livre du Citoyen,' 1864 ; and other works.

DELAPORTE, Michel, French dramatic writer, b. at Paris, 1802. Author of 'Le Parisien,' 1838 ; 'Le Masque de Velours,' 1860 ; 'Ah ! que l'Amour est agréable !' 1862 ; and numerous other dramas.

DELARUE, Joseph Ame de'e, French architect, b. at Lille, 1790 ; studied at Paris under Huyot, Alavoine, and Guénépin. Designed l'Hôtel de Ville and le Palais de Justice at Mézières ; and numerous churches and chapels.

DE LA RUE, Warren, English astronomer, b. 1815 ; educated at the College of St. Barbe, Paris ; acted as juror and reporter in the Great Exhibition of 1851 ; president of the Royal Astronomical Society.

DELARUE BEAUMARCHAIS, Edouard Charles, French general, b. Oct. 9, 1799 ; entered the army, 1814, and became a colonel, 1847 ; general of brigade, 1852 ; commander of the Légion d'honneur, 1858.

DELASIAUVE, Louis Jean François, French physician, b. at Garennes, Eure, 1804 ; graduated M.D. at Paris, 1830. Author of 'Examen de diverses Critiques de la Phrénologie,' 1844 ; 'Des Pseudomanies,' 1859 ; and other medical works.

DELATRE, Louis Michel James Lacour, French writer, b. at Paris, May 9, 1815. Author of 'Chants de l'Exil,' 1843 ; 'Marathon ; Promenade à Cheval,' 1853 ; and numerous other works.

DELAUNAY, Charles Eugene, French mathematician, b. at Lusigny, Aube, April 9, 1816 ; entered the École Polytechnique, 1834 ; elected member of the Institute, 1855 ; and member of the Bureau of Longitudes, 1862. Author of 'Cours élémentaire de Mécanique,' 1854 ; and other scientific works.

DELAVAL, Pierre Louis, French painter, b. in Paris, April 27, 1790 ; studied under Girodet. Exhibited 'Sainte Clotilde exhortant Clovis à embrasser la Religion chrétienne,' 1817 ; 'St. Louis portant l'Oriflamme,' 1841 ; and other paintings.

DELAVIGNE, Germain, French dramatic writer, b. at Giverny, Eure, Feb. 1, 1790 ; studied at the College of St. Barbe. Author of 'La Somnambule,' 1819 ; 'Le Diplomate,' 1827 ; 'La Nonne Sanglante,' 1854 ; and other dramas and comedies.

DELAWARR, George John Sackville West, Earl of, English administrator, b. in London, 1791 ; educated at Harrow and Oxford ; graduated D.C.L. 1834 ; high steward of Stratford-on-Avon ; was lord chamberlain to the Queen, 1841–46 ; reappointed, Feb. 1858 ; resigned, 1859.

DELEHAYE, Josse, Belgian politician, b. at Gand, 1800 ; elected representative of his native town in Congress, 1831 : king's counsel to the tribunal of Gand, 1839 ; vice-president of the Chamber of Representatives, 1849 ; burgomaster of Gand, 1858.

DELEPIERRE, Octave, Belgian writer, b. at Bruges, 1804 ; studied law at the *University of Gand ;* appointed secretary of legation, and consul-general of Belgium in *London, 1849. Author of 'Précis des Annales de Bruges,' 1835 ; and numerous other, chiefly antiquarian* and bibliographical, works.

DELESSERT, Alexandre Henri Edouard, French writer, b. in Paris, Dec. 15, 1828. Author of 'Voyage aux Villes maudites,' 1853; 'Le Chemin de Rome, s'il vous plaît?' 1860; 'Toujours tout droit,' 1862; and other works.

DELHASSE, Felix Joseph, Belgian writer, b. at Spa, Feb. 5, 1809. Author of 'Les Bords de l'Amblève,' Liege, 1853; contributor to the *Libéral, Radical, Débat Social,* and the *Nation.*

DELIGNY, Edouard Jean Etienne, French military commander, b. 1812; second lieutenant, 1835; first lieutenant, 1840; captain, 1844; lieutenant-colonel, May 1852; colonel, Dec. 1852; general of brigade, July 1855; general of division, Dec. 1859.

DELISLE, Leopold Victor, French historian, b. at Valognes, Manche, Oct. 24, 1826; entered the Ecole des Chartes, 1847; member of the Institute and of the Academy of Inscriptions, 1857. Author of 'Recherches sur la Condition de la Classe agricole en Normandie au Moyen Age,' 1846.

DE L'ISLE AND DUDLEY, Philip Sidney, Baron, English magistrate, b. 1828; educated at Eton; deputy-lieutenant of Kent; magistrate for the North Riding of Yorkshire.

DELITZSCH, Franz, German Protestant theologian, b. at Leipsic, Feb. 23, 1813; appointed professor of theology at the University of Erlangen, 1850. Author of 'Geschichte der jüdischen Poesie,' Leipsic, 1836; 'Vom Hause Gottes oder der Kirche,' ib. 1848; and numerous theological works.

DELOCHE, Jules Edouard Maximin, French writer, b. at Tulle, Corrèze, Oct. 27, 1817. Author of 'Étienne Baluze, sa Vie et ses Œuvres,' Limoges, 1858; 'Description des Monnaies Mérovingiennes du Limousin,' 1863; and other works.

DELORD, Taxile, French writer, b. at Avignon, Nov. 25, 1815; studied at Marseilles from 1830 to 1834; was long one of the chief contributors to the *Charivari.* Author of 'Physiologie de la Parisienne,' 1851; 'Les Troisième Pages du Journal le Siècle,' 1861; and of numerous contributions to French journals.

DELPIT, Martial, French writer, b. at Cahuzac, Lot-et-Garronne, Feb. 25, 1813; studied at the Ecole des Chartes. Author of 'Notice sur le Manuscrit intitulé Recognitiones feudorum,' 1841; and other works.

DELTHEIL, Jean, French politician, b. Sept. 2, 1795; member of the Chamber of Deputies, 1836–42; and of the Legislative Assembly, 1849; member of the Corps Législatif for the department of Lot since 1852.

DELTUF, Paul, French writer, b. at Paris, 1825. Author of 'Idylles Antiques,' 1851; 'Les Pigeons de la Course,' 1857; 'La Comtesse de Silva,' 1864; and numerous other works of fiction.

DELVAN, Alfred, French writer, b. at Paris, 1825; secretary to M. Ledru Rollin; minister of the interior, 1848. Author of 'Le Roué Innocent,' 1850; 'Les Barrières de Paris,' 1857; 'Bibliothèque Bleue,' 1859–60; and many other novels.

DEMANGEAT, Joseph Charles, French lawyer, b. at Nantes, Sept. 2, 1820; studied law at Paris; called to the bar, 1841; obtained the degree of LL.D. 1843; appointed supplementary professor to the faculty of law at Paris, 1851; professor, 1862. Author of 'Cours Élémentaire de Droit Romain,' 1864; and other legal works.

DEMANTE, Auguste Gabriel, French lawyer, b. at Paris, March 3, 1821; appointed supplementary professor to the faculty of law at Toulouse, 1850; and professor, 1856. Author of 'De la Loi et de la Jurisprudence en Matière de Donations déguisées,' 1855; and other legal works.

DE MAULEY, Charles Frederick Ashley Cooper Ponsonby, Baron, English magistrate, b. 1815; M.P. for Poole, 1837 to 1847; for Dungarvan, 1851 to 1852; deputy-lieutenant and magistrate of Gloucestershire and Oxfordshire.

DEMESMAY, Camille, French sculptor, b. at Besançon, Aug. 23, 1815; licentiate in law at Paris, 1839. Executed 'La Vierge et l'Enfant Jésus,' 1859; 'Naïs,' 1863; and a great number of statues.

DEMETZ, Frederic Auguste, French social reformer, b. May 12, 1796; studied law at Paris; appointed court counsel, 1832; founded the agricultural colony and penitentiary of Mettray, near Tours, 1840.

DEMOGEOT, Jacques Claude, French writer, b. at Paris, July 5, 1808; studied at the Seminary of St. Nicolas of Chardonnet, and professor there from 1826 to 1828; appointed *professor of rhetoric* at the Lycée de St. Louis of Paris, 1843. Author of 'Histoire du Collége de Lyon,' 1840; 'Contes et Nouvelles,' 1862; and other works.

DEMOLIE'RE, Hippolyte Jules, French dramatic writer, b. at Nantes, Aug. 3, 1802; studied law at Rennes, and medicine at Paris. Author of 'La Famille Renneville,' 1843; 'De Paris à Corbeil et à Orléans,' 1854; 'Le Revers de la Medaille,' 1861; and many other works.

DEMOLOMBE, Jean Charles Florent, French legal writer, b. at Fère, Aisne, July 22, 1804; studied law at Paris, and received the degree of LL.D. 1826; appointed professor of civil law to the faculty of Caen, 1831, and dean of the faculty, 1853. Published 'Cours de Code Napoléon,' 1845–63.

DE MORGAN, Augustus, English mathematician, b. at Madura, Southern India, 1806; educated at Trinity College, Cambridge, where he graduated B.A. 1827; appointed professor of mathematics at the University of London, 1828. Author of the 'Book of Almanacs;' and numerous mathematical and other scientific works.

DENIS, Jean Ferdinand, French traveller, b. at Paris, Aug. 13, 1798. Author of 'Buenos-Ayres et le Paraguay,' 1823; 'Luiz de Souza,' 1835; 'Une Fête Brésilienne,' 1850; and numerous romances and works of travel.

DENISON, Edward, English politician, b. 1840; educated at Eton, and Christ Church, Oxford; called to the bar of Lincoln's Inn, 1867; returned M.P. for Newark, 1868.

DENISON, Ven. George Anthony, English theological writer, b. 1805; educated at Eton, and Christ Church, Oxford, where he graduated B.A. 1826; curate of Cuddesden, Oxfordshire, 1832 to 1838; vicar of East Brent, Somerset, 1845; archdeacon of Taunton. Editor of the *Church and State Review;* and author of several sermons.

DENISON, Right Hon. John Evelyn, English statesman, b. 1800; educated at Eton, and Christ Church, Oxford, where he graduated B.A. 1823; M.P. for Newcastle-under-Lyne, 1824; for Hastings, 1830; for Notts, 1831; for South Notts, 1833 to 1837; for Malton, 1841–57; for North Nottinghamshire since 1857; elected speaker of the House of Commons, 1857; a magistrate and deputy-lieutenant of Notts.

DENJOY, Jean François Polynice, French politician, b. at Lectoure, Gers, June 6, 1809; studied law at Paris, and was called to the French bar; member of the Council of State for the Interior, 1851.

DENMAN, Hon. George, English politician, b. 1819; educated at Repton, and Trinity College, Cambridge, where he graduated M.A. 1842; called to the bar of the Inner Temple, 1846; made Q.C. 1860; M.P. for Tiverton since 1859.

DENMAN, Joseph, English naval officer, b. in London, 1810, brother of the preceding; entered the royal navy, 1823, and captain, 1841; lord-chamberlain to the Queen, 1848 to 1852; commodore, 1853; vice-admiral, 1863.

DENMAN, Thomas Denman, Baron, English magistrate, b. in London, 1805, brother of the two preceding; called to the bar, 1827; a magistrate for Derbyshire; succeeded his father, 1854.

DENNERY, or D'ENNERY, Adolphe Philippe, French dramatist, b. in Paris, June 17, 1811; director of the Théâtre Historique, 1850. Author of 'Le Changement d'Uniforme,' 1836; 'L'Ile du Prince Touton,' 1854; 'Le Sacrifice d'Ephigénie,' 1861; and numerous other dramas.

DENOIX DES VERGUES, Marie François Descampeaux, Lady, French authoress, b. at Beauvais, Oise, May 7, 1798; married to M. Laverguat, 1818. Authoress, under the name of Fanny Denoix, of 'Heures de Solitude,' 1837; 'Épitre à M. Proudhon,' 1858; and a great number of poems.

DENOUVILLIERS, Charles Pierre, French physician, b. Feb. 4, 1808; studied at Paris, and received the degree of M.D. 1837; appointed professor of anatomy at the École de Medicine, 1846; surgeon to the Hospital of St. Louis. Author of 'Des Cas dans lesquels le Trépan est applicable aux Os du Crâne,' 1836; and other works.

DENT, John, English politician, b. 1826; educated at Eton, and Trinity College, Cambridge, where he graduated B.A. 1848; called to the bar of Lincoln's Inn, 1851; M.P. for Knaresborough, 1852–57; M.P. for Scarborough since 1857.

DEPE'RY, Jean Ire'ne'e, French writer, b. at Chellex, Ain, March 16, 1796; studied at the College of Geneva, and at the Seminary of St. Sulpice; canon and grand vicar of Belley, 1827; bishop of Gap, 1844. Author of 'Biographie du Département de l'Ain,' *1835;* and other works.

DE'PRET Louis, French writer, b. at Lille, Oct. 9, 1837; studied at the Lycée of the *same town.* Author of 'Cloche,' 1854; 'Rosine Passmore,' 1861; 'Windsor, le Château, *son Histoire,* Récits et Souvenirs,' 1863; and many other works.

DERBY, Edward Geoffrey Smith Stanley, Earl of, English statesman, b. March 29, 1799 ; eldest son of the thirteenth Earl of Derby ; educated at Eton, and at Christ Church, Oxford ; sat as M.P. for Stockbridge, 1820–26 ; for Preston, 1826–30 ; for Windsor, 1830–32 ; for North Lancashire, 1832–46 ; summoned to the Upper House as Lord Stanley of Bickerstaffe, 1846 ; chief secretary for Ireland, 1830–33 ; secretary of state for the colonies, 1833–34, and again 1841–45 ; succeeded to the earldom, 1851 ; first lord of the Treasury from March to December 1852, and again from Feb. 26, 1858, to June 18, 1859 ; for the third time first lord of the Treasury, July 5, 1866, to Feb. 25, 1868. Author of a translation of Homer.

DERGER, Ernst, German painter, b. at Bockenheim, near Frankfort, April 15, 1809 ; studied at the Academy of Dusseldorf, and under Schadow ; professor at the School of Fine Arts, Munich. Executed 'The Saviour carrying His Cross ;' the 'Garden of Olives ;' the 'Infant Jesus,' 1857 ; and numerous other paintings.

DERING, Sir Edward Cholmeley, English politician, b. 1807 ; magistrate and deputy-lieutenant of Kent ; M.P. for Romney, 1831–32 ; M.P. for East Kent, 1852–57, and 1863–68.

DE ROS, William Lennox Lascelles Fitz-Gerald De Ros, Baron, English military commander, b. at Thames Ditton, 1797 ; educated at Westminster College, and graduated at Christ Church, Oxford ; lieutenant-general in the army ; deputy-lieutenant, and lieutenant-governor of the Tower ; magistrate for the Tower Liberties, and for the county of Down ; quartermaster-general of the army, 1856.

DERRY, Right Rev. William Higgin, Lord Bishop of, English divine, b. 1793 ; educated at Trinity College, Cambridge, where he graduated B.A., and at Trinity College, Dublin, where he took the degrees of M.A. and D.D. ; consecrated bishop of Limerick, 1849 ; translated to the see of Derry, 1853.

DERVICH, Pasha, Turkish statesman and diplomatist, b. at Eyoub, Constantinople, 1815 ; director of the Military School of Constantinople, with the grade of brigadier-general, 1841 ; general of division, 1849 ; ambassador at the Congress at Paris, 1856 ; chief of the administration of mines and forests, 1861.

DESARBRES, Nere'e, French dramatic writer, b. at Villefranche, Feb. 12, 1822. Author of 'Madame Diogène, deux Femmes en Cage,' 1854 ; 'Deux Hommes pour un Placard,' 1860 ; 'Sept Ans à l'Opera : Souvenirs anecdotiques,' 1864.

DESCAT, Louis Theodore Joseph, French politician, b. at Roubaix, Nord, Jan. 18, 1800 ; representative of the department of Nord, 1848 ; deputy to the Legislative Assembly after Dec. 10, 1851, and to the Corps Législatif, 1852–57.

DESCHAMEL, Emile Augustin Etienne Martin, French writer, b. in Paris, Nov. 14, 1819 ; studied at the College of Louis-le-Grand, 1839–42. Author of ' Les Courtisanes de la Grèce,' 1854 ; ' Causeries de Quinzaine,' 1861 ; and numerous other works. Contributor to the *Revue des Deux Mondes* and the *Journal des Débats*.

DESCHAMPS, Antoine, French writer, b. in Paris, March 12, 1800, brother of the following ; studied at Orleans. Author of ' Trois Satires politiques,' 1831 ; ' Resignation,' 1839 ; ' Études sur l'Italie,' 1832 ; and other works.

DESCHAMPS, Emile, French author, b. at Bourges, Feb. 20, 1791 ; studied at Paris. Author of ' Le Tour de Faveur,' 1818 ; ' Études Françaises et Étrangères,' 1829 ; ' Poésies des Crèches,' 1852 ; and numerous translations from Sir Walter Scott, Shakespeare, and other English authors.

DESCHAMPS, Fre'de'ric, French writer, b. at Rouen, 1806 ; called to the bar in the same town, 1829. Author of ' Bohême en Normandie,' Rouen, 1854 ; ' La Vendéenne,' ib. 1859 ; and other works.

DESCOURS, Laurent, French politician, b. at Lyons, Jan. 20, 1814 ; member of the General Council for the canton of Mornant ; member of the Corps Législatif for the 4th circonscription of the Rhone since 1857.

DESESSARTS, Alfred Stanislas Langlois, French writer, b. at Passy, Seine, Aug. 9, 1814 ; studied at the College of Henri IV. Author of ' Donjon de Vincennes,' 1830 ; ' Une Perle dans la Mer,' 1841 ; ' Valentin, ou la Femme de Mousse,' 1863 ; and numerous other works.

DESESSERT, De la Manche, French magistrate, b. at Coutances, May 4, 1802 ; studied law, was procureur du roi in his native town, the same at Bayeux, and at the royal court of Caen ; elected to represent the department of Manche, 1848.

DESGOFFE, Alexandre, French painter, b. at Paris, March 2d, 1805; studied under M. Ingres. Exhibited 'Site près d'Arbonne,' 1834 ; 'Chemin à Montmorency,' 1861 ; 'Résurrection de Jésus-Christ,' 1856 ; and numerous other paintings.

DESHAYES, Gerard Paul, French naturalist, b. at Nancy, May 13, 1795 ; studied at Strasburg. Author of 'Descriptions des Coquillages fossiles des Environs de Paris,' 1824–37 ; 'L'Histoire des Animaux sans Vertèbres,' 1836–46 ; and other works on natural history.

DESJARDINS, Abel, French historian, b. at Paris, 1814 ; obtained the degree of doctor, 1844 : appointed professor of history to the faculty of Dijon, 1847 ; at Caen, 1856 ; at Douai, 1857. Author of 'Études sur Saint Bernard,' 1859 ; 'L'Esclavage dans l'Antiquité,' 1857 ; and other works.

DESJARDINS, Ernest, French professor and historian, b. at Noisy-sur-Oise, Sept. 30, 1823 ; brother of the preceding ; appointed lecturer on geography at the Ecole Normale, 1861. Author of 'Le Grand Corneille, Historien,' 1861 ; and numerous historical and geographical works.

DESLANDES, Raymond, French dramatic writer, b. at Yvetot, July 12, 1825 ; studied at the College of Rouen. Author of 'Méridien,' 1852 ; 'Une Chasse à Saint Germain,' 1860 ; 'Un Mari qui lance sa Femme,' 1864 ; and numerous other dramas.

DESLYS, Charles, French writer, b. at Paris, 1820 ; studied at the College of Charlemagne. Author of 'Les Bottes vernies de Cendrillon,' 1846 ; 'La Mère Rainette,' 1851 ; 'L'Héritage de Charlemagne,' 1864 ; and many other works.

DESMAREST, Ernest Leon Joseph, French writer, b. in Paris, May 17, 1815 ; called to the bar, 1837. Author of 'Constantine, et de la Domination Française en Afrique,' 1837 ; and, with M. H. Rodrigues, of 'Les Principes et les Hommes : Esquisses retrospectives,' 1840.

DESMAROUX DE GUALMIN, Gilbert Desirat, French politician, b. at Montmarault, Allier, Feb. 11, 1815 ; studied at the École Polytechnique ; member of the Corps Législatif for the 2d circonscription of Allier since 1852.

DESNOIRESTERRES, Gustave le Brisoys, French writer, b. at Bayeux, Calvados, June 2, 1817. Author of 'La Pensionnaire et l'Artiste,' 1839 ; 'La Chambre Noire,' 1843 ; 'Les Cours Galantes,' 1859–64 ; and numerous other romances.

DESNOYERS, Jules Pierre François Stanislas, French geologist, b. at Nogent le Rotron, Oct. 8, 1800 ; member of the Institute ; secretary to the Society of Natural History of Paris, 1825, and to the Society of Geology of France, 1830. Author of 'Recherches geologiques et historiques sur les Cavernes à Ossements,' 1845 ; and numerous historical and geological works.

DESNOYERS, Louis Claude Joseph Florence, French writer, b. at Replonges, Ain, 1805. Founded, with M. Charles Philipon, *Le Charivari*, Dec. 1, 1832. Author of 'Les Aventures de Jean Paul Choppart,' 1836 ; 'De l'Opéra en 1847,' 1847 ; and of many dramas.

DESOLME, Laurent Pierre Charles, French journalist, b. in Paris, Dec. 15, 1817 ; studied at the Bourbon College. Established *L'Esprit du Peuple*, 1848 ; the *Courrier de l'Industrie*, 1853 ; and several other French periodicals. Author of 'Un Mari dans les Nuages,' 1855 ; 'Pongo,' 1859.

DESPREZ, Louis, French sculptor, b. at Paris, July 7, 1799 ; studied under Bosio, and at the École des Beaux Arts. Executed 'L'Innocence,' 1831 ; 'Diane au Bain,' in bronze, for the Champs Élysées ; 'Jacques Desbrosses,' 1852 ; and numerous busts and statues.

DESSALLES, Jean Leon, French philologist, b. at Bugue, Dordogne, May 18, 1803 ; studied at Perigeaux. Author of 'Études sur l'Origine et la Formation du Roman et de l'ancien Français,' 1854 ; 'Rapport sur l'État present des Archives de Sarlat,' 1855 ; and other works.

DESVAUX, Nicolas Gilles Toussaint, French general, b. Nov. 1, 1810 ; second lieutenant, 1830 ; captain, 1840 ; colonel, Dec. 1851 ; brigadier-general, March 17, 1855 ; general of division, March 12, 1859.

DE TABLEY, George Warren, Baron, English magistrate, b. at Tabley House, Cheshire, 1811 ; studied at Oxford ; was lord-in-waiting to the Queen ; is a deputy-lieutenant of Cheshire.

DEVAUX, Paul Louis Isidore, Belgian politician, b. at Bruges, April 10, 1801 ; called to the bar at Liege ; elected deputy to the National Congress, 1830 ; member of the Chamber of Representatives since 1831.

DE VERE, Aubrey Thomas, English writer, b. 1814 ; educated at the University of Dublin. Published 'The Waldenses and other Poems,' 1842 ; 'Poems Miscellaneous and Sacred,' 1856 ; 'Wanderings in Greece and Turkey,' 1850 ; and other works.

DEVEREUX, Richard Joseph, English politician, b. 1829 ; educated at Oscott ; a merchant in Wexford ; M.P. for Wexford since 1865.

DE VESCI, Thomas Vesey, Viscount, English politician, b. in Dublin, Sept. 21, 1803 ; graduated at Christ Church, Oxford ; M.P. for Queen's County, 1835 to 1852 ; succeeded his father, 1855 ; elected a representative peer of Ireland, 1856.

DEVIENNE, Louis, French magistrate, b. 1800 ; appointed procureur-général at Lyons, 1858 ; first president of the Imperial Court of Paris, 1858 ; created senator, March 15, 1865.

DEVOILLE, l'Abbe' Achille, French poet, b. at Besançon, 1815. Author of 'Voix de la Solitude,' 1839 ; 'Andreas, ou le Prêtre-Soldat,' 1843 ; 'La Cloche de Louville,' 'Les Echos de ma Lyre,' 1859 ; and other poems.

DEVON, William Reginald Courtenay, Earl of, English statesman, b. 1807 ; eldest son of the tenth Earl of Devon ; educated at Christ Church, Oxford ; sat as M.P. for South Devonshire, 1841–48 ; secretary to the Poor Law Board, 1850–59 ; succeeded to the earldom, 1859 ; chancellor of the Duchy of Lancaster, July 6, 1866, to May 17, 1867 ; president of the Poor Law Board, May 1867 to Dec. 1868.

DEVONSHIRE, William Cavendish, Duke of, English statesman, b. 1808 ; educated at Trinity College, Cambridge, where he graduated B.A. 1829 ; M.P. for the University of Cambridge, 1829–30 ; M.P. for Malton, 1830 ; and for North Derbyshire, 1832–34 ; succeeded to the peerage, Jan. 1858 ; is lord-lieutenant of Derbyshire ; chancellor of the London University, 1836 to 1856 ; chancellor of the University of Cambridge.

DEWEY, Rev. Chester, American writer, b. at Sheffield, Massachusetts, Oct. 25, 1784 ; graduated at William's College, 1806 ; appointed professor of chemistry and natural philosophy in the University of Rochester, 1850. Author of 'History of the Herbaceous Plants of Massachusetts ;' contributor to the *American Journal of Science and Art.*

DEWEY, Rev. Orville, D.D., American writer, b. at Sheffield, Massachusetts, March 28, 1794 ; graduated at William's College, 1814 ; studied at Andover Theological Seminary, 1816 to 1819. Author of 'The Old World and the New,' 1836 ; 'On the Education of the Human Race,' 1855 ; and other works.

DIAS, Gonçalvez, Brazilian poet, b. at Cachias, province of Maranha, Aug. 10, 1823 ; studied at the University of Coimbra. Author of 'Primeiros Cantos,' Rio de Janeiro, 1846 ; 'Leonor de Mendonça,' 1847 ; and other poems.

DICEY, Edward Stephen, English writer, b. 1829 ; educated at Trinity College, Cambridge, where he graduated B.A. 1854. Author of 'Memoir of Cavour ;' 'Rome in 1860 ;' and other works : contributor to *Fraser's* and *Macmillan's Magazines.*

DICK, William Wentworth Fitzwilliam, English politician, b. 1805 ; justice of the peace and deputy-lieutenant of Wicklow ; high sheriff, 1844 ; assumed the name of *Dick* in 1865 ; M.P. for Wicklow since 1852.

DICKENS, Charles, English novelist, b. at Portsmouth, Feb. 7, 1812. Author of 'Sketches by Boz,' 1836–37 ; 'Posthumous Memoirs of the Pickwick Club,' 1837–38 ; 'Oliver Twist,' 1838 ; 'Martin Chuzzlewit,' 1844 ; 'Bleak House,' 1853 ; 'Our Mutual Friend,' 1864 ; and numerous other works of fiction. Editor of *All the Year Round.*

DICKENSON, Daniel Stevens, American politician, b. at Goshen, Connecticut, U.S. Sept. 11, 1800 ; called to the New York bar, 1828 ; elected to the State Senate, 1836 ; lieutenant-governor and president of the State Senate ; member of the Federal Senate, 1844 to 1851.

DICKENSON, Samuel Henry, American physician, b. at Charleston, South Carolina, Sept. 1798 ; graduated at Yale College, 1814, and at the University of Pennsylvania, 1818–19 ; professor of medicine at the College of Charleston, 1824–32 ; appointed to the Jefferson Medical College, Philadelphia, 1850. Author of 'Elements of Medicine,' and numerous medical works.

DICKSON, Alexander George, English politician, b. 1834 ; educated at Rugby ; formerly major in the army ; M.P. for Dover, 1865.

DIDAY, Francis, Swiss painter, b. at Geneva, 1812 ; studied painting in France. Executed 'Un Chalet dans les Hautes Alpes ;' 'Le Soir dans la Vallée ;' 'Un Torrent dans les Alpes ;' the 'Glacier de Rosenheim ;' and other paintings, principally landscapes.

DIDIER, Henry, French politician, b. Jan. 1, 1823 ; is an advocate and member of the General Council for the canton of Aix ; member of the Corps Législatif for Ariege since 1857.

DIDIOT, Charles Nicolas Pierre, French theologian, b. at the village of Esnes, Meuse, 1797; appointed professor at Verdun, 1822; grand vicar of the diocese, 1837; bishop of Bayeux, 1856.

DIESTERWEG, Friederich Adolph Wilhelm, German educational writer, b. at Sieger, Westphalia, Oct. 29, 1790; studied at the Universities of Herborn and Tubingen; teacher at the Seminary of Berlin, 1832 to 1850. Author of 'Lehrbuch der mathem. geogr. und popul. Himmelskunde,' Berlin, 1840; and other scholastic works.

DIETRICH, David Nathaniel Friederich, German botanist, b. at Ziegenhain, near Jena, 1800. Author of 'Deutschlands Giftpflanzen,' Jena, 1826; 'Encyclopädie der Pflanzen,' ib. 1841–51; and other botanical works.

DIEZ, Friederich Christian, German philologist, b. at Giessen, March 15, 1794; studied at the College and University of his native town; graduated Ph.D. at Giessen, 1821; appointed professor at Bonn, 1830. Author of 'Altspanische Romanzen,' Berlin, 1821; 'Etymologische Wörterbuch der romanischen Sprachen,' Bonn, 1853; and numerous other works.

DIGBY, Kenelm Henry, English writer, b. 1800; educated at Trinity College, Cambridge, where he graduated B.A. 1823. Author of 'The Broad Stone of Honour; or, Rules for the Gentlemen of England,' 1829; 'Compitum, or the Meeting of Ways in the Catholic Church;' and other works.

DIGBY, Kenelm Thomas, English politician, b. 1843, son of the preceding; returned M.P. for Queen's County, 1868.

DILKE, Sir Charles Wentworth, English politician, b. in London, 1810; educated at Westminster, and Trinity Hall, Cambridge; graduated LL.B. 1834; M.L. 1860; magistrate of Middlesex and Westminster, and one of the royal commissioners for the International Exhibition of 1862; created a baronet, Jan. 1862; M.P. for Wallingford, 1865–68.

DILKE, Christopher Wentworth, English politician, b. 1843; educated at Trinity Hall, Cambridge; called to the bar of the Middle Temple, 1866; returned M.P. for Chelsea, 1868. Author of 'Greater Britain,' 1868.

DILLON, John Blake, English politician, b. 1814; educated at Trinity College, Dublin; graduated B.A. 1841; called to the Irish bar, 1842; alderman of the city of Dublin; M.P. for Tipperary, 1865–68.

DILLWYN, Louis Llewelyn, English politician, b. 1814; a magistrate and deputy-lieutenant of Glamorgan; M.P. for Swansea since 1855.

DINDORF, Wilhelm, German philologist, b. at Leipsic, 1804; educated at the University of his native town; professor of literary history at Leipsic, 1828–33. Edited critical editions of Demosthenes, Aristotle, Athenæus, and many other classical works.

DINGELSTEDT, Franz, German poet, b. at Halsdorf, Hesse, 1814; appointed professor at Cassel, 1836; councillor to the Royal Court of Wurtemberg, 1841. Author of 'Gedichte,' Cassel and Leipsic, 1848; 'Wanderbuch,' ib. 1839–43; and numerous other poems.

DIRCKINCK HOLMFELD, Constant Peter Walpurgis, Baron, Danish writer, b. at Bochold, 1799; studied at Copenhagen, 1813 to 1819; took the degree of LL.D. 1840. Author of 'Om den aandelige Sandheds Anerkjendelse,' Copenhagen, 1827; 'Tanker som Bidrag til et monarkisk Regjerings-Program,' &c., 1853; and other works.

DISRAELI, Right Hon. Benjamin, English author and statesman, b. Dec. 31, 1805, eldest son of Isaac Disraeli, author; articled as a solicitor's clerk, and subsequently devoted himself to literature; sat as M.P. for Maidstone, 1837–41, and for Shrewsbury, 1841–47; returned for Buckinghamshire at the elections from 1847 to 1868; chancellor of the Exchequer from February to December 1852, and from February 1858 to June 1859; for the third time chancellor of the Exchequer, July 1866 to Feb. 1868; first lord of the Treasury, Feb. 25 to Dec. 8, 1868. Author of numerous works of fiction, and several political essays.

DIX, John Adams, American general, b. at Boscawen, New Hampshire, 1798; entered the army, 1812; adjutant-general of the State of New York, 1830; member of the State Assembly, 1842; elected to the Senate at Washington, 1845; military commandant of New York, 1863.

DIXON, William Hepworth, English author, b. June 30, 1821; called to the bar of the Inner Temple. Author of 'John Howard, a Memoir,' 1849; 'Life of William Penn,' 1851; 'Robert Blake, Admiral and General at Sea,' 1852; 'New America,' 1867; 'Spiritual Wives,' 1868; and numerous other works. Editor of the *Athenæum* since 1854.

DOBBIN, Rev. Orlando, English philologist, b. in the county of Armagh, 1816; graduated at Trinity College, Dublin, 1837; took the degrees of LL.D. and B.D.; incumbent of Ballivor, in the diocese of Meath. Published Diodati's 'De Christo Græce loquente,' with a translation; 'Codex Montfortianus;' and numerous sermons: also contributed to the *London Quarterly*, and other periodicals.

DOBELL, Sydney, English writer, known by the pseudonym of 'Sydney Yendys,' b. at Peckham Rye, 1824. Author of 'The Roman,' 1850; 'Balder,' first part published in 1854; 'England in time of War,' and other poems.

DODDS, Joseph, English politician, b. 1819; a solicitor, and mayor of Stockton, in 1857–58; returned M.P. for Stockton, 1868.

DODSON, John George, English politician, b. 1821; educated at Eton, and Christ Church, Oxford, where he graduated B.A. 1847; called to the bar of Lincoln's Inn, 1851; magistrate of Sussex; M.P. for East Sussex since 1857.

DOELLINGER, Johann Joseph Ignaz, German theological writer, b. at Bamberg, Bavaria, Feb. 28, 1799; appointed chaplain of the diocese of Bamberg, 1822; represented the University of Munich in the Bavarian Parliament, 1845; delegate to the Parliament of Frankfort, 1851. Author of 'Die Reformation,' 1846–48; and other theological works.

DOENHOFF, August Herman, Count von, Prussian statesman, b. at Potsdam, Oct. 10, 1797; studied at Königsberg, Göttingen, and Heidelberg, 1816 to 1819; attaché to the Prussian embassy at Paris, 1823; secretary of legation in London, 1828; ambassador at Munich, 1833; elected member of the Diet of Frankfort, 1842; minister of foreign affairs, 1848–49; member of the Upper Chamber of Prussia since 1849.

DOENNIGES, Wilhelm, German writer, b. near Stettin, 1814; studied at the Universities of Bonn and Berlin; appointed professor to the University of Berlin, 1841; teacher of political economy to the Prince Maximilian, afterwards King of Bavaria, 1842 to 1845; represented Bavaria at the Parliament of Frankfort, 1848; ambassador and plenipotentiary to the conferences of Dresden, 1851. Author of 'Altschott, und altengl. Volksballaden,' Munich, 1852; and other philological works.

DONALDSON, Thomas Leverton, English architect, b. in London, 1795; professor of architecture in the London University. Author of 'Pompeii Illustrated,' 1837; 'Architectural Maxims and Theories,' 1847; 'Architectura Numismatica,' 1859; and other works on architecture. Elected president of the Royal Institute of British Architects, 1864.

DONEGALL, George Hamilton Chichester, Marquis of, Irish magistrate, b. 1798; studied at the University of Oxford; M.P. for Carrickfergus, Belfast, and Antrim, 1818 to 1837; lord-lieutenant of Antrim; vice-chamberlain from 1830 to 1834.

DONERAILE, Hayes St. Leger, Viscount, Irish magistrate, b. 1818; educated at Eton and Oxford; deputy-lieutenant of the county of Cork, of which he was high sheriff in 1845; succeeded his father, 1854; elected a representative peer of Ireland in 1855.

DONNET, Ferdinand François Auguste, French prelate, b. at Bourg-Argental, Loire, Nov. 16, 1795; studied at the Seminary of St. Irénée; ordained, 1819; appointed curé of Villefranche, 1827; created a cardinal, 1852, and senator, 1853.

DONOUGHMORE, Richard John Hely Hutchinson, Earl of, English statesman, b. in Dublin, 1823; educated at Harrow; succeeded his father, 1851; vice-president of the Board of Trade, Feb. 1858 to 1859; president, Feb. to June, 1859; deputy-lieutenant of Tipperary.

DOO, George Thomas, English engraver, b. 1807. Engraved 'The Duke of York,' after Sir Thomas Lawrence,' 1823; appointed historical engraver in ordinary to William IV. 1836; to Queen Victoria, 1842; elected A.R.A. 1855, and R.A. 1856. Exhibited 'The Raising of Lazarus,' after Sebastian del Piombo, in the Royal Academy, 1864; and published numerous engravings of celebrated paintings.

DORA D'ISTRIA, Helena Ghika, Princess KOLTZOFF MASSALSKY, Wallachian authoress, b. at Bucharest, Jan. 22, 1829; daughter of the Grand Ban Michel Ghika; married to the Prince Koltzoff Massalsky, 1849. Author of 'Monastic Life in an Eastern Church,' Paris and Geneva, 1855; 'Women, by a Woman,' 1864; and numerous other works.

DORAN, John, English author, b. 1807. Published 'History and Antiquities of the Town and Borough of Reading, in Berkshire,' 1835; 'Lives of the Queens of the House of Hanover,' 1855; 'Lives of the Princes of Wales,' 1860; 'Their Majesties' Servants,' 1864; and many other, chiefly historical, works.

DORÉ, Paul Gustave, French artist, b. at Strasburg, Jan. 1833; studied at the Lycée Charlemagne, Paris, in 1845   Exhibited 'La Bataille d'Alma,' 1855; 'La Bataille d'Inkerman,' 1857; illustrated the Bible, 'The Wandering Jew,' 'The Divine Comedy' of Dante in 1861, 'Don Quixote,' 1863, the poems of Alfred Tennyson, and many other works.

DORIAN, Pierre Frederic, French politician, b. Jan. 24, 1814; mayor of Enieux; elected member of the Corps Législatif for the department of Loire, 1863.

DORMER, Joseph Thaddeus, Baron, English magistrate, b. at Gran, Hungary, 1790; served in the Austrian army; succeeded his cousin, 1826; deputy-lieutenant of the county of Warwick.

DORN, Heinrich Ludwig Egmont, German musical composer, b. at Königsberg, Nov. 14, 1804; appointed professor to the School of Music of Frankfort on the Maine, 1827. Composed 'Artaxerxes,' 1831; and other operas.

DORN, Johann Albert Bernard, German writer, b. at Schenerfeld, Coburg, May 11, 1805; studied at Halle and Leipsic; appointed professor of history and geography at St. Petersburg, 1835. Author of 'Grammat. Bemerk. ungen über die Sprache der Afghanen,' St. Petersburg, 1840; 'Geschichte Tabaristans,' ib. 1850; and numerous other works.

DORNER, Johann August, German Protestant theologian, b. at Neuhausen-ob-Eck, Wurtemberg, June 20, 1809; studied at Tubingen, and obtained the degree of D.D. 1836; appointed professor of theology at Tubingen, 1838; at Kiel, 1839; at Königsberg, 1840–49; professor in ordinary to the faculty of theology at Bonn. Author of 'Darstellung der Lehre von Christus,' 1845–46; and numerous theological works.

DOUCET, Charles Camille, French dramatic writer, b. in Paris, May 16, 1812; studied law, and was called to the bar; appointed director of the administration of Paris theatres, 1863.   Author of 'Un Jeune Homme,' 1841; 'La Considération,' 1860; and many other works of fiction.

DOUGLASS, Frederick Bailey, American writer, b. in Talbot, Maryland, 1816, of slave parents; obtained his freedom, 1838. Lectured in England and America in support of the abolition of slavery; published 'Memoirs of Douglass,' Boston, 1845.

DOULTON, Frederick, English politician, b. 1824; member of the Metropolitan Board of Works; formerly a manufacturer in London and Liverpool; M.P. for Lambeth, 1862–68.

DOVE, Heinrich Wilhelm, German writer, b. at Liegnitz, Silesia, 1803; studied at Breslau and Berlin, and M.D. 1826; professor of natural philosophy at Berlin. Author of 'Ueber die nicht periodischen Aenderungen der Temperaturvertheilung,' Berlin, 1840–47; 'Tafeln der Temperatur,' ib. 1848; and other meteorological works.

DOWDESWELL, William Edward, English politician, b. 1841; educated at Westminster, and Christ Church, Oxford; a magistrate for the county of Worcester; M.P. for Tewkesbury, 1865–68.

DOWN, CONNOR, and DROMORE, Right Rev. Bent Knox, Lord Bishop of, Irish divine, b. 1808; educated at Trinity College, Dublin; formerly prebendary of Limerick, and chancellor of Ardfert and Aghadoe; bishop of Down, Connor, and Dromore, 1849.

DOWSE, Richard, English politician, b. 1818; educated at Trinity College, Dublin; called to the Irish bar, 1852; returned M.P. for Londonderry, 1868.

DOYLE, Richard, English artist, b. in London, 1826. Contributed to *Punch* until 1850; illustrated the 'Fairy Ring,' Leigh Hunt's 'Jar of Honey,' 'The Continental Tour of Messrs. Brown, Jones, and Robinson,' 1854; contributor of illustrations to the *Cornhill Magazine*, and other works.

DRAEXLER-MANFRED, Carl Ferdinand, German writer, b. at Lemberg, in Galicia, June 17, 1806; studied law at Vienna and Leipsic. Author of 'Romanzen und Lieder,' Leipsic, 1826–28; and numerous novels and poems.

DRAKE, Friederich, German sculptor, b. at Pyrmont, June 23, 1805; professor of sculpture to the Academy of Fine Arts of Berlin. Executed 'Madonna with the Infant;' 'Warrior crowned by Victory,' 1850; and numerous busts, groups, and statues.

DRAKE, Samuel, American writer, b. at Pittsfield, New Hampshire, Oct. 10, 1798. *Author of 'The Book of the Indians,' 1833; 'History of Boston,' 1852. Commenced the New York Register,* 1847.

DRAPER, John William, American chemist, b. in Liverpool, May 11, 1805; studied in the London University, and the University of Pennsylvania, U.S., where he graduated M.D. 1836; appointed professor of chemistry and natural history in the University of the City of New York, 1839. Author of 'Textbook on Chemistry,' 1846; and numerous other scientific works.

DRAPIEZ, Auguste, Belgian writer, b. at Brussels, 1790; studied in Paris. Author of 'Annales des Sciences physiques et naturelles,' Brussels, 1819–21; and numerous other works.

DREUX-BRE'ZE', Pierre Simon Louis Marie de, French prelate, b. at Brézé, Maine-et-Loire, June 2, 1811; studied at the Seminary of St. Sulpice; ordained, 1835; appointed to the diocese of Moulins, Oct. 28, 1849. Author of a published sermon on the 'Encyclical of the Pope of Dec. 8, 1864,' 1865.

DREW, Andrew, English naval officer, b. 1792; entered the royal navy, 1806; lieutenant, 1814; commander, 1824; appointed to the command of H.M. sloop *Wasp*, 1842; post-captain, 1843; rear-admiral, 1863.

DROGHEDA, Henry Francis Seymour Moore, Marquis of, Irish magistrate, b. at Bath, 1825; educated at Eton, and Trinity College, Dublin; deputy-lieutenant and magistrate of Kildare and Queen's County; succeeded his uncle, 1837.

DROUOT, Joseph Antoine, French politician, b. at Nancy, April 14, 1816; member of the General Council for the canton of Toul; member of the Corps Législatif for the department of Meuerthe since 1852.

DROUYN DE LHUYS, Edouard, French statesman, born at Paris, Nov. 10, 1805; studied jurisprudence, 1823–29; attaché to the embassy of Madrid, 1830–32; attaché at the Hague, 1833–36; first secretary of embassy at Madrid, 1836–40; director of the commercial department of the ministry of foreign affairs, 1840; deputy for Melun, 1842; elected member of the Constituent Assembly for Paris, 1848; secretary of state for foreign affairs, Dec. 20, 1848, to June 2, 1849; ambassador to Great Britain, July 1849 to Jan. 1851; minister of state for foreign affairs, July 28, 1852, to May 1855; nominated senator, Dec. 1851, and resigned his seat in the Senate, 1856; again minister of state for foreign affairs, Oct. 15, 1862, to Sept. 1, 1866.

DROYSEN, Johann Gustav, German historian, b. at Treptow, in Pomerania, July 6, 1808; studied at Stettin, and at Berlin, where he was professor from 1829 to 1840; professor of history at Kiel. Author of 'History of Danish Politics,' Hamburg, 1850; 'History of Alexander the Great,' Berlin, 1833; and many other historical works.

DUBAN, Jacques Felix, French architect, b. at Paris, Oct. 14, 1797; studied under Debret, and at the Paris École des Beaux Arts; appointed architect to the Louvre, 1854; elected member of the Institute, 1854.

DUBLIN, Rev. Richard Chenevix Trench, Archbishop of, English author and divine, b. Sept. 9, 1807; graduated at Trinity College, Cambridge, in 1829; appointed theological professor and examiner to King's College, London, 1847; dean of Westminster, 1856; consecrated archbishop of Dublin, Jan. 1, 1864. Author of 'Sabbation, Honor Neale, and other Poems,' 1837; 'The Epistles to the Seven Churches of Asia Minor;' 'The Study of Words;' and numerous other works.

DUBOIS, Jean Nicolas Louis Eugene, Comte, French administrator, b. at Paris, 1812; studied at the École Polytechnique, and the École de St. Cyr; called to the bar at Paris, 1839; appointed director-general of railways, and councillor of state, 1853; member of the General Council for the department du Nord.

DUBOIS, Paul François, French writer, b. at Rennes, Ille-et-Villaine, June 2, 1793; studied in his native town, and entered the École Normale, 1812; appointed professor of rhetoric to the College of Charlemagne, 1820; director of the École Normale, 1840; contributor to the *Globe*, and other French papers.

DU CANE, Charles, English administrator, b. 1825; educated at Charterhouse, and Exeter College, Oxford, where he graduated B.A. 1847; magistrate and deputy-lieutenant of Essex; M.P. for North Essex, 1857–68; appointed governor of Tasmania, Aug. 1868.

DU CASSE, Emmanuel Albert, Baron, French military writer, b. 1815; admitted to the School of St. Cyr; chief of a squadron and aide-de-camp to Prince Jerome, 1854. Author of 'Récit historique des Operations de l'Armée de Lyon en 1814,' 1849; and other works on military tactics.

DUCHATEL, Charles Marie Tanneguy, Comte, French statesman, b. in Paris, Feb. 19, 1803; one of the editors and proprietors of the Globe, 1827; appointed councillor of state, 1830, and elected deputy, 1832; minister of commerce, 1834–36; minister of the interior, 1838–45; retired from public service, 1851.

DUCIE, Henry John Moreton, Earl of, English administrator, b. at Sherborne, Gloucester, June 25, 1827 ; lord-lieutenant of Gloucestershire and a magistrate and deputy-lieutenant of Oxfordshire ; appointed captain of the Yeomen of the Guard, June 1859 ; succeeded to the peerage, 1853.

DUCKETT, Sir George Floyd, English writer, b. 1811 ; educated at Harrow, and Christ Church, Oxford ; served in the navy ; succeeded his father in the baronetcy, 1856. Author of 'Technological Military Dictionary,' in German, English, and French.

DUDEVANT, Madame Amantine Lucile Aurore, French authoress writing under the *nom de plume* of *George Sand*, b. in Paris, July 5, 1804. Author of 'Indiana,' 1832 ; 'La Mare au Diable ;' 'La Famille de Germandre,' 1861 ; 'Tamaris,' 1862 ; and numerous other works of fiction, dramas, essays, and political pamphlets.

DUDLEY, William Ward, Earl of, English administrator, b. 1817 ; educated at Trinity College, Oxford ; is deputy-lieutenant of Staffordshire and Worcestershire ; colonel of the Worcestershire Yeomanry Cavalry.

DUFAURE, Jules Armand Stanislas, French statesman, b. at Soiyon, Charente Inférieur, Dec. 4, 1798 ; studied law, and called to the bar ; councillor of state, 1834 ; minister of public works, 1839–40 ; minister of the interior, 1849 ; elected member of the French Academy, 1863.

DUFF, Rev. Alexander, Scottish missionary, b. near Pitlochry, Perthshire, 1806 ; studied at the University of St. Andrew ; first missionary to India from the Established Church of Scotland, 1829 ; quitted India, July 1863. Author of 'India and Indian Missions,' 1839 ; 'Letters on the Indian Rebellion,' 1858 ; and other works.

DUFF, Mountstuart Elphinstone Grant, English statesman, b. 1829 ; educated at Edinburgh, and Balliol College, Oxford, where he graduated B.A. 1850 ; called to the bar of the Inner Temple, 1853 ; deputy-lieutenant of Elgin, 1858 ; appointed under-secretary of state for India, Dec. 1868 ; M.P. for Elgin since 1857. Author of 'A Few Words on France, by a Scottish M.P.'

DUFF, Robert William, English politician, b. 1835 ; is deputy-lieutenant of the county of Banff, and lieutenant R.N. ; M.P. for Banffshire since 1861.

DUFFERIN, Frederick Temple Blackwood, Baron, English statesman, b. at Florence, June 21, 1826 ; educated at Eton, and Christ Church, Oxford ; was a lord-in-waiting to the Queen, and resigned, 1858 ; commissioner on a mission to Syria, 1860–61 ; appointed chancellor of the Duchy of Lancaster, Dec. 1868. Author of 'Letters from High Latitudes,' 1860.

DUFFY, Charles Gavan, Irish politician, b. 1816 ; founded *The Nation*, 1842 ; imprisoned with O'Connell for sedition, 1844 ; M.P. for the borough of New Ross, 1852–56 ; subsequently minister in Victoria.

DUFOUR, Guillaume Henri, Swiss general, b. 1787 ; officer in the Swiss army, 1809 ; staff major, 1831 ; quartermaster-general ; president of the war administration, 1864. Author of several military works.

DUHAMEL, Jean Marie Constant, French mathematician, b. at St. Malo, 1797 ; appointed professor to the Faculty of Sciences, 1851 ; member of the Institute. Author of 'Cours de Mécanique de l'École Polytechnique,' 1845–46 ; and other works.

DUKE, Sir James, English politician, b. 1792 ; sheriff of London and Middlesex, 1836 ; alderman of London, 1840 ; lord mayor, 1848–49 ; created a baronet, 1849 ; M.P. for Boston, 1837 to 1849 ; M.P. for the city of London, 1849 to 1865.

DULAURIER, Jean Paul Louis François Edouard, French writer, b. at Toulouse, Jan. 25, 1807 ; appointed professor of Armenian to the Paris École des Langues Orientales vivantes, 1862 ; elected member of the French Academy, 1864. Author of 'Histoire, Dogmes, Traditions et Liturgie de l'Eglise Armenienne Orientale,' 1859 ; and other works.

DUMANOIR, Philippe François Pinel, French dramatic writer, b. at Guadaloupe, July 31, 1806 ; studied at the Bourbon College, Paris. Author of 'Les Vieux Péchés,' 1833 ; 'Les Femmes Terribles,' 1858 ; 'Les Drames du Cabaret,' 1864 ; and numerous other dramas.

DUMAS, Alexandre, French dramatist and novelist, b. at Villers Cotterets, July 24, 1803. Author of 'Monte Cristo ;' 'Les Trois Mousquetaires ;' 'Les Memoires de Garibaldi,' 1860 ; 'La San Felice,' 1863–64 ; and a vast number of novels, dramas, and romances.

DUMAS, Alexandre, French author, b. in Paris, July 28, 1824, son of the preceding ; studied at the Bourbon College. Author of 'Les Aventures de quatre Femmes et d'un Perroquet,' 1846–47 ; 'La Dame aux Camélias,' 1848 ; 'La Boîte d'Argent,' 1855 ; and numerous other dramas and romances.

DUMAS, Jean Baptiste, French statesman, b. at Alais, Gard, July 1800; studied at Geneva; appointed teacher of chemistry to the École Polytechnique, Paris, 1823; elected to the National Assembly, 1849; minister of agriculture and commerce, Oct. 31, 1850, to Jan. 9, 1851; vice-president of the Council of Education, 1861 to 1863. Author of 'Traité de Chimie appliquée aux Arts,' 1828–43; and other works on chemistry.

DUMIRAL, Francisque Rudel, French politician, b. 1812; advocate at the Imperial Court of Paris; member of the Corps Législatif for the department of Puy de Dôme since 1852.

DUMON, Pierre Sylvain, French statesman, b. at Agen, Lot-et-Garonne, 1797; studied at the Lycée Napoleon, and called to the bar at Paris, 1820; appointed councillor of state, 1832; vice-president of the Committee of Legislation, 1840; minister of finance, 1847; elected member of the French Academy, 1859.

DUMONT, Augustin Alexandre, French sculptor, b. in Paris, Aug. 14, 1801; studied at St. Barbe. Executed 'Nicolas Poussin' for the hall of the Institute; 'Van Praet' for the Royal Bibliothèque, 1854; 'La Prudence et la Verité,' 1865; and numerous busts, statues, and groups. Elected member of the Institute, 1838.

DUNBAR, Sir William, English statesman, b. 1812; educated at the University of Edinburgh; called to the Scottish bar, 1835; succeeded to the baronetcy at the death of his uncle, 1841; M.P. for Wigton Burghs, 1857 to 1865; one of the lords of the Treasury, 1859–65; keeper of the great seal of the Prince of Wales, 1863.

DUNCKER, Maximilian Wolfgang, German historian, b. at Berlin, 1812; studied at the College of Frederick William at Berlin, 1825 to 1830, and at the Universities of Berlin and Bonn, 1834. Author of 'Die Krisis der Reformation,' Leipsic, 1846; 'Geschichte des Alterthums,' Berlin, 1852–53; and other historical works.

DUNCOMBE, Hon. Arthur, English politician, b. 1806; rear-admiral in the British navy; J.P. for Middlesex and Westminster; J.P. and deputy-lieutenant of the East Riding of Yorkshire; has been a lord of the Admiralty and a groom-in-waiting; M.P. for Retford, 1830–31, and 1835–51; M.P. for the East Riding of Yorkshire, 1851–66.

DUNCOMBE, Hon. William Ernest, English politician, b. 1829; deputy-lieutenant of the North Riding of Yorkshire; M.P. for East Retford, 1852–57, and for the North Riding of Yorkshire, 1859–68.

DUNDAS, Right Hon. Sir David, English politician, b. 1799; educated at Westminster, and Christ Church, Oxford, and graduated B.A. 1820; M.A. 1822; called to the bar of the Inner Temple, 1823; has been solicitor-general and judge advocate-general; M.P. for the county of Sutherland, 1840–52, and 1861–66.

DUNDAS, Frederick, English politician, b. 1802; lord-lieutenant of the Isle of Orkney; M.P. for the county, 1837–47; and for Orkney and Shetland since 1852.

DUNFERMLINE, Right Hon. Ralph Abercromby, Baron, English diplomatist, b. 1803; educated at Eton, and Peterhouse College, Cambridge; entered the diplomatic service; secretary of legation to Brazil, 1828; to Brussels, 1830; and to Berlin, 1831; minister at Florence, 1835–39; to the Germanic Confederation, 1839–40; at Turin, 1840; and at the Hague, 1851; retired, 1858.

DUNGLISON, Robley, American author, b. at Keswick, Cumberland, 1798; appointed professor of medicine to the University of Virginia, 1824 to 1833; and to Jefferson College, Philadelphia, since 1836. Author of 'Dictionary of Medical Science,' 1833; 'New Remedies,' 1839; and other medical works.

DUNLOP, Alexander Murray, English legal writer, b. at Greenock, 1798; educated at Greenock, and the University of Edinburgh; called to the Scottish bar, 1820; M.P. for Greenock, 1852–68. Author of 'Scottish Poor Law,' and other legal works.

DUNLOP, Madeline, English authoress, b. in India, 1835. Author of 'The Timely Retreat;' 'What we saw in Brittany;' and other works.

DUNNE, Francis Plunkett, English politician, b. 1802; educated at Trinity College, Dublin, where he graduated B.A. 1827; a magistrate and deputy-lieutenant of Queen's County; and a colonel in the army; was clerk of the Ordnance, 1852; M.P. for Portarlington, 1847–57; and for Queen's County, 1859–68.

DUNTZER, Johan Heinrich Joseph, German writer, b. at Cologne, July 11, 1813; studied at Bonn and Berlin, and obtained the degree of Ph.D. 1836. Author of 'Die Sage vom Doctor Joh. Faust.' Leipsic, 1848; and other works.

DUPANLOUP, Felix Antoine Philibert, French prelate, b. at St. Felix, Jan. 3, 1802; studied in Paris; ordained, 1825; appointed professor of theology at Sorbonne, 1841; bishop of Orleans, April 1849. Author of several theological and scholastic works,

DUPENTY, De'sire' Charles, French dramatic writer, b. at Paris, Feb. 6, 1798. Author of 'Le Hussard de Feltheim,' 1827; 'La Vie de Café,' 1850; 'Le Marquis d'Argencourt,' 1857; and numerous other dramas.

DUPIN, François Pierre Charles, Baron, French writer, b. at Varzy, Oct. 6, 1784, brother of the preceding; appointed professor of mechanics to the Conservatoire des Arts et Métiers, 1819; councillor of state, 1831; peer of France, Oct. 3, 1837; senator, Jan. 25, 1852. Author of 'Force commerciale de la Grande Bretagne,' 1826; 'Industries comparées de Paris et de Londres,' 1852; and numerous other works.

DUPLAN, Joseph, French politician, b. at Paris, March 17, 1791; studied at the École Polytechnique; member of the General Council for the canton of Aspet; member of the Corps Législatif for the department of Haute Garonne since 1852.

DUPONT, Pierre, French song writer, b. at Lyons, April 23, 1821. Author of 'The Two Angels,' 1844; 'The Oxen,' 1846; 'Song of Bread,' 1847; 'Song of the Workers,' 1847; 'Dix Églogues,' 1864; and numerous other poems.

DU PRE', Caledon George, English politician, b. 1803; a magistrate and deputy-lieutenant of Bucks; M.P. for Bucks since 1839.

DURANDO, Giacomo, Italian statesman, b. at Mondovi, 1807; studied law at Turin, 1831; entered the Spanish army, and made colonel in 1845; minister of war under Count Cavour, 1856; envoy to Constantinople, 1860; minister of foreign affairs, 1862.

DURANDO, Giovanni, Italian general, b. at Mondovi, 1809, brother of the preceding; entered the Spanish army, and became general, 1845; took part in the Italian war of independence, 1848; commander of a division, 1859; governor of Naples, 1861; military commander of Milan, 1862.

DURBIN, John, American writer, b. in Bourbon County, Kentucky, 1800; studied at the College of Cincinnati, 1824; graduated in 1825; elected president of Dickinson College, Carlisle, 1834. Author of 'Observations in Europe, principally in France and Great Britain,' 1845; and other works.

DURHAM, Right Rev. Charles Baring, Lord Bishop of, English divine, b. 1807; graduated at Christ Church, Oxford, 1829; consecrated Bishop of Gloucester and Bristol, 1856; translated to the see of Durham, 1861.

DURHAM, Joseph, English sculptor, b. in London, 1821; studied under E. H. Bailey, R.A. Executed a bust of Jenny Lind, 1848; of Queen Victoria, 1856; statue of the late Prince Consort in the gardens of the Horticultural Society, in memory of the Great Exhibition, 1863; and a great number of other statues, groups, and busts.

DURUY, Victor, French statesman and author, b. at Paris, 1811; studied at the College of St. Barbe, 1823; and at the Paris École Normale, 1830, and took the degree of D.C.L. 1853; inspector of the Academy of Paris, 1861 to 1862; appointed minister of public instruction, June 23, 1863. Author of 'Geographie politique de la Republique Romaine et de l'Empire,' 1838; 'Introduction générale à l'Histoire de France,' 1865; and other works.

DUSEIGNEUR, Bernard Jean, French sculptor, b. at Paris, June 23, 1808; studied in the Paris École des Beaux Arts, 1822 to 1826; and under Bosio, Duparty, and Cortot. Executed 'Saint Michel, Vainqueur de Satan, annonçant le Règne de Dieu,' 1834; 'La Crucifiement de N.S. Jésus-Christ,' for the Church of St. Roch, Paris, 1863; and numerous colossal groups and statues.

DUTTON, Hon. Ralph Heneage, English politician, b. 1821; educated at Trinity College, Cambridge; graduated.M.A. 1842; is a magistrate and deputy-lieutenant of Hants; M.P. for South Hants, 1857–65; and for Cirencester, 1865–68.

DUVAL, Jules, French writer, b. at Rodez, Aveyron, 1813; studied law, and called to the bar of his native town, 1836. Author of 'Les Colonies, et la Politique coloniale de la France,' 1864; and numerous other works: also contributor to the *Journal des Débats*, the *Revue des Deux Mondes*, and other French periodicals.

DUVERGIER DE HAURANNE, Prosper, French statesman and historian, b. at Rouen, Aug. 3, 1798; elected to the Constituent Assembly after Feb. 24; and to the *Legislative Assembly in 1850*. Author of 'Des Principes du Gouvernement représentatif, et de leur Application,' 1838; 'Histoire du Gouvernement parlementaire en France,' 1857–62.

DUVEYRIER, Charles, French novelist, b. at Paris, April 12, 1803; studied at the Lycée of Henri IV., and called to the bar at Paris. Author of 'Michel Perrin,' 1834; 'Oscar, ou le Mari qui trompe sa Femme,' 1842; 'Pourquoi des Propriétaires à Paris?' 1857; and numerous other works of fiction.

DYCE, Rev. Alexander, English writer, b. in Edinburgh, 1798; educated at Exeter College, Oxford, and graduated B.A. 1821. Author of 'Recollections of the Table Talk of Samuel Rogers;' edited 'Shakspeare, Beaumont, and Fletcher;' and many other works.

DYCE, Nichol, English politician, b. 1805; educated at the University of Glasgow; resided for many years in Bombay; a county magistrate of Kincardine; M.P. for Kincardineshire, 1865-68.

DYHRN, Conrad Adolph, Count von, Prussian politician, b. at Reesewitz, Nov. 21, 1803; studied at the University of Berlin; elected member of the Diet of Silesia, 1845; member of the Second Prussian Chamber, 1850-52. Published 'Conradin's Tod,' and other dramas.

DYKE, William Hart, English politician, b. 1837; educated at Harrow, and Christ Church, Oxford, where he graduated B.A. 1861, M.A. 1863; J.P. and deputy-lieutenant of Kent; M.P. for West and Mid-Kent since 1865.

DYNEVOR, George Rice Rice Trevor, Baron, English politician, b. 1795; studied at the University of Oxford; received the degree of LL.D. 1830; sat in the House of Commons, 1820 to 1831, and from 1832 to May 1852, when he succeeded his father, third baron.

DYOTT, Richard, English politician, b. 1808; educated at Westminster, and Trinity College, Cambridge; J.P. and deputy-lieutenant of the county of Stafford; high sheriff, 1856; M.P. for Lichfield since 1865.

E.

EADIE, Rev. John, English theological writer, b. in Stirlingshire, 1813; educated at the University of Glasgow. Edited the 'Biblical Cyclopædia;' author of 'Commentaries on St. Paul's Epistles,' 'Life of Dr. Kitto,' and other biographical and theological works.

EARLE, Ralph Anstruther, English politician, b. 1835; educated at Harrow; was attaché to the embassy at Paris, 1854-58; at Vienna, 1859; private secretary to the Right Hon. B. Disraeli, 1858-59; M.P. for Berwick, May to August 1859, and for Maldon, 1865-68.

EASTBURN, Manton, American divine, b. in England, 1801; studied at Columbia College, New York, where he graduated B.A. 1817, M.A. 1820; ordained deacon, 1822; rector of the Church of the Ascension, New York, and graduated D.D. 1835; consecrated bishop of Massachusetts, 1842. Author of 'Lectures on the Epistle to the Ephesians,' 1833; and other works.

EASTLAKE, Elizabeth Rigby, Lady, English authoress, b. 1816; married to the late Sir Charles Eastlake in 1849. Author of 'Letters from the Shores of the Baltic,' 1841; 'Livonian Tales,' 1846; and other works.

EASTMAN, Mrs. Mary, American authoress, b. 1814; married to Captain S. Eastman, 1835. Author of 'Dacotah, or Life and Legends of the Sioux,' 1849; 'Romance of Indian Life,' 'Aunt Phillis' Cabin,' 1852; and other works.

EASTWICK, Edward Blackhouse, English author, b. at Warfield, Berkshire, 1814; studied at the Charterhouse, and University of Oxford; appointed interpreter of Hindostanee at Bombay, 1836; professor of Hindostanee to the Company's College at Haileybury, 1845. Author of 'Dry Leaves from Young Egypt,' 1849; and numerous works on the East.

EATON, Henry William, English politician, b. 1816; educated at Enfield, and Collége Rollin, Paris; fellow of the geographical, horticultural, and botanical societies; a merchant in London; M.P. for Coventry since 1865.

EBLE, Charles, French general, b. 1799; studied at the École Polytechnique, 1818, and at the École d'Application of Metz, 1820; entered the army, 1838; Chief of a squadron, 1843; colonel and director of artillery at Metz; brigadier-general, 1854; nominated general of division, Aug. 1860.

EBORALL, Cornelius Willes, English railway manager, b. at Knowle, Warwickshire, Sept. 16, 1820, the son of Lieut. Sam. Eborall, R. N. ; goods manager of Manchester, Sheffield, and Lincolnshire Railway, 1847–49 ; manager of East Lancashire Railway, 1849–55 ; appointed general manager of South Eastern Railway, 1855 ; lieutenant-colonel of the railway volunteer staff corps.

EBRARD, Johan Heinrich August, German Protestant theologian, b. at Erlangen, Jan. 18, 1818 ; studied at Berlin ; professor at the University of Erlangen, 1842 ; professor of theology at Zurich, 1844 ; and counsellor of the Consistory of Spire. Author of ' Kritik der evangelischen Geschichte,' Frankfort, 1842 ; 'Die Zukunft der Kirche,' 1845–47 ; and other theological works.

EBURY, Right Hon. Robert Grosvenor, Baron, English statesman, b. April 24, 1801 ; educated at Westminster, and Christ Church, Oxford ; M.P. for Shaftesbury, 1822 to 1826 ; for Chester, 1826 to Jan. 1847 ; for Middlesex, 1847 to 1857, when he was elevated to the peerage ; was comptroller of the household, Nov. 1830 to Nov. 1834 ; groom of the stole to Prince Albert, Feb. 1840 to Aug. 1841 ; treasurer of the household, July 1846 to July 1847 ; president of the Sanitary Commission, 1847–48 ; deputy-lieutenant of Cheshire and Middlesex.

EDEN, Rev. Robert, English theological writer, b. at Whitehall, near Bristol, 1803 ; studied at Corpus Christi College, Oxford, where he graduated B.A. 1825, M.A. 1827 ; examiner for Haileybury College, 1829–56 ; vicar of North Walsham, 1851–54 ; vicar of Wymondham, 1854. Author of ' Some Thoughts on the Inspiration of the Holy Scriptures,' 1864 ; and other theological works.

EDHEM, Pasha, Turkish statesman, b. 1823 ; studied in France ; entered the Turkish army ; was colonel and aide-de-camp to the Sultan, 1849 ; general of division, 1850 ; minister of foreign affairs, 1856 ; minister of public instruction, 1863–65.

EDMONDS, John Worth, American jurist, b. at Hudson, New York, March 13, 1799 ; graduated at Union College, 1816 ; called to the bar, 1819 ; appointed inspector of prisons in the State of New York, 1843 ; state judge, 1845 ; judge of the Supreme Court of the U.S. 1847 ; retired from the bench, 1853. Published a work on ' Spiritualism,' 1853.

EDMONDSTONE, Sir Archibald, English writer, b. 1795 ; educated at Christ Church, Oxford, where he graduated B.A. 1816. Author of ' A Journey to the Oasis of Upper Egypt ;' ' The Christian Gentleman's Daily Walk ;' and other works.

EDWARDES, Hon. William, English politician, b. 1835 ; captain and lieutenant-colonel Coldstream Guards ; deputy-lieutenant of Pembrokeshire ; elected M.P. for Haverfordwest, 1868.

EDWARDS, Amelia Blandford, English authoress, b. 1831. Author of ' My Brother's Wife,' 1855 ; ' Barbara's History,' 1864 ; ' Half a Million of Money,' 1865 ; and other novels.

EDWARDS, Edward, English writer, b. in London, 1812 ; was principal librarian of the Free Library of the City of Manchester, 1851 to 1858. Author of ' Economy of the Fine Arts in England,' 1840 ; ' Life of Sir Walter Ralegh,' 1868 ; and many other works.

EDWARDS, Henri Milne, French writer, b. at Bruges, Oct. 23, 1800 ; studied medicine at Paris, and graduated M.D. 1823 ; appointed dean to the Museum and Faculty of Sciences, 1841 ; professor of zoology to the Museum, 1862 ; admitted to the Academy of Sciences, as successor of Cuvier, 1838. Author of ' Recherches anatomiques sur les Crustacés,' 1828 ; and numerous works on zoology and natural history.

EDWARDS, Sir Henry, English politician, b. 1812 ; a magistrate and deputy-lieutenant of the West Riding of Yorkshire, and lieutenant-colonel commandant 2d West York Yeomanry Cavalry ; M.P. for Halifax, 1847–52 ; and for Beverley since 1857.

EFFINGHAM, Henry Howard, Earl of, English administrator, b. at Southampton, 1806 ; deputy-lieutenant of the West Riding of Yorkshire ; was M.P. for Shaftesbury, 1841 to 1845, when he succeeded his father in the earldom.

EGAN, Pierce, English novelist, b. in London, 1815 ; entered as a student at the Royal Academy. Author of ' Robin Hood ;' ' The Black Prince ;' ' Clifton Grey ;' and numerous other works of fiction. Editor of the London Journal.

EGERTON, Hon. Algernon Fulke, English politician, b. 1825 ; educated at Harrow ; M.P. for South Lancashire since 1859.

EGERTON, Edward Christopher, English politician, b. 1816; educated at Harrow, and Christ Church, Oxford, where he graduated B.A. 1837; fellow of All Souls College; barrister-at-law, called in 1840; M.P. for Macclesfield, 1852–68.

EGERTON, Sir Philip de Malpas Grey, English politician, b. 1806; educated at Christ Church, Oxford, where he graduated B.A. 1828; deputy-lieutenant of Cheshire; M.P. for Chester, 1830–31; and for South Cheshire since 1835.

EGERTON, Hon. Wilbraham, English politician, b. 1832, son of the following; educated at Eton and Christ Church, Oxford, where he graduated B.A. 1853; magistrate of Cheshire; M.P. for North Cheshire since 1858.

EGERTON OF TATTON, William Tatton Egerton, Baron, English politician, b. 1806; magistrate and deputy-lieutenant of Cheshire; M.P. for Lymington, 1850–52, and for North Cheshire, 1852–58.

EGGER, Emile, French writer, b. at Paris, July 18, 1813; elected member of the French Academy, 1845. Author of 'Latini Sermonis vetustioris Reliquiæ selectæ,' Paris, 1843; 'Mémoires d'Histoire ancienne et de Philologie,' 1863; and numerous other critical works.

EGLINTON and WINTON, Archibald William Montgomery, Earl of, b. 1841; educated at Eton; served in the royal navy; succeeded his father, Oct. 1861; deputy-lieutenant of Ayrshire.

EGMONT, George James Perceval, Earl of, English naval commander, b. 1794; M.P. for Surrey, 1837 to 1840; admiral, 1863; succeeded his cousin in the peerage, 1841.

EHNINGER, John Whetton, American artist, b. in New York, July 20, 1827; graduated at Columbia College, 1847; studied under Couture, in Paris, and at Dusseldorf. Painted 'Peter Stuyvesant,' 1850; 'Lady Jane Grey;' 'Christ healing the Sick,' in pencil, 1857; and numerous other pictures.

EHRENBERG, Christian Gottfried, German naturalist, b. at Delitzsch, in Prussia, April 19, 1795; studied at the University of Leipsic. Author of 'Naturgeschicht-liche Reise durch Nordafrika und Westasien,' 1820–25; 'Passat Staub und Blutregen,' 1849; and numerous other works. Principal secretary to the Berlin Academy of Sciences since 1842.

EICHENS, Friedrich Eduard, Prussian engraver, b. at Berlin, May 27, 1804; studied under M. Buchhorn. Exhibited an engraving of the 'Vision of Ezekiel,' 1842; 'Macbeth and the Witches,' 1855; and many others.

EICHHOFF, Frederic Gustave, French philologist, b. at Havre, Aug. 17, 1799; studied at Paris, and obtained the degree of LL.D. 1826; appointed professor of litera-ture at Lyons, 1842. Author of 'Études Grecques sur Virgile,' 1825; 'Poésie héroïque des Indiens comparée à l'Épopée Grecque et Romaine,' 1860; and other philological works.

EICHWALD, Eduard, Russian naturalist, b. at Mitau, in Courland, July 4, 1795; studied at Berlin; was private tutor in the University of Dorpat, 1821; professor of zoology and mineralogy at the Academy of St. Petersburg, 1838–51. Author of 'A Journey to the Caspian and the Caucasus,' 1834–37; 'Palæontology of Russia,' 1851.

ELCHO, Right Hon. Francis Wemyss Charteris, Lord, English politician, b. 1818; educated at Eton, and Christ Church, Oxford, where he graduated B.A. 1841; M.P. for East Gloucestershire, 1841–46; and for Haddingtonshire, 1847–68; was a lord of the Treasury, 1852–55; deputy-lieutenant of Haddingtonshire.

E'LIE DE BEAUMONT, Jean Baptiste Armand Louis Leone, French geologist, b. at Cannon, Calvados, Sept. 25, 1798; studied at the College of Henri IV., at the École Polytechnique, and entered the École des Mines, 1819; elected member of the French Academy, Dec. 31, 1835, and perpetual secretary to the same. Author of 'Sur la Formation du Cône du Vésuve,' 1837; and a great number of scientific works.

ELIOT, Samuel, American writer, b. at Boston, U.S. Dec. 22, 1821; graduated in Harvard College, 1839; professor of history and political science in Trinity College, Hartford, 1864. Author of 'The Liberty of Rome,' 1849; 'A Manual of the United States' History between the Years 1492 and 1856,' 1856.

ELLENBOROUGH, Edward Law, Earl of, English statesman, b. 1790; edu-cated at Eton and the University of Cambridge; M.P. for St. Michael's, 1814 to 1818; has been first lord of the Admiralty; president of the Board of Control, and governor-general of India; reappointed president of the Board of Control, Feb. 1858; resigned, June 1858.

ELLET, Elizabeth Lummis, American authoress, b. at Sodus Point, Lake Ontario, 1818. Author of 'The Women of the American Revolution,' New York, 1848; 'The Pioneer Women of the West;' 'Watching Spirits;' and other works.

ELLICE, Edward, English politician, b. 1810; educated at Eton; M.P. for Huddersfield, May to July 1837; and for St. Andrew's since 1837.

ELLIOT, Sir Charles, English diplomatist, b. 1810; was chief superintendent of trade and her Majesty's plenipotentiary in China, 1830 to 1841, and subsequently chargé d'affaires in Texas, and governor of Bermuda and Trinidad; created K.C.B. 1856.

ELLIOT, Very Rev. Gilbert, English divine, b. 1800; educated at St. John's College, Cambridge, where he graduated B.A. 1822, and M.A. 1824; appointed dean of Bristol, 1850; prolocutor in the Lower House of Convocation, 1857 to 1864. Author of some volumes of sermons.

ELLIOT, Hon. Henry George, English diplomatist, b. 1817; educated at Eton; appointed clerk in the foreign office, 1840; attaché at St. Petersburg, 1841; secretary of legation at the Hague, 1848; at Vienna, 1853; minister at Denmark, 1858; sent on a special mission to the King of the Two Sicilies, 1859; to the King of Greece, 1862; envoy to the King of Italy, 1863.

ELLIOTT, Rev. Charles, American writer, b. in Killybergs, Donegal, Ireland, May 16, 1792; appointed professor of languages in Madison College, Union-town, Pennsylvania, 1827. Author of 'Treatise on Baptism,' 1834; 'History of the great Secession from the Methodist Episcopal Church,' 1855; and other works.

ELLIOTT, Charles Wyllys, American writer, b. at Guildford, Connecticut, May 27, 1817; one of the founders of the Children's Aid Society, 1853. Author of 'Mysteries, or Glimpses of the Supernatural,' 1852; 'The New England History, from the Discovery of the Country by the Northmen, A.D. 986, to 1776,' 1857; and other works.

ELLIOTT, Rev. Edward Bishop, English divine, b. 1795; educated at Trinity College, Cambridge, where he graduated B.A. 1816, and M.A.; appointed vicar of Tuxford, Notts, 1824–40; prebendary of Heytesbury, 1826; incumbent of St. Mark's Chapel, Brighton, 1853. Author of 'The Warburtonian Lectures,' 1849–52.

ELLIOTT, William, American author and politician, b. in Beaufort, South Carolina, April 27, 1788; entered Harvard College, 1806; was senator in the Upper House; resigned, 1832. Author of 'Carolina Sports by Land and Water,' 1856; 'Fiesco: a Tragedy,' 1850; and numerous other works.

ELLIS, George Edward, American divine, b. at Boston, 1815; graduated at Harvard College, 1833; studied at Cambridge Divinity School until 1836; ordained pastor of Harvard Church, Charlestown, Massachusetts, 1840. Author of 'Half a Century of the Unitarian Controversy,' 1857; and numerous theological works.

ELLIS, Hon. Leopold George Frederick Agar, English politician, b. 1829; captain of the Kilkenny Militia; M.P. for Kilkenny since 1857.

ELLIS, Sir Samuel Burden, English military commander, b. 1787; entered the royal marine forces, 1804; served at Trafalgar, 1805; at the taking of the island of Guadaloupe, 1810; actively employed in India, 1839–40; in the China war of 1840–41; became a lieutenant-general, 1857.

ELLIS, William, English writer, b. in London, 1800. Author of 'Outlines of the History and Formation of the Understanding;' 'Education as a Means of preventing Destitution;' contributed to the *Westminster Review* and other periodicals.

ELLIS, Rev. William, English writer, b. in London towards the end of the last century; was missionary to the islands of the Southern Ocean. Author of 'Polynesian Researches,' 1829; 'Vindication of the South Sea Missions,' 1831; and other works.

ELLIS, Sarah Stickney, English authoress, b. 1812; wife of the preceding, married in 1837. Author of 'Pictures of Private Life;' 'The Women of England;' 'Social Distinction,' and other works.

ELLISSEN, Adolph, German novelist, b. at Cartow, duchy of Lüneburg, March 14, 1815; studied at the University of Göttingen. Author of 'Thee und Asphodelosblüten,' Göttingen, 1840; 'Der alte Ritter,' Leipsic, 1846; and numerous other works of fiction.

ELMORE, Alfred, Irish painter, b. at Clonakilty, county of Cork, 1815; first exhibited at the Royal Academy, 1834. Painted 'The Crucifixion,' 1838; 'The Martyrdom of à Becket,' 1839; 'Rienzi in the Forum,' 1844; 'Hotspur and the Fop,' 1851; and numerous other paintings, chiefly historical. Elected A.R.A. 1845.

ELPHINSTONE, Sir Howard, English politician, b. in the county of Devon, 1804; studied at the University of Cambridge; received the degree of D.C.L. from Oxford; called to the bar, 1840; M.P. for Hastings, 1835–37; for Lewes, 1841–47; succeeded his father, 1846; deputy-lieutenant of Sussex.

ELSHOLTZ, Franz von, German author, b. at Berlin, Oct. 1, 1791; appointed secretary of administration at Cologne, 1815; secretary of legation from the duchy of Saxe-Coburg Gotha to the court of Munich, 1840–51. Author of 'Wanderungen durch Köln,' 1820; and many dramas.

ELSNER, Johan Gottfried, German political economist, b. at Gottesberg, Silesia, Jan. 14, 1784; studied at the Universities of Halle and Königsberg, and received the degree of D.D. at Breslau, 1807. Author of 'Der angehende rationelle Landwirth,' Prague, 1852; and a great number of works on political economy.

ELTON, Sir Arthur Hallam, Bart., English writer, b. 1818; educated at the Royal Military College, Sandhurst, and served in the army; M.P. for Bath, 1857 to 1859; a magistrate and deputy-lieutenant of Somersetshire. Author of 'Below the Surface: a Story of English Country Life.'

ELVENICH, Peter Joseph, German Catholic theologian, b. at Embken, near Aix-la-Chapelle. Jan. 29, 1796; studied at the University of Bonn, 1820; appointed director of the College of Leopold, 1830; conservator of the royal library, 1838. Author of 'Actenstücke zur geheimen Geschichte des Hermesianismus,' Breslau, 1845.

ELWART, Antoine Amable Elie, French musical composer, b. at Paris, Nov. 18, 1808. Composed 'Les Trois Jérusalem;' 'La Naissance d'Eve;' 'Ruth et Booz;' and other operas and oratorios. Published 'Petit Traité d'Instrumentation,' 1864; and other works.

ELWIN, Rev. Whitwell, English clergyman, b. Feb. 26, 1816; educated at Caius College, Cambridge, where he graduated B.A. 1839; ordained deacon, 1839, and priest, 1840; appointed rector of Boston, Norfolk, 1849. Editor of the *Quarterly Review*, 1853 to 1860.

ELWYN, Rev. Richard, English clergyman, b. 1827; educated at the Charterhouse, and at Trinity College, Cambridge, where he graduated, 1849; appointed second master of the Charterhouse, 1855, and head master, 1858; resigned, 1863.

ELY, Right Rev. Edward Harold Browne, Bishop of, English divine, educated at Eton, and at Emmanuel College, Cambridge, where he graduated in 1832; appointed canon residentiary of Exeter Cathedral, 1857; consecrated bishop of Ely, March 1864. Author of two volumes of sermons, and 'The Pentateuch and Elohistic Psalms, in reply to Bishop Colenso,' 1863.

EMBURY, Emma Catherine Manley, American authoress, b. at New York, 1808; married to Mr. D. Embury, 1828. Author of 'Guido, and other Poems,' New York, 1828; 'Constance Latimer, or the Blind Girl;' and many other works of fiction.

EMERSON, Ralph Waldo, American author, b. at Boston, 1803; graduated at Harvard College, 1821. Author of 'Literary Ethics: an Oration,' 1838; 'Man the Reformer,' 1841; 'Representative Men;' 'English Traits,' 1856; 'The Conduct of Life,' 1860; and numerous other works.

EMPIS, Adolphe Dominique Florent, French writer, b. at Paris, March 29, 1795; elected member of the French Academy, 1847; director of the Comédie Française, 1856. Author of 'Romulus,' 1822; 'Bothwell,' 1824; 'Les Femmes de Henri VIII.: Scènes historiques,' 1854.

ENAULT, Louis, French writer, b. at Isiguy, Calvados, 1824; studied in Paris, and called to the bar. Author of 'Promenade en Belgique et sur les Bords du Rhin,' 1852; 'La Norvège,' 1857; 'La Mediterranée, ses Iles et ses Bords,' 1862; and numerous romances and works of travel.

ENCKE, Johann Franz, German astronomer, b. in Hamburg, Sept. 23, 1791; studied at Göttingen under Gauss; appointed director of the Observatory at Berlin, and secretary to the mathematical class in the Royal Academy, 1825. Published 'Concerning the Comet of Pons,' 1831–32; 'The Distance of the Sun,' 1822–24; 'A New Method for discovering the Movements of the Planets;' and other astronomical works.

ENFIELD, George Henry Charles, Viscount, English politician, b. 1830; educated at Eton, and Christ Church, Oxford; a deputy-lieutenant of Middlesex; M.P. for Tavistock, 1852–57, and for Middlesex since 1857; secretary to the Poor Law Board, 1865–66.

ENGEL, Ludwig, composer, and harmonium-player, b. at Vienna, Jan. 9, 1828; studied music at the Conservatoire of Pesth; gave concerts at Paris, 1853–55; came to England to popularize the harmonium, 1856. Author of 'Piano-Harmonium School;' 'Studies for the Harmonium;' 'Harmonium Album;' and numerous other compositions.

ENGELSTOFT, Christiern Thorning, Danish theologian, b. at Næsberg, Aug. 8, 1805; appointed lecturer on theology to the University of Copenhagen, 1835; rector of the University, 1847–48; elected member of the Academy of Sciences of Copenhagen, 1847; of the Royal Academy of History, 1850. Author of 'Taler ved forskjellige Leiligheder,' Odense, 1853; and other works.

ENGLAND, Sir Richard, English military commander, b. in Canada, 1793; entered the army, 1809; held the chief military command in Caffraria, 1832–33; served in India, 1836, and was nominated K.C.B.; served in the Crimea; general in the army, and colonel of 41st Foot.

ENGSTROEM, John, Swedish writer, b. at Kærnebo, Calmar, April 7, 1794; graduated licentiate in medicine, 1817. Author of 'Resa genom Norrland och Lappland år 1834,' Stockholm, 1834; 'Förbundsbröderna,' ib. 1833–34; and other works.

ENNIS, Sir John, English politician, b. 1809; educated at Stonyhurst College; a deputy-lieutenant and county magistrate, and a governor of the Bank of Ireland; M.P. for Athlone, 1857–65; re-elected, 1868.

ENNISKILLEN, William Willoughby Cole, Earl of, b. 1807; educated at Harrow and Oxford; is deputy-lieutenant for the county of Fermanagh; trustee of the Hunterian Museum, Royal College of Surgeons; M.P. for Fermanagh, 1831–40.

EOTVOS, Joseph, Baron, Hungarian statesman and author, b. at Buda, in Hungary, Sept. 3, 1813; studied jurisprudence at the University of Pesth; minister of public instruction of the Republic of Hungary, 1848–49; appointed a second time minister of education by royal rescript, Feb. 24, 1867. Author of the 'Village Notary,' 1844; 'Hungary in 1514,' 1847; 'The Influence of the Leading Ideas of the Nineteenth Century upon Government and Society,' 1851; and other dramas, romances, and political essays.

ERBEN, Carl Jaromir, Bohemian historian, b. at Miletin, Bohemia, 1811; appointed archivist of the town of Prague, 1851. Author of 'Pisne Narodin,' 1842–45; 'Bartosova Kronika Praska,' 1851; and other works.

ERDELYI, Johann, Hungarian writer and poet, b. at Kazos, 1814; studied at the University of Pesth. Author of 'Nepdalok Esmondak,' Pesth, 1845–48; and other works.

ERDMANN, Johan Eduard, German writer, b. at Molmar, Livonia, June 13, 1805; studied at the University of Dorpat, 1823–26, and at Berlin; appointed professor of philosophy to the University of Halle, 1836. Author of 'Ueber Glauben und Wissen,' Berlin, 1837; 'Ueber den poetischen Reiz des Aberglaubens,' Halle, 1851; and numerous philosophical works.

ERDMANN, Otto Linne', German chemist, b. at Dresden, April 11, 1804; studied at Dresden and Leipsic, where he graduated licentiate in chemistry and Ph.D.; appointed supplementary professor of chemistry to the University of Leipsic, 1827; and professor, 1830. Author of 'Ueber den Nickel,' Leipsic, 1827; 'Waarenlexicon,' Leipsic, 1833–35; and other scientific works.

ERICSSON, John, American engineer, b. in the province of Vermeland, Sweden, 1803; entered the Swedish army, and became a lieutenant; emigrated to the United States, 1831; constructed the ship *Ericsson*, fitted with a 'caloric' engine, 1849; built the first *Monitor* for the United States, May 1862.

ERLE, Right Hon. Sir William, English judge, b. at Fifehead, Dorset, 1793; educated at Winchester, and New College, Oxford, where he graduated B.C.L. 1818; called to the bar, 1819; was made king's counsel, 1834; M.P. for Oxford, 1837 to 1841; appointed one of the judges of the Court of Common Pleas, 1844; of the Court of Queen's Bench, 1846; chief justice of the Common Pleas, 1859; retired 1866.

ERNE, John Crichton, Earl of, b. at Dublin, 1802; succeeded his uncle, 1842; lord-lieutenant of the county of Fermanagh.

ERNEST I., Duke of Saxe-Altenburg, b. Sept. 16, 1826, the son of Duke Georg of Saxe-Altenburg and Princess Marie of Mecklenburg-Schwerin; succeeded to the throne, at the death of his father, Aug. 3, 1853; married, April 28, 1853, to Agnes, the daughter of Duke Leopold of Anhalt Dessau.

ERNEST II., Duke of Saxe-Coburg Gotha, b. June 21, 1818, the son of Duke Ernest I. of Saxe-Saalfeld-Coburg and of Princess Louise of Saxe-Altenburg; studied philosophy and political economy at the University of Bonn, 1834–36; entered into the military service of Saxony, 1836; travelled in Spain, Portugal, Italy, and Northern Africa, 1838–40; succeeded to the throne, at the death of his father, Jan. 29, 1844. Composer of numerous musical pieces, and of the operas 'Zaïre,' 'Casilda,' and 'Santa-Chiara;' the latter represented at Paris, 1855.

ERROLL, William Harry Hay, Earl of, English military commander, b. 1823; hereditary lord high constable of Scotland; major in the rifle brigade; served with his regiment in the Crimea, and was wounded at the battle of Alma, Sept. 20, 1854.

ERSKINE, George, English officer, b. at Worthing, 1815 ; educated at the Royal College of Caen, and at the Royal Military College, Sandhurst ; entered the army as ensign, 1832 ; was lieutenant, 1836 ; major, 1854 ; lieutenant-colonel, 1854 ; colonel, 1860 ; appointed inspector-general of volunteers, 1865.

ERSKINE, John Elphinstone, English politician, b. 1806 ; educated at the Royal Naval College ; entered the navy, 1819 ; and became vice-admiral, 1864 ; M.P. for Stirlingshire since 1865.

ERSKINE, Thomas Americus Erskine, Baron, English diplomatist, b. 1802 ; educated at Cambridge ; was attaché at Turin, 1807 ; at Naples, 1824 ; succeeded his father, 1855.

ESAAD, Effendi Mahommed, Turkish historian, b. at Constantinople, Dec. 16, 1790 ; ambassador from the Sultan to the Shah of Persia, 1836 ; received the title of grand judge of Roumelia ; inspector-general of schools and counsellor of public instruction. Author of ' Uss-i-Tzafer,' Constantinople, 1828 ; 'Sefer-Namei-Klair,' ib. 1834.

ESCAYRAC DE LAUTURE, Comte d', French traveller, b. 1822 ; appointed by the Viceroy of Egypt to conduct an expedition to discover the source of the Nile, 1856. Author of ' Notice sur le Kordofan,' 1851 ; 'Mémoires sur la Chine,' 1844 ; and other works of travel.

ESCHASSERIAUX, Rene François Eugene, Baron, French politician, b. at Arènes, Charente Inférieure, July 25, 1823 ; studied law at Paris, and was called to the bar ; elected representative of Charente Inférieure to the Legislative Assembly, 1849 ; and member of the Corps Législatif for the same department since 1852.

ESCHER, Johan Heinrich Alfred, Swiss politician, b. at Zurich, Feb. 20, 1819 ; studied law in his native town, and at the Universities of Berlin and Bonn, and obtained the degree of LL.D. 1842 ; deputy to the Federal Diet, 1848 ; burgomaster of Zurich, 1848 ; one of the founders of the Federal Polytechnic School of Zurich ; vice-president of the National Council, 1856–59.

ESCOSURA, Patricio de la, Spanish statesman and author, b. at Madrid, Nov. 5, 1807 ; studied at Valladolid ; was an officer in the Spanish army, 1829 ; aide-de-camp and secretary to General Cordova, 1835–36 ; political chief of the town of Guadalaxara, 1838–40 ; secretary of state, 1843 to 1846. Author of ' La Corte del buen Retiro,' 1837–44 ; ' El Conde de Candespina,' Madrid, 1832 ; and other works.

ESMONDE, John, English politician, b. 1826 ; educated at Clongowes, and Trinity College, Dublin ; called to the Irish bar, 1850 ; is a magistrate for the counties of Waterford and Wexford ; M.P. for the county of Waterford since 1852.

ESPARTERO, Baldomero, Duke of Victory, Spanish statesman, b. at Granatula, in La Mancha, Feb. 27, 1793 ; entered the Sacred Battalion as a volunteer, 1808 ; studied in the Military School and became sub-lieutenant, 1815 ; field-marshal and lieutenant-general, 1833 ; regent of Spain, May 8, 1841, to July 22, 1843 ; commissioned by Queen Isabella to form a ministry, July 1854 ; dismissed, 1856 ; resigned his post as senator, and retired from active political life, 1857.

ESQUIROS, Henri Alphonse, French author, b. in Paris, 1814 ; elected to the Legislative Assembly for the Saône-et-Loire, 1850 ; exiled from France since Dec. 2, 1851. Author of ' Les Anglais chez Eux,' 1861 ; and numerous poems and works of fiction.

ESSEN, Peter, Count of, Russian statesman, b. in Livonia, 1780 : appointed military governor of the province of Orenburg, 1817 ; general, 1830 ; military governor-general of St. Petersburg, and created a count of the empire, 1833 ; entered the Council of State, 1842 ; chamberlain to the emperor, 1845 ; civil governor of the province of Livonia.

ESTCOURT, Right Hon. Thomas Sutton Sotheron Bucknall, English statesman, b. 1801 ; educated at Harrow, and Oriel College, Oxford ; M.P. for Marlborough, 1829 to 1832 ; for Devizes, 1835–44 ; and for North Wilts, 1844 ; president of the Poor Law Board, 1848 ; secretary of state for the Home Department, 1859–60.

ESTERHAZY DE GALANTHA, Paul Anton, Austrian statesman, b. March 10, 1786 ; Austrian minister at Dresden, 1810–11 ; ambassador to England, 1830–38 ; joined the Hungarian ministry of Count Louis Batthyani, 1848 ; privy councillor and chamberlain to the Emperor of Austria.

ETEX, Antoine, French sculptor and architect, b. in Paris, March 20, 1808 ; studied under M. Ingres and M. Duban. Executed ' Le jeune Hyacinthe tué par Apollon,' 1828 ; 'Cain,' 1833 ; ' La Vierge Immaculée,' 1864 ; and numerous groups, busts, and statues.

ETTMULLER, Ernst Moritz Ludwig, German philologist, b. at Gersdorf, near Läbau, Oct. 5, 1802; studied at the University of Leipsic, 1823 to 1826; appointed professor of languages and German literature to the University of Zurich, 1833. Editor of 'Kunech Laurin,' Jena, 1829; 'Heinrich von Weldecke's Eneide,' Zurich, 1852; and numerous other works.

EUGENIE, Empress of the French, b. at Granada, Spain, May 5, 1826, the second daughter of the Count de Montijo, grandee of Spain, and of Marie Manuela Kirkpatrick de Closeburn; married to the Emperor Napoleon III. Jan. 29, 1858.

EVANS, David Morier, English financial writer, b. 1819. Author of the 'Commercial Crisis, 1847–48;' 'City Men and City Manners;' 'Facts, Failures, and Frauds,' 1859. Has been City correspondent to the *Times*, the *Morning Herald*, and *Standard*.

EVANS, John, English geologist, b. 1823; educated at Bosworth School. Author of 'Ancient British Coins,' 1864; 'Flint Implements of the Drift.' Is honorary secretary of the Numismatic Society.

EVANS, Marian, English authoress, b. 1820; published under the *nom de plume* of *George Eliot* 'Adam Bede,' 1858; 'The Mill on the Floss,' 1859; 'Silas Marner, the Weaver of Ravenhoe,' 1861; 'Romola,' 1863; 'Felix Holt, the Radical,' 1866; and many other works of fiction.

EVANS, Ven. Robert Wilson Evans, English divine, b. at Shrewsbury, Aug. 30, 1789; educated at the Grammar School in his native town, and graduated at Trinity College, Cambridge, 1811; vicar of Tarvin, near Chester, 1836 to 1842; archdeacon of Westmoreland, 1856. Author of 'The Ministry of the Body;' 'England under God;' and other religious works.

EVANS, Thomas William, English politician, b. 1821; educated at Trinity College, Cambridge; a magistrate and deputy-lieutenant of Derby; M.P. for South Derbyshire, 1857–68.

EVERSLEY, Right Hon. Charles Shaw Lefevre, Viscount, English statesman, b. 1794; educated at Winchester, and Trinity College, Cambridge, where he graduated M.A.; called to the bar of Lincoln's Inn, 1819; M.P. for Downton, 1830; for Hampshire, 1831; for North Hants, Dec. 1832 to 1857; speaker of the House of Commons, 1839 to 1857, when he was created Viscount Eversley.

EWALD, Heinrich Georg August, German philologist, b. at Göttingen, Nov. 16, 1803; educated at the University of his native town; professor of philosophy and Oriental languages and theology at the University of Göttingen, 1831 to 1837; at Tubingen, 1838 to 1848; and again at Göttingen, 1848. Author of 'The Composition of Genesis,' 1823; 'The Prophets of the Old Testament,' 1840; and numerous other works.

EWART, William, English politician, b. 1798; educated at Eton, and Christ Church, Oxford, where he graduated B.A. 1821; called to the bar, 1827; M.P. for Bletchingley, 1828–30; for Liverpool, 1830–37; for Wigan, 1839–41; and for Dumfries, 1841–68.

EWBANK, Thomas, American writer, b. at Barnard Castle, Durham, England, 1792; commissioner of patents to the Government of the United States. Author of 'The World a Workshop,' 1855;' 'Life in Brazil,' 1858; and other works.

EWING, Archibald Orr, English politician, b. 1819; magistrate and deputy-lieutenant of Stirlingshire; returned M.P. for Dumbartonshire, 1868.

EWING, Humphrey Ewing Crum, English politician, b. 1803; is a magistrate and deputy-lieutenant of the county of Dumbarton, and a merchant in Glasgow; M.P. for Paisley since 1857.

EWING, Thomas, American statesman, b. in Ohio, Virginia, Dec. 28, 1789; graduated at Ohio University, B.A. 1815; called to the bar, 1816; appointed U.S. senator, 1831; secretary to the Treasury, 1840; minister of the interior, 1849; retired from political life, 1851.

EXETER, Henry Philpotts, Bishop of, English divine, b. at Gloucester, May 1779; studied at Corpus Christi College, Oxford, where he graduated B.A. 1795, and M.A. 1798; appointed prebendary of Durham, 1809; degree of D.D. 1821; dean of Chester, 1828; consecrated bishop of Exeter, 1830. Author of a great number of sermons and religious pamphlets.

EYRE, Edward John, traveller and colonial governor, b. 1817; travelled in Australia, 1840–41; lieutenant-governor of New Zealand, 1846–53; governor of Jamaica, 1862–65.

EYRE, Vincent, English military writer, b. 1810; educated at the Military College, Addiscombe; entered the Bengal Artillery, 1828; served in Affghanistan, 1841–42; also *during the Indian Mutiny*; colonel and C.B. 1858. Author of 'Military Operations in *Cabul,' 1843;* and a pamphlet on 'Metallic Boats and Floating Waggons for Naval and *Military Service; with Observations on American Life-preserving Cars,' 1856*.

F.

FABRE, Paul Andre', French lawyer, b. at Paris, July 23, 1809 ; advocate to the Council of State and to the Court of Cassation, 1839 ; president of the Order of Advocates, 1856 to 1859 ; legal adviser to the family of Orleans since 1852.

FAED, John, English painter, b. at Burley Mill, Kirkcudbright, 1820. Exhibited 'Shakespeare and his Contemporaries ;' 'The Cotter's Saturday Night ;' 'Tam O'Shanter ;' and 'The Soldier's Return.'

FAED, Thomas, English painter, b. at Burley Mill, 1826, brother of the preceding ; associate of the Royal Scottish Academy, 1849. Exhibited 'The Mitherless Bairn,' 1855 ; 'Home and the Homeless,' 1857 ; 'From Dawn to Sunset ;' and other paintings.

FAGAN, William Addis, English politician, b. 1832 ; educated at the College of Stonyhurst ; captain in the 12th Lancers ; elected M.P. for Carlow, 1868.

FAIDER, Charles, Belgian statesman, b. at Brussels, 1805 ; called to the bar at Brussels, 1832 ; minister of justice, Nov. 1852 to March 1855 ; advocate-general of the Court of Cassation at Brussels. Author of 'Paroles d'un Voyant,' Brussels, 1834 ; 'De la Nationalité littéraire en Belgique,' 1840 ; and other works.

FAIDHERBE, Louis Leon Cesar, French officer, b. at Lille, June 3, 1818 ; entered the École Polytechnique, 1838 ; and that of Metz, 1840 ; entered the army, and served in Algeria, 1844 to 1846 ; at Guadaloupe, 1848–49 ; and in the province of Constantine, 1849 to 1852 ; appointed governor of Senegal, 1854.

FAILLY, Pierre Louis Charles Achille de, French officer, b. 1808 ; studied at St. Cyr, 1826 ; second lieutenant, 1828 ; captain, 1837 ; lieutenant-colonel, 1848 ; colonel, 1851 ; brigadier-general, 1854 ; was general of division in the Crimea, 1855 ; and on his return aide-de-camp to the Emperor, and held command in the Italian campaign.

FAIRBAIRN, William, English civi engineer, b. at Kelso, Roxburghshire, 1789 ; studied at Newcastle-on-Tyne ; aided Stephenson in the erection of the bridge across the Menai Straits ; one of the founders and first members of the British Association for the Advancement of Science. Author of 'Mills and Mill-work ;' 'Iron ; its History, Properties, and Process of Manufacture,' second edition, 1865.

FAIRHOLT, Frederick William, English artist and author, b. in London, 1818. Illustrated 'History of the Silver Coinage of England ;' 'England under the House of Hanover,' 1848 ; 'Antiquities of Richborough,' 1850 ; and numerous historical and antiquarian works. Author of 'Costume in England,' 1846 ; 'Up the Nile,' 1861 ; and other works.

FALKENSTEIN, Johan Paul von, German statesman, b. at Pegau, Saxony, 1802 ; studied at the University of Leipsic, where he received the diploma of LL.D., and was professor of law, 1824–40 ; minister of the interior of the kingdom of Saxony, 1844 to 1848 ; president of the General Council, 1851 ; minister of public instruction of Saxony, 1853.

FALLOUX, Alfred Frederic Pierre, Comte de, French statesman and author, b. at Angers, May 7, 1811 ; member of the Chamber of Deputies, 1846–48 ; minister of public instruction, 1848–49 ; elected member of the French Academy, March 1856. Author of 'L'Histoire de Louis XVI.,' Paris, 1840 ; 'Madame Swetchine, sa Vie et ses Œuvres,' 1859 ; 'La Convention du 15 Septembre,' 1864 ; and other historical works.

FALMOUTH, Evelyn Boscawen, Viscount, English administrator, b. 1819 ; educated at Eton ; a magistrate of Kent and Cornwall ; deputy-lieutenant of Cornwall.

FANE, Henry Edward Hamlyn, English politician, b. 1817 ; educated at the Charterhouse ; a magistrate for Devon, Lincolnshire, and for Hants, and lieutenant-colonel R. S. Lincolnshire Militia ; M.P. for South Hants, 1865–68.

FANE, John William, English politician, b. 1804 ; educated at Rugby ; J.P. and deputy-lieutenant of Oxon ; and lieutenant-colonel of the Oxfordshire Militia ; M.P. for Oxfordshire, 1862–68.

FARINI, Carlo Luigi, Italian statesman, b. at Russi, in the Roman States, Oct. 22, 1822 ; studied medicine at Bologna ; was suspended and ordered to leave the Papal States, 1841 ; minister of the interior of Sardinia, 1847–48 ; director-in-chief of the sanitary and prison department of Rome, 1848 ; dictator of Modena, 1859 ; commissioner at Naples, 1860 ; president of the Italian Council of Ministers, Dec. 8, 1862, to March 24, 1863. Author of ' History of Italy,' and other works.

FARNHAM, Eliza Burhans, American authoress, b. in Albany County, New York, Nov. 17, 1815 ; married to Mr. Farnham, traveller, 1835 ; devoted herself to prison visiting, 1841 ; appointed matron of the state prison at Sing-Sing, 1844. Author of ' Life in Prairie Land ;' 'California Indoors and Out,' 1856 ; ' My Early Days,' 1859.

FARQUHAR, Sir Walter Minto Townshend, English politician, b. 1809 ; educated at Eton, and Christ Church, Oxford, where he graduated B.A. 1829 ; formerly attaché at Vienna ; M.P. for Hertford, 1857–68.

FARR, William, English statistician, b. 1803 ; licentiate of the Society of Apothecaries, London, 1832, and graduated M.D. at the University of New York ; chief superintendent of the registrar-general's department. Author of 'The Medical Annual,' 1835-39 ; ' Report to the Registrar-general on Cholera in England,' 1852 ; and of other statistical works.

FARRAGUT, David, American naval commander, b. at Knoxville, Tennessee, 1801 ; entered the naval service as midshipman, 1811 ; lieutenant, 1821 ; appointed to the command of the *Saratoga*, 1847 ; on the outbreak of the civil war, took command of the Gulf squadron, and reduced New Orleans, April 28, 1862 ; admiral of the United States navy, 1862.

FARRINGTON, Sarah Payson Willis, American authoress, b. at Portland, Maine, July 9, 1811 ; married to Dr. Eldridge, of Boston, 1837, who died 1846 ; and to Mr. Farrington, of Boston, from whom she separated. Published, under the pseudonym of *Fanny Fern*, 'Fern Leaves from Fanny's Portfolio ;' ' Ruth Hall ;' 'Rose Clark,' New York, 1856 : contributor to many American periodicals.

FAUCIT, Helen, English actress, b. 1817 ; made her début in London at Covent Garden as Julia in the 'Hunchback,' Feb. 5, 1836 ; was a member of Mr. Macready's companies ; appeared in the 'Lady of Lyons ;' in Shakespeare's plays as Juliet, Imogen, Lady Macbeth, and many others. Married to Theodore Martin, author, Aug. 25, 1851.

FAUGERE, Armand Prosper, French writer, b. at Bergerac, Dordogne, Feb. 10, 1810 ; appointed chief secretary to the minister of public instruction, 1839. Author of 'Pensées, Fragments et Lettres de Blaise Pascal,' 1844 ; 'Mémoires de Mme. Roland,' 1864 ; and numerous other works.

FAUGIER, Victor Auguste, French politician, b. Oct. 27, 1801 ; has been mayor, and member of the General Council for the canton of Vienne ; member of the Corps Législatif for the department of the Isère since 1852.

FAVRE, Gabriel Claude Jules, French advocate and politician, b. at Lyons, March 31, 1809 ; studied law, and was called to the bar at Lyons, 1830 ; secretary-general of the ministry of the interior, 1848 ; under-secretary for foreign affairs, 1848–49 ; elected to the General Council, of the Rhone and Loire, 1851, but refused to take the oath to the new constitution ; defended Orsini, 1858 ; member of the Corps Législatif since 1858. Author of 'Contemporaneous Biography,' 1837 ; and numerous political pamphlets.

FAWCETT, Henry, English politician, b. 1833 ; educated at King's College, London, and Trinity Hall, Cambridge, where he graduated B.A. 1856, and M.A. 1859 ; fellow of Trinity Hall, and professor of political economy in the University of Cambridge ; called to the bar of the Middle Temple, 1862 ; M.P. for Brighton since 1865. Author of 'Manual of Political Economy,' London, 1866.

FAY, Theodore Sedgwick, American diplomatist, b. in New York, Feb. 10, 1807 ; called to the bar, 1828 ; appointed United States secretary of legation at the court of Berlin, 1837 ; resident minister at Berne, Switzerland, 1840–60. Author of the 'Countess Ida,' 1840 ; ' Ulric, or the Voices : a Poem,' 1851 ; 'History of Switzerland ;' and other works.

FAYE, Herve Auguste Etienne Albany, French astronomer, b. at St. Benoît du Sault, Indre, Oct. 5, 1814 ; studied at the École Polytechnique, 1832–34 ; discovered a new comet, Nov. 22, 1843 ; elected member of the Institute, Jan. 18, 1841, and of the Bureau of Longitudes, March 26, 1862 ; appointed rector of the Academy of Nancy, 1854 ; member of the Imperial Council of Public Instruction, 1864. Author of 'Sur les Déclinaisons absolues,' 1850 ; and other astronomical works.

FAZY, Jean Jacques, Swiss political economist, b. in Geneva, May 12, 1796 ; studied in France. Editor of *La Revolution ; Revue de Genève,* and one of the founders of *La France Chrétienne.* Author of 'The Bank of France ;' 'La Mort de Levrier,' Geneva, 1826 ; and numerous political pamphlets.

FECHNER, Gustav Theodor, German author, b. at Gross Sährchen, near Muskau, in Niederlausitz, April 19, 1801; studied at the Colleges of Sorau and Dresden, and medicine at Leipsic; appointed professor at the same University, 1834. Author of 'Massbestimmungen über die galvanische Kette,' 1831; 'Das Räthselbüchlein,' 1850; and numerous other works.

FECHTER, Charles, English actor, b. in London, 1823; educated in France, and studied painting and sculpture; made his début at the Salle Molière; appeared in Berlin, 1846, and in England at the Princess's Theatre as Hamlet, 1860, and as Othello, 1861. Lessee and manager of the Lyceum Theatre, 1862–67.

FEE, Antoine Laurent Apollinaire, French naturalist, b. at Ardentes, Indre, Nov. 7, 1789; founded the Pharmaceutical Society of the department of the Seine, 1819; admitted to the Academy of Medicine, 1824; appointed professor of Military Instruction at Lille, 1824, and at Strasburg, 1832; director of the Jardin des Plantes. Author of 'Flore de Virgile,' 1823; and 'Souvenirs de la Guerre d'Espagne,' 1857.

FELLOWES, Edward, English politician, b. 1809; educated at the Charterhouse; a magistrate and deputy-lieutenant of Norfolk and Hunts; formerly lieutenant in the 15th Hussars; M.P. for Hunts since 1837.

FELON, Joseph, French painter, sculptor, and lithographer, b. at Bordeaux, Aug. 22, 1818; studied painting under M. Court. Painted 'La Mort de Mgr. Affre,' 1849; 'Andromède,' a statuette at the Universal Exhibition, 1855; and executed in marble for the new Louvre the Allegories of 'La Vérite,' 'L'Histoire,' 'La Justice,' 'La Fermeté,' 'La Prudence,' 'La Force;' and many other pieces of sculpture.

FELSING, Jacob, German engraver, b. at Darmstadt, 1802; studied at the Academy of Milan, and at Florence, and under Torchi at Parma. Engraved 'Christ in the Garden of Olives,' after Carlo Dolce; 'The Holy Family,' after Overbeck, 1839; 'St. Geneviève' of Steinbruck; and the works of many other celebrated painters.

FENWICK, Edward Matthew, English politician, b. 1812; assumed the name of Fenwick by royal licence, 1854; called to the bar of the Middle Temple, 1854; a J.P. and deputy-lieutenant of the county of Lancaster, and magistrate for the West Riding of Yorkshire; M.P. for Lancaster, 1864–68.

FERGUSON, Robert, English physician, b. 1799; educated in England, and at the University of Edinburgh, where he graduated M.D. 1823; consulting physician to King's College Hospital, and physician-extraordinary to the Queen. Author of a treatise 'On Puerperal Fever.'

FERGUSSON, James, English architect, b. in Ayr, Scotland, 1808; architect of the Nineveh Court in the Crystal Palace at Sydenham; one of the commissioners to inquire into the defences of the United Kingdom, appointed 1859. Author of 'Illustrations of the Rock-cut Temples of India,' 1845; 'The Palaces of Nineveh and Persepolis restored,' 1851; and other works on architecture.

FERGUSSON, Sir James, English administrator, b. 1832; educated at Rugby, and University College, Oxford; formerly captain in the Grenadier Guards, and served in the Crimea; M.P. for Ayrshire, 1854–57, and 1859–68; appointed governor of South Australia, Aug. 1868.

FERGUSSON, William, English surgeon, b. near Edinburgh, 1808; educated at the High School and the University of Edinburgh; professor of surgery at King's College, London; surgeon to King's College Hospital; surgeon-extraordinary to her Majesty. Author of 'System of Practical Surgery.'

FERNAN, Sebastian Franz Daxenberger, German statesman and poet, b. at Munich, Oct. 3, 1809; studied at the Universities of Göttingen and Berlin; counsellor of state, 1843; deputy to the National Assembly of Frankfort, 1849. Author of 'Edgar, oder Blüthe aus dem Leben eines Dichters,' Munich, 1838; 'Gedichte,' Ratisbon, 1845; and of several dramas.

FERRAND, William Busfield, English politician, b. 1809; a J.P. and deputy-lieutenant of the West Riding of Yorkshire; M.P. for Knaresborough, 1841–47, and for Devonport, 1863–68.

FERRARA, Francesco, Italian statesman, b. at Palermo, Dec. 10, 1810; studied political economy, and founded the *Giornale di Statistica;* imprisoned in the citadel of Palermo, 1847–48; member of the Provisional Government of the kingdom of Naples, 1848–49; professor of political economy at the University of Turin, 1849–67; minister of finance of the kingdom of Italy, April 7 to Oct. 28, 1867.

FERRARI, Giuseppe, Italian writer, b. at Milan, 1811; studied at the University of Pavia, and took the degree of LL.D. 1831; appointed professor of philosophy to the

College of Rochefort, 1840; at Strasburg, 1841. Author of 'Ideas on the Politics of Plato and Aristotle,' 1842; 'Histoire des Révolutions d'Italie, ou Guelfs et Gibelins,' Paris, 1856–58; and other historical and philosophical works.

FESSENDEN, William Pitt, American statesman, b. in Merrimac County, New Hampshire, Oct. 16, 1806; graduated at Bowdoin College, 1823; admitted to the bar, 1827; member of Congress, 1838; member of the United States House of Representatives, 1840; elected to the Senate; secretary of finance, 1864–65.

FETIS, François Joseph, Belgian musical composer, b. at Mons, March 25, 1784; studied under Haydn and Mozart; entered the Conservatoire, and received lessons from Roy and Boieldieu; appointed director of the Conservatoire of Brussels, 1833; member of the Belgian Academy, 1845. Published 'Traité du Contrepoint et de la Fugue,' 1818; 'Biographie universelle des Musiciens, et Biographie générale de la Musique,' Paris and Brussels, 1835–44; and numerous other works.

FEUERBACH, Ludwig, German author, b. at Anspach, Bavaria, July 28, 1804; studied theology at Heidelberg, under Professors Paulus and Daub. Author of 'Gedanken über Tod und Unsterblichkeit,' Nuremberg, 1830; 'Das Wesen der Religion,' Leipsic, 1845; and numerous other philosophical works.

FEUILLET, Octave, French dramatic writer, b. at St. Lo, Manche, Aug. 11, 1812; studied at the College of Louis-le-Grand, Paris. Author of 'La Nuit Terrible;' 'Bellah,' 1850; 'Histoire de Sibylle,' 1862; 'La Belle au Bois dormant,' 1865; and numerous other dramas, romances, and poems. Elected member of the French Academy, 1862.

FE'VAL, Paul Henri Corentin, French novelist, b. at Rennes, Sept. 27, 1817; studied in his native town, and was called to the bar. Author of 'Loup Blanc,' 1843; 'Histoire des Tribunaux secrets,' 1851; 'Annette Laïs,' 1864; and numerous other works of fiction.

FEVERSHAM, William Duncombe, Baron, English administrator, b. 1798; studied at Christ Church, Oxford; M.P. for York, 1826 to 1841, when he succeeded to the title; deputy-lieutenant of Yorkshire.

FEZENSAC, Raimond Emery Philippe Joseph de Montesquiou, Duc de, French diplomatist, b. at Paris, Feb. 26, 1784; brigadier-general, 1812; duke of Fezensac, 1832; ambassador at Madrid, 1838. Published 'Journal de la Campagne de Russie in 1812,' 1850.

FFEILDEN, Joseph, English politician, b. 1792; J.P. and deputy-lieutenant of Lancashire; high sheriff, 1818; M.P. for Blackburn since 1865.

FICHTE, Immanuel Hermann, German philosophical writer, b. at Jena, July 18, 1797; studied at the University of Berlin; professor at the College of Saarbrücken, 1822, and at Dusseldorf, 1836; at the University of Bonn, 1839, and at Tubingen, 1842. Author of 'Sätze der Vorschule zur Theologie,' Stuttgart, 1826; 'Anthropologie, oder die Lehre von der menschlichen Seele,' Leipsic, 1856; and other philosophical works.

FIELD, Cyrus West, American electrician, b. at Stockbridge, Massachusetts, Nov. 30, 1819; accompanied the expeditions of 1857 and 1858 to lay the telegraph cable in the Atlantic from England to America, and took a leading part in the third expedition of 1864.

FIELD, David Dudley, American jurist, b. at Haddam, Connecticut, Feb. 13, 1805, brother of the preceding; educated at Williams College, Massachusetts; called to the bar, 1828; appointed by the State of New York as president of a commission to prepare a new political, penal, and civil code, 1857.

FIELD, Rev. Frederick, English philologist, b. 1800; educated at Trinity College, Cambridge, where he graduated B.A. 1823; was elected fellow of his college; rector of Reepham, Norfolk, 1842; resigned, 1863. Edited the Greek text of St. Chrysostom's Homilies on St. Matthew, 1839; the Septuagint version of the Old Testament, according to the Alexandrian codex; and other works.

FIELDS, James, American author, b. at Portsmouth, New Hampshire, 1820. Edited and published an edition of De Quincey's writings in 21 vols.: author of 'A Few Verses for a Few Friends,' 1858; and other poems.

FIFE, James Duff, Earl of, English administrator, b. at Edinburgh, 1814; K.T. and lord-lieutenant of Banffshire; M.P. for Banffshire, 1837 to 1857; succeeded his uncle, third earl, March 1857.

FIGUIER, Guillaume Louis, French writer, b. at Montpellier, Feb. 15, 1819; took the degree of M.D. at Paris, 1841; appointed professor to the School of Pharmacy at Montpellier, 1846. Author of 'Du Tissu adipeux et des Matières grasses dans la Série animale,' 1844; 'La Terre avant le Déluge,' 1862; and numerous other works.

FILLIAS, Achille Etienne, French writer, b. at Aubusson, March 25, 1821; studied at St. Cyr, and entered the army, 1841. Author of ' Études sur l'Algérie,' 1849 ; 'Histoire de la Conquête et de la Colonisation de l'Algérie, 1850–60,' 1860 ; and other works.

FILLMORE, Millard, American statesman, b. at Summer Hill, State of New York, Jan. 7, 1800; apprenticed to a wool-carder ; elected to the State Assembly as representative of the county of Erie, 1829 ; member of Congress, 1832 and 1837 ; comptroller of the State of New York, 1847 ; vice-president of the United States, 1849–50 ; president of the United States, 1850 to 1853.

FINGALL, Archibald James Plunkett, Earl of, Irish administrator, b. 1791 ; lord-lieutenant of the county of Meath ; visitor and trustee of Maynooth College ; sat in the House of Commons as Lord Killeen till 1831.

FINLAY, Alexander Struthers, English politician, b. 1806; educated at Harrow and Glasgow ; a commissioner of supply, and magistrate and deputy-lieutenant of the county of Argyle; deputy-lieutenant of Bute ; M.P. for Argyleshire, 1857–68.

FINLAY, George, English historian, resident for many years at Athens. Author of ' History of the Greek Revolution,' and several other works on the history of Greece.

FINNIE, William, English politician, b. 1828 ; called to the bar of the Inner Temple, 1852 ; elected M.P. for North Ayrshire, 1868.

FITZGERALD, Right Hon. John David, Irish judge, b. in Dublin, 1815 ; educated at Trinity College, Dublin ; called to the Irish bar, 1838 ; appointed solicitor-general for Ireland, 1855 ; attorney-general, 1856 ; one of the judges of the Court of Common Pleas in Ireland, 1860.

FITZGERALD, Otho Augustus, Lord, English politician, b. 1827: formerly master of the horse to the lord-lieutenant of Ireland ; appointed comptroller of the royal household, Dec. 1868 ; M.P. for the county of Kildare since 1865.

FITZMAURICE, Lord Edmond George, English politician. b. 1846; educated at Eton, and Trinity College, Cambridge ; returned M.P. for Calne, 1868.

FITZMAURICE, Hon. William Edward, English author, b. 1805 ; educated at Oriel College, Oxford ; was captain in the 2d Life Guards ; M.P. for Bucks from 1842 to 1847. Author of 'A Cruise in Egypt, Palestine, and Greece.'

FITZPATRICK, Right Hon. John Wilson, English politician, b. in London, 1800 ; educated at Eton, and Trinity College, Dublin ; lord-lieutenant of Queen's County; captain in the army ; M.P. for Queen's County, 1837–41, 1847–52, and since 1865 ; sworn privy councillor for Ireland, 1848.

FITZPATRICK, William John, English writer, b. in Ireland, Aug. 31, 1830 ; educated at the Roman Catholic College of Clongowes Wood; a magistrate and grand juror of the county of Dublin. Author of 'The Life, Times, and Correspondence of Bishop Doyle ;' and many other biographical works.

FITZWILLIAM, Hon. Charles William Wentworth, English politician, b. 1826; educated at Trinity College, Cambridge ; formerly attaché at Vienna ; M.P. for Malton since 1858.

FITZWILLIAM, Hon. William Henry Wentworth-Fitzwilliam, English politician, b. 1840, second son of Earl Fitzwilliam ; returned M.P. for County Wicklow, 1868.

FITZWILLIAM, William Thomas Spencer Wentworth Fitzwilliam, Earl, English administrator, b. Oct. 12, 1815 ; educated at Trinity College, Cambridge, where he graduated M.A. 1837 ; a magistrate and lord-lieutenant of the West Riding of Yorkshire, and K.G. ; M.P. for Malton, 1837 to 1841, and again from 1846 to 1847 ; M.P. for Wicklow, 1847–57 ; succeeded his father, 1857.

FLACHAT, Eugene, French engineer, b. 1802 ; studied at the School of Nîmes, and at Havre and Paris, 1823 to 1830 ; appointed chief engineer of the railways of the West, 1857 ; founded the Union des Constructeurs, 1841 ; the Conference des Chemins de Fer, 1844 ; and the Société des Ingénieurs Civils, 1848. Author of ' De la Traversée des Alpes par un Chemin de Fer,' 1860 ; and numerous other works on railroads and engineering.

FLAGG, Edmund, American writer, b. at Wicasset, Maine, U.S., November 24, 1815; graduated at Bowdoin College, 1835 ; called to the bar, 1837 ; appointed United States consul for the port of Venice, 1850. Author of ' Venice, the City of the Sea;' ' Carrero, or the Prime Minister ;' and several novels and dramas.

FLAHAULT DE LA BILLARDERIE, Auguste Charles Joseph, Count de, French diplomatist, b. at Paris, April 20, 1785; created brigadier-general, and general of division with the title of count, 1813; appointed ambassador plenipotentiary at Berlin, 1831; ambassador at Vienna, 1841; ambassador to Great Britain, 1860 to 1862.

FLANDIN, Euge'ne Napoleon, French painter and traveller, b. at Naples, Aug. 15, 1809; accompanied M. de Sercey, the ambassador, to Persia, 1839, and M. Botta to the ruins of Nineveh, 1843. Published 'Voyage en Perse,' 1843; 'Voyage en Ninive,' 1845: painted 'La Ville de Venise,' 1836; 'Intérieurs de Bazar à Téhéran,' 1861; and many other pictures, principally landscapes.

FLAUBERT, Gustave, French novelist, b. 1821. Author of 'Madame Bovary,' 1857; 'Salammbo,' 1862.

FLAUDIN, Louis Hugues, French politician, b. at Paris, May 6, 1804; admitted to the bar, 1827; appointed advocate-general at the Paris Court of Appeal, 1848; member of the Council of State, 1852.

FLEISCHER, Heinrich Lebrecht, German philologist, b. at Schandau on the Elbe, Feb. 21, 1801; studied at the University of Leipsic, 1819 to 1824; appointed professor of the Kreuzschule of Dresden, 1831; professor of the University of St. Petersburg, and of Leipsic, 1835. Author of 'Samachscharis goldene Halsbänder,' Leipsic, 1835; 'Grammatik der lebenden persischen Sprache,' ib. 1847; and other philological works.

FLEMING, Charles, English linguistic writer, b. at Perth, 1806; studied in Edinburgh, and at the University of Glasgow; teacher of English at the College of Louis-le-Grand, Paris, 1829–31; at the École Polytechnique, 1844–48; at the Collége Bourbon, Paris, 1841–52. Published 'Dictionary of English and French, and French and English,' 1839–40; and several elementary works.

FLEMING, Sir Valentine, English colonial judge, b. 1809; educated at Trinity College, Dublin, where he graduated, 1834; called to the English bar; appointed commissioner of the Insolvent Court for Hobart Town, 1841; was successively solicitor and attorney-general for Tasmania, and chief justice of that colony.

FLETCHER, Isaac, English politician, b. 1827; coalowner and ironmaster, and a magistrate of Cumberland; returned M.P. for Cockermouth, 1868.

FLEURY, Anselme, French politician, b. Feb. 14, 1820; member of the Corps Législatif for the department of Loire Inférieure since 1852.

FLEURY, Emile Fe'lix, French general, b. at Paris, Dec. 23, 1815; studied at the Collége Rollin; entered the corps of Spahis, 1837; sub-lieutenant, 1840; captain, 1844; chief of a squadron, 1848; appointed aide-de-camp to the Emperor, colonel of the Guides, and grand equerry of the Crown, Dec. 31, 1852; general of brigade, 1856; general of division, 1868; senator, 1865.

FLOCARD DE MEPIEN, Adolphe, French politician, b. July 20, 1802; member of the General Council for the canton of Morestel; member of the Corps Législatif for the third circonscription of the Isère since 1852.

FLOCON, Ferdinand, French politician, b. in Paris, Nov. 1, 1800; reporter to the *Courrier Français,* 1820; fought at the barricades, 1830; wrote for the *Tribune National,* and was one of the founders of the *Réforme;* member of the Provisional Government of France, and minister of commerce, 1848; exiled after the coup d'état of Dec. 2, 1851.

FLORENCOURT, Franz Chassot von, German political writer, b. at Brunswick, July 4, 1804; studied at the University of Marburg. Author of 'Kirchliche, politische und literarische Zustände Deutschlands,' Leipsic, 1840; 'Zur preussischen Verfassungsfrage,' Hamburg, 1847; and other political works.

FLOTOW, Friedrich Ferdinand Adolph von, German musical composer, b. at Tentendorf, Mecklenburg, April 27, 1812; studied under Reicha. Composed 'Rob Roy,' 1832; the 'Duchess of Guise,' 1838; 'L'Esclave de Camöens,' 1843; 'Martha,' 1858; and many other operas and smaller musical pieces.

FLOURENS, Marie Jean Pierre, French physiologist, b. at Maureilhan, Hérault, April 15, 1794; received the degree of M.D. at Montpellier, 1813; created a peer of *France, 1846;* professor in the College of France, 1855; professor of comparative physiology in the Museum of Natural History in Paris; perpetual secretary of the French Academy of Sciences. Author of 'De la Longevité humaine,' Paris, 1854; and numerous other scientific works.

PLOYER, John, English politician, b. 1811; educated at Winchester, and Balliol College, Oxford, where he graduated B.A. 1831; a J.P. and deputy-lieutenant of Dorset; was high sheriff, 1844; M.P. for Dorset, 1846–57, and since 1864.

PLUGEL, Gustav Lebrecht, German philologist, b. at Bautzen, Feb. 18, 1802; educated at the University of Leipsic, and at Vienna, where he studied under Von Hammer; appointed professor in the College of Meissen, 1832. Author of 'Arabic Anthology: Collection of fugitive Pieces of Poetry of Tháalibi,' Vienna, 1829; 'History of the Arabs,' 1833; and other works.

POERSTER, Ernst Joachim, German writer and painter, b. at Munchengosserstadt, April 8, 1800, brother of the following; studied at Munich, in the school of Cornelius. Executed a great number of frescoes. Author of 'Beiträge zur neuern Kunstgeschichte,' Leipsic, 1835; 'Denkmale deutscher Baukunst, Bildnerei und Malerei,' ib. 1855; and many other works.

POERSTER, Friederich, German military writer, b. at Munchengosserstadt, Sept. 15, 1792; entered the volunteer corps of Lützow, 1813. Author of 'Beiträge zur neuern Kriegsgeschichte,' Berlin, 1816; 'Preussen's neuere und neueste Geschichte,' ib. 1850; and numerous other works.

POGARASSY, Johann, Hungarian jurist, b. at Kasmark, Abaujvar, 1801; called to the bar, 1829; and became a magistrate, 1835; elected member of the Hungarian Academy, 1838; councillor to the minister of finance, 1848; judge of the Tribunal of Pesth during the revolution. Author of 'Magyarhoui maganos Törvenytudomany elemei,' Pesth, 1839; and numerous other works on jurisprudence.

POLEY, John Henry, English sculptor, b. in Dublin, 1818; studied at the Dublin Royal Society, and in the schools of the Royal Academy, London. Exhibited 'The Death of Abel,' 1839; 'Ino and Bacchus,' 1840; 'Egeria,' 1854; and numerous statues, busts, and groups. Elected A.R.A. 1849; R.A. 1858.

POLEY, John Henry Wentworth Hodgetts, English politician, b. 1828; educated at Eton, and Christ Church, Oxford; a magistrate and deputy-lieutenant of Worcestershire and Staffordshire; M.P. for South Staffordshire, 1857–68.

POLEY, Thomas Henry Foley, Baron, English politician, b. 1808; M.P. for Worcestershire, 1830 to 1833; captain of the gentlemen-at-arms from July 1846 to March 1852, and Dec. 1852 to Feb. 1858; reappointed, June 1859; succeeded his father, 1833.

FOLJAMBE, Francis John Savile, English politician, b. 1830; educated at Eton, and Christ Church, Oxford; is a J.P. and deputy-lieutenant of Notts; M.P. for East Retford since 1857.

FONBLANQUE, Albany, English journalist and statistician, b. 1797; chief of the statistical department of the Board of Trade; for many years proprietor and editor of the *Examiner.* Author of 'England under Seven Administrations,' 1837.

FOOT, Solomon, American politician, b. at Addison County, Vermont, Nov. 19, 1802; graduated at Middleburg College, 1826; appointed professor of natural philosophy in the Vermont Academy of Medicine at Castleton, 1828 to 1831; called to the bar, 1831; returned to Congress, 1842 to 1844; member of the U.S. Senate, 1850–56.

FOOTE, Henry Stuart, American politician, b. in Fauquier County, Virginia, Sept. 20, 1800; graduated at Washington College, Lexington, 1819; commenced practice as a lawyer, 1822; elected to the United States Senate, 1847; governor of Mississippi, 1851.

FORBES, Right Rev. Alexander Penrose, Scottish divine, b. at Edinburgh, 1817; educated at Brasenose College, Oxford, where he graduated B.A. 1844; consecrated bishop of Brechin, in Scotland, 1847; and received the degree of D.C.L. Author of numerous devotional works.

FORBES, Charles Stuart, English naval commander, b. at Richmond, Surrey, 1829; entered the navy, 1841; served during the first China war, and in New Zealand, 1844–45; joined the first expedition in search of Sir John Franklin, and promoted to a lieutenancy, 1848; took the *Algerine* gunboat to China, 1857; commander in the navy, 1858. Author of 'Garibaldi's Campaign in the Two Sicilies,' 1861.

FORBES, Hon. Francis Reginald, English diplomatist, b. 1791; educated at Eton; entered the diplomatic service; was secretary of legation at Rio Janeiro, Copenhagen, and Lisbon, and secretary of embassy at Vienna; appointed minister at Dresden, 1832; envoy extraordinary to Brazil, 1858.

FORBES, James David, American naturalist, b. in Edinburgh, 1809; educated at the University of Edinburgh, where he was professor of natural philosophy, 1833 to 1860; *principal of St. Salvator's and St. Leonard's Colleges, St. Andrew's, New Brunswick.* Author of 'Travels in the Alps of Savoy;' and numerous scientific works.

FORCADE, Euge'ne, French writer, b. at Marseilles, 1820 ; founded the journal *Semaphore*, 1837 ; the *Messager de l'Assemblée*, Paris, 1851 ; director of the *Semaine Financière*, 1856 to 1862. Author of 'Historical Studies,' 1853 ; and other works.

FORCADE-LAROQUETTE, Jean Louis Victor Adolphe de, French statesman, b. in Paris, 1820 ; studied law in Paris, and called to the bar at the Royal Court, 1841 ; LL.D. 1846 ; minister of finance, Nov. 28, 1860, to Nov. 12, 1861 ; member of the Senate, Nov. 14, 1861 ; vice-president of the Council of State, 1863 ; minister of agriculture, commerce, and public works, 1867–68 ; appointed minister of the interior, Dec. 18, 1868.

FORCE, Peter, American journalist, b. in New Jersey, Nov. 26, 1790 ; educated in the trade of a printer ; mayor of Washington, 1836 to 1840. Published a documentary history of the American colonies, and several historical tracts.

FORCHHAMMER, Johan Georg, Danish chemist and geologist, b. at Husum, Schleswig, July 26, 1794 ; studied at Kiel, and at Copenhagen, under Oersted ; took the degree of M.D. 1820 ; appointed lecturer on mineralogy at the University of Copenhagen, 1823 ; professor, 1850 ; member of the Academy of Sciences of Copenhagen, 1825 ; and secretary, 1851. Author of 'Skandinaviens geognostiske Natur,' 1843 ; and numerous works on geology and chemistry.

FORCHHAMMER, Paul Wilhelm, German archæologist, b. at Husum, Schleswig, 1800 ; studied at Lubeck, and at the University of Kiel ; degree of Ph.D. 1828 ; appointed professor at Kiel, 1836. Author of 'Zur Topographie von Athen,' Göttingen, 1833 ; and numerous other works.

FORDE, William Brownlow, English politician, b. 1823 ; magistrate and deputy-lieutenant of the county of Down ; formerly colonel in the 67th Foot ; high sheriff, 1851 ; M.P. for Downshire since 1857.

FORESTER, Right Hon. George Cecil Weld, English politician. b. 1807 ; educated at Westminster ; colonel in the Royal Horse Guards ; groom of the bedchamber to George IV. and William IV. ; comptroller of the household, 1852, and 1858–59 ; M.P. for Wenlock since 1830.

FOREY, Elie Frederic, French military commander, b. in Paris, Jan. 10, 1804 ; educated at Dijon, and admitted to the Military School of St. Cyr, 1822 ; took part in the first expedition to Algeria ; colonel, 1844 ; general, 1848 ; took part in organizing the coup d'état of Dec. 1851 ; general of division, 1852 ; senator, 1859 ; marshal of France, May 17, 1863 ; commanded the French expedition to Mexico.

FORGACH, Graf Anton von, Hungarian politician, b. 1819 ; chancellor of Ofen and of Fiume, 1849 ; appointed vice-governor of Prague, 1853 ; governor of Moravia, 1860 ; and of Bohemia, Oct. 1860 ; chancellor of Hungary, 1861 ; resigned, April 1864.

FORGUES, Paul Emile Daurand, French writer, b. at Paris, April 20, 1813 ; studied law at Toulouse, and called to the bar at Paris, 1834. Contributor under the pseudonym of *Old Nick* to the *Charivari*, the *Revue des Deux Mondes*, and many other French periodicals : translated into French 'Jane Eyre ;' 'Shirley ;' 'Macaulay's Essays ;' and other works by English authors.

FORNEROD, Constant, Swiss statesman, b. at Avenches, Canton Vaud, 1820 ; studied at the Universities of Lausanne, Tubingen, and Heidelberg ; secretary to the government of Vaud, 1845 ; member of the Council of State for the same canton, 1848 ; president of the council, 1851 ; member of the Council of State of the Confederation, 1853 ; president, 1855 ; president of the Swiss Confederation, 1857 ; commissioner of the Confederation in the canton of Geneva, 1864.

FORREST, Edwin, American actor, b. in Philadelphia, March 9, 1806 ; made his début at the Walnut-street Theatre, Nov. 1820 ; played in some of the principal theatres in America and England.

FORRESTER, Alfred Henry, English writer, b. in London, 1805. Contributed, under the *nom de plume* of *Alfred Crowquill*, to the *Humorist*, 1828 ; *Bentley's Miscellany*, *Punch*, and the *Illustrated London News*. Author of 'Leaves from my Memorandum Book ;' 'The Wanderings of a Pen and Pencil ;' and other works.

FORSTER, Charles, English politician, b. 1815 ; educated at Worcester College, Oxford, where he graduated B.A. 1840 ; called to the bar of the Inner Temple, 1843 ; a magistrate and deputy-lieutenant of Staffordshire M.P. for Walsall since 1847.

FORSTER, Rev. Charles, English divine, b. 1790 ; educated at Trinity College, Dublin ; entered holy orders in Ireland ; rector of Stisted, near Braintree, Essex, 1828 ; appointed one of the six preachers in Canterbury Cathedral, 1835. Author of 'The Apostolical Authority of the Epistle to the Hebrews vindicated,' 1838 ; 'The One Primeval Language traced experimentally through Ancient Inscriptions,' 1851.

FORSTER, François, French engraver, b. at Locle, Neufchâtel, Aug. 22, 1790; studied at Paris under Langlois, Leopold Robert, and at the École des Beaux Arts; elected member of the Academy of Fine Arts, 1844. Engraved 'Sainte Cécile,' after Paul Delaroche; 'Queen Victoria,' after M. Winterhalter; and many other works.

FORSTER, John, English historian, b. at Newcastle, 1812; appointed commissioner in lunacy, 1861. Author of 'Lives of the Statesmen of the Commonwealth;' 'Sir John Eliot, a Biography, 1590–1632,' 1864; and other historical works. Editor for a time of the *Examiner* and *Daily News*, and contributor to the *Edinburgh* and *Quarterly Reviews*.

FORSTER, William Edward, English statesman, b. 1818; J.P. and deputy-lieutenant of the West Riding of Yorkshire; under-secretary of state for the colonies, 1865–66; appointed vice-president of the Council of Education, Dec. 1868; M.P. for Bradford since 1861.

FORSYTH, William, English author, b. 1812; educated at Trinity College, Cambridge, where he graduated B.A. 1834; called to the bar of the Inner Temple, 1839; a bencher of the Inner Temple, and standing counsel to the secretary of state in the Council of India; M.P. for Cambridge, 1865–68. Author of 'Hortensius, or the Duty and Office of an Advocate,' 1849; 'Life of Cicero,' 1864; and other works.

FORTESCUE, Right Hon. Chichester Samuel Parkinson, English statesman, b. 1823; educated at Eton, and Christ Church, Oxford, where he graduated B.A. 1844; a magistrate and deputy-lieutenant of the county of Louth; lord of the Treasury, 1844–45; under-secretary for the colonies, 1857–58, and 1859–66; appointed chief secretary for Ireland, Dec. 1868; M.P. for County Louth since 1847.

FORTESCUE, Hon. Dudley Francis, English politician, b. 1820; educated at Harrow, and Trinity College, Cambridge; a deputy-lieutenant of Devon, and magistrate of the county of Waterford; M.P. for Andover since 1857.

FORTESCUE, Right Hon. Hugh Fortescue, Earl, English statesman, b. 1818; educated at Harrow; M.P. for Plymouth, 1841–52; M.P. for Marylebone, 1854–59; succeeded his father, 1861; a lord of the Treasury, 1846–47; secretary to the Poor Law Board, 1847–51. Author of 'Public Schools for the Middle Classes,' 1864; and several political pamphlets.

FORTUNE, Robert, English botanist, b. in Berwickshire, 1813; appointed collector of plants in Northern China by the Botanical Society of London, 1842. Author of 'Three Years' Wandering in China,' 1847; 'Residence among the Chinese, Inland, on the Coast, and at Sea; being the Third Visit, from 1853 to 1856;' and other works.

FOSS, Edward, English author, b. 1787; a magistrate of Kent and Surrey, and of the borough of Dover. Author of 'The Grandeur of the Law, or the Legal Peers of England,' 1843; 'The Judges of England,' 1848–57.

FOSTER, Birket, English artist, b. at North Shields, Northumberland, 1812; studied wood-engraving under Mr. Landells. Contributor of sketches for the *Illustrated London News;* illustrated Longfellow's 'Evangeline;' 'Goldsmith's Poetical Works;' and other publications.

FOSTER, John, American military commander, b. in New Hampshire, 1824; educated at West Point, and entered the army as lieutenant, 1846; served in the Mexican war; was first lieutenant and captain at the outbreak of the civil war; took part with the North, and became major, 1861; major-general, 1862; placed in charge of the departments of Virginia and North Carolina, July 16, 1863.

FOSTER, La Fayette, American statesman, b. at Franklin, New London, Connecticut, Nov. 22, 1806; studied at the University of President Brown, Rhode Island; elected to the Senate of the United States, 1855; re-elected to Congress, 1860; president of the Senate, and on the death of Abraham Lincoln assumed the office of vice-president of the United States, April 14, 1865.

FOSTER, William Orme, English politician, b. 1814; a magistrate and deputy-lieutenant of the counties of Stafford and Worcester; M.P. for South Staffordshire, 1857–68.

FOTHERGILL, Richard, b. 1830, English politician; ironmaster, and magistrate and deputy-lieutenant of Glamorganshire; returned M.P. for Merthyr Tydvil, 1868.

FOUCHÉ LEPELLETIER, Edouard Edmund François, French politician, b. at Havre, 1809; member of the Corps Législatif for the department of the Seine since 1852; member of the Municipal Commission of Paris.

FOWLER, Robert Nicholas, English politician, b. 1825; a partner in the banking-house of Dimsdale & Co. Cornhill, London; returned M.P. for Penryn, 1868.

FOWLER, William, English politician, b. 1828; educated at University College, London; called to the bar of the Inner Temple, 1852; returned M.P. for Cambridge, 1868.

FOX, Sir Charles, English civil engineer, b. at Derby, 1810; constructed the building for the Great Exhibition of 1851 in Hyde Park, for which he was knighted; and the Crystal Palace at Sydenham.

FOX, Charles Richard, English politician, b. 1798; entered the army, 1815; M.P. for Horsham and Calne before the Reform Bill; for Stroud, 1832–33; for the Tower Hamlets, 1841–47. Published 'Engravings of unedited and rare Greek Coins, with Descriptions,' 1856–62.

FRASER, Alexander Campbell, English writer, b. in Argyleshire, 1818; studied at the University of Edinburgh; appointed professor of metaphysics and logic in his university, 1846. Editor of the *North British Review,* 1849; author of 'Essays in Philosophy.'

FRANCIS, George Henry, English writer, b. 1817. Author of 'Opinions of Lord Brougham,' 1857; 'Critical Biographies of Mr. B. Disraeli, Sir Robert Peel, Lord Brougham, and Lord Palmerston:' contributor to *Fraser's* and other magazines.

FRANCIS JOSEPH I., Emperor of Austria and King of Hungary, b. Aug. 18, 1830, the son of Archduke Franz Carl and of Archduchess Sophia, Princess of Bavaria; appointed governor of Bohemia, April 5, 1848; declared of age, Dec. 1, 1848; proclaimed Emperor of Austria in consequence of the abdication of his uncle, Ferdinand I., and the renunciation of the crown by his father, December 2, 1848; crowned King of Hungary, and took the oath on the Hungarian Constitution, June 8, 1867; married, April 24, 1854, to Elizabeth, Princess in Bavaria, the daughter of Duke Maximilian in Bavaria.

FREEMAN, Edward Augustus, English historical writer, b. at Harborne, Staffordshire, 1823; elected scholar of Trinity College, Oxford, 1841, and fellow, 1845; graduated M.A.; examiner in law and modern philosophy, 1857–58 and 1863–64. Author of 'History of Architecture,' 1849; 'History of Federal Government,' 1863; 'History of the Norman Conquest,' 1867; and other works.

FREER, Martha Walker, English authoress, b. at Leicester, Oct. 25, 1822; married to the Rev. John Robinson, rector of Windmerpool, near Nottingham, 1861. Author of 'Life of Marguerite d'Angoulême, Queen of Navarre,' 1854; 'The Married Life of Anne of Austria,' 1864; and other biographical works.

FREILIGRATH, Ferdinand, German poet, b. at Detmold, Northern Germany, June 17, 1810; educated for a mercantile career. Author of numerous lyrical poems.

FREMANTLE, Sir Thomas Francis, English statesman, b. 1798; educated at Oriel College, Oxford, where he graduated in 1819; M.P. for Buckingham, 1826–46; deputy-chairman of the Board of Customs, 1846, and chairman of the board, 1850; was secretary at war, 1844–45; chief secretary for Ireland, 1845–46.

FREMONT, John Charles, American officer and statesman, b. in South Carolina, Jan. 21, 1813; graduated at Charleston College, 1830; explored the South Pass of the Rocky Mountains, 1842; captain, 1845; colonel, 1850; unsuccessful candidate for the Presidency of the United States, 1856; took part with the Union Government in the civil war, and appointed lieutenant-general, 1861.

FREMY, Edmond, French chemist, b. at Versailles, Feb. 28, 1814; studied at the École Polytechnique; professor in the same from 1843 to 1850; elected member of the Academy of Sciences, 1857. Author of several works on chemistry.

FRENCH, Benjamin, American writer, b. in Virginia, June 8, 1799. Published 'Memoirs of Eminent Female Writers,' 1825; 'Historical Collections of Louisiana,' 1844 to 1853; and other works.

FRENCH, Right Hon. Fitz-Stephen, English politician, b. 1801; educated at Trinity College, Dublin; a magistrate and deputy-lieutenant of the county of Roscommon; M.P. for county of Roscommon since 1832.

FRERE, Sir Henry Bartle Edward, English colonial administrator, b. 1815; educated at Haileybury; entered the Bengal Civil Service, 1833; appointed British resident in Scinde, 1856; created K.C.B. civil division, 1859; governor of Bombay, 1862–68.

FRERE, Rev. John Alexander, English theological writer, b. 1814; educated at Trinity College, Cambridge, where he graduated B.A. 1838, and M.A.; appointed vicar of Shillington, Beds, 1853. Author of 'The Inspiration of Scripture,' 1850; 'The Testimony of the Spirit to the Incarnation,' 1853.

FRERE-ORBAN, Hubert, Belgian statesman, b. at Liege, April 24, 1812; studied law, and after 1830 entered the journalistic career; elected member of the Chamber of Deputies for Liege, June 1847; minister of finance in 1847, and again 1848–52; minister of public works, 1847–48; appointed a third time minister of finance, Oct. 26, 1861.

FRERICHS, Friedrich Theodor, German physician, b. at Aurich, in Hanover, March 24, 1819; studied at the University of Göttingen, where he graduated M.D.; physician to the King of Prussia, 1854. Author of a 'Practical Treatise on Diseases of the Liver;' and other medical works.

FRESHFIELD, Charles Kaye, English politician, b. 1812; educated at the Charterhouse; is deputy-lieutenant of London, and solicitor to the Bank of England; M.P. for Dover, 1865.

FRIEDRICH I., Grand Duke of Baden, b. Sept. 9, 1826, second son of Grand Duke Leopold I. and of Princess Sophia of Sweden; ascended the throne of Baden at the death of his father, April 24, 1852; married, Sept. 20, 1856, to Louise, b. Dec. 3, 1838, the daughter of King Wilhelm I. of Prussia.

FRIEDRICH FRANZ I., Grand Duke of Mecklenburg-Strelitz, b. Oct. 17, 1819, the son of Grand Duke Georg and Princess Marie of Hesse-Cassel; succeeded to the throne at the death of his father, Sept. 6, 1860; married, June 24, 1843, to Augusta, b. July 19, 1822, the daughter of the late Duke Adolphus of Cambridge.

FRIEDRICH FRANZ II., Grand Duke of Mecklenburg-Schwerin, b. Feb. 28, 1823, the son of Grand Duke Paul Friedrich and Princess Alexandrine of Prussia; studied philosophy and theology at the University of Bonn, 1840–42; succeeded to the throne at the death of his father, March 7, 1842.

FRISWELL, James Hain, English writer, b. at Newport, Shropshire, 1827. Author of 'Houses with the Fronts Off,' 1855; 'A Daughter of Eve;' 'The Gentle Life;' and other works of a miscellaneous character.

FRITH, William Powell, English painter, b. at Studley, near Ripon, 1819; entered the Art Academy, 1835. Exhibited 'Malvolio before the Countess Olivia,' 1840; 'English Merrymaking a Hundred Years Ago,' 1847; 'A Child at its Evening Prayers,' 1852; 'A Dream of the Future,' 1856; and numerous other paintings. Elected A.R.A. and R.A. 1852.

FROST, William Edward, English painter, b. at Wandsworth, Surrey, 1810; was admitted as student at the Royal Academy, 1829. Painted 'Diana and Actæon,' 1846; 'The Syrens,' 1849; 'Chastity,' 1854; 'The Glacis,' 1863; and many others. Elected A.R.A. 1846.

FROTHINGHAM, Richard, American author and politician, b. at Charlestown, Massachusetts, Jan. 31, 1812; member of the Massachusetts House of Representatives, 1839 to 1850; mayor of Charlestown, 1850 to 1853. Author of 'History of Charlestown,' 1848; and other works.

FROUDE, James Anthony, English historian, b. at Dartington, Devonshire, April 23, 1818; educated at Westminster, and Oriel College, Oxford; took deacon's orders, 1844. Author of 'Lives of the English Saints,' 1844; 'The Nemesis of Faith,' 1848; 'History of England, from the Fall of Wolsey to the Death of Elizabeth,' vols. 1–8, 1856–65. Editor of *Fraser's Magazine.*

FUAD, Mehmed Pasha, Turkish statesman, b. in Constantinople, 1814; studied medicine in the Schools of Galata; nominated second interpreter to the Porte, 1843; Ottoman commissioner at Bucharest, 1848; commissioner at the head-quarters of Omar Pasha in the Crimea; minister of foreign affairs, 1856; Grand Vizier, 1861–66. Author of 'The Alhambra,' a poem, and 'The Truth upon the Question of the Holy Places,' 1853.

FUERST, Julius, German philological writer, b. at Zerkowa, duchy of Posen, May 12, 1805. Author of a 'Hebrew Concordance;' 'Biographical Dictionary of eminent Hebrew Literati and Savans, past and present;' and other philological and biographical works.

FULLERTON, Lady Georgiana, English authoress, b. 1814; married to Captain Alexander Fullerton, 1833. Author of 'Ellen Middleton,' 1844; 'Lady Bird,' 1852; 'Laurentia, a Tale of Japan,' 1861; 'Too Strange not to be True,' 1864; and other works of fiction.

FURSTENBERG, Carl Egon Leopold Maximilian, Prince of, German military commander, b. March 4, 1820; succeeded his father, Oct. 22, 1854; lieutenant-general in the service of Baden, and aide-de-camp to the Grand Duke of Baden.

FURSTENBERG, Johann Nepomuck Joachim Egon, Landgrave of, Austrian statesman, b. March 21, 1802; succeeded his father, Feb. 4, 1856; chamberlain at the court of Austria; privy councillor and grand master of ceremonies to the Emperor.

G.

GABELENTZ, Hans Conon von, German philologist, b. at Altenburg, Oct. 13, 1807 ; studied at the Universities of Leipsic and Göttiugen ; privy councillor of the Duke of Saxe-Altenburg, 1843–48 ; president of the Cabinet of Altenburg, 1848–49 ; represented Altenburg at the parliament of Erfurt, 1850 ; president of the Diet of Altenburg, 1851. Author of ' Beiträge zur Sprachenkunde,' Leipsic, 1852 ; and other works.

GAERTNER, Friedrich von, German architect, b. at Coblentz, 1792 ; studied at Munich, and in England and Italy ; appointed professor of architecture in the Munich Academy, 1820 ; director of the Academy of Fine Arts at Munich ; furnished the design for the royal palace at Athens, 1836 ; superintended the restoration of the cathedrals of Regensburg and Bamberg ; architect of the principal public buildings at Munich.

GAGERN, Heinrich Wilhelm August, Baron von, German statesman, b. at Bayreuth, Aug. 20, 1799 ; studied at the Military School of Munich, and at Göttingen, Jena, and Heidelberg ; entered the service of the Grand Duke of Hesse-Darmstadt, 1821 ; deputy to the Legislative Chamber of Hesse-Darmstadt, 1832–48 ; member of the German Parliament at Frankfort, and one of the authors of the Federal Constitution, 1848–49 ; retired into private life, 1852. Published ' A Life of General Friedrich von Gagern,' 1856.

GAGNE, Paulin, French writer, b. at Montoison, Drôme, June 8, 1806 ; studied law, and was called to the bar at Paris. Author of ' Le Suicide,' 1841 ; ' Le Supplice du Mari,' 1865 ; ' Le Congrès Sauveur des Rois et des Peuples,' 1864 ; and other works.

GALLAIT, Louis, Belgian historical painter, b. at Tournay, 1810 ; studied at Antwerp and Paris. Painted ' Tasso in his Cell, visited by Montaigne,' 1836 ; ' The Last Moments of Egmont,' 1853 ; and exhibited at the International Exhibition of 1862 ' The Abdication of Charles V.' and ' The Last Honours paid to Egmont and Horn.'

GALLOWAY, Randolph Stewart, Earl of, English administrator, b. in Sussex, 1800 ; educated at Harrow, and Christ Church, Oxford ; M.P. for Cockermouth, 1826 to 1831 ; succeeded his father, 1834 ; a magistrate of Kirkcudbrightshire and Wigtonshire.

GALLWEY, Sir William Payne, English politician, b. 1808 ; deputy-lieutenant of the North Riding of Yorkshire ; M.P. for Thirsk since 1851.

GALWAY, George Edward Arundell Monckton Arundell, Viscount, English politician, b. March 1, 1805 ; educated at Harrow, and Christ Church, Oxford, where he graduated B.A. ; was a lord-in-waiting to the Queen, Feb. to Dec. 1852 ; deputy-lieutenant of Notts ; M.P. for East Retford since 1847.

GAMBIER, Sir Edward John, English colonial judge, b. 1796 ; educated at Trinity College, Cambridge, where he graduated ; called to the bar at Lincoln's Inn ; appointed recorder of Prince of Wales Island, 1828 ; transferred as puisne judge to Madras, 1836 ; chief judge, 1840 to 1849.

GARBETT, Ven. James, English divine, b. 1800 ; educated at Brasenose College, Oxford, where he graduated B.A. 1822 ; appointed public examiner at Oxford, 1829 ; rector of Clayton, Sussex, 1835 ; prebendary of Chichester, 1843 ; archdeacon of Chichester, 1851. Published ' Bampton Lectures ' and ' Prælectiones Academicæ.'

GARDNER, John, English physician, b. at Coggeshall, Essex, 1804 ; educated at London, Edinburgh, and Giessen ; graduated M.D. 1844 : founded the Royal College of Chemistry and the General Apothecaries' Company. Author of ' The Great Physician,' 1843 ; ' Treatise on Consumption,' 1854 ; ' Household Medicine,' 1863 ; and other works.

GARIBALDI, Giuseppe, Italian general and politician, b. at Nice, July 22, 1807 ; entered the Sardinian navy, 1825 ; engaged in a conspiracy, and took refuge in France, 1834 ; returned to Rome, 1848 ; commanded at Varese, Camerlata, &c. in the campaign against Austria, 1859 ; landed at Marsala, May 1860, and conquered Sicily and Naples ; attacked by the Italian troops at Aspromonte and severely wounded, Aug. 27, 1862 ; visited England, 1864 ; defeated at Mentana, 1867.

GARLIES, Lord Stewart, English politician, b. 1835, eldest son of the Earl of Galloway ; educated at Harrow, and Christ Church, Oxford ; a captain in the Royal Horse Guards Blue ; returned M.P. for Wigtonshire, 1868.

GARNIER, Jean Louis Charles, French architect, b. in Paris, Nov. 6, 1825; entered the École des Beaux Arts, 1842; designed the hall of the new Opéra at Paris.

GARNIER, Joseph Clement, French political economist, b. at Beuel, Nice, Oct. 3, 1813; studied at Draguignan, and at the École Supérieure du Commerce at Paris. Author of 'Éléments d'Économie politique,' 1846; 'Premières Notions d'Économie politique ou sociale,' 1864; and numerous other works. Founder of the *Nouveau Journal des Connaissances Utiles.*

GARNIER PAGE'S, Louis Antonin, French politician, b. at Marseilles, July 18, 1803; mayor of Paris, and minister of finance under the Provisional Government, 1848; elected member of the Corps Législatif for the fifth circonscription of Paris, 1864. Author of 'History of the Revolution of 1848,' 1860–62.

GARRETT, Sir Robert, English officer, b. 1794; entered the army, 1811; served in the Peninsula; was lieutenant-colonel during the war in the Crimea; appointed to command a brigade at Gibraltar, 1856, and in China, 1857; created K.C.B. for services in suppressing the Indian Mutiny.

GASC, Jean, French lawyer, b. at Toulouse, 1800; studied law, and was called to the bar of his native town, 1823; appointed councillor of state, 1855.

GASELEE, Stephen, English politician, b. 1807; educated at Winchester, and Balliol College, Oxford, where he graduated B.A. 1828, M.A. 1832; called to the bar of the Inner Temple, 1832; serjeant-at-law, 1840; M.P. for Portsmouth, 1865–68.

GASPARIN, Agenor E'tienne, Comte de, French writer, b. at Orange, July 10, 1810. Author of 'De l'Amortissement,' 1834; 'L'Amérique devant l'Europe,' 1862; and other historical and financial works.

GATTY, Margaret, English authoress, b. in Essex, 1809; married to the Rev. Alfred Gatty, D.D., vicar of Ecclesfield, near Sheffield, 1839. Author of 'The Fairy Godmothers, and other Tales,' 1851; 'Old Folks from Home;' and numerous works of fiction.

GAUME, Jean Joseph, French theological writer, b. at Fuans, Doubs, 1802; appointed professor of theology at the Seminary of Nevers, 1827; took the degree of D.D. from the University of Prague; vicar-general of Rheims, Montauban, and Aquila. Author of 'Le Signe de la Croix au XIX. Siècle,' 1863; and other theological works.

GAUTIER, The'ophile, French poet, novelist, and critic, b. at Tarbes, Aug. 31, 1808; entered the Collége Charlemagne, 1822. Author of 'Poésies' and 'Albertus,' 1830; 'La Comédie de la Mort,' 1838; 'Une Larme du Diable,' 1839; 'Trésors d'Art de la Russie ancienne et moderne,' 1860–63; 'Loin de Paris,' 1864; and other works.

GAVAZZI, Alessandro, Italian priest and politician, b. at Bologna, 1809; admitted into holy orders in the Church of Rome, 1825; appointed chaplain-general of the forces, and accompanied the Roman army to Vicenza, 1848. Published a 'Life' of himself, in English and Italian; and 'Orations,' 1851.

GAVIN, George O'Halloran, English politician, b. 1810; entered the 16th Lancers, 1827; became a major in the army, 1846; retired, 1850; a magistrate of the county of Limerick; M.P. for Limerick since 1859.

GAVINI, Sampiero, French politician, b. at Bastia, May 18, 1823; advocate at the Imperial Court of that town, and member of the General Council for the canton of Campile; elected to the Corps Législatif for the department of Corsica, 1863.

GAYANGOS, Pascual, Spanish historian, b. June 21, 1809; studied Oriental languages under Silvestre de Sacy, in France; appointed professor in the University of Madrid, 1843. Author of 'History of the Mohammedan Dynasties of Spain;' and of a Spanish translation of Ticknor's 'History of Spanish Literature,' 1851–56.

GAYARRE, Charles Arthur, American writer, b. at Louisiana, Jan. 3, 1805; studied at the College of New Orleans. Author of 'History of Louisiana;' the 'School for Politics;' and other works.

GEIGER, Abraham, German writer, b. at Frankfort-on-the-Maine, May 24, 1810, of Jewish parents; studied at the Universities of Heidelberg and Bonn; appointed Rabbi of the Jewish community of Wiesbaden, 1832. Author of 'Was hat Mohammed aus dem Judenthum aufgenommen?' Bonn, 1833; and other works in Jewish literature.

GEIKIE, Archibald, English geologist, b. at Edinburgh, 1835; educated at the High School and University of Edinburgh; appointed to the Geological Survey, 1855. Author of 'The Story of a Boulder,' 1858; 'The Phenomena of the Glacial Drift of Scotland,' 1863; and other geological works.

GEMEAU, Auguste Pierre Walbourg, French general, b. at Paris, Jan. 4, 1790; left the *Military School* as sub-lieutenant, 1808; colonel, 1825; lieutenant-general, 1845; senator, 1852.

GENDRON, Auguste, French historical painter, b. in Paris, 1818 ; studied under Paul Delaroche. Painted 'Le Dante commenté par Boccace,' 1844 ; 'Les Nymphes au Tombeau d'Adonis,' 1864 ; and numerous other pictures.

GENTEUR, Simon Maximilian, French statesman, b. at St. Germain Mont, Ardennes, 1815 ; studied at the Lycée of Rheims, and law at Paris ; called to the bar of Orleans, 1840 ; mayor of Orleans, 1854 ; appointed secretary-general of the Ministry of Public Instruction, and councillor of state, 1863.

GEORGE I., King of the Hellenes, b. Dec. 24, 1845, the second son of Prince Christian of Schleswig-Holstein-Sonderburg-Glücksburg ; elected King of the Hellenes by the National Assembly at Athens, March 18 (30), 1863 ; accepted the crown, through his father and the King of Denmark, acting as his guardians, June 4, 1863 ; declared of age by decree of the National Assembly, June 27, 1863 ; landed in Greece, Nov. 2, 1863.

GEORGE II., Duke of Saxe-Meiningen, b. April 2, 1826, the son of Duke Bernhard I. ; succeeded, on the abdication of his father, Sept. 20, 1866 ; married, May 18, 1850, to Princess Charlotte of Prussia, who died March 30, 1855 ; married again, Oct. 23, 1858, to Princess Theodora of Hohenlohe-Langenburg, b. July 7, 1839.

GEORGE Victor, Prince of Waldeck, b. Jan. 14, 1831, the son of Prince Georg Friederich and Princess Emma of Anhalt-Bernburg ; succeeded to the throne at the death of his father, under the guardianship of his mother, May 14, 1845 ; married, Sept. 26, 1853, to Helena, b. Aug. 12, 1831, daughter of the late Duke of Nassau.

GEORGE, John, English politician, b. 1804 ; educated at Trinity College, Dublin, where he graduated B.A. 1822, M.A. 1824 ; called to the Irish bar, 1826 ; to the English bar, 1828 ; magistrate of the county of Wexford ; formerly crown-prosecutor for the Leinster circuit ; solicitor-general for Ireland, 1858–59 ; M.P. for county of Wexford, 1852–57, and 1859–68.

GERLACH, Georg Daniel, Danish general, b. at Eckernforde, Schleswig, Aug. 31, 1798 ; entered the army as ensign, 1813 ; major, 1848 ; lieutenant-colonel, 1849 ; colonel, 1850 ; major-general, 1854 ; lieutenant-general, 1863 ; chief of the Danish army, 1864.

GERMINY, Charles Gabriel Le Be'gue, Comte de, French statesman, b. at Cliponville, Seine Inférieure, Nov. 3, 1799 ; minister of finance, 1848 ; governor of the Bank of France, 1857–63 ; vice-president of the General Council of the Seine Inférieure.

GE'ROME, Jean Le'on, French painter, b. at Vesoul, Haute-Saône, May 11, 1824 ; studied in Paris, 1841, under Paul Delaroche, and at the École des Beaux Arts ; appointed professor of painting to the École des Beaux Arts, 1863. Exhibited 'Bacchus et l'Amour,' 1848 ; 'Phryne,' 'Cléopatre,' 1863 ; and numerous other paintings.

GERSTAECKER, Friedrich, German traveller and author, b. at Hamburg, May 16, 1816. Author of 'Streif-und Jagdzüge durch die Vereinigten Staaten von Nordamerica,' Dresden, 1844 ; 'Pirates of the Mississippi,' 1858 ; 'A Wife to Order,' 1860 ; and other works of travel and fiction.

GERVINUS, Georg Gottfried, German historian and critic, b. at Darmstadt, May 20, 1805 ; studied at Heidelberg, 1826 ; professor of German literature at the University of Göttingen. Author of 'A History of Europe since 1815 ;' 'History of German Poetry,' Leipsic, 1853 ; treatises on Shakspeare and Handel ; and other works.

GESNER, Abraham, American geologist, b. at Cornwallis, Nova Scotia. Author of 'On the Mineralogy and Geology of Nova Scotia ;' 'On the Industrial Resources of Nova Scotia ;' and other geological works.

GETTY, Samuel Gibson, English politician, b. 1817 ; a magistrate of the county of Antrim ; was mayor of Belfast, 1856–58 ; M.P. for Belfast, 1860–68.

GIBSON, Right Hon. Thomas Milner, English statesman, b. at Trinidad, 1807, the son of Major T. Milner Gibson ; educated at Trinity College, Cambridge ; vice-president of the Board of Trade from July 1846 to May 1848 ; president of the Poor Law Board, 1859 ; sat for Ipswich from July 1837 to July 1839 ; and for Manchester from 1841 till 1857 ; M.P. for Ashton, 1857–68 ; president of the Board of Trade, 1859–66.

GIBSON, William Sidney, English antiquarian, b. at Fulham, 1815 ; called to the bar of Lincoln's Inn, 1845 ; appointed registrar of the Court of Bankruptcy, 1852. Author of 'The History of Tynemouth,' and other historical and antiquarian works.

GILBERT, Jacques Emile, French architect, b. in Paris, Sept. 3, 1793 ; entered the École Polytechnique, 1811 ; and the École des Beaux Arts, 1813 ; directed the construction of the Hôtel de la Préfecture de Police, 1856, and numerous other public buildings ; elected member of the French Académie des Beaux Arts, 1853.

GILBERT, John, English artist, b. at Blackheath, Kent, 1817. Exhibited paintings *in water-colour of 'Don Quixote giving Advice to Sancho Panza,' 1841 ; 'Peace and War,' 1852. Draftsman on wood for the Illustrated London News, the British Workman, and numerous other illustrated works.*

GILBERT, William, English novelist. Author of 'Shirley Hall Asylum;' 'Dr. Austin's Guests,' 'Life of Lucrezia Borgia;' and many other works.

GILES, Rev. John Allen, English author, b. 1802; educated at Corpus Christi College, Oxford, where he graduated B.A. 1824; appointed head master of the City of London School, 1836; resigned, 1840. Author of 'Life and Times of Alfred the Great;' 'History of the Ancient Britons;' and other historical works.

GILPILLAN, Rev. George, English author and critic, b. at Comrie, Scotland, 1813; appointed minister of the Schoolwynd Church at Dundee, 1837. Author of 'A Gallery of Literary Portraits;' 'The History of a Man,' 1856; 'Alpha and Omega,' 1860; and other works of miscellaneous literature.

GILLIES, Margaret, English artist, b. in Scotland, 1803; studied under Frederick Cruikshank and Henry Scheffer; elected lady member of the old Society of Painters in Water Colours, 1853; a constant contributor to the exhibitions of that institution.

GILLMORE, Quincy Adams, American military commander, b. in Loraine County, Ohio, 1825; admitted to the Academy of West Point, 1845, where he graduated, 1849; lieutenant, 1849; captain on the outbreak of civil war, 1861; brigadier-general and major-general, 1863.

GILPIN, Charles, English politician, b. at Bristol, 1815; educated for a mercantile career, and became member of the Common Council of London; secretary of the Poor Law Board, 1859-65; M.P. for Northampton since 1857.

GILPIN, Richard Thomas, English politician, b. 1801; educated at Rugby, and Christ's College, Cambridge; colonel of the Beds Militia; deputy-lieutenant and magistrate of Beds and Bucks; M.P. for Bedfordshire since 1851.

GIL Y ZARATE, Antonio, Spanish dramatic poet, b. Dec. 1, 1793; member of the Spanish Academy. Author of 'Un Año despues de la Boda,' played at Madrid, 1825; 'Don Pedro de Portugal,' 1828; 'Rosmunda,' 1840; and numerous other works.

GIRARDET, Karl, French painter, b. at Locle, Neufchâtel, May 13, 1810. Painted 'Le Mont Righi;' 'Le Retour du Soldat,' 1850; 'Vue prise dans les Landes de Gascogne,' 1864; and numerous other landscapes.

GIRARDIN, Emile de, French journalist, b. in Switzerland, 1806. Author of 'Emile,' 1827; 'Au Hasard,' 1828; founded La Presse, 1836; member of the Chamber of Deputies, 1834-48; retired from the direction of La Presse, 1856; subsequently established La Liberté.

GIRARDIN, Jean Pierre Louis, French chemist, b. in Paris, Nov. 16, 1803; correspondent of the Académie des Sciences de l'Institut. Author of 'Éléments de Minéralogie appliquée aux Sciences chimiques,' Paris, 1826; 'Leçons de Chimie élémentaire faites le Dimanche à l'École municipale de Rouen,' ib. 1860; and many other works on chemistry.

GIRAUD, Charles Joseph Barthelemy, French legal writer, b. at Pernes, Vaucluse, Feb. 20, 1802; studied law at Aix; vice-rector of the Académie de Paris, 1845 to Feb. 25, 1848; appointed inspector-general of the Order of Advocates, 1861. Author of 'Essai sur l'Histoire du Droit Français au Moyen Age,' 1845; and other legal works.

GIRAUD, Pierre François Eugene, French painter, b. at Paris, Aug. 9, 1806; entered the Ecole des Beaux Arts, 1821. Exhibited 'Les Enrôlements Volontaires,' 1835; 'Incendie à Constantinople,' 1853; 'Debordement du Nil,' 1863; and many other paintings.

GIRDLESTONE, Rev. Charles, English author, b. March 6, 1797; educated at Wadham College, Oxford, where he graduated B.A. 1818, and M.A.; vicar of Sedgley, Staffordshire, 1826-47; rector of Kingswinford, Staffordshire, 1847. Author of 'Family Commentary on the Bible,' 1832-42; and other religious works.

GLADSTONE, Right Hon. William Ewart, English statesman, b. at Liverpool, Dec. 29, 1809, the fourth son of Sir John Gladstone, Bart., a Liverpool merchant; educated at Eton, and at Christ Church, Oxford; a lord of the Treasury, Dec. 1834; under-secretary for the Colonial Department, Jan. 1835 to April 1835; vice-president of the Board of Trade and master of the Mint from Sept. 1841 to May 1843; president of the Board of Trade, May 1843 to Feb. 1845; secretary of state for the colonies, July 1846; chancellor of the Exchequer in Lord Aberdeen's ministry, Dec. 28, 1852; resigned with the Aberdeen ministry, Jan. 30, 1855; accepted the same office under Lord Palmerston, Feb. 5, but resigned, Feb. 21, 1855; M.P. for Newark, 1832-45; chancellor of the Exchequer, June 18, 1859, to July 5, 1866; M.P. for South Lancashire, 1865-68; returned M.P. for Greenwich, Nov. 1868; appointed first lord of the Treasury, Dec. 8, 1868. Author of 'The Church considered in its relation with the State,' 1840; and several other political treatises.

GLADSTONE, William Henry, English politician, b. 1840; educated at Eton, and Christ Church, Oxford, where he graduated B.A. 1862, M.A. 1865; deputy-lieutenant of the county of Flint; M.P. for Chester, 1865–68, for Whitby, 1868..

GLAIRE, l'Abbe' Jean Baptiste, French theologian, b. at Bordeaux, April 1, 1798; studied at St. Sulpice; entered holy orders, 1822; appointed to the chapter of Notre Dame de Paris, 1840; nominated councillor of the University, 1845. Author of 'Lexicon manuale Hebraïcum et Chaldaïcum,' 1830; 'Concordances Arabes du Coran;' 'Principes de Grammaire Arabe,' 1857 and 1861; and other theological and philological works.

GLAIS-BIZOIN, Alexander, French politician, b. at Quintin, Côtes du Nord, March 9, 1800; was called to the bar, 1822; member of the Corps Législatif for the department of Côtes du Nord, 1863.

GLASGOW, James Carr Boyle, Earl of, English administrator, b. 1792: studied at Oxford; was lieutenant R.N.; lord-lieutenant and principal sheriff of Renfrewshire; a deputy-lieutenant of the county of Bute; was M.P. for Ayrshire, as Lord Kilburn, 1839 to 1843, when he succeeded his father.

GLASS, Sir Richard Atwood, English politician, b. 1820; educated at King's College, London; created baronet for his services in laying the Atlantic Telegraph, 1866; returned M.P. for Bewdley, 1868, unseated, 1869.

GLEIG, Rev. George Robert, English author, b. at Stirling, April 20, 1796; educated at Glasgow, and Balliol College, Oxford; obtained a commission, 1812; joined the army of the Duke of Wellington, 1813; entered holy orders, and became rector of Ivychurch, Kent, 1822; prebendary of St. Paul's; chaplain-general of the forces. Author of 'The Subaltern,' 1825; 'The Life of the Duke of Wellington;' and numerous other works.

GLOCKER, Ernst Friedrich, German mineralogist, b. at Stuttgart, May 1, 1793; studied theology at Tübingen, and was ordained, 1815; studied botany and mineralogy at Halle and Berlin; professor of mineralogy at Breslau. Author of 'Charakteristik der schlesischen mineralogischen Literatur,' Breslau, 1827–32; 'Ueber die Geschiebe der Oderebene,' 1854; and numerous other scientific works.

GLOUCESTER AND BRISTOL, Right Rev. Charles John Ellicott, Bishop of, English divine, b. at Whitwell, 1819; educated at St. John's College, Cambridge, where he graduated, 1841; appointed professor of divinity in King's College, London, 1858; dean of Exeter, 1861; consecrated to the see of Gloucester and Bristol, 1863. Author of 'Critical and Grammatical Commentaries;' and other theological works.

GLYN, George Carr, English politician, b. 1797; educated at Westminster; a commissioner of lieutenancy for London; M.P. for Kendal, 1846–68.

GLYN, George Grenfell, English statesman, b. 1824; educated at Rugby, and University College, Oxford; appointed joint-secretary of the Treasury, Dec. 1868; M.P. for Shaftesbury since 1857.

GLYN, Isabella, English actress, b. at Edinburgh, May 22, 1823; first appeared on the stage in 1847; married to Mr. E. Dallas.

GOBAT, Samuel, German missionary, b. at Cremme, canton of Berne, 1799; went as missionary to Abyssinia, 1825; vice-principal of Malta Protestant College; consecrated missionary bishop of Jerusalem, 1846, on the nomination of the King of Prussia. Author of 'A Journal of Three Years in Abyssinia,' 1847.

GODARD DESMARETS, Hippolyte, French politician, b. at Paris, Oct. 8, 1796; member of the General Council for the canton of Trélon; member of the Corps Législatif for the departement du Nord since 1853.

GODDARD, Ambrose Lethbridge, English politician, b. 1819; educated at Harrow, and St. John's College, Cambridge; deputy-lieutenant of Wilts, and captain of Wilts Yeomanry; M.P. for Cricklade, 1847–68.

GODDARD, Arabella, English pianist, b. at St. Servan, near St. Malo, Brittany, Jan. 1836; studied under Kalkbrenner and Thalberg, and G. A. Macfarren; made her début at the National Concerts, Oct. 1850; married to Mr. Davidson, musical critic, 1860.

GODKIN, James, English writer, b. at Gorey, county of Wexford, 1806; minister of a dissenting congregation at Armagh, 1834; was editor of the *Christian Patriot*, the *Londonderry Standard*, and *Dublin Daily Express,* for several years; Irish correspondent of the *Times* since 1860. Author of 'The Outcast; a Story of the Modern Reformation;' 'Illustrated History of England from 1820 to 1852;' and other works.

GODWIN, George, English architect, b. at Brompton, Middlesex, Jan. 28, 1815; *designed* St. Mary's Church, West Brompton; and restored Redcliff Church, Bristol. *Author of 'Churches of London,' 1838; 'History in Ruins,' 1853; 'London Shadows,' 1854; and numerous other works* on architecture.

GODWIN, Parke, American journalist, b. at Paterson, New Jersey, Feb. 25, 1816; took his degrees at the College of Princetown, 1834, and studied law; was one of the principal editors of the New York *Evening Post*, 1837 to 1853. Author of 'Political Essays,' 1856; and other works.

GOERGEI, Arthur, Hungarian general and statesman, b. at Toporcz, in the comitat of Zips, Upper Hungary, Feb. 5, 1818; admitted as cadet to the School of Pioneers at Tulu, 1832; lieutenant, 1842; captain, 1844; took part in the Revolution of 1848; dictator of Hungary, Aug. 11, 1849. Published 'My Life and Acts in Hungary in the Years 1848 and 1849,' Leipsic, 1852.

GOLDNEY, Gabriel, English politician, b. 1813; a magistrate of Wilts, and governor of Christ's Hospital; was formerly a solicitor; M.P. for Chippenham since 1865.

GOLDSCHMIDT, Hermann, German astronomer and painter, b. at Frankfort, June 17, 1802; studied painting at Munich, under Schnorr and Cornelius. Painted 'A Woman in Algerine Costume,' 1836; 'The Deaths of Romeo and Juliet,' 1857. Engaged in constant astronomical observations, and discovered seven planets.

GOLDSCHMIDT, Madame, Swedish singer, b. at Stockholm, Oct. 21, 1821; studied under Croelius and Garcia; first appeared in London as **Jenny Lind,** May 1847; visited the United States, 1850; married to M. Otto Goldschmidt, and retired from the stage, 1851; reappeared for a short time in 1855, 1861, 1863, and 1864.

GOLDSCHMIDT, Meyer Aaron, Danish novelist, b. at Vordingbord, Jutland, Oct. 26, 1819; founded the *Corsair* at Copenhagen, 1840. Published, under the name of Adolph Meyer, 'A Jew,' 1845; 'The Homeless One,' 1853–57; and other works of fiction.

GOLDSMID, Sir Francis Henry, English politician, b. 1808; called to the bar of Lincoln's Inn, 1833; J.P. and deputy-lieutenant of Berks, and a baron of the kingdom of Portugal; M.P. for Reading since 1860.

GOLDSMID, Frederick David, English politician, b. 1812; educated at University College, London; a magistrate of Kent; M.P. for Honiton, 1865–68.

GOLOVIN, Ivan, Prince Hovna, Russian author, b. 1813; exiled from Russia on political grounds, and took refuge in England, 1843. Author of 'The Caucasus, from an Historical, Political, and Physical Point of View,' 1853; 'History of Alexander I.' 1858; 'Progress in Russia,' 1859; and other political works.

GOLOWINE, Eugene Alexandrowitch, Russian general and statesman, b. 1795; lieutenant-general, 1831; governor-general of the provinces of the Baltic, 1845; appointed minister of public instruction, Dec. 20, 1862.

GOMM, Sir William Maynard, English military commander, b. 1784; entered the army as ensign, 1798; served in Holland and the Peninsula; was quartermaster-general at Waterloo, and created K.C.B.; appointed governor and commander-in-chief of the Mauritius, 1842; commander-in-chief of India, 1850; retired, 1855; appointed colonel in the Coldstream Guards, 1863.

GONDRECOURT, Henri Ange Alfred de, French novelist, b. at Guadaloupe, March 22, 1816; entered the Military School of St. Cyr, 1832, and fought in Africa; lieutenant-colonel, 1855; colonel, 1859. Author of 'Médine,' 1845; 'Le Pays de la Soif,' 1864; and many other romances.

GONZALES, Louis Jean Emmanuel, French writer, b. at Saintes, Oct. 25, 1815. Author of 'Les Chercheurs d'Or,' 1857; 'Les Trois Fiancées,' 1864; and numerous other works; also contributor to a great number of French periodicals.

GOOCH, Sir Daniel, English politician, b. 1818; studied engineering, and took a leading part in laying the Atlantic telegraph; created baronet, 1866; M.P. for Cricklade since 1865.

GOODALL, Frederick, English painter, b. in London, Sept. 17, 1822, son of the preceding. Painted 'French Soldiers Drinking at a Cabaret,' 1839; 'Village Festival,' 1847; 'Raising the Maypole,' 1851; 'The Swing,' 1854; and many others. Elected A.R.A. 1852, and R.A. 1863.

GOODFORD, Rev. Charles Old, English divine, b. 1812; educated on the foundation at Eton, and at King's College, Cambridge; was assistant master at Eton; appointed head master, 1853; provost of Eton, 1862.

GOODSON, James, English politician, b. 1810; called to the bar of Gray's Inn, 1855; a magistrate of Middlesex and Westminster; M.P. for Great Yarmouth, 1865–68.

GOODWIN, Charles Wycliffe, English author, b. at King's Lynn, 1817; educated at St. Catherine's College, Cambridge, where he graduated B.A. 1838; called to the bar of Lincoln's Inn, 1848. Author of 'Hieratic Papyri,' 1858; 'The Mosaic Cosmogony,' published in the 'Essays and Reviews;' and editor of Anglo-Saxon and Greek works.

GOODWIN, Very Rev. Harvey, English author, b. at King's Lynn, Norfolk, 1818; entered Caius College, Cambridge, 1836, and graduated, 1840; incumbent of St. Edward's Church, Cambridge, from 1848 to 1858; dean of Ely. Author of 'Lectures on the Church Catechism;' 'Problems and Solutions in Mathematics;' and other works.

GORE, John Ralph Ormsby, English politician, b. 1816; educated at Eton, and Christ Church, Oxford; J.P. and deputy-lieutenant of the counties of Salop and Carnarvon; late groom-in-waiting to the Queen; M.P. for county of Carnarvon, 1837–41, and for North Shropshire since 1859.

GORE, William Richard Ormsby, English politician, b. 1819; educated at Eton; deputy-lieutenant of Salop, and a magistrate of Sligo; was captain in the 13th Light Dragoons; M.P. for County Sligo, 1841–52, and for County Leitrim since 1858.

GORE-LANGTON, William Henry Powell, English politician, b. 1824; educated at Eton, and Christ Church, Oxford, where he graduated B.A. 1845, M.A. 1848; magistrate and deputy-lieutenant of Somerset; M.P. for West Somerset, 1851–59, and since 1863.

GORSE, Joseph Augustin, Baron, French general, b. Sept. 20, 1784; entered the École Polytechnique, 1802; captain in the army, 1810; lieutenant-colonel, 1825; general, 1841; member of the Corps Législatif for the department of Tarn since 1863.

GORTSCHAKOFF, Alexander Michaelovich, Russian statesman, b. 1798; educated at the Lyceum of Zarskoe-Selo; entered the diplomatic service, 1818; secretary of embassy at London, 1824; minister at Florence, 1830; plenipotentiary at Vienna, 1832; ambassador-extraordinary at Stuttgart, 1841; ambassador at Vienna, 1854; appointed minister of foreign affairs, and chancellor of the empire, April 17, 1856.

GÖSCHEN, Right Hon. George Joachim, English statesman, b. 1831; educated at Rugby, and Oriel College, Oxford; a deputy-lieutenant of London, and late director of the Bank of England: vice-president of the Board of Trade, 1865–66; chancellor of the Duchy of Lancaster, Feb. to July 1866; appointed president of the Poor Law Board, Dec. 9, 1868; M.P. for the city of London since 1863.

GOSS, John, English musical composer, b. at Fareham, Hants, 1800; appointed organist of St. Paul's, April 1838. Composed the anthem, 'If we believe;' and numerous glees and other musical pieces, chiefly sacred.

GOSSE, Louis François Nicolas, French painter, b. in Paris, Oct. 4, 1787; entered the École des Beaux Arts, 1805, and studied under André Vincent. Exhibited 'Ex Voto,' 1808; 'La Mort de Saint Vincent de Paul,' 1845; and other paintings.

GOSSE, Philip Henry, English naturalist, b. at Worcester, 1810. Author of 'The Canadian Naturalist,' 1840; 'A Naturalist's Sojourn in Jamaica;' 'A Naturalist's Rambles on the Devonshire Coast;' 'Actinologia Britannica : a History of the British Sea Anemones and Corals,' 1860; and other works on natural history.

GOUGH, Hugh Gough, Viscount, English military commander, b. 1779; entered the army, 1791; commanded the 87th regiment through the Peninsular war; commanded the expeditionary force in China, and concluded a peace with that country; commanded the army of India in the Gwalior, Sutlej, and Punjaub campaigns; field-marshal in the army.

GOUGH, John, English lecturer, b. at Sandgate, Kent, 1817. Travelled through the Northern and Southern States of America, Canada, and England, lecturing on temperance. Published his 'Autobiography' and 'Orations,' 1855.

GOUIN, Alexandre, French politician, b. at Tours, Jan. 26, 1792; elected deputy for the department of Indre-et-Loire, 1831; minister of commerce, 1840–44; elected to the Constituent Assembly, 1848; member of the Legislative Assembly, and of the Corps Législatif for the department of Indre-et-Loire since 1852.

GOULBURN, Rev. Edward Meyrick, English divine, b. 1818; educated at Eton, and Balliol College, Oxford, where he graduated B.A. 1839; appointed head master of Rugby School, 1848; minister of Quebec Chapel and prebendary of St. Paul's, 1858; one of the Queen's chaplains in ordinary, and incumbent of St. John's, Paddington, 1859; *dean of* Norwich.

GOULD, Edward, American writer, b. at Lichfield, Connecticut, May 11, 1808. Published an abridgment of Alison's 'History of Europe,' New York, 1845; 'The Very Age;' ib. 1850; and numerous translations from French authors.

GOULD, John, English ornithologist, b. at Lyme, Dorset, Sept. 14, 1809. Author of 'A Century of Birds from the Himalaya Mountains,' 1838; 'The Birds of Australia;' 'Mammals of Australia;' 'Monograph of the Trochilidæ of Humming Birds;' and numerous other works on ornithology.

GOULHOT DE SAINT GERMAIN, Achille Felicite' de, French politician, b. at Paris, March 27, 1809; entered the army, and was captain, staff-major, and officer of ordnance to Marshal Oudinot; sub-prefect of Romorantin, 1835; and of Bernay, 1838; appointed senator, Jan. 25, 1852.

GOUNOD, Charles François, French musical composer, b. at Paris, June 17, 1818; studied under Reicha, Lesneur, and M. Halévy.   Composed 'Sapho,' 1850; 'La Nonne Sanglante,' 1854; 'Faust,' 1859; 'La Reine de Saba,' 1862; and many other operas.

GOURLEY, Edward Temperley, b. 1828; shipowner of Sunderland, and proprietor of the Maltese Cross line of steamers; elected M.P. for Sunderland, 1868.

GOUSSET, Thomas Marie Joseph, French divine, b. at Montigny les Cherlieux, Haute-Saône, May 1, 1792; studied in the School of Amance, near Vesoul; ordained, 1817; appointed bishop of Perigeux, Oct. 6, 1835; vicar-general of Besançon, 1830; archbishop of Rheims, May 26, 1840; cardinal, Sept. 30, 1850.

GOWER, Hon. Edward Frederick Leveson, English politician, b. 1819; educated at Eton, and Christ Church, Oxford, where he graduated B.A. 1840, M.A. 1844; called to the bar, 1845; J.P. and deputy-lieutenant of Staffordshire; M.P. for Derby, 1847, for Stoke, 1851–57, for Bodmin since 1859.

GOYON, Charles Marie Auguste, Comte de, French general, b. Nov. 19, 1802; studied at the Military School of St. Cyr; became lieutenant, 1821; captain, 1831; major, 1839; lieutenant-colonel, 1843; colonel, 1846; brigadier-general, 1850; general of division, 1853; charged with the command of the division of occupation at Rome, 1859; and received the title of general-in-chief of the French in Rome, 1861; recalled and created a senator, 1862.

GOZLAN, Le'on, French writer, b. at Marseilles, Sept. 21, 1806.   Author of 'Les Mémoires d'un Apothicaire,' 1828; 'Le Notaire de Chantilly,' 1836; 'Aristide Froissard,' 1843; 'Pluie et le Beau Temps,' 'Le Diamant et le Verre,' 1861; and numerous novels, romances, and dramas.

GRABOW, Johann, German politician, b. at Prenzlau, Prussia, April 15, 1802; studied law at Berlin, and was burgomaster of his native town; elected deputy to the Prussian Diet, 1847; and to the National Assembly for the town of Prenzlau, 1848; elected president of the Prussian Chamber of Deputies, 1849, and again 1861.

GRAEPE, Heinrich, German politician, b. at Buttstadt, March 3, 1802; studied at Weimar and at the University of Jena; director of the Municipal School of Jena, 1825; professor at the University of Jena, 1840; deputy to the German National Assembly, 1849.   Author of 'Der Verfassungskampf in Kurhessen,' Leipsic, 1851; and of several educational works.

GRAESSE, Johann Georg Theodor, German bibliographer, b. at Grimma, Jan. 31, 1814; studied at Leipsic, Halle, and Dresden; appointed librarian to the King of Saxony, 1843; inspector of the Royal Numismatic Cabinet, 1848.   Author of 'Lehrbuch einer allgemeinen Literaturgeschichte,' Dresden and Leipsic, 1837 to 1855; 'Handbuch der alten Numismatik,' ib. 1852; and numerous other works.

GRAFSTROEM, Andrew Abraham, Swedish poet, b. at Sundswall, 1790; took the degree of Ph.D. from the University of Upsal, 1815; was ordained, 1830; appointed pastor of Umea, 1835; dean of the district, 1837.   Author of 'Skaldeförsök,' Stockholm 1826–32; 'Sanger frau Norrland,' 1848; and other poetical works.

GRAFTON, William Henry Fitzroy, Duke of, b. Aug. 4, 1819; educated at Harrow; was attaché to the British Legation at Naples, 1841; M.P. for Thetford, 1847 to 1863; is deputy-lieutenant and magistrate of Northamptonshire, and magistrate of Suffolk; succeeded his father, 1863.

GRAHAM, Sir Frederick Ulrick, English diplomatist, b. 1820; attaché to the British Embassy at Vienna, 1842; deputy-lieutenant of Cumberland, 1856; succeeded his brother, 1861.

GRAHAM, Thomas, English chemist, b. at Glasgow, Dec. 20, 1805; educated at the Grammar School and the University of Glasgow, where he graduated M.A. 1826; appointed professor of chemistry at the London University, 1837; master of the Mint, 1855.   Author of 'Elements of Chemistry,' and other works.

GRAHAM, William, English politician, b. 1817 ; educated at the University of Glasgow ; a magistrate for the county of Lanark; merchant at Glasgow ; M.P. for Glasgow since 1865.

GRAHAMSTOWN, Right Rev. Henry Cotterill, Bishop of, English divine, b. 1812 ; educated at St. John's College, Cambridge, where he graduated, 1835 ; principal of Brighton College ; consecrated to the see of Grahamstown, South Africa, 1859. Author of 'The Seven Ages of the Church,' and other theological works.

GRAMMONT, Ferdinand, Marquis de, French politician, b. at Villersexel, June 6, 1805 ; was deputy for the arrondisement of Lure, 1837 ; elected for the Haute-Saône, 1848; member of the Corps Législatif for the department of Haute-Saône since 1852.

GRAMONT, Antoine Age'nor Alfred, Duc de, French diplomatist, b. at Paris, Aug. 14, 1819 ; entered the École Polytechnique, 1837 ; minister plenipotentiary to Cassel, and Stuttgart, 1852 ; to Turin, April 1853 ; ambassador to Rome, 1857 to 1861 ; ambassador to Austria, 1861–66.

GRANARD, George Arthur Hastings Forbes, Earl of, English administrator, b. 1833 ; was attaché at Dresden, 1852 to 1854 ; lord-lieutenant of the county of Leitrim ; succeeded to the earldom, 1837.

GRANIER DE CASSAGNAC, Adolphe de, French writer and politician, b. at Cassagnac, Gers, 1808 ; educated at the Lyceum of Toulouse ; contributor to the *Journal des Débats* and the *Revue de Paris*, 1832 to 1850, when he joined the *Constitutionnel* ; member of the Corps Législatif for the department of Gers since 1852. Author of 'Histoire des Classes ouvrières et des Classes bourgeoises,' 1837 ; and numerous other works.

GRANT, Albert, English politician, b. at Dublin, 1830 ; educated in London and Paris ; assumed the name of Grant in lieu of Gottheimer, 1863 ; M.P. for Kidderminster, 1865–68.

GRANT, Sir Francis, English painter, president of the Royal Academy, b. 1803. Exhibited 'Meet of his Majesty's Staghounds,' 1837; the 'Melton Hunt;' and many others, especially portraits of celebrated persons. Elected A.R.A. 1842, R.A. 1851, P.R.A. 1867.

GRANT, Hon. James, English politician, b. 1817 ; magistrate for Banff, Elgin, and Inverness ; elected M.P. for Elgin and Nairnshire, 1868.

GRANT, James, English journalist, b. at Elgin, Morayshire, 1805 ; editor of the *Morning Advertiser* since 1850. Author of 'Random Recollections of the House of Lords ;' 'The Bench and the Bar;' 'Our Heavenly Home ;' 'The End of all Things,' 1866 ; and numerous other works.

GRANT, James, English novelist, b. at Edinburgh, Aug. 1, 1822 ; ensign in the 62d Foot, 1839. Author of 'The Romance of War, or Highlanders in Spain,' 1846 ; 'Philip Rollo, or the Scottish Musketeers,' 1854 ; 'Mary of Lorraine,' 1860 ; 'Second to None,' 1864 ; and many other works of fiction.

GRANT, James Augustus, English traveller, b. at Nairn, 1827 ; educated at the Grammar School and Marischal College, Aberdeen ; appointed to the Indian army, 1845 ; took part in the relief of Lucknow under Gen. Havelock, where he was wounded, 1857 ; explored the sources of the Nile with the late Captain Speke, 1863–65.

GRANT, Sir Alexander, English author, b. 1826 ; educated at Harrow, and Balliol College, Oxford ; elected fellow of Oriel College, 1849 ; appointed one of the examiners for the Indian Civil Service appointments, 1855 ; inspector of schools in Madras presidency, 1858 ; professor of history and political economy in Elphinstone College, Madras, 1860. Author of 'The Ethics of Aristotle with English Notes,' 1854.

GRANT, Sir James Hope, English military commander, b. 1808 ; entered the army, 1826 ; served in China and India ; became brevet-colonel, 1854 ; served in India through the Mutiny of 1857–58 ; appointed to the command of the military forces during the war with China, 1860 ; appointed commander-in-chief and governor of Madras, Dec. 1861.

GRANT, Sir John Peter, English colonial administrator, b. 1808; entered the East India service, 1826 ; was lieutenant-governor of Bengal during the Indian Mutiny of 1857–59 ; K.C.B. civil division, 1862 ; governor of Jamaica, 1867.

GRANT, Sir Patrick, English officer, b. 1804 ; entered the military service of the East India Company, 1819 ; served on the staff in India ; was made C.B. for services at Sobraon ; appointed commander-in-chief of the Madras army, 1856 ; K.C.B. and aide-de-camp to the Queen.

GRANT, Ulysses Simpson, American general and statesman, b. at Point Pleasant, Ohio, April 27, 1822 ; entered at West Point, 1839 ; graduated with the brevet of lieutenant, June 30, 1843 ; first lieutenant, 1847 ; captain, Aug. 1853 ; resigned, 1854 ; took part with the North in the civil war; appointed brigadier-general, July 1861; commander-in-chief of the U.S. army, 1864; secretary of war, Aug. 1867 to Feb. 1868; elected President of the United States, Nov. 1868.

GRANTLEY, Fletcher Norton, Baron, English officer, b. 1798; served for some years in the Guards, and was wounded at Waterloo; succeeded to the title, 1822.

GRANVILLE, George Leveson Gower, Earl, English statesman, b. 1815; educated at Eton, and Christ Church, Oxford, where he graduated in 1834; attaché to the Embassy at Paris, 1835; M.P. for Morpeth, 1836–40, and for Lichfield, 1840–46, when he succeeded to the peerage; under-secretary of state for foreign affairs, 1840; vice-president of the Board of Trade, 1848; secretary of state for foreign affairs, Dec. 1851 to March 1852; lord president of the council, Dec. 21, 1852; resigned, April 1854; reappointed, Feb. 5, 1855; resigned, Feb. 1858; reappointed, June 1859, and resigned, July, 1866; appointed secretary of state for the colonies, May 9, 1868.

GRATTAN, Thomas Colley, Irish novelist, b. at Dublin, 1796; entered the army, and fought at the battle of Waterloo. Author of 'Highways and Byways,' London, 1827; 'Legends of the Rhine,' 1837; 'History of the Netherlands;' and numerous other works of fiction.

GRAVES, Samuel Robert, English politician, b. 1818; member of the Royal Commission of Lights, Buoys, and Beacons, and commodore of the Royal Mersey Yacht Club; mayor of Liverpool, 1860; M.P. for Liverpool since 1865.

GRAY, Asa, American botanist, b. at Paris, Oneida County, New York, Nov. 1810; graduated at Fairfield College, 1831; appointed professor of natural history at Cambridge, Massachusetts, 1842. Author of 'Elements of Botany,' 1836; 'Botany of the United States;' 'Pacific Exploring Expedition under Captain Wilkes,' 1854; and other works on botany.

GRAY, George Robert, English ornithologist, b. 1808; entered the Zoological department of the British Museum, 1831. Author of 'A List of the Genera of Birds,' 1840; 'The Genera of Birds,' 1837–49; and other works.

GRAY, John Edward, English naturalist, b. at Walsall, 1800, brother of the preceding; appointed assistant to the natural history department of the British Museum, 1824; keeper of the zoological collection, 1840. Author of 'Illustrations of Indian Zoology;' 'A Manual of British Land and Freshwater Shells;' and other works.

GRAY, Sir John, English politician, b. 1815; educated at Trinity College, Dublin; called to the Irish bar, and appointed magistrate of the city of Dublin; M.P. for Kilkenny since 1865. Editor and proprietor of the *Freeman's Journal*.

GRAY, William, English politician, b. 1814; J.P. and deputy-lieutenant of Lancashire, and manufacturer near Bolton; mayor of Bolton, 1850–52; M.P. for Bolton since 1857.

GRAY, Wilson, English administrator, b. 1815; educated at University College, Dublin; appointed one of the assistant commissioners of the Irish Poor Laws, 1835; called to the bar in America, and to the Irish bar, 1844; member of the Colonial Legislature of Sydney, Australia.

GREAVES, Edward, English politician, b. 1803; banker at Warwick, and mayor of the borough, 1840; M.P. for Warwick since 1855.

GREELEY, Horace, American journalist, b. at Amherst, New Hampshire, Feb. 3, 1811; apprenticed to a printer, 1825 to 1830. Founded *The New Yorker*, 1834; the *New York Tribune*, 1841. Author of 'History of the Struggle for Slavery Extension or Restriction in the United States from 1787 to 1856;' and other works.

GREENALL, Gilbert, English politician, b. 1806; deputy-lieutenant of Lancashire; M.P. for Warrington, 1847–68.

GREENE, Edward, English politician, b. 1815; educated at Bury St. Edmunds' School; magistrate of Suffolk; M.P. for Bury St. Edmunds since 1865.

GREENE, George Washington, American writer, b. at Rhode Island, U.S. of America, April 8, 1811; educated at Brown University; was United States consul at Rome, 1837 to 1842; professor of modern languages at Brown University, 1847. Author of 'History and Geography of the Middle Ages,' and other works.

GREENE, Mary Anne Everett, English authoress, b. at Sheffield, 1818; married to Mr. George P. Greene, artist, 1845. Published 'Lives of the Princesses of England,' 1849–55; 'Letters of Queen Henrietta Maria,' 1857; and other biographical works.

GREEN-PRICE, Richard, English politician, b. 1803; educated at Eton; a J.P. and deputy-lieutenant of the county of Radnor; M.P. for Radnor, 1863–69.

GREENWELL, Dora, English authoress. Author of 'Christina, and other Poems,' 1848; 'Stories that might be True,' 1851; 'The Power of Faith exemplified in Life,' 1849; 'Two Friends,' 1862; and other works.

GREG, William Rathbone, political and miscellaneous writer, b. about 1810. Author of 'The Creed of Christendom, 1851; 'Literary and Social Judgments,' 1868; and other works. Head of the Stationery Office.

GREGORY, Charles Hutton, English civil engineer, b. 1817; appointed resident engineer of the London and Croydon Railway, 1840; chief engineer of the Bristol and Exeter Railway, 1846; appointed a member of the Ordnance Select Committee, 1855; president of the Institution of Civil Engineers.

GREGORY, George Barrow, English politician, b. 1813; educated at Eton, and Trinity College, Cambridge; elected M.P. for East Sussex, 1868.

GREGORY, William Henry, English politician, b. 1817; a magistrate and deputy-lieutenant of the county of Galway; M.P. for Dublin, 1842–47, and for County Galway since 1857.

GRENFELL, Henry Riversdale, English politician, b. 1824; educated at Harrow, and Christ Church, Oxford; a partner in the firm of P. Grenfell & Sons; was private secretary to Lord Panmure at the War Office, and to Sir Charles Wood at the India Office; M.P. for Stoke-on-Trent, 1862–68.

GRENVILLE, Ralph Neville, English politician, b. 1817; educated at Eton, and Magdalen College, Cambridge, where he graduated M.A. 1837; J.P. and deputy-lieutenant of Somerset; M.P. for Windsor, 1841–47; a lord of the Treasury, 1846–52; M.P. for East Somerset, 1865–68; returned M.P. for Mid Somerset, 1868.

GRESLEY, Rev. William, English writer, b. 1801; educated at Christ Church, Oxford, where he graduated B.A. 1822; ordained, 1823; appointed prebendary of Lichfield Cathedral, 1840; incumbent of a district church at Boyne Hill, near Maidenhead, 1857. Author of 'Bernard Leslie,' and several novels.

GRESWELL, Rev. Edward, English theologian, b. at Manchester, 1797; entered Brasenose College, Oxford, 1815; graduated at Corpus Christi. B.A. 1819. Author of 'Harmonia Evangelica;' 'Fasti Temporis Catholici;' 'Origines Kalendariæ Italicæ;' and other works.

GREVILLE, Algernon William Fulke, English politician, b. 1841; captain in the 1st Life Guards; M.P. for the county of Westmeath since 1865.

GREVILLE, Fulke Southwell, English politician, b. 1821; deputy-lieutenant of the county of Longford; vice-lieutenant of Westmeath, and colonel of Westmeath Militia; M.P. for county of Longford since 1852.

GREY, Hon. Charles, English general, b. 1804; educated at Cambridge; entered the army, 1821; major-general, 1854; lieutenant-general, 1861.

GREY, Right Hon. Sir Charles Edward, English colonial administrator, b. 1785; educated at University College, Oxford, where he graduated B.A. 1806; appointed commissioner in bankruptcy, 1817; judge at Madras, 1820; chief judge of Bengal, 1825; governor of Barbadoes, 1841–46; governor of Jamaica, 1846.

GREY, Hon. Frederick William, English naval commander, b. 1805; entered the royal navy; fought in China; admiral of the blue, 1855; vice-admiral of the red, 1863; a lord of the Admiralty, 1861.

GREY, Sir George, English colonial administrator, b. 1812; educated at Sandhurst College, and entered the army as ensign in the 83d regiment, 1830; lieutenant, 1833, and captain, 1839; left England in 1837 with instructions from Government to explore the north-west part of Australia, during 1837–39; appointed governor of South Australia, Dec. 1840; governor of New Zealand, 1846; governor of the Cape of Good Hope, 1854; again governor of New Zealand, 1861–67.

GREY, Right Hon. Sir George, English statesman, b. at Gibraltar, 1799, the eldest son of Sir George Grey, Bart., resident commissioner of Portsmouth Dockyard; studied jurisprudence, and was called to the bar of Lincoln's Inn, 1826; under-secretary of state for the colonies, July to Nov. 1834; judge-advocate-general, 1839, and chancellor of the Duchy of Lancaster, 1841; secretary of state for the Home Department, July 1846 to March 1852; secretary of state for the colonies, June 1854 to Jan. 1855; home secretary under Lord Palmerston, Feb. 1855 to Feb. 19, 1858; chancellor of the Duchy of Lancaster, June 1859; secretary of state for the Home Department, July 1861 to July 1866.

GREY, Right Hon. Henry George, Earl, English statesman, b. 1802; educated at Trinity College, Cambridge; M.P. for Winchelsea, 1826; for Higham Ferrars, 1830;

for Northumberland, 1831 to 1841 ; for Sunderland, 1841 to 1845, when he succeeded to the peerage ; was under-secretary for the colonies, Nov. 1830 to Mar. 1835 ; for the Home Department, Jan. to July 1834 ; secretary at war, April 1835 to Sept. 1839 ; secretary of state for the colonies, July 1846 to Feb. 1852 ; lord-lieutenant of Northumberland.

GRIDLEY, Henry Gillett, English politician, b. 1820 ; called to the bar of the Middle Temple, 1856 ; captain in the King's Own Light Infantry Regiment Militia ; M.P. for Weymouth, 1865–68.

GRIER, Robert Cooper, American judge, b. in Cumberland County, Pennsylvania, March 5, 1794 ; studied at Dickinson College ; called to the bar, 1817 ; appointed president judge of the district court of Alleghany County, 1838 ; one of the justices of the Supreme Court of the United States, 1848.

GRIESHEIM, Karl August Julian von, German politician, b. at Berlin, 1798 ; entered the army ; lieutenant in the Guards, and staff-major, 1824 to 1831 ; deputy to the Prussian National Assembly, 1848 ; elected to the Second Chamber, 1850 ; appointed military commander of Coblentz, and major-general, 1853. Author of ' Lebensfragen der Landwehr,' 1851 ; and other political works.

GRIEVE, James Johnston, English politician, b. 1810 ; magistrate for Renfrew-shire, and provost of Greenock, 1868 ; returned M.P. for Greenock, 1868.

GRIFFITH, Christopher Darby, English politician, b. 1805 ; educated at Eton, and Christ Church, Oxford, where he graduated B.A. 1826 ; J.P. and deputy-lieutenant of Berks ; M.P. for Devizes, 1857–68.

GRIFFITH, Sir Richard John, Bart., English civil engineer, b. in Dublin, 1784 ; appointed commissioner for the general valuation of land and tenements in Ireland, 1825 ; chairman of the Board of Public Works, 1851 ; created a baronet, 1858. Author of ' The Geological Map of Ireland.'

GRISI, Giulia, Italian singer, b. May 22, 1812 ; educated at a convent in Italy ; made her début in London, 1834 ; was prima donna of her Majesty's Theatre till 1846, and at the Royal Italian Opera, Covent Garden, till 1861 ; has been twice married, first to M. Gérard de Melcy in 1836, and secondly to Signor Mario.

GROS, Jean Baptiste Louis, Baron, French diplomatist, b. at Ivry-sur-Seine, Feb. 8, 1793 ; created a baron, 1829 ; was secretary of legation in Mexico, 1834 ; ambassador at Athens, 1850 ; minister to Spain, 1854 ; signed the Treaty of Bayonne, 1856 ; signed the Treaty of Tietsin, Canton, June 27, 1858 ; called to the French Senate, 1858 ; French ambassador to Great Britain, 1862–63.

GROSVENOR, Lupus, Earl, English politician, b. 1825, second son of the Marquis of Westminster ; educated at Eton, and Balliol College, Oxford ; magistrate of Cheshire ; M.P. for Chester since 1847.

GROSVENOR, Lord Richard de Aquila, English politician, b. 1837 ; educated at Westminster, and Trinity College, Cambridge, where he graduated M.A. 1858 ; a magis-trate of the counties of Flint and Dorset ; M.P. for Flintshire since 1861.

GROSVENOR, Hon. Robert Wellesley, English politician, b. 1834 ; educated at Harrow, and King's College, London ; captain in the 1st Life Guards ; M.P. for West-minster since 1865.

GROTE, George, English author, b. at Beckenham, Kent, 1794 ; educated at the Charterhouse ; M.P. for the City of London, 1832 to 1841. Author of ' The History of Greece,' 1846–56 ; ' Plato and the other Companions of Socrates,' 1864 ; and other historical works.

GROUCHY, Ernest Henri, Vicomte de, French politician, b. at Paris, Jan. 26, 1806 ; studied at the École Polytechnique ; sub-prefect at Cambrai, 1830 ; at Bayeux, 1832 ; at Montargis, 1833 ; prefect of Gers, Jan. 10, 1849 ; member of the Corps Législatif for the department of Loire since 1857.

GROVE, George, English author, b. at Clapham, Surrey, 1820 ; educated for the engineering profession ; charged with the erection of an iron lighthouse on Morant Point, Jamaica, 1841, and of a similar tower on Gibbs' Hill, Bermuda, 1844 ; secretary to Society of Arts from 1849 to 1852 ; appointed secretary to the Crystal Palace Company, 1852. Editor of *Macmillan's Magazine;* a leading contributor to the *Dictionary of the Bible.*

GROVE, Thomas Fraser, English politician, b. 1823 ; J.P. and deputy-lieutenant of Wilts ; high sheriff, 1863 ; M.P. for South Wiltshire since 1865.

GROVE, William Robert, English author, b. at Swansea, July 14, 1811 ; educated at Brasenose College, Oxford, where he graduated B.A. 1832 ; called to the bar of Lincoln's Inn, 1835 ; *professor* of experimental philosophy at the London Institution, 1840 to 1846. *Author of ' On the Correlation of Physical Forces,'* 1846 ; and several other scientific works.

GRUNER, Wilhelm Heinrich, German engraver, b. at Dresden, Feb. 24, 1801: studied under Klinger, and at the Academy at Dresden. Engraved Raffaelle's cartoons at Hampton Court for the Berlin Museum, 1842. Published 'Fresco Decorations and Studies,' London, 1844 ; and other works.

GRUNERT, Johann August, German mathematician, b. at Halle, Feb. 7, 1797 ; studied at the University of Göttingen, where he graduated Ph.D. 1820 ; appointed professor of mathematics at Brandenburg, 1828 ; at the Academy of Eldena, 1838. Author of 'Lehrbuch der Kegelschnitte,' Leipsic, 1824 ; 'Lehrbuch der Mathematik und Physick,' ib. 1841–51 ; and other works.

GRUNNE, Karl Ludwig, Count, Austrian military commander, b. at Vienna. Aug. 25, 1808 ; entered the army, and became major, 1838 ; chamberlain and aide-de-camp to the emperor Franz Joseph, 1848, and created major-general ; field-marshal, 1850.

GUDIN, The'odore, French marine painter, b. in Paris, Aug. 15, 1802 ; studied under Girodet Trioson. Painted 'Sauvetage des Passagers du Columbus,' 1831 ; the 'Coup de Vent dans la Rade d'Alger,' 1835 ; commissioned by King Louis Philippe to paint the principal events in the naval history of France, for the chateau of Versailles, 1838–48.

GUELL-Y-RENTE, Don Jose', Spanish poet and politician, b. at Havannah, 1819 ; educated at the College of St. Charles, in Cuba ; and graduated D.C.L. at the University of Barcelona, 1840 ; sat in the Cortes for the city of Valladolid, 1855. Author of 'The Virgin of the Lily ;' 'The Granddaughter of a King ;' 'American Traditions ;' and other poetical works.

GUERICKE, Heinrich Ernst Ferdinand, German theologian, b. at Vettin, Prussia, Feb. 23, 1803 ; studied theology at Halle, and was assistant professor, 1829 ; appointed examiner at the University, 1833 to 1838, and again 1840. Author of 'A Manual of Church History,' 1833 ; 'History of the Reformation,' 1855 ; and other theological works.

GUE'RIN, Jules, French physician, b. at Boussu, Jemappes, March 11, 1801 ; studied at Louvain and Paris, and was admitted M.D. 1826 ; became proprietor and editor of the *Gazette Medicale de Paris.* Author of 'Détermination rigoureusement scientifique des Principes, Méthodes et Procédés de l'Orthopédie, sous le double Rapport de la Pratique et de la Théorie,' in sixteen volumes ; and other medical works.

GUERRAZZI, Francesco Domenico, Italian writer and politician, b. in Livonia, 1805 ; studied law at the University of Pisa ; took part in the conspiracies of 1831 ; imprisoned in the fortress of the isle of Elba, 1847 ; regained his freedom, and a member of the ministry of M. Montanelli, 1848 ; proclaimed dictator at Rome, April 12, 1849. Author of 'Isabella Orsini ;' 'Beatrice Cenci ;' 'Apology of my Life,' 1851.

GUEST, Arthur, English politician, b. 1841 ; educated at Harrow, and Trinity College, Cambridge ; deputy-lieutenant of Glamorganshire ; elected M.P. for Poole, 1868.

GUES-VILLER, Philippe Antoine, French military commander, b. at Paris, March 10, 1791 ; studied at the Military School of Fontainebleau, 1810 ; served in Spain, and at the battle of Leipsic ; colonel, 1836 ; general of division, June 1848 ; senator, 1852.

GUIGNIANT, Joseph Daniel, French historical writer, b. at Paray-le-Monial, Saône-et-Loire, May 15, 1794 ; studied at the École Normale, 1818 ; master of conferences at the École Normale : teacher of history at the College of France, 1854 ; professor, 1857. Author of 'Sur le Dieu Sérapis et son Origine,' 1828 ; and other works.

GUILLAUME, Jean Baptiste Claude, French sculptor, b. at Montbard, Feb. 1822 ; studied at Paris under M. Pradier, at the École des Beaux Arts. Executed bas-relief of 'An Amazon ;' 'Monument de Colbert,' at Rheims, 1856 : a statue in marble of Napoleon I. 1861 ; and other works. Member of the Institute, 1862.

GUILLAUMIN, Jacques François Augustin, French politician, b. at Brescia, Italy, Feb. 5, 1802 ; member of the Legislative Assembly for the department of Cher since 1856.

GUILLOUTET, Louis Adhemar, Marquis de, French politician, b. Aug. 6, 1819 : mayor of Parlebose, and member of the General Council for the canton of Gabaret ; member of the Corps Législatif for the department of Landes since 1863.

GUINNESS, Sir Arthur, English politician, b. 1839 ; educated at Eton, and Trinity College, Dublin ; succeeded his father, first baronet, 1868 ; returned M.P. for Dublin, 1868, unseated, 1869.

GUISTIERE, Amand Gautbier de la, French politician, b. at Rennes, May 2, 1825 ; mayor of Rennes, and counsellor of the prefecture of Ille-et-Vilaine, 1858 ; resigned, 1863 ; *elected member* of the Corps Législatif for the department of Ille-et-Vilaine, 1863.

GUIZOT, François Pierre Guillaume, French author and statesman, b. at *Nîmes, Oct. 4, 1787;* educated at Geneva ; elected member of the Chamber of Deputies.

1829; appointed minister of the interior, 1830; minister of public instruction, 1832; minister of foreign affairs, 1840 to Feb. 1848. Author of 'History of the English Revolution of 1640,' 1826–55; 'Love in Marriage,' 1854;' 'L'Église et la Société Chrétienne,' 1861; 'Méditations sur l'Essence de la Religion Chrétienne,' 1864; and numerous other historical and political works.

GUNTHER II., Prince of Schwarzburg-Sondershausen, b. Sept. 24, 1801; succeeded to the throne in consequence of the abdication of his father, Prince Günther I., Aug. 19, 1835; married, in first nuptials, in 1827, to Princess Marie of Schwarzburg-Rudolstadt, who died in 1833; and secondly, in 1835, to Princess Mathilda of Hohenlohe-Oehringen, from whom he was divorced in 1852.

GURDON, Rebow John, English politician, b. 1799; educated at Eton; J.P. and deputy-lieutenant of Essex; high sheriff, 1852; M.P. for Colchester, 1857–59, and since 1865.

GURNEY, Rev. Archer, English author, b. 1820; ordained, 1849; chaplain to an English congregation in Paris. Author of 'Charles I.,' a dramatic poem dedicated to the memory of 'The Royal Martyr' of the Established Church; and numerous sermons.

GURNEY, Russell, English politician, b. 1804; educated at Trinity College, Cambridge, where he graduated B.A. 1826; called to the bar of the Inner Temple, 1828; appointed Q.C. 1845; recorder of London, 1856; M.P. for Southampton, 1865–68.

GURNEY, Samuel, English politician, b. 1816; magistrate for Surrey; M.P. for Penrhyn and Falmouth, 1857–68.

GUTHRIE, Rev. Thomas, English author, b. at Brechin, Forfarshire, 1800; studied at the University of Edinburgh; ordained minister of the parish of Arbirlot, 1830; minister of St. John's, Edinburgh, 1840; assisted to establish the Edinburgh Original Ragged or Industrial School, 1847. Editor of the *Sunday Magazine.*

GUTZKOW, Karl Ferdinand, German dramatic poet, b. at Berlin, March 17, 1811; studied at the University of his native town. Author of 'König Saul,' 1839; 'Richard Savage;' 'Die Ritter vom Geist,' 1850–52; and numerous other dramas and works of fiction.

GYULAY, Franz, Count, Austrian military commander, b. at Pesth, 1799; entered the army, and became major-general, 1839; lieutenant field-marshal, 1846, and held command of the province of Trieste, 1847; minister of war, June 1849 to July 1850; commanded in the Italian campaign of 1859, and was commander-in-chief at the battle of Magenta, June 1859.

H.

HAASE, Christian, German philologist, b. at Magdeburg, Prussia, Jan. 4, 1808; studied at the Universities of Halle and Berlin; professor at Schulpforta, 1835; professor of philology at the University of Breslau, 1840; deputy to the National Assembly of Berlin, 1848. Author of 'Vergangenheit und Zukunft der Philologie,' Berlin, 1835; and other works.

HACKLAENDER, Friederich Wilhelm, German traveller and author, b. at Borcette, near Aix la-Chapelle, Nov. 1, 1816. Author of 'Bilder aus dem Soldatenleben im Frieden,' Stuttgart, 1841; 'Soldatenleben im Kriege,' ib. 1859–60; 'Ein Winter in Spanien,' ib. 1855; and numerous novels and comedies.

HADDINGTON, George Baillie, Earl of, English administrator, b. 1802; succeeded his cousin, ninth earl, Dec. 1858; elected a representative peer of Scotland, May 1859; deputy-lieutenant of the county of Haddingtion.

HADFIELD, George, English politician, b. 1787; was a solicitor in Manchester, and member of the Anti-Corn-Law League; M.P. for Sheffield since 1852.

HAENTJENS, Alfred Alphonse, French politician, b. at Nantes, June 11, 1824; member of the Corps Législatif for the department of the Sarthe since 1863.

HAGENBACH, Karl Adolph, German Protestant theologian, b. at Basel, May 4, 1801; studied at the Universities of Bonn and Berlin; appointed professor of theology at the University of Basel, 1828. Author of 'A Guide to Christian Instruction,' Leipsic, 1850; and numerous theological works.

HAGHE, Louis, Belgian painter, b. at Tournay, Belgium, 1802; chiefly residing in England, and member of the new Water Colour Society. Painted 'Hall of Courtray;' 'The Hall of Audience at Bruges;' and numerous other works.

HAHN-HAHN, Ida, Countess von, German authoress, b. at Tressow, Duchy of Mecklenburg-Schwerin, June 22, 1805; married to Count von Hahn, 1826; divorced, 1829. Author of 'Oriental Letters,' 1844; 'From Babylon to Jerusalem;' and numerous works of fiction.

HALDEMAN, Samuel, American naturalist, b. near Columbia, Pennsylvania, 1812; educated at Dickinson College, and employed on the New Jersey and Pennsylvania geological surveys, 1836–37; appointed professor of natural history in Delaware College, Newark, Delaware, 1855. Author of 'Analytic Orthography,' 1858; and other works.

HALE, John Parker, American politician, b. in Rochester, New Hampshire, U.S. March 31, 1806; called to the bar, 1830; elected to the State Legislature, 1832; appointed U.S. attorney for New Hampshire, 1834; returned to Congress, 1843; returned to the U.S. Senate, 1847; re-entered the Senate, 1855.

HALE, Sarah, American authoress, b. at Newport, New Hampshire, 1795: married to Mr. David Hale, 1814, who died, 1822. Author of 'The Genius of Oblivion,' 1823; 'Flora's Interpreter;' 'Woman's Record;' or Sketches of Distinguished Women, from the Creation to A.D. 1854;' and other works.

HALE, Ven. William, English divine, b. 1795; educated at the Charterhouse, and Oriel College, Oxford, where he graduated, 1817; rector of Cripplegate, 1847 to 1857; archdeacon of London, 1842. Author of 'Some Account of the Hospital of King Edward VI., called Christ's Hospital.' Editor of 'The Four Gospels;' and other works.

HALEVY, Leon, French author, b. at Paris, Jan. 14, 1802; studied at the Lycée Charlemagne; appointed professor of literature at the École Polytechnique, 1831 to 1834; entered the Ministry of Public Instruction, 1837 to 1853. Author of 'La Peste de Barcelone,' 1822; 'Ce que Fille veut,' 1858; and numerous poems and dramas.

HALL, Anna Maria, English authoress, b. in Wexford County, 1805; married to Mr. Samuel Carter Hall (see below), 1824. Published 'Sketches of Irish Character,' 1828; 'The Buccaneer,' 1832; 'The Whiteboy,' 1845; 'Can Wrong be Right?' and numerous other works of fiction.

HALL, James, American novelist, b. at Philadelphia, Aug. 19, 1793; took part in the war with England as volunteer, 1818. Author of 'Letters from the West,' 1820; 'Border Tales,' New York, 1853; 'History and Biography of the Indians of North America;' and other works.

HALL, James, American geologist, b. at Hingham, Massachusetts, U.S. 1811; studied at New York; appointed on the New York Survey, 1837; geologist of the State of Iowa, 1855. Author of 'Palæontology of New York,' 1847–52 and 1859.

HALL, Sir John, English surgeon, b. 1795; entered the medical department of the army, 1815; staff-surgeon, 1827; deputy-inspector of hospitals, 1846; chief medical officer of the army in the Crimea, 1854–56; and inspector-general of hospitals since 1854.

HALL, Rev. Newman, English theologian, b. 1816; educated at Highbury College, and graduated at the London University, B.A. and LL.B.; minister of the Albion Congregational Church, Hull, 1842 to 1854; minister of Surrey Chapel since 1854. Author of 'Come to Jesus;' and numerous devotional tracts.

HALL, Samuel Carter, English author, b. at Topsham, Devon, 1801; barrister-at-law; editor of the *Art Journal* since 1839. Edited the 'Book of Gems;' 'Book of British Ballads;' and other works.

HALLE, Charles, musical performer and composer, b. in Germany; director of the Musical Institution at Manchester.

HALLECK, Henry Wager, American military commander, b. in New York, 1816; entered West Point as a cadet, 1835, and graduated, 1839; lieutenant, 1839; captain, 1847; captain of engineers, 1853, and retired from service, Aug. 1854; commissioned major-general of the U.S. army, Aug. 19, 1861; placed at the head of the United States armies, July 11, 1862; resigned in favour of Lieutenant-general Grant, 1864; commander of the Pacific military department, 1865.

HALLIDAY, Sir Frederick James, English colonial administrator, b. near Epsom, Surrey, 1806; educated at St. Paul's School, Rugby, and Haileybury College; entered the civil service of the East India Company, 1825; member of the Supreme Council of India, 1853; appointed lieutenant-governor of Bengal, 1854; created K.C.B. civil division, 1860.

HALLIWELL, James Orchard, English bibliographical writer, b. at Chelsea, 1820. Author of 'A Life of Shakespeare;' 'Skeleton Hand List of the Early Quarto Editions of Shakespeare,' 1860 ; 'Popular Rhymes and Nursery Tales,' 1849; and numerous other works.

HAMILTON, Right Hon. Lord Claude, English politician, b. 1813 ; educated at Trinity College, Cambridge ; was M.P. for county of Tyrone, 1835–37, and since 1839 ; was treasurer of the Household, 1852, and 1858–59 ; a deputy-lieutenant of Tyrone, and lieutenant-colonel Donegal Militia.

HAMILTON, Lord Claude John, English politician, b. 1843 ; educated at Harrow ; lieutenant and captain Grenadier Guards ; M.P. for Londonderry, 1865–68.

HAMILTON, Edward William Terrick, English politician, b. 1809 ; educated at Eton, and Trinity College, Cambridge, where he graduated B.A. 1832, M.A. 1835 ; M.P. for Salisbury since 1865.

HAMILTON, Very Rev. Henry Parr, English divine, b. 1794; educated at Trinity College, Cambridge, where he graduated B.A. 1816; appointed dean of Salisbury, 1850. Author of 'The Principles of Analytical Geometry;' 'Remarks on Popular Education;' and several other works, and sermons.

HAMILTON, Ion Trant, English politician, b. 1839 ; educated at Trinity College, Cambridge; a magistrate for the county of Dublin ; M.P. for county of Dublin since 1863.

HAMILTON, James, Viscount, English politician, b. 1838 ; educated at Harrow, and Christ Church, Oxford, where he graduated B.A. 1860 ; a magistrate for the county of Donegal ; M.P. for county of Donegal since 1860.

HAMILTON, Sir Robert Collie, English diplomatist, b. in India, 1802 ; educated at Haileybury ; entered the Bengal Civil Service, 1819 ; political agent to the Governor-General in Central India, 1842 ; accompanied General Sir Hugh Rose through the whole campaign in the Indian Mutiny ; and created K.C.B. civil division, 1858.

HAMILTON, William Alexander, Duke of, Scottish administrator, b. 1845 ; premier peer of Scotland ; hereditary keeper of the palace of Holyrood ; succeeded his father, eleventh peer, July 1863.

HAMMERICH, Peder Adolph, Danish author, b. at Copenhagen, Aug. 9, 1809 ; studied at the University of Copenhagen, and graduated Ph.D. 1834 ; pastor in Jutland, 1839 ; pastor of Trinity Church, Copenhagen, 1845. Author of 'Heroic Songs,' 1841 ; 'Gustavus Adolphus in Germany,' 1844 ; 'The War of Three Years in Schleswig,' 1852 ; and numerous other works.

HAMMETT, Samuel, American writer, b. at Jewett City, Connecticut, 1816 ; graduated at the University of New York. Published, under the pseudonym of P. Paxton, 'A Stray Yankee in Texas,' New York, 1853 ; 'The Wonderful Adventures of Captain Priest,' 1854.

HAMMOND, James Hamilton, American statesman, b. in Newbury, South Carolina, U.S. Nov. 15, 1807 ; graduated at the South Carolina College ; admitted to the bar, 1828 ; elected to Congress, 1835 ; general of brigade, 1841 ; governor of South Carolina, 1842 ; elected to the Senate of the United States, 1857. Author of several papers on politics, military tactics, agriculture, and slavery.

HANBURY, Robert Culling, English politician, b. 1823 ; deputy-lieutenant of Middlesex and the Tower Hamlets, and a magistrate for Herts, Middlesex, and East Sussex ; M.P. for Middlesex, 1857–68.

HANBURY-TRACY, Hon. Charles Richard, English politician, b. 1840 ; a barrister-at-law of Lincoln's Inn ; late lieutenant in the Royal Navy ; M.P. for Montgomery since 1863.

HANCOCK, Winfield Scott, American military commander, b. in Pennsylvania, 1824 ; entered West Point Academy, 1840 ; graduated and received a commission as lieutenant, 1844 ; served in the Mexican war, and made assistant quartermaster-general ; brigadier-general, 1861 ; major-general, 1863.

HANKEY, Thomson, English politician, b. 1805 ; a West India merchant, and director of the Bank of England, of which he was governor, 1851 to 1853 ; M.P. for Peterborough, 1853–68.

HANMER, Sir John, English politician, b. 1809 ; educated at Christ Church, Oxford ; a magistrate and deputy-lieutenant of Flintshire ; M.P. for Shrewsbury, 1832–37 ; for Hull, 1841–47; and for Flintshire since 1847.

HANNA, Rev. William, English author, b. in Belfast, 1808; educated at the University of Glasgow, and ordained to the ministry of the Presbyterian Church, 1835. Author of 'Wycliffe and the Huguenots,' and a 'Biography of the late Rev. Thomas Chalmers.'

HANNAH, Rev. John, English theologian, b. 1819; educated at Corpus Christi College, Oxford, where he graduated B.A. 1840; rector of the Academy at Edinburgh, and warden of Trinity College, Glenalmond. Author of 'Discourses on the Fall and its Results.' Edited 'The Poems and Psalms of Harry King,' 1843; and other works.

HANNAY, James, English author, b. at Dumfries, 1827; served in the Royal Navy, 1840 to 1845. Author of 'Singleton Fontenoy,' 1854; 'Eustace Conyers,' 1855; 'Satire and Satirists;' and other works.

HANSEMANN, David, German politician and writer, b. at Firckenwerder, near Hamburg, July 12, 1790; member of the Provincial Diet of the Rhine, 1846; and of the Prussian Diet, 1847; appointed minister of finance of Prussia, March 1848; resigned, Sept. 10, 1848. Author of 'The German Constitution of March 28, 1849;' and numerous other political works.

HARDCASTLE, Joseph Alfred, English politician, b. 1815; educated at Bury, and Trinity College, Cambridge, where he graduated B.A. 1838, and M.A. 1841; called to the bar of the Inner Temple, 1841; M.P. for Colchester, 1847–52, and for Bury St. Edmund's since 1857.

HARDINGE, Charles Stewart, Viscount, English statesman, b. 1822; educated at Eton, and Christ Church, Oxford, where he graduated B.A. 1844; M.P. for Downpatrick, 1851 to 1856; under-secretary of state for the War Department, Feb. 1858 to June 1859; succeeded his father, first viscount, 1856. Author of 'Views in India,' 1847.

HARDWICK, Philip, English architect, b. 1793. Designed the buildings at St. Katharine's Docks; the Goldsmiths' Hall, London; the Grand Entrance to the North-Western Railway Station, Euston Square; the Great Hall at Lincoln's Inn; and other public buildings in London.

HARDWICKE, Right Hon. Charles Yorke, Earl, English admiral, b. 1799; educated at Harrow, and the Royal Naval College, Portsmouth; M.P. for Reigate, 1831–32, and for Cambridgeshire, 1832–34, when he succeeded his uncle, third earl; sworn privy councillor, 1852; lord privy seal, 1858–59; admiral, and lord-lieutenant of Cambridgeshire.

HARDY, Gathorne, English statesman, b. 1814; educated at Shrewsbury, and Oriel College, Oxford, where he graduated B.A. 1836; called to the bar of the Inner Temple, 1840; M.P. for Leominster, 1858; under-secretary of state for the Home Department, 1858–59; returned M.P. for Oxford University, 1865; president of the Poor Law Board, July 6, 1866, to May 17, 1867; secretary of state for the Home Department, May 17, 1867, to Dec. 9, 1868.

HARDY, John, English politician, b. 1809; educated at Oriel College, Oxford, where he graduated B.A. 1831; M.A. 1834; magistrate and deputy-lieutenant of Staffordshire, and for the West Riding of Yorkshire; M.P. for Midhurst, March to April 1859; and for Dartmouth, 1860–68.

HARDY, Thomas Duffus, English antiquarian, b. at Port Royal, Jamaica, 1804; entered the public service as junior clerk in the Record Office, Tower, 1819; appointed deputy-keeper of the Public Rolls, 1861. Edited 'Rotuli Literarum Clausarum in Turri Londinensi asservati,' 1833–34; 'Modus tenendi Parliamentum,' 1846; and other ancient MSS. in the Rolls collection.

HAREWOOD, Henry Thynne Lascelles, Earl, English administrator, b. 1824; a deputy-lieutenant of the West Riding of Yorkshire; succeeded his father, third earl, 1857.

HARGRAVES, Edmund Hammond, English traveller, b. at Gosport, Sussex, 1816; settled in Australia, 1834; sailed to the Californian Gold Diggings, 1849; returned to Australia, and made the discovery of gold fields, 1851; appointed commissioner of Crown lands, 1850. Published 'Australia, and its Gold Fields,' 1854.

HAERING, Wilhelm, German novelist, b. at Breslau, June 1798; fought in the campaign of 1815 as a volunteer; studied at Berlin and Breslau after 1817. Author, under the *nom de plume* of 'Wilibald Alexis,' of 'Die Treibjagd;' 'Walladmor,' 1823; 'Schloss Avalon,' 1827; and numerous other works of fiction.

HARINGTON, Rev. Edward Charles, English author, b. 1807; educated at Worcester College, Oxford, where he graduated B.A. 1828; appointed chancellor of Exeter Cathedral, 1847, and residentiary canon, 1857. Author of 'The Reformers of the Anglican Church;' 'Macaulay's History of England;' 'Rome's Pretensions tested;' and other works.

HARLESS, Theophilus Christoph, German Protestant theologian, b. at Nürnberg, Nov. 21, 1806; studied at Erlangen and Halle; professor of theology at the University of Erlangen, 1836; appointed private ecclesiastical councillor to the minister of worship at Munich, 1852. Author of 'Commentary on the Epistle to the Ephesians,' 1834; 'Treatise on Plastic Anatomy,' 1857; and numerous other works.

HARNESS, Rev. William, English author, b. 1790; educated at Harrow, and Christ's College, Cambridge, where he graduated B.A. 1813; incumbent of All Saints, Knightsbridge. Author of 'Welcome and Farewell,' a drama, 1837; 'Claims of the Church of Rome considered;' and numerous sermons and pamphlets.

HARRIS, Hon. Edward Alfred, English diplomatist, b. 1808; educated at Eton, and the Royal Naval College; entered the navy, 1823; captain, 1843; M.P. for Christ Church, Hants, 1844 to 1852; appointed consul at Elsinore, 1852; transferred to Peru as consul-general and chargé d'affaires, 1852, and to Chili, 1853; consul at Venice, 1858; minister-plenipotentiary at Berne, 1861–66.

HARRIS, George Francis Robert, Baron, English administrator, b. 1810; educated at Christ Church, Oxford, where he graduated B.A. 1831; succeeded his father, second baron, 1845; lieutenant-governor of Trinidad, 1846–54; governor of Madras, 1854–59; returned to England, 1861; chamberlain of the Princess of Wales.

HARRIS, John Dove, English politician, b. 1809; J.P. and deputy-lieutenant of the county of Leicester; M.P. for Leicester, 1857–59, and since 1865.

HARRISON, Ven. Benjamin, English divine, b. 1809; educated at Christ Church, Oxford, where he graduated B.A. 1830; appointed archdeacon of Maidstone, and preacher in Canterbury Cathedral, 1845. Author of 'An Historical Enquiry into the True Interpretation of the Rubrics relating to the Sermon and Communion Service,' 1845.

HARRISON, Thomas, English civil engineer, b. 1810; employed in the construction of docks in London; engineer of the North-Eastern Railway.

HARROWBY, Right Hon. Dudley Ryder, Earl, English statesman, b. 1798; educated at Christ Church, Oxford, where he graduated B.A. 1819; was M.P. for Tiverton, 1819 to 1830, and for Liverpool, 1832 to 1847, when he succeeded his father, first earl; has been secretary to the India Board, chancellor of the Duchy of Lancaster, and lord privy seal.

HART, Joel, American sculptor, b. in Clark County, Kentucky, 1810; executed a marble statue of Henry Clay, 1859; a statue in bronze of the same for the city of New Orleans, 1861; and busts of several other distinguished persons.

HART, Solomon Alexander, English painter, b. at Plymouth, April 1806; entered the Royal Academy as student, 1823; appointed professor of painting in the Royal Academy, 1857. Exhibited 'The Elevation of the Law,' 1830; 'Wolsey and Buckingham,' 1834; 'Simchath Torah, or the Rejoicing of the Law,' 1845 and 1850; 'The Three Inventors of Printing;' and numerous other paintings. Elected A.R.A. 1835, R.A. 1840.

HARTINGTON, Right Hon. Spencer Compton, Marquis of, English statesman, eldest son of the Duke of Devonshire, b. 1833; educated at Trinity College, Cambridge, where he graduated M.A. 1854; under-secretary for war, 1863–66; secretary for war, 1866; appointed postmaster-general, Dec. 9, 1868; M.P. for North Lancashire, 1857–68; for the Radnorshire boroughs, 1869.

HARTLEY, Sir Charles Augustus, English civil engineer, b. at Hepworth, county of Durham, 1825; served in the Crimea as captain in the Turkish Contingent Engineers, 1855–56; appointed engineer-in-chief to the European Commission for improving the Navigation of the Danube, 1857; knighted, 1862.

HARTLEY, James, English politician, b. 1811; educated at Bristol; a magistrate for the county of Durham, and an alderman of Sunderland; M.P. for Sunderland, 1865–68.

HARTMANN, Moritz, German author, b. at Duschink, Bohemia, Oct. 15, 1821; studied at the Universities of Prague and Vienna. Author of 'Kelch und Schwert,' Leipsic, 1845; 'Sie sind arm;' 'Reimchronik des Pfaffen Mauritius,' Frankfort, 1849; 'Briefe aus Irland,' 1851; and numerous other, chiefly poetical, works.

HARTOPP, Edward Bourchier, English politician, b. 1809; educated at Eton, and Christ Church, Oxford; a magistrate for the county of Leicester; was high sheriff, 1833; M.P. for North Leicestershire, 1859–68.

HARTSHORNE, Rev. Charles Henry, English author, b. 1803; educated at St. John's College, Cambridge, where he graduated B.A. 1825; appointed rector of Holdenby, near Northampton, 1850. Author of 'Book Rarities in the University of Cambridge,' 1829; 'Home of the Working Man,' 1856; and other works.

HARVEY, George, Scottish painter, b. at St. Ninian's, near Stirling, 1805; studied at the Trustees' Academy, Edinburgh, 1823 to 1825; associate of the Royal Edinburgh Academy, 1826; and academician, 1829. Exhibited the 'Covenanters Preaching,' 1830; 'The Wise and Foolish Builders,' 1849; and numerous other paintings.

HARVEY, Robert Bateson, English politician, b. 1824; a J.P. and deputy-lieu-tenant of Bucks; M.P. for Bucks, 1864–68.

HARVEY, Robert John Harvey, English politician, b. 1817; a J.P. and deputy-lieutenant of Norfolk; high sheriff, 1862; M.P. for Thetford, 1865–68.

HASSAN ALI KHAN, Persian statesman, b. at Bidjar, 1821; nominated colonel in the army by Mohammed Schah, 1839; general, 1851; governor of the city of Herat, 1856; envoy-extraordinary and minister-plenipotentiary to France, Aug. 1859 to Oct. 1864.

HASTINGS, Sir Charles, English physician, b. 1794; educated at Edinburgh, where he graduated M.D. 1818; knighted, 1850; deputy-lieutenant of Worcestershire. Author of 'Treatise on Inflammation of the Mucous Membrane of the Lungs;' 'Illustra-tions of the Natural History of Worcestershire;' and other works.

HASTINGS, Jacob Henry Astley, Baron, English administrator, b. 1822; educated at Eton, and Christ Church, Oxford; a deputy-lieutenant and magistrate of Norfolk; lieutenant in the 2d Life Guards, 1848–51.

HASTINGS, Sir Thomas, English administrator, b. 1790; entered the navy, 1808; principal storekeeper and member of the Board of Ordnance, 1845 to 1855; knighted, 1855; nominated K.C.B. 1859; J.P. for the counties of Hereford and Brecon, and deputy-lieutenant of Hereford.

HATCHELL, Right Hon. John, Irish administrator, b. in Wexford County, 1788; educated at Trinity College, Dublin; called to the Irish bar, 1809; solicitor-general for Ireland, 1847; attorney-general, and sworn in the privy council for Ireland, 1850; M.P. for Windsor, 1850–52; appointed commissioner of national education, and charitable donations and bequests in Ireland, 1853; resigned, 1861.

HATHERLEY, William Page Wood, Baron, English judge, b. 1801; vice-chancellor, 1852; lord justice of appeal, 1867; raised to the peerage and made lord chancellor, Dec. 1868.

HATHERTON, Edward Richard, Baron, English administrator, b. at Teddesley, Dec. 31, 1815; educated at Eton; M.P. for Walsall, 1847 to 1852, and for South Stafford-shire, 1853 to 1857; deputy-lieutenant and magistrate of Staffordshire.

HAUREAU, Jean Barthelemy, French author, b. in Paris, Nov. 9, 1812; studied at the College of Louis-le-Grand and the Collége Bourbon. Author of 'La Montagne,' 1832; 'Histoire de la Pologne,' Paris, 1844; 'Charlemagne et sa Cour,' 1852–55; 'Cata-logue chronologique des Œuvres de J. P. Gerbier,' 1863; and many other works.

HAUSSER, Ludwig, German historical writer, b. at Cleebourg, Lower Alsace, Oct. 26, 1818; studied at Mannheim and Jena; member of the Second Baden Chamber, 1849; appointed titular professor of history at the University of Zurich, 1850. Author of 'History of Germany from the Death of Frederick the Great,' 1863; and other works.

HAUSSMANN, Georges Eugene, Baron, French statesman, b. in Paris, March 27, 1809; entered the Conservatoire of Music, and subsequently studied law in Paris, and was called to the bar; sub-préfet of Nérac, 1833, of St. Girons, 1840, of Blaye, 1842; appointed préfet de la Seine, June 23, 1853; created senator, Aug. 1857.

HAVEGAL, Rev. William Henry, English divine, b. 1792; educated at St. Ed-mund's Hall, Oxford, where he graduated B.A. 1815, and M.A. 1819; rector of Astley, in Worcestershire, 1829–42; rector of St. Nicholas, Worcester, 1845; rector of Shareshill, near Wolverhampton, 1860. Author of several sermons and musical compositions.

HAVELOCK, Sir Henry Marsham, English military commander, b. at Chin-sura, Bengal, 1830; entered the army, 1846; quartermaster-general in the expedition to Persia, 1857; aide-de-camp to his father, the late General Havelock, in Oude and Cawnpore, Aug. 1857; lieutenant-colonel, 1859; assistant adjutant-general at Alder-shot, 1861.

HAVIN, Leonor Joseph, French politician, b. at St. Lô, 1799; judge of the peace at St. Lô, 1835; member of the Constituent Assembly for the department of La Manche, 1849; elected to the Corps Législatif for the 1st circonscription of the department of La Manche, 1863; director of Le Siècle newspaper.

HAVRINCOURT, Alphonse Pierre, Marquis d', French politician, b. Sept. 12, 1806; entered the École Polytechnique, 1826; lieutenant, 1832; elected to the Legislative Assembly, 1849; member of the Corps Législatif for the department of Nord, 1863.

HAWKINS, Benjamin Waterhouse, English, geologist, b. in London, Feb. 8, 1807; educated at St. Aloysius College. Author of 'Popular Comparative Anatomy,' 1840; 'Comparative View of the Human and Animal Frame,' 1860; and other works.

HAWKINS, Cæsar Henry, English surgeon, b. near the end of the last century; elected surgeon to St. George's Hospital, 1829; resigned, 1861; consulting surgeon and trustee to St. George's Hospital. Author of 'Lectures on Tumours;' and other medical works.

HAWKINS, Rev. Edward, English divine, b. 1789; educated at St. John's College, Oxford, where he graduated B.A. 1811; provost of Oriel College, 1828; appointed Dean Ireland's professor of the Exegesis of Holy Scripture at Oxford, 1847; resigned, 1861. Author of 'Discourses on the Historical Scriptures of the Old Testament;' and sermons.

HAWKSHAW, John, English civil engineer, b. at Leeds, 1811; educated at Leeds Grammar School; engineer of the Lancashire and Yorkshire Railway; the Charing Cross, and a great number of English and foreign railroads; one of the metropolitan commissioners of sewers.

HAY, Lord John, English politician, b. 1827; a captain in the Royal Navy, and captain of 1st Middlesex Rifle Volunteers; M.P. for Wick, 1857–59, and returned for Ripon, 1866; appointed lord of the Admiralty, Dec. 1868.

HAY, Sir John Charles Dalrymple, English naval officer, b. 1821; educated at Rugby, 1821; served as midshipman during the siege of Acre, 1841; flag-lieutenant, 1846; commanded the *Columbine,* 1849; commander of the *Hannibal,* in the Black and Mediterranean Seas, during the Russian war, 1854–56; M.P. for Wakefield, 1862.

HAY, Lord William Montague, English politician, b. 1826; educated at Hailey-bury College; formerly in the Civil Service at Bengal; M.P. for Taunton, 1865–68.

HAYES, Augustus Allen, American, chemist, b. at, Windsor, State of Vermont, Feb. 28, 1806; graduated at the Military Academy of Norwich, Vermont, 1823; state assayer of Massachusetts. Author of 'The Existence of a Deposit of Iron on the African West Coast;' and other works.

HAYTER, Arthur Divett, English politician, b. 1835; educated at Eton, and Brasenose College, Oxford, where he graduated B.A. 1857, and M.A. 1859; captain in the Grenadier Guards; M.P. for Wells, 1865–68.

HAYTER, Sir George, English painter, b. in London, 1792; appointed midshipman in the Royal Navy, 1809; studied painting in Rome, 1816 to 1819; member of the Imperial Academies of Parma, 1826; appointed historical painter in ordinary to her Majesty, 1841; knighted, 1842. Author of 'Hortus Ericæus Woburnensis.'

HAYTER, Right Hon. Sir William, English politician, b. 1792; educated at Winchester, and Trinity College, Oxford; called to the bar of Lincoln's Inn, 1819; M.P. for Wells, 1837–64; judge-advocate, 1847–49; financial secretary of the Treasury, 1849–50; parliamentary secretary, 1850–58; created a baronet, 1858.

HAZLITT, William Carew, English author, b. Aug. 22, 1834; educated at Merchant Taylors' School: called to the bar, 1861. Author of 'The History of the Venetian Republic: her Rise, her Greatness, and her Civilization,' 1860; and other works.

HEAD, Sir Francis Bond, English author, b. 1793; served in a corps of Royal Engineers at Waterloo; governor of Upper Canada, 1835; resigned, March 1838; created a baronet, 1838. Author of 'Rough Notes of a Journey across the Pampas;' 'A Faggot of French Sticks;' 'The Horse and his Rider;' and numerous other works.

HEADLAM, Right Hon. Thomas Emerson, English administrator, b. in Yorkshire, 1813; educated at Trinity College, Cambridge, where he graduated M.A. 1839; called to the bar of the Inner Temple, 1839; appointed judge-advocate-general, 1859; chancellor of Ripon and Durham, 1854; M.P. for Newcastle-on-Tyne since 1847.

HEADLEY, Joel Tyler, American author, b. at New York, Dec. 30, 1814; studied at Auburn Theological Seminary, and became pastor of a church at Stockbridge, Massachusetts. Author of 'Letters from Italy;' 'Napoleon and his Marshals,' 1846; 'History of the Second War between England and the United States;' and other works.

HEATH, Rev. Dunbar Isidore, English theologian, b. 1817; graduated at Trinity College, Cambridge, 1838; appointed vicar of Brading, Isle of Wight, 1846; deprived of his benefice, 1861. Author of 'The Future Kingdom of Christ,' 1852–53; 'The Proverbs of Aphobis, B.C. 1900,' 1858; and other works.

HEATHCOTE, Hon. Gilbert Henry, English politician, b. 1830; educated at Harrow, and Trinity College, Cambridge; a deputy-lieutenant of the counties of Lincoln and Rutland; M.P. for Boston, 1852–56; and for Rutlandshire, 1856–68.

HEATHCOTE, Sir William, English politician, b. 1801 ; educated at Winchester, and Oriel College, Oxford, where he graduated B.A. 1821 ; elected fellow of All Souls, 1822 ; magistrate and deputy-lieutenant of Hants ; M.P. for Hants, 1826–32, for North Hants, 1837–49, and for Oxford University, 1854–68.

HEDGE, Rev. Frederick Henry, American author, b. in Cambridge, Massachusetts, Dec. 12, 1805 ; ordained, 1829 ; minister of the Congregational Church in Brooklyn, Massachusetts. Author of ' Prose Writers in Germany,' 1848.

HEINRICH XIV., Prince of Reuss-Schleiz, b. May 28, 1832, the son of Prince Henry LXVII. and of Princess Adelaide ; succeeded to the throne at the death of his father, Prince Henry LXVII., July 10, 1867 ; married, Feb. 6, 1858, to Princess Louise of Würtemberg.

HEINTZELMAN, Samuel, American military commander, b. in Pennsylvania, 1807 ; admitted as cadet to West Point, 1822 ; major, 1847 ; lieutenant-colonel, 1861 ; wounded at the battle of Bull Run, July 21, 1861 ; brigadier-general, and commander of a division, 1861–62 ; major-general, July 1862.

HELMERSEN, Gregor von, Russian traveller, b. near Dorpat, Sept. 29, 1803 ; studied at St. Petersburg, and at the University of Dorpat ; professor of geology to the School of Mines of St. Petersburg. Author of ' Geognostiche Untersuchung des Südural-gebirgs,' Berlin, 1831 ; ' Beiträge zur Kenntniss des russischen Reichs.'

HELMORE, Rev. Thomas, English theologian, b. May 7, 1811 ; educated at Magdalen Hall, Oxford, where he graduated B.A. 1840 ; appointed priest in ordinary of her Majesty's Chapels Royal, 1847. Author of ' The Canticles noted :' and other works.

HELPS, Arthur, English author, b. 1817 ; educated at Trinity College, Cambridge, where he graduated B.A. 1838 ; appointed clerk of the privy council, 1859. Author of ' Catherine Douglas ;' ' The Conquerors of the New World and their Bondsmen ;' ' The Spanish Conquest of America ;' and other works.

HENDERSON, Edmund Yeamans Walcott, English administrator, b. 1820 ; studied at Woolwich, and entered the army, 1838 ; lieutenant-colonel Royal Engineers, 1862 ; appointed surveyor-general of prisons, 1863.

HENDERSON, John, English politician, b. 1807 ; educated at Durham Grammar School ; a magistrate of Durham, and carpet manufacturer in that city ; M.P. for Durham since 1864.

HENEAGE, Edward, English politician, b. 1840 ; educated at Eton ; a J.P. and deputy-lieutenant of the county of Lincoln ; was lieutenant 1st Life Guards ; M.P. for Lincoln, 1865–68.

HENGSTENBERG, Ernst Wilhelm, German theologian, b. at Fraudenberg, Oct. 20, 1802 ; educated at Bonn ; appointed professor and doctor of theology at Berlin, 1829. Editor of ' Aristotle's Metaphysics,' 1824 ; conductor of the *Evangelische Kirchen Zeitung*, 1827. Author of ' Commentaries on the Apocalypse and the Psalms.'

HENLEY, Anthony Henley Henley, Lord, English politician, b. in London, 1825 ; educated at Eton, and Christ Church, Oxford ; a magistrate and deputy-lieutenant of the county of Northampton ; was high sheriff, 1854 ; M.P. for Northampton since 1859.

HENLEY, Right Hon. Joseph Warner, English statesman, b. 1793 ; educated at Magdalen College, Oxford, where he graduated B.A. 1815 ; a magistrate and deputy-lieutenant of Oxon ; president of the Board of Trade, March to Dec. 1852, and 1858–59 ; M.P. for Oxfordshire since 1841.

HENNIKER, Lord John, English politician, b. 1801 ; educated at St. John's College, Cambridge, where he graduated M.A. 1822 ; called to the bar of Lincoln's Inn, 1826 ; deputy-lieutenant of Suffolk ; M.P. for East Suffolk, 1832–46, and since 1856.

HENRIQUEL-DUPONT, Louis Pierre, French engraver, b. in Paris, June 13, 1797 ; studied under Pierre Guerin. Engraved ' The Interment of Christ,' after Paul Delaroche ; ' The Abdication of Gustavus Vasa,' after Hersent ; and other works.

HENRY, Caleb Sprague, American author, b. at Rutland, Massachusetts, Aug. 2, 1804 ; graduated at Dartmouth College, 1825 ; appointed professor of philosophy and history in the University of New York, 1839. Author of ' A Compendium of Christian Antiquities ;' and other works.

HENRY, Joseph, American electrician, b. in Albany, New York, Dec. 17, 1797 ; learnt the trade of a watchmaker in his native city ; appointed professor of mathematics in the Albany Academy, 1826 ; professor of natural philosophy in the College of New Jersey, Princetown, 1832 ; first secretary of the Smithsonian Institution at Washington, 1846. Author of ' Contributions to Electricity and Magnetism,' 1839 ; and other works.

HERAUD, John Abraham, English author, b. in London, 1799. Author of 'Tottenham,' 1820; 'The Descent into Hell,' 1830; 'The Judgment of the Flood,' 1834; 'Videna,' a tragedy acted in 1854; and numerous other poems and dramas.

HERBERT, John Rogers, English painter, b. at Maldon, Essex, Jan. 23, 1810; entered the Royal Academy as a student, 1816. Exhibited 'The Appointed Hour,' 1834; 'Christ and the Woman of Samaria,' 1843; 'Lear disinherits Cordelia,' 1849; and numerous other paintings, chiefly of religious subjects. Elected A.R.A. 1841, R.A. 1846.

HERCULANO DE CARVALHO ETRANJO, Alexander, Portuguese author, b. at Lisbon, March 28, 1810; studied in Paris. Author of 'A Voz do Propheta,' 1836; 'Historia de Portugal,' Lisbon, 1848–52; 'History of the Origin and Establishment of the Inquisition in Portugal;' and other works.

HERRING, John Frederick, English painter, b. in Surrey, 1795. Painted 'Returning from Epsom;' 'Derby Day;' 'The Scene near the Windmill Inn on Clapham Common;' a 'Horse Fair;' and numerous other paintings, chiefly of horses and dogs.

HERSCHEL, Sir John Frederick, English astronomer, b. at Slough, near Windsor, 1792; educated at St. John's College, Cambridge; created a baronet, 1838; lord rector of Marischal College, Aberdeen, 1842; president of the Astronomical Society, 1848; appointed master of the Mint, 1850; resigned, Feb. 1855. Author of 'Outlines of Astronomy,' 1850.

HERTFORD, Richard Seymour Conway, Marquis of, b. 1800; attaché at Paris, 1817–19, and at Constantinople, 1829; formerly in the army; succeeded his father, third marquis, 1842; created K.G. 1855.

HERVEY, Lord Angus Henry, English politician, b. 1837; honorary M.A. of Trinity College, Cambridge, 1859; M.P. for West Suffolk since 1864.

HERVEY, Eleonora Louisa, English authoress, b. at Liverpool, 1811; married to Mr. T. K. Hervey, 1843. Author of 'The Landgrave,' 1839; 'The Double Claim;' 'The Feasts of Camelot,' 1863; and of numerous essays and tales.

HESKETH, Sir Thomas George, Bart., English politician, b. 1825; educated at Christ Church, Oxford; a deputy-lieutenant of Lancashire; high sheriff, 1848; M.P. for Preston since 1862.

HESSEY, Rev. James Augustus, English divine, b. in London, 1814; educated at St. John's College, Oxford, where he graduated B.A. 1836; elected head-master of Merchant Taylors' School, 1845; preacher of Gray's Inn, 1850; appointed to the prebendal stall of Oxgate in St. Paul's Cathedral, 1860.

HEURTLEY, Rev. Charles Abel, English divine, b. 1806; educated at Corpus Christi College, Oxford, where he graduated B.A. 1827; rector of Fenny Compton, Warwickshire, 1840; elected Margaret professor of divinity, and canon in Christ Church Cathedral, 1853; member of the Hebdomadal Council of the University of Oxford, 1864. Author of numerous sermons and lectures.

HEWITSON, William, English naturalist, b. at Newcastle-on-Tyne, Jan. 6, 1806. Published 'The British Oology,' 1831; 'Exotic Butterflies,' 1852; and 'Illustrations of Diurnal Lepidoptera.'

HEYGATE, Sir Frederick William, English politician, b. 1822; educated at Eton, and Trinity College, Cambridge; deputy-lieutenant of Leicestershire, and lieutenant of Leicestershire Yeomanry; M.P. for county of Londonderry since 1859.

HEYGATE, Rev. William Edward, English author, b. 1817; studied at St. John's College, Oxford, where he graduated B.A. 1839. Author of 'Godfrey Davenant, or School Life;' 'Sir Henry Appleton;' 'The Good Shepherd;' and other works.

HEYTESBURY, William Henry Ashe, Baron, English administrator, b. 1809; educated at Eton, and St. John's College, Cambridge; a deputy-lieutenant and magistrate of Wilts, Hants, and the Isle of Wight; M.P. for the Isle of Wight, 1837–47.

HEYWOOD, James, English politician, b. May 28, 1810; educated at Trinity College, Cambridge, and graduated B.A. 1837; called to the bar, 1838; M.P. for North Lancashire, 1847 to 1857. Author of 'History of University Subscription Tests,' 1853; 'The State of Biblical Revision,' 1860; and other works.

HIBBERD, Shirley, English horticulturist. Author of 'Summer Songs,' 1851; 'Fresh Water Aquaria,' 1856; 'Garden Favourites,' 1858; 'Epitome of the [Russian] War,' 1857; and other works.

HIBBERT, John Tomlinson, English politician, b. 1824; educated at St. John's College, Cambridge, where he graduated B.A. 1847, M.A. 1851; called to the bar of the Inner Temple, 1849; M.P. for Oldham since 1862.

HIGGINSON, Sir James Macaulay, English colonial governor, b. 1805; educated at Trinity College, Dublin; entered the Bengal army, 1824; governor and commander-in-chief of the Leeward Islands, 1846 to 1850; governor of Mauritius, 1850; retired, 1857.

HILDRETH, Richard, American author, b. at Deerfield, Massachusetts, 1807; graduated at Harvard College; called to the bar, 1830; U.S. consul at Trieste. Author of 'History of the United States of America;' 'Japan as it is,' 1855; and other works.

HILDYARD, Rev. James, English author, b. 1809; educated at Shrewsbury School, and Christ's College, Cambridge, where he graduated B.A. 1833; appointed rector of Ingoldsby, Lincolnshire, 1846. Author of 'Ingoldsby Legends,' 1858–62.

HILL, Ambrose, American general, b. at Culpepper, Virginia, 1825; entered West Point Military Academy as a cadet, 1842; lieutenant, 1847; appointed assistant on the U.S. Coast Survey, Nov. 1855; joined the Confederate Army, March 1861; appointed brigadier-general, May 1862; lieutenant-general, 1863–66.

HILL, David Octavius, English artist, b. at Perth, 1802; studied in Edinburgh. Exhibited 'Windsor Castle—Summer Evening;' 'Old and New Edinburgh—from the Castle;' 'The River Tay from the Bridge at Perth;' and numerous other landscapes.

HILL, Matthew Davenport, English administrator, b. 1792; called to the bar of Lincoln's Inn, 1819; M.P. for Kingston upon Hull, 1832 to 1834; recorder of Birmingham, and commissioner in bankruptcy for the Bristol district. Author of 'Suggestions for the Repression of Crime;' and several pamphlets on Reformatories.

HILL, Rowland Hill, Viscount, English administrator, b. 1800; lord-lieutenant of Shropshire; colonel of the North Shropshire Yeomanry; sat in the House of Commons as Sir R. Hill, 1821 to 1842, when he succeeded his uncle, first viscount, in the peerage.

HILLARD, George Stillman, American author, b. in the State of Maine, 1808; educated at Harvard College; studied law, and was called to the bar. Published 'Six Months in Italy,' 1853; was editor of the *North American Review*.

HILL-TREVOR, Lord Arthur Edwin, English politician, b. 1819; educated at Eton, and Balliol College, Oxford; a J.P. and deputy-lieutenant of the counties of Denbigh, Down, and Salop; M.P. for the county of Down since 1845.

HINCKS, Francis, English colonial administrator, b. in Cork, 1795; studied at Trinity College, Dublin; member of the Provincial Parliament of Canada, and subsequently prime minister for some years under Lord Elgin; governor of Barbadoes, 1856–61; governor of British Guiana, 1861–66.

HIND, John Russell, English astronomer, b. at Nottingham, 1822; foreign secretary of the Royal Astronomical Society, and superintendent of the *Nautical Almanac*. Published 'The Solar System,' 1846; 'The Unexpected Return of the Great Comet,' 1848; 'Astronomical Vocabulary,' 1852; and other works on astronomy.

HINDS, Right Rev. Samuel, English divine, b. in Barbadoes, 1793; educated at Queen's College, Oxford, where he graduated in 1815; appointed dean of Carlisle, 1848; consecrated bishop of Norwich, 1849; resigned, 1857. Author of a 'Treatise on Logic;' 'History of the Rise and Early Progress of Christianity;' 'Inquiry into the Nature and Extent of Inspiration;' several sonnets and sacred poems.

HINGESTON, Rev. Francis Charles, English author, b. March 31, 1833; educated at Exeter College, Oxford, where he graduated B.A. 1855, and M.A. 1858; appointed rector of Ringmore, Devon, 1860. Author of 'Specimens of Ancient Cornish Crosses, Fonts, &c.' 1850; edited 'A Collection of Royal and Historical Letters during the Reign of Henry IV.' 2 vols. for the Master of the Rolls, 1860; and numerous other works.

HINTON, Rev. John Howard, English author, b. at Oxford, March 24, 1791; graduated at Edinburgh; minister of a Baptist chapel in Devonshire-square, Bishops-gate, London. Author of 'History of the United States of North America;' 'Elements of Natural History;' and other works.

HIRSCHER, Johann Baptist von, German theologian, b. at Alt-Ergarten, June 20, 1788; educated at the University of Freiburg: ordained, 1810; appointed professor of Christian morals at the University of Tübingen, 1817; transferred in the same capacity to Freiburg, 1837; resigned, 1863. Author of 'Christian Ethics;' 'Treatise on the Present State of the Church,' 1850; and other works.

HIS DE BUTENVAL, Charles Adrien, Baron, French diplomatist, b. 1805; *entered the diplomatic service,* 1830; successively secretary of legation at Lisbon and *secretary of embassy at Constantinople* till 1842; minister-plenipotentiary to Brazil, *1847; to Sardinia, 1851;* to Belgium, 1852; councillor of state, June 23, 1853.

HITZIG, Ferdinand, German philologist, b. at Hüningen, Baden, June 23, 1807; studied theology at the Universities of Halle and Heidelberg; appointed professor of Exegesis at Zurich, 1833. Author of 'Translation and Commentary of the Prophet Isaiah,' 1832; 'Commentary on the Psalms,' 1833; and other critical works on the Old Testament, Oriental mythology, philology, and archæology.

HOARE, Sir Henry Ainslie, English politician, b. 1824; educated at Eton, and Trinity College, Cambridge; a J.P. and deputy-lieutenant of Somerset, and a magistrate of Wilts; M.P. for Windsor, 1865–68.

HODGES, James, English civil engineer, b. at Queenborough, Kent, 1816; assistant engineer to the late Sir William Cubitt, at Dover, 1839 to 1844; constructed the new harbour at Lowestoft, 1844 to 1848, and the great Victoria Bridge across the St. Lawrence, at Montreal, opened 1860.

HODGKINSON, Grosvenor, English politician, b. 1818; educated at King Edward's School, Louth; a solicitor in practice at Newark; M.P. for Newark since 1859.

HODGSON, Kirkman Daniel, English politician, b. 1814; educated at the Charterhouse; a merchant, one of the directors of the Bank of England, and a commissioner of Public Works Loan Office; M.P. for Bridport, 1857–68.

HODGSON, William Nicholson, English politician, b. 1801; a J.P. and deputy-lieutenant of Cumberland; was high sheriff, 1863; M.P. for Carlisle, 1847–48, 1857–59, and 1865–68.

HOFFMAN, Charles Fenno, American author, b. in New York, 1806; studied at Columbia College. Author of 'A Winter in the Far West,' 1835; 'Wild Scenes in the Forest and the Prairie,' 1837; 'Grey Slaves;' and a volume of poems. Founder of the *Knickerbocker Magazine.*

HOFFMANN VON FALLERSLEBEN, August Heinrich, German poet, b. at Fallersleben, Hanover, April 2, 1798; studied theology at Rome. Author of 'Fragments of Ottfried,' 1820; 'Deutsche Lieder aus der Schweiz,' 1843; 'Horæ Belgicæ,' in 8 vols. 1850–52; and numerous other poetical works.

HOFMANN, August Wilhelm, German chemist, b. at Giessen, Hesse, 1817; studied chemistry under Liebig; successively professor of chemistry at the University of Bonn, and manager and director of the College of Chemistry in London; appointed professor of chemistry in the University of Berlin, 1864. Edited 'Fowne's Manual of Chemistry,' and other works.

HOGG, James Macnaghten, English politician, b. 1823; educated at Eton, and Christ Church, Oxford; formerly lieutenant-colonel 1st Life Guards; M.P. for Bath, 1865–68.

HOGG, Sir James Weir, English administrator, b. 1799; called to the bar, went to India, and became registrar of the Supreme Court of Calcutta; M.P. for Beverley and Honiton, 1835–57; director of the East India Company, 1839–58, and chairman of the same, 1846–47.

HOGG, Robert, English botanist, b. at Dunse, Scotland, 1818. Author of the 'Vegetable Kingdom and its Products;' 'British Pomology.' Editor of the *Florist and Pomologist,* and of the *Journal of Horticulture.*

HOLBROOK, John Edwards, American naturalist, b. at Beaufort, South Carolina, 1795; graduated at Brown University, Massachusetts; studied medicine in Europe; appointed professor of anatomy in the Medical College of South Carolina, 1824. Author of 'American Herpetology;' 'Description of the Reptiles inhabiting the United States;' and 'Ichthyology of South Carolina.'

HOLDEN, Rev. Hubert Aston, English author, b. 1822; educated at Trinity College, Cambridge, and graduated B.A. 1845; vice-principal of Cheltenham College, 1853; head-master of Queen Elizabeth's Grammar School, Ipswich, 1858. Edited 'Foliorum Silvula,' and numerous other works.

HOLFORD, Robert Stayner, English politician, b. 1808; educated at Oriel College, Oxford, where he graduated B.A. 1829; a magistrate and deputy-lieutenant of Gloucestershire, and a magistrate of Wilts; M.P. for East Gloucestershire since 1854.

HOLLAND, Edward, English politician, b. 1805; a magistrate and deputy-lieutenant of Gloucestershire and Worcestershire; M.P. for East Worcestershire, 1835–37; M.P. for Evesham, 1855–68.

HOLLAND, Sir Henry, English author and physician, b. at Knutsford, Cheshire, 1788; studied medicine at the University of Edinburgh, and graduated M.D. 1811; appointed physician in ordinary to the late Prince Consort, 1840, and to the Queen, 1852; created a baronet, 1853. Author of 'Medical Notes and Reflections;' and other works.

HOLMES, John, b. 1830; is a deputy-lieutenant for the Tower Hamlets, and a magistrate for Lanarkshire; elected M.P. for the new borough of Hackney, 1868.

HOLMES, Oliver Wendell, American author, b. at Cambridge, Massachusetts, Aug. 29, 1809; entered Harvard College, and graduated in 1829; received the degree of M.D. 1836; appointed professor of anatomy and physiology in Harvard College, 1847. Author of 'Report on Medical Literature,' 1848; 'The Autocrat of the Breakfast Table;' 'Elsie Venner;' and numerous songs and poems.

HOLMESDALE, William Archer Amherst, Viscount, English politician, b. 1836; educated at Eton; a magistrate of Kent; formerly captain in the Coldstream Guards; served in the Crimea, 1854–55; M.P. for West Kent, 1859–68.

HOLST, Hans Peder, Danish author, b. at Copenhagen, Oct. 22, 1811; appointed master of Danish language and logic at the Academy of Cadets, 1836. Author of 'National Romances,' 1832; and several novels and poems.

HOLT, James Maden, b. 1829; a magistrate for Lancashire; elected for North-East Lancashire, 1868.

HOME, Cospatrick Alexander Home, Earl, English administrator, b. 1799; entered the diplomatic service, and was attaché to the embassy at St. Petersburg, 1822; under-secretary of state, 1828–30; succeeded his father, tenth earl, 1841; deputy-lieutenant of Berwickshire.

HOME, Daniel Douglas, spiritualist, b. March 1833. Author of 'Incidents of my Life,' 1863.

HONE, Ven. Richard Brindley, English divine, b. 1805; educated at Brasenose College, Oxford, where he graduated B.A. 1827; honorary canon of Worcester, 1845; archdeacon of Worcester, 1849. Author of 'Lives of Eminent Christians,' in 4 vols.; and several sermons.

HONOLULU, Right Rev. Thomas Staley, Bishop of, English divine, b. at Sheffield, Yorkshire, 1823; educated at Queen's College, Cambridge, where he graduated in 1844, and was elected fellow, 1846; consecrated first missionary bishop of Honolulu, Sandwich Islands, 1861.

HOOD, Sir Alexander Ackland, English politician, b. 1819; educated at Rugby; a deputy-lieutenant of Somerset; formerly captain in the Royal Horse Guards; M.P. for West Somersetshire, 1859–68.

HOOD, Rev. Edwin Paxton, English author, b. at Weston, 1820; minister of an Independent chapel at Brighton. Author of 'The Age and its Architects;' 'Life of Swedenborg;' 'Genius and Industry;' 'Mental and Moral Philosophy of Laughter;' and numerous other works.

HOOK, James Clarke, English painter, b. 1818; studied in the schools of the Royal Academy. Painted 'Bassanio commenting on the Caskets,' from the Merchant of Venice, 1847; 'Times of the Persecution of the Reformers in Paris,' 1854; 'Luff Boy,' 1859; and numerous other works. Elected A.R.A. 1854; R.A. 1859.

HOOK, Very Rev. Walter Farquhar, English divine, b. 1798; educated at Winchester College, and at Christ Church, Oxford, where he graduated in 1821; vicar of Leeds, 1837; dean of Chichester, 1859. Author of 'Lives of the Archbishops of Canterbury,' 1861–64; and several theological works.

HOOKER, Joseph, American military commander, b. at Hadley, Massachusetts, 1819; cadet at West Point, 1833; lieutenant, 1837; captain, 1846; major, June 1847; lieutenant-colonel, Sept. 1847; resigned, Feb. 1858; appointed lieutenant-colonel and brigadier-general of Volunteers, 1861; major-general of Volunteers, Aug. 1862; major-general of the U.S. army, Jan. 1863.

HOOKER, Joseph Dalton, English botanist, b. 1817; graduated M.D. 1841; appointed assistant director of Kew Gardens, 1855. Author of 'Flora Antarctica;' 'Himalayan Journals,' 1852; 'Flora Indica;' and other botanical works.

HOPE, Alexander Beresford, English politician, b. 1820; educated at Harrow, and Trinity College, Cambridge, where he graduated B.A. 1841; M.P. for Maidstone, 1841 to 1852, and 1857 to 1859; returned for Cambridge University, 1868.

HOPE, Sir James, English naval commander, b. at Edinburgh, 1808; entered the Royal Naval College, and became a midshipman, 1822; captain, 1838; commander-in-chief of the English naval forces on the East India station and the Chinese coast, 1859–60; on the West India station, 1863.

HOPETOWN, John Alexander Hope, Earl of, English administrator, b. at Edinburgh, 1831; educated at Harrow, and Christ Church, Oxford; lord-lieutenant of Linlithgowshire.

HOPKINS, Edward John, English musical composer, b. 1818; studied music in the choir of the Chapel Royal, St. James's, 1826 to 1833; appointed organist of the Temple Church, 1843. Composed the anthems, 'Let us now go even unto Bethlehem;' 'Why seek ye the living among the dead?' and numerous chants and anthems.

HOPKINS, John Larkin, English musical composer, b. 1820, cousin of the preceding; educated in the choir of Westminster Abbey; successively organist of Rochester Cathedral and of Trinity College, Cambridge. Author of a great number of chants and services.

HOPKINS, John Henry, American theologian, b. in Dublin, 1792; called to the bar, 1817; ordained to the American Episcopal Church, 1823; appointed rector of Trinity Church, Pittsburg, 1824; elected first bishop of Vermont, 1832. Author of 'Christianity Vindicated,' 1833; and numerous theological works.

HORNBY, Sir Phipps, English admiral, b. 1785; entered the navy, 1797; attained flag rank, 1846, and full admiral, 1858; commander-in-chief on the Pacific station, 1847 to 1851; made a K.C.B. 1852, and G.C.B. 1861.

HORNBY, William Henry, English politician, b. 1805; a magistrate and deputy-lieutenant of Lancashire; M.P. for Blackburn since 1857.

HORNE, Richard Henry, English author, b. 1807; educated at the Royal Military College, Sandhurst; entered the Mexican navy as a midshipman; appointed commander of the Gold Escort, at Melbourne, 1852. Author of 'The Death of Marlowe;' 'Orion;' 'Judas Iscariot,' a miracle play; and other poetical and dramatic works.

HORSFALL, Thomas Berry, English politician, b. 1805; a magistrate and deputy-lieutenant of Lancashire and Staffordshire; was first president of Liverpool Chamber of Commerce; mayor of Liverpool, 1847; M.P. for Derby, 1852–53; and for Liverpool, 1853–68.

HORSLEY, John Callcott, English painter, b. in London, Jan. 19, 1817. Exhibited 'Rent-day at Haddon Hall in the Sixteenth Century;' 'Winning Gloves,' 1842; and numerous other paintings. Elected A.R.A. 1864.

HORSMAN, Right Hon. Edward, English statesman, b. 1807; educated at Rugby; called to the Scottish bar, 1832; a lord of the Treasury, June to Sept. 1841; chief secretary for Ireland, 1855–57; M.P. for Cockermouth, 1836 to 1852, and for Stroud, 1853–68.

HOSMER, Harriett, American sculptor, b. at Watertown, Massachusetts, Oct. 9, 1830; studied at the Medical College of St. Louis, and in Rome, under Gibson. Sculptured 'Daphne' and 'Medusa,' 1852; 'Puck,' 1855; and other statues and busts.

HOTHAM, Beaumont, Baron, English administrator, b. Aug. 9, 1794; general on half-pay, unattached; served in the Peninsula and at Waterloo; a magistrate and deputy-lieutenant of the East Riding of Yorkshire; M.P. for Leominster, 1820 to 1841, and for the East Riding of Yorkshire, 1841–66.

HOUGHTON, Right Hon. Richard Monckton Milnes, Baron, English author, b. 1809; educated at Trinity College, Cambridge, where he graduated M.A. 1831; D.C.L. Oxford, 1856; M.P. for Pontefract, 1837 to 1863, when he was elevated to the peerage. Author of 'Life of Keats;' 'Poems;' and many articles in the leading Reviews.

HOUSSAYE, Arsène, French dramatist, b. at Bruyères, near Laon, March 28, 1815; appointed director of the Théâtre Française, 1852; resigned, 1856. Author of 'Couronne de Bluets,' 1836; 'History of Dutch and Flemish Painting,' 1846; 'Le Roi Voltaire,' 1858; 'Histoire de l'Art française,' 1860; and numerous other works.

HOWARD, Hon. Charles Wentworth George, English politician, b. 1814; educated at Eton, and Trinity College, Cambridge, where he graduated M.A. 1836; a magistrate for Cumberland; M.P. for East Cumberland since 1840.

HOWARD, Lord Edward George, English administrator, b. 1818; educated at Trinity College, Cambridge; deputy-lieutenant of Derbyshire; was vice-chamberlain of the Household, 1846–52; M.P. for Horsham, 1848–52; and for Arundel, 1852–68.

HOWARD, Sir Henry Francis, English diplomatist, b. 1809; educated at Stonyhurst, and the University of Edinburgh; secretary of legation at the Hague, 1845; transferred to Berlin, 1846; envoy-extraordinary and minister-plenipotentiary to the Emperor of Brazil, 1832, to Lisbon, 1855, and to Hanover, 1859; made a K.C.B. 1863.

HOWARD, Hon. Henry George, English diplomatist, b. 1818; entered the diplomatic service as attaché to the embassy at Paris, 1838; secretary of legation at the Hague, 1846; chargé d'affaires at Lisbon, 1848; secretary of embassy at Paris, 1853; appointed envoy-extraordinary and minister-plenipotentiary at Florence, March 1858; resigned, May 1858.

HOWARD, James, partner in the firm of the eminent agricultural implement makers, b. 1821; elected M.P. for Bedford, 1868.

HOWARD DE WALDEN, Right Hon. Charles Augustus, Baron, English diplomatist, b. 1799; educated at Eton; was under-secretary of state for foreign affairs under Canning; minister at Stockholm, 1832; at Lisbon, 1833; and at Brussels, 1846.

HOWDEN, Right Hon. John Hobart, English diplomatist, b. 1799; lieutenant-general in the army; entered the diplomatic service, 1825; successively minister at Rio Janeiro, Monte Video, and Buenos Ayres; ambassador at the court of Madrid, 1850 to 1852; M.P. for Dundalk, 1830–32.

HOWE, Elias, American mechanician, b. at Spencer, Massachusetts, U.S. 1819; inventor of the sewing machine, first produced in 1846.

HOWE, Joseph, British colonial administrator, b. at Halifax, Nova Scotia, 1804; apprenticed to a printer, and became editor and proprietor of the *Nova Scotia*, 1828; member of the provincial government, 1840; for several years colonial agent in Great Britain. Published 'Speeches and Public Letters,' 1858.

HOWE, Samuel Gridley, American oculist, b. at Boston, Massachusetts, Nov. 10, 1801; graduated at Brown University, 1821; joined the Greek army as military surgeon, 1824; appointed physician of the Institution for the Blind at Boston, 1831.

HOWES, Edward, English politician, b. 1813; educated at Trinity College, Oxford, where he graduated B.A. 1825; called to the bar of Lincoln's Inn, 1839; a J.P. and deputy-lieutenant of Norfolk, and chairman of Quarter Sessions; M.P. for South Norfolk since 1859.

HOWITT, Mary, English authoress, b. at Uttoxeter, Staffordshire, 1804; married to Mr. William Howitt, 1823. Author of 'The Seven Temptations,' 1830; 'Ballads and other Poems,' 1847; the 'Stories of Stapleford,' 1863; 'The Coast of Caergwyn,' 1864; and many other works of fiction.

HOWITT, William, English author, b. at Heanor, Derbyshire, 1795; educated at a Quakers' school. Author of 'The Forest Minstrel,' 1823; 'History of Priestcraft,' 1833; 'The Rural Life of England,' 1837; the 'Illustrated History of England,' in 6 vols. 1861; and numerous other works.

HOWSON, Rev. John Saul, English theologian, b. 1816; educated at Trinity College, Cambridge, where he graduated B.A. 1837; ordained, 1845; principal of the Collegiate Institution at Liverpool in 1849; dean of Chester, 1867. Author of numerous lectures and sermons; contributor to the *Quarterly Review.*

HUBBARD, John Gillibrand, English administrator, b. 1805; a magistrate and deputy-lieutenant of Bucks; one of the directors of the Bank of England, and chairman of the Public Works Exchequer Loan Commission; M.P. for Buckingham, 1859–68. Author of 'Vindication of a Fixed Duty on Corn,' 1842; 'The Currency of the Country,' 1843; and other pamphlets.

HUDDLESTON, John Walter, English politician, b. 1817; educated at Trinity College, Dublin; called to the bar of Gray's Inn, 1839; appointed Q.C. 1857; one of the members of the Council of Legal Education, and a bencher of Gray's Inn; M.P. for Canterbury, 1865–68.

HUDSON, George, English railway administrator, b. at York, 1800; a magistrate for York, and was three times lord mayor of that city; formerly chairman of the Eastern Counties, the Midland, and the York, Newcastle, and Berwick Railways, and of the Sunderland Dock Company; M.P. for Sunderland, 1845 to 1859.

HUDSON, Sir James, English diplomatist, b. 1810; educated at Rugby and Westminster; was private secretary to King William IV.; entered the diplomatic service, and was appointed secretary of legation at Washington, 1838, to the Hague, and to Rio Janeiro; minister at Rio Janeiro, 1850–51; transferred to Florence; minister-plenipotentiary at Turin, 1852–63; created K.C.B. 1855; and G.C.B. 1863.

HUEBNER, Joseph, Baron von, Austrian diplomatist, b. at Vienna, Nov. 26, 1811; studied at the University of Vienna; appointed to a post in the ministry of foreign affairs, 1833; attaché to the embassy at Paris, 1837; secretary to the embassy in Portugal, 1840; chargé d'affaires at Leipsic, 1844; Austrian ambassador to Paris, 1849; signed the Treaty of Paris, 1856.

HUGESSEN, Edward Knatchbull, English administrator, b. 1829; educated at Eton, and Magdalen College, Oxford; a magistrate and deputy-lieutenant of Kent; appointed a lord of the Treasury, 1859; M.P. for Sandwich since 1857.

HUGHES, Sir Frederick, English diplomatist, b. 1814 ; entered the Madras Cavalry, and served in Persia ; employed on a political mission in Circassia and the Crimea during the Russian war, 1854-55 ; knighted, 1858.

HUGHES, Thomas, English author, b. 1823 ; educated at Rugby and Oriel College, Oxford, where he graduated B.A. 1845 ; called to the bar of Lincoln's Inn, 1848 ; M.P. for Lambeth, 1865–68 ; returned M.P. for Frome, 1868. Author of 'Tom Brown's School-days,' 1856 ; 'Tom Brown at Oxford,' 1861 ; and other works.

HUGHES, William Bulkeley, English politician, b. 1797 ; educated at Harrow ; called to the bar of Lincoln's Inn, 1825 ; a magistrate of Anglesey, and J.P. and deputy-lieutenant of the county of Carnarvon ; M.P. for Carnarvon, 1837–59, and since 1865.

HUGO, Rev. Thomas, English historical writer, b. at Taunton, 1820 ; educated at Worcester College, Oxford, where he graduated B.A. 1842 ; appointed rector of All Saints, Skinner-street London, 1858. Author of 'Memoir of Gundulph, Bishop of Rochester,' 1853 ; and numerous other works.

HUGO, Victor, French poet and novelist, b. at Besançon, Feb. 26, 1802 ; admitted to the French Academy, 1841 ; created a peer of France by Louis Philippe ; exiled from France and resident in the Isle of Guernsey since 1852. Author of 'Odes and Ballads,' 1822 ; 'Last Days of a Condemned Criminal,' 1829 ; 'Hernani,' first played at the Théâtre Français, 1830 ; 'Notre Dame de Paris,' 1831 ; 'Les Misérables,' 1863 ; 'Les Travailleurs de la Mer,' 1866 ; and numerous other works.

HULL, Edward, English geologist, b. 1810 ; employed upon the Geological Survey of Great Britain under the late Sir H. de la Beche. Author of 'History, Structure, and Resources of the Coal-fields of Great Britain ;' 'Geological Survey of the United Kingdom,' 1860–62 ; and other works on geology.

HULLAH, John, English musical composer, b. at Worcester, 1812 ; studied music under Horsley, 1829, and under Crivelli at the Royal Academy of Music, 1832 ; established the system of singing known by his name in 1840 ; professor of vocal music in King's College, and in Queen's College, London. Composer of the opera of 'The Village Coquettes,' and many other musical pieces. Author of 'The History of Modern Music.'

HUME, Rev. Abraham, English writer, b. 1815 ; educated at Belfast College, at Glasgow University, and Trinity College, Dublin ; ordained, 1843 ; appointed incumbent of a parish in Liverpool, 1847. Published 'The Learned Societies and Printing Clubs of the United Kingdom,' 1847 ; 'Results of the Irish Census, with a special reference to the Church in Ireland,' 1864 ; and numerous other works.

HUME, Hamilton, Australian traveller, b. at Humewood, New South Wales, 1797 ; discovered the district of Cowpasture River, 1810 ; led a party across the Blue Mountains, 1824, and accomplished the first overland journey from New South Wales to Victoria. Author of 'A Brief Statement of Facts in connexion with an Overland Expedition from Lake George to Port Phillip in the year 1824,' 1855.

HUMPHERY, William Henry, English politician, b. 1828 ; educated at Winchester, and at Wadham College, Oxford, where he graduated B.A. 1850, and M.A. 1853 ; called to the bar of the Inner Temple, 1852 ; M.P. for Andover, 1863–68.

HUMPHREYS, Henry Noel, English author, b. at Birmingham, 1810 ; educated at King Edward's Grammar School, Birmingham, and on the Continent. Author of 'Literary Sketches ;' 'Goethe in Strasburg ;' and other works.

HUMPHRY, Rev. William Gilson, English theological writer, b. 1815 ; educated at Trinity College, Cambridge, where he graduated B.A. 1837 ; appointed vicar of St. Martin's-in-the-Fields, 1855. Author of 'The Doctrine of a Future State,' 1849 ; 'The Miracles,' 1857 ; and many sermons and lectures.

HUNT, Right Hon. George Ward, English statesman, b. 1825 ; educated at Eton, and Christ Church, Oxford, where he graduated B.A. 1848 ; called to the bar of the Inner Temple, 1851 ; secretary to the Treasury, 1866–68 ; chancellor of the Exchequer, Feb. 1 to Dec. 1868 ; M.P. for North Northamptonshire since 1857.

HUNT, Robert, English geologist, b. at Devonport, Sept. 6, 1807 ; keeper of mining records at the Museum of Practical Geology. Author of 'Researches on Light ;' 'The Poetry of Science ;' and numerous other works. Editor of 'Ure's Dictionary of Arts, Manufactures, and Mines.'

HUNT, Thomas Sterry, American chemist, b. in Norwich, Connecticut, Sept. 5, 1826 ; was chemical assistant to Professor Silliman in Yale College ; appointed professor of chemistry in the University of Quebec, 1857. Author of 'Solution ;' 'Chemical Changes ;' and other scientific works.

HUNT, William Holman, English painter, b. in London, 1827. Exhibited 'Dr. Rochecliffe performing Divine Service in the Cottage of Joceline Joliffe at Woodstock,' 1847 ; 'Our English Coasts,' 1853; 'The Light of the World,' and the 'Awakening Conscience,' 1854 ; 'The Scapegoat,' 1856 ; 'Finding of the Saviour in the Temple,' 1860 ; and numerous other paintings.

HUNTER, Robert Mercer, American statesman, b. in Essex County, Virginia, April 21, 1809; graduated at the University of Virginia, and called to the bar, 1830 ; elected to Congress, 1837 ; Speaker in the Congress of 1841 ; elected to the Senate, 1847 ; chairman of the Finance Committee, 1850 ; returned for the third time to the Senate, 1858.

HUNTINGTON, Daniel, American painter, b. in New York, 1816; studied under Professor Morse. Painted the 'Toper Asleep ;' the 'Bar Room Politician ;' 'The Roman Penitents,' 1845 ; 'The Communion of the Sick ;' 'Queen Mary signing the Death Warrant of Lady Jane Grey ;' and numerous other, chiefly historical, pictures.

HURLSTONE, Frederick Yeates, English painter, b. in London, 1801 ; studied at the Royal Academy : president of the Society of British Artists. Executed 'Arthur and Constance,' and 'The Farewell of Bobadil to Granada,' exhibited at the International Exhibition at Paris, 1855 ; and numerous other paintings.

HURST, Robert Henry, English administrator, b. 1817 : educated at Westminster, and Trinity College, Cambridge ; called to the bar of the Middle Temple, 1842 ; deputy-lieutenant of Sussex ; recorder of Rye and Hastings, 1862 ; M.P. for Horsham since 1865.

HUTT, Right Hon. Sir William, English statesman, b. 1803 ; educated at Trinity College, Cambridge, where he graduated B.A. 1827 ; M.A. 1831 ; vice-president of the Board of Trade and paymaster-general, 1860–65 ; M.P. for Hull, 1832–41, and for Gateshead since 1841.

HUXLEY, Thomas Henry, English naturalist, b. at Ealing, Middlesex, 1825 ; educated at Ealing School, and studied medicine at the Medical School of the Charing Cross Hospital ; appointed professor of natural history in the Government School of Mines, London, 1854. Author of 'Man's Place in Nature ;' and numerous memoirs and papers for the Geological and other societies.

HUXTABLE, Rev. Anthony, English agricultural writer, b. 1808 ; studied at Trinity College, Cambridge, where he graduated B.A. 1833 ; ordained, 1834 ; appointed prebendary of Torleton in Salisbury Cathedral, 1854. Published 'Lectures on the Science and Application of Manures,' 1847 ; 'The Present Prices,' 1850.

HYMERS, Rev. John, English mathematician, b. 1803 ; educated at St. John's College, Cambridge, where he graduated B.A. 1826 ; appointed rector of Brandsburton, Yorkshire, 1852. Author of 'The Elements of the Theory of Astronomy ;' 'Treatise on Conic Sections ;' and numerous other works.

I.

IANKOWITSCH, Alexis, Servian statesman, b. at Temesvar, 1810 ; entered the administration of Servia, 1829 ; secretary to Prince Michel, 1839 ; one of the promoters of the Revolution of 1842 ; chancellor of Servia, 1843 ; minister of justice, 1847–48 ; senator and coadjutor of the minister of foreign affairs, 1850 ; chancellor of state, 1855 ; resigned, 1856.

ILCHESTER, William Strangways, Earl of, English diplomatist, b. 1795 ; studied at the University of Oxford ; entered the diplomatic service, 1815 ; secretary of embassy at Vienna, 1832 ; under-secretary of state for foreign affairs, 1835 to 1840 ; British envoy at Frankfort, 1840 to 1849 ; succeeded his brother, third earl, 1858.

INCHIQUIN, Lucius O'Brien, Baron, Irish administrator, b. 1800 ; educated at Harrow, and Trinity College, Cambridge, where he graduated B.A. 1825, M.A. 1828 ; lord-lieutenant of the county of Clare ; M.P. for that county, 1826 to 1830, and from 1847 to 1852 ; succeeded his cousin, twelfth baron, 1855.

INDUNO, Domenico, Italian painter, b. at Milan, 1815 ; studied at the Academy of his native town. Painted 'Samuel and David,' in the museum of Vienna ; and many others, principally historical pictures.

INGELOW, Jean, English authoress, b. 1830. Author of 'A Story of Doom ;' and numerous poems and works of fiction.

INGERSOLL, Charles Jared, American author, b. at Philadelphia, Oct. 3, 1782; elected to the House of Representatives, 1812. Author of 'Chismara,' 1800; 'Julian,' 1831; 'Historical Sketch of the Second War between the United States and Great Britain,' 1845; and 'History of the Territorial Acquisitions of the United States.'

INGHAM, Robert, English politician, b. 1793; educated at Oriel College, Oxford, where he graduated B.A. 1815; called to the bar, 1820; attorney-general for the county of Durham, and recorder of Berwick; sat for the borough of Berwick, 1832–41, and for South Shields, 1852–68.

INGLIS, Right Hon. John, Scottish judge, b. 1810; educated at Glasgow, and Balliol College, Oxford, where he graduated B.A. 1834; called to the Scottish bar, 1835; nominated solicitor-general for Scotland, 1852; lord-advocate, 1852 and 1858; elevated to the bench as lord justice clerk of session, 1858; sworn privy councillor, 1859.

INGRAHAM, Duncan, American naval officer, b. 1803; entered the United States Navy, 1812; commanded the frigate *Sommers*, in the war with Mexico; commander of the *St. Louis*, and stationed in the Mediterranean, 1853; joined the South at the outbreak of the civil war, 1861, and was appointed commodore by the Government at Richmond.

INNES, Arthur Charles, English politician, b. 1834; educated at Eton; a magistrate of the county of Down; M.P. for Newry, 1865–68.

IRONS, Rev. William Josiah, English theologian, b. 1812; educated at Queen's College, Oxford, where he graduated B.A. 1833; appointed vicar of Brompton, Middlesex, 1842. Author of 'An Epitome of the Bampton Lectures of Dr. Hampden;' and numerous sermons and lectures.

IRVING, Theodore, American author, b. 1810; appointed secretary of embassy in London, 1840; ordained a minister in the Episcopal Protestant Church, 1854. Author of 'The Conquest of Florida,' New York, 1835; 'The Fountain of Living Waters,' 1849; and other works.

ISABELLE, Charles Édouard, French architect, b. at Havre, Feb. 24, 1800; studied at the École des Beaux Arts, 1818–22. Constructed at Angers the École des Arts et Métiers, 1835–42. Published 'Les Edifices circulaires, et les Dômes,' 1843–50; and other works.

ISABEY, Eugene, French painter, b. at Paris, July 22, 1804. Exhibited 'La Plage de Honfleur;' 'L'Ouragan devant Dieppe,' 1827; 'Vue de Boulogne,' 1834; 'Incendie du Steamer l'Austria,' 1859; and numerous landscapes and marine scenes.

ISELIN, Henri Frédéric, French sculptor, b. at Clairegoutte, Haute Saône, 1825; studied sculpture under Rude, and at the École des Beaux Arts. Executed 'Jean Goujon' for the minister of the interior, 1852; 'Le Genie du Feu,' a group for the new Louvre; 'Augustin Thierry' for the galleries of Versailles, 1864; and numerous groups and busts.

ISMAIL PACHA, Turkish statesman, b. near Smyrna, 1812; studied at the School of Medicine at Constantinople, and graduated at Pisa, 1840; appointed physician-in-chief to the Sultan, and member of the council of ministers, 1865.

ISMAIL PACHA, Viceroy of Egypt, b. 1828; succeeded his brother, Said, Jan. 18, 1863.

ISTURITZ, Xavier d', Spanish statesman, b. at Cadiz, 1790; deputy to the Cortes, 1812–18; president of the Cortes, 1823; minister of state for foreign affairs and president of the council, 1836; president of Congress, 1832; replaced Narvaez as minister, Feb. to March 1846; ambassador to St. Petersburg, 1856; accredited to London, 1858; Spanish ambassador to France, 1863–64.

ITIER, André Jules, French author, b. 1805; appointed by the ministers of commerce and finance to proceed on a commercial mission to China, 1842. Author of 'Journal d'un Voyage en Chine pendant les Années 1843, 1844, 1845 and 1846,' 1853, in 3 vols.

IVORY, James, Scottish judge, b. at Dundee, 1792; called to the bar, 1816; solicitor-general for Scotland, 1839; one of the senators of the College of Justices, 1840, when he took the courtesy title of Lord Ivory; a lord justiciary, 1849–62.

J.

JACINI, Pietro, Italian statesman, b. at Milan, 1827; minister of public works in the cabinet of Count Cavour, July 21, 1860, to June 12, 1861; reappointed minister of public works, 1864; resigned, 1867.

JACKSON, Sir Charles Mitchell, English colonial judge, b. 1814; called to the bar of Lincoln's Inn, 1836; advocate-general at Calcutta, 1848; puisne judge at Bombay, 1852; judge of the High Court of Judicature of Calcutta, 1862–63.

JACKSON, Charles Thomas, American geologist, b. at Plymouth, Massachusetts, June 21, 1805; graduated M.D. in Havard University, 1829; engaged on a geological survey of Maine, Rhode Island, and New Hampshire, 1836–40. Author of many works on geology and chemistry.

JACKSON, Rev. Thomas, English divine, b. 1812; educated at St. Mary's Hall, Oxford, where he graduated B.A. 1834; nominated to a bishopric in New Zealand, 1849, but was not consecrated; rector of Stoke Newington, and prebendary of St. Paul's Cathedral. Author of 'A Manual of Logic,' and other works.

JACKSON, William, English politician, b. 1805; a magistrate and deputy-lieutenant of Cheshire; formerly a merchant at Liverpool; M.P. for Newcastle-under-Lyne, 1847–65; returned for North Derbyshire, 1865.

JACOBS, Paul, German painter, b. at Leipsic, 1800; studied at the Academy of Munich. Painted 'The Resurrection of Lazarus;' 'Sampson and Delilah,' 1850; 'Luther at the Diet of Worms;' and numerous others, chiefly historical pictures.

JACOBSON, Heinrich, German jurist, b. at Marienwerder, 1804; studied law at Königsberg, Berlin, and Göttingen; appointed professor of jurisprudence at Königsberg, 1836. Author of 'Kirchenrechtliche Versuche,' Königsberg, 1831–33; 'Geschichte der Quellen des Kirchenrechts des preussischen Staates,' ib. in 3 vols. 1837–44.

JACOBSON, Rev. William, English divine, b. 1805; educated at Lincoln College, Oxford, and graduated B.A. 1827; vice-president of Magdalen Hall, 1832 to 1848, when he was appointed regius professor of divinity, and created D.D. by decree of Convocation; bishop of Chester, 1865. Edited, for the Oxford University Press, 'The Remains of the Apostolic Fathers,' and other works.

JACOBY, Johann, German politician, b. at Königsberg, 1805; studied medicine at Berlin and Heidelberg; member of the first Parliament of Frankfort, 1848, and of the National Assembly at Berlin, 1849; retired to Switzerland, 1850; re-elected to the Prussian Parliament, 1862; condemned to imprisonment for his political opinions, 1864.

JACQUAND, Claude, French painter, b. at Lyons, 1805; studied at the Academy of his native town, and under Fleury Richard. Painted for the Hôtel de Ville at Boulogne-sur-Mer 'Le Maire de Boulogne refusant la Capitulation de Henry VIII. en 1544,' 1852 to 1855; 'The Baptism of Clovis,' 1860; 'Dante at Rome,' 1864; and numerous other works, chiefly historical.

JACQUES, Ame'de'e Florent, French author, b. at Paris, July 4, 1813; studied at the Bourbon College; one of the founders of *La Liberté de Penser*, 1847. Author of 'Manuel de Philosophie,' 1847; 'Excursion au Rio Salado et dans le Chaco,' 1857; and other works.

JADIN, Louis Godefroy, French landscape and animal painter, b. at Paris, 1805; studied under Hersent and Abel de Pujol. Exhibited 'Les Plaines de Montfort-l'Amaury;' 'La Vision de St. Hubert,' 1859; 'Douze Chiens, Race de Virelade,' 1864; and many other paintings.

JAEGER, Gustav, German painter, b. at Leipsic, June 12, 1808; studied at the Academy of Dresden, and at Munich, under Julius Schnorr, of Carolsfeld, 1830; appointed to execute a number of frescoes to decorate the new royal palace at Munich. Painted 'The Election of Frederick to the Empire;' 'The Coronation of Charlemagne at Rome;' 'The Death of Moses;' and many other historical pictures.

JAHN, Otto, German archæologist, b. at Kiel, Holstein, June 16, 1813; studied at Berlin, 1833, under Lachmann and Gerhard; graduated Ph.D. 1836; appointed professor of archæology and philosophy at Greifswald, 1842; the same at Leipsic, 1847; director of the Leipsic Archæological Museum, 1851–52. Author of 'W. A. Mozart,' Leipsic, 1856; and other works.

JAL, Auguste, French author, b. at Lyons, April 12, 1795; studied at the École de Brest, 1811–15. Author of ' Mes Visites au Musée du Luxembourg,' 1818; 'Archéologie navale,' 2 vols. 1839; 'Glossaire nautique,' 1850; and numerous other works.

JALABERT, Charles François, French painter, b. at Nîmes, 1819; studied under P. Delaroche. Painted 'Virgile lisant ses Géorgiques,' 1847; 'Le Christ aux Oliviers,' 1855; 'Le Christ marchant sur la Mer,' 1863; and many other pictures.

JALEY, Le'on Louis Nicolas, French sculptor, b. at Paris, Jan. 27, 1802; studied at the École des Beaux Arts, 1820. Executed 'Le Duc d'Orléans' for the Chamber of Peers, 1844; 'La Révélation,' 1863; and many other statues, busts, and groups.

JAMAICA, George Spencer, Bishop of, English divine, b. 1795; educated at Magdalen Hall, Oxford; was consecrated bishop of Newfoundland, 1839; translated to Jamaica, 1843. Published a volume of sermons, and contributed poems to *Blackwood's Magazine* and other periodicals.

JAMES, Sir Henry, English military engineer, b. in Cornwall, 1803; educated at the Royal Military Academy, Woolwich; entered the corps of Engineers, 1825; colonel, 1857; successively director of the Geological Survey in Ireland, of the Admiralty engineering works at Portsmouth, of the Ordnance Survey of the United Kingdom, and of the topographical and statistical department of the War Office; knighted in 1860. Author of several works on geology and engineering.

JAMES, Sir William Milbourne, English judge; appointed vice-chancellor, Dec. 1868.

JANET, Paul, French philosophical writer, b. at Paris, April 30, 1823; studied at the Lycée St. Louis, and the École Normale; appointed professor of history and philosophy at the Sorbonne, 1864; elected member of the French Academy, Feb. 13, 1864. Author of ' Essai sur la Dialectique de Platon,' 1848; 'La Philosophie du Bonheur,' 1862; and numerous other works.

JANIN, Jules, French author, b. at Condrieu, Loire, Dec. 24, 1804; studied at the College of St. Étienne, and in Paris at the College of Louis le Grand; one of the founders of the *Revue de Paris.* Author of 'L'Ane mort et la Femme guillotinée,' 1829; 'Le Mariage du Critique,' 1841; 'L'Histoire de la Litterature dramatique,' 6 vols. 1850; and numerous other works.

JANMOT, Jean Louis, French painter, b. at Lyons, May 2, 1814; studied under Victor Orsel, at the École des Beaux Arts in Paris, and under Ingres. Painted 'La Cène' for the chapel of the Hospice de l'Antiquaille, 1845; 'La Resurrection du Fils de Naim,' 1849; 'Ophélie,' 1863; 'Eve,' 1864; and many other, principally religious and historical, pictures.

JANZE, Charles, Baron de, French politician, b. at Paris, Aug. 15, 1822; member of the General Council for the canton of Loudéac; member of the Corps Législatif for the fifth circonscription of the department des Côtes du Nord since 1863.

JARDINE, Robert, English politician, b. 1826; educated at Edinburgh; formerly a merchant in China; elected M.P. for Ashburton, 1865.

JARDINE, Sir William, English naturalist, b. 1800; educated at Edinburgh; a magistrate of Dumfriesshire. Edited Wilson's 'North American Ornithology;' the 'Naturalist's Library,' in 40 vols.; editor of the *Edinburgh Philosophical Journal.*

JARRETT, Rev. Thomas, English divine, b. 1805; educated at St. Catherine's College, Cambridge, where he graduated B.A. 1827; appointed professor of Arabic in the University of Cambridge, 1831; regius professor of Hebrew, and canon in Ely Cathedral, 1854. Author of a 'Grammatical Index to the Hebrew Text of the Book of Genesis;' and other works.

JAUCOURT, François, Count de, French politician, b. 1825; formerly secretary of embassy, and secretary to M. de Persigny; minister of the interior; elected to the Corps Législatif for the second circonscription of the department of Seine-et-Marne, 1863.

JAVAL, Le'opold, French politician, b. at Mulhouse, Dec. 1, 1804; took part in the campaign in Algeria of 1830, as second lieutenant; member of the Corps Législatif for the department of the Yonne since 1857.

JEAFFRESON, John Cordy, English author, b. at Framlingham, Suffolk, Jan. 10, 1831; studied at Pembroke College, Oxford, where he graduated B.A. 1852; called to the bar of Lincoln's Inn, 1859. Author of 'Crewe Rise,' 1854; 'Novels and Novelists from Elizabeth to Victoria;' 'Live it Down,' 1863; 'Not Dead Yet;' and numerous other works.

JEANRON, Philippe Auguste, French painter, b. at Boulogne-sur-Mer, May 10, 1809. Painted 'Les petits Patriotes,' 1831 ; 'Les Criminels cueillant le Poison de l'Upas,' 1840 ; 'à Solferino,' 1861 ; 'Bains des Bonnettes,' 1863 ; 'Le Phare,' view near Marseilles, 1864 ; and many other pictures.

JEBB, Rev. John, English theologian, b. 1805 ; educated at Trinity College, Dublin, where he graduated B.A. 1826 ; rector of Peterstow, Herefordshire, and prebendary of Hereford Cathedral. Author of 'The Divine Economy of the Church ;' 'Six Letters on the Present State of the Church,' 1851 ; and other theological works.

JELF, Rev. Richard William, English divine, b. about 1799 ; educated at Christ Church, Oxford, and graduated B.A. 1820 ; preceptor to Prince George of Cumberland, 1826–30 ; appointed canon of Christ Church, Oxford, 1839, and principal of King's College, London, 1844–64. Author of 'The Means of Grace,' 1844 ; and several sermons.

JELF, Rev. William Edward, English divine, b. at Gloucester, 1811 ; educated at Eton, and Christ Church, Oxford, and graduated B.A. 1833 ; one of the preachers at Whitehall, 1846–48 ; preached the Bampton Lectures before the University, 1857. Author of a 'Greek Grammar,' 1861 ; and other works.

JELLINEK, Adolph, German author, b. at Orslowitz, Moravia, June 26, 1820 ; studied at the University of Prague ; appointed Rabbi to the Jewish community of Leipsic, 1845. Author of ' Beiträge zur Geschichte der Kabbala,' Leipsic, 1851–52 ; 'Zur Geschichte des Kreuzzüge,' 1854 ; and numerous other works.

JENKYNS, Rev. Henry, English divine, b. 1795 ; educated at Corpus Christi College, Oxford, and graduated B.A. 1816 ; appointed professor of Greek language and literature in the University of Durham, 1833 ; canon in Durham Cathedral, 1839 ; and professor of divinity in the same University, 1841. Edited 'Cranmer's Remains,' 4 vols.

JENNER, William, English physician, b. at Chatham, 1815 ; educated at University College, London, and graduated M.D. 1844 ; became a member of the Royal College of Physicians, 1848 ; elected fellow of the same, 1852 ; appointed physician extraordinary to the Queen, 1861, and in ordinary, 1862. Author of several publications on fever and other diseases.

JEREMIE, Very Rev. James Amiraux, English divine, b. 1802 ; educated at Trinity College, Cambridge, and graduated in 1824 ; ordained, 1830 ; professor of classical literature in the East India College, Haileybury, 1830 ; elected regius professor of divinity at Cambridge, 1849 ; appointed dean of Lincoln, 1864. Author of articles on the 'History of Rome from Constantine to the Death of Julian,' 'History of the Church in the second and third Centuries,' in the ' Encyclopædia Metropolitana ;' and numerous sermons and pamphlets on theological and ecclesiastical subjects.

JERICHAU, Adam, Danish sculptor, b. 1815 ; studied under Thorwaldsen at Rome, 1839. Executed 'The Marriage of Alexander with Roxana,' a bas-relief for the frieze of the royal castle at Copenhagen ; 'Hercules and Hebe,' a colossal group, 1846 ; and other works.

JERROLD, William Blanchard, English author, b. in London, 1826. Author of 'The Disgrace to the Family,' 1847 ; 'The Chronicles of a Crutch,' 1860 ; 'The Children of Lutetia,' 1863 ; and many other works, chiefly of fiction.

JERVIS, Henry White, English politician, b. 1825 ; educated at Harrow and Woolwich ; a captain R.A. and former director of the Great Eastern Railway ; M.P. for Harwich since 1859.

JERVISWOODE, Hon. Charles Baillie, Scottish judge, b. 1804 ; called to the Scottish bar, 1830 ; appointed solicitor-general for Scotland and lord-advocate, 1858 ; appointed judge of the Supreme Court in Scotland, 1859, when he took the courtesy title of Lord Jerviswoode ; was M.P. for Linlithgowshire, 1859.

JERVOIS, William Francis Drummond, English military engineer, b. 1822 ; studied at Woolwich, and entered the Royal Engineers, 1839 ; major of brigade to the garrison of Cape Town, 1846 ; major in the army, 1852 ; appointed assistant inspector-general of fortifications, 1856.

JERVOISE, Sir Jervoise Clarke, English politician, b. 1804 ; a magistrate and deputy-lieutenant of Hants ; M.P. for South Hants since 1857.

JESSE, John Heneage, English historical writer, b. 1815. Author of 'Memoirs of the Court of England during the Reign of the Stuarts,' 1839 ; 'Memoirs of the Pretenders and their Adherents,' 1845 ; 'London and its Celebrities,' 1847–50 ; 'Memoirs of King Richard III. ;' and other works.

JEWSBURY, Geraldine, English authoress, b. at Measham, Warwickshire, 1820. Author of 'Zoe, or the History of Two Lives,' 1845 ; 'The Half-Sisters,' 1848 ; 'Right or Wrong,' 1859 ; and other works of fiction.

JOANNE, Adolphe, French topographical writer, b. at Dijon, Sept. 15, 1813; studied at the Collége Charlemagne; called to the bar at Paris, 1836; was one of the founders of *L'Illustration*, 1843. Author of 'Les Bords du Rhin illustrés,' 1863; 'La Suisse,' 1865; and many other works.

JOBBE-DUVAL, Amand, French painter, b. at Carhaix, Finistère, July 16, 1821; studied under Paul Delaroche, and at the École des Beaux Arts. Exhibited 'Marguerite dans le Jardin de Marthe,' 1845; 'Marthe et Marie Madeline au Tombeau du Christ,' 1863; and many other, chiefly religious and historical, paintings.

JOBERT DE LAMBALLE, Antoine, French physician, b. at Lamballe, Côtes du Nord, 1799; graduated M.D. in Paris, 1828; surgeon in ordinary to the Emperor Napoleon III.; elected member of the French Academy, March 31, 1856. Author of 'Études sur le Système nerveux,' 1838; 'Traité de la Réunion des Plaies dans tous les Organes,' 1864; and other medical works.

JOCHMUS, Adolph, German military commander, b. at Hamburg, 1808; entered the Greek army as a volunteer, 1828; staff-major, 1832; colonel, 1836; general-in-chief at the siege of Acre, Dec. 1840; under-secretary of state to the minister of war at Constantinople, 1841 to 1848; returned to Germany at the Revolution of 1848; appointed chancellor of the empire; minister of foreign affairs, and of the navy, May 17, 1849; resigned, Dec. 1849.

JOHANN I., King of Saxony, b. Dec. 12, 1801; second son of Duke Maximilian of Saxony, and of Princess Caroline of Parma; studied jurisprudence, and in 1822 entered the ministry of finance, of which he was nominated president in 1830; commander-in-chief of the National Guards of the kingdom, 1831–46; travelled in Italy, and published under the name of *Philalethes* a German translation of Dante's 'Divina Commedia,' 3 vols. Leipsic, 1839–49; succeeded to the throne at the death of his brother, King Frederick Augustus II., Aug. 9, 1854.

JOHNS, Rev. Bennet George, English historical writer, b. 1820; appointed chaplain of the Blind School in St. George's-in-the-Fields, 1841. Author of 'History of Spain;' 'History of the Jews between the Old and New Testament;' 'History of England;' and other writings.

JOHNS, Rev. Charles Alexander, English botanist, b. 1811; educated at Trinity College, Dublin, where he graduated B.A. 1841. Author of 'Botanical Rambles;' 'The Forest Trees of Britain;' 'British Birds in their Haunts;' and other works.

JOHNSON, Andrew, American statesman, b. at Raleigh, North Carolina, Dec. 29, 1808; apprenticed to a tailor at Raleigh, 1818–24; established himself as master tailor at Greenville, Tennessee, 1827; elected alderman of Greenville, 1828, and mayor, 1830; member of the State Legislature, 1835–37, and 1839–41; elected member of the State Senate, 1840; member of the Lower House of Congress of the United States, 1843; elected governor of Tennessee, 1853, and re-elected, 1855; senator of the United States, 1857–63; elected vice-president of the United States, Nov. 8, 1864; president from April 14, 1865, to March 4, 1869.

JOHNSON, Cuthbert William, English agricultural writer, b. Sept. 28, 1799: called to the bar, 1836. Editor of *The Farmer's Almanack*, commenced 1841; 'On the Uses of Salt for Agricultural Purposes,' 1820; 'The English Rural Spelling-Book,' 1846; and other works on agriculture.

JOHNSON, Very Rev. George Sacheverell, English divine, b. 1807; educated at Queen's College, Oxford, where he graduated B.A. 1828; appointed dean of Wells, 1854. Author of a 'Treatise on Optics;' and a volume of sermons.

JOHNSTON, Alexander, English painter, b. in Edinburgh, 1816; studied at the Royal Academy. Exhibited 'The Gentle Shepherd,' 1840; 'The Covenanter's Burial,' 1852; 'Lord and Lady Russell receiving the Sacrament in Prison,' 1846; 'Tyndal Translating the Bible,' 1856; and other paintings.

JOHNSTON, Alexander Keith, English geographer, b. at Kirkhill, near Edinburgh, Dec. 28, 1804; educated at the High School, and was apprenticed to an engraver. Published his 'National Atlas,' 1843; 'Physical Atlas of Natural Phenomena,' 1848; 'The Dictionary of Geography,' 1850; 'General and Geological Maps of Europe,' 1856; and other works.

JOHNSTON, Joseph Eccleston, American general, b. in Virginia, Feb. 1807; admitted to the U.S. Military Academy, 1825; lieutenant, 1829; captain, 1838; major, 1847; colonel, 1847; quartermaster-general of the U.S. army, June 1860; joined the South on the outbreak of civil war; general in the Confederate army, 1861–65.

JOHNSTONE, Henry Butler, English politician, b. 1837; educated at Eton, and Christ Church, Oxford, where he graduated B.A. 1860; M.P. for Canterbury since 1862.

JOIGNEAUX, Pierre, French author, b. at Varennes, Côte d'Or, 1815; member of the Constituent Assembly and Legislative Assembly, 1848–49; exiled after the coup d'état of Dec. 2, 1851. Author of 'Les Prisons de Paris,' Paris, 1841; 'Le Livre de la Ferme et des Maisons de Campagne,' 1861–64; and other works.

JOLLIFFE, Hedworth Hylton, English politician, b. 1829; educated at Eton, and Oriel College, Oxford; a magistrate of Surrey, Sussex, and Somerset, and captain of North Somerset Yeomanry; formerly lieutenant in the 4th Light Dragoons; served in the Crimea, 1854–55; M.P. for Wells since 1855.

JOLLIFFE, Right Hon. Sir William Hylton, English politician, b. 1800; a magistrate of Surrey, Sussex, and Hants; under-secretary of state for the Home Department, 1852, and 1858–59; M.P. for Petersfield, 1830–32, and 1837–38, and since 1841.

JOLLIVET, Pierre Jules, French painter, b. at Paris, June 27, 1803; studied under Baron Gros, and at the École des Beaux Arts, 1822–25. Exhibited 'Le Massacre des Innocents,' 1845; 'L'Installation de la Magistrature en 1849,' 1861; and numerous other religious and historical paintings.

JONES, David, English politician, b. 1810; educated at Charterhouse, and Christ Church, Oxford; a magistrate and deputy-lieutenant of Middlesex, Brecon, and Carmarthen; high sheriff, 1845; M.P. for Carmarthenshire since 1852.

JONES, George, English painter, b. 1786; admitted as student of the Royal Academy, 1801; served as captain in the Peninsular war in France, 1808–15; resumed his practice as a painter after the war; elected A.R.A. 1822; R.A. 1824; librarian to the Royal Academy, 1834 to 1840, and keeper from 1840 to 1850. Painted 'The Battle of Waterloo;' 'The Battle of Borodino;' and many other pictures.

JONES, Rev. Harry Longueville, English archæologist, b. 1806; educated at Magdalen College, Cambridge, where he graduated B.A. 1828, and M.A.; appointed one of her Majesty's inspectors of schools, 1848. Edited 'Archæologia Cambriensis.'

JONES, Sir Harry David, English general, b. 1792; educated at Woolwich; entered the Royal Engineers, 1808; served in the campaign in Spain, 1810–14; chairman of the Board of Works in Ireland, 1845–50; commanded the English forces at Bomarsund, 1854, and the engineering operations at Sebastopol, 1855; appointed governor of the Military College at Sandhurst, 1856; president of the Royal Commission on National Defences, 1859.

JONES, Henry Bence, English physician, b. 1814; educated at Harrow, and Trinity College, Cambridge, where he graduated B.A. 1836; appointed physician to St. George's Hospital, 1840. Author of 'Animal Chemistry;' 'Animal Electricity;' and other medical works.

JONES, John Winter, English bibliographer, b. in Lambeth, 1805; educated at St. Paul's School, and studied for the bar; appointed assistant keeper of the printed books in the British Museum, 1850, and keeper, 1856, principal librarian, 1866. Edited for the Hakluyt Society 'Divers Voyages touching the Discovery of America,' 1850; translated 'The Travels of Ludovico di Varthema in Egypt, Syria, Arabia Deserta and Felix, in Persia, India, and Ethiopia, A.D. 1503 to 1508,' 1863; and other works.

JONES, Owen, English architect, b. 1809; decorated the interior of the Great Exhibition building in Hyde Park, 1851; and the Crystal Palace at Sydenham; designed and erected St. James's Hall, Piccadilly. Author of 'The Grammar of Ornament,' 1856; 'An Attempt to define the Principles which should regulate the Employment of Colours in Decorative Art,' 1851; and other works.

JONES, Thomas Rymer, English anatomist, b. 1809; studied medicine in London, and became a member of the College of Surgeons, 1833; appointed professor of comparative anatomy in King's College, London, on its establishment; Fullerian professor of physiology in the Royal Institution, 1840. Author of 'A General Outline of the Animal Kingdom,' 1838; and other scientific works.

JONES, Thomas Wharton, English oculist, b. at St. Andrew's, 1808; educated at the University of Edinburgh; professor of ophthalmic medicine and surgery in University College, London, and surgeon to the Ophthalmic Hospital. Author of 'The Physiology and Philosophy of Body, Sense, and Mind;' and other works.

JONES, Rev. William Basil, English divine, b. 1822; educated at Shrewsbury School, and Trinity College, Oxford; elected fellow and tutor of University College, 1851; incumbent of Haxby, Yorkshire, and examining chaplain to the Archbishop of York.

JOSIKA, Nicholas, Baron, Hungarian novelist, b. 1796. Author of 'Irany;' 'The Last Bathori;' and many other works of fiction.

JOUAGE, Ce'sar, Comte de, French politician, b. April 24, 1798 ; studied at the College of Tournon, and served in the army until 1830 ; member of the Corps Législatif for the department de l'Ain since 1852.

JOUFFROY, François, French sculptor, b. at Dijon, Feb. 1, 1806; studied under Ramey, and at the École des Beaux Arts ; appointed professor of sculpture to the École des Beaux Arts, Dec. 1863. Executed 'Caïn maudit,' 1838 ; 'La Rêverie,' 1848 ; 'L'Abandon,' 1853 ; 'Châtiment,' and 'La Protection ;' and many other statues and busts.

JOURDAIN, Charles Gabriel, French author, b. at Paris, Aug. 24, 1817 : studied law and obtained the diploma of LL.D. 1838 ; appointed minister of public instruction, 1849. Author of 'Notions de hogique,' 1852–63 ; 'Histoire de l'Université de Paris aux XVII. et XVIII. Siécles,' 1862–64 ; and many other works.

JOURDAN, Louis, French novelist, b. at Toulon, 1810 ; studied at Aix. Author of 'Contes industriels,' 1859 ; 'Hermaphrodite,' 1861 ; 'Les Martyrs de l'Amour,' 1862 ; and other works of fiction.

JOWETT, Rev. Benjamin, English divine, b. at Camberwell, 1817 ; educated at St. Paul's School ; elected scholar of Balliol College, Oxford, 1835, and fellow, 1838 ; tutor of Balliol College since 1842 ; regius professor of Greek at the University, 1855. Author of 'Commentary on the Epistles of St. Paul to the Thessalonians, Galatians, and Romans,' 1855 ; second edition, 1859 ; contributed an essay on the 'Interpretation of Scripture' to the 'Essays and Reviews.'

JUAREZ, Benito, Mexican general and statesman, b. at Ixtlan, State of Oaxaca, in 1807, descendant of the Indian race of Tapatecos ; studied jurisprudence, and became advocate at Ixtlan, 1830 ; elected deputy to the House of Representatives, 1846 ; governor of the State of Oaxaca, 1848–52 ; exiled by President Santa Anna, 1853 ; returned to Mexico, 1855 ; minister of justice under President Alvarez, 1856–58 ; minister of the interior under President Comonfort, 1858 ; head of the insurrectionary forces of the Constitutional party against President Zuloaga, 1858–59, and against President Miramon, 1859–61 ; entered the city of Mexico, Jan. 12, 1861 ; elected president of the Republic, June 11, 1861 ; driven from the city of Mexico by French troops, May 31, 1863 ; ordered the execution of the Emperor Maximilian, June 16, 1867 ; re-entered the city of Mexico, July 10, 1867 ; re-elected president of the Republic, Nov. 1867.

JUBINAL, Michel Louis Achille, French author, b. at Paris, Oct. 24, 1810 ; studied at the École des Chartes ; appointed professor of foreign literature to the Faculté des Lettres de Montpellier, 1839 ; member of the Corps Législatif for the district of Bagnères since 1852. Author of 'Jongleurs et Trouvères,' 1835 ; and other works.

JUGELET, Jean, French marine painter, b. at Brest, 1805 ; studied at Paris under M. Gudin. Exhibited 'Environs de Brest,' 1833 ; 'Jésus-Christ apaisant la Tempête,' 1845 ; 'Environs d'Alassio près Nice,' 1852 ; 'Italie,' 1863 ; and numerous other paintings, chiefly sea views.

JUKES, Joseph, English geologist, b. near Birmingham, Oct. 1811 ; educated at St. John's College, Cambridge, where he graduated B.A. 1836, and M.A. 1841 ; appointed lecturer on geology to the Irish Museum of Industry, 1854. Author of 'Report on the Geology of Newfoundland ;' 'Sketch of the Physical Structure of Australia ;' and many other geological works.

JULIEN, Stanislas Aignan, French philologist, b. at Orleans, Sept. 20, 1799 ; educated at a seminary in Orleans, and in the College of France, 1823 ; appointed assistant curator to the Imperial Library, 1839; professor at the College of France, 1832. Translated from the Chinese 'The Book of Rewards and Punishments,' 1835 ; 'The Book of the Way of Virtue,' 1841 ; and numerous other Chinese works.

JURIEU LA GRAVIERE, Jean Pierre, French admiral, b. Nov. 19, 1812 ; entered the navy, 1828 ; captain, 1841 ; employed in the Black and Adriatic seas, and promoted rear-admiral, Dec. 1, 1855 ; vice-admiral, Jan. 15, 1862 ; appointed aide-de-camp to the Emperor, and member of the Board of Admiralty, June 29, 1863. Published 'Souvenirs d'un Amiral,' 1860 ; 'Voyage en Chine pendant les Années, 1847, 48, 49, and 50;' 1864 ; and other works.

K.

KAHNIS, Karl Auguste, German theologian, b. at Greiz, Dec. 22, 1814; studied at the University of Halle, and graduated at Berlin, 1842; professor of theology at Breslau, 1844; appointed professor of theology at Leipsic, and vice-president of the Missionary College, 1850. Author of 'Ruge und Hegel,' Guedlinbourg, 1888; 'Der Gang des deutschen Protestantismus,' 1854; and other theological works.

KALERGIS, De'me'trius, Greek statesman, b. at the Isle of Candia, 1803 or 1804; took part in the Greek war of independence; one of the promoters of the Revolution of September 3–15, 1843; general and aide-de-camp to King Otho, 1844–45; minister of war, 1854–56; appointed minister-plenipotentiary to Paris, 1861.

KANARIS, Constantine, Greek statesman, b. at the isle of Ipsara, 1795; served as captain in the Greek war of independence, and commanded the frigate *Hellas,* 1826; represented Ipsara in the Greek National Assembly, 1827; minister of marine, and president of the council, 1848–49; and again May 26, 1854, to May 1855; prime minister, 1862–64; minister of marine, 1864–65.

KANE, Sir Robert, English administrator, b. in Dublin, 1810; studied at Trinity College, and graduated, 1832; fellow of King and Queen's College of Physicians, Ireland, 1841; knighted, 1846; appointed member of the Irish Relief Commission, 1846; president of Queen's College, Cork. Author of 'The Elements of Chemistry,' 1841–42.

KARR, Alphonse, French author, b. at Paris, Nov. 24, 1808; studied at the Collége Bourbon. Editor-in-chief of *Figaro,* 1839, and founded *Les Guépes,* 1839; author of 'Sous les Tilleuls,' 1832; 'Une Heure trop tard,' 1833; 'La Pénélope normande,' 1858; and numerous other novels; contributor to the *Revue des Deux Mondes,* and other French periodicals.

KASTNER, Jean Georges, French musical composer, b. at Strasburg, 1812; elected member of the Institute, 1859. Composed 'Gustave Wasa;' 'Le Sarrazin;' 'La Danse de Morts,' 1852; published 'Histoire musicale des Cris de Paris,' 1855; and other works.

KAULBACH, Wilhelm von, German painter, b. at Arolsen, Westphalia, Oct. 15, 1805; studied at the Academy of Düsseldorf, and at Munich; appointed director of the Royal Academy of Fine Arts in Munich, 1849. Painted the 'Madhouse,' 1828–29; 'Battle of the Huns,' 1837; 'Bedouins,' the 'Fall of Jerusalem,' and many others; also executed a series of frescoes for the Museum of Berlin and new palace at Munich.

KAVANAGH, Julia, English authoress, b. at Thurles, county of Tipperary, 1824. Author of 'The Three Paths,' 1847; 'Women in France during the Eighteenth Century,' 1850; 'Daisy Burns,' 1853; 'Rachel Gray,' 1855; 'French Women of Letters;' and many works of fiction.

KAYE, John William, English historical writer, b. 1814; served as lieutenant of Artillery in the East India Company's service, Bengal, 1835–45; entered the Home Civil Service of the same Company, 1856; appointed secretary to the Political and Secret Department of the India Office. Author of 'The History of the War in Affghanistan;' 'Christianity in India;' 'History of the Indian Mutiny;' and other works.

KEANE, Edward Arthur, Baron, b. 1815; entered the army, 1833; aide-de-camp to his father during the campaign in Affghanistan, 1839; and retired with the rank of captain; took his seat in the House of Lords, 1844.

KEARSLEY, Robert, English politician, b. 1822; a magistrate for Ripon, and thrice mayor of that borough; captain in the 1st West Yorkshire Rifle Volunteers, 1864; elected M.P. for Ripon, 1865.

KEATING, Sir Henry Singer, English judge, b. near Dublin, 1804; educated at Trinity College, Dublin, where he graduated M.A.; called to the bar of the Inner Temple, 1832; M.P. for Reading, 1852; solicitor-general and knighted, 1857; judge of the Common Pleas.

KEATINGE, Right Hon. Richard, Irish judge, b. 1793; called to the bar at Dublin, 1813; judge of the Prerogative Court of Ireland, and sworn privy councillor, *1843; appointed* judge of the Court of Probate in Ireland, 1858.

KEIGHTLY, Thomas, English historical writer, b. in Dublin, 1789; educated at Trinity College, Dublin. Published a 'History of Rome;' 'History of England;' 'The Mythology of Greece and Italy,' 1854; 'History of India;' and other works.

KEITH, Rev. Alexander, English theologian, b. at Keithall, N.B. 1791; educated at Marischal College, Aberdeen; minister of the Established Church of Scotland at St. Cyrus, Kincardineshire, 1816–43. Author of 'The Signs of the Times,' 1831; 'The History and Destiny of the World and of the Church, according to Scripture,' Part I. 1861; 'A Narrative of the Mission to the Jews;' and other theological works.

KEKEWICH, Samuel Trehawke, English politician, b. 1796; educated at Eton, and Christ Church, Oxford; a magistrate and deputy-lieutenant for Devon; high sheriff, 1834; M.P. for Exeter, 1826–30, and for South Devon since 1858.

KELK, John, English politician, b. 1816; a J.P. and deputy-lieutenant for Middlesex, and a railway contractor; returned M.P. for Harwich, 1865.

KELLER, Emile, French politician, b. 1828; studied at the École Polytechnique; elected to the Corps Législatif for the third circonscription of the department of the Haut Rhin, 1857, and re-elected for the fourth circonscription of the same department, 1863. Author of 'L'Encyclique et les Libertés de l'Église gallicane,' 1860; and other works.

KELLER, Joseph, German engraver, b. at Linz-on-the-Rhine, 1815; studied at the Academy of Düsseldorf. Executed 'The Madonna' of Deger; 'The Evangelists,' after Ary Scheffer; 'The Trinity,' after Raffaelle; and numerous other engravings after celebrated paintings.

KELLER VON STEINBOCK, Friedrich Ludwig, Swiss jurist, b. at Zurich, Oct. 17, 1799; studied at the University of Göttingen, and graduated LL.D. 1822; professor of law at Zurich, 1825; judge and president of the Superior Court; professor of law at Halle, 1848, and at Berlin, 1847; member of the second Prussian Chamber. Author of several legal works.

KELLY, Sir Fitzroy, English judge, b. 1796; called to the bar of Lincoln's Inn, 1824; king's counsel and bencher of Lincoln's Inn, 1835; a deputy-lieutenant of Suffolk; solicitor-general, 1845–46, and in 1852; attorney-general, 1858–59; chief baron of the Exchequer, 1866.

KEMAL, Effendi, Turkish diplomatist, b. at Constantinople, 1809; entered the department of finance, 1828; member of the Council of Education, and inspector-general of schools of the empire, 1839–49; ambassador to Berlin, 1854–57. Author of 'Guide to Conversation in Persian and Turkish,' Constantinople, 1842; and several elementary works for schools.

KEMBLE, Adelaide, English actress, b. 1816, younger daughter of the late Charles Kemble; sang at the York festival, 1834; made her début in Italy, at Venice, as 'Norma;' appeared in London, in 'Norma,' in 1841, and numerous other operas. Married to Mr. Frederick N. Sartoris, 1843.

KEMBLE, Frances Anne, English actress and authoress, b. in London, 1811, sister of the preceding; made her début at Covent Garden Theatre, Oct. 5, 1829. Authoress of 'Francis I.' a tragedy, 1828; 'Journal,' 1835; 'A Year of Consolation;' a volume of poems, and several translations. Married to Mr. Pierce Butler, 1835, from whom she obtained a divorce, 1849.

KEMENY, Sigismund, Baron, Hungarian statesman, b. in Transylvania, 1816; studied at the Catholic and the Reform Colleges; member of the Diet of Clausenburg, 1834; deputy to the National Hungarian Assembly, 1848; councillor and minister of the interior, April 1849; chancellor of Transylvania, 1859; resigned, Sept. 1861. Author of 'After the Revolution,' Pesth, 1850; 'Men and Women,' ib. 1852; and other works.

KENDALL, George Wilkins, American author, b. at Vermont, 1810. Author of 'Narrative of Texan Expedition,' New York, 1844; 'History of the War between the United States and Mexico,' ib. 1850; and several works of fiction.

KENDALL, Nicholas, English politician, b. 1800; educated at Trinity College, Oxford, where he graduated B.A. 1830; a magistrate and deputy-lieutenant of Cornwall, and special deputy-warden of the Stannaries; M.P. for East Cornwall since 1852.

KENNARD, Robert William, English politician, b. 1800; commissioner of lieutenancy of London, and a magistrate of Westminster, Middlesex, and Herts; was sheriff of London and Middlesex, 1846–47; engaged as an ironmaster in South Wales and Scotland; M.P. Newport, Isle of Wight, since 1859.

KENNEDY, Rev. Benjamin, English author, b. at Summer Hill, Birmingham, Nov. 6, 1804; educated at St. John's College, Cambridge, and graduated B.A. 1827; appointed head-master of Shrewsbury School, 1836; prebendary of Lichfield, 1841; and select preacher to the University of Cambridge, 1860; president of the Royal College of Preceptors. Author of a 'Latin Vocabulary;' and other educational works.

KENNEDY, John Pendleton, American novelist, b. at Baltimore, Oct. 25, 1795; studied at the College of his native town, and entered the legal profession, 1812. Author of 'The Red Book,' 1817–19; 'Horse-Shoe Robinson,' 1835; 'The Annals of Quodlibet,' 1840; 'The Life of William Wirt,' 1849; and other works.

KENNEDY, Tristram, English politician, b. 1805; called to the Irish bar, 1834; high sheriff of Londonderry, 1828; founder of the Dublin Law Institute; returned M.P. for the county of Louth, 1852–57, and 1865.

KENRICK, Francis Patrick, American Catholic theologian, b. in Dublin, Dec. 3, 1797; entered the College of the Propaganda of Rome, 1815, and was ordained a priest, 1821; appointed professor to the College of St. Joseph, at Bardstown, Kentucky, U.S. 1821; consecrated bishop of Philadelphia, 1830; and archbishop of Baltimore, 1851. Author of 'Theologia Dogmatica,' 1839–40; 'A Vindication of the Catholic Church,' 1856; and numerous theological works.

KENT, William Charles Mark, English poet, b. in London, Nov. 1823; educated at Prior Park and Oscott Colleges; called to the bar of the Middle Temple, 1859. Author of 'Aletheia;' 'The Vision of Cagliostro, a Tale of the Five Senses;' and other works.

KEOGH, Right Hon. William, Irish judge, b. at Galway, 1817; educated at Trinity College, Dublin; entered as a student at Lincoln's Inn; was called to the Irish bar, 1840; appointed Q.C. 1849; solicitor-general, 1852, attorney-general, and sworn a privy-councillor, 1855; appointed one of the judges of the Common Pleas in Ireland, 1856. Author of some political pamphlets, and a work on the 'Practice of the Court of Chancery in Ireland.'

KEPPEL, Hon. Sir Henry, English naval commander, b. 1809; entered the navy, 1828; served on the East India, Mediterranean, and Cape of Good Hope stations, and on the coast of China, where he commanded the *Dido*, 1841–45; commanded the *St. Jean d'Acre* in the Baltic during the Russian war, and the forces in China, 1857–58; attained flag rank, 1857. Author of 'An Expedition to Borneo;' and other works.

KEPPLE, Hon. George Thomas, English author, b. 1799; entered the army; fought at Waterloo, and in India; lieutenant-colonel, 1841; M.P. for Lymington, 1832–35, and 1847–52. Author of 'Journey across the Balkan;' 'Journey from India to England.'

KER, David Stuart, English politician, b. 1820; educated at Eton, and Christ Church, Oxford, where he graduated B.A. 1841; a magistrate for Down and Antrim, and deputy-lieutenant for Down; M.P. for county of Down, 1852–57, for Downpatrick, 1841–47, and since 1859.

KERCADO, Alexis Thomas, French politician, b. Aug. 31, 1809; mayor of Roche Bernard, and member of the general council of the same canton; elected to the Corps Législatif for the first circonscription of the department of Morbihan, 1863.

KERN, Conrad, Swiss statesman, b. at Berlingen, near Arenenberg, 1808; studied at the Universities of Berlin, Heidelberg, and Paris; appointed president of the Supreme Court of Judicature, and of the canton of Thurgau, 1837; member of the Diet for the same canton, 1833; Swiss plenipotentiary at the Court of France, 1861.

KERRISON, Sir Edward Clarence, Bart., English politician, b. 1821; lieutenant of Suffolk Yeomanry Cavalry; M.P. for Eye since 1852.

KERVE'GUEN, Philippe Auguste, Vicomte de, French politician, b. at Toulon, Nov. 17, 1811; served in the French navy; member of the general council of the canton of Toulon; member of the Corps Législatif for the department of Var since 1852.

KETTELER, Wilhelm Emmanuel, Baron von, German Catholic theologian, b. at Münster, 1811; admitted to the bar, but entered the Church, 1837; ordained priest, and appointed to the parish of Hopster, in Westphalia, 1838; deputy to the National Assembly at Frankfort, 1848; consecrated bishop of Mayence, 1850. Author of 'Liberty and Authority of the Church,' 1861; and numerous sermons.

KEY, Thomas Hewitt, English philologist, b. 1799; educated at Trinity College, Cambridge, where he graduated, 1821; professor of comparative grammar and head-master of the junior school in London University. Author of a 'Latin Grammar;' and contributed numerous articles to the *Penny Cyclopædia*.

KEYSER, Nicaise de, *Belgian painter, b. at Sandvliet, province of Antwerp, Aug. 26, 1813; studied at the Academy of Antwerp; director of the Academy of Antwerp. Painted 'Christ on the Cross,' for the Catholic Church of Manchester, 1834; 'The Battle of Woringen,' in the National Palace at Brussels, 1839; and numerous other paintings.*

KIEPERT, Heinrich, German geographer, b. at Berlin, July 31, 1818; studied under Carl Ritter; appointed director of the Geographical Institute of Weimar, 1845. Published 'Atlas of Greece and her Colonies,' Berlin, 1840–46; second edition, 1851; 'Historical Atlas of the Ancient World,' Weimar, 1848; 'Atlas of Asia,' Berlin, 1853; and numerous maps and geographical works.

KILIAN, Hermann, German physician, b. at Leipsic, Feb. 5, 1800; studied medicine at Wilna, and in England and Scotland; appointed professor of medicine to the University of Bonn, 1828; dean of the faculty, 1853. Author of numerous medical works.

KILLALOE, Right Rev. William Fitzgerald, Bishop of, Irish divine, b. in Ireland, 1815; educated at Trinity College, Dublin, where he graduated B.A. 1837; consecrated bishop of Cork, 1857; translated to Killaloe, 1862. Edited Constable's 'Ethics;' Butler's 'Analogy;' and other works.

KILMORE, Right Rev. Hamilton Verschoyle, Bishop of, Irish divine, b. 1803; educated at Trinity College, Dublin; ordained, 1829; chancellor of Christ Church Cathedral, Dublin, 1855; dean of Ferns, 1862; consecrated to the see of Kilmore, Elphin, and Ardagh, Dec. 1862.

KIMBALL, Richard, American novelist, b. at Lebanon, New Hampshire, 1815; studied at the College of Dartmouth, where he graduated, 1834. Author of 'St. Leger, or the Threads of Life,' 1849; 'Cuba and the Cubans,' 1849; 'Student Life Abroad,' 1853; and other works of fiction.

KINDERSLEY, Sir Richard Torin, English judge, b. 1792; educated at Trinity College, Cambridge, where he graduated B.A. 1814; called to the bar of Lincoln's Inn, 1818; master in Chancery, 1848–51; one of the vice-chancellors, 1851; retired, 1866.

KING, James King, English politician, b. 1806; educated at Balliol College, Oxford, where he graduated B.A. 1829; a magistrate and deputy-lieutenant for Hereford; high sheriff, 1845; M.P. for Herefordshire since 1852.

KING, John Gilbert, English politician, b. 1823; educated at Trinity College, Dublin; a J.P. and deputy-lieutenant for King's County; high sheriff, 1852; returned M.P. for King's County, 1865.

KING, Hon. Peter John Locke, English politician, b. at Ockham, Surrey, 1811; educated at Harrow, and Trinity College, Cambridge, where he graduated M.A. 1833; a magistrate of Surrey; M.P. for East Surrey since 1847.

KINGLAKE, Alexander William, English author, b. near Taunton, 1811; educated at Eton, and Trinity College, Cambridge, where he graduated B.A. 1832; called to the bar of Lincoln's Inn, 1837; retired, 1856; a deputy-lieutenant for Somerset; M.P. for Bridgewater, 1857; unseated, 1869. Author of 'Eöthen,' 1849; 'History of the Russian War of 1854–56,' vols. I. II. in 1863, III. IV. 1868.

KINGLAKE, John Alexander, English politician, b. 1805; educated at Eton and Trinity College, Cambridge, where he graduated B.A. 1826; called to the bar of Lincoln's Inn, 1830; serjeant-at-law; recorder of Bristol; M.P. for Rochester since 1857.

KINGSCOTE, Robert Nigel Fitz-Hardinge, English politician, b. 1830; formerly lieutenant-colonel Scots Fusilier Guards, and was aide-de-camp to Lord Raglan in the Crimea, 1854–55; M.P. for West Gloucestershire since 1852.

KINGSLEY, Rev. Charles, English author, b. at Dartmoor, Devon, June 12, 1819; educated at King's College, London, and Magdalen College, Cambridge; appointed professor of modern history in the University of Cambridge, 1859. Author of 'Alton Locke,' 1850; 'Saint's Tragedy,' 1846; 'Alexandria and her Schools,' 1854; 'Westward Ho!' 1854; and numerous other works of fiction.

KINGSLEY, Henry, English author, b. 1830, brother of the preceding; educated at King's College, London, and Worcester College, Oxford. Author of 'Geoffry Hamlyn,' 'Ravenshoe,' and other works.

KINKEL, Johann Gottfried, German poet and political writer, b. at Obercassel, Rhenish Prussia, Aug. 11, 1815; studied at the University of Bonn; elected to the Berlin Parliament, 1848; joined the Badish insurrection, was taken prisoner by the Prussian troops, tried and sentenced to imprisonment in a fortress for life, 1849; escaped, 1850; appointed professor of literature at the University of Berne, Switzerland, 1867. Author of 'Otto der Schutz,' 1846; and numerous other works.

KINNAIRD, Hon. Arthur Fitzgerald, English politician, b. 1814; a J.P. and deputy-lieutenant for the county of Perth; a partner in Messrs. Ransom's bank, London; formerly held a diplomatic appointment; M.P. for the borough of London, 1837–39; returned for Perth, 1852.

KINNOUL, Thomas Robert Hay Drummond, Earl of, English administrator, b. 1785 ; Lord Lyon king-at-arms ; lord-lieutenant of Perthshire and colonel of the Perthshire Militia.

KIP, Right Rev. William, American author, b. at New York, Oct. 3, 1811 ; entered holy orders, 1832 ; consecrated missionary bishop of California, 1853. Author of 'History of the Early Jesuits ;' 'The Double Witness of the Church,' New York, 1844 ; 'The Catacombs of Rome,' 1854 ; and other works.

KIRWAN, Andrew Valentine, English author, b. 1804 ; called to the Irish bar, 1825, and to the English bar, 1828. Author of the 'Ports, Arsenals, and Dockyards of France,' 1839 ; 'Army and Garrisons of France,' separately, 1841 ; 'Modern France : its Journalism and Literature,' 1863 ; and other works.

KISS, August, German sculptor, b. at Pless, Upper Silesia, Oct. 11, 1802 ; studied under Rauch, at Berlin, 1822. Executed a colossal model of an 'Amazon on horseback attacked by a Panther,' 1839 ; an equestrian group of 'St. George and the Dragon ;' and numerous other works.

KISSELEFF, Nicholas de, Russian diplomatist, b. 1800 ; entered the diplomatic service, 1824 ; secretary of legation at Berlin and at Paris, 1826 ; chargé d'affaires in Paris ; Russian ambassador in France, 1852–54.

KLAPKA, George, Hungarian general, b. at Temeswar, April 7, 1820 ; entered the military service, 1838 ; took part in the Revolution of 1848 ; chief of the staff of General Kiss, 1848 ; minister at war under Kossuth, 1849 ; commander of Komorn, 1849. Published 'Memoirs,' Leipsic, 1856 ; 'The National War in Hungary and Transylvania,' 1851.

KNAUS, Ludwig, German painter, b. at Wiesbaden, Nassau, Oct. 5, 1829 ; studied at Düsseldorf under Schadow. Exhibited 'The Rustic Fête,' 1847 ; 'Gipsy Encampment,' 1857 ; and numerous other paintings.

KNIGHT, Charles, English author and publisher, b. at Windsor, 1790. Author of 'Knowledge is Power ;' 'Once upon a Time ;' 'Popular History of England ;' 'Passages of a Working Life during Half a Century ;' and numerous other works.

KNIGHT, Frederick Winn, English administrator, b. 1812 ; educated at the Charterhouse ; a family trustee of the British Museum ; parliamentary secretary to the Poor Law Board, 1852 ; M.P. for West Worcestershire since 1841.

KNIGHT, John Prescot, English portrait-painter, b. at Stafford, 1803 ; appointed secretary to the Royal Academy ; exhibited at the Royal Academy from 1827 ; elected A.R.A. 1836 ; R.A. 1844.

KNIGHTLEY, Sir Rainald, English politician, b. 1819 ; a magistrate and deputy-lieutenant for Northamptonshire ; M.P. for South Northamptonshire since 1852.

KNOX, Brownlow, English politician, b. 1806 ; a lieutenant-colonel unattached ; formerly major 2d Bucks Yeomanry ; M.P. for Great Marlow, 1847–68.

KNOX, Hon. William Stuart, English politician, b. 1826 ; major in the 51st Foot, and a magistrate and deputy-lieutenant for Tyrone ; M.P. for Dungannon since 1851.

KOBELL, Franz von, German mineralogist and poet, b. at Munich, July 19, 1803 ; educated at Munich University ; appointed assistant professor of mineralogy at the University, 1828 ; head keeper of the mineralogical collection at Munich. Author of 'Characteristics of Minerals,' 1830–31 ; 'Hochdeutsche Gedichte,' 1852 ; and numerous poems and works on mineralogy.

KOCH, Karl Heinrich, German naturalist, b. at Weimar, 1809 ; studied medicine at Würtzburg and Jena. Author of 'A Journey across Russia to the Isthmus of the Caucasus,' 2 vols. 1842–43 ; 'Wanderings in the East,' 1846–7 ; 'The Crimea and Odessa,' 1854 ; and numerous other works of travel and natural history.

KOCK, Charles Paul de, French novelist, b. at Passy near Paris, 1794. Author of 'L'Enfant de ma Femme,' 1811 ; 'Le Muletier,' 1823 ; 'La Fille aux trois Jupons,' 1863 ; 'Enfants du Boulevard,' 1864 ; and a vast number of other works of fiction.

KOCK, Henri de, French novelist, son of the preceding, b. 1821. Author of 'L'Amant de Lucette ;' 'Les Buveurs d'Absinthe ;' and many other novels.

KOECHLY, Hermann August, German philologist, b. at Leipsic, Aug. 5, 1815 ; studied at Berlin ; professor at the Königschule of Dresden, 1840 ; member of the second Chamber of Dresden, 1849 ; professor of Greek and Roman languages and literatures at Zurich, 1851. Editor of 'Quintus Smyrnæus,' Leipsic, 1850 ; and other works.

KOELLIKER, Albert, German anatomist, b. 1817 ; professor of anatomy and physiology at the University of Würtzburg. Author of 'Handbuch der Gewebelehre des Menschen,' 1852–55 ; and numerous other works on anatomy.

KOENIG, Heinrich Joseph, German novelist, b. at Fulda, Hesse Cassel, March 19, 1790; appointed secretary to the superior tribunal at Fulda, 1835. Author of 'Die hohe Braut,' Leipsic, 1833; 'Auch eine Jugend,' ib. 1852; 'König Jerome's Carnaval,' ib. 1853; and numerous other works of fiction.

KOENIG-BEY, Mathieu Auguste, Egyptian statesman, b. at Paris, 1802; studied rhetoric and Oriental languages at the College of Henry IV.; appointed professor of French language at the school of Djihad-Abad near Cairo, 1827; charged by Mehemet Ali with the education of the young princes of his family, 1834; member of the Egyptian council of ministers, 1862.

KOHL, Johann Georg, German traveller and geographical writer, b. at Bremen, April 28, 1808; studied at the Universities of Heidelberg and Munich. Author of 'Sketches and Pictures in St. Petersburg,' 1846; 'British Isles and their Inhabitants,' 1842; 'Kitchi-Gami, or Tales from Lake Superior,' 1857; 'Geographical History of America,' 1866; and numerous other works of travel.

KOLB-BERNARD, Charles, French politician, b. at Dunkirk, Jan. 16, 1798; member of the municipal council of Lille, and president of the Chamber of Commerce for the same town; member of the Corps Législatif for the second circonscription of the department du Nord since 1859.

KOSSUTH, Louis, Hungarian statesman, b. at Monok, county of Zemplin, April 27, 1802; educated at the Protestant College of Sarospatak, where he studied law and became an advocate, 1826; sat in the National Diet, 1832; imprisoned, 1837; minister of finance, March 17, 1848; governor of Hungary, May 14 to Aug. 11, 1849; took refuge in Turkey, Aug. 17, 1849; took up his residence in England, June 1852.

KRASZEWSKI, Joseph Ignaz, Polish author, b. at Varsovia, July 26, 1812; studied at Wilna. Author of 'Literary Studies,' Wilna, 1842; 'Voyage to Odessa,' ib. 1845; 'Pod wloskiem Niebem,' Leipsic, 1846; and other works in prose and verse.

KUECKEN, Friedrich Wilhelm, German musical composer, b. at Blekede, Lüneburg, Nov. 10, 1800; studied under Rombach at Berlin, and Halévy at Paris; composed 'The Swiss Flight;' 'The Pretender;' and numerous operas, sonatas, songs, and ballads.

KUEHNE, Gustav, German author, b. at Magdeburg, Prussia, Dec. 27, 1806; studied at the University of Berlin, where he graduated Ph.D. 1825. Author of 'Die beiden Magdalenen,' Leipsic, 1833; 'German Men and Women,' ib. 1851; 'Death of Fröbel, and Continuation of his Doctrine,' 1852; and numerous other works.

KUETZING, Friedrich Traugott, German naturalist, b. at Ritteburg, Thuringia, Dec. 8, 1807; studied at the University of Halle; professor of natural sciences at the College of Nordhausen. Author of 'Compendium of Natural History,' Nordhausen, 1837; 'Elements of Geography,' ib. 1853; 'Elements of Philosophical Botany,' Leipsic, 1851–52; and other works.

KUHLMANN, Carl Friedrich, French chemist, b. at Colmar, May 22, 1803; studied chemistry at the University of Strasbourg; president of the Chamber of Commerce of Lille, and member of the sanitary committee, and of the General Council du Nord. Author of 'Expériences chimiques et agronomiques,' 1847; 'Application des Silicates alcalins solubles au Durcissement des Pierres calcaires poreuses, à la Peinture et à l'Impression,' 1855; and numerous papers on chemistry.

KUPER, Sir Augustus Leopold, English naval commander, b. 1809; entered the Royal Navy, 1823; served in South America, the Mediterranean stations, and in China; attained flag rank, 1861; appointed commander-in-chief on the East India and China stations, with the rank of vice-admiral, 1862.

KURTZ, Johann Heinrich, German theologian, b. at Montjoie, Rhenish Prussia, 1809; studied theology at Halle and Bonn; appointed professor of ecclesiastical history at the University of Dorpat, 1850. Author of 'The Bible and Astronomy,' Mittau, 1842; 'Introduction to the History of the Church,' ib. 1852; third edition, 1856; and other theological works.

KYNASTON, Rev. Herbert, English divine, b. at Warwick, 1809; educated at Westminster, and Christ Church, Oxford, where he graduated B.A. 1831; ordained, 1834; appointed head-master of St. Paul's School, London, 1838; prebendary of St. Paul's Cathedral. Author of 'Miscellaneous Poems,' and translator of Damiani's 'Glory of Paradise.'

L.

LABARRE, François Theodore, French musical composer, b. at Paris, April 8, 1805; studied under Cousineau, Bochsa, and Naderman, 1812–20; entered the Conservatoire, 1820. Composed 'Les Deux Familles,' performed 1831; 'L'Aspirant de Marine,' 1834; 'Graziosa,' 1861; and numerous pieces of music, chiefly for the harp.

LABARRE, Louis, Belgian journalist, b. at Dinan, Namur, 1810. Edited the Belgian *Charivari*, the *Tribune* of Liège, and the *Nation* of Brussels. Author of 'Satires and Elegies,' 1836; 'Souvenirs du Drapeau,' 1855; and other works.

LA BE'DOLLIE'RE, Emile Gigault de, French author, b. in Paris, 1814. Author of 'Vie politique du Marquis de la Fayette,' 1833; 'Histoire de la Garde nationale,' 1848; 'Histoire de la Guerre du Mexique,' 1863; and numerous other historical and political works.

LABICHE, Euge'ne Marin, French dramatist, b. at Paris, May 5, 1814; studied at the Bourbon College, the Lycée Bonaparte, and the École de Droit. Author of 'Deux Papas très-bien,' 1845; 'En avant les Chinois!' 1858; 'Un Mari qui lance sa Femme,' 1864; and numerous other comedies.

LABINTZOFF, Ivan, Russian military commander, b. at Toula, 1800; entered the Caucasian army, 1826; lieutenant, 1828; major-general, 1839; lieutenant-general, 1845; appointed to the chief command of the forces in the Caucasus, 1856.

LABORDE, Emmanuel Joseph, Comte de, French archæologist, b. in Paris, June 12, 1807; studied at the University of Göttingen; elected member of the French Academy, 1842; appointed curator of the museum of antiquities in the Louvre, 1847. Author of 'Voyage en Orient,' 1838–55; 'Athens in the XV. XVI. and XVII. Centuries,' 1864; and numerous other works.

LABORDE, Henri, Vicomte de, French painter, b. at Rennes, May 2, 1811; studied under Paul Delaroche. Painted 'Hagar in the Desert,' in the museum of Dijon, 1836; 'La Passion du Christ,' in the Cathedral of Amiens, 1848; and other historical paintings.

LABORDE, Louis Jules, Comte de, French jurist, b. in Paris, Jan. 13, 1806, brother of the preceding; admitted as an advocate at the Court of Cassation, 1836; president of the Order of Advocates, 1853–56. Published 'Traité des Avaries particulières sur Merchandises,' 1836; and other works.

LABOUCHERE, Henry, English politician, b. 1831; educated at Eton, and Trinity College, Cambridge; was in the diplomatic service, 1854–64; M.P. for Windsor, 1865–66; for Middlesex, 1867–68.

LABOULAYE, Edouard Rene', French jurist, b. at Paris, Jan. 18, 1811; studied law, and was admitted as advocate at the Royal Court of Paris, 1842; appointed professor of legislation to the College of France, 1849. Author of 'Études sur la Propriété littéraire en France et en Angleterre,' 1858; 'Paris en Amérique,' 1863; 'Abdallah,' 1859; 'Contes bleus,' 1863; and other works.

LABROUSSE, Fabrice, French dramatic writer, b. 1810. Author of 'Fleurette,' 1833; 'Pauline,' 1841; 'Un Enfant du Peuple,' 1847; 'Consulat et l'Empire,' 1853; 'L'Armée d'Orient,' 1855; and other works.

LABROUSTE, François Marie Theodore, French architect, b. in Paris, March 21, 1799, brother of the following; studied under Vaudoyer and Hippolyte-Lebas, and at the École des Beaux Arts; architect to the Government, and to the College of St. Barbe.

LABROUSTE, Pierre Victor Alexandre, French administrator, b. in Paris, March 4, 1790; studied at the College of St. Barbe, and the School of Law, and called to the bar; appointed director of the College of St. Barbe, 1838.

LABROUSTE, Pierre François Henri, French architect, b. in Paris, May 11, 1801, brother of the two preceding; studied at the College of St. Barbe, and the École des Beaux Arts; appointed architect of the Bibliothèque St. Geneviève, 1838; architect of the new Bibliothèque St. Geneviève, commenced 1843, and finished 1849; vice-president of the Central Society of Architects.

LACAUSSADE, Auguste, French writer, b. at the Ile Bourbon, 1820; studied at Nantes. Published a translation of 'Ossian,' 1842. Author of 'Poëmes et Paysages,' 1852; 'Les Épaves,' 1861. Founder of the *Revue Européene,* 1859.

LACON, Sir Edmund Knowles, English politician, b. 1807; educated at Emmanuel College, Cambridge, where he graduated B.A. 1828; a deputy-lieutenant of Norfolk, and major in the Norfolk Militia; M.P. for Yarmouth, 1852–57, and 1859–68.

LACROIX, Jules, French writer, b. in Paris, May 7, 1809, brother of the following, Author of 'Une Grossesse,' 1833; 'Le Mauvais Ange;' 'La Testament de César,' 1849; and numerous romances and dramatic works.

LACROIX, Paul, French author, b. at Paris, Feb. 27, 1806; studied at the Collége Bourbon; appointed curator of the library of the Arsenal in Paris, 1855. Author, as *Bibliophile Jacob,* of 'Dissertations sur quelques Points curieux de l'Histoire de France, et de l'Histoire littéraire,' 1834–38; and numerous other works.

LACROIX, Paul Euge'ne, French architect, b. at Paris, March 19, 1814; studied at the École des Beaux Arts; appointed architect of the Élysée Impérial, 1852; architect to the Tuileries; and inspector of imperial palaces.

LACROIX ST. PIERRE, Pierre Henri, French politician, b. Aug. 9, 1817; member of the Administrative Council of the Railways of Ouest; elected to the Corps Législatif for the department de la Drôme, 1863.

LADOUCETTE, Louis Charles de, French politician, b. at Gap, Feb. 11, 1809; studied at the Military School of St. Cyr; left the army as officer of cavalry, 1837; appointed senator, Jan. 27, 1852.

LADREITT DE LA CHARRIE'RE, Jules, French military commander, b. at Coux, Ardèche, March 30, 1806; entered the Military School of St. Cyr, 1825; lieutenant, 1831; captain, 1827; chef de bataillon, 1844; lieutenant-colonel, 1848; colonel, 1851; brigadier-general, 1855; commanded in Italy, at Magenta and Solferino, 1859.

LAFOND DE LURCY, Gabriel, French traveller, b. at Lurcy Lévy, Allier, March 25, 1802; studied at the Lycée of Nantes. Published 'Quinze Ans de Voyages autour du Monde,' 1839; 'Voyages autour du Monde et Naufrages célèbres,' 1842; and other works.

LAFOND DE SAINT-MUR, Remi, French politician, b. at Roche Cavillac, near Tulle, Dec. 8, 1817; councillor, and secretary-general to the prefecture of Corrèze, 1847–57; member of the Corps Législatif for the department of Corrèze since 1857.

LA GRANDIE'RE, Paul Pierre Marie de, French naval commander, b. June 28, 1807; entered the navy, 1820; ensign, 1827; lieutenant, 1833; captain, May 1, 1849; rear-admiral, Dec. 24, 1861; vice-admiral, Dec. 5, 1865.

LAGRANGE, Fre'de'ric, Comte de, French politician, b. 1816; member of the General Council of the Eure for the canton of Gisors; deputy to the Corps Législatif for the department of Gers since 1852.

LA GRANGE ET DE FOURILLES, Edouard, Marquis de, French diplomatist, b. Dec. 18, 1796; studied at the Lycée Napoléon, and entered the diplomatic service; successively attaché at Madrid, secretary of legation at Carlsruhe and Vienna, and chargé d'affaires in Holland, 1821–30; made a senator, 1852. Author of 'La Délivrance de Bude,' 1829; and other works.

LA GUE'RONNIE'RE, Louis Etienne Arthur, Vicomte de, French statesman, b. 1816; held a post in the ministry of foreign affairs, 1848; appointed editor of the *Pays,* 1850; made a senator, 1861; ambassador at Brussels, 1868. Author of 'De la Politique intérieure et extérieure de la France,' 1862; and numerous other works.

LAINE', Pierre Jean, French naval commander, b. Dec. 4, 1796; studied at the Naval School of Brest; ensign, 1817; lieutenant, 1821; captain, 1831; rear-admiral, 1840; commander-in-chief of the navy at Algiers, 1841; préfet of the arrondissement of Cherbourg, 1842; member of the Imperial Council of Admiralty.

LAING, Samuel, English politician, b. 1812; educated at Harrow, and St. John's College, Cambridge, where he graduated B.A. 1832; called to the bar of Lincoln's Inn, 1840; a J.P. and deputy-lieutenant for the Isle of Orkney; M.P. for Wick, 1852–57, 1859–61, and 1865–68; appointed financial secretary in India, 1860; chairman of the London and Brighton Railway.

LAIRD, John, English politician, b. at Greenock, Scotland, 1805; a magistrate and deputy-lieutenant for the county of Chester; formerly head of the firm of Laird and Sons, shipbuilders of Birkenhead; M.P. for Birkenhead since 1861.

LAITY, Armand François Ruperch, French naval officer, b. at Lorient, 1812; admitted to the École Polytechnique; lieutenant, 1836; appointed préfet of the Basses Pyrénées, 1854; made a senator, 1857.

LAKE, Colonel Henry Atwell, English military engineer, b. 1809; appointed to the Madras Engineers, 1826; captain, 1842; lieut.-colonel, Nov. 1855; served in Turkey during the Russian war; nominated aide-de-camp to her Majesty, and appointed to a military command in Ireland, 1857. Author of 'Kars, and our Captivity in Russia.'

LAKE, Rev. William, English educational writer, b. June 1817; educated at Rugby, and Balliol College, Oxford, where he graduated B.A. 1835; appointed to report on Popular Education in England, 1858; rector of Huntspill, Somerset, and preacher at the Chapel Royal of Whitehall.

LAKEMAN, Sir Stephen Bartlett, Turkish military commander, b. in England, 1825; educated at the College of Louis le Grand, in Paris; knighted, 1853; entered the Turkish army and served in the Crimean war, 1854–55; lieut.-general in the Turkish service, under the title of Misa Pasha.

LA MARMORA, Alphonso, Marquis de, Italian general and statesman, b. Nov. 17, 1804; entered the Military Academy at Turin, 1816; lieutenant of artillery, 1823; captain, 1831; major, 1845; general of brigade, Oct. 27, 1848; appointed minister of war, Nov. 3, 1849; resigned, Feb. 1855; commander-in-chief of the Italian army in the Crimea, 1855; minister of war, Oct. 31, 1855; president of the Council of Ministers, July 19, 1859, to July 21, 1860; minister of foreign affairs, and president of the Council of Ministers, Sept. 30, 1864, to June 16, 1866.

LAMBINET, Emile, French painter, b. at Versailles, near 1808; studied under Drolling and Horace Vernet. Exhibited 'Sites du Dauphiné,' 1837; 'Les Bords de la Seine à Bougival,' 1861; 'Le Matin à Yoré-l'Evêque,' 1864; and many other landscapes.

LAMBRECHT, Felix, French politician, b. April 4, 1819; elected to the Corps Législatif for the fifth circonscription of the department du Nord, 1863.

LAME', Gabriel, French mathematician, b. at Tours, July 22, 1795; studied at the École Polytechnique, 1817; appointed professor of physics in the same school, 1832, and examiner in the same, 1845; resigned, 1863. Author of 'Leçons sur la Théorie mathématique de l'Elasticité,' 1852; and other mathematical works.

LAMONT, James, English politician, b. 1830; educated at Rugby; a magistrate for the county of Argyll, and a deputy-lieutenant for the county of Bute; M.P. for Buteshire, 1865–68. Author of 'Seasons with the Sea-horses.'

LA MOTTEROUGE, Joseph Edouard de, French military commander, b. Feb. 3, 1802; entered the College of St. Cyr, 1819; lieutenant, 1830; captain, 1832; chef de bataillon, 1841; colonel, 1848; general of brigade, 1852; served in the Crimea, and nominated general of division, June 22, 1855.

LANCE, Adolphe, French architect, b. at Littry, Calvados, Aug. 3, 1813; studied at the École des Beaux Arts; appointed inspector of works for the restoration of the Abbey of St. Denis, 1850; member of the Commission of Historical Monuments, 1854. Author of several works on architecture.

LANDSEER, Charles, English painter, b. 1799; studied under Haydon, and entered as student at the Royal Academy, 1816. Exhibited 'Dorothea,' 1828; 'The Monks of Melrose,' 1843; 'Return of the Dove to the Ark,' 1842; and other paintings. Elected A.R.A. 1837, and R.A. 1845; appointed 'Keeper' of the Royal Academy, 1851.

LANDSEER, Sir Edwin, English painter, b. in London, 1802, brother of the preceding; entered as student at the Royal Academy, 1816. Exhibited at the Academy 'The Dog and the Shadow,' 1826; 'A Highland Breakfast,' 1834; 'The Old Shepherd's Chief Mourner,' 1857; 'Deer Stalking,' 1858; 'Doubtful Crumbs,' 1859; 'The Shrew Tamed,' 1863; 'Man Proposes and God Disposes,' 1864; and numerous other paintings. Elected A.R.A. 1827; and R.A. 1830; knighted, 1850.

LANE, Edward William, English philologist, b. at Hereford, 1801. Translated 'The Thousand and One Nights,' 1841. Author of an 'Arabic Lexicon,' first part published 1863.

LANGALERIE, Pierre Henri de, French theologian, b. at St. Foy, Gironde, 1810; was professor of physics and mathematics to the Grand Seminary of Bordeaux; professor of law and canon to the Faculty of Theology; appointed vicar-general to the Archbishop of Bordeaux, 1852; consecrated bishop of Belley, 1857.

LANGENN, Friedrich von, German author, b. at Merseburg, Saxony, Jan. 26, 1798; studied at the University of Leipsic, and appointed professor, 1820; commissioner of the Government at Leipsic, 1831; president of the High Court of Appeal at Dresden, 1849. Author of 'Life of Albert the Brave,' 1838; and other works.

LANGIEWICZ, Maryan, Polish general, b. at Krotosczin, grand duchy of Posen, Aug. 5, 1827; studied at the University of Breslau; appointed Dictator by the Provisional Government of Poland, 1862–63; defeated by the Russians in the battle of Chrobrze, March 18, 1863, and took refuge in Austria, retiring subsequently to Switzerland.

LANGLAIS, Jacques, French politician, b. at Mamers, Sarthe, Feb. 27, 1810; educated at the Seminary of Mans; studied law in Paris, and called to the bar, 1837; elected member of the Legislative Assembly for Mamers, 1852–57; councillor of state, 1857; minister of finance of the Mexican empire, 1865–66.

LANGLOIS, Charles, French painter, b. at Beaumont-en-Ange, Calvados, July 22, 1789; studied at the École Polytechnique, and under Girode, Baron Gros, and Horace Vernet; entered the army, 1830; colonel, 1849. Painted 'La Bataille de la Moskowa,' 1835; 'Le Combat des Pyramides,' 1849; 'La Bataille de Solferino,' 1864; and numerous other battle scenes.

LANGSDORFF, Emile, Baron de, French diplomatist, b. at Fumel, Lot-et-Garonne, 1804; studied at the College of Heuri IV.; attaché to the Legation at Florence, 1828; secretary to the embassies at Rome, Turin, Munich, and Constantinople, Berlin, and Vienna, 1830–40; minister plenipotentiary to Brazil, 1841; minister at Baden and at the Hague, 1842–48; retired into private life after the Revolution of Feb. 1848.

LANJUINAIS, Victor Ambrose, Vicomte, French politician, b. Nov. 5, 1802; studied law at Paris, and was called to the bar, 1821; member of the Chamber of Deputies, 1837–39, 1842, and 1846; and of the Constituent Assembly for Loire Inférieur. 1849; elected to the Corps Législatif for the department of the Loire Inférieur, 1863. Author of 'Nouvelles Recherches sur la Question de l'Or,' 1855; and other works.

LANKESTER, Edwin, English author, b. at Melton, Suffolk; educated at Woodbridge, and studied medicine at University College, London, 1834–37; member of the College of Surgeons, 1837; graduated M.D. at Heidelberg, 1839; appointed professor of natural history at the New College of London, 1850; elected coroner for Central Middlesex, 1862. Author of 'Lives of Naturalists,' 1842; Lectures on Animal Food;' and numerous other works.

LANNO, François Gaspard, French sculptor, b, at Rennes, Jan. 7, 1800; studied under Frederic Lemot, 1818, Cartillier, and at the Ecole des Beaux Arts. Executed 'Prométhée enchaîné,' 1825; 'Le Maréchal Brune,' 1843; a bronze bust of Montaigne, 1864; and other statues and busts.

LANNOY, Antoine de, French architect, b. at Paris, June 28, 1800; studied under Vandoyer, Delespine, and M. H. Lebas; architect of the Banque de France, 1849. Published 'Projet d'Agrandissement de la Bibliothèque royale,' 1827; 'Le Tombeau de Robert de Naples,' 1852; and other works on architecture.

LANOUE, Felix Hippolyte, French painter, b. at Versailles, Oct. 14, 1812; studied under Victor Bertin, 1830, Horace Vernet, and at the École des Beaux Arts. Exhibited 'Saint Benoît fondaut ses Monastères dans les Déserts du Subiaco,' 1853; 'Les Bords de la Nerva,' 1861; 'Vue du Tibre,' 1864; and many other paintings, chiefly landscapes.

LANZA, Federico, Italian statesman, b. 1814; studied medicine; appointed minister of finance in the cabinet of Count Cavour, 1859; minister of the interior, Sept. 30, 1864; resigned, Oct. 20, 1865.

LAPLACE, Charles Emile, Marquis de, French general, b. at Paris, April 15, 1789; studied at the École Polytechnique and the École de Metz; entered the army, 1809; took part in the wars with Spain, Russia, and Germany; lieutenant-general, April 9, 1843; made a senator, Dec. 31, 1852.

LAPLACE, Cyrille Pierre Theodore, French naval commander, b. Nov. 7, 1793; entered the Imperial Navy as ensign, 1812; lieutenant, 1819; captain, 1828; rear-admiral, 1841; vice-admiral, June 11, 1853; member of the Council of Admiralty, 1857; appointed maritime préfet of Brest, and placed on half-pay, 1858. Author of 'Voyage autour du Monde par les Mers de l'Inde et de la Chine,' 1833–39; and other works.

LAPRADE, Pierre Richard de, French poet, b. at Montbrison, Loire, Jan. 13, 1812; studied at Lyons, and was called to the bar. Author of 'Les Parfumes de Madeleine,' 1839; 'Poëmes évangéliques,' 1852; 'Les Symphonies,' 1855; 'Questions d'Art et de Morale,' 1861; and other works.

LARABIT, Denis, French politician, b. at Roye Somme, Aug. 15, 1792; studied at the École Polytechnique, and served in the French army; represented the department of the Yonne at the Constituent Assembly, 1848; appointed senator, March 4, 1853.

LARCHEY, François Etienne, French general, b. at Cambrai, Jan. 20, 1795; studied at the School of St. Cyr; lieutenant, 1814; major, 1843; general of brigade, 1852; general of division, 1855; entered the reserve, 1860.

LARCOM, Sir Thomas Aiskew, English military engineer, b. 1801; educated at the Royal Military Academy, Woolwich, and obtained a commission, 1820; director of the Irish Ordnance Survey Office, 1828–46; under-secretary for Ireland, 1853; major-general in the Engineers and C.B. 1858.

LARIVE, Auguste de, Swiss medical writer, b. at Geneva, Oct. 9, 1801. Author of ' Mémoires sur les Caustiques,' 1824 ; 'Traité d'Électricité théorique appliquée,' Paris, 1854–58 ; and other scientific works.

LA RONCIE'RE LE NOURY, Cle'ment, Baron de, French naval officer, b. at Turin, Oct. 31, 1813 ; entered the Naval School, 1829 ; captain of a frigate, 1851 ; rear-admiral, 1861.

LARRABURE, Raymond, French politician, b. at St. Jean Pied de Port, Basses Pyrénées, Jan. 16, 1799 ; member of the Legislative Assembly, 1849 ; deputy to the Corps Législatif for the department des Basses Pyrénées since 1857.

LARREY, Felix Hippolyte, Baron, French physician, b. at Paris, Sept. 1808 ; entered the medical service of the French army ; received the degree of M.D. at Paris, 1832 ; appointed professor of pathology at Val de 'Grâce, 1841. Author of ' Medical History of the Siege of Antwerp,' 1831 ; and other medical works.

LARRIEN, Guillaume Lucien E'mile, French naval commander, b. July 5, 1809 ; entered the navy, 1824 ; rear-admiral, Oct. 12, 1855 ; commander of the naval station of Oceania, 1861 ; vice-admiral and préfet of the fourth maritime arrondissement, 1864.

LARROQUE, Patrice, French philosophical writer, b. at Beaune, Côte d'Or, March 27, 1801 ; graduated LL.D. 1827 ; inspector of the Academy of Toulouse, 1830–36 ; rector of the academies of Cahors, Limoges, and Lyons, 1836–49. Author of ' Opinion des Déistes rationalistes sur la " Vie de Jésus," selon M. Renan,' 1863 ; and other works.

LA RUE, Aristide, Comte de, French general, b. March 11, 1795 ; entered the army, 1812 ; captain, 1816 ; lieutenant-colonel, 1836 ; colonel, 1839 ; general of division, 1851 ; appointed senator, Feb. 13, 1860.

LAS-CASES, Charles Barthe'lemy, Marquis de, French politician, b. at Paris, Aug. 1, 1811 ; entered the navy, 1830 ; mayor of Chalons-sur-Loire, and member of the general council of the same canton, 1859 ; member of the Corps Législatif for the department of Maine-et-Loire since 1857.

LASNONIER, Euge'ne, French politician, b. Sept. 1, 1807 ; called to the bar of Niort ; member of the General Council for the canton of Lecondigny ; elected to the Corps Législatif for the department des Deux Sèvres, 1863.

LASSEN, Christian, German philologist, b. at Bergen in Norway, Oct. 22, 1800 ; studied at Christiania, Heidelberg, and Bonn, where he graduated Ph.D. 1827 ; appointed professor of Oriental languages and literature at Bonn, 1840. Author of ' Indian Archæology,' 1844–58 ; 'The Ancient Persian Cuneiform Writings,' 1836 ; and other works.

LASTEYRIE, Ferdinand, Comte de, French politician, b. June 15, 1810 ; studied at the École des Mines, 1827–30 ; represented the city of Paris at the Constituent and Legislative Assemblies ; elected member of the French Academy, April 1860. Author of ' History of Painting on Glass from the Monuments of France,' 1837–56 ; and other works.

LATHAM, Robert Gordon, English philologist and ethnologist, b. 1812 ; educated at Eton, and King's College, Cambridge, where he graduated B.A. 1835 ; studied medicine, graduated M.D. and became assistant-physician to the Middlesex Hospital. Author of ' The Varieties of Mankind ;' ' The Ethnology of Europe ;' ' The English Language ;' and other works. Editor of a new edition of ' Johnson's Dictionary.'

LATHBURY, Rev. Thomas, English theologian, b. 1798 ; educated at St. Edmund's Hall, where he graduated B.A. 1824, and M.A. 1827 ; appointed incumbent of St. Simon's, Bristol, 1848. Author of ' History of the Nonjurors ;' ' History of the Book of Common Prayer ;' and other works.

LA TOUR, Gustave, Comte de, French politician, b. in the Côtes du Nord, 1809 ; served in the Austrian army in Hungary, and retired with the rank of captain ; elected to the Corps Législatif for the arrondissement of Lannion since 1851.

LATOUR-DUMOULIN, Pierre, French politician, b. at Paris, Feb. 18, 1823 ; studied at the College of St. Louis, and was called to the bar ; member of the Corps Législatif for the department of Doubs since 1853. Author of 'Lettres sur la Constitution de 1852,' 1861 ; and other works.

LAUBE, Heinrich, German author, b. at Sprottau, Silesia, Sept. 18, 1806 ; educated at Halle and Breslau ; appointed director of the Theatre at Vienna, 1849. Author of ' Die Schauspielerin,' Mannheim, 1837 ; ' Geschichte der deutschen Litteratur,' Stuttgart, 1840 ; ' Das erste deutsche Parlament,' Leipsic, 1849 ; and other, chiefly dramatic, works.

LAUDER, Robert Scott, English painter, b. at Silver Mills, near Edinburgh, 1803 ; *studied at the Trustees' Academy, Edinburgh. Painted 'The Bride of Lammermuir ;'* '*The Trial of Effie Deans ;' ' Christ walking on the Waters,' 1847 ; and other works.*

LAUGIER, Auguste Paul, French astronomer, b. at Paris, Dec. 22, 1812; studied at the École Polytechnique, 1834; elected to the French Academy of Sciences, 1843; member of the Bureau des Longitudes, 1862. Author of 'Recherches sur la Rotation du Soleil autour de son Centre de Gravité,' 1841; and numerous works on astronomy.

LAURENTIE, Pierre, French writer, b. at Houga, Gers, Jan. 21, 1793; professor of history at the École Polytechnique, 1818–22. Author of 'Etudes littéraires et morales sur les Historiens latins,' 1822; 'Histoire des Ducs d'Orléans,' 1832–34; 'Histoire de l'Empire romain,' 1861–62; 'Les Rois et le Pape,' 1860; and other works.

LAURIANO, Augustin, Roumanian author, b. in Transylvania, 1815; studied at Vienna; appointed inspector of Moldavian schools by Prince Gregory Ghika, 1851. Author of 'Tentamen criticum in Linguam romanicam,' Vienna, 1840; 'Magazinu historicu pentra Dacia,' Bucharest, 1844–47; and other works.

LA VALETTE, Charles Jean, Marquis de, French statesman, b. at Senlis, Nov. 25, 1806; entered the diplomatic career, 1837; consul-general at Alexandria, 1841–45; minister at Cassel, 1846–49; ambassador extraordinary at Constantinople, 1851–53, and at Rome, 1862–63; minister of the interior, March 29, 1865, to Nov. 13, 1867; appointed minister of foreign affairs, Dec. 18, 1868.

LAVALLE'E, Theophile, French historian, b. at Paris, Oct. 13, 1804; appointed professor of history and literature at the Military School of St. Cyr, 1852. Author of 'History of the French,' 1838–39; 'History of the Ottoman Empire,' 1855–59; and other works.

LAVALLETTE, Samuel Welles, Comte de, French politician, b. at Boston, May 22, 1834; entered the diplomatic service; adopted by the Marquis La Vallette, and naturalized a Frenchman, 1863; elected to the Corps Législatif for the departement de la Dordogne, 1863.

LAWOESTINE, Alexandre Charles, Marquis de, French general, b. Dec. 25, 1786; lieutenant, 1805; lieutenant-general, 1841; made a senator, Jan. 1852; appointed governor of the Invalides, Oct. 22, 1863.

LAWRENCE, George Alfred, English author, b. 1827; educated at Balliol College, Oxford, where he graduated in 1848; called to the bar, 1852. Author of 'Guy Livingstone,' 'Sword and Gown,' 'Barren Honour;' and other works of fiction.

LAWRENCE, Sir John Laird Mair, English statesman, b. March 4, 1811, the fourth son of Lieutenant-colonel Alex. Wm. Lawrence, of Londonderry; educated at Haileybury for the Indian Civil Service, 1827–29; assistant, agent, collector, and magistrate at Delhi, 1831–48; chief commissioner of the Punjaub, 1849–58; nominated member of the Council of State for India, 1858; governor-general of India, Nov. 28, 1863, to Sept. 30, 1868; returned home, Jan. 1869.

LAWRENCE, William, English politician, b. 1818; a magistrate of Middlesex and an alderman of London; was sheriff of London and Middlesex, 1857–58; lord mayor of London, 1863–64; M.P. for London since 1865.

LAWSON, Right Hon. James Anthony, English politician, b. 1817; educated at Trinity College, Dublin, where he graduated B.A. 1839, LL.D. 1840; called to the Irish bar, 1840; appointed solicitor-general for Ireland, 1861; attorney-general, 1865; M.P. for Portarlington, 1865–68.

LAYARD, Austin Henry, English statesman, b. in Paris, March 5, 1817; formerly attaché at Constantinople; M.P. for Aylesbury, 1852–57; under-secretary of state for foreign affairs, Jan. to Feb. 1852, and again 1861–66; commissioner of public works and buildings, Dec. 1868; president of the Board of Works, Dec. 1868; M.P. for Southwark since 1860. Author of 'Nineveh and its Remains,' 1849.

LEADER, Nicholas Philpot, English politician, b. 1814; educated at Trinity College, Dublin; a magistrate of the county of Cork; M.P. for Cork County, 1861–68.

LEATHAM, William Henry, English politician, b. 1815; a J.P. and deputy-lieutenant of the West Riding of the county of York; formerly a banker at Wakefield, Pontefract, and Doncaster; M.P. for Wakefield, 1865–68.

LE BARBIER DE TINAN, Charles Adelbert, French naval commander, b. Aug. 30, 1803; studied at the Naval School at Brest; captain, 1837; member of the Council of Admiralty, and rear-admiral, 1851; vice-admiral, 1855.

LEBOENT, Edmond, French military commander, b. Nov. 5, 1809; studied at the École Polytechnique and the École d'Artillerie of Metz; served in the Crimea; general of brigade, 1854; general of division, 1857; aide-de-camp to the Emperor.

LECLERC D'OSMONVILLE, Jules Olivier, French politician, b. at Laval, April 27, 1797; member of the General Council for the canton of Ouest; deputy to the Corps Législatif for the department of Mayenne since 1853.

LECLERQ, Mathieu Joseph, Belgian statesman, b. at Herve, near Liege, 1796; counsellor at the Superior Court of Justice, 1830; member of the National Congress, 1831; procureur-général at the Court of Cassation, 1831 and 1840; minister of justice, 1840–41; procureur-général to the Supreme Court of Brussels.

LECOMTE, Eugène, French politician, b. 1805; studied at Paris in the École de Droit; lieut.-colonel in the National Guard, 1830; deputy of the Yonne to the National Assembly, 1848; member of the Corps Législatif for the Yonne since 1852.

LECOMTE-VERNET, Charles, French painter, b. in Paris, 1821; studied under H. Vernet and Léon Cogniet. Exhibited 'Ecce Homo;' 'La Reine de Navarre,' 1855; 'Expedition de Syrie,' 1863; and numerous other paintings.

LECONTE, John, American naturalist, b. at New York, 1825; studied at the Medical College, and graduated M.D. 1846; contributed numerous papers on entomology to the *Journal of the Academy of Sciences, The Journal of Natural History of Boston,* and to other American scientific journals.

LECOQ, Henri, French naturalist, b. at Avesnes, Nord, April 14, 1802; graduated M.D. at Paris, 1827; professor of natural history at the Preparatory School of Medicine at Clermont-Ferrand. Author of 'Éléments de Minéralogie appliquée aux Sciences,' 1826; 'Des Glaciers et des Climats,' 1847; and other scientific works.

LECOURTIER, François Joseph, French theologian, b. Dec. 19, 1799; studied at Paris; arch-priest and canon of Notre Dame, 1848; consecrated bishop of Montpellier, June 5, 1861. Author of 'Le Dimanche,' 1839; and other works.

LEDEBUR, Leopold August von, German author, b. at Berlin, July 2, 1799; entered the army as lieutenant, 1827; captain, 1828: director of the new museum at Berlin. Author of 'Blicke auf die Literatur des letzten Jahrzehends, &c.' 1837; 'Erlebnisse aus den Kriegsjahren, 1806 und 1807,' 1855; and other works.

L'EDIER, Stanislas, French politician, b. at Bacqueville, Dec. 30, 1798; entered the General Council for the canton of Bacqueville, and became mayor of the town, 1849; member of the Corps Législatif for the department of Seine Inférieure since 1852.

LEDRU ROLLIN, Auguste, French statesman, b. in Paris, Feb. 2, 1808; studied law, and was called to the bar, 1830; minister of the interior in the Provisional Government, 1848; accused of a conspiracy against President Louis Napoleon, and obliged to seek refuge in England, 1849. Author of 'La Décadence de l'Angleterre,' 2 vols. 1850; 'La Loi anglaise,' 2 vols. 1853; and numerous legal and political works.

LEE, Frederick Richard, English painter, b. at Barnstaple, Devon, June 1798; received a commission in the 56th Foot, and served in the Netherlands. Exhibited 'The Fisherman's Haunt;' 'The Bay of Biscay;' 'Plymouth Breakwater;' and numerous other landscapes and sea views. Elected A.R.A. 1834, R.A. 1838.

LEE, Rev. Robert, English author, b. at Tweedmouth, North Durham, 1804; studied at St. Andrew's; minister of the Grey Friars church, Edinburgh, 1843; professor of Biblical criticism at the University of Edinburgh, 1846. Author of 'The Family and its Duties,' 1863; and numerous lectures, sermons, and other religious works.

LEE, Robert Edmund, American military commander, b. in Virginia, Jan. 1807; admitted as a cadet at West Point, 1825; second lieutenant in the United States army, 1829; first lieutenant, Sept. 1836; captain, July 1838; appointed chief engineer of the army in Mexico, 1846; major, April 1846; lieut.-colonel, Aug. 20, 1847; colonel, Sept. 13, 1847; superintendent of West Point Military Academy, 1852 to March 1855; appointed commander-in-chief of the Confederate forces in Virginia, 1861; after the termination of the civil war, appointed president of Washington College, Pennsylvania, 1866.

LEE, William, English politician, b. 1801; a magistrate and deputy-lieutenant for Kent, and a merchant in London and Rochester; M.P. for Maidstone, 1853–57, and since 1859.

LEE, Ven. William, English divine, b. 1815; educated at Trinity College, Dublin, where he was appointed professor of ecclesiastical history, 1857; Archbishop King's lecturer in divinity, 1863; archdeacon of Dublin. Author of 'Donnellan Lectures' of 1852; 'Inspiration of Holy Scripture, its Nature and Proof;' and other works.

LEES, Edwin, English naturalist, b. at Worcester, May 12, 1800. Author of 'The *Botanical Looker-out in England and Wales;'* 'Pictures of Nature around the Malvern *Hills and Vale of Severn;'* and other works.

LEESER, Isaac, American author, b. of Jewish parents at Neukirch, Westphalia, 1806; studied at Munster, and went to the United States, 1825; Rabbi of the synagogue of Philadelphia. Author of 'The Jews and the Mosaic Law,' 1833; 'Descriptive Geography of Palestine,' 1852; and other works.

LEFE'BURE, Charles Euge'ne, French politician, b. April 15, 1808; member of the General Council for the canton of Lapoutroye; deputy to the Corps Législatif for the departement du Haut Rhin since 1852.

LEFE'VRE, Andre', French author, b. at Provins, Seine-et-Marne, Nov. 9, 1834; studied at the College of St. Barbe. Author of 'Le Rêve d'une Reine d'Asie,' 1861; 'La Vallée du Nil,' 1863; 'La Lyre intime,' 1865.

LEFEVRE, Sir George Shaw, English statesman, b. in London, 1797; educated at Eton, and Trinity College, Cambridge, where he graduated in 1818; called to the bar of the Inner Temple, 1824; under-secretary of state for the colonies, 1833; commissioner of the poor laws, 1834; vice-chancellor of the University of London; deputy-clerk of Parliament.

LEFEVRE, John Shaw, English politician, b. 1832, son of the preceding; educated at Eton, and Trinity College, Cambridge; M.P. for Reading since 1863.

LEFROY, Anthony, English politician, b. 1800; educated at Trinity College, Dublin, where he graduated B.A. 1821; a deputy-lieutenant of Longford; M.P. for the county of Longford, 1830-37, and 1841-47; and for Dublin University since 1858.

LEFUEL, Hector Marin, French architect, b. at Versailles, Nov. 14, 1810; studied at the École des Beaux Arts, 1829-30; appointed architect of the Palais de Fontainebleau, and charged to connect the Louvre and the Tuileries, 1853; chief architect of the Palais des Beaux Arts, and of numerous public buildings in Paris.

LEGH, George Cornwall, English politician, b. 1804; educated at Christ Church, Oxford, where he graduated B.A. 1826; magistrate and deputy-lieutenant of Cheshire; M.P. for Mid-Cheshire, 1841-47, and since 1848.

LEGOUVE', Gabriel, French author, b. at Paris, Feb. 15, 1807. Author of 'Max,' 1833; 'Édith de Falsen,' 1840; 'La Croix d'Honneur et les Comédiens,' 1863; and numerous poems, romances, and dramas.

LEGOYT, Alfred, French statistical writer, b. at Clermont-Ferrand, Puy de Dôme, Nov. 18, 1815; studied at the College of his native town and at Paris; appointed director of the Statistical Bureau of France, 1852. Assisted in the compilation of the 'Collection de la Statistique générale de France,' 1854; and author of numerous statistical works.

LEHARIVEL DUROCHER, Victor, French sculptor, b. at Chann, Orne, Nov. 20, 1816; studied at the École des Beaux Arts, 1838-44. Executed 'La Vierge,' a bust in marble, 1863; 'Colin Maillard,' a statue in bronze, 1864.

LEHMANN, Charles, French painter, b. at Kiel, Holstein, April 14, 1814; studied in France under M. Ingres, and exhibited 'Tobias and the Angel,' 1835; 'Jephthah's Daughter,' 1837; 'Profil sur Fond d'Or,' 1863; 'Le Repos,' 1864; and other paintings.

LEIGHTON, Frederick, English painter, b. at Scarborough, Dec. 3, 1830; studied painting at the Royal Academy of Berlin. Exhibited 'Cimabue,' 1855; 'Dante in Exile,' 1864; 'Helen of Troy,' 1865; and numerous other paintings.

LEITRIM, William Sydney Clements, Earl of, English administrator, b. in Dublin, 1806; served in the army as Lord Clements, and retired with the rank of lieutenant-colonel, 1855; M.P. for Leitrim, 1839-47; colonel of the Leitrim Militia.

LE JEUNE, Henry, English painter, b. 1819; head-master of the Government School of Design, 1845-48; appointed curator of the painting school of the Royal Academy, 1848. Painted 'Samson bursting his Bonds,' 1841. Elected A.R.A. 1863.

LELEUX, Adolphe, French painter, b. at Paris, Nov. 15, 1812. Painted 'Chasseur des Côtes de Picardie,' 1836; 'La Danse des Djinns,' 1849; 'L'Arrivée au Champ de Foire,' 1855; 'Noce en Bretagne,' 1863; 'La Rentrée du Troupeau,' 1864; and other works.

LELEUX, Armand, French painter, b. at Paris, 1818, brother of the preceding; studied under M. Ingres, 1832. Exhibited 'St. Jérôme lisant la Bible,' 1839; 'Un Guide du Saint-Gothard,' 1850; 'Cuisine du Convent des Franciscains de Sassuolo,' 1864; and numerous other paintings.

LE'LUT, Louis François, French author, b. at Gy, Haute Saône, April 15, 1804; studied at Paris; member of the Constituent Assembly, 1848; member of the Corps Législatif for his native department since 1852. Author of 'Qu'est-ce que la Phrénologie?' 1835; 'L'Amulette de Pascal,' 1846; 'Petit Traité de l'Égalité,' 1857; and other works.

LEMAIRE, Philippe Henri, French sculptor, b. at Valenciennes, 1798; studied under Cartellier. Exhibited 'Jeune Fille effrayée par un Serpent,' 1831, in the museum of the Luxemburg; 'Frontons,' for the city of Strasburg, 1859; and numerous busts, groups, monuments, and bas-reliefs.

LE MARCHANT, Sir Denis, English statesman, b. 1795; educated at Eton, and Trinity College, Cambridge; called to the bar of Lincoln's Inn, 1823; principal secretary to Lord-chancellor Brougham, 1830; secretary of the Board of Trade, 1836–41; secretary to the Treasury, 1841; created a baronet, 1841; M.P. for Worcester, 1846–47; under-secretary for the Home Department, 1847–50; appointed chief clerk to the House of Commons, 1850. Edited Walpole's 'Memoirs of George III.'

LE MARCHANT, Sir John Gaspard, English officer, b. 1803, brother of the preceding; educated at Sandhurst, and entered the army, 1821; served in Spain as brigadier and adjutant-general of the Anglo-Spanish legion; governor and commander-in-chief of Newfoundland, 1847–52; lieutenant-governor of Nova Scotia, 1852–57; commander-in-chief of the forces of Malta and lieutenant-general, 1858–63; knighted, 1838.

LE MAROIS, Jules, Comte, French politician, b. in Paris, Dec. 25, 1802; represented the department of La Manche in the Legislative Assembly; made a senator, 1852.

LEMELOREL DE LA HAICHOIS, Joseph, French politician, b. at Rennes, Feb. 17, 1807; studied law, and was called to the bar; mayor of Lorient, 1850; member of the Corps Législatif for the department of Morbihan since 1852.

LEMON, Mark, English author, b. in London, Nov. 30, 1809; one of the founders of *Punch* in 1841. Author of 'The Enchanted Doll;' 'Wait for the End;' 'Loved at Last;' and a great number of dramatic pieces; contributor to *Household Words*, the *Illustrated London News*, and other periodical publications.

LENNOX, Lord Arthur, English politician, b. 1806; entered the army as ensign, 1822; lieutenant-colonel, 1842; M.P. for Chichester, 1831–46; and for Yarmouth, 1847; a lord of the Treasury, 1844–45.

LENNOX, Lord George Gordon, English politician, b. 1829, nephew of the preceding; educated at Eton; entered the Royal Horse Guards as cornet, 1846; retired, 1853; J.P. and deputy-lieutenant of Sussex; M.P. for Lymington since 1860.

LENNOX, Lord Henry Gordon, English politician, b. 1821, brother of the preceding; educated at Westminster, and Christ Church, Oxford, where he graduated B.A. 1843, M.A. 1847; a magistrate of Sussex; was a lord of the Treasury, 1852; M.P. for Chichester since 1846.

LENNOX, Lord William Pitt, English author, b. 1799, uncle of the two preceding; educated at Westminster; was for some time on the staff of the late Duke of Wellington, whom he accompanied to Brussels, Waterloo, Paris, and Vienna; retired from the army, 1829. Author of 'Compton Audley;' 'Three Years with the Duke of Wellington in Private Life;' 'Fifty Years' Biographical Reminiscences;' and numerous other works.

LENSTRÖM, Carl Julius, Swedish writer, b. at Gefle, 1811; studied at Upsal; and was appointed professor of theology in the College of his native town. Author of 'History of the Theories of Art,' 1839; 'History of the Church Universal, and the Swedish Church,' 1843; 'Sigurd and Brynhild,' an epic poem; and other works.

LEO, Heinrich, German historical writer, b. at Rudolstadt, March 19, 1799; studied at Breslau and Göttingen; graduated Ph.D. at Jena, 1820; appointed professor of history at Halle, 1830. Author of 'Handbuch der Geschichte des Mittelalters,' Halle, 1830; 'Die Hegelingen,' ib. 1838; second edition, 1839; 'Leitfaden für den Unterricht in der Universalgeschichte,' Halle, 1828–40; and numerous other works.

LEOPOLD, Duke of Anhalt, b. Oct 1, 1794, the son of Prince Friedrich of Anhalt-Dessau and of Princess Amelia of Hesse-Homburg; succeeded to the throne at the death of his grandfather, Duke Leopold Friedrich, Aug. 9, 1817; married, April 18, 1818, to Princess Frederica of Prussia, who died Jan. 1, 1850.

LEOPOLD II. King of the Belgians, b. April 9, 1835, the son of King Leopold I., former Duke of Saxe-Coburg, and of Princess Louise, daughter of Louis Philippe, King of the French; ascended the throne at the death of his father, Dec. 10, 1865; married, Aug. 22, 1853, to Marie, Archduchess of Austria, b. Aug. 23, 1836.

LE PLAY, Pierre Frédéric, French civil engineer, b. at Honfleur, April 11, 1806; studied at the École Polytechnique, 1825–27; commissioner-general for the Universal Exhibition of 1855; councillor of state, Dec. 1855; commissioner of France to the International Exhibition in London, 1862. Author of 'Description des Procédés metallurgiques dans le Pays de Galles,' 1848; and other works.

LEPSIUS, Karl Richard, German philologist, b. at Naumburg, Dec. 20, 1813 ; studied philology at Leipsic and Berlin, graduated Ph.D. 1833 ; nominated professor at the University of Berlin, 1846, and member of the Academy of Sciences, 1850. Author of 'Monuments of Egypt and Ethiopia,' 1853–57 ; 'Universal Linguistic Alphabet,' 1855 ; and numerous works on the languages and monuments of Egypt.

LEQUIEN, Arthur, French politician, b. 1813 ; called to the bar of Douai ; represented Pas de Calais in the Legislative Assembly, 1849 ; deputy to the Corps Législatif since 1852.

LEROUX, Charles Guillaume, French painter, b. at Nantes, April 25, 1814 ; studied painting in Paris, under M. Corot ; member of the Corps Législatif for the department of Deux-Sèvres since 1860. Exhibited 'Bords de la Loire,' 1857 ; 'Bords de l'Erdre,' 1859 ; and other landscapes.

LEROUX, Paul, French politician, b. Dec. 11, 1815 ; member of the Corps Législatif for the department of the Vendée since 1852 ; vice-president of the Corps Législatif, 1863. Author of 'Poems,' 1842 ; and other works.

LEROUX, Pierre, French author, b. at Rennes, 1798 ; formerly a compositor and corrector of the press in Paris ; member of the Legislative Assembly of 1848. Author of 'De l'Humanité, de son Principe et de son Avenir,' 1849 ; 'La Grève de Samarez,' 1863–64, a philosophical poem ; and numerous philosophical and political works.

LEROY DE SAINT ARNAUD, Louis, French politician, b. in Paris, 1802 ; studied law, and was called to the bar of the Royal Court of Paris, 1825 ; mayor of the twelfth arrondissement of Paris, 1851 ; created senator, Dec. 26, 1857. Published 'Lettres du Maréchal de Saint Arnaud,' 2 vols. 1855.

LESLIE, Charles Powell, English politician, b. 1821 ; lord-lieutenant of the county of Monaghan, and colonel of the militia ; M.P. for County Monaghan since 1842.

LESLIE, George Robert, English painter, son of C. R. Leslie, b. July 2, 1835 ; A.R.A. 1867.

LESLIE, Hon. George Waldegrave, English politician, b. 1825 ; called to the bar of the Middle Temple, 1849 ; J.P. and deputy-lieutenant for the county of Fife, and captain of the 1st Cinque Ports Rifle Volunteers ; M.P. for Hastings, 1864–68.

LESLIE, Henry David, English musical composer, b. in London, June 18, 1822 ; studied music under Charles Lucas, 1838 ; founded the choral society known by his name, 1856 ; principal of the College of Music. Composed 'Let God arise,' 1849 ; 'Immanuel,' 1853 ; 'Judith,' 1857 ; 'The Daughter of the Isles,' 1861 ; and other works.

LESLIE, William, English politician, b. 1814 ; educated at Aberdeen University, where he graduated M.A. 1832 ; magistrate and deputy-lieutenant of the county of Aberdeen ; formerly a merchant in China ; M.P. for Aberdeenshire, 1861–68.

LESPE'RUT, François, Baron de, French politician, b. at Paris, Oct. 5, 1813 ; elected to the Legislative Assembly, 1849 ; member of the Corps Législatif for the department of Haute Marne since 1852.

LESSEPS, Ferdinand, Vicomte de, French diplomatist, b. at Versailles, Nov. 19, 1805 ; attaché to the French consulate at Lisbon, 1825, and at Tunis, 1828 ; consul at Barcelona, 1842 ; minister at Madrid, 1848, and at Rome, 1849 ; obtained a concession from the Viceroy of Egypt to construct a canal through the Isthmus of Suez, Jan. 1856. Author of numerous 'Notes,' 'Documents,' and 'Rapports,' bearing upon and describing the progress of the Suez Canal undertaking.

LESSING, Karl Friedrich, German painter, b. at Wartenburg, Silesia, Feb. 15, 1808 ; studied at the Academy of Arts, Berlin. Painted the 'Battle of Iconium,' 1829 ; 'The Brigand and his Son,' 1831 ; 'Pope Pascal II. Prisoner of Henry V. ;' 'Huss before the Council of Constance ;' and numerous other historical paintings.

LETHEBY, Henry, English medical writer, b. 1816 ; graduated M.B. 1843, Ph.D. and M.A. 1858 ; lecturer on chemistry and toxicology at the London Hospital ; chemical analyst to the Corporation of London. Author of 'Reports on the Sanitary Condition of the City of London ;' contributor to the *Lancet*, the *Medical Times*, and other medical journals.

LETTE, Wilhelm, German politician, b. at Kienitz, Prussia, March 10, 1799 ; studied philosophy and law at the Universities of Berlin and Göttingen, 1814–20 ; member of the National Assembly of Frankfort, 1848 ; member of the first Prussian Chamber since 1851. Author of 'The Prussian Constitution,' 1857 ; and several works on political economy.

LEVER, Charles James, English novelist, b. in Dublin, 1809 ; studied at Trinity College, Cambridge, where he graduated M.D., and at Göttingen ; physician to the British legation at Brussels, 1833. Author of 'Harry Lorrequer ;' 'The Dod Family Abroad ;' 'The O'Donoghue ;' and numerous other works of fiction.

LEVER, John Orrell, English politician, b. 1824; established the Atlantic Royal Mail Steam Navigation Company; M.P. for Galway, 1859–65.

LE VERRIER, Urbain, French astronomer, b. at St. Lô, Manche, April 11, 1811; studied at the École Polytechnique; discovered the planet Neptune simultaneously with Mr. Adams; elected to the Legislative Assembly for the department of Manche, 1849; made a senator, 1852; succeeded Arago at the Observatory of Paris, 1854.

LEVESON-GOWER, Granville William, English politician, b. 1838; educated at Eton, and Christ Church, Oxford; a magistrate and deputy-lieutenant of Surrey; M.P. for Reigate, 1863–67.

LEVI, Leone, English political economist, b. at Ancona, Italy, June 6, 1821; naturalized a British subject, 1847; called to the bar of Lincoln's Inn, 1859. Author of 'International and Commercial Law,' 1864; and other works.

LEWALD, Fanny, German authoress, b. at Königsberg, March 24, 1811. Author of 'The Substitute,' 1834; 'A Question of Life;' 'Diogena,' 'The Italian Sketch-Book,' 'England and Scotland,' 1852; and other works, chiefly of fiction.

LEWES, George Henry, English author, b. in London, April 18, 1817; educated at Greenwich, and on the Continent. Author of 'Biographical History of Philosophy;' 'The Noble Heart,' a tragedy; 'Life of Goethe;' 'Physiology of Common Life;' 'Studies in Animal Life;' and other works.

LEWIN, Thomas, English author, b. 1805; educated at Merchant Taylors' School, at Worcester College and Trinity College, Oxford, where he graduated B.A. and M.A.; called to the bar, 1833; one of the conveyancing counsel to the Court of Chancery, 1853. Author of 'Life and Epistles of St. Paul,' 1851; 'Jerusalem, a Sketch of the City and Temple,' 1861; 'Cæsar's Invasion of Britain,' 1862; and other works.

LEWIS, John Frederick, English painter, b. in London, July 14, 1805. Exhibited 'The Harem,' 1852; 'Roman Peasants at a Shrine;' 'Scenes in the Desert;' 'Armenian Lady at Cairo,' in oil colours, 1855; 'A Frank Encampment, Desert of Mount Sinai,' 1856. President of the Water Colour Society, 1855–58; elected A.R.A. 1859.

LEWIS, John Harvey, English politician, b. 1814; educated at Trinity College, Dublin, where he graduated M.A. 1837; a magistrate of Westminster and Middlesex, and deputy-lieutenant of the Tower Hamlets; M.P. for Marylebone since 1861.

LEWIS, Lady Maria Theresa, English authoress, b. March 1803; married first to Mr. Thomas Henry Lister, 1830, and secondly, 1844, to Sir George Cornewall Lewis, Bart. M.P., who died 1863. Author of 'The Semi-Detached House,' and 'The Semi-Attached Couple;' 'The Lives of the Friends and Contemporaries of Lord-Chancellor Clarendon.'

LEWIS, Taylor, American author, b. at Northumberland, State of New York, 1802; appointed professor of Greek at the University of New York, 1833; and at Union College, Schnectady, New York. Author of 'The Six Days of Creation, or Scriptural Cosmology,' 1855; 'Science and the Bible,' New York, 1856; and other works.

LEYS, Jean Henri, Belgian painter, b. 1815; studied under M. de Braekelec, 1830. Exhibited 'Combat d'un Grenadier contre un Cosaque,' 1833; 'Albert Durer à Anvers,' 1856; 'Margaret of Austria receiving the Oaths of the Archers of Antwerp;' 'Young Luther singing in the Streets of Eisenach,' 1862; and numerous other pictures.

LIBRI CARRUCCI, Guglielmo, Comte, French mathematician, b. at Florence, Jan. 2, 1803; professor of mathematics at the University of Pisa, 1826; took refuge in France, and was naturalized, 1833. Author of 'Histoire des Sciences mathématiques en Italie depuis la Renaissance jusqu'à la Fin du XVII. Siècle,' 1838–41; and other works.

LICHFIELD, Right Rev. George Augustus Sylwyn, Bishop of, English divine, b. 1809; educated at St. John's College, Cambridge, where he graduated B.A. 1831, M.A. 1834, B.D. and D.D. 1841; appointed bishop of New Zealand, 1841; consecrated bishop of Lichfield, 1867. Author of a number of sermons and theological works.

LICHFIELD, Thomas George Anson, Earl of, English administrator, b. Aug. 15, 1825; précis writer to Lord Palmerston at the Foreign Office, 1846–47; M.P. for Lichfield, 1847–54, when he succeeded his father, first earl; lord-lieutenant of Staffordshire.

LIDDELL, Hon. Henry George, English politician, b. 1821; educated at Eton; magistrate of Durham, and deputy-lieutenant of Northumberland; M.P. for South Northumberland since 1852.

LIDDELL, Sir John, Scottish physician, b. at Dumblane, Scotland, 1794; educated at the University of Edinburgh; entered the Royal Navy as assistant surgeon, 1812; appointed inspector of fleets and hospitals, 1844; director-general of the medical department of the navy, 1854; honorary physician to her Majesty, 1859; knighted, 1850.

LIDDELL, Very Rev. Henry George, English divine, b. 1811; educated at Charterhouse, and Christ Church, Oxford; was domestic chaplain to the late Prince Consort, and chaplain-extraordinary to the Queen; appointed dean of Christ Church, Oxford, 1855. Author of 'A History of Rome.' Editor of 'Liddell and Scott's Greek Lexicon.'

LIEBER, Francis, American author, b. at Berlin, March 18, 1800; entered the Russian army as a volunteer, 1815; graduated at Jena, 1820; took part in the war of independence in Greece, 1821; appointed professor in Columbia College, South Carolina, 1835. Author of 'Journal of my Residence in Greece in 1822,' Leipsic, 1823; 'Civil Liberty and Self-Government,' Philadelphia, 1853; and other works.

LIEBIG, Justus, Baron, German chemist, b. at Darmstadt, May 12, 1803; studied at Bonn and Erlangen, 1819–22, and at Paris, 1822–24; appointed professor of chemistry at Giessen, 1826; created a baron by the Grand Duke of Hesse, 1845; appointed president of the chemical laboratory at the University of Munich, 1852. Author of 'Organic Chemistry in its Application to Agriculture,' Brunswick, 1840; 'Familiar Letters;' and numerous other works on chemistry.

LIEDTS, Auguste Charles, Belgian statesman, b. at Audenarde, 1803; was one of the secretaries of Congress, 1830; president of the Tribunal of Antwerp, 1831–40; envoy-extraordinary to Holland, 1839; minister of the interior, 1840–41; president of the Belgian Chamber, 1843–48; governor of Hainault, 1841–45; minister of finance, 1852–55; Belgian plenipotentiary to France, 1860–61.

LIFFORD, James Hewitt, Viscount, English administrator, b. 1811; graduated at Christ Church, Oxford; deputy-lieutenant of the counties of Warwick and Donegal; succeeded his father, third viscount, 1855.

LIGNE, Euge'ne, Prince de, Belgian statesman, b. at Brussels, Jan. 23, 1804; charged to represent Belgium at the coronation of Queen Victoria, 1838; ambassador to France, 1842–48; and to Italy, 1848–49; member of the Senate, 1851, and president of that body, 1852–56.

LILFORD, Thomas Lyttelton Powys, Baron, English administrator, b. 1833; educated at Harrow, and Christ Church, Oxford, where he graduated B.A. 1855; a deputy-lieutenant of Northamptonshire; succeeded his father, third baron, March 1861.

LINCOLN, Right Rev. Christopher Wordsworth, Bishop of, English divine, b. 1808; educated at Trinity College, Cambridge, where he graduated B.A. 1830, M.A. 1830, B.D. and D.D. 1839; head-master of Harrow School, 1836–44; canon-resident and archdeacon of Westminster, 1844–68; consecrated bishop of Lincoln, Feb. 1869. Author of 'Correspondence of Richard Bentley;' 'Memoirs of William Wordsworth;' 'Athens and Attica;' and numerous theological works.

LINDLEY, John, English botanist, b. at Catton, Norfolk, 1799; was secretary of the Horticultural Society, London; professor of botany in University College, London, and appointed examiner in the same, 1860. Author of 'Natural System of Botany;' 'Synopsis of the British Flora;' 'Vegetable Kingdom;' 'Fossil Flora of Great Britain;' and numerous other works on botany.

LINDSAY, Lord Alexander Crawford, English author, b. 1812; educated at Eton, and Trinity College, Cambridge, where he graduated M.A. 1833. Author of 'Letters on Egypt, Edom, and the Holy Land,' 1838; 'Sketches of the History of Christian Art,' 1847; 'The Lives of the Lindsays,' 1849; and other works.

LINDSAY, Hon. Charles Hugh, English politician, b. 1816; a colonel in the army; was formerly in the 43d Regiment and the Grenadier Guards; elected M.P. for Abingdon, 1865.

LINDSAY, Hon. James, English politician, b. 1815; educated at Eton; a magistrate and deputy-lieutenant for Lancashire; late lieut.-colonel Grenadier Guards; M.P. for Wigan, 1845–57, and since 1859.

LINDSAY, William Schaw, English author, b. at Ayr, Scotland, 1816; was cabin-boy in the *Isabella* West Indiaman, 1831; second mate, 1834; appointed agent for the Castle Eden Coal Company, 1841; M.P. for Tynemouth, 1854 and 1857; for Sunderland, 1859. Author of 'Our Navigation and Mercantile Marine Laws;' 'Our Merchant Shipping;' and numerous pamphlets and letters on the shipping interest.

LINGEN, Ralph Robert Wheeler, English administrator, b. in Birmingham, 1819; educated at Trinity College, Oxford, where he graduated B.A. 1840; entered the *educational department* of the Privy Council, 1845; appointed chief secretary to the *Committee* of the Privy Council for Education, 1849.

LINNELL, John, English painter, b. in London, June 1792. Exhibited 'Fishermen, a Scene from Nature,' 1807; 'The Morning Walk,' 1847; 'The Return of Ulysses,' 1849; 'Christ and the Woman of Samaria at the Well;' 'The Disobedient Prophet;' 'Under the Hawthorn;' and numerous other landscape paintings and portraits of celebrated persons.

LINWOOD, Rev. William, English author, b. 1817; educated at Birmingham, and Christ Church, Oxford, where he graduated B.A. 1839; was assistant master in Shrewsbury School. Author of 'Lexicon to Æschylus;' edited 'Anthologia Oxoniensis,' 1847; and the plays of Sophocles, with English notes.

LIONVILLE, Joseph, French mathematician, b. at St. Omer, March 24, 1806; studied at the École Polytechnique, 1825–27; professor at the École Polytechnique, 1831; and professor of mathematics at the College of France, 1837; member of the Bureau of Longitudes, March 26, 1862. Author of 'Notes and Memoirs,' and other works.

LIPRANDI, Paul Petrowitsch, Russian military commander, b. 1796; took part in the campaigns of 1812–15; appointed lieut.-general, 1848; held a command in the Crimea, 1854–55; appointed to the command of the 1st Corps of the Russian army in Poland, 1861.

LISZT, Franz, Hungarian pianist and composer, b. at Reiding, in Hungary, Oct. 22, 1811; studied under Czerny and Salieri; assumed monastic orders in the Church of Rome, 1864. Composed 'Don Sanche, ou le Château des Amours,' 1825; and numerous preludes, symphonies, and fantasias.

LITTLE, William John, English physician, b. 1810; graduated M.D. 1827; formerly lecturer on medicine to the London Hospital; a founder of the Royal Orthopædic Hospital. Author of a 'Course of Lectures on Deformities' in the *Lancet*, 1843–44; 'Oration of the Hunterian Society,' 1852; and other works.

LITTRE', Maximilien, French philologist, b. in Paris, Feb. 1, 1801. Author of 'Œuvres d'Hippocrate,' 10 vols. 1839–61; 'Histoire de la Langue française,' 1862; 'Auguste Comte et la Philosophie positive,' 1863; 'Dictionnaire de la Langue française;' and numerous philosophical and philological works.

LIVINGSTONE, Rev. David, English traveller, b. at Blantyre, near Glasgow, 1817; worked in the cotton-mills of his native town; admitted a licentiate of the Faculty of Physicians and Surgeons, Glasgow, 1838; ordained a missionary, 1840. Published 'Missionary Travels and Researches in South Africa,' 1857; 'Exploration of the Zambesi,' 1865.

LLANDAFF, Right Rev. Alfred Ollivant, Bishop of, English divine, b. at Manchester, 1798; educated at St. Paul's School, London, and Trinity College, Cambridge; vice-principal of St. David's College, Lampeter, 1827–43; regius professor of divinity at Cambridge, 1843–49; consecrated bishop of Llandaff, 1849.

LLOYD, Sir Thomas Davies, English politician, b. 1820; educated at Harrow, and Christ Church, Oxford; formerly cornet 13th Light Dragoons, and served in Canada with 22d Regiment, 1840–44; a J.P. and deputy-lieutenant for the counties of Cardigan, Carmarthen, and Pembroke; elected M.P. for Cardiganshire, 1865.

LOCH, Henry Brougham, English officer, b. 1827; entered the Bengal Cavalry, 1844; sent to Bulgaria under General Beatson, 1854; retired from the Indian army, and attached to the late Earl of Elgin's special mission to China, 1857; appointed lieut.-governor of the Isle of Man, 1863.

LOCKE, John, English politician, b. 1805; educated at Trinity College, Cambridge, where he graduated B.A. 1826, and M.A. 1829; called to the bar of the Inner Temple, 1833; appointed recorder of Brighton, 1861; M.P. for Southwark since 1857.

LOCOCK, Sir Charles, English physician, b. 1799; educated at the University of Edinburgh, where he graduated M.D.; appointed first physician accoucheur to her Majesty, 1840; retired from the medical profession, 1857; created a baronet, 1857.

LOENNROT, Elias, Finlandish philologist, b. at Sammati, Helsingfors, April 9, 1802; entered the University of Abo, 1822, where he graduated M.D. 1832; appointed professor of Finnish language and literature at the University of Helsingfors, 1853; president of the Academy of Sciences of Finland, 1854. Author of 'Kalevala,' Helsingfors, 1835; 'Om Finnarnes magiska Medicin,' 1832; 'Om nordtschudiska Spraket,' ib. 1853; and numerous poetical, medical, and philological works.

LOGAN, Sir William Edmond, American geologist, b. 1798; educated at Montreal, and at the University of Edinburgh; appointed director of the Geological Survey of Canada, 1840; knighted, 1856; one of the jurors of the scientific department of the International Exhibition of 1862.

LONDESBOROUGH, William Henry Forester Denison, Baron, English administrator, b. 1834; educated at Eton, and Christ Church, Oxford; was M.P. for Beverley, 1857–59; for Scarborough, 1859–60; succeeded his father, first baron, 1860.

LONDON, Right Rev. John Jackson, Bishop of, English divine, b. 1811; rector of St. James's, Westminster, 1846; canon of Bristol, 1852; bishop of Lincoln, 1853; of London, 1868.

LONDONDERRY, Frederick William Robert, Marquis of, English administrator, b. in London, 1805; M.P. for the county of Down, 1825–52; a lord of the Admiralty, 1828; vice-chamberlain of the Household from Dec. 1834 to April 1835; privy councillor; colonel of the Royal North Down Militia, 1837; succeeded his father, third marquis, March 1854.

LONG, George, English historical writer, b. at Poulton, Lancashire, 1800; educated at Macclesfield School, and Trinity College, Cambridge, where he graduated B.A. 1822; called to the bar of the Inner Temple, 1837; professor of Greek and Latin in the University of London. Author of 'A History of France and its Revolutions,' 1850; 'Decline of the Roman Republic;' and other works.

LONG, Richard Penruddocke, English politician, b. 1825; educated at Harrow, and Trinity College, Cambridge, where he graduated B.A. 1848, and M.A. 1852; a magistrate for Wilts, and a deputy-lieutenant for the county of Montgomery; M.P. for Chippenham, 1859–65; returned for North Wiltshire, 1865.

LONGFELLOW, Henry Wadsworth, American poet, b. at Portland, Maine, United States, Feb. 27, 1807; entered Bowdoin College, 1821, where he graduated, 1825; appointed professor of modern languages at Bowdoin College, 1829, and at Harvard College, 1835. Author of 'Voices of the Night,' 1841; 'Evangeline,' 1847; 'The Golden Legend,' 1851; 'Miles Standish,' 1858; 'Tales of a Wayside Inn,' 1863; and numerous other poems.

LONGFORD, William Lygon Packenham, Earl, English administrator, b. 1819; educated at Winchester; entered the army, 1837; colonel, 1855; served in the Crimea, 1854–56, and in India and China, 1857–59; succeeded his brother, third earl, March 1860; deputy-lieutenant for Westmeath, and a magistrate for Westmeath and Longford.

LONGPE'RIER, Adrien Pre'vost de, French antiquarian, b. at Paris, Sept. 21, 1816; appointed under-keeper of the Egyptian antiquities in the museum of the Louvre, 1847, and head-keeper, 1848. Author of 'Des Rois arsacides;' 'Le Musée Napoléon III.: Architecture, Sculpture, &c.' 1864; and numerous papers and memoirs.

LONGRIDGE, James Atkinson, English civil engineer, b. 1817; consulting engineer to the Calcutta and South-Eastern Railway, and engaged in railway undertakings in Trinidad and the Mauritius. Author of several papers on the ventilation of mines, and other subjects connected with engineering.

LONGSTREET, James, American military commander, b. in South Carolina, 1821; entered West Point Academy, 1838; lieutenant, 1842; captain, 1852; major, 1858; resigned his commission, June 1, 1861, and joined the South; appointed to a command in the Confederate army, July 1861; major-general, 1862; lieut.-general, Oct. 1862.

LONSDALE, William Lowther, Earl of, English statesman, b. 1787; educated at Trinity College, Cambridge, where he graduated M.A. 1808; M.P. for Cockermouth, and for the county of Westmoreland from 1808 to 1841, when he entered the House of Lords as Baron Lowther; has been a lord of the Treasury; chief commissioner of woods and forests; treasurer of the navy; vice-president of the Board of Trade, and postmaster-general; was president of the council from March to Dec. 1852; lord-lieutenant of the counties and vice-admiral of the coasts of Cumberland and Westmoreland; succeeded his father, first earl, 1844.

LOOMIS, Elias, American mathematician, b. 1818; studied at Yale College, Connecticut; appointed professor of mathematics and physics at the University of New York, 1844. Author of 'Elements of Geometry and Algebra;' 'Recent Progress of Astronomy, especially in the United States,' 1850; 'A Treatise on Arithmetic, Theoretical and Practical,' 1856; and other elementary works.

LOPES, Sir Massey, English politician, b. 1818; educated at Winchester and Oriel College, Oxford; M.P. for Devon and Wilts; a deputy-lieutenant for Devon, and captain of the 2d Devon Militia; M.P. for Westbury, 1857; for South Devon, 1868.

LOPEZ, Don Francisco Solano, Paraguayan statesman, b. 1827; the eldest son of Don Carlos Lopez, president of the Republic of Paraguay; succeeded to the presidency at the death of his father, by the will of the latter, Sept. 10, 1862; engaged in a war with Brazil, 1865–68.

—————[170]—————

LOS HERREROS, Manuel Breton de, Spanish author, b. at Quel, province of Logroño, Dec. 19, 1800; studied at Madrid, and entered the army as a volunteer, 1814; keeper of the National Library, 1834–44; elected member of the Royal Academy of Spain, 1837. Author of 'El Carnaval,' Madrid, 1833; 'La Desvergüenza, Poema jocoseria,' ib. 1858; and numerous other works in verse and prose.

LOSSING, Benson, American author, b. at Bickman, Dutchess County, New York, 1819. Published 'An Outline of the History of the Fine Arts,' 1841; 'Lives of the Signers of the Declaration of Independence,' 1847; 'Pictorial Field-Book of the Revolution,' 1848–52; 'Illustrated History of the United States,' 1857; and numerous other works.

LOUGH, John Graham, English sculptor, b. at Greenhead, Northumberland, 1804; executed the statue of Queen Victoria for the Royal Exchange, London, 1845; 'Comus,' in the Egyptian Hall at the Mansion House; and numerous busts, groups, and statues.

LOUVET, Charles, French politician, b. at Saumur, Maine-et-Loire, Oct. 22, 1806; studied law; represented Maine-et-Loire in the Legislative Assembly, 1848; member of the Corps Législatif for the department of Maine-et-Loire since 1852.

LOVE, Sir James Frederick, English military commander, b. 1789; entered the army, 1804; served in Sweden, the Peninsula, at Antwerp, New Orleans, and Waterloo; commanded a division in Canada in the Rebellion of 1835–36; employed in suppressing the Rebecca and Chartist riots, 1838–39; lieutenant-governor of Jersey, 1851–57; inspector-general of infantry; and colonel of the 57th Foot.

LOVELACE, William King Noel, Earl of, English administrator, b. 1805; educated at Eton, and Trinity College, Cambridge; lord-lieutenant of Surrey; a magistrate for Surrey and Somerset; colonel of the 2d Surrey Royal Militia.

LOVER, Samuel, Irish painter and author, b. in Dublin, 1797; elected Academician of the Royal Hibernian Society of Arts, 1828. Painted the portraits of the Marquis Wellesley, Lord Brougham, and of numerous celebrated persons. Author of 'Legends and Tales illustrative of Irish Character,' 'Handy Andy,' 'The May Dew,' 'Rory O'More,' 'The Happy Man;' and other songs, poems, and sketches of Irish life.

LOWE, Rev. Richard Thomas, English naturalist, b. Dec. 1801; educated at Christ College, Cambridge, where he graduated B.A. 1825; was British chaplain in Madeira; appointed rector of Lea, Lincolnshire, 1852. Author of 'The Fishes of Madeira,' 1843; 'A Manual of the Flora of Madeira;' and numerous memoirs on zoological and botanical subjects.

LOWE, Right Hon. Robert, English statesman, b. 1811; educated at Winchester, and University College, Oxford, where he graduated B.A. 1833; called to the bar of Lincoln's Inn, 1842; a member of the Council at Sydney, 1843–50; joint secretary of the Board of Control, 1852–55; paymaster of the forces and vice-president of the Board of Trade, 1855–58; M.P. for Kidderminster, 1852–59; vice-president of Committee of Council on Education, 1859–64; M.P. for Calne, 1859–68; for the University of London, 1868; chancellor of the Exchequer, Dec. 1868.

LOWELL, James Russell, American author, b. at Boston, United States, 1819; studied law, and graduated at Harvard University. Author of 'A Year's Life,' 1841; 'A Legend of Brittany,' and 'Prometheus,' 1844; 'The Biglow Papers,' 1848; 'A Fable for Critics,' 1848; and other works in prose and verse.

LOWER, Mark Antony, English antiquarian, b. at Chiddingley, Sussex, 1813; conductor of a boarding-school at Lewes. Author of 'English Surnames, an Essay on Family Nomenclature,' 1842; 'Curiosities of Heraldry,' 1845; 'Patronymica Britannica,' 1860; and other works.

LOWTHER, Henry, English politician, b. 1818; educated at Westminster, and Trinity College, Cambridge, and graduated M.A. 1838; formerly captain in the 1st Life Guards; M.P. for West Cumberland since 1847.

LOWTHER, Hon. Henry Cecil, English politician, b. 1790; deputy-lieutenant for Rutland; a lieutenant-colonel in the army; formerly captain in the 7th Hussars and major in the 10th Hussars; M.P. for Westmoreland since 1812.

LOWTHER, James, English politician, b. 1840; educated at Westminster and Trinity College, Cambridge, where he graduated B.A. 1862; called to the bar of the Inner Temple, 1864; elected M.P. for York, 1865.

LOYD-LINDSAY, Robert James, English politician, b. 1832; educated at Eton; a magistrate for Berks and county of Northampton, and a lieutenant-colonel Scots Fusilier Guards; assumed the additional surname of Loyd by royal licence, 1858; elected M.P. for Berkshire, 1865.

LUARD, Rev. Henry Richard, English author, b. 1825; educated at Trinity College, Cambridge, where he graduated B.A. 1847, M.A. 1850; fellow and assistant-tutor of Trinity College, and registrar of the University of Cambridge. Author of 'The Life of Porson,' 1857. Edited 'Lives of Edward the Confessor,' 1858; 'Annales Monastici,' 1864; and other works.

LUBBOCK, Sir John William, English mathematician, b. in London, 1803; educated at Trinity College, Cambridge, and graduated B.A. 1825, and M.A. 1833; high sheriff of Kent, 1852; one of the vice-presidents of the Royal Society.

LUBONIS, Louis Ignace, French politician, b. at Nice, Aug. 9, 1816; studied law at the University of Turin, and graduated LL.D. 1837; was counsellor and procureur-général to the court of Nice; appointed governor of the province of Nice, 1860; member of the Corps Législatif for the first circonscription of the department of Alpes Maritimes since 1860.

LUCAN, George Charles Bingham, Earl of, English military commander, b. 1800; educated at Westminster; M.P. for Mayo, 1826–30; elected one of the representative peers for Ireland, 1840; commanded the British cavalry in the Crimea, 1844–45; a lieutenant-general in the army.

LUCAS, Charles, English musical composer, b. at Salisbury, 1808; educated at the Cathedral Grammar School in that city, and at the Royal Academy of Music; conductor of the orchestra of the R.A. of Music, 1832; appointed principal of the R.A. of Music, 1859. Author of several overtures, anthems, operas, songs, and glees.

LUCAS, Charles Jean, French political economist, b. at St. Brieuc, May 3, 1803; admitted advocate at the Royal Court of Paris, 1825; appointed inspector of prisons, 1833. Author of 'On the Penitentiary System in Europe and America,' 1826–30; 'Theory of Imprisonment,' 1836–38; and numerous other works.

LUCAS, Hippolyte Julien, French author, b. at Rennes, Dec. 20, 1807; educated at the College of his native town, and studied law in Paris, 1826. Author of 'Caractères et Portraits de Femmes,' 1836; 'Le Portefeuille d'un Journaliste,' 1856; 'La Pêche d'un Mari,' 1862; and numerous poems and dramas.

LUDERS, Alexander Nicolaiewitch von, Russian general, b. 1790; entered the army, 1807; commanded a Russian army corps in Hungary, 1849; held a command in the Crimea, 1854–55; created a count of the Russian empire, June 1862.

LUDWIG II. King of Bavaria and Count Palatine of the Rhine, b. Aug. 24, 1845, the son of King Maximilian II. and his consort, Queen Maria, daughter of the late Prince William of Prussia; succeeded to the throne at the death of his father, March 10, 1864.

LUDWIG III. Grand Duke of Hesse-Darmstadt, b. June 9, 1806, the son of Grand Duke Ludwig II. and of Princess Wilhelmine of Baden; appointed co-regent of Hesse-Darmstadt in consequence of an insurrection, March 5, 1848; succeeded to the throne at the death of his father, June 16, 1848; married, Dec. 26, 1833, to Princess Mathilde, daughter of King Ludwig of Bavaria; widower, May 25, 1862.

LUGARD, Sir Edward, English military commander, b. at Chelsea, 1810; educated at the Military College, Sandhurst; entered the army, 1821, and served in India; brigade-major, 1842; adjutant-general to the Queen's forces in the Punjaub campaigns, 1848–49; adjutant-general in India, 1857; brigadier-general and major-general, 1858.

LUGY PELLISSAC, Louis Henri, Marquis 'de, French general and politician, b. Aug. 13, 1797; colonel, April 14, 1844; general of brigade, 1848; general of division, 1854; elected deputy to the Corps Législatif for the second circonscription de la Drôme, 1863.

LUIZ I. King of Portugal, b. Oct. 31, 1838; the son of Queen Maria II. and of Prince Ferdinand of Saxe-Coburg; succeeded his brother, King Pedro V., Nov. 11, 1861; married, Oct. 6, 1862, to Pia, b. Oct. 16, 1847, the youngest daughter of King Victor Emmanuel of Italy.

LUKIS, Rev. William Collings, English author, b. 1817; educated at Trinity College, Cambridge, where he graduated in 1840; rector of Wath-juxta-Ripon, Yorkshire. Author of 'Specimens of Ancient Church Plate,' 1845; 'Danish Cromlechs and Burial Customs, compared with those of Brittany, Great Britain, &c.' 1861; and other works.

LUND, Rev. Thomas, English mathematician, b. Dec. 2, 1805; educated at St. John's College, Cambridge, where he graduated B.A. 1828; appointed rector of Morton, Derbyshire, 1841, and of Brindle, Lancashire, 1864. Author of 'The Elements of Geometry and Mensuration;' 'A Key to Bishop Colenso's Biblical Arithmetic,' 1863; and various mathematical works.

LUSK, Andrew, English politician, b. 1813; a magistrate for Middlesex, an alderman of London, and a merchant in the City; was sheriff of London and Middlesex, 1861; elected M.P. for Finsbury, 1865.

LUYNES, Joseph d'Albert, Duc de, French archæologist, b. at Paris. Dec. 15, 1802; represented the department of the Seine-et-Oise in the Constituent Assembly, 1848; and in the Legislative Assembly, 1849. Author of 'Études numismatiques,' 1835; 'Essai sur la Numismatique des Satrapies,' 1846; and other works.

LYELL, Sir Charles, English geologist, b. at Kinnordy, Forfarshire, 1797; educated at Exeter College, Oxford, where he graduated M.A. 1821; called to the bar; appointed a deputy-lieutenant for Forfarshire, 1831; president of the Geological Society, 1836–37, and 1850–51; knighted, 1848; created a baronet, 1864. Author of 'The Principles of Geology,' 1833; 'Travels in North America,' 1841; and numerous geological works.

LYONNET, Jean Baptiste, French divine, b. at St. Étienne, Loire, June 4, 1801; studied at the College of St. Chamond and the Seminary of Argentière; ordained, 1824; consecrated bishop of Algiers, 1846; bishop of St. Fleur, Oct. 15, 1851; appointed to the see of Valence, June 24, 1857. Author of 'Tractatus de Contractîbus,' 1837; and other works.

LYONS, Richard Bickerton, Baron, English diplomatist, b. 1823; educated at Winchester, and Christ Church, Oxford; attaché at Athens, 1849; at Dresden, 1852; at Florence, 1853; secretary of legation at Florence, 1856; chargé d'affaires, 1857; envoy extraordinary and minister plenipotentiary to the United States, Dec. 1858; resigned, Nov. 1864; nominated K.C.B. 1859; G.C.B. 1862; British ambassador at Paris.

LYTTELTON, George William, Baron, English administrator, b. 1817; educated at Eton, and Trinity College, Cambridge, where he graduated in 1838; under-secretary of state for the colonies, Jan. to July 1846; lord-lieutenant of Worcestershire; high steward of Bewdley, and a magistrate for Staffordshire and Shropshire.

LYTTON, Right Hon. Edward Lytton Bulwer, Baron, English statesman and author, b. 1805; educated at Trinity College and at Trinity Hall, Cambridge, where he graduated B.A. 1826, M.A. 1835; created a baronet, 1838; assumed the surname of Lytton, 1844; M.P. for St. Ives, 1831–32; for Lincoln, 1832–41; and for Hertfordshire, 1852 to July 1856, when he was elevated to the peerage; secretary of state for the colonies, 1858–59. Author of 'Ismael,' an Oriental tale, 1820; 'Pelham, or the Adventures of a Gentleman,' 1827; 'Zanoni,' 1843; 'A Strange Story,' 1862; and a great number of novels, romances, and dramas.

LYTTON, Edward Robert Bulwer, English diplomatist, b. 1831, only son of the preceding; educated at Harrow and Bonn; entered the diplomatic service, 1849; first secretary of the British legation at Copenhagen, 1864. Author, under the *nom de plume* of 'Owen Meredith,' of 'Clytemnestra, and other Poems,' 1855; 'The Wanderer, a Collection of Poems in Many Lands,' 1859; 'Lucile,' a novel in verse, 1860; and other poetical works.

LYVEDEN, Robert Vernon Smith, Baron, English statesman, b. 1800; educated at Eton, and Christ Church, Oxford; was M.P. for Tralee, 1829–31; for Northampton, 1831–59, when he was elevated to the peerage; was a lord of the Treasury, 1830–35; secretary of the Board of Control, 1835–39; under-secretary of state for the colonies, 1839–41; president of the Board of Control, 1855–58.

M.

MACCABE, William Bernard, English writer, b. in Dublin, Nov. 23, 1801; consul in London for the Republic of Uruguay, 1847–51. Author of 'A Catholic History of England;' 'Bertha, a Romance of the Dark Ages;' both in 1856; 'A True History of the Hungarian Revolution,' 1851; 'Agnes Arnold,' a novel, 1860; and other works.

MACCHI, Mauro, Italian politician, b. at Milan, 1815; founded the journal *L'Italia* at Genoa, 1850; elected to represent Cremona in the Italian Parliament, 1860. Published 'Les Contradictions de M. Vincent Gioberti,' 1853.

McCLELLAN, George, American military commander, b. at Philadelphia, Dec. 3, 1826; educated at West Point, which he left as second lieutenant, 1846; a member of the commission sent by the United States Government to the seat of war in the Crimea, 1854–55; received the commission of major-general of Volunteers on the outbreak of the civil war, 1861; appointed commander-in-chief, Nov. 1861; commander of the army of the Potomac, March 1862; relieved from his command, Nov. 1862.

MACCLESFIELD, Thomas Augustus Parker, Earl of, English administrator, b. 1811; was M.P. for Oxfordshire as Lord Parker, 1837–41; succeeded his father, fifth earl, 1850; lord high steward of Henley.

McCLINTOCK, Sir Francis Leopold, English naval commander, b. at Dundalk, 1819; entered the navy, 1831; post-captain, 1854; knighted for services in the Arctic regions in searching after Sir John Franklin; appointed commander of the screw frigate *Aurora,* 1864.

McCLURE, Sir Robert John Le Mesurier, English naval commander, b. at Wexford, Ireland, Jan. 28, 1807; educated at Winchester and Sandhurst; volunteered to join the expedition under Captain Back to the Arctic seas, 1836; joined Sir J. Ross's expedition to discover Sir J. Franklin, 1848; nominated commander in the navy, 1849; commanded the *Investigator* and discovered the north-west passage, 1850; knighted, and received the reward of £5,000 offered for the discovery, 1851.

McCONNELL, John, American novelist, b. at Illinois, Nov. 11, 1826; studied at the Law School of Lexington, Kentucky; and subsequently fought as volunteer in the war with Mexico, and received the commission of captain. Author of 'Talbot and Vernon,' New York, 1850; 'The Gleens, a Family History,' ib. 1851; 'Western Characters,' 1858; and other works of fiction.

McCORMIC, Robert, English author, b. 1804; studied medicine, and nominated fellow of the Royal College of Surgeons, 1844; commanded the boat expedition in search of Sir J. Franklin, 1852. Author of 'Narrative of a Boat and Sledge Expedition up Wellington Channel in search of Franklin, with Plans of Search in the Arctic Ocean;' and other works.

McCOSH, James, English theologian, b. in Ayrshire, 1811; educated at the Universities of Glasgow and Edinburgh; minister of the Church of Scotland in Arbroath, 1835–50; appointed professor of logic and metaphysics in Queen's College, Belfast, 1851; at Princeton, 1868. Author of 'The Method of Divine Government, Physical and Moral,' 1850; 'The Supernatural in relation to the Natural,' 1862; and other theological works.

McCRIE, Rev. Thomas, English theologian, b. at Edinburgh, 1798; educated at Edinburgh University; appointed professor of theology at the English Presbyterian College, 1856. Author of 'Sketches of Scottish Church History,' and of many contributions to religious periodicals.

McCROHON, Jose', Spanish military commander, b. at Ferrol, 1803; lieutenant, 1817; colonel, 1841; general of brigade, 1843; field-marshal, 1846; commanding general of the eastern district of Cuba and governor of Santiago, 1847; under-secretary to the minister of war, 1851; lieutenant-general, 1855; captain-general of New Castile, 1858; of the Philippine Isles, 1860.

McCULLOCH, Horatio, English landscape painter, b. in Glasgow, 1806; studied art at Edinburgh. Exhibited 'A View on the Clyde,' 1826; 'Highland Loch;' 'A View in Cadzow Forest,' 1838; 'Mist rising off the Mountains,' 1861; and numerous other paintings. Elected associate of the Scottish Academy, 1836, and member, 1838.

MACDONALD, George, English novelist, b. in Scotland about 1824. Author of 'Phantastes,' 'Alec Forbes of Howglen,' 'Unspoken Sermons,' and many other works.

MACDONNELL, Sir Richard Graves, English colonial administrator, b. 1815; educated at Trinity College, Dublin, and graduated B.A. 1835, and M.A. 1838; called to the bar in Ireland, 1838, and at Lincoln's Inn, London, 1840; chief justice of the Gambia colony, 1843–47; governor of Gambia, 1847–51; governor of St. Lucia and St. Vincent in 1852; captain-general and governor-in-chief of South Australia, 1855–62; governor of Nova Scotia, 1864–65; of Hong Kong, 1865.

McDOWELL, Irwin, American military commander, b. in Ohio, 1818; educated in France and at the Military Academy, West Point; appointed brigadier-general on the outbreak of the civil war, 1860; major-general, March 14, 1862; commander of the department of the Rappahannock, April 14, 1862; relieved from his command, Sept. 5, 1862; commander of the department of California, Sept. 1863.

MACDOWELL, Patrick, English sculptor, b. at Belfast, Aug. 1789. Executed 'Loves of the Angels,' 'A Girl Reading,' 'Love Triumphant,' 'The Death of Virginia;' statue of Lord Exmouth for Greenwich Hospital; statues of Pitt and Chatham for the House of Lords; and numerous other groups and statues in bronze and marble. Elected A.R.A. and R.A. 1846.

McEVOY, Edward, English politician, b. 1826; a magistrate for the county of Meath; formerly lieutenant in the 6th Dragoon Guards, and captain of Longford Rifles; M.P. for the county of Meath since 1855.

MACFARREN, George Alexander, English musical composer, b. in London, March 2, 1813; educated at the Royal Academy of Music; appointed member of the board of professors of the R.A. of Music, 1860. Author of 'The Devil's Opera,' at the Lyceum, 1838; 'Don Quixote,' Drury Lane, 1846; 'Robin Hood,' her Majesty's, 1860; 'She Stoops to Conquer,' Covent Garden, 1864; and numerous other operas and songs. Author of 'Rudiments of Harmony,' 1860; and other works.

McGHEE, Rev. Robert James, English theological writer, b. in Ireland, 1790; educated at Trinity College, Dublin, and graduated B.A. 1811; appointed rector of Holywell, Hunts, 1846. Author of 'A History of the Douay and Rhemish versions of the Bible;' and other theological works.

McGREGOR, Sir John, English physician, b. at Perth, 1791; educated at the University of Edinburgh, and entered the medical department of the army, 1809; served under the Duke of Wellington in the Peninsula, and during the Mutiny in India; appointed inspector-general of hospitals, 1856; honorary physician to the Queen, and created K.C.B. military division, 1859; changed his name by royal licence from McAndrew to McGregor, 1863.

McILVAINE, Right Rev. Charles Petit, American theologian, b. at Burlington, New Jersey, Jan. 18, 1798; graduated at Princeton College, 1816; admitted to deacon's orders, 1820; professor of history and ethics at West Point, 1825–27; consecrated bishop of Ohio, 1832. Author of 'Evidences of Christianity,' which passed through thirty editions.

MACINTOSH, Maria, American authoress, b. at Sunbury, Georgia, 1802. Author of 'Aunt Kitty's Tales,' 1837; 'Conquest and Self-Conquest,' New York, 1844; 'Violet, or the Cross and the Crown,' Boston, 1856; and other works of fiction.

MACKAY, Charles, English author, b. in Perth, 1812; was editor of the *Glasgow Argus,* 1844–47; and subsequently of the *Illustrated London News.* Author of 'The Hope of the World,' 1837; 'Voices from the Crowd,' 1844; 'Voices from the Mountains,' 1846; 'Egeria,' 1850; 'The Lump of Gold,' 1855; 'A Man's Heart,' 1860; 'Studies from the Antique, and Sketches from Nature,' 1864; 'History of Popular Delusions;' and other works in prose and verse.

McKENNA, Sir Joseph Neale, English politician, b. 1819; educated at Trinity College, Dublin; called to the Irish bar, 1848; M.P. for Youghal, 1865–68.

MACKENZIE, Thomas, Scottish judge, b. 1807; educated at Perth and the Universities of St. Andrew's and Edinburgh; called to the Scottish bar, 1832; appointed sheriff of Ross and Cromarty, 1851; solicitor-general of Scotland, and a judge of the Court of Session, 1855; retired from the bench, 1864.

MACKIE, James, English politician, b. 1821; educated at Oriel College, Oxford, where he graduated B.A. 1844, and M.A. 1847; advocate of the Scottish bar, and a magistrate of Kirkcudbright; M.P. for Kirkcudbrightshire since 1857.

MACKIE, John Milton, American writer, b. at Wareham, Massachusetts, 1813; graduated at Brown University, Rhode Island, 1832. Author of 'Life of Leibnitz,' 1845; 'Life of Samuel Gorton,' 1848; 'Going to Spain,' 1855; and other works.

MACKINNON, Lachlan Bellingham, English politician, b. 1815; a magistrate of Surrey; formerly captain in the Royal Navy; elected M.P. for Rye, 1865.

MACKINNON, William Alexander, English author and politician, b. 1789; studied at Lincoln; was M.P. for Lymington, 1831–52, and for Rye, 1857–65. Author of 'Thoughts on the Currency Question;' 'The History of Civilization;' and other works.

MACKINNON, William Alexander, English politician, b. 1813, son of the preceding; educated at St. John's College, Cambridge, and graduated B.A. 1836; a magistrate of Hants and Middlesex; M.P. for Rye, 1852–53; returned for Lymington, 1857.

McLAGAN, Peter, English politician, b. 1814; educated at Edinburgh University; a magistrate of the counties of Edinburgh and Linlithgow; and member of the Council of the University of Edinburgh; elected M.P. for Linlithgowshire, 1865.

McLAREN, Duncan, English politician, b. 1800; deputy-lieutenant of Edinburgh; and president of the Chamber of Commerce, Edinburgh; elected M.P. for Edinburgh, 1865.

MACLEAN, John, English colonial administrator, b. 1810; chief commissioner for British Kaffraria, 1852–60; lieutenant-governor of British Kaffraria, 1860–64; appointed lieutenant-governor of Natal, April 6, 1864.

MACLEOD, Rev. Norman, English author, b. 1812; educated at Edinburgh, *Glasgow,* and in Germany; appointed minister of Loudoun, Ayrshire, 1838; and the *Barony parish, Glasgow,* 1851. Author of 'The Home Education;' 'The Earnest Student;' *and other works.* *Editor of Good Words.*

MACLISE, Daniel, English painter, b. in Cork, Jan. 25, 1811; studied in the schools of the Royal Academy. Exhibited 'Mokanna unveiling his features to Zelica,' 1833; 'The Banquet Scene in Macbeth,' 1840; 'The Play Scene in Hamlet,' 1842; 'The Sacrifice of Noah,' 1847; 'The Death of Nelson,' in the New Houses of Parliament, 1866; and numerous other paintings. Elected A.R.A. 1835, and R.A. 1841.

McMURDO, William, English military commander, b. 1819; entered the army as ensign, 1837; lieutenant, 1841; captain, 1843; major, 1843; lieutenant-colonel, 1853; colonel in the army, 1854; created C.B. after the Crimean war, 1856; was inspector-general of Volunteer forces for five years.

McNEILE, Rev. Hugh, English theologian, b. at Ballycastle, county of Antrim, 1795; studied at Trinity College, and graduated B.A. 1815; ordained, 1820; honorary canon in Chester Cathedral, 1845–48; appointed incumbent of St. Paul's, Princes Park, Liverpool, 1848; dean of Ripon, 1868. Author of 'The Church and the Churches,' 1846; and other theological works.

MACNEILL, Sir John, English engineer, b. at Mount Pleasant, near Dundalk, 1788; professor of practical engineering at Trinity College, Dublin; knighted on the opening of the railway from Dublin to Drogheda, 1844. Author of several works on engineering.

McNEILL, Right Hon. Duncan, Scottish judge, b. 1793; educated at the Universities of St. Andrew's and Edinburgh; called to the Scottish bar, 1816; one of the junior counsel for the Crown, 1820–24; sheriff of Perthshire, 1824–34; solicitor-general for Scotland, 1835–41; lord-advocate, 1842; dean of the Faculty of Advocates, 1843–51; M.P. for Argyllshire, 1843–51; lord chief justice-general and president of the Court of Session, 1852; sworn in the Privy Council, 1853.

McNEILL, Sir John, English diplomatist, b. 1795; assistant envoy to the court of Persia, 1831; envoy extraordinary and minister plenipotentiary to Persia, 1836; president of the commission of inquiry into the administration of the commissariat of the army in the Crimea, 1855; appointed member of the Privy Council, 1856.

MACREADY, William Charles, English actor, b. in London, March 3, 1793; educated at Rugby; made his début as Romeo, at Birmingham, June 1813; made his first appearance in London at Covent Garden, Sept. 16, 1816; performed Shakespeare's principal plays in England and America.

MADDEN, Sir Frederick, English author, b. 1801; knighted, 1833; keeper of manuscripts in the British Museum, 1837–66. Editor of 'The Wycliffite Version of the Holy Scriptures;' 'Layamon's Brut, or History of Britain;' and author of numerous historical, literary, and genealogical works.

MADDEN, Richard Robert, English colonial administrator, b. 1798; fellow of the Royal College of Surgeons; special magistrate in Jamaica, 1833–46; appointed colonial secretary of Western Australia, 1847. Author of 'Travels in Turkey and Egypt,' 1829; 'Shrines and Sepulchres of the Old and New World,' 1851; 'The Lives and Times of the United Irishmen,' 1863; and other works.

MADDOCK, Sir Thomas Herbert, English politician, b. 1792; entered the East India Civil Service in the Bengal Presidency, 1811; assistant magistrate at Moorshedabad, 1815; knighted by patent, 1844; deputy-governor of Bengal, and president of the Council of India, 1845–49; M.P. for Rochester, 1852–57.

MADOZ, Pascual, Spanish statesman and author, b. at Pampeluna, May 17, 1806; studied law at the University of Saragossa; successively civil governor of Barcelona and president of the Cortes; minister of finance, 1855. Author of 'A Geographical, Statistical, and Historical Dictionary of Spain,' Madrid, 1848–50.

MADRAZO, Federico, Spanish painter, b. in Rome, Feb. 12, 1815; studied at Paris under Winterhalter. Painted 'Godfrey proclaimed King of Jerusalem,' in the museum of Versailles, 1839; 'La Comtesse de Vilchés;' and numerous portraits of celebrated persons.

MADVIG, Israel, Danish philologist, b. 1800; professor of Latin literature at Copenhagen. Author of 'Opuscula Academica,' 1834–42; 'Syntax der griechischen Sprache,' Brunswick, 1847; and other philological works.

MAEDLER, Johann Heinrich, German astronomer, b. at Berlin, May 29, 1794; appointed professor of astronomy and director of the Observatory at Dorpat, in Russia, 1840. Author of 'Popular Astronomy,' Berlin, 1849; 'The Existence of a Central Sun,' Dorpat, 1846; 'Letters on Astronomy,' Mittau, 1845–47; and other works on astronomy.

MAGENIS, Sir Arthur Charles, English diplomatist, b. 1810; educated at the University of Dublin, and entered the diplomatic service, 1839; minister plenipotentiary in Switzerland, 1851; envoy extraordinary and minister plenipotentiary at Lisbon, 1859; nominated K.C.B. civil division, 1860.

MAGIN, Alfred Joseph Auguste, French author, b. at Modena, Italy, Dec. 31, 1806 : educated at the Lyceum of Turin, 1812–15 ; rector of the Academy of the Seine-et-Oise, 1852–62 ; rector of the Academy of Rheims, 1862. Author of ' Précis de Géographie universelle,' 1840 ; 'Histoire de France abrégée,' 1848 ; new edition, 1864 ; and other works.

MAGNE, Pierre, French statesman, b. at Perigueux, Dec. 3, 1806 ; under-secretary of finance, 1849 ; minister of public works, April 10 to Oct. 26, 1851 ; reappointed, Dec. 1, 1851 ; minister of finance, 1854 to Nov. 1860 ; made a senator, Dec. 31, 1852.

MAGNIN, Joseph, French politician, b. at Dijon, Jan. 1, 1824 ; member of the Constituent Assembly, 1849 ; member of the Corps Législatif for the first circonscription of the department of Côte d'Or since 1863.

MAGNUS, Edward, Prussian painter, b. at Berlin, Jan. 7, 1799 ; studied successively medicine, philosophy, and painting, the last under Schlesinger. Painted 'The Return of the Pirate ;' the portrait of Jenny Lind ; and portraits of all the members of the Royal Family of Prussia, and of numerous other celebrated persons.

MAGUIRE, John Francis, English politician, b. 1815 ; called to the Irish bar, 1843 ; mayor of Cork, 1853 and 1862–63 ; principal editor and proprietor of the *Cork Examiner ;* a magistrate and alderman of the city of Cork ; M.P. for Dungarvon, 1852–65, and returned for Cork, 1865. Author of ' Rome and its Rulers,' 1857 ; 'Father Mathew,' 1863.

MAGUIRE, Rev. Robert, English author, b. in Dublin, 1826 ; educated at Trinity College, Dublin, and graduated, 1847 ; curate of St. Nicholas, Cork, 1849–52 ; appointed incumbent of Clerkenwell, 1857. Author of 'The Seven Churches of Asia ;' 'Things Present and Things to Come ;' and other religious and controversial works.

MAILLET, Jacques Le'onard, French sculptor, b. at Paris, July 12, 1823 ; studied under Pradier, at the Ecole des Beaux Arts. Executed ' Agrippine et Caligula,' a group in marble ; 'Une Novice de Vesta,' 1853 ; 'La Primavera della Vita,' 1864 ; 'Chasseurs,' a group in bronze ; and numerous statues, groups, and busts.

MAINDRON, Etienne Hippolyte, French sculptor, b. at Champtoceaux, Maine-et-Loire, Nov. 16, 1801 ; studied at the Ecole des Beaux Arts, and under David of Angers. Exhibited 'Jeune Pâtre mordu par un Serpent,' 1834 ; 'Christ en Croix,' 1842 ; 'Sœur Rosalie,' 1861 ; and numerous groups, busts, and statues.

MAINWARING, Townshend, English politician, b. 1807 ; educated at Rugby ; M.P. for Denbigh, 1841–47, and since 1857.

MAITLAND, Rev. Samuel Roffey, English author, b. in London, 1795 ; educated at Trinity College, Cambridge, and graduated B.A. 1816 ; formerly barrister of the Inner Temple ; ordained, 1821, and became librarian and keeper of the MSS. at Lambeth Palace. Author of ' An Attempt to elucidate the Prophecies concerning Antichrist,' 1830 ; ' Chatterton, an Essay,' 1857 ; and numerous theological works.

MAJOR, Rev. John Richardson, English educational writer, b. in London, 1797 ; educated at Trinity College, Cambridge, and graduated B.A. 1819 ; appointed headmaster of the Grammar School at King's College, London, 1830. Author of 'Latin Grammar and Exercises ;' 'Guide to the Greek Tragedians ;' and other schoolbooks.

MAJOR, Richard Henry, English antiquarian, b. in London, 1818 ; appointed to the department of maps and charts in the British Museum, Jan. 1844 ; was honorary secretary of the Hakluyt Society, 1849–58. Edited, for the same society, Select Letters of Christopher Columbus,' 1847 ; 'Notes on Russia, translated from the Latin of Herbertstein,' 1851–52 ; ' Early Voyages to Terra Australis,' 1859 ; and other works. Author of 'The Life of Prince Henry the Navigator,' 1868.

MAJORIBANKS, Dudley Coutts, English politician, b. 1820 ; educated at Harrow, and Christ Church, Oxford ; a magistrate of Middlesex, and deputy-lieutenant of the county of Inverness ; was M.P. for Berwick, 1843–49 ; returned for Berwick-on-Tweed, 1859.

MALAN, Rev. Solomon Cæsar, English philologist, b. 1812 ; educated at St. Edmund's Hall, Oxford, and graduated B.A. 1837 ; appointed classical professor in Bishop's College, Calcutta, 1838 ; ordained and appointed vicar of Broadwindsor, Dorset, 1845. Author of 'The Coasts of Tyre and Sidon ;' ' The Threefold San-tsze-King, or Triliteral Classic of China, with critical notes ;' and numerous other works.

MALCOLM, John Wingfield, English politician, b. 1833 ; educated at Eton, and Christ Church, Oxford, where he graduated B.A. 1854 ; M.P. for Boston since 1860.

MALDEN, Henry, English philologist, b. 1800 ; educated at Trinity College, *Cambridge,* and graduated B.A. 1822 ; appointed professor of Greek in University College, London, 1861. Author of 'Evening,' a poem ; 'Origin of Universities and Academical Degrees,' 1834 ; contributor to the Transactions of the Philological Society.

MALET, Sir Alexander, Bart., English diplomatist, b. 1800; educated at Christ Church, Oxford, and graduated B.A. 1822; successively attaché to the embassies at St. Petersburg, Paris, and Lisbon; secretary of legation at Turin, 1835; and at the Hague, 1836; envoy-extraordinary and minister-plenipotentiary to the Germanic Confederation, 1852. Translator from the Norman of Master Wace's 'Chronicle of the Conquest of England.'

MALINS, Sir Richard, English judge; vice-chancellor, 1867.

MALLOUF, Nassif, Turkish philologist, b. at Zabouga, Mount Lebanon, 1823; studied Turkish and Persian at Beyrouth and Constantinople; professor of Oriental languages in the College of the Propaganda at Smyrna, 1845; first secretary and interpreter to the commanding general of the Anglo-Ottoman contingent in the Crimean campaign, 1854–55. Author of several grammars and books of conversation for teaching Turkish, Arabic, Persian, and other Oriental languages.

MALMESBURY, James Howard Harris, Earl of, English statesman, b. 1807, eldest son of the second Earl of Malmesbury; educated at Eton, and Oriel College, Oxford; sat as M.P. for Wilton in July 1841; succeeded to the earldom, August 1841; secretary of state for foreign affairs from February to December 1852, and from February 1858 to June 1859; privy seal, July 6, 1866, to Dec. 1868.

MALTE BRUN, Victor Adolphe, French geographer, b. at Paris, 1816; member of the Geographical Society, and secretary-general of the same, 1855–61. Author of 'Les jeunes Voyageurs en France,' 1840; second edition, 1844; 'La France illustrée,' 1855–57; 'Les nouvelles Acquisitions des Russes dans l'Asie orientale,' 1861; 'Les États Unis et le Mexique, Histoire et Géographie,' 1862; and other works.

MAME, Charles Auguste, French politician, b. at Angers, Nov. 4, 1805; mayor of Tours, 1851; president of the chamber of commerce, and member of the General Council for the canton of Tours-Centre; member of the Corps Législatif for the third circonscription of the department of Indre-et-Loire since 1859.

MAMIANI, Terenzio Della Rovere, Count, Italian statesman and author, b. at Pesaro, Roman States, 1800; member of the Provisional Government constituted in Bologna, and president of the cabinet of Rome, 1848; minister of foreign affairs in the Roman ministry of Galletti, 1849; member of the Italian Parliament, 1859; minister of public instruction of the kingdom of Italy, 1860; ambassador at Athens, 1861. Author of 'Del Papato,' Paris, 1851; 'Nuovo Diritto Europeo,' Turin, 1859; and numerous poetical, philosophical, and political works.

MANCHESTER, Right Rev. James Prince Lee, Bishop of, English divine, b. 1804; educated at Trinity College, Cambridge, and graduated B.A. 1828; head-master of King Edward's Grammar School, Birmingham, 1838–48; consecrated bishop of Manchester, 1848.

MANCHESTER, William Drogo Montagu, Duke of, English administrator, b. at Bampton Park, Huntingdon, Oct. 15, 1823; educated at Sandhurst for the army; retired, 1850; M.P. for Bewdley, April 1848 to June 1852; for Huntingdonshire, June 1852 to Aug. 1855; succeeded his father, Aug. 1855; major of the Huntingdon Militia and deputy-lieutenant of Huntingdonshire.

MANN, Dudley, American diplomatist, b. in Virginia, United States, 1805; minister-plenipoteniary to Hanover, Oldenburg, and Mecklenburg, 1845, and to all the German states, 1847; minister to Switzerland, 1850; secretary of state of the United States, 1853; resigned the same year; one of the commissioners to represent the Confederate Government in Europe, 1860–61.

MANNERS, Lord George John, English politician, b. 1820; educated at Eton, and Trinity College, Cambridge; lieutenant-colonel Royal Horse Guards; M.P. for Cambridgeshire, 1847–57, and since 1863.

MANNERS, Right Hon. Lord John James Robert, English administrator, b. 1818; educated at Eton, and Trinity College, Cambridge, where he graduated M.A. 1839; commissioner of works and buildings, March to Dec. 1852, and 1858–59; M.P. for Newark, 1841–47; for Colchester, 1850–57; and for North Leicestershire since 1857. Author of 'Poems,' 'A Cruise on Scotch Waters,' and other works.

MANNING, Anne, English authoress, b. 1812. Author of 'Mary Powell,' 'The Duchess of Trajetto,' 'Good Old Times,' 'A Noble Purpose Nobly Won,' 'Tasso and Leonora,' and other works of fiction.

MANNING, Rev. Henry Edward, English Roman Catholic theologian, b. 1808; educated at Harrow, and Balliol College, Oxford, where he graduated B.A. 1830; appointed archdeacon of Chichester, 1840; joined the Roman Catholic Church and entered the priesthood, 1851; received the degree of D.D. at Rome, 1852; appointed to succeed Cardinal Wiseman as titular archbishop of Westminster, 1865. Author of 'Unity of the Church,' and other theological works.

MANNING, Sir William Montague, English administrator, b. 1811; educated at University College, London; called to the bar of Lincoln's Inn, 1832; successively chairman of the Quarter Sessions in New South Wales, solicitor-general, acting judge of the Supreme Court, attorney-general, and a member of the Executive Council; knighted, 1858. Author of 'Notes on Proceedings in Electoral Revision Courts.'

MANSEL, Rev. Henry Longueville, English theologian, b. at Cosgrove, Oct. 6, 1820; educated at St. John's College, Oxford, where he graduated B.A. 1843; ordained deacon, 1844, and priest, 1845; appointed Waynflete professor at Magdalen College, Oxford, 1859; dean of St. Paul's, 1868. Published 'Aldrich's Logic, with Notes,' 1849; 'The Limits of Religious Thought,' 1858; and other theological works.

MANSFIELD, William David Murray, Earl of, English politician, b. 1806; sat in the House of Commons as Lord Stormont, 1830–40, when he succeeded his father, third earl; lieutenant-colonel of the Perthshire Militia and lord high commissioner to the General Assembly of the Church of Scotland.

MANSFIELD, Sir William Rose, English military commander, b. 1819; educated at the Royal Military College, Sandhurst, and entered the army, 1835; lieutenant, 1838; captain, 1843; major, 1847; lieutenant-colonel, 1851; colonel, 1854; brigadier-general, 1855; chief of the staff in India, 1857; major-general and K.C.B. 1858; nominated to the command of the Bombay army, 1860; gazetted colonel of the 38th Regiment, March 1862; appointed commander-in-chief in India with the rank of general, Feb. 1865.

MANTEUFFEL, Otto Theodor, Baron von, Prussian statesman, b. at Lübben, Brandenburg, Feb. 3, 1805; studied law at the University of Halle; minister of the interior, 1848; minister of foreign affairs, 1850; president of the Council of Ministers, 1852; one of the peace plenipotentiaries at Paris, 1856; ceased to hold office, Nov. 6, 1858.

MANVERS, Sydney William Herbert Pierrepoint, Earl, English administrator, b. March 12, 1825; educated at Christ Church, Oxford, where he graduated B.A. 1845; was M.P. for South Notts, 1852–60; succeeded his father, second earl, Oct. 1860.

MAQUET, Auguste, French author, b. at Paris, Sept. 13, 1813; appointed assistant professor at the College of Charlemagne, 1831. Author of 'Le Beau d'Angennes,' 1843; 'Histoire de la Bastille,' 1844; 'La Maison du Baigneur,' 1856; and numerous novels and dramatic works.

MARECHAL, Charles Laurent, French painter, b. at Metz, 1800; studied under Regnault. Painted 'Les Sœurs de Misère,' 1840; 'Le petit Gitano,' 1841; 'L'Apothéose de Sainte Catherine,' 1842, for the cathedral of Metz; and numerous paintings on religious subjects for the churches and cathedrals of France.

MAREY MONGE, Guillaume Felix, French politician, b. at Nuits, Côte d'Or, Aug. 30, 1818; member of the General Council for the canton of Gevry; deputy to the Corps Législatif for the second circonscription of the department of Côte d'Or since 1861.

MARGOLIOUTH, Rev. Moses, English, b. 1805, of Jew parents; converted to Christianity and sent as missionary to Asia and Africa; ordained, 1844. Author of 'The Antiquities of the Jews in Great Britain;' 'The Hebrew Old Testament, with Critical, Historical, Philological, Polemical, and Expository Comments;' and other works.

MARIE, Alexandre Thomas, French statesman, b. at Auxerre, Yonne, Feb. 15, 1797; studied law in Paris; called to the bar of the Royal Court, 1819; member of the Chamber of Deputies for the fifth arrondissement of Paris, 1842–46; minister of justice in the Provisional Government, 1848; elected member of the Corps Législatif for the fourth circonscription of the department of Bouches du Rhône, 1863. Author of 'Code des Avocats,' 1841.

MARIETTE, Auguste Edouard, French archæologist, b. at Boulogne sur Mer, Feb. 11, 1821; appointed to a post in the Egyptian Museum of the Louvre, 1848; charged with a scientific mission to Egypt, 1851; and on his return appointed keeper of the Egyptian Museum of the Louvre. Published 'Choix de Monuments et des Dessins découverts ou exécutés pendant le Déblayement du Sérapeum de Memphis,' 1856; 'Le Sérapeum de Memphis, dédié à S. A. I. le Prince Napoleon, et publié sous les auspices du Ministère d'État,' 1857–64; and other works.

MARLBOROUGH, John Winston Spencer Churchill, Duke of, English statesman, b. June 2, 1822, eldest son of the fifth duke of Marlborough; educated at Eton; M.P. for Woodstock, 1844–57; succeeded to the dukedom, July 1857; president of the council, 1857–58, and again 1866–68.

MARMIER, Alfred Ferdinand, Duc de, French politician, b. May 7, 1805; member of the Corps Législatif for the third circonscription of the department of Haute Saône since 1863.

MARMIER, Xavier, French author, b. at Pontalier, Doubs, June 24, 1809; appointed keeper of the library of St. Geneviève, Nov. 22, 1846. Author of 'Choix de Paraboles de Krummacher,' Strasburg, 1833; 'Lettres sur le Nord, Danemark, Suède, Laponie et Spitzberg,' 1840; 'Du Rhin au Nil,' 1847; 'Voyages et Littérature,' 1862; and many other, principally works of travels.

MARRAST, François, French politician, b. at Bayonne, Basses Pyrénées, 1800; member of the Constituent and Legislative Assemblies, 1848–49; and deputy to the Corps Législatif for the circonscription of Mont de Marsan since 1852.

MARSH, Catherine, English authoress, b. 1820. Published 'English Hearts and English Hands;' 'Memorials of Captain Hedley Vicars;' 'Light for the Line, or the Story of Thomas Ward, a Railway Workman;' and other works.

MARSH, George, American diplomatist, b. at Woodstock, Vermont, 1801; member of the Congress of the United States, 1843–49; United States minister to Constantinople, 1850–53; and at Turin, 1854–61. Author of a 'Compendious Grammar of the Old Northern Languages,' Burlington, 1838; and other works.

MARSH, Matthew Henry, English politician, b. 1810; educated at Westminster, and Christ Church, Oxford; called to the bar of the Inner Temple, 1836; late member of the Legislative Council of New South Wales; M.P. for Salisbury since 1857.

MARSH CALDWELL, Anne, English authoress, b. 1796. Published 'Two Old Men's Tales,' 1834; 'The Triumphs of Time,' 1836; 'Norman's Bridge,' 1847; 'Time, the Avenger;' 'Evelyn Marston;' 'The Rose of Ashurst;' and numerous other novels.

MARSHALL, Sir Charles, English colonial judge, b. 1788; educated at Jesus College, Cambridge; where he graduated B.A. 1810; called to the bar of the Inner Temple, 1815; chief justice of Ceylon, 1832–36, when he retired; knighted, 1832. Author of 'Marshall on Insurance;' and other legal works.

MARSHALL, William, English politician, b. 1796; a magistrate of Cumberland and Westmoreland; was M.P. for Petersfield, 1826–30; for Leominster, 1830–31; for Beverley, 1831–32; for Carlisle, 1835–47; returned for East Cumberland, 1847.

MARSHALL, William Calder, English sculptor, b. in Edinburgh, 1813; studied in London under Chantrey and Bailey, and in Rome. Exhibited 'The Broken Pitcher,' 1842; 'First Whisper of Love,' 1845; 'Sabrina,' 1847; executed the statue of Lord Clarendon for the Houses of Parliament, 1847; and numerous other groups and statues. Elected A.R.A. 1844, R.A. 1852.

MARSTON, Westland, LL.D., English author, b. at Boston, Lincolnshire, Jan. 30, 1820. Author of 'The Patrician's Daughter;' 'A Life's Ransom;' 'Death Ride at Balaklava;' and many other dramas and poems.

MARSTRAND, William Nicholas, Danish painter, b. at Copenhagen, 1810; studied at the Academy of his native town, at Munich, and Rome; professor and director of Academy of Fine Arts at Copenhagen; painter of many scenes from the comedies of Holberg, and other Danish authors.

MARTENSEN, Hans Lassen, Danish theologian, b. at Flensborg, Aug. 19, 1808; licentiate in theology, 1836; D.D. at Kiel, 1840; appointed bishop of Seeland, 1843; elected member of the Danish Academy of Sciences, 1841. Author of 'Plan of a System of Moral Philosophy,' 1841; 'Meister Eckart,' 1840; second edition, 1857; and other works.

MARTIMPREY, Ange Auguste de, French military commander, b. 1809; was colonel, 1851; general of brigade, Aug. 1854; commanded a brigade in Italy, and made general of division, July 23, 1859.

MARTIMPREY, Edmond Charles de, French military commander, b. June 16, 1808; studied at the Military School of St. Cyr; captain, 1835; lieut.-colonel, 1848; colonel, July 1849; general of brigade, 1852; general of division, June 11, 1855; appointed to the command of the forces in Algiers, and governor of Algeria on the death of Marshal Pelissier; nominated senator, Sept. 1, 1864.

MARTIN, Charles Wykeham, English politician, b. 1801; educated at Eton, and Balliol College, Oxford; a magistrate of Kent and Hants, and deputy-lieutenant of Kent; was M.P. for Newport, 1841–52; for West Kent, 1857–59; returned for Newport, Isle of Wight, 1865.

MARTIN, Henri, French historical writer, b. at St. Quentin, Aisne, Feb. 20, 1810; studied at the College of St. Quentin. Author of 'La vieille Fronde,' 1832; 'Tancrède de Rohan,' 1855; 'Histoire de France,' Paris, 1833–36; 'De la France, de son Génie et de ses Destinées,' 1847; 'L'Unité Italienne et la France,' 1861; 'Pologne et Moscovie,' 1863; and other historical works.

MARTIN, Nicolas, French author, b. at Bonn, on the Rhine, July 7, 1814. Author of 'Les Harmonies de la Famille,' Lille, 1837; 'Les Cordes graves,' ib. 1845; 'Les Poëtes contemporains de l'Allemagne,' 1860; 'Poésies nouvelles,' 1863; and other works in prose and verse.

MARTIN, Philip Wykeham, English politician, b. 1829; educated at Eton, and Balliol College, Oxford; M.P. for Rochester since 1856.

MARTIN, Robert Montgomery, English historical writer, b. at Tyrone, Ireland, 1803; studied medicine at Dublin; was surgeon in the Royal Navy, 1820–30. Author of 'The British Colonial Library,' 1836–37; 'The Colonies of the British Empire,' 1834–38; 'The History, Antiquities, Topography, and Statistics of Eastern India,' 1838; 'China, Political, Commercial, and Social,' 1847; and other works.

MARTIN, Sir Samuel, English judge, b. 1801; educated at Trinity College, Dublin; called to the bar of the Middle Temple, 1830; appointed Q.C. 1843; M.P. for Pontefract, 1847–50; nominated a baron of the Exchequer, and knighted, 1850.

MARTIN, Theodore, English author, b. in Edinburgh, 1816; educated at the High School and University of Edinburgh; practised as a solicitor in London since 1846. Author of translations from the Danish: Henrik Hartz's play, 'King René's Daughter;' Oehlenschläger's dramas—'Correggio,' 1854, and 'Aladdin,' 1857: also 'Odes of Horace, with Notes,' 1860; 'Translations from Goethe, Schiller, and Uhland,' 1863; and other works.

MARTINEAU, Harriet, English authoress, b. at Norwich, June 12, 1802. Author of 'Devotional Exercises for the Use of Young Persons,' 1823; 'Traditions of Palestine,' 1831; 'Society in America,' 1837; 'Deerbrook,' 1839; 'Eastern Life, Past and Present,' 1848; 'History of England during the Thirty Years' Peace,' 1850; and numerous other works, chiefly on social and political subjects.

MARTINEAU, Rev. James, English theological writer, b. 1806; appointed pastor of the Unitarian Chapel in Little Portland Street, London, 1859. Author of 'The Rationale of Religious Enquiry;' 'Endeavours after the Christian Life;' 'Studies of Christianity;' and other works.

MASKELL, William, English theological writer, b. 1814; educated at University College, Oxford, where he graduated B.A. 1836, and M.A. 1838; ordained, 1837; chaplain to the Bishop of Exeter, and vicar of St. Mary's Church, Devon, 1847; entered the Roman Catholic Church, 1850. Author of 'The Ancient Liturgy of the Church of England,' 1844; 'First and Second Letters on the Position of the High Church Party in the Church of England,' 1850; and other works.

MASSEY, Gerald, English author, b. at Tring, Hertfordshire, 1828; formerly employed in a silk-mill, and as a straw-plaiter. Author of 'Poems and Chansons,' 1845; 'Babe Christabel,' 1853; 'Craigcrook Castle,' 1856; 'Havelock March,' 1861; and other works in prose and verse.

MASSEY, Right Hon. William Nathaniel, English statesman, b. 1810; called to the bar, 1844; recorder of Portsmouth, 1851; M.P. for Newport, Isle of Wight, 1852–57, and for Salford, 1857–65; under-secretary of state for the Home Department, Aug. 1855 to Feb. 1858; chairman in Parliament of the Committees of Ways and Means, 1859–65; finance minister in India, 1865–68. Published 'Common Sense versus Common Law;' and 'A History of England during the Reign of George III.'

MASSINGBERD, Rev. Francis Charles, English historical writer, b. 1800; educated at Magdalen College, Oxford, where he graduated, 1822; appointed incumbent of South Ormsby, 1825; prebendary of Lincoln, 1847, and chancellor of Lincoln Cathedral, 1862. Author of 'History of the English Reformation.'

MASSON, Auguste, French novelist and dramatic writer, b. at Paris, July 31, 1800. Author of 'La Conquête de Perou;' 'Le Maçon,' 1829; 'Héloïse et Abeilard,' 1850; 'Marie Rose,' 1853; 'De la Gerbée,' 1861; 'Une Couronne d'Epines,' 1861; and other novels and dramas.

MASSON, David, English author, b. at Aberdeen, Dec. 2, 1822; educated at Marischal College, Aberdeen, and at the University of Edinburgh; professor of English language and literature at University College, London, 1842–66; appointed professor of literature at the University of Edinburgh, 1866. Author of 'Essays, Biographical and Critical; chiefly on English Poets,' 1856; 'British Novelists, and their Styles; a Critical Sketch of the History of British Prose Fiction,' 1859; and numerous other works.

MASSON, Victor, French judge, b. at Baume, April 2, 1807; studied law and medicine; founded the libraries of 'Langlois' and 'Leclerq,' 1847; and the *Gazette hebdomadaire de Médecine et de Chirurgie,* 1854; appointed assistant-judge to the Tribunal of Commerce of the Seine, 1857; judge, 1860.

MATHESON, Alexander, English politician, b. 1805; educated at the University of Edinburgh; a director of the Bank of England, and of the East and West India Docks; deputy-lieutenant of Ross, Cromarty, Inverness, and London; M.P. for Inverness since 1847.

MATHESON, Sir James, English politician, b. 1796; is a deputy-lieutenant of London, Ross, and Sutherland; formerly a merchant in China; was M.P. for Ashburton, 1843–47; returned for Ross and Cromarty, 1847; created a baronet, 1851.

MATHEWS, Cornelius, American novelist, b. at Port Chester, New York, Oct. 28, 1817. Author of 'Behemoth,' 1839; 'The Politicians,' 1840; 'Poems on Man in the Republic,' 1843; 'Money Penny, or the Heart of the World,' 1850; and other works of fiction.

MATHIEU, Auguste, French politician, b. at Airze, Marne, Nov. 24, 1814; studied at the College of Epernay; called to the bar at Paris, 1837; member of the General Council of Marne for the canton of Airze; and of the Corps Législatif for the second circonscription of the department of Corrèze since 1863.

MATHIEU, Jacques Adrien, French theologian, b. at Paris, Jan. 20, 1796; entered the Seminary of St. Sulpice, was ordained a priest, and became secretary to the Bishop of Evreux, 1823; bishop of Langres, 1833; appointed archbishop of Besançon, June 11, 1834, and cardinal, Sept. 30, 1850. Author of 'Pouvoir temporel des Papes justifié par l'Histoire, etc.' 1863; and other theological works.

MAURICE, Rev. John Frederick Denison, English divine, b. 1805; studied at Trinity College and Trinity Hall, Cambridge, and graduated B.A. at Exeter College, Oxford, in 1831; chaplain and reader at Lincoln's Inn, 1846; incumbent of St. Peter's Chapel, Vere Street, Marylebone. Author of 'Eustace Conway,' 1831; 'Theological Essays,' 1853; 'The Conscience,' 1868; and numerous essays, lectures, sermons, and pamphlets.

MAURY, Louis Ferdinand, French writer, b. at Meaux, Seine-et-Marne, March 23, 1817; studied at the École Polytechnique; appointed keeper of the library of the Tuileries, 1860; professor of history and morality to the College of France, 1862. Author of 'La Terre et l'Homme,' 1856; 'La Magie et les Magiciens,' 1860; 'Histoire des Religions de la Grèce antique,' 1857–60; and numerous other works.

MAURY, Matthew, American hydrographer, b. in Spottsylvania County, Virginia, 1806; served in the navy; was promoted lieutenant, and appointed astronomer to the South Sea Exploring Expedition, 1840. Author of 'The Physical Geography of the Sea,' 1854; and other works.

MAXSE, Henry Fitzhardinge Berkeley, English colonial administrator, b. 1830; educated at Eton, and entered the Royal Navy; was naval aide-de-camp to Lord Raglan in the Crimean campaign; governor and commander-in-chief of the island of Heligoland, 1864–67.

MAY, Thomas Erskine, English historian, b. 1815; educated at Bedford School; assistant-librarian of the House of Commons, 1831; called to the bar of the Middle Temple, 1839; examiner of petitions for private bills, 1846; and taxing-master of the House of Commons, 1847; appointed clerk-assistant of the House of Commons, 1856; created C.B. 1860. Author of 'Constitutional History of England since the Accession of George III. 1760–1860;' 1861–63; and other historical works.

MAYER, Brantz, American author, b. at Baltimore, Sept. 27, 1809; educated at St. Mary's College, and studied law; United States secretary of legation to Mexico, 1841–43. Author of 'Mexico as it was, and as it is,' 1844; 'Mexico, Aztec, Spanish, and Republican,' Philadelphia, 1851; and other works.

MAYO, Richard Southwell, Earl of, English statesman, b. 1822; succeeded his father, 1868; secretary for Ireland, 1858–59, and 1866–68; governor-general of India, Nov. 1868.

MAYO, Thomas, English physician, b. in London, 1790; educated at Oriel College, Oxford, where he graduated M.D. 1818; president of the Royal College of Physicians of London since 1856. Author of 'Elements of the Pathology of the Mind,' 1838; 'Outlines of Medical Proof revised,' 1850; and other medical works.

MAYO, William Starbuck, American novelist, b. at Ogdensburg, State of New York, 1812; studied at the Medical College of New York, where he graduated M.D. 1832. Author of 'Kaloolah, or Journeyings to the Djebel Kumri,' New York; second edition, 1851; 'The Berber, or the Mountaineer of the Atlas,' ib. 1850; and other works.

MAZZINI, Giuseppe, Italian politician, b. at Genoa, June 28, 1808; studied at the University of Genoa, where he graduated LL.D.; joined the 'Carbonari' revolt, 1830; organized an expedition into Savoy, 1833; took refuge in England, 1837; triumvir of the Roman Republic, 1849. Author of several works on Italy, and many political pamphlets.

MEADE, George Gordon, American military commander, b. at Cadiz, Spain, 1815; educated at West Point, 1832–35; lieutenant of artillery, 1836; lieutenant of topographical engineers, 1842; major, 1862; brigadier-general of volunteers, 1862–63; commander-in-chief of the army of the Potomac, June 28, 1863, to April 1864.

MEATH, William Brabazon, Earl of, Irish administrator, b. 1803; colonel of the Dublin Militia, and a deputy-lieutenant of the county of Dublin.

ME'GE, Jacques Philippe, French politician, b. at Riom, Sept. 15, 1817; studied law, and graduated LL.D.; practised at the bar of Clermont Ferrand, 1844–45; appointed assistant-judge, 1845; mayor of Clermont, 1862; member of the General Council, and of the Corps Législatif for the first circonscription of the department of Puy de Dôme, 1863.

MEHEMET DJEMIL, Pacha, Turkish diplomatist, b. at Constantinople, 1823; accompanied his father, Reschid Pacha, to the embassies in Paris and London, 1834–45, and received a European education; appointed secretary to the Sultan, 1849; represented the Porte at Paris, 1855, and at the Congress at Paris, 1856; accredited ambassador to Turin, 1857; chancellor of the Divan, Aug. 8, 1861; ambassador to Paris, 1862.

MEHEMET KIBRISLI, Pacha, Turkish statesman, b. at Cyprus, 1810; educated in France, England, and Germany; appointed military governor of St. Jean d'Acre, 1846, and of Belgrade, 1848; governor-general of Aleppo, 1850; minister of marine, and grand vizier, 1854; governor of Adrianople, 1861.

MEIGNAN, Guillaume Rene', French theologian, b. at Ranaze, Mayenne, April 1, 1817; studied at Angers; ordained priest, 1840; professor to the College of Tessé, 1841; vicar of St. Clotilde, 1857–62; appointed bishop of Châlons, Sept. 17, 1864. Author of 'Prophéties messianiques,' 1858; 'Evangiles et la Critique au XIX. Siècle,' 1864; and other works.

MEINICKE, Karl Eduard, German geographer, b. at Brandenburg, Prussia, Aug. 31, 1803; studied at the University of Berlin; appointed professor in the College of Prenzlau, 1835, and director of the same, 1846. Author of 'The Continent of Australia,' 1837; 'Ethnographical Studies on Asia,' ib. 1837; and other geographical works.

MEISSNER, Alfred, German author, b. at Toplitz, Oct. 15, 1822; studied medicine, and graduated M.D. 1846. Author of 'Poems,' Leipsic, 1845; 'Im Jahre des Heils,' ib. 1848; 'Henrich Heine, Erinnerungen,' Hamburg, 1856; and other works in verse and prose.

MEISSONIER, Ernest, French painter, b. at Lyons, 1813. Exhibited 'Petit Messager,' a microscopic painting, 1836; 'La Partie de Boules,' 1848; 'Napoléon III. à Solferino,' 1861; and numerous other paintings, chiefly historical.

MELLER, Walter, English politician, b. 1818; a J.P. and deputy-lieutenant of the Tower Hamlets, and captain-commander 1st Surrey Light Horse Volunteers; elected M.P. for Stafford, 1865.

MELLIN, Gustaf, Swedish author, b. at Revolax, Finland, April 23, 1803; appointed pastor of Clara, 1829. Author of 'The Flower of Kinnekulla,' Stockholm, 1829; 'The Princess of Angola,' 1839; 'The Slave,' a poem, 1840; 'History of North Scandinavia,' 1850; and numerous works of fiction, poetry, and history.

MELLINET, E'mile, French military commander, b. at Nantes, June 11, 1798; educated for a military career; lieutenant, 1815; general of brigade, 1850; general of division, June 22, 1855; held a command in the campaign in Italy, 1859; chief commander of the National Guard of the Seine, Oct. 23, 1863; created senator, March 15, 1865.

MELLOR, Sir John, English judge, b. at Hollingwood, near Oldham, 1808; called to the bar of the Inner Temple, 1833; appointed Q.C. 1851; recorder of Leicester, Feb. 1855; elevated to the bench, 1861; returned M.P. for Great Yarmouth, 1857, and for Nottingham, 1859.

MELVILL, Rev. Henry, English author, b. 1800; educated at St. John's College, Cambridge, and graduated B.A. 1821; appointed incumbent of Camden Chapel, Camberwell, 1830; chaplain to the Tower of London, 1840; canon of St. Paul's, 1856. Author of 'Sermons preached before the University of Cambridge,' and other works.

MELVILLE, George John Whyte, English author, b: 1821; entered the army, 1839; captain in the Coldstream Guards, 1846; retired, 1849. Author of 'Digby Grand;' 'General Bounce;' 'The Interpreter;' 'Good for Nothing, or All Down Hill;' 'The Gladiators;' and numerous other works of fiction.

MELVILLE, Henry Dundas, Viscount, English military commander, b. 1801; a colonel in the army, and formerly aide-de-camp to the Queen; commanded the 83d Foot during the Canadian rebellion of 1838; and a brigade at Goojerat, 1849; commanded a division in India, 1853; lieutenant-general and governor of Edinburgh Castle, 1860; sat in the House of Commons as Hon. H. Dundas, 1826–31; succeeded his father, second viscount, 1851.

MELVILLE, Herman, American novelist, b. at New York, Aug. 1, 1819; educated in the State of Massachusetts. Author of 'Typee,' 1846; 'Omoo, or Adventures in the South Seas,' 1847; 'White Jacket,' 1850; 'Israel Potter,' 1854; 'Piazza Tales,' 1856; and other works.

MENSDORFF POUILLY, Alexander, Count, Austrian statesman, b. 1813; entered the Austrian army, 1830; general, 1849; ambassador at the court of St. Petersburg, 1854–60; governor of Galicia, 1862–64; appointed minister of foreign affairs, and president of the Council of Ministers, Oct. 27, 1864; resigned, July 27, 1865.

MENZEL, Wolfgang, German historical writer, b. at Waldenberg, Silesia, June 21, 1798; studied at Breslau, Jena. Author of 'History of the Germans,' 1824–25; 'German Literature,' 1828; second edition, 1836; 'The Spirit of History,' 1835; 'History of Europe from 1798–1815,' 1853; 'History of Nature, in a Christian Point of View,' 1856; and numerous other historical works.

MERCIER, Theodore, Baron, French politician, b. 1804; member of the Corps Législatif for the second circonscription of the department of Mayenne since 1852.

MEREDITH, George, English author, b. in Hampshire, 1828; educated partly in Germany. Author of 'Poems,' 1853; 'Farina, a Legend of Cologne,' 1858; 'The Ordeal of Richard Feverel,' 1859; 'Evan Harrington,' 1860; and other works in prose and verse.

MEREDITH, Louisa, English authoress, b. at Birmingham, 1812: married to Mr. C. Meredith, 1839. Author of 'Poems,' 1832; 'Autumn Tour on the Wye,' 1838; 'Notes and Sketches of New South Wales,' 1843; 'Over the Straits,' 1856; 'Loved and Lost,' 1860; and numerous other works.

MERIMEE, Prosper, French author, b. at Paris, Sept. 23, 1803; elected member of the French Academy, 1844; created senator, 1853. Author of 'Theâtre de Clara Gazul, Comédienne Espagnole,' 1825; 'Voyage dans le Midi de la France,' 1835; 'Mélanges historiques et littéraires,' 1855; and numerous other works.

MERIVALE, Rev. Charles, English author, b. 1808; educated at St. John's College, Cambridge, and graduated B.A. 1830; select preacher before the University of Cambridge, 1838–40, and one of the preachers at Whitehall, 1840–42; rector of Lawford, Essex, and chaplain to the Speaker of the House of Commons. Author of 'History of the Romans under the Empire,' 1850–62, in 7 vols.; and of a translation of the Iliad, 1869.

MERIVALE, Herman, English political economist, b. 1806; educated at Trinity College, Oxford, where he graduated B.A. 1827; called to the bar of the Inner Temple, 1832; professor of political economy in the University of Oxford, 1837; appointed permanent under-secretary of state for the colonies, 1848; and for the Indian Department. Author of 'Lectures on the Colonies and Colonization,' 1841; and other works.

MERLE D'AUBIGNE, Jean Henri, Swiss author, b. at Geneva, Aug. 16, 1794; studied at the Universities of Leipsic and Berlin; pastor of the French Protestant church at Hamburg, 1828–31; professor of church history to the Theological School of Geneva since its foundation, 1830. Author of 'History of the Reformation of the Sixteenth Century,' Paris, 1835–53; new edition, 1861–62; 'Life of Cromwell;' 'Histoire de la Reformation en Europe au Temps de Calvin,' 1862; and other historical works.

MERRY, James, English politician, b. 1805; educated at Glasgow; an ironmaster in Lanark and Ayrshire; M.P. for Falkirk, &c., March to July 1857, and since 1859.

MERY, Joseph, French author, b. at Aygalades, near Marseilles, Jan. 21, 1798; studied at Marseilles. Author of 'L'Insurrection,' a poem; 'Sciences de la Vie Italienne,' 1837; 'Les Nuits de Londres,' 1840; 'Napoléon en Italie,' 1859; and numerous other works in prose and verse.

MESLIN, Jacques Felix, French politician, b. at Briquebec, Manche, March 1, 1785; educated for the army; lieutenant, 1809; colonel, 1835; lieutenant-general, 1845; entered the section of reserve, 1849; member of the Corps Législatif for the fourth circonscription of the department of La Manche since 1852.

METCALFE, Rev. Frederick, English author, b. 1817; educated at St. John's College, Cambridge, where he graduated B.A. 1838. Author of 'A History of German Literature,' 1858; 'The Oxonian in Iceland;' and other works.

METEYARD, Eliza, English authoress, b. 1801. Published, chiefly under the pseudonym of 'Silverpen,' 'Struggles for Fame,' 1845; 'The Doctor's Little Daughter,' 1850; 'Lilian's Golden Hours,' 1856; 'The Hallowed Spots of London,' 1862; 'The Little Museum Keepers,' 1863; 'The Life of Wedgwood,' 1866; and other works.

METHUEN, Frederick Henry, Baron, English administrator, b. 1818; lord in waiting and aide-de-camp to the Queen; colonel of the Royal Wiltshire Militia and deputy-lieutenant of Wilts and Gloucestershire.

METTERNICH, Richard Clement, Prince von, Austrian diplomatist, b. at Vienna, Jan. 7, 1829; Austrian ambassador at the court of Saxony, 1854; charged with a special mission to Paris, 1859; appointed hereditary councillor of the Austrian empire, April 18, 1861; Austrian ambassador to the court of France, 1862.

MEURICE, François Paul, French novelist and dramatic writer, b. in Paris, Feb. 1820; studied at the College of Charlemagne. Author of 'Benvenuto Cellini,' 1852; 'Schamyl,' 1855; with G. Sand, 'Le Drac,' 1864; and other dramas and works of fiction.

MEYRICK, Rev. Frederick, English author, b. 1826; educated at Trinity College, Oxford, and graduated B.A. 1847; appointed one of her Majesty's Whitehall preachers, 1856, and one of her Majesty's inspectors of schools, 1859. Author of 'Practical Working of the Church in Spain;' 'The Outcast and Poor of London;' 'The Wisdom of Piety;' and other works.

MIALL, Edward, English writer and politician, b. at Portsmouth, 1809; educated at the Protestant Dissenters' College, at Wymondley, Herts; was minister of an Independent congregation at Ware for three years, and at Leicester; editor and founder of the *Nonconformist*; M.P. for Rochdale, 1852–57; for Bradford, 1869. Author of 'Ethics of Nonconformity;' 'Bases of Belief;' and other works.

MICHELET, Jules, French author, b. in Paris, Aug. 21, 1798; professor of history at the Collège Rollin, 1821–26; professor of history at the Collège de France, 1838. Author of 'History of France,' 1833–68, in 15 vols.; 'History of the French Revolution,' 1847–53, in 7 vols.; 'La Mer,' 1861; 'La Bible de l'Humanité,' 1864; and numerous other works, chiefly historical.

MICHELET, Karl Ludwig, German philosophical writer, b. at Berlin, Dec. 4, 1801; studied in the University of Berlin, and graduated Ph.D. 1824. Author of 'System of Moral Philosophy,' Berlin, 1828; 'Anthropology and Psychology,' ib. 1840; 'Eine Italienische Reise in Briefen,' ib. 1856; and other philosophical works.

MICHELL, Richard, English divine, b. 1805; educated at Wadham College, Oxford, where he graduated B.A. 1824; professor of logic in the University of Oxford, 1839–49; public orator of the University, and vice-principal and tutor of Magdalen Hall; appointed rector of South Moreton, Berks, 1856.

MIDDLETON, Henry Willoughby, Baron, English administrator, b. Aug. 28, 1817; educated at Eton, and Trinity College, Cambridge; a deputy-lieutenant and magistrate of the East Riding of Yorkshire; colonel 1st Brigade East Yorkshire Artillery Volunteers; succeeded his cousin, seventh baron, 1856.

MIDDLETON, Rev. William John Brodrick, Viscount, English divine, b. 1798; educated at Balliol College, Oxford, and graduated B.A. 1820, M.A. 1823; entered holy orders, 1826; canon of Wells, and chaplain to the Queen; was rector of Bath, 1839–54; succeeded his brother, sixth viscount, Dec. 1863.

MIEROSLAWSKI, Louis, Polish general, b. at Nemours, France, 1814; educated at the Military School of Kalitz, and received a commission as ensign, 1830; joined the Secret Democratic Society of Poland, 1844; arrested, 1846; condemned to death at Berlin; liberated in the Revolution of 1848. Author of 'History of the Polish Revolution,' 1835; 'A Critical Analysis of the Campaign of '31,' 1845; and other works.

MIGNET, François Auguste, French historical writer, b. at Aix, May 8, 1796; educated at Avignon; called to the bar of his native town, 1818; director of the archives of the Foreign Ministry, 1822; elected member of the French Academy, 1836; and perpetual secretary of the same, 1837. Author of 'History of the French Revolution of 1789–1814,' 1824; 'History of Marie Stuart,' 1851.

MILBANK, Frederick Acclom, English politician, b. 1820; educated at Harrow; a *deputy-lieutenant* of the county of Durham; high sheriff and a magistrate of the *North Riding* of York, 1852; formerly an officer in the 79th Highlanders; elected M.P. for *the North Riding* of Yorkshire, 1865.

MILES, Sir William, English politician, b. 1797; educated at Eton, and Christ Church, Oxford; was M.P. for Chippenham, 1820; for Romney, 1829–32; for East Somerset, 1834–65; made a baronet, 1859.

MILEY, Rev. John, Irish Roman Catholic theologian, b. in Ireland, 1805; educated at St. Patrick's College, Maynooth; parish priest of Bray, County Wicklow. Author of 'Rome under Paganism and the Popes,' 1832–34; 'History of the Papal States from their Origin down to the Present Day,' 1850.

MILL, John Stuart, English political economist, b. 1806; entered the East India House, 1823; chief examiner of Indian correspondence, 1856–58; elected rector of St. Andrew's University, 1865; M.P. for Westminster, 1865–68. Author of 'A System of Logic,' 1843; 'Essays on Political Economy;' 'A Treatise on Liberty;' 'Utilitarianism;' and other works.

MILLAIS, John Everett, English painter, b. at Southampton, 1829; studied in the schools of the Royal Academy. Exhibited 'Pizarro seizing the Inca of Peru,' 1846; 'The Tribe of Benjamin seizing the Daughters of Shiloh,' 1848; 'The Order of Release,' 1853; 'The Rescue,' 1855; 'Vale of Rest,' 1860; 'My First Sermon,' 1863; 'Charley is my Darling,' 1864; and numerous other paintings. Elected A.R.A. 1853, and R.A. Dec. 1863.

MILLER, Emmanuel, French philologist, b. at Paris, 1812; assistant in the manuscript department of the Bibliothèque Royale, 1834; appointed librarian to the National Assembly, 1849, and to the Corps Législatif, 1858. Published 'Supplément aux dernières Éditions des petits Géographes Grecs,' 1839; and other works.

MILLER, Rev. John Cale, English theologian, b. at Margate, 1814; educated at St. John's College, Oxford, and graduated B.A. at Lincoln College, 1835; ordained, 1837; appointed rector of Birmingham, 1846, and honorary canon of Worcester Cathedral, 1852; vicar of Greenwich, 1867. Author of 'Sermons,' and several controversial and religious works.

MILLER, Stearne Ball, English politician, b. 1813; called to the Irish bar, 1835; became a Q.C. 1852; M.P. for Armagh, 1857–59, and since 1865.

MILLER, Taverner John, English politician, b. 1804; a merchant in Westminster; a magistrate and deputy-lieutenant of Middlesex; was M.P. for Maldon, 1852; returned for Colchester, 1857.

MILLER, Thomas, English author, b. at Gainsborough, Lincolnshire, Aug. 31, 1808. Author of 'Song of the Sea Nymphs;' 'Royston Gower,' 'A Day in the Woods,' 1836; 'History of the Anglo-Saxons;' 'Lights and Shadows of London Life;' 'Sketches of English Country Life;' and numerous other works in prose and verse.

MILLER, William, English politician, b. 1815; educated at Edinburgh; formerly a merchant and British vice-consul at St. Petersburg; M.P. for Leith since 1859.

MILLER, William Allen, English chemist, b. at Ipswich, Dec. 17, 1817; educated at the Quakers' Seminary in Yorkshire; studied medicine and chemistry at King's College, London, and in Professor Liebig's laboratory at Giessen, 1840; appointed professor of chemistry in King's College, London, 1845; Government commissioner to report on the water supply of the metropolis; assayer to the Mint and Bank of England. Author of 'Elements of Chemistry, Theoretical and Practical;' and other works.

MILLER, William Hallows, English mineralogist, b. 1803; graduated at St. John's College, Cambridge, 1826; appointed professor of mineralogy in his college, 1832; vice-president of the Cambridge Philosophical Society. Author of papers 'On Spurious Rainbows,' 'On the Crystals of Boracic Acid,' 'On the Construction of the Imperial Standard Pound,' and other scientific subjects.

MILLET, Baptiste Pierre, French politician, b. at Orange, Jan. 16, 1796; member of the General Council for the canton of Orange, and mayor of the town; deputy of the Corps Législatif for the second circonscription of the department of Vaucluse since 1852.

MILLON, Claude, French politician, b. Oct. 13, 1828; member of the General Council of Vaubecourt; deputy to the Corps Législatif for the first circonscription of the department of the Meuse since 1860.

MILLS, John Remington, English politician, b. 1798; a magistrate of Middlesex and Herts; formerly a silk manufacturer; elected M.P. for Wycombe, 1862.

MILTON, William, Viscount, English politician, eldest son of Earl Fitzwilliam, b. 1839; educated at Eton, and Trinity College, Cambridge; lieutenant in the 1st West York Yeomanry Cavalry; elected M.P. for the South-West Riding of Yorkshire, 1865.

MINGHETTI, Marco, Italian statesman, b. at Bologna, Sept. 8, 1818; member of the Committee of Finance at Rome, 1847; and minister of public works, March 10 to April 29, 1848; appointed by Count Cavour secretary-general to the minister of foreign affairs, 1859; minister of the interior, Oct. 1860; president of the council and minister of finance, March 1863 to 1866.

MINIE', Claude E'tienne, French mechanician, b. at Paris about 1805; entered the army as a private soldier; chef de battaillon, 1852; appointed inspector of the foundries and gun-manufacturer to the Viceroy of Egypt, 1858.

MINTO, William Hugh Elliott, Earl, English administrator, b. 1814; educated at Eton, and Trinity College, Cambridge; a deputy-lieutenant of Roxburgh; was M.P. for Hythe, 1837–41; for Greenock, 1847–52; and for Clackmannan, 1857–59; succeeded his father, second earl, Aug. 1859.

MIOLAN-CARVALHO, Caroline Felix, French operatic singer, b. at Marseilles, 1829; studied at the Conservatoire of Paris; made her first appearance in Paris at the Grand Opera in 'Lucia di Lammermoor,' 1849; married to M. Carvalho, director of the Théâtre Lyrique, 1853.

MIRE'S, Jules, French banker, b. at Bordeaux, 1809; manager of the Gas Company of Arles, 1848; obtained the concession of the works of the port of Marseilles and for supplying Marseilles with gas, 1851; founded successively the Crédit Foncier, the Caisse générale des Chemins de Fer; tried for fraud and condemned to six years' imprisonment, Feb. 1861; decision annulled, April 1862.

MIRZA, Mahommed-Ah, Persian writer, b. at Retch, Ghilau, Persia, Aug. 3, 1803; entered the service of Russia, and became interpreter of Turco-Tartar at Omsk, Siberia, 1825; lecturer at the University of Kazan, 1826; professor of Persian language and literature in the University of St. Petersburg. Author of 'On the Distinctive Merits of Christianity compared to Islam,' in Arabic, Astrakan, 1821; 'Derbend Nameh, or History of Derbend and Caghestan,' Kazan, 1852; and other works.

MITCHELL, Alexander, English politician, b. 1831; educated at Eton, and Christ Church, Oxford; deputy-lieutenant of the county of Berwick, and a magistrate of Midlothian and the county of Selkirk; formerly captain in the Grenadier Guards; elected M.P. for Berwick-on-Tweed, 1865.

MITCHELL, Donald, American writer, b. at Norwich, Connecticut, April 1822; graduated at Yale College, 1841; appointed consul at Venice, 1853. Author of 'Fresh Gleanings, a new Sheaf from the Old Fields,' New York, 1847; 'Reveries of a Bachelor,' ib. 1851; 'Dream Life,' ib. 1852; 'Fudge Doings,' ib. 1855.

MITCHELL, Thomas Alexander, English politician, b. 1812; a merchant in London, and partner in the house of Sampson, Mitchell, and Co., New Broad Street; M.P. for Bridport since 1841.

MITFORD, William Townley, English politician, b. 1817; educated at Eton, and Oriel College, Oxford, where he graduated B.A. 1839; a magistrate and deputy-lieutenant of Sussex; M.P. for Midhurst since 1859.

MITRE, Bartolome, Argentine statesman, b. 1820; entered the army as officer of artillery in Monte Video, 1839; took part in the campaigns against General Oribe and Urquiza, 1840–45; entered the service of Chili with the rank of colonel, 1846; led the insurrectionary movement against General Rosas, 1851; commander of the forces of the city of Buenos Ayres, 1852; promoted to the rank of general, 1859; elected governor of the province of Buenos Ayres, 1860; defeated General Urquiza in the battle of Pavon, Sept. 17, 1861; appointed provisionally governor-general of the Argentine Republic, Oct. 1861; president of the republic, 1862–66.

MOBERLY, Rev. George, English author, b. 1803; educated at Winchester, and Balliol College, Oxford, where he graduated B.A. 1825; has been head-master of Winchester School since 1835. Author of 'An Examination of Mr. Newman's Theory of Development,' 'Sermons preached at Winchester College,' 'Sayings of the Great Forty Days,' and other works.

MOELLER, Peder Louis, Danish author, b. at Aalborg, Jutland, April 18, 1814. Author of 'Kritiske Skizzer,' Copenhagen, 1847; 'Biedermann, Neue Utopie,' Berlin, 1850; 'Modern French Comedy and its Influence on Danish Theatres,' Copenhagen, 1857; and other critical and poetical works.

MOFFAT, George, English politician, b. 1814; a partner in the house of Moffat and Co., merchants in London; M.P. for Dartmouth, 1845–52; for Ashburton, 1852–59; for Honiton, 1860–65; returned for Southampton, 1865.

MOFFAT, Robert, English missionary, b. 1795; a missionary in South Africa since 1816. Published 'History of Missionary Labours in South Africa,' 1840; translated the Psalms and New Testament into the Bechuana language.

MOHL, Jules de, French philologist, b. at Stuttgardt, Oct. 25, 1800; studied theology at Tübingen; naturalized in France, 1844; appointed professor of Persian at the Collége de France, 1847; and inspector of Oriental typography at the Imprimerie Impériale, 1852. Published a Latin translation of 'Y-King,' Stuttgardt, 1834; and other works.

MOHL, Robert von, German statesman and author, b. at Stuttgardt, Aug. 14, 1799, brother of the preceding; studied law and political economy at the Universities of Tübingen and Heidelberg, 1817–21; professor of law at Tübingen, 1824; of political economy, 1829; keeper of the library of the University, 1836; professor of law at the University of Heidelberg, 1847; member of the Parliament and National Assembly of Frankfort, 1848; minister of justice of the German empire, Sept. 25, 1848, to May 17, 1849; represented the grand duchy of Baden at the Federal Diet, 1861. Author of 'History of Literature and Political Economy,' Erlangen, 1855; and numerous legal and political works.

MOLESCHOTT, Jacob, German medical writer, b. at Herzogenbusch, Netherlands, Aug. 9, 1822; studied at Heidelberg, where he graduated M.D.; professor of physiology at Zurich. Author of 'Physiologie der Nahrungsmittel,' Darmstadt, 1850; second edition, 1859; and other medical works.

MOLESWORTH, Rev. John Nassau, English author, b. 1790; educated at Trinity College, Oxford, where he graduated B.A. 1812; vicar of Rochdale, Lancashire, 1849. Author of several theological works; contributor to the *Penny Sunday Reader* and numerous periodicals.

MOLTKE, Adam Wilhelm, Count, Danish statesman, b. Aug. 25, 1785; was minister of finance under King Charles VIII.; president of the Council of Ministers, March 22, 1848; resigned office, 1852.

MOLTKE, Helmuth Carl Bernhard, Baron von, Prussian general, b. Oct. 26, 1800; served with the Turkish army in Syria, 1839; chief of staff to the Prussian army since 1858; directed the campaign of 1866.

MOMMSEN, Johann Tycho, German philologist, b. 1819. Author of a translation of Pindar, and distinguished as a critic on Shakspeare.

MOMMSEN, Theodor, German historian, brother of the preceding, b. at Garding, Schleswig, Nov. 30, 1817; studied at the Universities of Altona and Kiel; appointed professor of law at the University of Zurich, 1852, and at that of Breslau, 1854. Author of 'Römische Geschichte,' Leipsic, 1854; third edition, 1862; and of numerous other works.

MONAHAN, Right Hon. James Henry, Irish judge, b. at Portumna, County Galway, 1800; educated at Trinity College, Dublin; called to the Irish bar; appointed Q.C. and solicitor-general for Ireland, 1846; attorney-general for Ireland, 1847; chief justice of the Common Pleas in Ireland, 1850; M.P. for Galway, 1847; and sworn a privy councillor for Ireland, 1848.

MONCK, Right Hon. Charles Stanley Monck, Viscount, English colonial administrator, b. 1819; educated at Trinity College, Dublin; called to the bar in Ireland, 1841; M.P. for Portsmouth, 1852–57; lord of the Treasury, 1855–58; commissioner of charitable donations and bequests in Ireland, 1851–60; governor-general of Canada, 1861–65.

MONCRIEFF, Right Hon. James, English politician, b. 1811; educated at the University of Edinburgh; called to the Scottish bar, 1833; solicitor-general for Scotland, 1850–51; lord-advocate, 1851–52 and 1853–57; reappointed, 1859; M.P. for Leith, 1851–59; and for Edinburgh since 1859.

MONIER DE LA SIZERANNE, Henri, French politician, b. in Dauphiné, 1796; represented the arrondissement of Die at the Chamber of Deputies, 1837–48; elected to the Corps Législatif, 1852–57; made a senator, May 7, 1863.

MONK, Charles James, English politician, b. 1824; educated at Eton, and Trinity College, Cambridge, where he graduated B.A. 1847, and M.A. 1850; called to the bar of Lincoln's Inn, 1850; chancellor of Bristol, 1855, and of Gloucester, 1859; a deputy-lieutenant for the county of Gloucester; M.P. for Gloucester, 1859–65, and since 1867.

MONRAD, Ditler Gothard, Danish author, b. at Copenhagen, Nov. 24, 1811; ordained to the ministry, 1836; pastor of Vester Ulsler, in the diocese of Laaland, 1846–49; bishop of Laaland, 1850. Author of 'Om Skolevæsenets Ordning i flere store protestantiske Stæder,' Copenhagen, 1844; and other works.

MONSELL, Right Hon. William, English administrator, b. 1812; educated at Oriel College, Oxford; J.P. and deputy-lieutenant of the county of Limerick; clerk to Ordnance, 1852–57; president of the Board of Health, 1857–58; vice-president of the Board of Trade, 1866.

MONSON, William John Monson, Baron, English administrator, b. 1829; educated at Christ Church, Oxford, where he graduated B.A. 1848; deputy-lieutenant of Surrey and Lincolnshire, and major of the North Lincoln Militia; chairman of the Liberal Association of North Lincolnshire, 1853–62; M.P. for Reigate, Oct. 1858–62; succeeded his father, sixth baron, Dec. 1862.

MONTAGNAC, Joseph Elisée de, French politician, b. Oct. 17, 1808; a cloth manufacturer at Sedan; member of the Corps Législatif for the first circonscription of the department of Ardennes since 1860.

MONTAGU, Lord Robert, English politician, b. 1825; educated at Trinity College, Cambridge, and graduated M.A. 1848; magistrate and deputy-lieutenant of the counties of Antrim and Derby; M.P. for Hunts since 1859.

MONTALEMBERT, Charles Forbes, Comte de, French statesman and author, b. in London, May 29, 1810; member of the Constituent Assembly for the department of Doubs, 1849; elected member of the French Academy, 1851; returned to the Corps Législatif for the department of Doubs, 1852. Author of 'An Essay on Gustavus Adolphus,' 1829; 'The Political Future of England,' 1856; 'Monks of the West,' 1860; 'The Pope and Poland,' 1864; and numerous other works.

MONTALIVET, Camille Bachasson, Comte de, French statesman, b. at Valence, April 25, 1801; studied at the Lycée Napoléon, and entered the École Polytechnique, 1820; appointed minister of the interior, Nov. 3, 1830; minister of public instruction, March 1831 to 1840; elected member of the French Academy, 1840. Author of 'Rien, Dix Années de Gouvernement parlementaire,' 1862.

MONTEAGLE OF BRANDON, Thomas Spring Rice, Baron, English statesman, b. at Limerick, 1790; educated at Trinity College, Cambridge; M.P. for Limerick, 1820–32, and for Cambridge, 1832–39, when he was elevated to the peerage; under-secretary of state for the Home Department, 1827–28; secretary of the Treasury, and secretary of state for the colonies, 1834; chancellor of the Exchequer, 1835; comptroller of the Exchequer, and a trustee of the National Gallery.

MONTEBELLO, Gustave Lannes, Comte de, French military commander, b. in Paris, Dec. 4, 1804, brother of the following; colonel, 1847; general of brigade, Dec. 22, 1851; general of division, Dec. 28, 1855; charged with a mission to the Pope, Oct. 1861; appointed to the command of the Corps of Occupation of Rome, May 1862.

MONTEBELLO, Napoléon Lannes, Duc de, French diplomatist, b. at Paris, July 30, 1801; appointed French ambassador to Switzerland, 1836–38; at Naples, 1838; appointed minister of foreign affairs, April 1, 1832; minister of marine, May 9, 1847; elected to the Legislative Assembly of the department of Marne, 1849; ambassador at St. Petersburg, 1858; made a senator, Oct. 5, 1864.

MONTE PIN, Xavier Aymon de, French novelist and dramatist, b. at Apremont, Haute Saône, March 18, 1824. Author of 'Les Étoiles, ou la Voyage de la Fiancée,' 1850; 'La Sirène de Paris,' 1860; 'Les Confessions d'un Bohême,' 1849–50; 'Les Marionnettes du Diable,' 1861; 'Les Pirates de la Seine,' 1864; and numerous other novels and dramas.

MONTGOMERY, Sir Graham Graham, English politician, b. 1823; educated at Christ Church, Oxford, where he graduated B.A. 1845; lord-lieutenant of Kinross, and a deputy-lieutenant of Peebles; late lieutenant of Midlothian Yeomanry Cavalry; M.P. for Peebles-shire since 1852.

MONTGOMERY, Sir Henry Conyngham, English colonial administrator, b. 1803; educated at Eton, and at Haileybury College, and entered the Civil Service in India; secretary to the Government of Madras, 1847–57; returned to England, and was nominated a member of her Majesty's Indian Council, 1858.

MONTGOMERY, Sir Robert, English colonial administrator, b. at Londonderry, 1809; entered the East India Civil Service, 1828; appointed to assist Sir John Lawrence in the administration of the Punjaub, 1849; held a judicial post at Lahore, 1857–58; appointed chief commissioner in Oude, 1858; chief commissioner of the Punjaub, 1859; appointed lieutenant-governor of the Punjaub, 1860; resigned, Jan. 1865.

MONTI, Raffaelle, Italian sculptor, b. at Milan, 1818; studied under his father, Gaetano Monti, of Ravenna. Exhibited 'Ajax defending the Body of Patroclus,' 1838; executed in England the 'Sister Anglers,' the 'Veiled Vestal,' 'Eve after the Fall,' 'Italy,' 'Truth,' and numerous other groups and statues.

MONTJOYEUX, Antoine Richard de, French politician, b. at Paris, Oct. 22, 1795; mayor of Annay, and member of the General Council for the canton of Cosne; deputy to the Corps Législatif for the second circonscription of the department of the Nièvre since 1858.

MONTPENSIER, Antoine Marie Philippe Louis, Duc de, French and Spanish prince, son of King Louis Philippe, and husband of the Infanta Luisa, b. 1824; married, 1846; banished from France, Feb. 1848; a resident at Seville until 1868; at present understood to be a candidate for the throne of Spain.

MONTREAL, Right Rev. Francis Fulford, Bishop of, English divine, b. 1803; educated at the Grammar School, Tiverton, and at Exeter College, Oxford, where he graduated; was chaplain to H.R.H. the late Duchess of Gloucester; consecrated bishop of Montreal, Lower Canada, 1850.

MONTREAL, Simon Allonveux de, French military commander, b. Sept. 14, 1790; colonel, 1840; general of brigade, 1848; general of division, May 10, 1852; commander of the army in Rome, 1853–56; made a senator, March 9, 1857.

MONTREUIL, Alfred, Baron de, French politician, b. at Paris, Feb. 18, 1802; elected to the Constituent Assembly for the department of Eure, and to the Corps Législatif for the same department since 1852.

MONTROSE, James Graham, fourth Duke and Marquis of, b. 1799; eldest son of the third Duke of Montrose; educated at the University of Glasgow; sat as M.P. for Cambridge, 1825–30; entered the House of Lords as Earl Graham, 1836; chancellor of the Duchy of Lancaster from March 1858 to June 1859; appointed postmaster-general, July 6, 1866.

MOODIE, Susannah, English authoress, b. 1805; married to Mr. John Dunbar Moodie, and resident in Canada. Author of 'Mark Hurdlestone,' 'Flora Lindsay,' 'Roughing it in the Bush,' and other works.

MOON, Sir Francis Graham, English administrator, b. 1796; was sheriff of London, 1843; alderman, 1844; lord mayor, 1854–55; created a baronet, 1855; magistrate of Middlesex, and a commissioner of lieutenancy for London.

MOORE, Charles, English politician, b. 1804; a magistrate for Tipperary; elected M.P. for Tipperary, 1865.

MOORE, George, English merchant, b. in Cumberland, 1807; became junior partner in the firm of Groucock, Copestake, and Co., 1830; assisted in founding the Commercial Travellers' Orphan School, the Royal Hospital for Incurables, and the Female Mission among Fallen Women; appointed by the Bishop of London a commissioner to inquire into the fund entitled 'Londoners over the Border,' 1861.

MOORE, Thomas, English botanist, b. 1806. Author of 'Cultivation of the Cucumber and Melon,' 1844; 'Ferns and Allied Plants,' 1856; 'Field Botanist's Companion: British Isles,' 1862; and other botanical works.

MORAY, John Stuart, Earl, English administrator, b. 1797; vice-lieutenant of Elgin; formerly a captain in the army; succeeded as twelfth earl, May 1859.

MORDAUNT, Sir Charles, Bart., English politician, b. 1836; educated at Eton, and Christ Church, Oxford; a magistrate and deputy-lieutenant of the county of Warwick; M.P. for South Warwickshire since 1859.

MORE, Robert Jasper, English politician, b. 1836; educated at Shrewsbury, and Balliol College, Oxford, where he graduated B.A. 1861; B.C.L. and M.A. 1862; called to the bar of Lincoln's Inn, 1863; a J.P. and deputy-lieutenant for the county of Salop; elected M.P. for South Shropshire, 1865.

MORGAN, Charles Octavius Swinnerton, English politician, b. 1803; educated at Westminster, and Christ Church, Oxford, where he graduated B.A. 1825; a magistrate and deputy-lieutenant of the county of Monmouth; M.P. for Monmouthshire since 1840.

MORGAN, Hon. Godfrey Charles, English politician, b. 1830; educated at Eton; a deputy-lieutenant of Brecon, and major of the Royal Gloucestershire Yeomanry Hussars; late captain in the 17th Lancers, and served in the Crimean war, 1854–55; M.P. for Brecon since 1858.

MORGAN, Marie Pierre E'douard de, French politician, b. at Amiens, Aug. 15, 1803; was mayor for Chaussoy Epagny, 1834; member of the General Council for the canton of Ailly sur Noye; deputy to the Corps Législatif for the fourth circonscription of the department of the Somme since 1857.

MORGAN, Rev. Richard William, English author, b. in Wales, 1815 ; educated at St. David's College, Lampeter ; appointed to an incumbency in North Wales, which he resigned, 1858. Author of 'North Wales, or Venedocia ;' 'Christianity and Modern Infidelity ;' and other works.

MORIN, Arthur Jules, French mathematician, b. Oct. 17, 1795 ; studied at the École Polytechnique, and the École d'Application de Metz, 1813–19 ; general of division, April 7, 1855 ; nominated president of the Society of Civil Engineers, 1862. Author of 'Leçons de Mécanique pratique,' 5 vols. ; second edition, 1858 ; and numerous works on mechanics and mathematics.

MORIN, Etienne François The'odore, French politician, b. at Dieu le Fit, Drôme, Nov. 10, 1814 ; a cloth manufacturer ; was member of the Chamber of Deputies ; member of the Constituent and Legislative Assemblies ; and of the Corps Législatif for the department of Drôme since 1852. Author of 'Essai sur l'Organisation du Travail,' 1845 ; and other works.

MORIN, Fre'de'ric, French historical writer, b. at Lyons, June 11, 1823 ; studied at the École Normale, 1844–47 ; professor of philosophy at the Lycée of Macon, 1847, and of Nancy, 1849. Author of 'Saint François d'Assises et les Franciscains,' 1853 ; 'Origine de la Démocratie,' 'La France au Moyen Age,' 1864 ; and numerous other works.

MORLEY, Edmund Parker, second Earl, English administrator, b. 1810 ; studied at Oxford ; colonel of the South Devon Militia ; succeeded his father, first earl, 1840.

MORLEY, Henry, English author, b. in London, 1822 ; educated at the Moravian School, Neuwied, on the Rhine, and at King's College, London ; professor of English literature at University College, London. Author of 'How to make Home Unhealthy,' 1850 ; 'Life of Palissy the Potter,' 1852 ; 'Fairy Tales,' 1859–60 ; 'English Writers,' 1864.

MORLEY, John, English political and miscellaneous writer, b. about 1833 ; editor of the *Fortnightly Review.* Author of 'Edmund Burke,' and of numerous contributions to periodical literature.

MORLEY, Samuel, English politician, b. 1809 ; J.P. for Middlesex ; M.P. for Bristol, 1868.

MORRIS, Rev. Francis Orpen, English author, b. March 25, 1810 ; educated at Worcester College, Oxford, where he graduated B.A. 1823 ; incumbent of Nunburnholme, Yorkshire, and chaplain to the Duke of Cleveland. Author of 'A History of British Birds,' 6 vols. ; 'A Book of Natural History ;' 'An Essay on the Eternal Duration of the Earth ;' and other works.

MORRIS, George, American author, b. at Philadelphia, 1802. Author of 'Brier Cliff,' 1842 ; 'The Maid of Saxony,' 1842 ; 'Complete Poetical Works,' 1853 ; 'Woodman, Spare that Tree ;' and other publications.

MORRIS, Louis Michel, French military commander, b. Oct. 17, 1803 ; admitted to the Military School of St. Cyr, 1821 ; colonel, 1843 ; general of division, Dec. 1851 ; took part in the campaign in Italy, 1859 ; appointed to the command of the regular cavalry in Algiers, 1863.

MORRIS, Michael, Irish administrator, b. 1827 ; educated at Galway College, and Trinity College, Dublin, where he graduated B.A. 1847 ; called to the Irish bar, 1849 ; appointed a Q.C. 1863 ; magistrate of the county of Galway ; formerly recorder of Galway ; elected M.P. for Galway, 1865.

MORRIS, William, English poet, b. 1834. Author of 'The Defence of Guenevere,' 1858 ; 'The Life and Death of Jason,' 1867 ; 'The Earthly Paradise,' 1868.

MORRIS, William, English politician, b. 1800 ; banker at Carmarthen, and a magistrate of the county of Carmarthen ; M.P. for Carmarthen since 1864.

MORRISON, Walter, English politician, b. 1836 ; educated at Eton, and Balliol College, Oxford ; a magistrate for the West Riding of Yorkshire ; M.P. for Plymouth since 1861.

MORSE, Samuel Finley Breese, American engineer, b. in Charleston, Massachusetts, April 27, 1791 ; educated at Yale College, where he graduated, 1810 ; studied painting. Exhibited 'The Dying Hercules' at the Royal Academy, London, 1813. Completed his 'Recording Electric Telegraph,' 1835, which he patented in Washington, 1837 ; perfected his patent, 1840.

MORTEMART, Rene' de Rochechouart, Marquis de, French politician, b. at Lyons, 1805 ; studied at the Military Schools of St. Cyr and Saumur ; deputy for Villefranche, Rhône, 1847 ; and represented the same department in the Constituent and Legislative Assemblies ; member of the Corps Législatif since 1852.

MOSELEY, Rev. Henry, English astronomer, b. 1801; educated at St. John's College, Cambridge, where he graduated B. A. 1826; was professor of natural history and astronomy in King's College, London; canon of Bristol Cathedral, 1853; vicar of Alveston, Gloucestershire, 1854; one of her Majesty's chaplains, 1855. Author of various scientific papers.

MOSEN, Julius, German poet and dramatic writer, b. at Mariency, Saxony, July 8, 1803; studied at the University of Jena, 1822; appointed dramatist in ordinary to the court of Oldenburg, with the title of councillor, 1844. Author of 'Lied von Ritter Wasa,' Leipsic, 1831; 'Georg Venlot,' ib. 1831; 'Bilder in Moose,' ib. 1846; and numerous other works of poetry and fiction.

MOSTYN, Edward Mostyn Lloyd Mostyn, Baron, English administrator, b. 1795; educated at Westminster, and Christ Church, Oxford; assumed the name of Mostyn in addition to that of Lloyd, 1831; lord-lieutenant of Merionethshire; a deputy-lieutenant of Flintshire, 1852; was M.P. for Flintshire, 1831–37, 1841–42, and 1847–54; and for Lichfield from Jan. 1846 to Aug. 1847.

MOTLEY, John Lothrop, American historical writer, b. at Dorchester, Massa-chusetts, United States, Aug. 15, 1814; educated at Harvard College, where he graduated, 1831; appointed secretary of the United States legation at St. Petersburg, 1841; and ambassador from the United States to the court of Vienna, 1861–67. Author of 'History of the Rise of the Dutch Republic,' London, 1856; 'The History of the United Netherlands, from the Death of William the Silent to the Synod of Dort,' 1860–68.

MOULTRIE, Rev. John, English author, b. 1804; educated at Trinity College, Cambridge, where he graduated B.A. 1823; ordained, 1825; and priest; rector of Rugby, Warwickshire. Author of 'My Brother's Grave, and other Poems,' 1837; 'The Dream of Life,' 1843; 'Altars, Hearths, and Graves,' 1853; and other poetical works.

MOULY, Joseph, French divine, b. at Figeac, Lot, about 1830; entered the congregation of the Lazaristes; successively bishop of Fessulah, apostolic administrator of Pekin, and superior visitor of the province of Petcheli, in China; appointed bishop of Petcheli, 1860.

MOURAVIEFF, Andrei, Russian author, b. 1797, titular councillor of the empire; councillor of state and minister of the administration of the Holy Synod. Author of 'Bitwa pri Tiweriade,' 1832; 'Biblische Geschichte,' 1842; 'Schilderung Armeniens,' 1848; and other works.

MOWATT, Anna Cora, American authoress, b. at Bordeaux, 1821; married to Mr. James Mowatt, 1836, who died, 1851. Author of 'The Fortune Hunter;' 'Fashion,' a comedy, 1845; 'The Autobiography of an Actress, or Eight Years on the Stage;' and other works.

MOWBRAY, Right Hon. John Robert, English politician, b. 1815; educated at Christ Church, Oxford, where he graduated B.A. 1837, M.A. 1839; a magistrate and deputy-lieutenant of Durham, and a magistrate of Berks; was judge advocate general, 1858–59; sworn in the Privy Council, 1858; M.P. for the city of Durham, 1853–68; for the University of Oxford in 1868.

MOZLEY, Rev. James Bowling, English theologian, b. in Lincolnshire, 1813; educated at Oriel College, Oxford, where he graduated B.A. 1834; appointed vicar of Shoreham, Sussex, 1856; Bampton lecturer at Oxford for 1865. Author of 'A Treatise on the Augustinian Doctrine of Predestination;' 'Review of the Baptismal Question,' 1862; and other works.

MOZLEY, Rev. Thomas, English author, b. in Lincolnshire, 1806, brother of the preceding; educated at the Charterhouse, and at Oriel College, Oxford, where he graduated B.A. 1828; appointed rector of Cholderton, Wilts, 1836; resigned, 1848. Contributor to the *British Critic*, 1838–42; contributor of 'leading articles' to the *Times* since 1843.

MUELLER, Charles Louis, French historical painter, b. at Paris, Dec. 22, 1815; studied under E. Léon Cogniet, Baron Gros, and at the École des Beaux Arts. Exhibited 'Le Lendemain de Noël,' 1837; 'Lady Macbeth,' 1849; 'L'Appel des Victimes de la Terreure,' 1850; 'L'Arrivée de la Reine d'Angleterre à Saint Cloud,' 1859; and numerous other paintings.

MUELLER, Friedrich Max, English philologist, b. at Dessau, Dec. 6, 1823; studied at the University of Leipsic, where he graduated in 1843; and at Berlin, 1844–45; Taylorian professor at Oxford, 1854; curator of the Bodleian Library, 1866. Author of 'A Survey of Languages,' 1855; 'History of Ancient Sanskrit Literature,' 1859; 'Chips from a German Workshop,' 1868; and numerous other philological works.

MUELLER, Julius, German Protestant theologian, b. at Brieg, Prussia, April 10, 1801; studied law at Breslau and Göttingen, and theology at the University of Berlin; became pastor of Schönbrunn and Rosen, Prussia, 1825; preacher at the University of Göttingen, 1831, and professor of theology, 1834. Author of 'Die christliche Lehre von der Sünde,' 1839; and other religious and theological works.

MUELLER, Wolfgang, German author, b. at Königswinter, on the Rhine; studied medicine at the University of Bonn, 1835–39; member of the Parliament at Frankfort, 1848. Author of 'Junge Lieder,' Dusseldorf, 1841; 'The May Queen,' Stuttgardt, 1852; 'The Rhine Book,' 1856; and numerous other works.

MUENCH-BELLINGHAUSEN, Eligius Franz Joseph, Baron, German dramatic author, known under the pseudonym of Friedrich Halm, b. at Cracow, April 2, 1806. Author of 'Der Fechter von Ravenna,' and many other plays.

MULOCK, Miss Dinah Maria. See **CRAIK, Mrs. George Lillie.**

MUNDY, George Rodney, English naval officer and author, b. in London, April 19, 1805; entered the Royal Naval College, 1818; lieutenant, 1826; commodore, 1828; vice-admiral, 1863. Author of 'Narrative of the Events in Borneo,' London, 1848; 'The *Hannibal* at Palermo and at Naples,' 1859–61.

MURAT, Joachim Joseph André, Comte, French diplomatist, b. at Paris, Dec. 12, 1828; entered the diplomatic service, 1847; successively attaché to the French legation in Tuscany and Sweden; chargé d'affaires at Florence, 1852; at Stockholm, 1853; member of the Corps Législatif for the first circonscription of the department of the Lot since 1854.

MURAT, Napoléon Lucien, Prince, b. at Milan, March 16, 1803, the second son of Joachim Murat, King of Naples; elected to the National Assembly for the department of the Lot, 1848; nominated minister-plenipotentiary at the court of Turin, Oct. 3, 1849; made a senator, Jan. 25, 1852.

MURCHISON, Sir Roderick Impey, English geologist, b. at Tarradale, Ross-shire, Feb. 19, 1792; educated at Durham Grammar School, and at the Military College of Marlow; was an officer in the army, 1807–16; knighted, Feb. 1846; appointed director-general of the Geological Survey of the British Isles, 1855. Author of 'The Silurian System;' 'Geology of Russia in Europe and the Oural Mountains,' London, 1845; 'Geological Atlas of Europe,' 1856; and other geological works.

MURE, David, Scottish judge, b. 1810; educated at the University of Edinburgh; called to the Scottish bar, 1831; appointed solicitor-general for Scotland, 1858, and lord-advocate, April 1859; deputy-lieutenant of Buteshire; was sheriff of Perthshire, 1853–58; was M.P. for Perthshire, 1859 to Jan. 1865, when raised to the Scottish bench.

MURRAY, Hon. Charles Augustus, English diplomatist, b. 1806; educated at Eton, and Oriel College, Oxford, where he graduated B.A. 1827; secretary of legation at Naples, 1845; British agent and consul-general in Egypt, 1846; British minister in Switzerland, 1853; envoy to Teheran, 1854; British minister in Saxony, 1859. Author of 'The Prairie Bird,' and other works.

MURRAY, Nicholas, American theologian, b. in Ireland, 1802; entered William College, Massachusetts, 1822, and studied theology at Princeton, New Jersey; appointed pastor of a Presbyterian church at Elizabethtown, 1833. Author, under the pseudonym of 'Kirwan,' of 'Letters to the Catholic Archbishop of New York,' 1847; 'The Decline of Popery, and its Causes;' 'Romanism at Home,' New York, 1852; 'Men and Things in Europe,' ib. 1853; 'Parish Pencillings,' ib. 1854; and other works.

MUSGRAVE, Rev. George, English author, b. 1798; educated at Brasenose College, Oxford; incumbent of Borden. Translator of the Hebrew Psalter into blank verse, 1833. Author of 'Rambles in Normandy;' 'Ten Days in a French Parsonage,' 1864; and other works.

MUSPRATT, James Sheridan, English chemist, b. in Dublin, 1821; studied at the Andersonian University of Glasgow, and at Giessen under Professor Liebig, 1843. Founded the College of Chemistry in Liverpool. Edited Plattner's 'Treatise on the Blow-pipe,' and is the author of numerous papers on chemistry published in the *Proceedings of the Royal Society*, the *Philosophical Magazine*, and in the *Chemical Society's Transactions*.

MUSSET, Paul Edme de, French writer, b. at Paris, Nov. 7, 1804. Author of 'Samuel,' 1833; 'La Tête et le Cœur,' 1834; 'Anne de Boleyn,' 1836; 'Les Femmes de la Régence,' 1841; 'Lui et Elle,' 1859; 'Christine, Roi de Suède,' 1857; and other novels and dramas.

MUSTAPHA FAZIL, Pasha, Egyptian statesman, b. 1816. Founded several schools in Egypt; minister of public instruction at Constantinople, 1862; minister of finance; appointed minister without a portfolio, 1864.

MUSURUS, Constantine, Turkish diplomatist, b. at Constantinople, Feb. 18, 1807; educated at Constantinople; secretary to Stephen Vogorides, Prince of Samos, 1832; governor of Samos, 1834; envoy-extraordinary and minister-plenipotentiary at Athens, 1840; represented Turkey at the court of Austria, 1848; envoy-extraordinary and minister-plenipotentiary to England, and ambassador at the court of St. James's since 1856.

N.

NADAR, Felix Tournachon, French writer and aeronaut, b. at Paris, April 5, 1820; studied medicine at Lyons. Founder of the *Revue Comique*, 1849, and contributor to the *Charivari* and numerous other French journals. Author of 'Le Miroir aux Alouettes,' 1858; 'A Terre et en l'Air, 1864; and other works.

NAPIER, Francis Napier, Baron, English diplomatist, b. 1819; succeeded his father, eighth baron, 1834; entered the diplomatic service, Aug. 1840; attaché at Constantinople, 1844–45; secretary of legation at Naples, 1846–52; at St. Petersburg, 1852–54; secretary of embassy at Constantinople, 1854; envoy-extraordinary and minister-plenipotentiary at Washington, 1857–58; at the Hague, 1858–60; at St. Petersburg, 1860; at Berlin, 1864.

NAPIER, Right Hon. Sir Joseph, English statesman, b. in Belfast, Dec. 26, 1804; educated at Trinity College, Dublin; called to the Irish bar, 1831; attorney-general for Ireland, and sworn in the Privy Council, 1852; lord-chancellor of Ireland, 1858–59; was M.P. for the University of Dublin, 1848–58.

NAPIER, Robert, Baron Napier of Magdala, English military commander, b. in Ceylon, 1810; educated at the Military College of Addiscombe; entered the corps of Bengal Engineers, 1826; chief engineer with the army of Lord Clyde during the Mutiny in India, 1857; served in China, and was made a major-general, K.C.B., and military member of the Council of India; nominated commander-in-chief at Bombay, with the rank of lieutenant-general, 1865; commander-in-chief of the Abyssinian expedition, 1868; raised to the peerage, 1868.

NAPOLEON III. Emperor of the French, b. April 20, 1808, the third son of Louis Napoléon, King of Holland, and of Queen Hortense, daughter of the Empress Josephine of France by her first husband, Viscount Beauharnais; educated at the Grammar School of Augsburg, and at Thun, Switzerland; attempted to raise an insurrection at Strasburg, Oct. 30, 1836; detained prisoner at Strasburg till Nov. 9, 1836, and transported to Lorient; sent in exile to America; returned to Europe in Sept. 1837; landed at Boulogne to raise an insurrection, Aug. 6, 1840; tried by the High Court of Justice of the Chamber of Peers, and condemned to perpetual imprisonment, Oct. 9, 1840; escaped from the fortress of Ham, May 24, 1846; elected member of the Constituent Assembly in five departments, Aug. 1848; returned to France, Sept. 21, 1848; elected President of the French Republic for four years, Dec. 10, 1848; took the oath on the Constitution, Dec. 20, 1848; dissolved the National Assembly by a coup-d'état, Dec. 2, 1851; elected President of the Republic for ten years, Dec. 20–21, 1851; chosen hereditary Emperor by a 'plebiscite' of 7,864,189 votes against 231,145 votes, Nov. 21–22, 1852; accepted the imperial dignity and assumed the title 'Napoléon III. Emperor of the French,' Dec. 1, 1852. Author of 'Idées Napoléoniennes,' 1839; 'Études sur le Passé et l'Avenir de l'Artillerie,' 4 vols. 1846–63; 'Vie de Jules César,' 2 vols. 1866–67; and other works.

NASH, Joseph, English painter, b. 1812. Exhibited at the Old Society of Water Colour Artists in 1835. Painted 'The Queen's Visit to Lincoln's Inn Hall,' 1846; 'Interior Views of the Great Exhibition,' 1851; and many others. Illustrated 'Architecture of the Middle Ages,' 1838; 'Mansions of England in the Olden Time,' 1839–49.

NASSER-ED-DIN, Shah of Persia, b. Nov. 1829; succeeded, Oct. 13, 1848.

NATAL, Right Rev. John William Colenso, Bishop of, English divine, b. 1814; educated at St. John's College, Cambridge, where he graduated in 1836; assistant-master of Harrow School, 1838–42; tutor of St. John's College, 1842–46; rector of Forncett St. Mary, Norfolk, 1846–54; consecrated first bishop of Natal, South Africa, 1854. Author of 'Treatise on Algebra,' 1849; 'Plane Trigonometry,' 1851; 'Ten Weeks in Natal,' 1855; 'A Translation of the Epistle to the Romans, commented on from a Missionary Point of View,' 1861; 'A Critical Commentary on the Pentateuch and Book of Joshua,' 1863–64; and other works.

NAVERY, Marie de, French authoress, b. at Ploermel, Morbihan, Sept. 1831. Published, under the pseudonym of 'Raoul,' 'Crèche et la Croix,' 1856; 'Le Bonheur dans le Mariage,' 1864; and other works of fiction.

NEAL, John, American novelist, b. at Portland, Maine, 1794. Author of 'Keep Cool,' 1817; 'Seventy-six,' 1822; 'Rachel Dyer,' 1828; 'Down-easters,' 1831; 'Ruth Elder;' and other romances and novels.

NEALE, Rev. Erskine, English author, b. 1805; educated at Emmanuel College, Cambridge, where he graduated B.A. 1828; vicar of Exning, Suffolk. Author of 'The Closing Scene;' 'The Dangers and Duties of a Christian;' 'Self-sacrifice, or the Chancellor's Chaplain;' 'The Life-book of a Labourer;' 'Scenes where the Tempter has triumphed;' and numerous other works.

NEATE, Charles, English political economist, b. at Adstock, Bucks, 1807; educated at Lincoln College, Oxford, where he graduated B.A. 1821, M.A. 1830; called to the bar of Lincoln's Inn, 1832; professor of political economy at Oxford; M.P. for Oxford, May to Aug. 1857, and 1863–65. Author of 'Lectures on the Currency,' 1859; 'Three Lectures on Taxation,' 1861; and other works.

NEAVES, Lord Charles Neaves, Scottish judge, b. in Scotland, 1800; educated at the High School and University of Edinburgh; studied law, and was called to the Scottish bar, 1822; sheriff of Orkney and Shetland, 1845; solicitor-general for Scotland, 1852; appointed lord of the Session, and received the title of Lord Neaves, 1854.

NEELD, Sir John, Bart., English politician, b. 1806; educated at Harrow, and Trinity College, Cambridge, where he graduated B.A. 1827, M.A. 1830; a J.P. and deputy-lieutenant of Wilts; M.P. for Cricklade, 1835–59; and for Chippenham since 1865.

NEGRETE, Santiago Fernandez, Spanish statesman, b. 1800; studied law at the Universities of Oviedo and Alcala de Henares; procureur-fiscal to the Supreme Tribunal of Cruzada, 1843; minister of public works in the cabinet of Bravo Murillo, 1851; minister of justice, 1858; representative in the Cortes of the province of Badajoz since 1843.

NEHER, Bernhard, German historical painter, b. at Biberach, 1806; studied art at the Academies of Stuttgardt and Munich, and in Italy; professor of painting at Stuttgardt. Painted 'The Death of Ulric at the Battle of Döffingen;' and numerous other historical pictures.

NELSON, Right Rev. Edmund Hobhouse, Bishop of, English divine, b. 1817; educated at Eton, and Balliol College, Oxford, where he graduated B.A. 1838; fellow of Merton College, 1841; vicar of St. Peter's, Oxford, 1843–58; consecrated bishop of Nelson, New Zealand, 1858. Author of 'Life of Walter de Merton, the Founder of Merton College.'

NELSON, Horatio Nelson, Earl, English administrator, b. 1823; succeeded his father, second earl, 1835; deputy-lieutenant of the county of Wilts.

NESLE, Louis Armand, Comte de, French politician, b. at Caen, May 3, 1803; entered the army, and retired with the rank of captain; member of the Corps Législatif for the department of the Cher since 1856.

NESTEROFF, Peter, Russian military commander, b. 1807; educated at Moscow; entered the army, 1823; staff-major, 1826; appointed commander of the fortress of Wladikawkas, 1842; major-general, and military governor of the district of Wladikawkas, 1846.

NETTEMENT, Alfred François, French historical writer, b. at Paris, July 22, 1805; studied at the Collége Rollin; founded *L'Opinion Publique,* 1848. Author of 'Histoire de la Révolution de Juillet,' 1833; 'Histoire de la Littérature française sous la Restauration,' 1852; 'Histoire de la Restauration,' 1860–63; and numerous other works.

NEWCASTLE, Henry James Alexander Pelham Clinton, Duke of, b. 1834; succeeded, 1864.

NEWDEGATE, Charles Newdigate, English politician, b. 1816; educated at Christ Church, Oxford; a magistrate and deputy-lieutenant of the county of Warwick; M.P. for North Warwickshire since 1843.

NEWMAN, Edward, English naturalist, b. 1815. Author of 'Letters on the Natural History of Godalming,' 1849; 'A History of British Ferns;' 'A List of British Ornithology;' 'A Natural History of British Butterflies;' and other works. Editor of the *Zoologist.*

NEWMAN, Francis William, English author, b. in London, 1805; educated at Worcester College, Oxford, and graduated B.A. 1826; elected fellow of Balliol College, Nov. 1826; resigned, 1830; appointed Latin professor in University College, London, 1846; resigned, 1863. Author of 'The Soul, her Sorrows and Aspirations;' 'Regal Rome;' 'A History of the Hebrew Monarchy;' 'Theism, or Didactic Religious Utterances,' 1858; and other works.

NEWMAN, Rev. John Henry, English theologian, b. in London, 1801, brother of the preceding; educated at Trinity College, Oxford, where he graduated B.A. 1820; appointed incumbent of St. Mary's, Oxford, 1828; seceded from the Established Church, Oct. 1845; appointed rector of the Roman Catholic University in Dublin, 1854; resigned, 1858. Author of 'The Arians of the Fourth Century,' 1833; 'Essay on the Development of Christian Doctrine,' 1845; 'Apologia pro Vitâ Suâ,' 1864; and many other works.

NEWMARCH, William, English statistician, b. in Yorkshire, 1820; one of the honorary secretaries of the Statistical Society, and editor of its 'journal.' Author of 'New Supplies of Gold,' 1853; 'Loans raised by Mr. Pitt during the First French War, 1793–1807,' 1855; and other works.

NEWTON, Charles Thomas, English antiquarian, b. 1816; educated at Christ Church, Oxford, where he graduated B.A. 1837; assistant in the department of Antiquities in the British Museum, 1840–52; vice-consul at Mitylene; made excavations at Cnidus and Branchidæ, Oct. 1856 to April 1859, and discovered a collection of sculptures now in the British Museum; appointed British consul at Rome, May 1860; appointed keeper of the Greek and Roman Antiquities in the British Museum, 1861.

NEY, Napoléon Edgar, Prince de la Moskowa, French general, b. at Paris, May 20, 1812; educated at the Military School of St. Cyr; chief of squadron, Dec. 1848; general of brigade, 1856; succeeded his brother, 1857; nominated a senator, Aug. 16, 1859; general of division, 1863.

NIBOYET, Eugénie, French authoress, b. 1804. Author of 'Dieu manifesté par les Œuvres de la Création,' 1842; 'Catherine II.' 1847; 'Le vrai Livre des Femmes,' 1862; and other works.

NICHOLS, John Gough, English archæologist, b. in London, 1806; educated at Merchant Taylors' School. Editor of the *Collectanea Topographica et Genealogica,* 1834–43, and of *Topographer and Genealogist,* 1850–57; commenced *The Herald and Genealogist,* Sept. 1862. Author of 'A Descriptive Catalogue of the Works of the Camden Society,' 1862; and other works.

NICHOLSON, Sir Charles, Bart., English physician, b. 1808; graduated M.D. at the University of Edinburgh; member of the first Legislative Council of New South Wales, 1843–50; vice-chancellor of the Sydney University, 1853, and chancellor, 1854; knighted by patent, 1852; created a baronet, 1858.

NICOL, James Dyce, English politician, b. 1805; a J.P. and deputy-lieutenant of the counties of Aberdeen and Kincardine; elected M.P. for Kincardineshire, 1865.

NIEL, Adolphe, French military commander, b. at Muret, Haute Garonne, Oct. 4, 1802; educated at the École Polytechnique, and entered the army as lieutenant of engineers, 1821; captain, 1831; chef de bataillon, 1837; lieutenant-colonel, 1842; colonel, 1846; chef d'état-major of engineers in the expedition to Rome, 1849; general of brigade, 1850; general of division, 1853; commander-in-chief of the corps of engineers at the siege of Bomarsund, 1854, and at the siege of Sebastopol, 1855; nominated senator, June 7, 1857; commander of the fourth corps d'armée in the Italian war, 1859; nominated marshal of France after the battle of Solferino, June 24, 1859; appointed minister-secretary of state for the War Department, Jan. 19, 1867. Author of 'Le Siège de Sebastopol,' Paris, 1858.

NIEPCE DE SAINT VICTOR, Claude Marie François, French chemist, b. at St. Cyr, July 26, 1805; entered the army, 1829; lieutenant of dragoons, 1842; chef d'escadron, 1854. Author of papers 'Sur l'Action de la Vapeur,' 1847 and 1853; 'La Photographie sur Verre,' 1847–48; 'Recherches photographiques,' 1855.

NIEUWERKERKE, Alfred Emilien, Comte de, French sculptor, director-general of the national museums, b. at Paris, April 16, 1811; appointed to preside over the reorganization of the École des Beaux Arts, Dec. 1863; nominated senator, Oct. 5, 1864. Executed 'Descartes,' a statue in bronze, for the town of Haye; 'Isabelle la Catholique entrant à Grenade,' 1846; statue of Napoléon I. at Lyons, 1852; 'La Princesse Murat,' 1859; and other statues in bronze and marble.

NIGHTINGALE, Florence, English authoress, b. at Florence, May 1820 ; entered the institution of the Protestant Sisters of Mercy at Kaiserswerth on the Rhine, 1851 ; undertook the organization of an establishment of lady nurses, to tend the sick and wounded soldiers in the Crimean campaign, 1854. Author of 'Hints on Hospitals,' 1859 ; and 'Notes on Nursing,' 1861.

NISARD, E'douard Charles, French author, b. Jan. 10, 1808, brother of the following. Author of 'Le Triumvirat littéraire au XVIᵉ Siècle,' 1852 ; 'Les Gladiateurs de la République des Lettres aux XVᵉ, XVIᵉ, et XVIIᵉ Siècles,' 1860 ; 'Curiosités de l'Étymologie française,' 1863 ; and other works.

NISARD, Jean De'sire', French author, b. at Chatillon-sur-Seine, Côte d'Or, March 20, 1806 ; studied at St. Barbe ; elected member of the French Academy, 1850. Author of 'Les Poëtes latins de la Décadence,' 1834 ; 'Histoire de la Littérature française,' 1844–49 ; new edition, 1861–63 ; 'Nouvelles Études d'Histoire et de Littérature,' 1864 ; and other works.

NISBET-HAMILTON, Right Hon. Robert Adam, English politician, b. 1804 ; M.P. for Ipswich, 1826–30 ; for Edinburgh, 1831–32 ; and for North Lincolnshire, 1837–57 ; took the name of 'Nisbet-Hamilton' by royal licence, 1855 ; chancellor of the Duchy of Lancaster, and sworn a privy councillor, 1852.

NOAILLES, Paul, Duc de, French historical writer, b. Jan. 4, 1802 ; elected member of the French Academy, 1849. Author of 'Histoire de la Maison royal de Saint Louis,' 1843 ; 'L'Histoire de Madame de Maintenon,' 1848 ; 'La Pologne et ses Frontières,' 1863.

NOBLE, John, English sculptor, b. 1820 ; studied under John Francis. Executed the 'Wellington Monument' in bronze for the city of Manchester, inaugurated 1856 ; a statue of 'Wellington' in the court-room of the East India Company in Leadenhall Street, 1855 ; 'Life, Death, and the Resurrection,' a monument in the church of Ashley, Staffordshire ; and other works.

NOEL, Hon. and Rev. Baptist Wriothesley, English theologian, b. 1799 ; educated at Trinity College, Cambridge ; was one of the chaplains to the Queen, and rector of St. John's Chapel, Bedford Row ; resigned, 1848, on leaving the English Church ; minister of the Baptist Chapel, John Street, Gray's Inn. Author of 'Essay on the Union of Church and State,' 1848 ; 'Essay on the External Act of Baptism,' 1850 ; 'Protestant Thoughts in Rhyme ;' and other religious and controversial works.

NOEL, Hon. Gerard James, English politician, b. 1823 ; a J.P. and deputy-lieutenant of the county of Rutland ; formerly captain 11th Hussars ; M.P. for Rutlandshire since 1847.

NOGENT SAINT-LAURENS, Jules Henri, French politician, b. at Orange, Vaucluse, Dec. 27, 1814 ; educated at the College of Avignon, and studied law at Aix ; called to the bar at Paris, 1836 ; member of the Corps Législatif for the first circonscription of the department of Loiret since 1853. Author of 'De la Législation des Théâtres,' 1842 ; and other works.

NORMANBY, George Augustus Constantine Phipps, Marquis of, English administrator, b. 1819 ; a magistrate and deputy-lieutenant of the North Riding of Yorkshire ; formerly lieutenant in the Scots Fusilier Guards ; was comptroller of the Household, 1851–52 ; treasurer of the Household, 1853–57 ; lieutenant-governor of Nova Scotia, 1858–63 ; M.P. for Scarborough, 1847–51, and 1852–58 ; succeeded his father, first marquis, 1863.

NORMAND, Pierre François, French politician, b. at Montfort-l'Amaury, Oct. 12, 1782 ; entered the army, 1803 ; colonel, 1834 ; member of the Corps Législatif for the circonscription of Chartres since 1852.

NORTH, John Sidney, English politician, b. 1804 ; educated at Sandhurst ; a magistrate and deputy-lieutenant of Oxfordshire, and lieutenant-colonel of Oxfordshire Rifle Volunteers ; formerly lieutenant-colonel in the Irish Fusiliers ; M.P. for Oxfordshire since 1852.

NORTHCOTE, Sir Stafford Henry, Bart., English statesman, b. 1818, the son of H. S. Northcote, Esq. ; educated at Eton, and Balliol College, Oxford ; called to the bar, 1847 ; created baronet, 1851 ; sat as M.P. for Dudley, 1855–57 ; financial secretary of the Treasury from Jan. to June 1859 ; returned M.P. for Stamford at the elections from 1858–65 ; president of the Board of Trade, July 6, 1866, to March 6, 1867 ; secretary of state for India from March 1867 to Dec. 1868.

NORTHWICK, George Rushout, Baron, English administrator, b. 1811 ; graduated M.A. at Oxford ; a magistrate and deputy-lieutenant of Shropshire and Worcestershire ; was M.P. for Evesham, 1837–41, and for East Worcestershire, 1847–59 ; succeeded his uncle, second baron, Feb. 1859.

NORTON, Caroline Elizabeth, English authoress, b. 1808; married to the Hon. G. C. Norton, 1827. Author of 'The Sorrows of Rosalie,' 1829; 'The Undying One,' a poem, 1831; 'The Dream, and other Poems,' 1840; 'Stuart of Dunleath,' a novel; 'The Lady of La Garaye,' 1862; and other novels and poetical works.

NORWICH, Right Rev. and Hon. John Pelham, Bishop of, English divine, b. 1811; educated at Westminster, and Christ Church, Oxford; rector of Marylebone, 1855–57; consecrated bishop of Norwich, 1857.

NORWOOD, Charles Morgan, English politician, b. 1825; a merchant and shipowner of London and Hull; was twice president of the Hull Chamber of Commerce and Shipping, and the first chairman of the Association of Chambers of Commerce of the United Kingdom; elected M.P. for Hull, 1865.

NOTHOMB, Jean Baptiste, Baron, Belgian statesman, b. at Messancy, Luxemburg, July 3, 1805; studied at the University of Liege, where he graduated LL.D. 1826; took part in the Revolution of 1830; elected to the National Assembly by three districts of the province of Luxemburg, 1831; envoy-extraordinary and minister-plenipotentiary to the Germanic Confederation, 1840; minister-plenipotentiary at Berlin, 1845; member of the Belgian Academy.

NOUALHIER, Jean Baptiste, French politician, b. at Limoges, May 1, 1803; judge of the Tribunal of Commerce, 1840–44; administrator of his native town, and mayor, 1853–60; member of the Corps Législatif for the first circonscription of the department of Haute Vienne since 1852.

NOUBEL, Raymond Henri, French politician, b. at Agen, June 2, 1822; was mayor of the town of Agen; member of the Corps Législatif for the first circonscription of the department of Lot-et-Garonne since 1852.

NOVA SCOTIA, Right Rev. Hibbert Binney, Bishop of, English divine, b. in Nova Scotia, 1819; educated at King's College, London, and at Worcester College, Oxford, and graduated 1842; consecrated fourth bishop of Nova Scotia, 1851.

NOVELLO, Clara Anastasia, English singer, b. in London, June 10, 1818; studied at the Conservatoire de Musique Sacrée at Paris, and in Italy; married to Count Gigliucci, Nov. 1848, and quitted the stage; reappeared, 1850, and again retired, 1860.

NUS, Eugène, French dramatic writer, b. at Châlon-sur-Saône, 1816; studied at the college of his native town. Author of 'L'Enseignement mutuel,' 1846; 'La Tour de Londres,' 1855; 'Les Médecins,' 1863; and other dramas.

O.

O'BEIRNE, James Lyster, Irish politician, b. 1820; educated at Trinity College Dublin; elected M.P. for Cashel, 1865.

O'BRIEN, Sir Patrick, Bart., Irish politician, b. 1823; educated at Trinity College, Dublin, where he graduated M.A. 1843; called to the Irish bar, 1844; M.P. for King's County since 1852.

OCHOA, Eugenio de, Spanish author, b. at Madrid, 1812. Author of 'Ecos del Ama,' Paris, 1841; 'España litteraria, scientifica, politica y artistica,' 1847; 'Parliamentary History of Spain,' 1860; and other works. Translator of the works of Sir Walter Scott.

OCHSENBEIN, Ulrich, Swiss politician, b. at Nidau, Berne, 1811; studied law; entered the army as officer of artillery, 1834; lieutenant-colonel, 1844; member of the National Council, and charged with the direction of the military affairs of the Confederation, 1848; entered the French army, and nominated general during the war in the Crimea, 1855.

O'CONOR DON, Denis, Irish politician, b. 1838; educated at St. Gregory's College, Downside, near Bath; a magistrate and deputy-lieutenant of the county of Roscommon; M.P. for the county of Roscommon since 1860.

O'DONOGHUE, Daniel, Irish politician, b. 1833; educated at Stonyhurst; formerly a magistrate of Cork and Kerry, and major of the Kerry Militia; M.P. for Tipperary, 1857–65; returned for Tralee, 1865.

OETTINGER, Eduard, German author, b. at Breslau, Nov. 19, 1808; studied at the University of Vienna. Author of 'Der Ring des Nostradamus,' Leipsic, 1838; eighth edition, 1853; 'Jérôme Napoléon und sein Capri,' Dresden, 1853; 'Das Buch der Liebe,' Berlin, 1832; fifth edition, Leipsic, 1850; and other poetical and dramatic works.

OFFENBACH, Jacques, French musical composer, b. at Cologne, June 21, 1819; studied at the Paris Conservatoire, 1833–34; chief of the orchestra of the Théâtre Français, 1847. Composed 'Les Deux Aveugles,' 1855; 'La Chanson de Fortunio,' 1861; 'Le Roman comique,' 1861; 'La belle Hélène,' 1864–65; and many other light comic operas.

OGILVIE, Rev. Charles Atmore, English divine, b. 1793; educated at Balliol College, Oxford, and graduated B.A. 1815; fellow of Balliol, 1816; appointed regius professor of pastoral theology at Oxford, 1842. Author of 'Divine Glory manifested in the Conduct and Discourses of our Lord,' Bampton Lectures for 1836; and several sermons.

OGILVY, Sir John, Bart., English politician, b. 1803; educated at Harrow, and Christ Church, Oxford; vice-lieutenant of the county of Forfar; late captain of the Forfar and Kincardine Artillery; was formerly in the 2d Life Guards; M.P. for Dundee since 1857.

O'HAGAN, Right Hon. Thomas, Irish judge, b. at Dublin, 1810; educated at the Institution, Belfast, and called to the Irish bar, 1836; appointed solicitor-general for Ireland, 1860; attorney-general for Ireland, and sworn in the Privy Council, 1861, to Jan. 1865, when he was appointed a judge; was M.P. for Tralee, May 1863, till his elevation to the bench; lord-chancellor of Ireland, Dec. 1868.

OLIPHANT, Lawrence, English author, b. in Ceylon, 1829; called to the bar of Lincoln's Inn, 1855; was civil secretary and superintendent-general of Indian affairs in Canada; accompanied Lord Elgin on a special mission to China, 1857; acted as secretary of embassy till April 1859; secretary of legation in Japan, 1861–62; elected M.P. for Stirling, 1865. Author of 'The Russian Shores of the Black Sea,' 1853; 'A Narrative of the Earl of Elgin's Mission to China and Japan in the Years 1857–58–59,' 1860; and other works.

OLIVIER, Juste Daniel, Swiss author, b. at Eysius, Canton du Vaud, Oct. 18, 1807. Author of 'Poëmes Suisses,' 1830; 'Les Deux Voix,' 1835; 'Etudes d'Histoire nationale,' Lausanne, 1842; and other works in prose and poetry.

OLLIVIER, Olivier E'mile, French politician, b. July 2, 1825; called to the bar at Paris, 1847; commissioner-general of the Republic at Marseilles, 1848; member of the Corps Législatif for the third circonscription of the department of the Seine since 1857. Author of 'Sur les Coalitions;' and other legal and political works.

OLMSTED, Denison, American author, b. at East Hartford, Connecticut, 1791; graduated at Yale College; was professor of chemistry and philosophy in the University of North Carolina; professor of mathematics, physics, and astronomy in Yale College since 1824. Author of 'Introduction to Natural Philosophy,' 1832; 'Journeys and Explorations in the Cotton Kingdom,' 1861; and other works.

O'LOGHLEN, Sir Colman Michael, Bart., Irish administrator, b. 1819; educated at London University, and graduated B.A. 1840; called to the Irish bar, 1840; chairman of Quarter Sessions of the county of Mayo, and a magistrate of the county of Clare; M.P. for the county of Clare since 1863; judge advocate, Dec. 1868.

OLOZAGA, Salustiano, Spanish politician, b. at Logron, 1800; elected to the Cortes, 1833; ambassador to France, 1840–43, and again in 1854 and 1868; prime minister for a short period in 1844; member of the Provisional Government in 1868.

OLSHAUSEN, Justus, German philologist, b. at Hohenfeld, Holstein, May 9, 1800, brother of the following; studied at the Universities of Kiel and Berlin; appointed professor of Oriental languages at the University of Kiel, 1830; nominated counsellor and member of the Academy of Copenhagen, 1845; elected deputy for Kiel at the Diet of Holstein, 1848; vice-president of the Diet, 1849; appointed keeper of the library and professor of Oriental languages at Königsberg. Author of 'Vendidad-zend-Avestæ Pars vicesima adhuc superstes,' Hamburg, 1829; and other philological works.

OLSHAUSEN, Theodor, German politician, b. at Glückstadt, Holstein, June 19, 1802; studied law at the Universities of Kiel and Jena; member of the Constituent Diet of Holstein, 1848; emigrated to America, 1851. Author of 'The Valley of the Mississippi,' 1853.

OMER PACHA, Lattas Michael, Turkish military commander, b. at Plaski, Ogulin, Servia, 1806; studied in the Military School of Thurm, in Transylvania; assistant-surveyor of roads and bridges at Zara, 1826; left the Austrian service, adopted the *Mahometan creed,* and assumed the name of Omer, 1838; colonel in the Turkish army, *1839;* general, June 1853; commander-in-chief of the Turkish army in the Crimean campaign, *1854–55;* appointed minister without a portfolio, March 1861; commander of the *Turkish forces in Crete,* 1866–68.

O'NEIL, Henry, English historical painter, b. 1807. Exhibited at the Royal Academy 'Martha and Mary informing Christ of the Death of Lazarus ;' 'By the Rivers of Babylon ;' 'Esther in Royal Robes ;' 'Catherine's Dream ;' 'Eastward Ho !' August 1857 ; 'Home Again !' 1858 ; 'The Landing of the Princess Alexandra at Gravesend ;' and numerous other paintings.

O'NEILL, Edward, English politician, b. 1839 ; educated at Eton, and Trinity College, Cambridge ; a J.P. for the county of Antrim ; M.P. for the county of Antrim since 1863.

ONSLOW, Guildford James Hillier, English politician, b. 1814 ; educated at Eton ; a deputy-lieutenant of Lincoln and the East Riding of Yorkshire ; formerly captain in the Scots Fusilier Guards and the 11th Foot ; M.P. for Guildford since 1858.

ONTARIO, Right Rev. James Lewis, Bishop of, English divine, b. 1825 ; educated at Trinity College, Dublin ; ordained, 1848 ; rector of Brookville, Canada, 1854 ; consecrated first bishop of Ontario, Upper Canada, 1861.

OPPERT, Jules, French philologist, b. at Hamburg, July 9, 1825 ; studied at Heidelberg, Bonn, and Berlin. Author of 'Lautsystem des Altpersischen,' 1847 ; 'Les Inscriptions des Achéménides,' 1852 ; 'Sanscrit Grammar,' Berlin, 1859 ; second edition, 1863 ; 'Elements of Assyrian Grammar,' 1860 ; 'The Great Inscription of Khorsabad,' 1864 ; and numerous other philological works.

O'QUIN, Patrick, French politician, b. at Pau, Feb. 21, 1821 ; member of the General Council of the canton Est de Pau, 1852 ; mayor of Pau, 1860 ; returned deputy to the Corps Législatif for the department of Basses Pyrénées, 1852. Author of several works on political economy.

ORBIGNY, Charles Dessalines d', French naturalist, b. at Coneron, Loire Inférieure, Sept. 1806 ; educated at La Rochelle ; appointed assistant in the Museum of Natural History, Paris, 1835. Author of 'Tableau synoptique du Règne végétal,' 1834 ; 'Manuel de Géologie,' 1852 ; 'La Géologie appliquée aux Arts, aux Mines et à l'Agriculture, &c.' 1855 ; and other works on natural history.

ORD, Edward Otto Cresap, American military commander, b. in the county of Alleghany, Maryland, 1822 ; entered the Military School of West Point, 1835 ; second lieutenant of infantry, 1839 ; captain, Sept. 7, 1850 ; took part with the North in the civil war, and commanded the Pennsylvanian Volunteers ; major-general at the siege of Corinth, 1862 ; replaced General Butler in the military command of Virginia, Jan. 8, 1865.

O'REILLY, Myles Patrick, English politician, b. 1825 ; educated at London University, where he graduated B.A. 1845 ; LL.D. of Roman University, 1847 ; a J.P. and deputy-lieutenant of the county of Louth, and captain of the Louth Militia ; commander of the Irish Brigade in the Papal service, 1860 ; M.P. for the county of Longford since 1862.

ORTOLAN, Joseph Louis Elze'ar, French legal writer, b. at Toulon, Var, Aug. 21, 1802 ; studied law at Aix and Paris, and called to the bar, 1826. Author of 'Explication historique des Institutes de Justinien,' 1827 ; 'Elements du Droit pénal,' 1856 ; and other legal works.

ORTS, Charles, Belgian politician, b. at Brussels, 1815 ; studied law, and called to the bar, 1831 ; appointed professor of public law at the University of Brussels, 1839 ; deputy for Brussels since 1848 ; vice-president of the Chamber of Deputies, 1856.

OSBORN, Sherard, English naval officer and author, b. 1820 ; entered the Royal Navy ; midshipman of the *Hyacinth* at the reduction of Canton, 1841 ; lieutenant, 1846 ; commander, 1852 ; captain, 1855 ; appointed to the command of the *Royal Sovereign,* 1864. Author of 'A Cruise in Japanese Waters ;' 'The Career, Last Voyage, and Fate of Sir John Franklin,' 1860 ; 'The Past and Future of British Relations in China,' 1860 ; and other works.

OSBORNE, Ralph Bernal, English politician, b. 1812 ; educated at the Charterhouse School ; assumed the name of Osborne, 1844 ; formerly a captain in the army ; secretary to the Admiralty, Dec. 1852 to Feb. 1858 ; M.P. for Wycombe, 1841–47 ; for Middlesex, 1847–57 ; for Dover, 1857–59 ; for Liskeard, 1859–65 ; for Nottingham, 1865–68.

OSBORNE, Rev. Lord Sydney Godolphin, English divine, b. 1808 ; educated at Brasenose College, Oxford, and graduated B.A. 1830 ; appointed rector of Durweston, Dorsetshire, 1841. Author of 'Hints to the Charitable for the Amelioration of the Condition of the Poor ;' 'Scutari and its Hospitals ;' 'Lady Eva ;' 'Immortal Sewerage ' and other works.

OSGOOD, Samuel, American theologian, b. at Charlestown, Massachusetts, Aug. 30, 1812 ; studied theology at Cambridge, where he graduated, 1835 ; appointed minister of the Unitarian Chapel in New York, 1849. Author of 'Studies in Christian Biography,' or Four Hours with Theologians and Reformers,' New York, 1850 ; 'Milestones in our Life Journey ;' and other theological works.

O'SHAUGHNESSY, Sir William Brooke, Irish physician, b. in Limerick, 1809; educated at the University of Edinburgh, where he graduated M.D.; entered the Bengal army as a surgeon; appointed superintendent of telegraphs in India, 1852; knighted, 1856.   Published a 'Memoir on the Electric Telegraph,' 1840.

OSSORY, FERNS, AND LEIGHLIN, Right Rev. James O'Brien, Bishop of, English divine, b. 1794; educated at Trinity College, Dublin, and graduated B.A. 1815; dean of Cork, 1842; consecrated bishop of Ossory, Ferns, and Leighlin, 1842.   Author of several volumes of sermons.

OTWAY, Arthur John, English politician, b. 1822; educated at Sandhurst College; called to the bar of the Middle Temple, 1850; a magistrate of Middlesex; formerly in the army; M.P. for Stafford, 1852–57; returned for Chatham, 1865; under-secretary of state for foreign affairs, Dec. 1868.

OUDINE', Euge'ne Andre', French sculptor, b. at Paris, Jan. 1, 1810; studied under André Galle, Petitot, and M. Ingres.   Executed 'Le Gladiateur blessé,' 1837; 'La Vierge à l'Enfant' and 'Les Quatre Evangélistes' for St. Gervais, 1845; 'Le Baptême de Clovis,' 1853; and numerous busts, groups, and statues.

OUSELEY, Sir Frederick Arthur Gore, Bart., English musical composer, b. in London, 1825; educated at Christ Church, Oxford, and graduated B.A. 1846, M.A. 1849, Mus. Bac. 1850, Mus. Doc. 1854; entered holy orders, 1854; precentor of Hereford Cathedral, 1855; incumbent of St. Michael's, Tenbury, 1856; appointed professor of music at the University of Oxford, 1855.   Author of 'How goodly are thy Tents, O Israel!' and other anthems and compositions of sacred music.

OUSELEY, Sir William Gore, English diplomatist, b. 1799, cousin of the preceding; entered the diplomatic service as attaché at Stockholm, 1817; secretary of legation at Rio Janeiro, 1832; minister-plenipotentiary at Buenos Ayres, 1844; sent on a special mission to Monte Video, 1846.   Author of several political pamphlets and works on foreign countries.

OUVRIE', Pierre Justin, French painter and lithographer, b. at Paris, May 9, 1806; studied under Abel de Pujol and Châtillon.   Exhibited 'La Cérémonie funèbre du Poëte Shelley,' 1831; 'Vue d'Amsterdam,' 1853; 'Sites du Rhin,' 1857; 'Le Kéreen Gracht à Amsterdam,' 1863; and numerous other works.

OVERBECK, Friedrich, German painter, b. at Lübeck, July 3, 1789; studied in Vienna, 1806; went in 1810, with Schadow, Veit, and Cornelius, to Rome, where he has since resided.   Exhibited 'Madonna,' 1811; 'The Entrance of Christ into Jerusalem,' 1824; 'Christ blessing Little Children;' 'John the Preacher in the Wilderness;' and numerous other paintings, chiefly of religious subjects.

OVERSKON, Thomas, Danish dramatic writer, b. at Copenhagen, Oct. 11, 1798. Author of 'Œstergade og Vestergade,' 1828; 'Diamant Korset,' 1847; 'Den danske Skueplads i dens Historie,' 1854–56; and other dramatic works.

OVERSTONE, Samuel Jones Loyd, Baron, English administrator, b. 1796; educated at Trinity College, Cambridge; was high sheriff of Warwickshire, 1838; M.P. for Hythe, 1819–26; formerly a partner in the firm of Jones Loyd & Co. bankers; member of the Senate of the University of London, and a trustee of the National Gallery.

OWEN, Sir Hugh Owen, Bart., English politician, b. 1803; a magistrate and deputy-lieutenant of the county of Pembroke, and lieutenant-colonel of Pembrokeshire Militia; was M.P. for Pembroke, 1826–38, and since 1861.

OWEN, Richard, English naturalist, b. at Lancaster, 1804; graduated at the University of Edinburgh, 1824; member of the Royal College of Surgeons of London, 1826; Hunterian professor and conservator of the museum of the College, 1835; superintendent of the natural history departments of the British Museum, 1856.   Author of 'Principles of Comparative Osteology,' published in French, 1855; 'On Palæontology,' 1860; and numerous other works.

OXENFORD, John, English dramatic writer, b. in Camberwell, Surrey, 1812; educated for the law, and articled to a London solicitor.   Translated from the German 'Eckermann's Conversations with Goethe;' 'The Autobiography of Goethe.'   Author of several songs and many dramatic pieces and criticisms.

OXFORD, Right Rev. Samuel Wilberforce, Bishop of, English divine, b. 1805; educated at Oriel College, Oxford, and graduated B.A. 1826, M.A. 1829, D.D. 1845; successively archdeacon of Surrey, canon of Winchester, and dean of Westminster; *consecrated* bishop of Oxford, 1845; chancellor of the Order of the Garter, and lord high almoner to the Queen.   Author of 'The Life of Wilberforce;' 'History of the American Church;' and of several volumes of sermons and pastoral addresses.

P.

PACCARD, Alexis, French architect, b. in Paris, June 19, 1813 ; studied at the École des Beaux Arts, 1830 ; architect of the Palais de Rambouillet, 1852 ; designed the Château de Pau, 1853 ; architect to the Museum of Fontainebleau, 1853-63 ; appointed professor of architecture at the École des Beaux Arts, 1863.

PACKE, George Hussey, English politician, b. 1796 ; was formerly in the army ; a magistrate and deputy-lieutenant of the county of Lincoln ; was high sheriff, 1842, and vice-chairman of the Great Northern Railway Company ; M.P. for South Lincolnshire since 1859.

PACKENHAM, Right Hon. Sir Richard, English diplomatist, b. 1797 ; attaché to the embassy at the Hague, 1817 ; minister-plenipotentiary in Mexico, 1835 ; sworn a privy councillor, 1843 ; envoy-extraordinary and minister-plenipotentiary at Washington, 1843-49, and at Lisbon, April 1851 to 1855.

PADMORE, Richard, English politician, b. 1789 ; a magistrate and alderman of Worcester, and chairman of the Worcester City and County Banking Company ; M.P. for Worcester since 1860.

PADOUE, Ernest Louis Arrighi de Casanova, Duc de, French statesman, b. in Paris, Sept. 26, 1814 ; studied at the École Polytechnique, 1833-35 ; created a senator, June 23, 1853 ; was minister of the interior from May 5 to Nov. 1, 1859.

PAGE, The'oge'ne François, French naval commander, b. March 31, 1807 ; studied at the École Polytechnique, 1825 to 1827 ; ensign in the navy, 1830 ; lieutenant, 1836 ; captain, 1845 ; rear-admiral, Aug. 12, 1858 ; vice-admiral, Aug. 10, 1861 ; maritime préfet of Rochefort, 1862 ; member of the Council of Admiralty, Oct. 20, 1863.

PAGE, Thomas, English civil engineer, b. 1810 ; engineer of the suspension bridge at Battersea, opened 1859, and of the new bridge across the Thames at Westminster, commenced 1860, and finished 1866 ; appointed architect and engineer of the new Blackfriars Bridge, 1865.

PAGET, Lord Alfred Henry, English politician, b. June 29, 1816 ; educated at Westminster ; deputy-lieutenant of Staffordshire and Suffolk, and a colonel in the army ; appointed chief equerry to the Queen, 1859 ; M.P. for Lichfield, 1837-65.

PAGET, Lord Clarence Edward, English naval commander and politician, b. 1811 ; educated at Westminster ; is vice-admiral R.N. ; appointed secretary to the Admiralty, 1859 ; M.P. for Sandwich, 1847-52, and since 1857.

PAGET, Rev. Francis Edward, English author, b. 1806 ; educated at Westminster, and Christ Church, Oxford, where he graduated B.A. 1832 ; rector of Elford, Staffordshire, since 1835. Author of 'St. Antholins,' 1842 ; 'The Warden of Berkenholt,' 1843 ; 'Luke Sharp, a Tale of Modern Education,' 1845 ; and other works.

PAGET, Lord George Augustus Frederick, English officer, b. in London, 1818 ; entered the army ; was lieutenant-colonel of dragoons, 1846 ; brigadier-general, 1855 ; major-general, 1861 ; appointed to the command of a division of the Bengal army, 1862 ; was M.P. for Beaumaris, 1847-57 ; created C.B. 1855, and received the cross of officer of the Legion of Honour, 1856.

PAGET, James, English surgeon, b. 1815 ; member of the Royal College of Surgeons, 1836 ; surgeon-extraordinary to the Queen, and assistant surgeon at St. Bartholomew's Hospital. Author of 'Lectures on Surgical Pathology ;' and other medical works.

PAGET, Richard Horner, English politician, b. 1832 ; educated at Sandhurst ; a magistrate of Somerset, and captain of the North Somersetshire Yeomanry Cavalry ; served in 66th Foot ; elected M.P. for East Somersetshire, 1865.

PAGE'ZY, David Jules, French politician, b. Sept. 20, 1803 ; mayor of Montpellier, and member of the General Council for the canton of Castries ; elected member of the Corps Législatif for the department of Hérault, 1863.

PAKINGTON, Right Hon. Sir John Somerset, English statesman, b. 1799, son of William Russell, Esq. of Powick Court, Worcestershire ; educated at Eton, and Oriel College, Oxford ; assumed the name of Pakington, 1831 ; created baronet, 1837 ; secretary of state for the colonies from March to Dec. 1852 ; first lord of the Admiralty from March 1858 to June 1859 ; returned M.P. for Droitwich in the elections from 1837 to 1865 ; first lord of the Admiralty, July 6, 1866, to March 6, 1867 ; appointed secretary of state for war, March 6, 1867, to Dec. 1868.

PALACKY, Franz, Bohemian writer, b. at Hodslawitz, in Moravia, June 1798; studied at Presburg and Vienna; appointed historiographer to the kingdom by the States of Bohemia, 1831. Author of 'History of Bohemia,' in German, 1836–54; 'The Invasion of the Mongols in the Thirteenth Century,' 1842; and other historical works.

PALEY, Frederick Apthorpe, English writer, b. at Easingwold, near York, 1816; educated at St. John's College, Cambridge, where he graduated B.A. 1836. Author of 'Illustrations of Baptismal Fonts;' 'Manual of Gothic Mouldings;' 'Guide to the Churches round Cambridge;' and other works. An eminent classical scholar; has edited Theocritus, Propertius, and other ancient writers.

PALFREY, John Gorham, American theologian, b. at Boston, May 2, 1798; studied theology and graduated at Harvard College, 1815; minister of a Unitarian Church at Boston, 1818–31. Editor of the *North American Review*, 1835–1843. Author of 'Evidences of Christianity,' Boston, 1843; and other works.

PALGRAVE, Francis Turner, English author, b. 1824; educated at the Charter-house, and at Balliol College, Oxford, where he graduated B.A.; was private secretary to Mr. W. E. Gladstone; employé in the Educational Department of the Privy Council. Edited 'The Golden Treasury of English Poetry.' Author of 'Idylls and Songs;' and other works.

PALGRAVE, William Gifford, English traveller, consul at Trebizond, b. 1826, brother of the preceding. Author of 'Travels in Arabia,' 1863.

PALIN, Rev. William, English author, b. 1802; educated at Trinity College, Cambridge, where he graduated B.A. 1833, and M.A. 1851; appointed rector of Stifford, Essex, 1834. Author of 'History of the Church of England, 1688 to 1717;' 'The Christian Month;' 'Bellingham,' a tale; and other works.

PALK, Sir Lawrence, Bart., English politician, b. 1818; educated at Eton; a magistrate and deputy-lieutenant of Devon; M.P. for South Devon since 1854.

PALLAVICINI, della Priola, Marquis Emilio, Italian military commander, b. at Ceva, province of Mondovi, 1823; studied at the Military Academy at Turin; fought as a volunteer in the campaign of Lombardy, 1848–49; served in the Crimea, 1855, and during the war in Italy, 1859; took Garibaldi prisoner at Aspromonte, for which he received the title of major-general.

PALLAVICINO-TRIVULZIO, Giorgo, Marquis, Italian politician, b. 1795; prefect of Palermo, April to July 1862; created a senator by Victor Emmanuel, 1859.

PALLISER, John, English traveller and author, b. 1817; a magistrate of the county of Waterford; engaged for the English Government to conduct the British North America Exploring Expedition, 1857–60, and published the account of it, 1861. Author of 'The Solitary Hunter, or Sporting Adventures in the Prairies.'

PALLU, Leopold Charles de la Barrie're, French naval commander and author, b. at Saintes, Aug. 19, 1829; lieutenant in the navy, 1858; appointed to command *Le Tancrède* in the Chinese Seas, 1864. Author of 'History of the Expedition in Cochin China in 1861,' 1864; and other works.

PALLUEL, Joseph Ferdinand, French politician, b. at Chambéry, April 10, 1796; called to the bar of his native town, 1822; deputy to the Parliament of Turin, 1848, and vice-president of the Sardinian Chamber, 1849; after the annexation of Savoy by France, became member of General Council for the canton of Bourg St. Maurice; elected member of the Corps Législatif for the second circonscription of the department of Savoy, 1862.

PALMER, Sir Roundell, English politician, b. 1812; educated at Rugby, Winchester, and Trinity College, Oxford; afterwards fellow of Magdalen College; graduated B.A. 1834, M.A. 1836; called to the bar of Lincoln's Inn, 1837; solicitor-general, 1861; attorney-general, 1863–66; was M.P. for Plymouth, 1847–52, and 1853–57, and returned for Richmond, 1861.

PALMER, Rev. William, English theologian, b. 1803; educated at Trinity College, Dublin, where he graduated B.A.; appointed vicar of Whitchurch Canonicorum, Dorset, 1846; rural dean and prebendary of Salisbury. Author of 'Origines Liturgicæ, or Antiquity of the English Ritual,' 1832; 'A Compendious Ecclesiastical History,' 1842; and other theological works.

PALUDAN-MÜLLER, Frederik, Danish poet, b. at Kjerteminde, Fionia, Feb. 7, 1809. Author of 'Fire Romanser,' Copenhagen, 1832; 'Danserinden,' 1833; 'Dryadens Bryllup,' 1844; 'Luftskipperen og Atheisten,' 1853; 'Tree Digte,' 1854; and numerous other poems.

PALUDAN MÜLLER, Caspar Peder, Danish historian, b. Jan. 25, 1805, brother of the preceding; appointed professor in 1829, and head-master in 1843, of the Cathedral School of Odense; elected member of the Academy of Sciences of Copenhagen, 1843. Author of 'Om St. Hans Kloster i Odense,' Odense, 1831; 'Grevens Feide,' 1853–54; 'Herredagene i Odense,' 1857; and other works.

PAMARD, Paul Antoine Marie, French politician, b. at Avignon, Aug. 24, 1802 mayor of Avignon; member of the General Council for the canton of the same town; elected member of the Corps Législatif for the department of Vaucluse, 1861.

PANIZZI, Antonio, English bibliographer, b. at Brescello, Modena, Italy, Sept. 16, 1797; studied at the University of Parma, where he graduated LL.D. 1818; professor of Italian at University College, London, 1828–30; assistant librarian of the British Museum, 1831–37; principal librarian, 1837–66. Editor of the 'Orlando Innamorato' of Bojardo, 1830; the 'Orlando Furioso' of Ariosto, 1832. Author of 'Chi era Francesco da Bologna?' 1858.

PAPE CARPANTIER, Marie, French authoress, b. at Flèche, Sarthe, Sept. 10, 1815; appointed directress of the Normal School of Paris, 1848. Author of 'Préludes,' 1841; 'Ce que dit un Grain de Sable,' 1862; 'Géométrie de la Nature,' 1863; and other works.

PAQUIS, Ame'de'e, French writer, b. 1800. Author of 'Nouvelle Grammaire latine,' 1828; 'Oui et Non,' 1830; 'Histoire d'Espagne et de Portugal,' 1846–48; and other works.

PARCHAPPE, Charles Jean, French military commander, b. at Épergnay, Marne, April 4, 1787; studied at the École de Fontainebleau; second lieutenant, 1806; colonel, 1837; general of division, 1848; elected member of the Corps Législatif for the second circonscription of the department of Marne, 1852.

PARIEU, Felix Esquirou de, French statesman, b. at Aurillac, March 13, 1815; studied law at Paris and Strasburg, and graduated LL.D.; represented the department of Cantal in the Constituent and Legislative Assemblies, 1848–49; was minister of public instruction, Oct. 31, 1849, to Feb. 13, 1851; vice-president of the Corps Législatif, 1855; elected member of the French Academy, 1856. Author of 'Traité des Impôts considérés sous le Rapport historique, économique et politique, en France et à l'Étranger,' 1862–64; and other works.

PARIS, Alexis Paulin, French author, b. at Avenay, Marne, March 25, 1800; appointed professor of language and literature at the College of France, 1853. Author of 'Apologie de l'École romantique,' 1824; 'Grandes Chroniques de Saint Denis,' 1836–38; 'Les Aventures de Maître Renart et d'Ysengrin, mises en nouveau Langage,' 1861; and other works.

PARISH, Sir Woodbine, English diplomatist, b. 1792; educated at Eton; entered the diplomatic service, 1815; concluded the first treaty with La Plata, 1825; chargé d'affaires at Buenos Ayres, 1840; brought to the British Museum the remains of the Megatherium, Glyptodon, and other antediluvian monsters of the Pampas. Author of 'Provinces of La Plata.'

PARKER, Sir Henry Watson, English colonial administrator, b. 1808; was successively colonial secretary, first minister, and principal secretary of New South Wales; knighted, 1858.

PARKER, John Henry, English author and publisher, b. 1806; educated at Dr. Haines' School, the Manor House, Chiswick; vice-president of the Oxford Architectural Society. Author of 'Glossary of Architecture,' 1836; fifth edition, 1850; 'Introduction to the Study of Gothic Architecture,' 1849; and other works.

PARKER, Sir William, English naval commander, b. 1781; entered the navy, 1793; rear-admiral, 1830; admiral of the blue, April 1851; commander-in-chief at Plymouth, 1854; admiral of the fleet, 1863; created a baronet, 1844; first naval aide-de-camp to the Queen, 1846; a lord of the Admiralty, July to December 1834, and from April 1835 to May 1845.

PARKER, Windsor, English politician, b. 1802; a magistrate and deputy-lieutenant of Suffolk, and major of the West Suffolk Militia; late captain in the Bengal Cavalry; M.P. for West Suffolk since 1859.

PARKES, Sir Harry Smith, English diplomatist, b. 1828; successively consul at Amoy, Shanghai, and Canton; British minister in Japan, 1865.

PARKMAN, Francis, American author, b. at Boston, Sept. 16, 1823; educated at Harvard College. Author of 'Prairie and Rocky Mountain Life,' New York, 1852; 'The History of the Conspiracy of Pontiac,' Boston, 1851; 'Vassall Morton,' ib. 1856.

PARLATORE, Filippo, Italian naturalist, b. at Palermo, Aug. 8, 1816; studied at the University of Palermo, and graduated M.D. 1834. Author of 'Monografia delle Fumarice,' Florence, 1844; 'Flora Italiana,' ib. 1850–58; 'Travels to the North of Europe,' ib. 1854; and other botanical works.

PARRY, Thomas, English politician, b. 1818; educated at Lincoln; M.P. for Boston, 1865–67.

PARTRIDGE, Richard, English surgeon, b. 1805; admitted a member of the Royal College of Surgeons, 1827; professor of anatomy at King's College, London, and to the Royal Academy of Arts.

PASSAGLIA, Carlo, Italian theologian, b. 1804; educated at Rome, and became professor of theology in the Roman University; appointed professor of moral philosophy at the University of Turin, 1861; elected deputy to the Italian Parliament, 1863. Author of 'Pro Causa Italica ad Episcopos Catholicos,' 1861; and numerous theological works.

PASSY, Antoine Fre'de'ric, French politician, b. 1792, brother of the following; préfet of the Eure, 1830; councillor of state, 1839; under-secretary to the minister of the interior, 1840; appointed professor of political economy at Montpellier, 1860. Author of 'Description of the Geology of the Department of the Seine Inférieure,' 1832; and other works.

PASSY, Hippolyte Philibert, French statesman, b. at Garches Villeneuve, near St. Cloud, Oct. 16, 1793; admitted to the School of Cavalry of Saumur, 1809; lieutenant, 1812; elected deputy for Louviers, 1830; minister of finance from 11 to 14 Nov. 1834; minister of commerce, Feb. 22 to Aug. 25, 1836; entered the Chamber of Peers, Dec. 16, 1843; took part in the first ministry of President Louis Napoléon, Dec 20, 1848, to Oct. 31, 1849; retired from public life after the coup d'état of Dec. 2, 1851. Author of 'Des Causes d'Inegalité des Richesses,' 1849; and other works.

PASTEUR, Louis, French chemist, b. at Dôle, Jura, Dec. 27, 1822; studied at the College of Besançon, and received the degree of M.D. 1847; professor of chemistry to the Faculty of Sciences, Strasburg, 1852–63; appointed professor of geology, physics, and chemistry at the Paris École des Beaux Arts, Dec. 1863. Author of several works on chemistry.

PATMORE, Coventry, English author, b. at Woodford, Essex, July 2, 1823; appointed one of the assistant librarians to the British Museum, 1846; retired, 1865. Author of 'Tamerton Church Tower, and other Poems,' 1853; 'The Angel in the House,' 1855; 'Faithful for Ever;' 'Victories of Love,' 1862; and other poems.

PATON, Andrew Archibald, Servian author, b. 1807. Author of 'The Modern Syrians by an Oriental Student,' 1843; 'Servia, the Youngest Member of the European Family,' 1844; 'The Goth and the Hun,' 1851; 'The Mamelukes, or Life in Grand Cairo,' 1851; and other works.

PATON, Sir Joseph Noel, English painter, b. at Dunfermline, Fifeshire, 1823; admitted as a student at the Royal Academy, 1843. Painted 'Christ bearing the Cross,' 1847; 'The Quarrel of Oberon and Titania,' 1849; 'The Dead Lady,' 1854; 'The Pursuit of Pleasure,' 1855; 'In Memoriam,' 1858; 'Dawn: Luther at Erfurt,' 1861; and other works of art.

PATTEN, Right Hon. John Wilson, English statesman, b. 1802, the eldest son of T. W. Patten, M.P. for Lancashire; educated at Eton, and Magdalen College, Oxford; M.P. for Lancashire since 1830; chairman of committees of the House of Commons, 1852–53; chancellor of the Duchy of Lancaster, 1867–68.

PATTERSON, Robert Hogarth, English author, b. in Edinburgh, 1821; was editor of the *Press* newspaper, 1859–62. Author of 'The New Revolution, or the Napoleonic Policy in Europe,' 1860; 'Essays in History and Art,' 1861.

PATTI, Adelina Juana Maria, Italian operatic singer, b. at Madrid, March 19, 1843; studied under her brother-in-law, Maurice Strakosch, and made her début at New York, Nov. 24, 1859; made her first appearance in London at the Italian Opera House, May 14, 1861.

PATTI, Carlotta, Italian operatic singer, b. at Florence, 1840, sister of the preceding; made her début at the Academy of Music, New York, 1861.

PAULL, Henry, English politician, b. 1822; studied law, and called to the bar of the Middle Temple, 1845; a deputy-lieutenant of Middlesex; M.P. for St. Ives since 1857.

PAVIE, The'odore Marie, French philologist, b. at Angers, Aug. 16, 1811. Author of 'Voyage aux États Unis et au Canada,' 1828–38; 'Krichna et sa Doctrine,' 1852; 'Scénes et Récits des Pays d'outre Mer,' 1853; 'Récits des Landes et des Grèves,' 1863; and other philological works.

PAYEN, Anselme, French chemist, b. at Paris, Jan. 6, 1795; studied chemistry under Vauquelin, Chevreul, and Thénard; directed a beetroot sugar manufactory, 1814–20; admitted a member of the Academy of Sciences, 1842. Author of 'Cours de Chimie appliquée,' 1847; and numerous other works on chemistry.

PEABODY, George, American philanthropist, b. at Danvers, Massachusetts, U.S. Feb. 18, 1795; came to England, 1837, and established himself in London as a merchant and money-broker; gave £25,000 to found an Institute at Danvers, U.S., and £100,000 to found another at Maryland; presented the City of London with £150,000 to erect comfortable and convenient lodging-houses for the working classes in 1859.

PEACOCK, Sir Barnes, English judge, b. 1810; legal member of the Council of India, 1852; chief justice of Calcutta, 1859.

PEARD, Colonel John Whitehead, English administrator, b. at Fowey, in Cornwall, 1811; educated at Ottery St. Mary, Devon, and at Exeter College, Oxford, where he graduated B.A. 1833, and M.A. 1836; called to the bar of Lincoln's Inn, 1837; offered his services as a volunteer to Garibaldi, 1859; fought with him during the Italian campaign, and at Palermo, 1860; a magistrate and deputy-lieutenant of Cornwall.

PEASE, Joseph Whitwell, English politician, b. 1828; a magistrate of the county of Durham and the North Riding of Yorkshire; elected M.P. for South Durham, 1865.

PEDRO II. Emperor of Brazil, b. Dec. 2, 1825, the son of Emperor Pedro I. and of Archduchess Leopoldina of Austria; succeeded to the throne at the abdication of his father, April 7, 1831; declared of age, July 23, 1840; crowned, July 18, 1841; married, Sept. 4, 1843, to Theresa, b. March 14, 1822, the daughter of the late King Francis I. of the Two Sicilies.

PEEL, Arthur Wellesley, English politician, b. 1829; educated at Eton, and Balliol College, Oxford, where he graduated B.A. 1852, M.A. 1865; a magistrate of Bedfordshire; elected M.P. for Warwick, 1865.

PEEL, Right Hon. Frederick, English statesman, b. 1823; educated at Harrow, and Trinity College, Cambridge; called to the bar of the Inner Temple, 1849; under-secretary of state for the colonies; under-secretary for war, 1855–57; M.P. for Leominster, Feb. 1849 to July 1852; and for Bury, Lancashire, April 1857; re-elected, May 1859 to 1865.

PEEL, John, English politician, b. 1804; educated at Manchester Grammar School; a magistrate of the counties of Stafford and Warwick; M.P. for Tamworth, 1863–68.

PEEL, Right Hon. Jonathan, English statesman, b. 1799; educated at Rugby; a major-general in the army; was surveyor-general of the ordnance, 1841–46; secretary of state for the War Department, 1858–59; M.P. for Norwich, 1826–30; and for Huntingdon, 1831–68.

PEEL, Right Hon. Sir Lawrence, English colonial judge, b. 1799; educated at St. John's College, Cambridge, where he graduated B.A. 1821; called to the bar of the Middle Temple, 1824; chief justice of the Supreme Court of Calcutta, 1842–55; vice-president of the Legislative Council of Madras.

PEEL, Right Hon. Sir Robert, Bart., English statesman, b. 1822; educated at Christ Church, Oxford, where he graduated B.A. 1843; was attaché at Madrid, June 1844 to May 1846; a lord of the Admiralty, 1855–57; chief secretary for Ireland, 1861–65; M.P. for Tamworth since 1850.

PEILE, Rev. Thomas Williamson, English author, b. 1806; studied at Trinity College, Cambridge; head-master of Repton School, 1841–58; vicar of Luton, Bedfordshire, 1858–61; incumbent of St. Paul's, Hampstead. Editor of 'Agamemnon,' 1839; 'Choephorœ' of Æschylus, 1840; and other classical publications.

PELHAM, Walter John, Lord, English administrator, b. 1838; educated at Harrow, and Trinity College, Cambridge, where he graduated M.A. 1860; a deputy-lieutenant of Sussex.

PELIGOT, Eugene Melchior, French chemist, b. in Paris, 1812; professor of chemistry to the Conservatoire des Arts et Métiers; and assayer to l'Hôtel des Monnaies. Author of 'Recherches sur l'Analyse et la Composition chimique de la Betterave à Sucre,' 1839; 'Traité pratique d'Analyse chimique,' 1843; and other works on chemistry.

PELLAT, Charles Auguste, French author, b. at Grenoble, Oct. 6, 1793; studied law in his native town, and received the degree of LL.D. 1819; dean of the Faculty of Law in Paris since 1847. Author of 'Textes choisis des Pandectes,' 1860–63; and numerous other works.

PELLETAN, Euge'ne, French writer and politician, b. at Royan, Charente Inférieure, Oct. 26, 1813; studied law at Paris; elected member of the Corps Législatif for the ninth circonscription of the department of Seine, 1864. Author of 'Le Lampe éteinte,' 1840; 'Les Droits de l'Homme,' 'Les Rois philosophes,' 1858; 'Décadence de la Monarchie française,' 1860; 'Adresse au Roi Coton,' 1863; 'Le Termite,' 1864; and other works.

PELOUZE, The'ophile Jules, French chemist, b. at Valognes, Manche, Feb. 26, 1807; studied under Gay Lussac, in Paris, 1827; appointed professor of chemistry at Lisle, 1830; assayer to the Mint of Paris, 1833, and president of the same, 1848. Published, with M. Frémy, 'Traité de Chimie, générale, analytique, etc.' 1853–56, in 6 vols.; third edition, 1860; and other works on chemistry.

PENCO, Rosina, Italian operatic singer, b. at Naples, 1830; made her début in Copenhagen, 1850, as 'Lucia,' in Donizetti's opera, and in London at Covent Garden Theatre, 1859.

PENGELLY, William, English geologist, b. in Cornwall, 1812; published, with Dr. Heer, of Zurich, a monograph on 'The Lignite Formation of Bovey Tracey, Devonshire,' 1863; author of several papers on the geology of Devonshire; collected and arranged the Devonian fossils in the Oxford University under the name of 'Pengelly Collection.'

PENNANT, Hon. Edward Gordon Douglas, English politician, b. 1800; assumed the name of Pennant, 1833; a deputy-lieutenant of Carnarvon, and lieutenant-colonel of the Carnarvon Militia; formerly lieutenant-colonel of the Grenadier Guards; M.P. for Carnarvonshire since 1841.

PENNEFATHER, Sir John Lysaght, English military commander, b. 1800; entered the army as cornet, 1818; lieutenant-colonel, 1839; colonel in the army, 1846; major-general, 1854; appointed colonel of the 46th Foot, 1854; created K.C.B. 1855; lieutenant-general, 1855; governor of Malta, 1856–57; nominated commander of the camp at Aldershot, 1860.

PEPOLI, Carlo, Italian statesman, b. at Bologna, 1801; studied at the university of his native city; chosen member of the Provisional Government, 1831, and prefect of the provinces of Urbino and Pesaro; professor of Italian literature in London University, 1839–48; member of the Roman Parliament, and vice-president of the Assembly, 1848; one of the commissioners employed in the pacification of Naples, 1860.

PEPOLI, Gioacchino Napoleone, Marquis, Italian statesman, b. at Bologna, 1825; colonel of the National Guard, 1848; minister of finance, 1859; deputy of Bologna and governor of Umbria, 1860; minister of agriculture and commerce, 1862; minister of the interior, Sept. 1863; minister-plenipotentiary at St. Petersburg, Jan. 1863 to 1864.

PERCY, Lord Henry Hugh Manvers, English officer and politician, b. 1817; educated at Eton; a major-general in the army; formerly in the Grenadier Guards, and aide-de-camp to the Queen; elected M.P. for Northumberland, 1865.

PERCY, John, English physician, b. at Nottingham, 1817; educated at Paris, and in Edinburgh, where he graduated M.D.; lecturer on metallurgy in the Government School of Mines since 1851. Author of 'Metallurgy, or the Art of extracting Metals from their Ores, and adapting them to the various Purposes of Manufacture.'

PERCZEL, Moritz, Hungarian politician, b. at Tolna, 1814; studied philosophy and law at Pesth; deputy from the county of Tolna to the Diets of 1840, 1844, and 1847; deputy from Buda to the Diet, and counsellor to the minister of the interior, 1848; one of the members of the Triumvirate Government of the Hungarian Republic, 1848–49.

PE'REIRE, E'mile, French banker and politician, b. at Bordeaux, Dec. 3, 1800; member of the General Council of the Gironde for the canton of Réole; member of the Corps Législatif for the third circonscription of the department of Gironde since 1863.

PE'REIRE, Isaac, French banker and politician, b. at Bordeaux, Nov. 25, 1806; brother of the preceding; member of the General Council for the canton of Perpignan; member of the Corps Législatif for the circonscription of the department of Pyrénées Orientales since 1863.

PEREZ, Jose' Joaquin, Chilian statesman, b. 1801; secretary of legation in France, 1829–31; minister-plenipotentiary at Buenos Ayres, 1832; subsequently councillor of state, minister of finance, of the interior, of foreign affairs; president of the Chamber of Deputies, and president of the Senate; elected president of the Republic of Chili, Sept. 7, 1861; re-elected, July 24, 1866.

PE'RIER, Auguste Casimir, French politician, b. at Paris, Aug. 20, 1811; entered the diplomatic service, 1831, and was successively secretary of embassy at London and Brussels; chargé d'affaires at Naples and St. Petersburg, and minister-plenipotentiary at Hanover; deputy for the first arrondissement of Paris to the Legislative Assembly, 1849. Author of 'Les Finances de l'Empire,' 1861; 'Les Sociétés de Co-opération,' 1864; and other works.

PERRAS, Benoit Hippolyte, French politician, b. at Régny, Loire, April 9, 18C4; an advocate at the Imperial Court of Lyons; member of the Corps Législatif for the third circonscription du Rhône since 1863.

PERRIN, Emile, French artist, b. at Rouen, Jan. 1815; studied under Gros and Delaroche; appointed director of the Imperial Academy of Music, 1862. Exhibited 'Louis XV. au Château de Crécy;' 'La Mort de Malfilâtre;' and other paintings.

PERRY, Sir Thomas Erskine, English judge, b. 1806; educated at Trinity College, Cambridge, where he graduated B.A. 1829; called to the bar of the Inner Temple; chief justice at Bombay, 1847–52; M.P. for Devonport, 1854–59; member of the Imperial Council for India.

PERSIGNY, Jean Gilbert Victor Fialin, Duc de, French statesman, b. at St. Germain Lespinasse, Loire, Jan. 11, 1808; entered the Cavalry School at Saumur, 1826; appointed aide-de-camp to President Louis Napoléon, 1848; ambassador to England. 1855; recalled to Paris, 1860; minister of the interior, 1860 to June 23, 1863; created a duke by the Emperor, Sept. 13, 1863.

PERTZ, Georg Heinrich, German historical writer, b. at Hanover, March 28, 1795; studied at Göttingen, and received the degree of Ph.D. 1816; privy councillor at the court of Berlin, 1842; director of the Royal Library, 1846. Author of 'Monumenta Germaniæ historica,' Hanover, 1826–54, in 13 vols.: and numerous other historical works.

PERUZZI, Ubaldino, Italian statesman, b. 1821; studied at the School of Mines in Paris, and in Germany; member of the Assembly of Tuscany, 1859; elected to represent Florence at the National Parliament at Turin, 1860; minister of public works, 1861; minister of the interior, 1863.

PETER I. Grand-duke of Oldenburg, b. July 8, 1827, the son of Grand-duke Augustus and of Princess Ida of Anhalt-Bernburg; succeeded to the throne at the death of his father, Feb. 27, 1853; married, Feb. 10, 1852, to Elizabeth, b. March 26, 1826, daughter of Prince Joseph of Saxe-Altenburg.

PETERBOROUGH, Right Rev. William Connor Magee, Bishop of, English divine, b. 1821; dean of Cork, 1866; bishop of Peterborough, 1868. Author of 'Sermons at Bath;' and other works.

PETERMANN, August Heinrich, German geographer, b. at Bleicherode, Prussia, April 18, 1822; educated at the College of Nordhausen; appointed professor of geography at Gotha, by the Duke of Saxe-Coburg Gotha, 1854. Published 'The Atlas of Physical Geography,' with the Rev. Thomas Milner; 'An Account of the Expedition to Central Asia.' Contributor to the *Encyclopædia Britannica.* Editor of *Geographische Mittheilungen.*

PETIT, Rev. John Louis, English architectural writer, b. 1806; educated at Trinity College, Cambridge, where he graduated B.A. 1823; entered holy orders, 1824. Author of 'Architectural Character,' 1846; 'Lectures on Architectural Studies,' 1854; and other works on architecture.

PETIT, Pierre Guillaume, French politician, b. Sept. 1, 1804; a manufacturer at Louviers; member of the Corps Législatif for the fourth circonscription of the department of the Eure since 1863.

PETO, Sir Samuel Morton, Bart., English civil engineer, b. 1800; constructed Hungerford Market, the Reform, Oxford, and Cambridge Clubhouses, Bloomsbury Chapel, Regent's Park Chapel, and a large portion of the railways in England, and lines in Canada and Norway; created a baronet, 1855; a deputy-lieutenant of Suffolk; M.P. for Norwich, 1847–54; for Finsbury, 1859–65; and for Bristol, 1865–68.

PETRE, William Bernard Petre, Baron, English administrator, b. 1817; a deputy-lieutenant and magistrate of Essex; succeeded his father, eleventh baron, 1850.

PEYRAT, Alphonse, French writer, b. at Toulouse, June 21, 1812. Published 'Correspondance d'Angleterre,' 1854; 'L'Empire jugé avec Indépendance,'1856; 'Histoire et Religion,' 1858; 'Histoire élémentaire et critique de Jésus,' 1864; and numerous other works.

PFEIFFER, Ludwig Georg, German physician, b. at Cassel, July 4, 1805; studied medicine at the Universities of Göttingen and Marburg; obtained the degree of M.D. 1825. Author of 'Enumeratio diagnostica Cactearum hucusque cognitarum,' Berlin, 1837; 'Monographia Heliceorum viventium,' Leipsic, 1847–48; 'Novitates Conchologicæ,' 1855; and other works on botany and natural history.

PFORDTEN, Ludwig Carl von der, Bavarian statesman, b. at Ried, on the Inn, Sept. 11, 1811; studied at Nürnberg and Heidelberg, and received the degree of LL.D.; professor of law at the University of Leipsic, 1843–47; minister of agriculture of Bavaria, 1848–49; minister of the Household and of foreign affairs, April 1849 to 1859; prime minister, 1866. Author of 'Abhandlungen aus dem Pandektenrechte,' Erlangen, 1840; and other legal works.

PHELPS, Samuel, English actor, b. at Devonport, 1806; apprenticed to a printer; made his first appearance on the stage at York, 1828; and in London at the Haymarket Theatre, in the character of 'Shylock,' 1829; manager of Sadler's Wells Theatre, London, 1844.

PHILIPPES, Charles Marie de Kerhullet, French naval writer, b. at Rennes, Sept. 17, 1809; entered the navy, 1825; lieutenant, 1837; captain, 1856. Author of 'Instructions pour remonter la Côte du Brésil depuis St. Luiz de Maranhâo jusqu'au Para,' Paris, 1841; 'Description de l'Archipel des Açores,' 1851–58; and numerous other works.

PHILIPPOTEAUX, Frédéric Emmanuel, French historical painter, b. at Paris, April 3, 1815; studied under M. Léon Cogniet. Exhibited 'La Retraite de Moscou,' 1835; 'Le Général Gourgaud sauvant la Vie à Napoléon,' 1848; 'Combat de Montebello,' 'Combat de Diernstein,' 1863; and numerous other, chiefly historical, paintings.

PHILIPS, Georg, German historical writer, b. at Königsberg, 1804; studied in Berlin and London; appointed professor of history and law at the University of Vienna, 1851. Author of 'Essay on the History of Anglo-Saxon Law,' Göttingen, 1825; 'History of England and of English Law since the Norman Conquest,' Berlin, 1827–28; 'History of Germany and German Law,' Munich, 1845; second edition, 1850; and other historical works.

PHILIPS, Robert Needham, English politician, b. 1815; educated at Rugby; a merchant and manufacturer, and J.P. and deputy-lieutenant of the county of Lancaster; elected M.P. for Bury, 1865.

PHILLIMORE, Sir Robert Joseph, English judge, b. 1810; educated at Christ Church, Oxford, where he graduated B.A. 1831; admitted at Doctors' Commons, 1839; called to the bar of the Middle Temple, 1841; chancellor of the dioceses of Oxford, Chichester, and Salisbury; advocate-general, and knighted, 1862; judge of the Court of Admiralty, and of the Court of Arches, 1866; was M.P. for Tavistock, 1853–57. Author of 'Commentaries on International Law;' and other works.

PHILLIPS, George Lort, English politician, b. 1811; educated at Harrow, and Trinity College, Cambridge; a magistrate and deputy-lieutenant of the county of Pembroke; M.P. for Pembrokeshire since 1861.

PHILLIPS, John, English geologist. b. Dec. 25, 1800; successively professor of geology in King's College, London, in Trinity College, Dublin, 1844, and at the University of Oxford since 1856. Author of 'A Treatise on Geology,' London, 1837; 'The Rivers, Mountains, and Sea-coasts of Yorkshire,' 1855; 'Three Years' Observations on Rain;' and numerous other works.

PHILLIPS, Sir Thomas, English antiquarian. b. 1792; educated at Rugby, and University College, Oxford; created a baronet, 1821; nominated one of the trustees of the British Museum, 1861.

PHILLIPS, Sir Thomas, English barrister, b. 1801; called to the bar of the Inner Temple, 1842; knighted, 1839; made a Q.C. Feb. 1865.

PICARD, Louis Joseph Ernest, French politician, b. at Paris, Dec. 24, 1821; called to the bar, 1844; elected member of the Corps Législatif for the fifth circonscription of the department of Seine, 1858.

PICCIONI, Vincent, French politician, b. at Pino, Corsica, Aug. 19, 1812; studied at the College of Sarrèze, and at the School of Law at Toulouse, and was called to the bar; elected member of the Corps Législatif for the third circonscription of the department of Haute Garonne, 1863.

PICCOLOMINI, Maria, Italian operatic singer, b. at Sienna, 1835; made her début in Florence in the character of 'Lucrezia Borgia,' 1852; appeared in London, 1856; sang in the principal cities of the United Kingdom, in Paris, and New York; married, and retired from the stage, 1861.

PICKERSGILL, Frederick Richard, English historical painter, b. in London, 1820; studied at the Royal Academy. Exhibited 'The Combat between Hercules and Achelous,' 1840; 'The Death of King Lear,' exhibited at Westminster Hall, 1843; the 'Burial of Harold,' 1847; and numerous other paintings. Elected A.R.A. 1847, and R.A. 1857.

PICKERSGILL, Henry William, English portrait painter, b. in London, 1781; exhibited at the Royal Academy from 1827–65; elected A.R.A. 1812, and R.A. 1827.

PIERCE, Franklin, American statesman, b. at Hillsborough, New Hampshire, Nov. 23, 1804; studied at Bowdoin College, Maine, and at Amherst; called to the bar, 1827; elected to Congress, 1833; member of the United States Senate, 1837; resigned, 1842; took part in the Mexican war, and made brigadier-general, 1847; president of the United States, 1853–57; appointed United States judge, 1863.

PIGOT, Right Hon. David Richard, Irish judge, b. 1805; called to the' Irish bar, 1826; solicitor-general for Ireland, 1839; attorney-general, 1840–41; chief baron of the Exchequer in Ireland, 1846; was M.P. for Clonmel, 1839–46; appointed one of the visitors of Maynooth College, 1845.

PIGOTT, Sir Gillery, English judge, b. 1813; called to the bar of the Middle Temple, 1839; serjeant-at-law, with patent of precedence, 1856; has been recorder of Hereford; M.P. for Reading, 1860–63; appointed judge in the Court of Exchequer, and knighted, 1863.

PILLET, Raymond François, French writer, b. at Paris, Dec. 6, 1803; studied at the Lycée Napoléon; French consul at Nice, 1849 to June 1860; consul at Palermo, 1861. Author of 'L'Obstiné, ou les Bretons,' 1837; 'De la Situation actuelle des Théâtres,' 1844; and other works.

PILS, Adrien Auguste, French painter, b. at Paris, July 19, 1813; studied under M. Picot, and at the École des Beaux Arts; appointed professor of painting at the École des Beaux Arts, 1863. Exhibited 'Le Christ prêchant dans la Barque de Simon,' 1846; 'Une Tranchée devant Sébastopol,' 1855; 'Bataille de l'Alma,' 1861; and numerous other, chiefly historical, paintings.

PIM, Bedford Capperton Trevylian, English naval officer, b. at Bideford, Devon, June 12, 1826; educated at the Royal Naval School; admitted in the Royal Navy, 1842; made a voyage round the world in H.M.S. *Herald*, 1845–51; engaged in the search for Sir John Franklin, and reached the *Investigator;* made a commander, 1858. Author of 'The Gate of the Pacific;' and various pamphlets.

PINE, Sir Benjamin Chilley Campbell, English colonial administrator, b. 1813; educated at Trinity College, Cambridge; called to the bar, 1841; Queen's advocate at Sierra Leone, 1848; lieutenant-governor of Natal, 1849–56; governor of the Gold Coast settlements, 1856–59; governor of Western Australia, 1860–69; appointed governor of Antigua, 1869. Author of articles in the *Encyclopædia Britannica* on African colonies.

PIORRY, Pierre Adolphe, French physician, b. at Poitiers, Dec. 31, 1794; studied medicine, and received the degree of M.D. 1816; appointed professor of Clinique Interne at the Hôtel-Dieu, 1864. Author of 'De l'Hérédité dans les Maladies,' 1840; 'Dieu, l'Ame, la Nature,' a poem, 1854; 'La Médecine du bon Sens,' 1864; and other works.

PIRE' DE ROSNYVINEN, Alexandre, Marquis de, French politician, b. at Rennes, July 12, 1809; member of the Corps Législatif for the department of Ile et Villaine since 1856.

PIROUX, Joseph, French administrator, b. at Hardigny, Vosges, Jan. 2, 1800; director of the institution for the Deaf and Dumb at Nancy. Author of 'Le Vocabulaire des Sourds-Muets,' Paris, 1830; and other works on the treatment of the deaf and dumb.

PIUS IX., sovereign pontiff of Rome, b. at Sinigaglia, May 13, 1792, the son of Count Mastai Ferretti; employed on a mission in Chili, 1823–25; bishop of Imola, Dec. 14, 1838; created cardinal, Dec. 24, 1839; elected sovereign pontiff as successor of Gregory XVI. June 16, 1846; crowned, June 21, 1846.

PLANAT, Oscar Abel, French politician, b. at Limoges, Haute-Vienne, May 14, 1826; studied law, and called to the bar at Paris, 1849; member of the Corps Législatif for the arrondissements of Cognac and Barbezieux since 1863.

PLANCHE', James Robinson, English author and dramatist, b. in London, Feb. 27, 1796. Author of 'Charles XII.' a drama, 1826; 'Lays and Legends of the Rhine,' 1826; 'Descent of the Danube,' 1827; 'History of British Costume,' 1834; 'Regal Records,' 1838; translator of the 'Fairy Tales' of the Countess d'Aulnoy, 1855; and other works.

PLANCY, Auguste, Baron de, French politician, b. at Paris, 1815; member of the Legislative Assembly, 1849; and member of the Corps Législatif for the department of Aube since 1862.

PLANCY, Charles, Vicomte de, French politician, b. at Paris, Jan. 4, 1809; brother of the preceding; member of the Legislative Assembly, 1849; and member of the Corps Législatif for the department of Oise since 1852.

PLATT, John, English politician, b. 1817 ; a magistrate of the county of Lancaster ; high sheriff of the county of Carnarvon, 1863 ; M.P. for Oldham since 1865.

PLAYFAIR, Lyon, English chemist and sanitary reformer, b. in Bengal, 1819 ; educated at St. Andrew's, North Britain, and at Giessen under Professor Liebig, 1838 ; professor of chemistry in the Royal Institution, 1843 ; special commissioner in charge of the department of juries in the Exhibition of 1851 ; and of the same department in the Exhibition of 1862 ; president of the Chemical Society, London, 1858 ; professor of chemistry at the University of Edinburgh, 1858 ; returned first M.P. for Edinburgh and St. Andrew's Universities, 1868.

PLOUVIER, E'douard, French dramatic writer, b. at Paris, Aug. 2, 1821. Author of 'Les Vengeurs,' 1851 ; 'Le Pays des Amours,' 1858 ; 'La Belle aux Cheveux bleus,' 1861 ; 'Le Comte de Saules,' 1864 ; and other dramas and romances.

PLUMPTRE, Charles John, English writer, b. 1818 ; called to the bar of Gray's Inn, 1844 ; lecturer on elocution to the University of Oxford. Author of ' Lectures on Elocution.'

POEZE, Olivier, Comte de la, French politician, b. June 25, 1821 ; honorary chamberlain to the Emperor ; member of the Corps Législatif for the department of Vendée since 1863.

POGGENDORF, Johann Christian, German physician, b. at Hamburg, Dec. 26, 1796 ; studied at the University of Berlin ; appointed professor of medicine at the same University, 1834. Author of 'A Treatise on Voltaic Electricity,' 1821 ; 'Biographical and Literary Dictionary of the History of the Exact Sciences, Chemistry, Mathematics, &c.' 1858 ; and other works.

POIRSON, Auguste Simon, French historical writer, b. in Paris, Aug. 20, 1795 ; studied at the École Normale ; professor of rhetoric at the College of Henri IV. and at the Collége. Charlemagne, 1837–53. Author of 'Histoire Romaine,' 1827–28 ; 'Histoire de Henri IV.' 1857 ; second edition, 1862 ; and other historical works.

POLAIN, Mathew Lambert, Belgian author, b. at Liége, June 27, 1808 ; obtained the degree of Ph.D. and was appointed professor of history in the University of Liége. Author of 'Le Massacre des Magistrats de Louvaine, 1379,' Liége, 1838 ; 'Henri de Dinant, Histoire de la Revolution communale de Liége,' ib. 1843 ; and other historical works.

POLLOCK, Sir Frederick, English judge, b. 1783 ; M.P. for Huntingdon, 1831–44 ; attorney-general, 1841–44 ; chief baron of the Exchequer, 1844–66.

POLLOCK, Sir George, English military commander, brother of the preceding, b. in London, 1786 ; entered the service of the East India Company, 1802 ; major, 1819 ; general, 1859 ; relieved Jellalabad, and captured Cabul, 1841 ; appointed honorary colonel 1st battalion Surrey Rifle Volunteers, 1861.

POLTIMORE, Augustus Frederick Bampfylde, Baron, English administrator, b. in London, April 12, 1837 ; educated at Harrow, and Christ Church, Oxford ; succeeded his father, first baron, Dec. 1858 ; a deputy-lieutenant of Devon, and captain of 1st Devon Yeomanry Cavalry.

POLWARTH, Henry Hepburn Scott, Baron, Scottish administrator, b. in 1800 ; lord-lieutenant of Selkirk, and deputy-lieutenant of the counties of Roxburgh and Berwick ; was a lord-in-waiting to the Queen from March to Dec. 1852, and from Feb. 1858 to June 1859.

POMFRET, George William Richard Fermor, Earl, English administrator, b. 1824 ; educated at Christ Church, Oxford ; deputy-lieutenant of Northamptonshire.

PONGERVILLE, Jean Baptiste Antoine Aime' Sanson de, French author, b. at Abbeville, May 3, 1792 ; appointed conservateur to the Bibliothèque Impériale, 1851. Author of 'Lucrèce,' a poem, 1823 ; 'Histoire de l'Invasion d'Édouard III. en France ;' and other works.

PONSARD, Francis, French dramatic author, b. at Vienne, Isère, June 1, 1814 ; studied at the college of his native town ; appointed librarian of the Senate, 1851 ; elected member of the French Academy, 1855. Translated Byron's 'Manfred' in verse, 1837. Author of 'Charlotte Corday,' 1850 ; 'La Bourse,' 1856 ; 'Ce qui plait aux Femmes,' July 1860 ; and other dramas and comedies.

PONSONBY, Hon. Ashley George, English politician, b. 1831 ; educated at Eton, and Trinity College, Cambridge ; a deputy-lieutenant and magistrate of Gloucestershire ; was captain in the Grenadier Guards, and served in the Crimean war ; M.P. for Cirencester, 1852–57, and 1859–65.

POOLE, Rev. George Ayliffe, English author, b. 1809; graduated at Emmanuel College, Cambridge, 1831; vicar of Welford, Northamptonshire, since 1843. Author of 'History of England from a Churchman's Point of View,' 1845; 'History of Ecclesiastical Architecture in England,' 1848; and other works.

POOLE, Paul Falconer, English painter, b. in Bristol, 1810. Exhibited 'The Well, a Scene at Naples,' 1830; 'The Emigrant's Departure,' 1838; 'The Visitation of Sion Monastery,' 1846; 'Edward III.'s Generosity to the People of Calais,' at Westminster Hall, 1847; 'The Goths in Italy,' 1850; and numerous other paintings. Elected A.R.A. 1846, R.A. 1861.

POPE, John, American military commander, b. at Kaskaskin, Illinois, March 1823; entered West Point, 1838, and graduated, 1842; lieutenant in the United States army, 1846; captain, 1847; appointed brigadier-general of volunteers at the outbreak of the civil war, 1861; major-general, 1862; brigadier-general United States army, July 1862; relieved from the command of the army of Virginia, Sept. 1862; subsequently employed in Minnesota and Alabama.

PORTAELS, Jean François, Belgian painter, b. at Vilvorde, Brabant, 1820; studied at the Academy of Brussels, and at Paris under Paul Delaroche; appointed director of the Academy of Gand, 1847. Painted 'Rébecca,' 'Ruth,' 'Jeune Juive de l'Asie Mineure,' 'Le Suicide de Judas,' the last two in the Paris Exhibition of 1855.

PORTARLINGTON, Henry Robert Reuben Dawson Damer, Earl, Irish administrator, b. 1822; succeeded his uncle, second earl, 1845; elected a representative peer of Ireland, 1855.

PORTER, David, American naval commander, b. in Pennsylvania, 1812; lieutenant, 1841; commander in the United States, 1861; appointed acting rear-admiral, Oct. 1862.

PORTMAN, Edward Berkeley Portman, Baron, English administrator, b.1797; lord-lieutenant of Somersetshire, and a member of the Councils of the Duchies of Cornwall and Lancaster; was M.P. for Dorsetshire and Marylebone, 1823–34.

PORTMAN, Hon. William Henry Berkeley, English politician, b. 1829, son of the preceding; educated at Eton, and Merton College, Oxford; a deputy-lieutenant of Somerset and Dorset, and colonel of West Somerset Yeomanry Cavalry; M.P. for Shaftesbury, 1852–57, and for Dorset since 1857.

PORTSMOUTH, Isaac Newton Wallop, Earl of, English administrator, b. Jan. 11, 1825; educated at Rugby and Cambridge; a deputy-lieutenant and magistrate of Devon, and a magistrate of Hants; was formerly in the 16th Lancers.

POSADA HERRERA, José de, Spanish statesman, b. at Llares, Oviedo, 1815; member of the Cortes, 1839–40; re-elected, 1853, and appointed vice-president; minister of the interior, 1858–63, and 1865–67.

POTTER, Cipriani, English composer, b. in London, 1792; studied music in Germany; principal of the Royal Academy of Music; composer of several symphonies, overtures, sonatas, and other musical pieces.

POTTER, Edmund, English politician, b. 1802; a manufacturer at Glossop and Manchester, and a magistrate and deputy-lieutenant of the county of Lancaster; M.P. for Carlisle since 1861.

POTTER, Thomas Bayley, English politician, b. 1817; educated at Rugby and the London University; a J.P. and deputy-lieutenant of Lancashire, and a magistrate of Manchester; M.P. for Rochdale since 1865.

POUILLET, Claude Servais Mathias, French physician, b. at Cuzance, Doubs, Feb. 16, 1791; professor of medicine at the Collége Bourbon, 1826; sub-director of the Conservatoire des Arts, 1829; and afterwards director of the same. Author of 'Éléments de Physique expérimentale et de Météorologie,' seventh edition 1856; and numerous scientific works.

POUJADE, Eugene, French diplomatist, b. at Ile de France, Jan. 15, 1815; French consul at Tarsus, 1843; consul at Malta, 1847; French consul-general at Rome, Aug. 1861. Author of 'Le Liban et la Syrie,' 1860; and other works.

POUJOULAT, Jean Joseph, French author, b. at Fare, Bouches du Rhône, Jan. 26, 1808; studied at Aix, and went to Paris, 1826; was member of the Constituent and Legislative Assemblies. Author of 'Histoire des Croisades,' 1840–48; 'Histoire de la Révolution française,' Tours, 1847; 'Examen de la Vie de Jésus de M. Renan,' 1863; and numerous other works.

POUYER-QUERTIER, Augustin Thomas, French politician, b. at Étouteville en Caux, Seine Inférieure; mayor of Fleury sur Audelle, 1854; member of the Corps Législatif for the first circonscription of Seine Inférieure since 1857.

POWELL, Francis Sharp, English politician, b. 1827; educated at St. John's College, Cambridge, where he graduated B.A. 1850, and M.A. 1853; called to the bar of the Inner Temple, 1853; J.P. for the West Riding of Yorkshire; M.P. for Wigan, 1857–59; and for Cambridge, 1863–68.

POWER, Sir James, Irish administrator, b. 1800; called to the Irish bar at Dublin; a J.P. and deputy-lieutenant of the county of Wexford; high sheriff of the city of Dublin, 1859; M.P. for the county of Wexford, 1835–47, and 1865–68.

POWERS, Hiram, American sculptor, b. at Woodstock, Vermont, July 29, 1805. Executed 'Eve,' 1838; the 'Greek Slave,' exhibited at the London Exhibition, 1851; 'The Young Fisherman;' a statue of Calhoun; busts of Webster, Jackson, Adams; and other works of art.

POWIS, Edward James Herbert, Earl, English administrator, b. 1818; high steward of the University of Cambridge; lieutenant-colonel of the South Salop Yeomanry, and a deputy-lieutenant of Shropshire and Montgomery; was M.P. for Montgomery as Lord Clive, 1843–48.

PRATI, Giovanni, Italian author, b. at Dascindo, Jan. 27, 1815; studied law at Padua; elected member of the Italian Parliament, 1862. Author of 'Edmenegarda,' Milan, 1841; 'Rodolfo,' 'La Battaglia d'Imera,' 'Satania e le Grazie,' 1855; 'Il Conte Riga,' 1856; 'Ariberto,' 1860; and other poems and ballads.

PRATT, John Tidd, English jurist and legal writer, b. 1798; called to the bar of the Inner Temple, 1824; registrar of Friendly Societies in England, and barrister appointed to certify the rules of Savings' Banks. Author of 'A Collection of the Public General Statutes;' 'The Laws of Highways;' and other legal works.

PRÉAULT, Antoine Augustin, French sculptor, b. at Paris, Oct. 8, 1809. Exhibited 'La Famine,' and 'Gilbert mourant à l'Hôpital,' 1833; 'La Rivière des Amazones' and 'La Reine de Saba,' two large bas-reliefs, 1835; 'Charlemagne,' a colossal statue, 1836; 'Sainte Catherine,' for the church of St. Louis, 1863; and other statues.

PRÉMARAY, Jules Martial Regnault, French author, b. at Pont d'Armes, Loire Inférieure, June 11, 1819. Author of 'Les Cendres de Napoléon,' 1840; 'Une Femme laide,' 1846; 'Donnez aux Pauvres,' 1854; 'La Jeunesse de Grammont,' 1862; and other odes, couplets, and dramatic pieces.

PRESCOTT, Admiral Sir Henry, English naval commander, b. 1783; entered the Royal Navy, 1799; governor and commander-in-chief of Newfoundland, 1834–41; admiral-superintendent of Portsmouth dockyard, 1847–52; admiral of the blue, 1860.

PRÉVOST-PARADOL, Lucien Anatole, French author, b. at Paris, Aug. 8, 1829; studied at the Collège Bourbon, and the École Normale; elected member of the French Academy, 1865. Author of 'Revue de l'Histoire universelle,' 1854; 'Les Anciens Partis,' 1860; 'Études sur les Moralistes françaises,' 1864; and other works.

PRICE, Rev. Bartholomew, English mathematician, b. 1818; educated at Pembroke College, Oxford, where he graduated B.A. 1840, and M.A.; appointed Sedleian professor of natural philosophy at Oxford, 1853: a curator of the Bodleian library and a delegate of the University press. Author of a work on the 'Infinitesimal Calculus,' 1854–58.

PRICE, William Philip, English politician, b. 1817; a J.P. and deputy-lieutenant of the county of Gloucester; was high sheriff, 1849; M.P. for Gloucester, 1852–59, and since 1865.

PRIM, Juan, Comte de Reus, Spanish military commander, b. at Reus, Catalonia, Dec. 6, 1814; took part in the civil war of 1833, and was made colonel, 1837; exiled to France, 1842; deputy to the Cortes for the city of Barcelona, 1843; governor of Madrid, 1844; joined the Ottoman army on the Danube, 1853; represented Barcelona in the Cortes, 1855; lieutenant-general in the Spanish army, 1856; commander-in-chief of the Spanish expedition against Mexico, 1861; exiled, 1866; minister of war, and one of the heads of the Provisional Government of Spain, Sept. 1868.

PRINSEP, Henry Thoby, English writer, b. 1792; educated at Haileybury, and entered the Bengal Civil Service; elected one of the directors of the East India Company, 1849; nominated one of her Majesty's Council for India, 1858. Author of 'A History of the Administration of the Marquis of Hastings;' 'Historical Results from Discoveries in Affghanistan;' and other works on India.

PRIOR, Sir James, English author, b. at Lisburn, Ireland, 1790; entered the medical service of the navy, and served in the East Indies; appointed deputy-inspector of hospitals, 1843; knighted, 1858. Author of 'A Voyage in the Indian Ocean,' several biographies, volumes of poems, and pamphlets.

PRITCHARD, Rev. Charles, English astronomer, b. 1808 ; educated at St. John's College, Cambridge, where he graduated B.A. 1830. Author of ' A Treatise on Statical Couples ;' ' On the Figure of the Earth ;' ' Paper on the Improved Method of using Mercury ;' and papers in the Transactions of the Royal Astronomical Society.

PRITCHARD, John, English politician, b. 1816 ; called to the bar, 1841 ; a banker in the city of London, and deputy-lieutenant of the county of Salop ; M.P. for Bridge-north, 1853–68.

PROBY, Granville Leveson, Lord, English politician, b. 1825 ; formerly captain in the 74th Foot ; a magistrate and deputy-lieutenant of Wicklow ; comptroller of the Household, 1859 ; M.P. for the county of Wicklow, 1858–68.

PROCTER, Bryan Waller, English author, b. 1790 ; educated at Harrow School ; was a commissioner of lunacy till 1861. Author, under the pseudonym of ' Barry Corn-wall,' of ' Mirandola,' a tragedy, 1821 ; ' Marcian Colonna ;' ' The Flood of Thessaly ;' and numerous other poetical and dramatic works.

PROKESCH-OSTEN, Anton, Baron von, Austrian diplomatist, b. at Gratz in Styria, Dec. 10, 1795 ; entered the Austrian army, 1813 ; and the diplomatic service, 1822 ; Austrian ambassador to the court of Athens, 1834–49 ; ambassador at the court of Berlin, 1849–52 ; at the city of Frankfort, 1853 ; and at Constantinople, 1857. Author of ' Erinnerungen aus Ægypten und Kleinasien,' Vienna, 1829–31 ; and other works.

PROTET, Auguste Le'opold, French naval commander, b. Feb. 20, 1808 ; educated at the Naval School of Angoulême, 1824–27 ; rear-admiral, and charged with the command of the French naval expedition to China and Japan, 1851 ; wounded in the action of Na-Kio, May 17, 1862 ; vice-admiral, 1867.

PRYSE, Edward Lewis, English politician, b. 1817 ; lord-lieutenant of Cardigan-shire ; formerly captain in the 1st Dragoon Guards ; M.P. for Cardigan, 1857–68.

PUGH, David, English politician, b. 1806 ; educated at Rugby, and Balliol College, Oxford ; called to the bar of the Inner Temple, 1837 ; a J.P. of the county of Carmarthen, and a deputy-lieutenant of the county of Cardigan ; M.P. for Carmarthen, 1857–68.

PUGIN, Edward Welby, English architect, b. March 11, 1834. Designed the church of Notre Dame de Dadezell, in Belgium ; the new College of St. Cuthbert, Ushaw ; St. Michael's Priory, Belmont, Herefordshire ; the church of St. Peter and St. Paul at Cork ; and a great number of other ecclesiastical edifices in England and on the con-tinent of Europe.

PULSZKY, Ferencz Aurel, Hungarian author and politician, b. at Eperies, county of Sáros, Sept. 17, 1814 ; studied law and theology in Germany and Italy ; elected to represent the county of Sáros in the Hungarian Diet, 1840 ; under-secretary for foreign affairs at Pesth, 1848. Author of ' White, Red, and Black,' 1852 ; ' Tales and Traditions of Hungary,' 1854 ; and other works.

PUNSHON, Rev. William Morley, English writer, b. at Doncaster, 1823 ; was ' local preacher' to the Wesleyan Methodists in Sunderland, 1840 ; appointed to the ministry of Whitehaven, Cumberland, 1845 ; removed to London, 1858, to Canada, 1868. Published lectures on ' John Bunyan ;' the ' Huguenots ;' a volume of poems ; and numerous sermons.

PUSEY, Rev. Edward Bouverie, English divine, b. 1800 ; educated at Christ Church, Oxford, where he graduated B.A. ; elected fellow of Oriel College, where he graduated M.A. ; appointed regius-professor of Hebrew in the University of Oxford, and canon of Christ Church, 1828 ; suspended from preaching before the University, 1843. Published numerous sermons ; contributed to ' Tracts of the Times ;' one of the working editors of the Oxford ' Library of the Fathers.' Author of ' Daniel the Prophet,' 1864 ; ' The Church of England, an Eirenicon,' 1865.

PYAT, Felix, French political writer, b. at Vierzon, Oct. 4, 1810 ; studied law at Paris, and called to the bar, 1831. Author of ' Le Chiffonier de Paris,' 1847 ; ' Diogène,' 1846 ; ' Le Droit du Travail,' 1848 ; ' The Letter of the Jersey Exiles to the Queen of England,' 1855 ; and other political works, as well as several dramas.

PYCROFT, Rev. James, English author, b. 1813 ; educated at Trinity College, Oxford, where he graduated B.A. 1836 ; incumbent of St. Mary's, Barnstaple, 1845–56. Author of ' Twenty Years in the Church ;' ' Elkerton Rectory ;' 'Agony Point ;' ' How and What to Study ;' and other works.

PYE, John, English engraver, b. at Birmingham, 1782. Engraved the ' Temple of Jupiter,' after Turner, and numerous other works. Author of ' Patronage of British Art,' 1845.

PYNE, James, English landscape painter, b. at Bristol, Dec. 5, 1800; vice-president of the Society of British Artists. Painted 'Lake Derwentwater;' 'Eton College;' 'View of Heidelberg,' exhibited at the Paris Exhibition of 1855; and other landscapes.

PYNE, Louisa, English operatic singer, b. 1832; studied under Sir George Smart, and made her début, 1842; sang at Paris, 1847; made her first appearance on the stage, 1849; sang at the Royal Italian Opera, 1851; joint lessee, with Mr. Harrison, of Covent Garden Theatre, 1858–66.

Q.

QUATREFAGES DE BRE'AN, Jean Louis Armand de, French naturalist, b. at Berthezeme, Gard, Feb. 10, 1810; studied at Strasburg, where he graduated M.D.; professor of natural history at the Lycée Napoléon, 1850; professor of anatomy and ethnology in the Museum of Natural History, Paris, 1855. Author of 'Recherches sur le Système nerveux, l'Embryogénie, les Organes des Sens et la Circulation des Annélides,' 1844–45; and other works.

QUEBEC, Right Rev. James William, Bishop of, English divine, b. in Hampshire, 1825; educated at Pembroke College, Oxford, where he graduated B.A. 1851, M.A. and D.D., and was ordained; was consecrated fourth bishop of Quebec, Canada, 1863.

QUECQ, Jacques Edouard, French painter, b. at Cambrai, 1796. Exhibited 'Les premiers Combats de Romulus et de Rémus,' 1828; 'Martyrs Chrétiens,' 1845; 'Première Chute de Jésus-Christ sous la Croix,' 1861; and other paintings.

QUESTEL, Charles Auguste, French architect, b. at Paris, Sept. 18, 1807; studied at the École des Beaux Arts, 1823–28; designed the church of St. Paul at Nimes, commenced 1838, finished 1849; and the large fountain of the esplanade in the same town, inaugurated 1851; appointed professor at the École des Beaux Arts, 1856.

QUETELET, Jules, Belgian statistician, b. 1796; secretary to the Royal Academy of Belgium. Author and compiler of a great number of statistical treatises.

QUINEMONT, Arthur, Marquis de, French politician, b. Aug. 18, 1808; formerly colonel in the National Guard of Tours; member of the General Council for the canton of Ile Bouchard; member of the Corps Législatif for the department of Indre et Loire, 1863.

QUINET, Edgar, French author, b. at Bourg, Ain, Feb. 17, 1803; studied in France, and at the University of Heidelberg; professor of foreign literature to the faculty in Lyons, 1839–42; professor of language and literature of Southern Europe in the College of France, 1842–46; member of the Constituent and Legislative Assemblies, 1848–52. Author of numerous dramatic and political works issued in 'Œuvres Complètes,' 10 vols. 1856–59.

QUINETTE DE ROCHEMONT, Baron, French politician, b. at Amiens, Sept. 7, 1802; mayor of Soissons, 1832; minister-plenipotentiary to Belgium, 1848–51; nominated councillor of state, 1854.

R.

RABAN, Louis François, French novelist, b. at Damville, Eure, Dec. 14, 1795. Author of 'Le petit Jésuite,' 1826; 'Le Valet du Diable;' 'Plus de Fraudes! les Falsificateurs dévoilés,' 1859; and other romances. •

RABOU, Charles Felix Henri, French author, b. at Paris, Sept. 6, 1803; studied at the College of Henri IV., and law at Dijon. Author of 'L'Histoire de tout le Monde,' 1829; 'Les Tribulations et Métamorphoses posthumes de Maitre Fabricius, Peintre liegeois,' 1860; and other works. One of the founders of the *Revue de Paris.*

RAGG, Rev. Thomas, English theological writer, b. at Nottingham, 1808; entered holy orders, 1858; appointed curate of Malins Lee, 1860. Author of 'Deity,' a poem, 1834; 'Heber,' 'Lays from the Prophets,' 1841; 'Man's Dreams and God's Realities,' 1858.

RAGLAN, Richard Henry Fitz-Roy Somerset, Baron, English administrator, b. 1817; was in the Ceylon Civil Service, and private secretary to the late King of Hanover; a lord-in-waiting to the Queen, 1858; succeeded his father, first baron, 1855.

RAMBOURGT, Amand Ambroise Charles, Vicomte de, French politician, b. at Ervy, Aube, Oct. 25, 1819; took the degree of LL.D., and became assistant-judge and secretary-general to the prefecture of the Aube; member of the Corps Législatif for the department of Aube since 1852.

RAMÉE, Daniel, French architect, b. at Hamburg, May 16, 1806; restored the cathedrals of Noyen, Senlis, and Beauvais. Author of 'Sculptures décoratives, Motifs d'Ornamentation, &c. du XIIe au XVIe Siècle,' 1864; translator of numerous works on architecture from the English and German.

RAMSAY, Very Rev. Edward Bannerman, English divine, b. 1793; educated at St. John's College, Cambridge, and graduated B.A. 1815, M.A. 1831; LL.D. from Edinburgh, 1859; appointed dean of St. John's, Edinburgh, 1841. Author of 'Reminiscences of Scottish Life and Character,' 1857.

RANDON, Jacques Ce'sar Alexandre, Comte, French military commander, b. at Grenoble, March 25, 1795; captain, 1813; colonel, 1838; created senator, 1852; nominated marshal of France, March 1856.

RANELAGH, Thomas Heron Jones, Viscount, English administrator, b. 1812; succeeded his father, sixth viscount, 1820; served under Don Carlos in the Spanish civil war, 1835–37; a magistrate of Middlesex and Norfolk.

RANGABE, Alexander Rizo, Greek statesman and poet, b. at Constantinople, 1810; sub-lieutenant in the service of Bavaria, 1829–30; professor of archæology at the University of Athens, 1844–56; minister of the Royal Household, 1856–58. Author of 'Poésies diverses,' Athens, 1837–40; and other works.

RANK, Joseph, German novelist, b. at Friedrichstal, Bohemia, July 10, 1815; studied law at the University of Vienna. Author of 'Aus dem Böhmerwalde,' Leipsic, 1851; 'Die Freunde,' Prague, 1854; 'Geschichten armer Leute,' Stuttgardt, 1853; and other novels.

RANKE, Leopold, German historical writer, b. at Wiehe, Thuringia, Dec. 21, 1795; appointed professor of history in the University of Berlin, 1825; and historiographer of the Prussian State, 1841. Author of 'The History of the Roman and Germanic Peoples, from 1494 to 1535,' 1824; 'German History in the Times of the Reformation,' 1839–43; 'History of the Popes;' and other works.

RANKINE, William John Macquorn, English civil engineer, b. 1805; educated at the University of Edinburgh; was professor of mechanics and civil engineering in the University of Glasgow, and first president of the Institution of Civil Engineers in Scotland. Author of 'Civil Engineering,' 1862; and other works.

RASPAIL, François Vincent, French chemist and politician, b. at Carpentras, Vaucluse, Jan. 29, 1794; studied medicine at Avignon; member of the Constituent Assembly, 1848. Author of 'Réforme pénitentiaire,' 1839; 'Manuel de la Santé,' 1846–64; and other scientific and political works.

RASTOUL, DE MONGEOT, Alphonse Simon, French historical writer, b. at Avignon, Sept. 12, 1800; appointed professor of history at the College of Avignon, 1831. Author of 'Histoire de la Nation française,' 1832–34; 'Histoire de Hollande,' Liége, 1850; 'Vienne et Bruxelles,' ib. 1854; and other works.

RATAZZI, Urbano, Italian statesman, b. at Alessandria, June 29, 1808; studied at a Government school, and was called to the Turin bar; member of the Chamber of Deputies of Turin, 1848; president of the Chamber, and minister of justice, 1852; appointed president of the cabinet, and minister of foreign affairs, March 1862; resigned, Dec. 1, 1862; again called to power, April 1867, and again resigned in October.

RAU, Karl Heinrich, German political economist, b. at Erlangen, Nov. 23, 1792; professor of political economy at the University of Heidelberg, 1822; member of the First Baden Chamber, 1837–40. Author of 'Treatise on Political Economy,' Heidelberg, 1826–37; and numerous other works, chiefly on political economy.

RAUMER, Friedrich Ludwig Georg von, German historian, b. 1781. Author of 'Geschichte der Hohenstaufen,' Leipsic, 1823; 'Geschichte Europas seit dem Ende des XVter Jahrhunderts,' 1832–58; and many other works.

RAVAISSON, Jean Gaspard Felix, French bibliographer, b. at Namur, Oct. 23, 1813; studied at the Collége Rollin; appointed professor of philosophy to the Faculty of Letters at Rennes, 1838–40; elected member of the French Academy, 1849. Author of 'Catalogue général des Bibliothèques publiques,' 1849.

RAVENSWORTH, Henry Thomas Liddell, Baron, English administrator, b. 1797; was M.P. for Northumberland, 1822–30; for North Durham, 1837–47; and for Liverpool, 1853–55; succeeded his father, first baron, March 7, 1855; a deputy-lieutenant of Northumberland and Durham.

RAVINEL, Henri Felix Dieudonne', Baron de, French politician, b. at Nossoncourt, Vosges, April 16, 1806; member of the Corps Législatif for the département des Vosges since 1857.

RAWLINSON, Sir Christopher, English colonial judge, b. 1806; educated at Trinity College, Cambridge; called to the bar of the Middle Temple, 1831; recorder of Portsmouth, 1840; recorder of Prince of Wales's Island, Singapore, and Malacca, and knighted, 1847; chief-justice of Madras, 1850–59.

RAWLINSON, Rev. George, English author, b. 1815; entered Trinity College, Oxford, 1835; fellow of Exeter College, 1840; Camden professor of Ancient History in the University of Oxford, 1861. Author, with Sir G. Wilkinson, of 'History of Herodotus,' 1858–60; 'The Five Great Monarchies of the Ancient and Eastern World,' 1862 and 1864; and several volumes of sermons and lectures.

RAWLINSON, Sir Henry Creswicke, English military commander and diplomatist, b. 1810; entered the Indian military service, 1827; and retired lieutenant-colonel of the Bombay army, with rank of major-general; crown-director of the East India Company, 1856; member of the Council for India, 1858; envoy-extraordinary and minister-plenipotentiary to Persia, 1859; M.P. for Reigate, 1858–59; and for Frome, 1865–68.

READ, Clare Sewell, English politician, b. 1826; a magistrate of Norfolk; elected M.P. for East Norfolk, 1865 and 1869.

READ, Thomas Buchanan, American poet and painter, b. in the county of Chester, Pennsylvania, March 12, 1822. Author of 'Lays and Ballads,' Philadelphia, 1848; 'The New Pastoral,' ib. 1855; 'The House by the Sea,' 1856; and other poems.

READE, Charles, English novelist and dramatist, b. 1814; educated at Magdalen College, Oxford, where he graduated B.A. 1835; called to the bar of Lincoln's Inn, 1843. Author of 'Never Too Late to Mend,' 1856; 'Love me little, Love me long;' 'Masks and Faces;' 'Hard Cash;' and other novels and dramatic works.

READE, John Edmund, English author, b. at Broadwell, Gloucestershire, 1806. Author of 'Cain the Wanderer,' 1830; 'Italy,' 1838; 'The Vision of the Ancient Kings,' about 1841; 'Man in Paradise,' 1856; 'The Laureate Wreath,' 1863; and other works.

REBELLE DA SILVA, Luiz Augusto, Portuguese historian, b. April 2, 1822; elected member of the Portuguese Parliament, 1848; secretary to the Council of State, 1849; member of the Academy of Sciences of Lisbon, 1853; member of the Council of Public Instruction, 1859; charged by the Government to write a History of Portugal of the Seventeenth and Eighteenth Centuries, 1861.

REBER, Napoleon Henri, French musical composer, b. at Mulhouse, Oct. 21, 1807; studied at the Paris Conservatoire; appointed professor of composition in the Conservatoire, 1862; elected member of the Académie des Beaux Arts, 1853. Composed 'La Nuit de Noël,' 1848; 'Les Dames Capitaines,' 1857; and other operas.

RECHBERG, Johann Bernhard, Count von, Austrian statesman, b. Aug. 17, 1806; educated for the diplomatic career; minister-plenipotentiary from Austria to the Germanic Confederation, and president of the Federal Diet at Frankfort, 1849–55; minister of foreign affairs, 1859–64.

REDDING, Cyrus, English author, b. at Penrhyn, Feb. 2, 1785; commenced writing for the press, in 1806, under Fox. Edited six newspapers in England, and one in France. Author of forty volumes in general literature, besides pamphlets.

REDESDALE, John Thomas Freeman Mitford, Baron, English statesman, b. 1805; studied at the University of Oxford; succeeded his father, first baron, 1830; chairman of the House of Lord's Committees since 1851.

REDGRAVE, Richard, English painter, b. in Pimlico, April 30, 1804; admitted as student in the Royal Academy, 1826. Exhibited 'Gulliver on the Farmer's Table,' 1837; 'Fashion's Slaves,' 1847; 'The Flight into Egypt,' 1851; and numerous other paintings. Elected A.R.A. 1840, R.A. 1851. Inspector-general of Art Schools.

REDWITZ SCHMELTZ, Oscar, Baron von, German author, b. at Lichtenau, near Anspach, June 28, 1823; studied philosophy and jurisprudence at the University of Munich. Author of 'Amaranth,' Mayence, 1849; 'Gedichte,' ib. 1852; 'Der Doge von Venedig,' Munich, 1861; and other poetical works.

REEVE, Henry, English author, b. 1815; registrar in the Privy Council Office; editor of the *Edinburgh Review* since 1855; translator of De Tocqueville's 'Democracy in America,' and of the same author's 'France before the Revolution of 1789.'

REEVES, Sims, English singer, b. at Woolwich, 1821; studied under J. B. Cramer and T. Cooke Hobbs; made his début on the stage at Newcastle, 1839; at Drury Lane Theatre, 1847; and subsequently appeared in concerts in the principal cities of England.

REGNAUD DE SAINT JEAN D'ANGELY, Auguste Michel Marie E'tienne, Comte, French military commander, b. in Paris, July 29, 1794; entered the Military School of St. Germain, 1811; sub-lieutenant, 1812; chef d'escadron at the battle of Waterloo; colonel, 1832; general of division, 1848; created senator, 1852; marshal of France, 1859; vice-president of the Senate and colonel of the Imperial Guard, 1862.

REGNAULT, E'lias Georges Soulange Oliva, French statesman and author, b. in London, April 22, 1801; studied law in Paris; admitted to the bar of the Royal Court, Paris; was minister of the interior, 1848. Author of 'La Presse et le Parlement,' 1838; 'Histoire du Gouvernement provisoire,' 1849; 'La Question européenne,' 1863; and other political and historical works.

REGNAULT, Henri Victor, French physician, b. at Aix-la-Chapelle, July 21, 1810; studied in the École Polytechnique, 1830–32; appointed engineer-in-chief of mines, 1847; director of the porcelain manufactory of Sèvres, 1854; professor of physics in the College of France, and of chemistry at the École Polytechnique, 1840; elected member of the French Academy, 1840. Author of 'Cours élémentaire de Chimie;' and several papers in the 'Mémoires de l'Académie des Sciences.'

REGNIER, Jacques Auguste Adolphe, French philologist, b. at Mayence, July 7, 1804; professor of Latin in the College of France, 1838; precentor to the Comte de Paris, 1843; elected member of the French Academy, March 9, 1855. Author of 'Studies on the Idiom of the Vedas, and the Origin of the Sanskrit Language,' 1855; and other philological works.

REICHENBACH, Heinrich Ludwig, German naturalist, b. at Leipsic, Jan. 8, 1793; studied at the University of his native town, where he graduated Ph.D. 1815, M.D. 1817; appointed professor of natural history at the Academy of Dresden, 1820; director of the Dresden Museum of Natural History. Author of 'Flora Germanica' and 'Iconographia Botanica,' Leipsic, 1823–54, in seventeen vols.; and other works on botany and natural history.

REID, Mayne, English novelist, b. in Ireland, 1818; captain in the army of the United States, 1845; was present at the siege of Vera Cruz, and resigned his commission at the close of the Mexican war. Author of 'The Desert Home,' 1851; 'The Bush Boys,' 1855; 'The Quadrupeds,' 1860; 'The Hunter's Feast,' 1861; 'The Maroon,' 1862; and numerous other works of fiction.

REIFFENBERG, Fre'deric Guillaume, Baron de, Belgian author, b. at Louvain, Aug. 28, 1830. Author of 'Juvenilia, Choix de Poésies,' Brussels, 1848; 'Les Femmes qu'on aime,' 1859; 'La Vie de Garnison,' 1863; 'Le Testament du Czar,' Brussels and Paris, 1848–64; and other novels and dramas.

REILLE, Gustave Charles, French politician, b. at Paris, Dec. 1, 1818; studied at the École Polytechnique, 1836–38; ensign in the navy, 1840; retired with the rank of captain, 1853; member of the Corps Législatif for the department of Eure et Loire since 1853.

REINAUD, Joseph Toussaint, French philologist, b. at Lambesc, Bouches du Rhône, Dec. 4, 1795; studied philology under Silvestre de Sacy, at Paris; appointed to the manuscript department of the Bibliothèque Royale, 1824; keeper of Oriental manuscripts, 1833, and head-keeper, 1855; elected member of the French Academy, 1832. Author of 'Notice sur Mahomet,' 1860; and numerous works on the history, geography, and languages of the East.

REINICK, Robert, German painter and author, b. at Dantzic, Feb. 22, 1807; studied at Berlin under Begas, and at Düsseldorf. Author of 'Liederbuch für deutsche Künstler,' Berlin, 1833; 'Gedichte,' ib. 1844; and other works.

REINSBERG, Ida von Duringsfeld, Baroness von, German authoress, b. at Militsch, Silesia, Nov. 12, 1815; married to Baron von Reinsberg, 1845. Author of 'Gedichte,' Leipsic, 1835; 'Margarethe von Valois und ihre Zeit,' ib. 1847; 'Niko Veliki,' Brussels, 1856; and other works.

REMILLY, Ovide, French politician, b. at Versailles, Nov. 18, 1800; studied law in his native town, and was called to the bar; mayor of Versailles, 1837; member of the Chamber of Deputies, 1839–48; member of the Legislative Assembly, 1849–51.

RE'MUSAT, Charles François, Comte de, French statesman, b. at Paris, March 14, 1797; studied law in Paris, and was called to the bar; deputy for Toulouse, 1830; under-secretary to the minister of the interior, 1836; minister of the interior, 1840; member of the Constituent and Legislative Assemblies, 1848–51; retired from public life after the coup d'état of Dec. 1851; elected member of the French Academy, 1846. Author of 'Essais de Philosophie,' 1842; 'De la Théologie naturelle en France et en Angleterre,' 1864; and numerous other works.

RE'MY, Jules, French naturalist, b. at Châlons-sur-Marne, Sept. 2, 1826; assistant-professor of natural history at the Collége Rollin, 1848–50. Author of 'Monografia de las Comquestas de Chile,' Paris, 1849; 'Voyage au Pays des Mormons,' ib. 1860; and other works of travel.

RENAN, Joseph Ernest, French philologist, b. at Trégnier, Côtes du Nord, Feb. 27, 1823; studied philosophy and theology at the Seminary of St. Sulpice; elected member of the French Academy, 1856. Author of 'Histoire générale et Systèmes comparés des Langues sémitiques,' 1845; second edition, 1858; 'Vie de Jésus,' 1863; 'Mission de Phénicie,' 1864; and other works.

RENAULT, Pierre Hippolyte, French military commander, b. Jan. 20, 1807; studied in the Military School of St. Cyr, and captain in the army, 1835; general· of division, July 1851; created senator, Aug. 1859.

RENDU, Euge'ne, French author, b. at Paris, Jan. 10, 1824. Author of 'De l'Instruction primaire en Angleterre dans ses Rapports avec l'Etat social,' 1852; 'La Souveraineté pontificale et l'Italie,' 1862; and numerous other works.

RENIER, Charles Alphonse Le'on, French archæologist, b. at Charleville. Ardennes, May 2, 1809; professor at the College of France, 1861; elected member of the Academy, 1856. Author of 'Mélanges d'Epigraphie,' 1854; and several papers on archæology.

RENNIE, Sir John, English civil engineer, b. 1796; builder of New London Bridge, after the designs of his father; superintendent of the drainage of the Lincolnshire coast at the Wash; designed the harbour at Ramsgate, the new docks at Whitehaven, and numerous other works; knighted, 1831.

REPTON, George William John, English politician, b. 1818; educated at University College, Oxford; was M.P. for St. Alban's, 1841–52; and for Warwick, 1852–68.

REUMONT, Alfred von, German author, b. at Aix-la-Chapelle, Prussia, Aug. 15, 1808; studied at Bonn and Heidelberg, and entered the diplomatic service; was sent to Florence, 1829, to Rome and London, 1836 to 1843; Prussian chargé d'affaires at the court of Tuscany, 1848. Author of 'Römische Briefe von einem Florentiner,' Leipsic, 1840–44; 'Ganganelli, seine Briefe und seine Zeit,' Berlin, 1847; and other historical works.

REUTERDAHL, Heinrik, Swedish theologian, b. at Malmoë, Sept. 10, 1795; studied at the University of Lund, and obtained the degree of D.D. 1830; keeper of the library of Lund, 1838; minister of public instruction, 1842; professor of theology at Lund, 1844. Author of 'History of the Swedish Church,' 1838; and other works.

RE'VEIL, Jacques, E'douard, French politician, b. 1797; mayor of Lyons, 1848; member of the Corps Législatif for the Rhône, 1852–57; appointed senator, 1863.

RE'VOIL, Be'ne'dict Henri, French author, b. at Aix, Bouches du Rhône, Dec. 16, 1816. Author of 'Histoire et Recherches succinctes sur l'Origine des Ports d'Armes,' 1839; 'Le Roi d'Oude, Mœurs de l'Inde,' 1857; and other works.

REYBAUD, Marie Roch Louis, French author, b. at Marseilles, Aug. 15, 1799; studied at the College of Juilly. Author of 'Histoire scientifique et militaire de l'Expedition française en Égypte,' 1830; 'Scènes de la Vie moderne,' 1855; 'Économistes modernes,' 1862; and other works.

REYNAUD, Aime Felix Sainte Elme, French naval commander, b. at Lyons, Sept. 16, 1808; lieutenant in the navy, 1840; captain, 1845; rear-admiral, 1850; appointed commander-in-chief of the naval station of the Antilles and Gulf of Mexico, 1861.

REYNOLDS, Rev. James, English philologist, b. 1803; educated at St. Catherine's Hall, Cambridge, where he graduated, 1826; incumbent of St. Mary's, Great Ilford, Essex. Published 'History of Jerusalem,' translated from the Arabic, 1837; 'Kitab-i-Yamini,' translated from the Persian, 1859. Secretary of the Oriental Translation Fund.

RHALLIS, George Alexander, Greek statesman, b. at Constantinople, April 30, 1804; studied in Paris, at the College of Henri IV.; appointed rector of the University of Athens, 1838; minister of justice, 1841, and again 1848; president of the Areopagus at Athens. Author of several legal works.

RICASOLI, Bettino, Baron, Italian statesman, b. in Tuscany, March 9, 1809; educated in Florence; minister of the interior of Tuscany, May 8, 1859; dictator of Tuscany, Aug 1, 1859; prime minister of Italy, June 7, 1861, to March 2, 1862; again premier from May 1866 to Oct. 1867.

RICCIARDI, Giuseppe Napoleone, Italian author, b. at Naples, July 19, 1808; elected deputy to the Italian Parliament. Author of 'Drammi Storici,' Paris, 1855; 'Martirologio italiano del 1792 à 1847,' Turin, 1856; and other poetical works.

RICHARD, Maurice, French politician, b. at Paris, Oct. 26, 1832; studied law, and became an advocate at the Imperial Court of Paris; member of the Corps Législatif for the department of Seine et Oise, 1863.

RICHARDS, Alfred Bate, English author, b. 1820. Author of 'Crœsus, King of Lydia;' 'Cromwell;' 'Poems, Essays, and Opinions;' and other dramas and poetical pieces.

RICHARDS, Brinley, English musical composer, b. 1819; studied at the Royal Academy of Music, to which he was appointed professor; composed 'The Pilgrim's Path;' 'The Harp of Wales;' 'The Angel's Song;' 'The Birds and the Rivulet;' and numerous other musical pieces.

RICHARDS, Right Hon. John, Irish judge, b. in Dublin, 1790; educated at Trinity College, Dublin; called to the Irish bar, 1811; was judge of the Supreme Court at Madras; solicitor-general for Ireland, 1835; attorney-general, 1836; baron of the Exchequer in Ireland, 1837; appointed chief commissioner for Ireland, 1849; returned to the Court of Exchequer, 1856.

RICHE, Jules, French politician, b. 1814; an advocate at Charleville; was member of the Legislative Assembly for the department of Ardennes, 1849; member of the Corps Législatif for the same department since 1852; entered the Council of State, 1860.

RICHEMONT, Louis Lemercier, Vicomte de, French politician, b. at Guadeloupe, Jan. 1, 1805; studied in the School of St. Cyr, and officer of cavalry; member of the Chamber of Deputies, 1835; and of the Corps Législatif for the department of Lot et Garonne since 1852.

RICHEMONT, Paul des Bassyns, Baron de, French politician, b. at Suresues, Seine, Oct. 29, 1809; member of the Corps Législatif for the arrondissement of Loches, 1852–59; created a senator, 1859; appointed governor of the Commercial and Industrial Company of Madagascar, 1863.

RICHMOND, Charles Henry Gordon Lennox, Duke of, b. Feb. 27, 1818, the eldest son of the fifth Duke of Richmond; educated at Westminster, and Christ Church, Oxford; lieutenant and captain in the Royal Horse Guards, and aide-de-camp to the commander-in-chief of the army, 1842–48; M.P. for West Sussex, 1841–60; succeeded to the dukedom, Oct. 1860; president of the Poor Law Board, March to June 1859; president of the Board of Trade, March 1867 to Dec. 12, 1868.

RICHMOND, George, English portrait painter, b. 1809; elected A.R.A. 1857; exhibited portraits of many celebrated persons in the Royal Academy.

RICHOMME, Jules, French painter, b. in Paris, 1812; studied under Drolling. Exhibited 'Abraham reçevant Agar,' 1842; 'Le Christ guérissant un Malade,' 1855; 'La Leçon de Lecture,' 1864; and other, chiefly historical, paintings.

RICHSON, Rev. Charles, English author, b. 1810; educated at St. Catherine's Hall, Cambridge, where he graduated B.A. 1841, M.A. 1844; rector of St. Andrew's, Ancoats; canon of Manchester Cathedral. Author of 'On the Observance of the Sanitary Laws;' and several schoolbooks, and pamphlets on educational and sanitary reform.

RICHTER, Adrian Ludwig, German painter, b. at Dresden, Sept. 28, 1803; appointed professor of landscape painting at the Academy of Dresden, 1836; president, 1841; member of the Council of the Academy, 1852. Painted 'The Valley of Lauterbrunn,' 1826; 'View of the Campagna of Rome,' 1835; and numerous other landscapes.

RICHTER, Emil Julius, German jurist, b. at Stolpen, Saxony, Feb. 15, 1808; studied philology and jurisprudence at the University of Leipsic, where he received the degree of LL.D. 1834; appointed professor of ecclesiastical law at Berlin, 1846; and superior councillor of the 'Consistorium' of Prussia, 1852. Author of 'Lehrbuch des katholischen und evangelischen Kirchenrechts,' Leipsic, 1841–42; and other legal works.

RICORD, Philippe, French physician, b. at Baltimore, U.S. Dec. 10, 1800; studied medicine in Paris, and received the degree of M.D. March 1826; appointed physician-in-ordinary to the household of Prince Napoleon, 1862. Author of 'De l'Emploi du Speculum,' 1833; and numerous other medical works.

RIDLEY, Sir Matthew White, English politician, b. 1807; is a deputy-lieutenant of Northumberland; was high sheriff, 1841; major of Northumberland Yeomanry Cavalry; M.P. for North Northumberland, 1859–68.

RIGAULT DE GENOUILLY, Charles, French statesman and naval commander, b. at Rochefort, Charente Inférieure, April 12, 1807; educated at the École Polytechnique, and entered the navy in 1827; lieutenant, 1834; capitaine de corvette, 1841; capitaine de vaisseau, 1848; rear-admiral, 1854; commander of a detachment of marines at the siege of Sebastopol, 1855; vice-admiral, 1858; nominated senator, 1860; commander-in-chief of the Mediterranean fleet, 1862; admiral of France, 1864; appointed minister of marine and the colonies, Jan. 19, 1867.

RIO, Alexis François, French theological writer, b. at the Ile d'Arz, Morbihan, 1806. Author of 'Essai sur l'Histoire de l'Esprit humain dans l'Antiquité,' 1828–30; 'De l'Art Chrétien,' 1841–55; second edition, 1861; 'Les Quatre Martyrs,' 1856; sixth edition, 1862; and other works on ecclesiastical art and history.

RIOS-Y-ROSAS, Antonio de Los, Spanish politician, b. at Ronda, Andalusia, 1812; was deputy to the Cortes, 1837; took part in the ministry presided over by the Duke de Rivas, 1854; minister of the interior, 1856; president of the Spanish Congress, 1863.

RIPON, Right Rev. Robert Bickersteth, Bishop of, English divine, b. at Acton, Suffolk, 1816; educated at Queen's College, Cambridge, where he graduated B.A. 1841, and M.A. 1846; rector of St. Giles'-in-the-Fields, 1851; canon-residentiary of Salisbury, 1854; consecrated bishop of Ripon, 1856. Author of 'Bible Landmarks;' 'Means of Grace;' and several sermons.

RISTORI, Adelaide, Italian tragic actress, b. at Cividale, 1821; married to the Marquis Capranica del Grillo, 1847, who died 1861; has acted in London, Paris, and all the principal cities of Europe and America.

RITSCHL, Friedrich Wilhelm, German philologist, b. at Grossvargula, Thüringen, April 26, 1806; studied philology at the Universities of Leipsic and Halle; received the degree of Ph.D. 1829; appointed professor of philology at the University of Bonn, 1839; received the title of privy-councillor from the king of Prussia, 1856. Author of 'Die Alexandrinischen Bibliotheken,' Breslau, 1838; and other philological works.

RIVERS, George Pitt Rivers, Baron, English administrator, b. 1810; lieutenant-colonel of the Dorset Yeomany; was a lord-in-waiting to the Queen, 1841–46, and 1853–58; reappointed, 1859; succeeded his father, third baron, 1831.

RIVOLI, Victor Massena, Duc de, French politician, b. 1826; formerly an officer in the army; member of the Corps Législatif for the department of Alpes Maritimes since 1861.

ROBARTES, Thomas James Agar, English politician, b. 1808; educated at Harrow, and Christ Church, Oxford, where he graduated B.A. 1830; assumed the additional name of Robartes, 1826; a special deputy-warden of the Stannaries; M.P. for East Cornwall, 1847–68.

ROBERT, Antoinette Henriette Cle'mence, French authoress, b. at Mâcon, Dec. 6, 1797. Author of 'Une Famille, s'il vous plaît,' 1837; 'Le Roi,' 1844; 'Les quatre Sergents de la Rochelle,' 1849; 'Daniel le Laboureur,' 1860; and other novels, romances, and dramas.

ROBERT, Auguste François, French author, b. at Paris, Feb. 28, 1813; studied at the College of Henri IV. Author of 'Louis XI. et St. François de Paule,' 1830; 'La Confession des Bandits,' 1831; 'La Réforme en Allemagne,' 1865; and other poetical works.

ROBERT-FLEURY, Joseph Nicolas, French painter, b. at Cologne, Aug. 8, 1797; studied in Paris. Exhibited 'Le Tasse au Convent de St. Onuphre,' 1827; 'Charles-Quint au Monastère de St. Just,' 1857; and other paintings. Elected member of the French Académie des Beaux Arts, Jan. 1850; appointed professor at the École des Beaux Arts, 1855.

ROBERTS, Rev. George, English author, b. 1808; educated at Trinity College, Cambridge, where he graduated in 1830; has been minister of St. John's, Cheltenham, since 1853. Author of 'The Duties of Subjects and Magistrates,' 1842; 'Strata Florida Abbey, Cardiganshire,' 1848; and other works.

ROBERTSON, David, English politician, b. 1797; educated at Edinburgh; lord-lieutenant of the county of Berwick; late sheriff of the county of Haddington; formerly a merchant in London; M.P. for Berwickshire since 1859.

ROBERTSON, Rev. James Craigie, English author, b. at Aberdeen, 1813; educated at Marischal College, Aberdeen, and at Trinity College, Cambridge, where he graduated B.A. 1834; canon of Canterbury, 1859; appointed professor of ecclesiastical history in King's College, London, 1864. Author of 'How shall we conform to the Liturgy?' 1843–44; 'A Biography of Thomas à Becket,' 1859; and other works.

ROBERTSON, Patrick Francis, English politician, b. 1807; educated at the University of St. Andrew's; a magistrate of Hastings, and deputy-lieutenant of Sussex; formerly a merchant at Canton; M.P. for Hastings, 1852–59, and 1865–68.

ROBIN, Charles Philippe, French physician, b. at Jafferon, Ain, June 4, 1821; studied medicine in Paris; received the degree of M.D. Aug. 31, 1846; appointed professor of histology in the Faculty of Medicine of Paris, April 12, 1862. Author of 'Histoire naturelle des végétaux Parasites qui croissent sur l'Homme et les Animaux vivants,' 1853; and numerous medical works.

ROBINSON, Rev. Edward, American author, b. at Southington, Connecticut, 1794; studied at Hamilton College, New York, where he graduated, 1815, and at Paris and Halle; professor of Biblical literature in the Union Theological Seminary of New York. Author of 'Biblical Researches in Palestine, Mount Sinai, and Arabia Petræa,' 1841; and other works.

ROBINSON, Rev. Hastings, English divine, b. 1793; educated at Rugby and Cambridge, where he graduated in 1815; appointed incumbent of Great Warley, Essex, 1827; and select preacher before the University, 1836. Edited 'The Acts of the Apostles,' 1824; 'Zurich Letters,' 1841–46; and other works.

ROBINSON, Sir Hercules Robert George, English colonial administrator, b. 1824; educated at the Royal Military College, Sandhurst; held a commission in the army, and retired, 1846; president of Montserrat, 1854; lieutenant-governor of St. Christopher, 1855; governor of Hong-Kong, and knighted, 1859; appointed governor of Ceylon, 1865.

ROBINSON, John Henry, English engraver, b. at Bolton, Lancashire, 1796; studied under James Heath. Engraved 'Napoleon and Pope Pius VII.,' after Wilkie; 'Little Red Riding Hood,' after Landseer; and the 'Spanish Flower Girl,' after Murillo. Elected associate engraver of the R. A. 1864.

ROBINSON, Rev. Thomas, English divine, b. 1790; educated at Rugby, and Trinity College, Cambridge; rector of Therfield, Herts, 1853–61; master of the Temple since 1845, and canon of Rochester since 1854. Author of 'The Last Days of Bishop Heber,' 1827; 'The Twin Fallacies of Rome,' 1851; and other theological works.

ROCHESTER, Right Rev. Thomas Legh Claughton, Bishop of, b. 1808; educated at Trinity College, Oxford, and graduated B.A. 1831, M.A. 1834; vicar of Kidderminster, 1841; hon. canon of Worcester Cathedral, 1845; professor of poetry at Oxford, 1852; consecrated bishop of Rochester, 1867.

ROCK, Rev. Daniel, Roman Catholic theologian, b. in Liverpool, 1799; educated at Old Hall, Herts, and at the English College, Rome; appointed canon of Southwark, 1852. Author of 'Hierurgia, or the Sacrifice of the Mass expounded;' and other works.

RODEN, Robert Jocelyn, Earl, English administrator, b. 1788; educated at Harrow; custos rotulorum of the county of Louth, and a deputy-lieutenant of the county of Down; formerly auditor-general of the Irish Exchequer.

ROEBUCK, John Arthur, English politician, b. at Madras, 1803; called to the bar of the Inner Temple, and went on the Northern Circuit, 1831; a bencher of the Inner Temple; M.P. for Bath, 1833–37, and 1841–47, and for Sheffield, 1849–68. Author of 'The Colonies of England,' and 'History of the Whig Party in 1830,' 1852.

ROENNE, Ludwig Peter von, German jurist, b. at Glückstadt, Holstein, Oct. 18, 1804; studied at the Universities of Bonn and Berlin; auditor in the Court of Justice of Berlin, 1825; deputy to the First Prussian Chamber, 1849–50. Author of 'Die Verfassung und Verwaltung des preussischen Staats,' Berlin, 1854; and other legal works.

ROER, Johann Eduard, German philologist, b. at Brunswick, Dec. 26, 1805; studied at the University of Königsberg; appointed professor of philosophy at Berlin, 1833. Published 'Bibliotheca Indica,' with English translations, 1846; and numerous other works translated from Hindostanee and Sanscrit.

ROGERS, Rev. Henry, English divine, b. 1814; studied at Highbury; was professor of English language and literature in University College, London; appointed principal of the Lancashire Independent College, 1858. Author of 'The Eclipse of Faith, or a Visit to a Religious Sceptic;' essays from the *Edinburgh Review.*

ROGERS, Henry Darwin, American naturalist, b. 1808; professor of chemistry and natural philosophy in Dickinson College, Pennsylvania, 1829–48; appointed regius professor of natural history in the University of Glasgow, 1857. Author of 'Geological Survey of the States of New Jersey and Pennsylvania.'

ROGERS, Rev. William, English clergyman, b. 1820; educated at Balliol College, Oxford, where he graduated B.A. 1842; appointed incumbent of St. Thomas', Goswell Street, London, 1844; rector of Bishopsgate, 1863; governor of Dulwich College, and one of her Majesty's chaplains.

ROGIER, Charles, Belgian statesman, b. at St. Quentin, France, Aug. 12, 1800; studied law at Liege; became editor and co-proprietor of the journal *Le Politique;* organized in the Revolution of 1830 a battalion of 300 volunteers, entered Brussels, Sept. 19, and took possession of the Hôtel de Ville; nominated member of the Provisional Government, Oct. 1830; governor of Antwerp, June 1831 till July 1832; minister of home affairs, 1832–35; governor of the Province of Antwerp, 1835–40; minister of public works, 1840–41; minister of the interior, and of war, 1847–52; president of the Council and minister of foreign affairs, 1861–68.

ROGUET, Christophe Michel, Comte, French military commander, b. at San Remo, Piedmont, April 28, 1800 ; studied at St. Cyr ; chef de bataillon, 1830 ; general of division, 1851 ; made a senator, Dec. 1852.

ROKITANSKY, Karl, German physician, b. at Königsgrätz, in Bohemia, Feb. 19, 1804 ; studied medicine at Prague and Vienna, and received the degree of M.D. 1828 ; rector of the University of Prague, and member of the Academy of Sciences of Vienna, 1848 ; rector of the University of Vienna, 1850. Author of 'Manual of Pathological Anatomy,' 1842–46 ; translated into English, London, 1845–50.

ROLLO, John Rogerson Rollo, Baron, English administrator, b. 1835 ; educated at Trinity College, Cambridge, where he graduated M.A. 1856 ; a deputy-lieutenant of Dumfriesshire, and a magistrate of Perthshire ; succeeded his father, ninth baron, 1852 ; elected a representative peer of Scotland, 1860.

ROLT, Sir John, English judge, b. 1804 ; called to the bar of the Inner Temple, 1837 ; became Q.C. 1846 ; a magistrate and deputy-lieutenant of Gloucestershire ; M.P. for West Gloucestershire, 1857–65 ; attorney-general, 1866 ; lord justice of appeal, 1867 ; resigned from ill-health, 1867.

ROMENT, Barthélemy de, French politician, b. at Voûte Gilhac, Haute Loire, May 17, 1799 ; was staff-major and aide-de-camp to Marshal Soult ; member of the Corps Législatif for the department of Haute Loire since 1852.

ROMILLY, Right Hon. Lord, English judge, b. 1802 ; educated at Trinity College, Cambridge, where he graduated M.A. 1826 ; called to the bar of Gray's Inn, 1827 ; has been solicitor and attorney-general ; was M.P. for Bridport, 1832–35 and 1846–47, and for Devonport, 1847–52 ; appointed Master of the Rolls, 1851 ; raised to the peerage, 1865.

ROMNEY, Charles Marsham, Earl, English administrator, b. 1808 ; educated at Christ Church, Oxford, where he graduated B.A. ; a magistrate and deputy-lieutenant of Kent ; governor of the Charterhouse ; was M.P. as Viscount Marsham for the county of Kent, 1841–45 ; succeeded his father, second earl, 1845.

RONGE, Johannes, German theological writer, b. at Bischofswalde, Silesia, 1813 ; educated at the University of Breslau ; Roman Catholic priest at Grottkau, 1840 : suspended from his functions and excommunicated, 1843 ; formed a 'German Catholic' congregation at Breslau, 1845. Author of 'Letter of a Catholic Priest to Bishop Arnoldi in relation to the Holy Coat of Trèves ;' and other works.

ROQUES SALVAZA, Paul Auguste, French politician, b. at Carcassonne, Dec. 18, 1793 ; member of the Corps Législatif for the first circonscription of the department of Aude since 1852.

ROS DE OLANO, Antonio, Count d'Almina, Spanish military commander, b. at Caracas, 1808 ; lieutenant, 1834 ; colonel, 1837 ; minister of instruction and public works, 1843 ; director-general of the sanitary department of the army, 1852–54 ; took part with General O'Donnell in the insurrection of June 1854 ; commander of the third corps of the Spanish army in the expedition to Africa, 1859 ; took an important part in the Revolution of 1868.

ROSE, Etienne Hugues, French general, b. Sept. 25, 1812 ; studied at St. Cyr ; captain, 1840 ; lieutenant-colonel, 1852 ; general of brigade, 1858 ; served in Africa and the Crimea ; commander of a brigade of infantry of the Imperial Guard.

ROSE, Gustav, German chemist, b. at Berlin, March 18, 1798 ; studied at the University of Berlin, and received the degree of Ph.D. 1821 ; professor in the University of Berlin, 1839. Author of 'Journey to the Ural, Altaï, and the Caspian Sea,' 1837–42 ; 'Elements of Crystallography,' 1838 ; and other scientific works.

ROSE, Hugh Henry, Baron Strathnairn, English general, b. 1803 ; educated at Berlin ; entered the army, 1820 ; major, 1826 ; lieutenant-colonel and K.C.B. 1855 ; was commissioner at the headquarters of the French army in the East, 1855–56 ; colonel, 1858 ; lieutenant-general, 1860 ; commander-in-chief in India, 1860–65, in Ireland since 1865.

ROSECRANS, William Starke, American military commander, b. in Kingston, Ohio, Sept. 6, 1819 ; entered West Point Military Academy, 1838, where he graduated, 1842 ; aide-de-camp and chief engineer to General McClellan, 1861 ; brigadier-general and commander of the army of Western Virginia, 1861 ; major-general, March 1862 ; commander of the army of the Cumberland, 1862–63, of Missouri, 1864 ; minister to Mexico, 1868–69.

ROSENKRANZ, Johann Friedrich, German philosophical writer, b. at Magdeburg, April 23, 1805 ; studied at Berlin, Halle, and Heidelberg ; appointed professor of philosophy at Königsberg, 1833 ; member of the First Prussian Chamber, 1849. Author of 'Notes on the System of Hegel,' Königsberg, 1840 ; 'Poetry and its History,' ib. 1855 ; and other philosophical works.

ROSETTI, Costantino, Roumanian politician, b. at Bucharest, 1816; served in the militiai 1836–38; member of the Revolutionary Committee of Roumania, 1846; chief of the police at Bucharest, and director of the ministry of the interior, 1848; minister of public instruction, 1861. Published a 'Collection of Songs' in the dialect of Roumania, 1840; and founded several newspapers in Roumania and Paris.

ROSNY, Le'on de, French philologist, b. 1835; appointed professor of the Japanese language in the Bibliothèque Impériale, 1863. Author of 'Aperçu général des Langues sémitiques et de leur Histoire,' 1858; 'Recueil de Textes japonais,' 1863; and other works on the language and literature of the East, chiefly of Japan.

ROSS, Rev. John Lockhart, English author, b. 1810; educated at Oriel College, Oxford, where he graduated B.A. 1833, and M.A. 1836; vice-principal of Chichester Theological College, 1840–51; appointed rector of St. George's in the East, London, 1863. Author of 'Lectures on the History of Moses,' 1837; 'Druidical Temples at Avebury,' 1859; and other works.

ROSSEEUW SAINT HILAIRE, Euge'ne François, French author, b. at Paris, June 30, 1805; appointed assistant professor of ancient history at Sorbonne, 1842; titular professor, 1856. Author of 'Rienzi et les Colonna, ou Rome au XIVᵉ Siècle,' in five vols. 1825; 'Études religieuses et littéraires,' 1863; and other, chiefly historical, works.

ROSSETTI, Christina, English authoress, b. 1827. Author of 'Goblin Market,' 1862; 'The Prince's Progress,' 1866; and other poetical works.

ROSSETTI, Dante Gabriel, English painter, brother of the preceding, b. 1828; has painted a great number of pictures, none of which have been publicly exhibited. Author of 'The Early Italian Poets,' 1861.

ROSSETTI, William Michael, English author, brother of the preceding, b. 1829; employed in the Inland Revenue Office. Author of 'Fine Art, chiefly contemporary,' 1867.

ROSSHIRT, Conrad Franz, German jurist, b. at Bamberg, 1793; studied law at Erlangen and Göttingen; received the degree of LL.D. 1812; appointed professor of law at Heidelberg, 1818. Author of 'Beitäge zum römischen Rechte und zum röm. deutschen Staatsrechte,' Heidelberg, 1820–22; 'Dogmengeschichte des Civilrechts,' ib. 1853; and other legal works.

ROSSI, Giovanni Battista de, Italian archæologist, b. at Rome, 1822. Author of a work on the Christian inscriptions in the Roman catacombs, and of numerous essays on archæology.

ROSSLYN, James Alexander St. Clair Erskine, Earl of, English administrator, b. 1802; educated at Eton; a major-general in the army; magistrate and deputy-lieutenant of the county of Fife; master of the buckhounds, 1841–47, and from Feb. to Dec. 1852; under-secretary for the War Department, March to June 1859.

ROTHERMAL, Peter, American artist, b. in Luzerne County, Pennsylvania, July 8, 1817; educated in Philadelphia as a land-surveyor; studied in France, Germany, and Italy, 1856–37. Painted 'St. Agnes,' 1837; 'Foscari;' 'De Soto discovering the Mississippi;' 'Columbus before the Queen;' and 'The Martyrs in the Coliseum.'

ROTHSCHILD, Lionel Nathan, Baron de, English banker, b. 1808; educated at Göttingen; succeeded his father as a Baron of the Austrian Empire, 1836; chief partner in the banking firm of Rothschild and Co.; a deputy-lieutenant of London and a J.P. for Middlesex; M.P. for London since 1847.

ROTHSCHILD, Meyer Amschel, Baron de, English banker, b. 1818; partner in the banking firm of Rothschild and Co., and a magistrate of Bucks; M.P. for Hythe since 1859.

ROTHSCHILD, Nathaniel Meyer de, English politician, b. 1840; educated at Trinity College, Cambridge; M.P. for Aylesbury since 1865.

ROTOURS, Alexandre Antoine des, French politician, b. June 29, 1806; mayor of Avelin; member of the Corps Législatif for the département du Nord since 1863.

ROUGE', Olivier Emmanuel, Vicomte de, French archæologist, b. at Paris, April 11, 1811; entered the Council of State in the section of the interior and of public instruction, 1854; appointed professor of archæology in the College of France, 1857; elected member of the French Academy, 1853; contributor to the Revue Archéologique.

ROUHER, Euge'ne, French statesman, b. at Riom, Nov. 30, 1814; studied jurisprudence, and was called to the bar of Riom, 1838; elected member of the Constituent Assembly for the department of Puy de Dôme, 1848; deputy to the Legislative Assembly for the same department, 1849; appointed minister of justice, Oct. 31, 1849; resigned, July 18, 1851; minister of justice, Dec. 2, 1851, to Jan. 22, 1852; vice-president of the Council of State, 1852; nominated senator, June 18, 1856; appointed minister and secretary of state of agriculture, commerce, and public works, Feb. 3, 1855; nominated minister of state, Oct. 19, 1863.

ROULAND, Gustave, French statesman, b. at Yvetot, Feb. 1, 1806; studied at the College of Rouen and at Louviers; procureur du roi at Dieppe,'1832–47; advocate-general at the Court of Cassation at Paris, 1847–48; minister of public instruction, 1856–57; minister and president of the Council of State, June 24 to Oct. 18, 1863; appointed governor of the Bank of France, Sept. 1864.

ROULLEAUX DUGAGE, Charles Henry, French politician, b. at Alençon, April 26, 1802; advocate at Caen, 1821, and at the bar of Paris from 1822 to 1830; subprefect of Domfront, 1830; prefect of Ardèche, 1835, of Loire Inférieure, 1847–48; member of the Corps Législatif for the department of Hérault since 1852.

ROUSSET, Camille Felix Michel, French author, b. at Paris, Feb. 15, 1821; professor of history at Grenoble, 1843–45, and at the Collége Bourbon, 1845–63; appointed historiographer to the ministry of war, 1864. Author of 'Histoire de Louvois et de son Administration politique et militaire,' 1861–63; and other historical works.

ROXBURGHE, James Henry Robert Innes Ker, Duke of, English administrator, b. 1816; succeeded his father, fifth duke, 1823; took his seat in the House of Lords, 1837.

ROY-BRY, Henri, French politician, b. at Rochefort, December 7, 1810; a banker at Rochefort; president of the Chamber of Commerce, and member of the General Council for the canton; member of the Corps Législatif for the department of Charente Inférieure since 1859.

ROYER, Paul Henri Ernest de, French statesman, b. at Versailles, Oct. 29, 1808; studied at Marseilles, and law at Grenoble and Paris, where he was called to the bar, 1829; procureur-général to the Court of Appeal of Paris, 1850–51; minister of justice, Jan. 25 to April 11, 1851; reappointed minister of justice, Nov. 16, 1857; senator, and vice-president of the Senate, May 5, 1859; nominated first president of the Cour des Comptes, Feb. 1, 1863. Author of several legal works.

ROYER, Pierre Marie Casimir, French politician, b. at St. Galmier, Loire, May 29, 1791; studied law, and was called to the bar at Grenoble, 1815; member of the Chamber of Deputies for Grenoble, 1846; member of the Corps Législatif for the department of the Isère since 1863.

ROYSTON, Charles Philip, Viscount, English politician, b. 1836; educated at Harrow, and Trinity College, Cambridge, where he graduated M.A. 1858; a magistrate of the county of Cambridge; formerly an officer in the 7th and 11th Light Dragoons; M.P. for Cambridgeshire since 1865.

RUCHDI, Pasha Me'he'met, Turkish statesman, b. at Constantinople, 1809; entered the Turkish army, 1825; chief of staff at Nezib, 1839; general of division and minister of war, 1853–56; grand vizier, 1857–58; minister of war, 1861–62; reappointed to the ministry, July 1865. Translator of several French works, principally on war and military tactics.

RUDDER, Louis Henri de, French painter, b. at Paris, Oct. 17, 1807; studied under Gros, Charlet, and at the École des Beaux Arts. Exhibited 'La Mort de Jehan d'Armagnac,' 1835; 'Les Proscrits des Cévennes,' 1848; 'Le Christ au Jardin des Olives,' 1863; 'Berger des Abruzzes,' 1864; and numerous other paintings, chiefly of religious or historical subjects.

RUFINO, Casimir Rufino Ruiz, Spanish political economist, b. at Soto de Cameros, July 21, 1806; took part in the civil war; was nominated deputy for Seville, 1836; obliged to leave Spain, 1838; appointed professor and director of the commercial classes of science and art at the University of Madrid, 1848. Author of 'La Historia mercantil universal,' Madrid, 1852–53.

RUGE, Arnold, German politician, b. at Bergen, island of Rügen, 1802; studied philosophy and philology at the Universities of Halle, Jena, and Heidelberg; professor of philosophy at the University of Halle, 1830–50. Author of 'Two Years in Paris,' 1845; and of numerous political and philosophical works.

RUNEBERG, Johann Ludwig, Finnish author, b. at Jacobstede, Feb. 5, 1804; studied at Abo; received his degree of doctor, 1827; appointed professor of eloquence at Helsingfors, 1830; nominated lecturer on poetry and eloquence at Borgo, and lecturer on Greek at the same college, 1842; appointed professor of the same, 1844. Author of 'Poems,' Helsingfors, 1851; 'Smærre Berrættelser,' 1854.

RUSCALLA, Juvenale Vegezzi, Italian politician, b. at Turin, 1799; employed in the ministry of foreign affairs of Piedmont, 1818; was secretary to the same, 1836; and took part in the Congress of Verona; appointed inspector-general of prisons; resigned, 1857; elected deputy for Scandiano to the Italian National Parliament, 1860; one of the chief contributors to the *Rivista Contemporanea*.

RUSCHENBERGER, William, American naturalist, b. in the county of Cumberland, New Jersey, Sept. 4, 1807; studied medicine at New York and Philadelphia; assistant-surgeon in the navy, 1826–31; appointed surgeon in the navy, 1831. Author of 'Three Years in the Pacific,' Philadelphia, 1835; 'Elements of Natural History,' 1850; and other works.

RUSKIN, John, English author, b. in London, Feb. 1819; educated at Christ Church, Oxford. Author of 'Modern Painters,' 1843–46; 'The Seven Lamps of Architecture,' 1849; 'The Stones of Venice,' 1851–53; 'King's Treasuries and Queen's Gardens,' 1865; and numerous other works on art and subjects connected therewith.

RUSSELL, Arthur John Edward, English politician, b. 1825, second son of Lord G. W. Russell; was private secretary to Lord John Russell; M.P. for Tavistock since 1857.

RUSSELL, Sir Charles, English politician, b. 1826; educated at Eton; a J.P. and deputy-lieutenant of Berks; captain and lieutenant-colonel Grenadier Guards; was deputy-assistant quartermaster-general in the East; M.P. for Berkshire, 1865–68.

RUSSELL, Francis Charles Hastings, English politician, b. 1819; a deputy-lieutenant of Beds; lieutenant-colonel Beds Rifle Volunteers; late major Beds Militia; formerly lieutenant in the Scots Fusilier Guards; M.P. for Bedfordshire since 1847.

RUSSELL, Francis William, English politician, b. 1800; educated at Fermoy, and at Trinity College, Dublin; called to the Irish bar, 1824; a partner in the firm of Russell and Sons, merchants, of Limerick and London; M.P. for Limerick since 1852.

RUSSELL, Rev. John Fuller, English author, b. 1816; educated at St. Peter's College, Cambridge, where he graduated S.C.L. 1837, B.C.L. 1838; incumbent of Greenhithe, Kent, since 1856. Author of 'Judgment of the Church on the Sufficiency of Holy Scripture,' 1838; 'Life of Dr. Johnson,' 1847; and other works.

RUSSELL, John Russell, Earl, English statesman, b. in London, Aug. 18, 1792; educated at Westminster and Edinburgh; paymaster of the forces, 1830–34; secretary of state for the Home Department, 1835–39; secretary of state for the colonies, 1839–41; first lord of the Treasury, 1846–52; secretary of state for foreign affairs, Dec. 1852 to March 1853; lord president of the Council, April 1854 to Jan. 1855; appointed on a special mission to Vienna, Feb. 1855; secretary of state for the colonies, Feb. to Jan. 1855; again secretary of state for foreign affairs, June 1859–61; was M.P. for Tavistock, 1813–19; for Huntingdonshire, 1820–26; Bandon Bridge, 1827–30; Devonshire, 1830–32; South Devon, 1832–35; Stroud, 1835–41; London, July 1841–61; elevated to the peerage, 1861; first lord of the Treasury, Oct. 23, 1865, to July 6, 1866.

RUSSELL, John Scott, English civil engineer, b. in the Vale of Clyde, 1808; educated at the Universities of Edinburgh, St. Andrew's, and Glasgow; vice-president of the Institution of Civil Engineers; one of the three promoters of the Great Exhibition of 1851; designed the *Great Eastern*, and numerous other large steamships. Author of 'The Modern System of Naval Architecture for Commerce and War.'

RUSSELL, Sir William, English politician, b. 1822; entered the army, 1841; served in the 14th Hussars in the Crimea and in India, 1857–59; a colonel unattached; was M.P. for Dover, 1847–49; M.P. for Norwich since 1860.

RUSSELL, William Howard, English author, b. at Lily Vale, county of Dublin, March 28, 1821; educated at Trinity College, Dublin; entered the Middle Temple, 1846; called to the bar, 1850; was special correspondent to the *Times* in the Crimea, India, and America. Author of 'Letters from the Crimea,' 1855–56; 'My Diary in India;' 'My Diary North and South,' 1863; 'Canada: its Defences, Condition, &c.' 1865; 'The Adventures of Dr. Brady,' 1868.

RUTLAND, Charles Cecil John Manners, Duke of, English administrator, b. in London, May 16, 1815; educated at Eton, and Trinity College, Cambridge; lord-lieutenant of Leicestershire; honorary colonel of the Leicestershire Militia; lord of the bedchamber to Prince Albert, Dec. 1843 to Aug. 1846; was M.P. for Stamford, 1837 to July 1852, and for North Leicestershire, 1852–57, when he succeeded as sixth duke.

RYAN, Right Hon. Sir Edward, English judge, b. 1793; educated at Trinity College, Cambridge; called to the bar of Lincoln's Inn. 1817; was puisne judge; chief justice at Calcutta, and one of the comptrollers of the Exchequer; sworn in the Privy Council, 1843; appointed a commissioner of railways, 1846; one of the Civil Service commissioners, and member of the Senate of the University of London.

RYLE, Rev. John Charles, English theological writer, b. near Macclesfield, 1816; educated at Eton, and Christ Church, Oxford, where he graduated B.A. 1836; appointed vicar of Stradbroke, Suffolk, 1861. Author of 'Expository Thoughts on the Gospels,' and of numerous tracts.

S.

SAAVEDRA, Angelo de, Duke de Rivas, Spanish statesman and author, b. at Cordova, March 1, 1791; studied at Madrid; entered the Guards, 1807, and retired with the rank of colonel; deputy to the Cortes for the province of Cordova, 1813; succeeded his brother in the dukedom, 1835; minister of the interior, 1836–38; ambassador to Naples, 1843–48; president of the Council of State, 1863–65. Author of 'Florinda,' 1824; and several poems, tragedies, and romances.

SABATIER, Raymond Gabriel Baptiste, French diplomatist, b. 1810; was captain in the army, 1836; colonel, 1852; appointed French consul-general at Alexandria, 1852.

SABINE, Edward, English general and author, b. 1786; second lieutenant in the army, 1803; lieutenant-colonel, 1841; major-general, 1859. Author of 'The Pendulum and other Experiments,' 1825; and of numerous 'Memoirs' contributed to the *Philosophical Transactions;* elected president of the Royal Society, 1861.

SACK, Karl Heinrich, German theologian, b. at Berlin, Oct. 17, 1790; studied law at Göttingen and theology at the University of Berlin; appointed professor of theology at the University of Bonn, 1823; took part in the General Synod of Berlin as deputy from the Faculty of Bonn, 1846. Author of 'Die Kirche von Schottland,' Heidelberg, 1844–45; and other theological works.

SACY, Samuel Ustazade Silvestre de, French author, b. at Paris, Oct. 17, 1801; studied at the Lyceum of Louis le Grand, and was called to the bar; appointed conservateur of the Bibliothèque Mazarine, 1836; and keeper of the same, 1848; nominated member of the Imperial Council for Public Education, July 2, 1864; elected member of the French Academy, 1854. Contributor to *Le Journal des Débats* since 1828.

SA DA BANDEIRA, Bernardo De Sa Nogueira, Viscount de, Portuguese statesman, b. 1796; served as a volunteer in the War of Independence, 1810; was governor of Oporto; minister of marine, and created Baron de Sã Da Bandeira, 1832; resigned, May 1833; minister of marine, Nov. 1835 to April 1836; was member of the Cortes, 1846–56; reappointed minister of marine, 1856; minister of war, Dec. 1860, and Feb. 1862; president of the Council, and minister of war and marine, 1865–67.

SAGRA, Ramon de la, Spanish political economist, b. at Corunna, 1798; studied at Madrid; appointed director of the Botanical Garden of Havana, 1820. Author of 'Historia economica, politica y estadistica de la Isla de Cuba,' Havana, 1831; 'Cuba in 1860,' 1862; 'Icones Plantarum in Flora Cubana descriptarum, &c.' 1863; and other works, especially on political economy.

ST. ALBAN'S, William Amelius Aubrey de Vere Beauclerk, Duke of, English administrator, b. 1840; educated at Eton, and Trinity College, Cambridge; hereditary grand falconer of England, and hereditary registrar of the Court of Chancery; succeeded his father, ninth duke, 1849.

ST. ASAPH, Right Rev. Thomas Vowler Short, Bishop of, English divine, b. 1790; educated at Westminster, and Christ Church, Oxford; rector of St. George's, Bloomsbury, 1834; appointed deputy-clerk of the closet to the Queen, 1837; consecrated bishop of Sodor and Man, 1842; translated to St. Asaph, 1846. Author of 'A Sketch of the History of the Church to the Revolution of 1688;' and other works.

ST. AUBYN, John, English politician, b. 1829; educated at Eton, and Trinity College, Cambridge, where he graduated B.A. 1842; a magistrate and deputy-lieutenant of Cornwall, and captain of the Royal Cornwall Rangers; M.P. for West Cornwall since 1858.

ST. DAVID'S, Right Rev. Connop Thirlwall, Bishop of, English divine, b. 1797 ; educated at the Charterhouse, and Trinity College, Cambridge ; called to the bar of Lincoln's Inn, 1825 ; ordained, 1828 ; consecrated bishop of St. David's, 1840 ; is dean of Brecon and visitor of St. David's College, Lampeter. Author of 'History of Greece ;' and other works.

SAINT-GENOIS, Jules Ghislain, Baron de, Belgian historian, b. at Lennick St. Quintin, Brabant, March 22, 1813 ; appointed professor and keeper of the library to the University of Gand, 1848 ; elected member of the Belgian Academy, 1846. Author of 'Histoire des Avoueries en Belgique,' Brussels, 1837 ; and other historical works.

SAINT GEORGES, Jules Henri Vernoy de, French dramatic writer, b. at Paris, 1801. Author of 'Nuits Terribles,' 1821 ; ' Pierre et Catherine,' 1829 ; 'Les Amours du Diable,' 1852 ; 'La Bohémienne,' 1862 ; and numerous other dramas.

SAINT GERMAIN, François Charles Herve' de, French politician, b. at Avranches, Feb. 16, 1803 ; deputy to the Legislative Assembly for the department of Manche, 1849 ; member of the Corps Législatif for the department of Manche since 1852.

ST. GERMANS, Edward Granville Eliot, Earl of, English statesman, b. 1798 ; educated at Christ Church, Oxford ; was a lord of the Treasury, 1828–32 ; ambassador to Spain, 1835 ; chief secretary for Ireland, 1841–45 ; postmaster-general, 1846 ; appointed lord-lieutenant of Ireland, Dec. 28, 1852 ; resigned, Feb. 24, 1855 ; lord-steward of the Household, Nov. 1857 to Feb. 1858 ; reappointed, June 1859 ; sat in the House of Commons as Lord Eliot, 1824–45, when he succeeded his father, second earl.

SAINT HILAIRE, E'mile Marc Hilaire, French author, b. 1790. Author of 'Le Donneur d'Eau bénite,' 1825 ; 'Les Habitations Napoléoniennes,' 1844 ; 'Les Deux Empereurs,' 1853 ; 'La Caserne du Quai d'Orsay,' 1856 ; 'Histoire des Armées françaises depuis 1792,' 1859 ; and numerous other works.

ST. JOHN, Horace, English author, b. in Normandy, July 5, 1830. Author of 'The Indian Archipelago ;' 'A History of the British Conquests in India ;' 'Life of Christopher Columbus ;' and other historical and biographical works.

ST. JOHN, James Augustus, English author, b. in Carmarthenshire, Sept. 24, 1801, father of the preceding. Author of 'History, Manners, &c. of the Hindoos,' 1831 ; 'Egypt and Mehemet Ali,' 1834 ; 'History of the Manners and Customs of Ancient Greece,' 1842 ; 'Isis, an Egyptian Pilgrimage,' 1852 ; 'Philosophy at the Foot of the Cross,' 1855 ; 'A History of the Four Conquests of England,' 1862 ; and other works.

ST. JOHN, Percy Bayle, English author, b. 1819, son of the preceding. Author of 'Two Years in a Levantine Family ;' 'Purple Tints of Paris ;' and numerous works of fiction ; contributor to the *London Journal*, and other periodical publications.

ST. JOHN, Spencer, English author, b. in London, Dec. 22, 1826, brother of the preceding ; appointed secretary to Sir James Brooke in Borneo, 1848 ; chargé d'affaires to the Republic of Hayti, 1860 ; received a consular appointment in the West Indies, 1863. Author of 'Life in the Forests of the Far East,' London, 1862.

ST. LEONARD'S, Edward Burtenshaw Sugden, Baron, English statesman, b. 1781 ; called to the bar of Lincoln's Inn, 1807 ; king's counsel, 1822 ; became solicitor-general, 1829 ; lord chancellor of Ireland, 1835, for three months, and again 1841–46 ; lord high chancellor, March to Dec. 1852 ; sat in the House of Commons as Sir Edward Sugden till 1841 ; elevated to the peerage as Baron St. Leonard's, 1852. Author of 'The Law of Vendors and Purchasers ;' 'The Handy-Book of Property Law ;' and other legal works.

SAINT MARC GIRARDIN, Marc, French author, b. at Paris, Feb. 12, 1801 ; studied in the Collége Napoléon, and the College of Henri IV. ; was called to the bar ; appointed professor of history to the Faculté des Lettres, and professor of French poetry, 1834 ; member of the Chamber of Deputies, 1834–48 ; elected to the French Academy, 1844. Author of 'Cours de Littérature dramatique,' 1843 ; 'Souvenirs et Voyages ;' and numerous other works.

ST. VINCENT, Carnegie Robert John Jervis, Viscount, English adminis trator, b. 1825 ; educated at Eton ; a magistrate and deputy-lieutenant of Staffordshire ; succeeded his grandfather, first viscount, Sept. 1859.

SAINTE BEUVE, Charles Augustin, French author, b. at Boulogne-sur-Mer, Dec. 23, 1804 ; studied at the Collége Charlemagne ; admitted to the French Academy, 1845 ; appointed master of conferences at the École Normale, 1857 ; created senator, 1865. Author of 'Historical and Critical Picture of French Poetry and of the French Theatre in the Sixteenth Century,' 1828 ; 'History of Port Royal,' 1840–60 ; 'Causeries du Lundi,' 1851–57 ; and other works : contributor to the *Revue des Deux Mondes*, the *Constitutionnel,* and the *Moniteur.*

SAINTE CLAIRE DEVILLE, Charles, French geologist, b. at St. Thomas, Antilles, 1814; studied at the Paris School of Mines; elected member of the French Academy, 1857. Author of 'Voyage géologique aux Antilles et aux Iles Ténériffe et De Fogo,' 1856–64; 'Recherches sur les principaux Phénomènes de Météorologie, &c., aux Antilles,' 1864; and other geological works.

SAINTE CLAIRE DEVILLE, Henri Etienne, French chemist, b. at St. Thomas, Antilles, March 11, 1818, brother of the preceding; studied in Paris; appointed professor of chemistry in the École Normale, 1851; elected member of the French Academy, Nov. 1861. Author of several papers relating to chemical discoveries in the 'Comptes Rendus' of the Académie des Sciences and the 'Annales de Chimie.'

SAINTE HERMINE, Jean Helie Emile, Marquis de, French politician, b. at Niort, Jan. 22, 1809; was secretary-general of the Prefecture of La Vendée, 1835–52; member of the Corps Législatif for the first circonscription of La Vendée since 1852. Author of 'Influence des Guerres entre la France et l'Angleterre dans les XIIe, XIIIe et XIVe, Siècles,' 1855.

SALA, George Augustus, English journalist and author, b. in London, 1826. Author of 'The Baddington Peerage;' 'Twice Round the Clock;' 'Down among the Dutchmen;' 'America in the midst of War,' republished from the *Daily Telegraph*, 1864; and other works.

SALISBURY, Robert Arthur Cecil, Marquis of, English statesman, b. 1830; educated at Eton, and Christ Church, Oxford, where he graduated B.A. 1850; chosen fellow of All Souls, Oxford, 1852; returned M.P. for Stamford, as Viscount Cranbourne, 1853; succeeded his father, second marquis, 1868.

SALISBURY, Walter Kerr Hamilton, Bishop of, English divine, b. in London, Nov. 16, 1808; educated at Eton, and Christ Church, Oxford, where he graduated B.A. 1830; elected fellow of Merton College, and graduated M.A. 1833; appointed vicar of St. Peter's in the East, Oxford, and examining chaplain to the bishop of Salisbury, 1837; canon-residentiary of Salisbury, June 1841; consecrated bishop of Salisbury, 1854.

SALLANDROUZE DE LAMORNAIX, Charles Jean, French politician, b. at Paris, March 27, 1809; a manufacturer at Aubusson, Creuse; elected representative of the department of Creuse, 1848; member of the Corps Législatif for Creuse since 1852. Author of 'Considérations sur la Législation des Brevets d'Invention,' 1829; and other works.

SALLES, Eusebe François, Comte de, French philologist, b. at Montpellier, Dec. 16, 1796; educated for the medical profession, and received the degree of M.D.; studied Arabic, Persian, Turkish, and Hindostanee at the College of France and the College of Oriental Languages; professor of Arabic at Marseilles since 1835. Author of 'Aly le Renard, ou le Conquête d'Alger,' 1832; 'Pérégrinations en Orient,' 1840–55; and other, chiefly philological, works.

SALOMONS, David, English politician, b. 1798; called to the bar of the Middle Temple, 1849; an alderman of London; lord-mayor, 1855–56; a deputy-lieutenant of Middlesex and Kent; was high sheriff, 1850; M.P. for Greenwich, 1851–52, and since 1859.

SALVADOR, Joseph, French historical writer, b. at Montpellier, 1796. Author of 'Loi de Moïse, ou Système religieux et politique des Hébreux,' 1822; 'Jesus devant Caïphe et Pilate,' 1829; 'Paris, Rome, Jérusalem, ou la Question religieuse au XIXe Siècle,' 1859; and other historical works.

SAMUDA, Joseph D'Aguilar, English politician, b. 1813; member of the Institute of Civil Engineers, and member of the Council of the Institute of Naval Architects; was a member of the Metropolitan Board of Works, 1860–65; M.P. for Tavistock, 1865–68; returned M.P. for the Tower Hamlets, 1868.

SAMUELSON, Bernhard, English politician, b. 1820; an ironmaster at Middlesborough on Tees; and manufacturer of agricultural machinery at Banbury; M.P. for Banbury, Feb. to April 1859, and since 1865. Author of a paper on technical education on the Continent, published as a 'Blue-book,' 1868.

SANDEAU, Jules, French author, b. at Aubusson, Feb. 19, 1811; studied law in Paris; elected member of the French Academy, 1858; assistant in the Imperial Library of Paris, and one of the conservators of the Mazarin Library since 1853; wrote, in conjunction with Madame Dudevant, 'Rose et Blanche,' 1831; also author of 'Madame de Sommerville,' 1834; 'Olivier,' 1854; 'Un Début dans la Magistrature,' 1862; 'La Maison de Penarvan,' 1863; and other novels and dramas.

SANDFORD, Edward, American writer, b. in New York, 1805; studied law; was elected to the Senate for the State of New York, 1843; contributor to the *Knickerbocker Magazine*, and other American periodicals.

SANDFORD, George Montagu Warren, English politician,. b. 1821; educated at Eton, and Magdalen College, Cambridge, where he graduated M.A. 1843; called to the bar of the Inner Temple, 1846; a magistrate and deputy-lieutenant of Essex, and a magistrate of Hants; assumed the surname of Sandford, instead of Peacocke, by royal licence, 1866; M.P. for Harwich, 1852–53; for Maldon, 1854–55, and 1859–63.

SANDFORD, Ven. John, English divine, b. 1805; educated at Balliol College, Oxford; and graduated B.D. 1846; appointed honorary canon of Worcester, 1844; archdeacon of Coventry, 1851; rector of Alve Church, 1854; Bampton Lecturer at Oxford, 1861; one of her Majesty's commissioners for revising the forms of clerical subscription, 1864. Author of 'Vox Cordis,' and other works.

SANDWICH, John William Montagu, Earl of, English administrator, b. 1811; lord-lieutenant of Huntingdonshire; was captain of the Gentlemen-at-Arms from March to Dec. 1852; and master of the buckhounds, Feb. 1858 to June 1859.

SANTA ANNA, Antonio Lopez de, Mexican statesman, b. in Jalapa, Feb. 21, 1798; appointed to the command of Vera Cruz, 1822; deposed, Nov. 1822; chosen president of Mexico, 1833; taken prisoner, April 21, 1836; was again president, 1841–45; reinstated, Feb. 1846; anew proclaimed president of the republic, Feb. 2, 1848; resigned, and escaped from the country, 1855.

SARDOU, Victorien, French dramatic writer, b. at Paris, 1831; studied medicine. Author of 'La Taverne des Étudiants,' 1854; 'La Perle noire,' 1862; 'Le Dégel,' 1864; 'La Famille Benoiton,' 1865; and numerous other dramatic works.

SARGENT, Epes, American author, b. at Gloucester, Massachusetts, Sept. 1816; studied at Boston,.and graduated at Harvard College. Author of 'The Bridge of Genoa,' 1836; 'Wealth and Worth;' 'Songs of the Sea, and other Poems,' 1845; 'Standard Speaker,' 1852.; 'The Priestess,' 1855; and other, chiefly dramatic, works.

SARRUT, Germain Marie, French politician and author, b. at Toulouse, April 20, 1800; elected to represent Loire-et-Cher at the Constituent Assembly, 1848; elected for the same department to the Legislative Assembly, but retired from political life after the coup d'état of Dec. 2, 1851. Author of 'Procès à l'Histoire,' 1832; with M. St. Edme, 'Biographie des Hommes du Jour,' 1835–42; 'Histoire de France de 1792 à nos Jours,' 1848; and other historical works.

SARTORIUS, Ernst Wilhelm Christian, German theologian, b. at Darmstadt, May 10, 1797; studied at Göttingen; appointed professor of theology in the University of Marburg, 1823; director of the Consistory of Königsberg, 1835. Author of 'Three Treatises on Matters of Exegetical and Systematic Theology,' 1820; 'Doctrine of the Person and Work of Christ,' 1831; and other theological works.

SARTORIUS, Sir George Rose, English naval commander, b. 1790; was present at the battle of Trafalgar and the siege of Cadiz; appointed to the command of the Portuguese fleet, 1832–33; knighted, 1841; made a K.C.B. 1865. Author of several pamphlets on naval warfare and engineering.

SARTORIUS, Luis Jose, Count de San Luis, Spanish statesman, b. about 1810; founded the *Heraldo*, 1841; was deputy to the Cortes, 1843–47; minister of the interior, 1847–50; prime minister from Sept. 1853 to July 1854; re-elected to the Cortes, 1857.

SAULCY, Louis Felicien Joseph Caignart de, French antiquarian, b. at Lille, March 19, 1807; entered the École Polytechnique, 1826, and became an officer of artillery; elected member of the French Academy, 1842; nominated senator, 1859. Author of 'Voyage autour de la Mer Morte, et dans les Terres Bibliques,' 1852–54; 'Histoire de l'Art Judaïque tirée des Textes sacrés et profanes,' 1858; and other antiquarian works.

SAUNDERS, Very Rev. Augustus Page, English divine, b. 1803; educated at Winchester, the Charterhouse, and at Christ Church, Oxford, where he graduated B.A. 1824; appointed head-master of the Charterhouse, 1834; dean of Peterborough, 1853. Author of several papers on Educational Reform.

SAUNDERSON, Edward James, English politician, b. 1837; a magistrate of the county of Cavan; was high sheriff, 1859; M.P. for the county of Cavan since 1865.

SAUZET, Paul Jean Pierre, French statesman, b. at Lyons, March 23, 1800; studied law, and was called to the bar of Lyons; minister of justice in the cabinet of M. Thiers, Feb. 22, 1836, to April 15, 1837; president of the Chamber, 1839–48, when he retired from public life. Author of 'Rome devant l'Europe,' 1860; 'Les deux Politiques de la France et le Partage de Rome,' 1862.

SAXE, John Godefroy, American author, b. at Highgate, Vermont, June 2, 1816; graduated at the College of Middleburg, 1839, and studied law. Author of 'Progress,' 1846; 'The New Rape of the Lock,' 1847; 'The Proud Miss McBride,' 1848; 'New England,' 1851; and other poetical works.

SAYE AND SELE, Rev. Frederick Benjamin Twisleton Wykeham Fiennes, Baron, English administrator, b. 1799; high steward of Banbury; treasurer and canon-residentiary of Hereford.

SCARBOROUGH, Richard George Lumley, Earl of, English administrator, b. at Tickhill Castle, Yorkshire, May 7, 1813; educated at Eton; formerly an officer in the 7th Hussars; lieutenant-colonel Yorkshire Yeomanry Cavalry.

SCARLETT, Hon. Sir James Yorke, English military commander, b. 1799; educated at Eton, and Trinity College, Cambridge; second lieutenant in the 18th Hussars, 1818; lieutenant-colonel, 1840; lieutenant-general, 1862; created K.C.B. at the close of the Crimean war; colonel of the 5th Dragoon Guards, and appointed to the command of Aldershot camp.

SCARLETT, Hon. Peter Campbell, English diplomatist, b. 1804; entered the diplomatic service, and was attaché at Constantinople, Paris, and at Rio Janeiro, and secretary of legation at Florence; envoy to Brazil, 1856; to the court of Tuscany, 1858; to the Emperor Maximilian of Mexico, 1864.

SCHACK, Adolf Friedrich von, German poet and historian of literature, b. at Brüsewitz, near Schwerin, Mecklenburg, Aug. 2, 1815; studied law at the Universities of Bonn, Heidelberg, and Berlin; entered the diplomatic service of the Grand Duke of Mecklenburg; retired, 1852. Author of 'Geschichte der dramatischen Litteratur und Kunst in Spanien,' Berlin, 3 vols. 1845–46; 'Poesie und Kunst der Araber in Spanien und Sicilien,' 1865; a translation of Firdusi; and other historical and critical works.

SCHAFF, Philip, American theologian, b. at Chur, Switzerland, Jan. 1, 1819; studied at the Gymnasium of Stuttgardt, and at the Universities of Tübingen, Halle, and Berlin; received the degree of Ph.D. from Berlin, 1841; appointed professor of sacred history to the Seminary of Mercersburg, United States, 1843. Author of 'What is Church History?' Philadelphia, 1846; 'The Political, Social, and Religious Condition of the United States of North America,' New York, 1855; and other theological works.

SCHALLER, Julius, German philosophical writer, b. at Magdeburg, 1810; studied theology at the University of Halle; appointed assistant-professor of philosophy at Halle, 1838. Author of 'The Philosophy of our Time,' Leipsic, 1837; 'Letters on the Cosmos of Alexander von Humboldt,' ib. 1850; and other philosophical works.

SCHAMYL, Imam, Circassian military commander, b. at the Aoul of Himry, in the Caucasian district of Daghestan, 1797; commenced his military career against the Russians, 1824; chosen chief of the Circassians, 1836; captured, with his son, by the Russians, Sept. 7, 1859.

SCHARF, George, English author and artist, b. 1820; admitted a student of the Royal Academy, 1838; appointed art secretary and keeper of the Gallery of Old Masters at the Manchester Exhibition of 1857; secretary and keeper of the National Portrait Gallery. Author of 'Catalogue of Pictures and Works of Art in Blenheim Palace,' 1860; and other works. Exhibited several oil paintings in the Royal Academy, and illustrated Macaulay's 'Lays of Ancient Rome' and other books.

SCHERER, Edmond, French Protestant theologian, b. April 8, 1815. Author of 'Mélanges religieuses;' and other works.

SCHLEIDEN, Matthias Jacob, German botanist, b. at Hamburg, April 5, 1804; studied at the University of Heidelberg, where he obtained the degree of LL.D. 1827; appointed assistant-professor at the University of Jena, 1839. Author of 'Scientific Elements of Botany,' Leipsic, 1842–43; and other works on botany.

SCHLEINITZ, Alexander, Baron von, Prussian statesman, b. 1807; entered the diplomatic career, and appointed councillor in the department of foreign affairs, 1832; ambassador at the court of Hanover; envoy-extraordinary to conclude the peace with Denmark, June 1849; minister of foreign affairs, July 29, 1849, to Sept. 26, 1850, and Nov. 6, 1858, to Oct. 12, 1861; appointed minister of the Royal House, Oct. 12, 1861.

SCHMERLING, Anton, Baron von, Austrian statesman, b. at Vienna, Aug. 23, 1805; studied law and became an advocate of the Court of Appeal, 1846; elected to the Council of State, 1846; member of the National Parliament of Germany held at Frankfort, 1848; minister of justice of Austria, 1849–51; minister of state, and chief of the Council of Ministers of the Austrian empire, 1860; resigned, June 1865.

SCHMITZ, Leonhard, English historical writer, b. at Eupen, near Aix-la-Chapelle, March 6, 1807; studied history and philology at the University of Bonn, 1828–32; appointed rector of the High School of Edinburgh, 1845. Author of a 'Popular History of Rome;' eleventh edition, 1859; 'Manual of the History of the Middle Ages,' 1859; and other historical works.

SCHNEIDER, Euge'ne, French statesman and mechanical engineer, b. at Nancy, April 1805; owner of the iron and locomotive establishment of Creuzot; member of the Chamber of Deputies, and of the Constituent and Legislative Assemblies, 1845–51; minister of agriculture and commerce, 1851; member of the Corps Législatif for the department of Sâone-et-Loire since 1852; one of the vice-presidents of the Chamber, 1865; president, 1867–69.

SCHNEIDER, Henry William, English politician, b. 1817; a merchant, ship-owner, and ironmaster; M.P. for Norwich, 1857–59, and for Lancaster, 1865–68.

SCHNETZ, Jean Victor, French painter, b. at Versailles, May 15, 1787; studied under David, Gros, Regnault, and Gérard; nominated director of the Academy of France at Rome, 1840; elected member of the Académie des Beaux Arts, 1837. Painted 'Jérémie pleurant sur les Ruines de Jérusalem,' 1819; 'Jeanne d'Arc revêtant les Armes,' 1834; 'La Leçon du Piferaro,' 1863; and many other historical works.

SCHNITZLER, Jean Henri, French statistical writer, b. at Strasburg, June 1, 1802; appointed professor of German to the Lyceum of Strasburg, 1856. Author of 'La Russie, la Pologne, et la Finlande,' Paris, 1835; 'L'Empire des Tzars au Point de Vue actuel de la Science,' 1856–62, and 1864; 'La Mission de l'Empereur Alexandre II. et le Général Rostoffsof,' 1860; and other historical and statistical works.

SCHNORR VON KAROLSFELD, Julius, German painter, b. at Leipsic, March 26, 1794; studied under his father, and at the Academy of Vienna; appointed professor of historical painting in the Academy of Munich, 1827; professor at the Academy of Dresden, and director of the Royal Museum, 1846. Painted 'The Marriage in Cana;' 'Ruth and Boaz;' executed eleven frescoes for the Villa Massimi from the 'Orlando Furioso;' and the illustrations for 'Die Bibel in Bildern,' 1854.

SCHOELCHER, Victor, French writer and politician, b. at Paris, July 21, 1804; studied at the College of Louis le Grand; was under-secretary in the Ministry of Marine, March 3, 1848; elected representative of Guadaloupe and Martinique to the Constituent Assembly, 1849; exiled, 1851. Author of a biography of Handel, and several works on slavery.

SCHOLL, Aure'lien, French author, b. at Bordeaux, July 14, 1833. Author of 'Lettres à mon Domestique,' 1854; 'Claude le Borgne,' 1859; 'Hélène Hermann,' 1863; and other works of fiction.

SCHOOLCRAFT, Henry Rowe, American author, b. in the county of Albany, March 28, 1793. Author of 'Narrative of an Expedition to Haska Lake, the actual Source of Mississippi River,' New York, 1834; 'Ethnological Researches respecting Red Man in America;' 'Historical and Statistical Information respecting the History, Condition, &c. of the Indian Tribes of the United States,' Philadelphia, 1852; and other works.

SCHOTT, Wilhelm, German philologist, b. at Mayence, Sept. 3, 1807; studied at the Universities of Giessen, Halle, and Berlin, 1830; appointed professor at the University of Berlin, 1838. Author of 'Essay on the Tartar Languages,' Berlin, 1836; 'Buddhism in Upper Asia and China,' 1844; and other philological works.

SCHREIBER, Charles, English politician, b. 1826; educated at Eton, and Trinity College, Cambridge, where he graduated B.A. 1850, M.A. 1853; fellow of Trinity, 1852–55; elected M.P. for Cheltenham, 1865.

SCHREIBER, Charlotte Elizabeth, English authoress, b. May 19, 1812; married first to Sir Josiah John Guest, Bart., 1833, who died 1852; and secondly to Charles Schreiber, Esq., M.P. 1855. Translator of the 'Mabinogion.'

SCHUMANN, Klara, German pianiste, b. Sept. 1819, widow of the celebrated composer, Robert Schumann.

SCHUSELKA, Franz, German author, b. at Budweis, Bohemia, Aug. 18, 1811; studied law at Vienna, and became advocate at the criminal tribunal; member of the German National Parliament at Frankfort, 1848. Author of 'Œstreichs Vor- und Rück-schritte,' Hamburg, 1847; 'Ein Stück Geschichte aus Russland,' Dresden, 1857; and other works.

SCHWEIGAARD, Anton Martin, Norwegian author, b. at Krageroe, April 11, 1808; studied at the University of Christiania; nominated lecturer on law in his university, 1835; deputy from Christiania to the National Assembly, 1842; director of the Bank of Christiania, 1845. Author of 'The Bank and Finances of Norway,' Christiania, 1836; 'Commentary on Norwegian Criminal Law,' 1844–46.

SCIALOJA, Antonio, Italian statesman, b. at Geduccio, near Naples, 1817; was advocate at the Court of Cassation, 1845; minister of agriculture and commerce, and deputy to the Chamber, 1848 to April 1849; elected for Moncalvo to the Italian National Parliament, 1859; appointed minister of finance, 1860; sent to Paris to negotiate a treaty of commerce between France and Italy, 1862. Author of 'Principles of Social Economy,' Naples, 1840; and other works.

SCLATER, Philip Lutley, English naturalist, b. 1829; educated at Winchester School, and at Corpus Christi College, Oxford, where he graduated in 1849; called to the bar of Lincoln's Inn, 1855; elected secretary of the Zoological Society of London, 1862. Author of 'Monograph of the Birds forming the Tanagrine Genus Calliste;' and other works on natural history.

SCOTT, Benjamin, English author, b. 1814; chief clerk in the Chamberlain's office, 1842; resigned, 1853; founded the Bank of London, of which he was secretary till 1858; elected to the office of city chamberlain, 1858. Author of 'The Catacombs at Rome;' and other historical works.

SCOTT, George Gilbert, English architect, b. at Gawcott, near Buckingham, 1811; designed the Martyrs' Memorial at Oxford, 1841; the Church of St. Nicholas at Hamburg; the cathedral church of St. John Newfoundland, erected 1848; and other churches and public buildings; appointed official architect of the dean and chapter of Westminster, 1849; architect to the new Foreign Office, and to the memorial of the late Prince Consort. Elected A.R.A. 1852, R.A. 1860.

SCOTT, Lord Henry John Douglas, English politician, b. 1832; educated at Eton; a magistrate of Midlothian, and captain of Midlothian Yeomanry Cavalry; M.P. for Selkirkshire since 1861-68; returned M.P. for Hampshire, 1868.

SCOTT, Rev. Robert, English divine, b. in Devonshire, 1810; educated at Shrewsbury, and at Christ Church, Oxford, where he graduated B.A. 1831; appointed master of Balliol College, 1854. Editor, with Dr. Liddell, of a Greek and English Lexicon.

SCOTT, Rev. William, English theological writer, b. 1812; educated at Queen's College, Oxford, where he graduated in 1835; was perpetual curate of Christ Church, Hoxton, 1839-60; appointed rector of St. Olave, Jewry, 1860; editor of the *Christian Remembrancer.*

SCOTT, Sir William, English politician, b. 1803; a deputy-lieutenant of Roxburgh; late lieutenant in the 2d Life Guards; M.P. for Carlisle, 1829-30; and for Roxburghshire since 1859.

SCOURFIELD, John Henry, English politician, b. 1808; educated at Harrow, and Oriel College, Oxford, where he graduated B.A. 1825, M.A. 1832; lord-lieutenant of Haverfordwest, and a magistrate and deputy-lieutenant of the county of Pembroke; assumed the name of Scourfield in lieu of Philipps, 1862; M.P. for Haverfordwest, 1852-68; returned M.P. for Pembroke, 1868.

SCROPE, George Poulett, English geologist, b. 1797; a magistrate and deputy-lieutenant of Wilts; M.P. for Stroud, 1833-65. Author of 'Considerations on Volcanoes,' 1825; 'The Geology of Central France,' 1827.

SCULLY, Vincent, English politician, b. Sept. 8, 1810; educated at Trinity College, Dublin, and at Cambridge; called to the Irish bar, 1833; M.P. for the county of Cork, 1852-57, and 1859-65. Author of works on the Irish Land Question, on Free Trade in Land, and Mutual Land Societies.

SEAFIELD, John Charles Ogilvie Grant, Earl of, Scottish administrator, b. 1815; a deputy-lieutenant of Inverness-shire, and for Banffshire; succeeded his father, sixth earl, 1853; elected a representative peer of Scotland, 1853.

SEATON, James Colborne, Baron, English politician, b. 1820; educated at Trinity College, Cambridge; a colonel in the army; served in Canada and the Ionian Islands; military secretary in Ireland, 1855-60; succeeded his father, first baron, 1863.

SECOND, Albéric, French author, b. at Angoulême, 1816. Author of 'Un Dragon du Vertu,' 1839; 'Contes sans Prétention,' 1857; and other novels and dramas.

SEDGWICK, Rev. Adam, English geologist, b. in Yorkshire, 1787; graduated at Trinity College, Cambridge, 1808; appointed Woodwardian professor of geology, 1818; and canon of Norwich, 1834. Author of 'Geology of the Lake District,' 1853; 'Discourse on the Studies of the University of Cambridge,' 1850; and other geological works.

SEDGWICK, Amy, English actress, b. at Bristol, Oct. 27, 1835; made her début at Richmond Theatre as 'Julia,' in 'The Hunchback,' 1853; first appeared in London at the Haymarket Theatre as 'Pauline,' in 'The Lady of Lyons,' 1857; married to W. B. Parkes, M.D. 1858, who died 1863.

SEDGWICK, Catherine Maria, American authoress, b. at Stockbridge, Massachusetts, 1790. Author of 'The New England Tale,' 1822; 'Hope Leslie, or Early Times in America,' 1827; 'Clarence, a Tale of our own Times,' 1830; 'The Poor Rich Man, and the Rich Poor Man,' 1836; and other works of fiction.

SEDILLOT, Louis Pierre, French philologist, b. at Paris, June 23, 1808; appointed secretary to the College of France and to the School of Oriental Languages, 1832. Author of 'Lettres sur quelques Points de l'Astronomie orientale,' 1834–59; 'Histoire des Arabes,' 1854; and other works.

SEELY, Charles, English politician, b. 1803; a magistrate and deputy-lieutenant of the county of Lincoln; was high sheriff of Hants, 1860–61; M.P. for Lincoln, 1847–48, and since 1861.

SEEMANN, Berthold, English naturalist, b. at Hanover, 1825; studied at the University of Göttingen, where he graduated Ph.D.; appointed naturalist on board H.M.S. *Herald*, 1846; appointed by the Colonial Office one of the royal commissioners to the Viti and Fiji Islands, 1860. Author of 'The Botany of the Voyage of H.M.S. *Herald*;' 'Popular History of the Palms;' and other works on natural history.

SEFTON, William Philip Molyneux, Earl of, English administrator, b. 1835; lord-lieutenant of the county of Lancaster; was lieutenant in the Grenadier, Guards, 1854, and served with his regiment in the Crimea until the peace.

SEGRIS, Emile Alexis, French politician, b. at Poitiers, March 4, 1811; advocate at the Imperial Court of Angers; member of the Corps Législatif for the department of Maine-et-Loire since 1859.

SEIDL, Johann Gabriel, German archæologist, b. at Vienna, June 21, 1804; studied law; appointed conservator of the Numismatic and Antiquarian Cabinet of Vienna, 1840; a member of the Academy of Sciences, 1847. Author of 'Dichtungen,' Vienna, 1826–28; 'Natur und Herz,' Stuttgardt, 1853; 'Beiträge zur Chronik,' Vienna, 1854; and other poetical and archæological works.

SEJOUR, Victor, French dramatic writer, b. at Paris about 1816. Author of 'Retour de Napoléon,' 1841; 'Le Fils de la Nuit,' 1857; 'Les Massacres de Syrie,' 1860; 'Le Marquis Caporal,' 1864; and other dramas.

SELKIRK, Dunbar James Douglas, Earl of, Scottish administrator, b. 1809; lord-lieutenant of the stewartry of Kirkcudbright; appointed keeper of the Great Seal of Scotland, April 1858; resigned, 1859.

SELWIN, Henry John, English politician, b. 1826; educated at St John's College, Cambridge, where he graduated B.A. 1849, M.A. 1852; a J.P. and deputy-lieutenant of Essex; M.P. for South Essex, 1865–68.

SELWYN, Sir Charles Jasper, English judge, b. 1813; educated at Eton, and Trinity College, Cambridge, where he graduated B.A. 1836, M.A. 1839; called to the bar of Lincoln's Inn, 1840; nominated commissary of the University of Cambridge, 1855; M.P. for the University of Cambridge, 1859–68; solicitor-general, 1867–68; one of the lords justices of appeal, 1868.

SELWYN, Rev. William, English divine, b. 1806; educated at Eton, and St. John's College, Cambridge, where he graduated B.A. 1828; canon of Ely Cathedral, 1833; Lady Margaret's reader in theology, 1855, and chaplain to her Majesty, 1859. Author of 'Horæ Hebraicæ,' 1848–60; 'Two Charts of Prophecy;' and other theological works.

SEMPER, Gottfried, German architect, b. at Hamburg, 1804; studied at the University of Göttingen, and at Munich; appointed professor to the Academy of Dresden, 1834; designed the new hall of the theatre at Dresden, and other buildings. Author of 'On Industry, Science, and Art,' 1852; 'The Four Elements of Architecture,' 1851.

SENARD, Antoine Marie Jules, French politician, b. at Rouen, April 9, 1800; studied law in Paris, and was called to the bar, 1821; took part in the Revolution of 1830; elected to the Constituent Assembly, of which he was chosen president, 1848; a member of the bar of Paris.

SE'NE'CA, Myrtil Joseph, French politician, b. at Abbeville, May 11, 1800; appointed magistrate, 1830; king's council at Arras, 1834; counsellor at the Court of Cassation, 1853; member of the Corps Législatif for the department of the Somme since 1863.

SERRANO, Francisco, Duke de la Torre, Spanish military commander, b. at Cadiz, Nov. 10, 1810; entered the army, 1825; captain-general of Grenada, 1850; exiled, 1854; returned and nominated captain-general of artillery, 1854; captain-general of New Castile, 1856; Spanish ambassador at Paris, 1857; director and colonel-general of artillery, 1859–61; captain-general of Madrid, 1865; president of the Senate, 1866; president of the Council of Ministers of the Provisional Government of Spain, Sept. 1868.

SERRET, Ernest, French writer, b. at Boulogne-sur-Mer, Dec. 3, 1821; studied law at Paris. Author of the 'Touristes,' 1846; 'Les Illustrations de l'Amour,' 1862; 'Neuf Filles et un Garçon,' 1864; and other novels and dramas.

SERRET, Joseph Alfred, French mathematician, b. 1819; studied at the École Polytechnique, and became lieutenant of artillery, 1840; examiner at the École Polytechnique, 1848; appointed professor of differential and integral calculus to the College of France, Dec. 20, 1863. Author of 'Sur l'Integration des Équations aux Dérivées partielles du premier Ordre,' 1861; and other works on mathematics.

SEVERNE, John Edmund, English politician, b. 1826; educated at Brasenose College, Oxford, where he graduated B.A. 1848; deputy-lieutenant of the counties of Northampton and Salop, and a magistrate of the county of Montgomery; formerly captain in the 16th Light Dragoons; M.P. for Ludlow, 1865-68.

SEWARD, William Henry, American statesman, b. in Orange County, New York, May 16, 1801; graduated at Union College, 1820; called to the bar, 1822; elected to the State Senate of New York, 1830; member of the Senate of the United States, 1849-61; was a candidate for the Presidency, 1860; secretary of state for foreign affairs, 1861-69. Author of 'Speeches, State Papers, and Miscellaneous Works,' New York, 1853.

SEWELL, Elizabeth Missing, English authoress, b. in the Isle of Wight, 1815. Author of 'Amy Herbert,' 1844; 'The Earl's Daughter;' 'Cleve Hall.'

SEWELL, Rev. William, English divine, b. in the Isle of Wight, 1805, brother of the preceding; educated at Harrow, and Merton College, Oxford, where he graduated B.A. 1827; appointed principal of St. Peter's College, Radley. Author of 'On the Dialogues of Plato;' 'Sacred Thoughts in Verse;' and other works.

SEYDOUX, Jean Jacques, French politician, b. at Vevey, Switzerland, July 6, 1796; a manufacturer of merinos at Cateau; representative of the département du Nord in the Legislative Assembly, 1849; member of the Corps Législatif for the département du Nord since 1852.

SEYFFARTH, Gustav, German philologist, b. July 13, 1796; graduated in philology and theology at the University of Leipsic, 1823; appointed professor of archæology in the same University, 1825. Author of 'Systema Astronomiæ Ægyptiorum quadripartitum,' Leipsic, 1833; 'Grammatica Ægyptiaca,' Gotha, 1855; 'Theological Writings of the Ancient Egyptians,' 1857; and other works on the language and literature of Egypt.

SEYMOUR, Alfred, English politician, b. 1824; educated at Christ Church, Oxford; a J.P. and deputy-lieutenant of Wilts; M.P. for Totnes, 1863-67.

SEYMOUR, Right Hon. Sir George, English diplomatist, b. 1797; graduated at Merton College, Oxford; appointed attaché at the Hague, 1817; resident minister at Florence, 1830; envoy-extraordinary and minister-plenipotentiary to Brussels, 1836, to Lisbon, Dec. 1846, and to St. Petersburg, 1851; ambassador at Vienna, 1855; retired from the diplomatic service, 1858.

SEYMOUR, George Henry, English naval commander, b. 1818; educated at the Royal Naval College, Portsmouth; a rear-admiral in the Royal Navy, and magistrate for Norfolk; M.P. for the county of Antrim since 1865.

SEYMOUR, Henry Danby, English politician, b. 1820; educated at Eton, and Christ Church, Oxford; a deputy-lieutenant of Wilts; was joint secretary to the Board of Control, 1855-58; M.P. for Poole, 1850-68.

SEYMOUR, Horatio, American politician, b. at Onondaga County, State of New York, 1811; studied for the bar, and practised as a lawyer in Utica; member of the Legislative Assembly, 1842-45; elected governor of the State of New York, 1852, and again 1862.

SEYMOUR, Sir Michael, English naval commander, b. 1802; educated at the Royal Naval College; a vice-admiral in the Royal Navy; has been commander-in-chief on the East India station; made K.C.B. for services against the Russians in the Baltic, 1855, and G.C.B. after the Chinese war, 1857-58; was secretary and registrar to the Order of the Bath; M.P. for Devonport, 1859-63; admiral in command at Portsmouth.

SEYMOUR, Rev. Michael Hobart, English author, b. 1802; educated at Trinity College, Dublin, where he graduated B.A. 1825, M.A. 1827; was ordained, 1825. Author of 'Mornings among the Jesuits,' 1850; 'Evenings with the Romanists,' 1854; and other theological works.

SHAFTESBURY, Anthony Ashley Cooper, Earl, English statesman, b. April 28, 1801; educated at Christ Church, Oxford, where he graduated M.A. 1832; created D.C.L. 1841; sat in the House of Commons as Lord Ashley, 1827–51; was a commissioner of the Board of Control, 1828–30; a lord of the Admiralty, Dec. 1834 to April 1835, and an ecclesiastical commissioner, 1841–47; chairman of the Lunacy Commission, and a commissioner of the Board of Health; succeeded his father, sixth earl, 1851.

SHAFTO, Robert Duncombe, English politician, b. 1806; a magistrate and deputy-lieutenant of Durham, and a magistrate of Wilts; M.P. for North Durham, 1847–68.

SHAW, Right Hon. Frederick, English politician, b. 1799; educated at Trinity College, Dublin, and at Brasenose College, Oxford; received the degree of LL.D. from Dublin; called to the Irish bar, 1822; appointed recorder of Dundalk, 1826; recorder of Dublin, 1828; member of the Privy Council in Ireland, 1835; was M.P. for Dublin City, 1830–32, and for the University of Dublin, 1832–48.

SHELTON, Frederick William, American author, b. at Jamaica, Long Island, 1814; graduated at the College of New Jersey, 1834; ordained a minister of the Episcopal Church, 1847; appointed incumbent of a parish in the State of Vermont, 1854. Author of 'The Rector of St. Bardolph's,' 1852; 'Peeps from a Belfry,' 1855; and other works.

SHERBORNE, James Henry Legge Dutton, Baron, English administrator, b. 1804; educated at Eton; a deputy-lieutenant and a magistrate of Gloucestershire; succeeded his father, second baron, Oct. 1862.

SHERIDAN, Henry Brinsley, English politician, b. 1820; called to the bar of the Inner Temple, 1851; J.P. for Middlesex and Kent, and lieutenant-colonel of the Sixth Cinque Ports Artillery; M.P. for Dudley since 1857.

SHERIDAN, Philip Henry, American military commander, b. in the State of Ohio, 1831; educated at West Point; admitted to the Military Academy, 1848, and graduated, 1853; lieutenant, 1855; captain, 1861; chief quartermaster-general of the Western Department, 1862; brigadier-general, 1862; major-general, 1863; gained the battle of Five Forks, March 30, 1865.

SHERIDAN, Richard Brinsley, English politician, b. 1809; a magistrate and deputy-lieutenant of Dorset; was high sheriff, 1838; M.P. for Shaftesbury, 1845–52; and for Dorchester, 1852–68.

SHERMAN, William Tecumseh, American military commander, b. in the State of Ohio, Feb. 8, 1820; entered West Point, 1836, and graduated, 1840; lieutenant, 1841; captain, 1848; appointed president of the State Military Institute of Louisiana, 1853; colonel, 1861; major-general, May 1, 1862; captured Atlanta, July 1864, and Savannah, Dec. 1864; general-in-chief of the United States forces, 1869.

SHERRIFF, Alexander Clunes, English politician, b. 1816; magistrate of the city of Worcester; deputy-chairman of the Metropolitan District Railway, and director of the Metropolitan Railway; M.P. for Worcester, 1865–68.

SHIRLEY, Evelyn Philip, English politician, b. 1812; educated at Eton, and Magdalen College, Oxford, where he graduated B.A. 1834, M.A. 1847; a magistrate and deputy-lieutenant of Warwickshire, and of the county of Monaghan; M.P. for the county of Monaghan, 1841, and for South Warwickshire, 1853–65. Author of 'The Noble and Gentle Men of England.'

SHREWSBURY AND TALBOT, Henry John Chetwynd Talbot, Earl of, English administrator, b. 1803; rear-admiral on the retired list; a magistrate and deputy-lieutenant of Staffordshire; was M.P. for Hertford, 1832–33, and for South Staffordshire, 1837–49; was a lord-in-waiting to the Queen, March to Dec. 1852; captain of the Hon. Corps of Gentlemen-at-Arms, Feb. 1858 to June 1859; succeeded as third Earl Talbot, 1849; made out his claim to the earldom (19th earl) of Shrewsbury, 1858.

SHUTTLEWORTH, Sir James Philipps Kaye, English politician, b. 1804; educated at Scottish and foreign Universities; formerly secretary to the Committee of Privy Council on Education; created a baronet, 1850; assumed the name of Shuttleworth by royal licence; a magistrate and deputy-lieutenant of the county of Lancaster.

SIBOUR, Le'on, French divine, b. at Istres, Bouches du Rhône, Feb. 9, 1807; studied at Aix, and entered the Grand Seminary; appointed professor of ecclesiastical history to the Faculty of Aix, 1845; represented Ardèche in the Constituent Assembly, 1849; consecrated bishop of Tripoli *in partibus infidelium*, 1855.

SIBTHORP, Rev. Richard Waldo, English theological writer, b. 1791; educated at Magdalen College, Oxford, where he graduated B.A. 1813, and M.A. and B.D.; was incumbent of St. James' Church, Ryde; resigned and joined the Roman Catholic Church, 1842; subsequently returned to the English communion. Author of 'Notes on the Book of Jonah;' and other theological works.

SIBUET, Joseph Prosper, Baron, French politician, b. at Thionville, Moselle, Feb. 7, 1811; studied law, and was called to the Paris bar, 1833; appointed auditor to the Council of State, 1838; member of the Corps Législatif for the department of Ardennes, 1863.

SICHEL, Jules, French medical writer, b. at Frankfort-on-the-Maine, 1802; received the degree of M.D. at Berlin, 1825, and at Paris, 1833; founded the Clinique Ophthalmologique, for gratuitous advice, in Paris, 1836. Author of 'Propositions générales sur l'Ophthalmologie,' 1833; 'Iconographie Ophthalmologique,' 1852–56; and other works on diseases of the eye.

SICKLES, Daniel, American military commander, b. in New York, 1822; elected to Congress, 1857; raised a brigade of 5,000 men on the outbreak of civil war, and received the commission of brigadier-general, 1861; major-general of Volunteers after the battle of Fair Oaks, 1862; appointed U.S. envoy to Spain, 1869.

SIGNOL, Emile, French painter, b. at Paris, March 11, 1804; studied at the École des Beaux Arts. Painted 'Joseph racontant son Rêve à ses Frères,' 1824; 'La Prise de Jérusalem,' 1848; 'Sainte Famille,' 1863; and many other, chiefly historical, works.

SIGURDSSON, Jon, Icelandic author, b. at Rafnseyri, June 17, 1811; studied philology at the University of Copenhagen, 1834; elected to the Althing, or Icelandic Parliament, 1845–47, and to the Danish Legislative Assembly, 1848. Author of 'Om Islands Statsreteige,' Forhold, 1856. Edited 'Islenzk Fornkvædi,' Copenhagen, 1854; and other works.

SIMEON, Sir John, English politician, b. 1815; educated at Christ Church, Oxford, where he graduated B.A. 1837, M.A. 1840; a magistrate of Hants, deputy-lieutenant of the Isle of Wight, and major 1st battalion Isle of Wight Rifle Volunteers; M.P. for the Isle of Wight, 1847–51, and since 1865.

SIMMS, William Gilmore, American author, b. at Charleston, South Carolina, April 17, 1807. Author of 'Lyrical and other Poems,' 1825; 'Atalantis, a Story of the Sea,' 1832; 'The Wigwam and the Cabin,' New York,' 1845; 'Poems, descriptive, dramatic, legendary, and contemplative,' ib. 1853; and numerous other works.

SIMON, John, English surgeon, b. 1810; elected fellow of the Royal College of Surgeons, 1844; medical officer of the Privy Council; surgeon to St. Thomas's Hospital, and lecturer on pathology. Author of several papers on the sanitary condition of England.

SIMON, Joseph François, French politician, b. at Guéméné, Loire Inférieure, Feb. 5, 1801; member of the Corps Législatif for the department of Loire Inférieure since 1857.

SIMON, Jules, French philosopher and politician, b. at Lorient, Morbihan, Dec. 31, 1814; studied in the college of his native town, and at the École Normale, 1832; elected to the Constituent Assembly, 1848; member of the Corps Législatif for the department of the Seine since 1863. Author of 'Histoire de l'École d'Alexandrie,' 1844–45; second edition, 1861; 'L'École,' 1864; and several works on philosophy and education.

SIMONDS, William Barrow, English politician, b. 1820; educated at Merchant Taylors' School; a magistrate of the city of Winchester; captain of 1st Hants Rifle Volunteers; auditor to King's College, Cambridge; M.P. for Winchester since 1865.

SIMPSON, Sir James Young, Scottish physician, b. at' Bathgate, Linlithgowshire, 1811; appointed professor of midwifery in the University of Edinburgh, 1840; introduced chloroform, 1847; elected president of the Edinburgh Royal College of Physicians, 1849. Author of 'Obstetric Memoirs;' and other medical works.

SIMROCK, Karl, German poet, b. at Bonn, Oct. 28, 1802; studied at the Universities of Bonn and Berlin, 1822; appointed professor of German literature and language at Bonn, 1850. Author of 'Gedichte,' Leipsic, 1844; 'Altdeutsches Lesebuch,' Stuttgardt and Tubingen, 1854; and other poetical works.

SIMSON, Martin Eduard, German statesman, b. at Königsberg, Nov. 10, 1810; studied in his native town, and received the degree of LL.D. 1829; appointed professor, 1836; and counsellor of the superior tribunal of Königsberg, 1846; represented Königsberg at the Parliament of Frankfort, 1848; charged with the leadership of the deputation to Berlin to offer the crown to the king of Prussia, 1849; member of the Parliament of Erfurt, 1852; president of the Second Prussian Chamber, 1861–64.

SINCLAIR, James St. Clair, Baron, Scottish administrator, b. at Herdmanston, Haddingtonshire, 1803; educated at Winchester College; a deputy-lieutenant of Berwickshire; a magistrate of Haddingtonshire and Berwickshire; was formerly captain in the Grenadier Guards; succeeded his father, twelfth baron, 1863.

SINCLAIR, Ven. John, English divine, b. 1796; educated at Pembroke College, Oxford, where he graduated B.A. 1819, M.A. 1822; appointed examining chaplain to the Bishop of London, 1839; archdeacon of Middlesex, 1843. Author of 'The Life and Times of Sir John Sinclair, Bart.,' 1837; and other works.

SINTENIS, Karl Friedrich, German politician, b. at Zerbst, June 25, 1804; studied law at the Universities of Leipsic and Jena; member of the Diet of Anhalt, 1849; president of the tribunal of the Duchy of Anhalt, 1853. Author of 'Corpus Juris Civilis,' 1829; and other legal works.

SKODA, Joseph, German physician, b. at Pilsen, Bohemia, Dec. 10, 1805; studied at the University of Vienna, and received the degree of M.D. 1831; second physician to the General Hospital of Vienna, 1833; physician-in-chief to the hospital, 1841. Author of 'Treatise on Auscultation and Percussion,' 1855.

SLADE, Sir Adolphus, English naval commander, b. 1807; appointed a commander in the navy, 1841; entered the Turkish service, and became vice-admiral in the Ottoman Navy, 1858; created K.C.B. 1858. Author of 'Records of Travels in Turkey,' and 'Turkey, Greece, and Malta.'

SMEE, Alfred, English author, b. 1818; admitted a member of the College of Surgeons, 1840. Author of 'The Potato Plant, its Uses and Properties;' 'The Principles of the Human Mind;' 'Lectures on Electro-metallurgy, delivered at the Bank of England,' and other works.

SMILES, Samuel, English author, b. at Haddington, N.B., Dec. 23, 1812; matriculated at Edinburgh University, 1829; diploma of the Royal College of Surgeons, Edinburgh, 1832; practised medicine for six years, and became afterwards secretary to two railway companies for twenty-one years. Author of 'Life of George Stephenson;' 'Lives of Engineers;' 'Self Help;' 'The Huguenots in England;' and other works.

SMIRKE, Sydney, English architect, b. 1805; architect of the Juvenile Reformatory in the Isle of Wight, the Carlton and Conservative Club Houses in London, the Reading Room and Roman and Assyrian Galleries of the British Museum, and of numerous other public buildings; architect to the Inner Temple, and surveyor-general to the Duchy of Lancaster. Elected A.R.A. 1848, R.A. 1860.

SMITH, Sir Andrew, English physician, b. 1797; educated at Edinburgh, where he graduated in 1819; M.D. of Trinity College, Dublin; inspector-general of hospitals, 1851; director-general of the Army Medical Department, 1853–59. Author of 'Illustrations of the Zoology of South Africa;' 'Origin and History of the Bushmen;' 'History of Secondary Small-pox;' and other works.

SMITH, Charles Roach, English antiquary, b. at Landguard, Isle of Wight, 1804. Author of 'Collectanea Antiqua,' 1848–63; 'Roman London,' 1859; edited the 'Inventorium Sepulchrale' of Bryan Faussett, 1856.

SMITH, Christopher Webb, English ornithologist, b. 1793; educated at Haileybury College, and nominated to the Indian Civil Service, 1811. Author, with Sir C. D'Oyly, of the 'Ornithology of Hindostan,' and of 'Indian Sport.'

SMITH, Francis Pettit, English engineer, b. at Hythe, Feb. 9, 1808; educated at a school at Ashford, Kent, and became a grazing farmer; constructed a model of the screw propeller for purposes of navigation, 1834, which was adopted by the Admiralty in the *Archimedes*, 1838; received a pension from the civil list of £200 per annum, 1855; appointed curator of the Patent Museum, South Kensington, 1860.

SMITH, Goldwin, English author, b. at Reading, 1823; educated at Eton, Christ Church and Magdalen College, Oxford, and graduated B.A. 1845; called to the bar of Lincoln's Inn, 1847; was a member of the Education Commission, 1859; professor of modern history in the University of Oxford, and subsequently professor at the Cornell University, Ithaca, New York. Author of 'The Empire;' 'Does the Bible sanction American Slavery?' and several historical works.

SMITH, James, English writer, b. near Maidstone, Kent, 1820. Author of 'Rural Records,' 1845; 'Lights and Shadows of Artist Life and Character;' founder of the *Melbourne Punch*. Appointed librarian to the Parliament of Victoria, 1863.

SMITH, John Abel, English politician, b. 1802; educated at Christ's College, Cambridge, where he graduated B.A. 1824. M.A. 1827; a magistrate of Middlesex and Sussex; M.P. for Midhurst, 1830–31, and for Chichester, 1831–59, and 1863–68.

SMITH, John Benjamin, English politician, b. 1792; was president of the Anti-Corn Law League, and of the Manchester Chamber of Commerce, 1839–41; M.P. for Stirling, 1847–52; and for Stockport since 1852.

SMITH, Sir John Mark Frederick, English military commander, b. 1792; entered the corps of Royal Engineers, 1805; general in the army, and colonel-commandant of the Royal Engineers; was M.P. for Chatham, 1852–53, and 1857–59. Translator of Marmont's 'Present State of the Turkish Empire.'

SMITH, Rev. Joseph Denham, English author, b. 1816; ordained minister of the Congregational Dissenters, 1837; minister of the Congregational church at Kingstown, near Dublin, 1849–62; and minister of Merrion Hall, Dublin, 1863. Author of 'Oliver Cromwell, or England Past and Present;' 'The Rhine and the Reformation;' and other works.

SMITH, Sir Montagu Edward, English judge, b. 1809; educated at the Grammar School, Bideford; called to the bar of the Middle Temple, 1835; made a Q.C. 1852; M.P. for Truro, April 1859 to Feb. 1865. when he was appointed a judge of the Court of Common Pleas, and knighted.

SMITH, Robert Angus, English chemist, b. near Glasgow, Feb. 15, 1817; educated at Glasgow, and studied chemistry at Giessen under Liebig, 1839–41; appointed inspector-general of alkali works for the United Kingdom, 1863. Author of 'Life of Dalton, and History of the Atomic Theory up to his Time;' and of numerous papers on the air of towns, of mines, and the constitution of the atmosphere.

SMITH, Rev. Robert Payne, English divine, b. 1819; educated at Pembroke College, Oxford, where he graduated in 1841; appointed regius professor of divinity in the University of Oxford, 1865. Author of 'Messianic Interpretation of the Prophecies of Isaiah,' 1862; and other theological works.

SMITH, Samuel George, English politician, b. 1822; educated at Rugby, and Trinity College, Cambridge, where he graduated B.A. 1844, M.A. 1847; a magistrate of Herts; M.P. for Aylesbury since 1859.

SMITH, Right Hon. Thomas Berry Cusack, English jurist, b. 1797; educated at Trinity College, Dublin; called to the Irish bar, 1819; appointed king's council, 1830; solicitor-general for Ireland, 1842; attorney-general, 1842; a bencher of King's Inn, 1843; master of the Rolls in Ireland since 1846; M.P. for Ripon, 1843–46.

SMITH, William, English author, b. in London, 1814; educated at the University of London; appointed classical examiner in the University of London, 1853. Editor of 'Dictionary of Greek and Roman Geography,' 1852–57; 'Dictionary of the Bible, comprising its Antiquities, Biography, Geography, and Natural History,' 1860–63; of 'Gibbon's Decline and Fall of the Roman Empire,' 1854; and other works.

SMOLLETT, Patrick Boyle, English politician, b. 1805; educated at Edinburgh, and Haileybury College; formerly in the East India Company's civil service at Madras; retired, 1858; M.P. for Dumbartonshire, 1859–68.

SOLLOHUB, Vladimir Alexandrowitch, Count, Russian author, b. at St. Petersburg, 1815; entered the diplomatic service, and was attaché to the Russian embassy at Vienna. Author of 'Na Son,' 1841; and several novels and dramas.

SOMERS, Charles Somers, Earl, English administrator, b. July 14, 1819; educated at Oxford; was M.P. for Reigate as Viscount Eastnor, 1841–47; appointed a lord-in-waiting to the Queen, Dec. 1852; resigned, 1857; a deputy-lieutenant of Herefordshire.

SOMERSET, Edward Adolphus St. Maur, Duke of, English statesman, b. Dec. 20, 1804, the eldest son of the eleventh duke; educated at Eton, and Christ Church, Oxford; sat in the House of Commons as Lord Seymour, 1834–55, when he succeeded to the dukedom; has been a lord of the Treasury, secretary of the Board of Control, under-secretary of state for the Home Department, and chief commissioner of woods and forests; first lord of the Admiralty, June 1859 to July 1866.

SOMERSET, Poulett George Henry, English politician, b. 1822; educated at Eton, and the Royal Military College, Sandhurst; late lieutenant-colonel Coldstream Guards; served in the Crimea, 1854–56; a magistrate and deputy-lieutenant of the county of Monmouth; M.P. for Monmouthshire since 1859.

SOMERVILLE, Mary, English authoress, b. in Scotland. Author of 'Mechanism of the Heavens,' 1831; 'The Connexion of the Physical Sciences,' 1834; 'Physical Geography,' 1848. Received a grant from the civil list of £300 per annum, 1835.

SOMMER, Jean E'douard Albert, French author, b. at Nancy, April 6, 1822; studied at the École Normale, 1841–46. Author of 'Méthode uniforme pour l'Enseignment des Langues,' 1861–65; 'Comédies de Plaute,' 1864; and other works, chiefly French and Latin lexicons.

SOTHERN, Thomas Edward, English actor and dramatic writer, b. in Liverpool, April 1, 1830; educated for the Church; went to America, 1851, and made his first appearance on the stage at Boston. Author of and actor in 'The American Cousin;' 'Lord Dundreary Married and Done For;' and other comedies.

SOULE', Pierre, American politician, b. in France, 1800 ; called to the bar of Paris ; elected senator of the American Congress, 1847–49 ; American ambassador at Madrid, 1853 to June 1855.

SOUTHWORTH, Emma, American authoress, b. at Washington, Dec. 26, 1818. Author of ' Retribution,' 1849 ; ' The Deserted Wife,' 1850 ; ' The Foster Sister,' 1852 ; ' Hickory Hall,' 1855 ; and other works of fiction.

SOWERBY, George Brettingham, English naturalist, b. 1812. Author of ' A Conchological Manual,' 1839 ; ' Popular British Conchology,' 1854 ; ' Popular Guide to the Aquarium,' 1857 ; and other works on natural history.

SPARKS, Jared, American writer, b. at Wellington, Connecticut, 1794 ; minister of Unitarian congregations, 1819–39 ; retired from the ministry, and was appointed professor of history at Harvard University, 1839 ; principal of the same, 1842–52. Author of ' Life and Writings of George Washington,' Boston, 1833–40 ; ' History of the American Revolution ;' and other works.

SPENCE, Sir James, English surgeon, b. 1808 ; licentiate of the Royal College of Surgeons at Edinburgh, 1832 ; fellow of the same, 1849 ; professor of surgery in the University of Edinburgh ; appointed surgeon-in-ordinary to the Queen, 1865.

SPENCER, Right Rev. George John Trevor, English divine, b. 1801 ; educated at the Charterhouse, and University College, Oxford, where he graduated B.A. 1822, M.A. 1825 ; consecrated bishop of Madras, 1837 ; resigned, 1849 ; appointed chancellor of St. Paul's Cathedral, 1860. Author of ' Journal of a Visitation to the Provinces of Travancore and Tinnevelly in the Diocese of Madras,' 1842 ; and several sermons.

SPENCER, John Poyntz Spencer, Earl, English administrator, b. 1832 ; educated at Harrow, and Trinity College, Cambridge ; was M.P. for South Northamptonshire, 1857 ; succeeded his father, fourth earl, Dec. 1857 ; a P.C. and deputy-lieutenant and magistrate of Northamptonshire ; appointed groom of the stole to the Prince of Wales, 1863.

SPEIRS, Archibald Alexander, English politician, b. 1840 ; educated at Eton ; a J.P. and deputy-lieutenant of the county of Renfrew, and captain of the Scots Fusilier Guards ; M.P. for Renfrewshire, 1865–68.

SPIERS, Alexander, English writer, b. at Gosport, Hampshire, 1808 ; studied in England, Germany, and at Paris ; appointed professor of English at the Lycée Bonaparte, 1833. Author of ' Studies of English Poetry,' 1835 ; ' General French and English Dictionary,' 1849 ; and other works.

SPONNECK, Wilhelm Carl Eppingen, Count von, Danish statesman, b. at Rinkjöbing, Feb. 16, 1815 ; studied law at the University of Sorö near Copenhagen, 1837 ; appointed minister of finance, Nov. 16, 1848 ; accompanied King George I. to Greece as chief councillor, 1863.

SPOTTISWOODE, William, English author and printer, b. in London, Jan. 11, 1825 ; educated at Eton, Harrow, and Balliol College, Oxford, where he graduated B.A. 1845 ; was public examiner in mathematics at Oxford, 1857–58 ; succeeded his father as Queen's printer, 1858. Author of ' Travels in Russia ;' and several scientific papers.

SPRENGER, Aloys, German philologist, b. at Nassereni, in the Tyrol, Sept. 3, 1818 ; studied at the College of Innspruck, and at the University of Vienna ; appointed director of the College of Delhi, 1844 ; appointed examiner at the College of Fort William, 1850. Published ' Masudi's Meadows of Gold, translated from the Arabic,' London, 1849 ; ' Life of Mohammed,' Allahabad, 1851 ; and other works.

SPURGEON, Rev. Charles Haddon, English dissenting minister, b. at Kelvedon, Essex, June 19, 1834 ; educated at Colchester, and was usher in a school at Newmarket ; became pastor of a Baptist chapel at Waterbeach, 1851 ; and of New Park Street Chapel, Southwark, 1853 ; subsequently preached at the Surrey Music Hall ; minister of the Baptist ' Tabernacle,' Kennington Road, 1861.

SQUIER, Ephraim George, American archæologist, b. in Bethlehem, Albany County, New York, June 17, 1821. Author of ' Nicaragua, its People, Scenery, Ancient Monuments, and proposed Interoceanic Canal,' 1852 ; ' Monograph of Authors who have written on the Aboriginal Languages of Central America,' 1861 ; and numerous other works on American antiquities.

STAAF, Ferdinand Nathaniel, Swedish author, b. at Stockholm, July 7, 1823 ; entered the Swedish army, 1841 ; staff-major and teacher of French literature in the Military Academy of Carlberg, 1853 ; appointed military attaché to the Swedish and Norwegian legation in Paris, 1862. Author of ' Urval ur franska Litteraturen,' Stockholm, 1859–62 ; and other works.

STACPOOLE, William, English politician, b. 1830; educated at Cheltenham, and Trinity College, Dublin; a magistrate of the county of Clare, and captain of the Clare Militia; M.P. for Ennis since 1860.

STAEMPFLI, Jacob, Swiss politician, b. at Schüpfen, Berne, 1820; studied law, and was called to the bar, 1843; editor of the *Berne Gazette*, 1845; member of the Federal Council, 1846; federal vice-president, 1858; president of the Council, 1859; chief of the military department of the Swiss Confederation, 1860; president of the Swiss Confederation, 1861.

STAHR, Adolf Wilhelm, German author, b. at Prenzlau, Prussia, Oct. 22, 1805; graduated at Halle; one of the directors of the College of Oldenburg, 1836. Author of 'Torso, oder Kunst, Künstler und Kunst-werke der Alten,' Brunswick, 1854–55; 'Tiberius;' and numerous other works.

STAIR, North Hamilton Dalrymple, Earl of, English administrator, b. 1795; studied at the University of Edinburgh; deputy-lieutenant and J.P. of the county of Edinburgh; was captain 25th Dragoons; left the army, 1817; succeeded his brother, eighth earl, 1853.

STALLBAUM, Gottfried, German philologist, b. at Zaach, near Delitsch, Sept. 25, 1793; studied at Leipsic; professor at the University of Halle, 1817; professor at Leipsic, 1840. Author of 'Ueber den innern Zusammenhang der musikalischer Bildung der Jugend mit dem Gesammtzwecke des Gymnasiums,' Leipsic, 1842; and other works.

STANHOPE, George Philip Cecil Arthur, Lord, English politician, b. 1831; educated at Eton; entered the army, 1849; lieutenant in the Royal Horse Guards Blue, 1853; retired, 1855; a magistrate of Notts, and captain of the South Notts Yeomanry Cavalry; M.P. for South Nottinghamshire, 1860–65.

STANHOPE, James Banks, English politician, b. 1821; educated at Westminster; a magistrate and deputy-lieutenant of the county of Lincoln; M.P. for North Lincolnshire, 1852–68.

STANHOPE, Philip Henry Stanhope, Earl, English statesman and historian, b. at Walmer, 1805; educated at Christ Church, Oxford, where he graduated B.A. 1827; was M.P. for Wootton Bassett, 1830–31; for Hertford till unseated, 1832, and from 1835 to 1852; under-secretary of state for foreign affairs, Dec. 1834 to Aug. 1835; secretary to the Board of Control, July 1845 to July 1846; president of the Society of Antiquarians, 1846; lord rector of Aberdeen University, 1858. Author of 'History of England from 1713 to 1783;' and numerous other works.

STANLEY, Very Rev. Arthur Penrhyn, English divine, b. 1815; educated at Rugby, and Balliol College, Oxford; canon of Canterbury, 1851–58; regius professor of ecclesiastical history at Oxford, canon of Christ Church, and chaplain to the Bishop of London, 1858–64; dean of Westminster, 1864. Author of 'Life of Dr. Arnold,' 1844; 'Sinai and Palestine,' 1855; and numerous other works.

STANLEY, Right Hon. Lord Edward Henry Smith, English statesman, b. at Knowsley Park, Lancaster, 1826, eldest son of the Earl of Derby; educated at Rugby, and Trinity College, Cambridge; M.P. for Lynn Regis since 1848; under-secretary of state for foreign affairs from February to December 1852; secretary of state for the colonies from February to May 1858; secretary of state for India, May 1858 to June 1859; secretary of state for foreign affairs, July 6, 1866, to Dec. 1868.

STANLEY, Hon. Frederick Arthur, English politician, b. 1841; educated at Eton; formerly lieutenant and captain Grenadier Guards; M.P. for Preston, 1865–68.

STANLEY, Hon. William Owen, English politician, b. 1802; educated at Eton; a magistrate and deputy-lieutenant of Anglesea; formerly captain Grenadier Guards; M.P. for Anglesea, 1837–47; for Chester, 1850–57; and for Beaumaris since 1857.

STANLEY OF ALDERLEY, Edward John Stanley, Baron, English statesman, b. 1802, the eldest son of the first Baron Stanley; sat in the House of Commons as Mr. Stanley, 1831–46; called to the House of Lords as Baron Eddioburg, 1859; under-secretary of state for the Home Department from July to November 1834; secretary of the Treasury from 1835 to June 1841, and paymaster of the forces from June to September 1841; under-secretary of state for foreign affairs from 1847 to Dec. 1851; paymaster of the forces, and vice-president of the Board of Trade till March 1852; reappointed to the same office, Dec. 1852; president of the Board in Lord Palmerston's ministry, from Feb. 24, 1855, to Feb. 19, 1858; postmaster-general, Aug. 1860 to July 1866.

STANSFELD, James, English statesman, b. 1820; educated at University College, London, and graduated LL.B. 1844; called to the bar of the Inner Temple, 1846; a junior lord of the Admiralty, 1863–64; under-secretary for India, 1866; third lord of the Treasury, 1868; M.P. for Halifax since 1859.

STANTON, Edwin, American statesman, b. in Steubenville, Ohio, 1815; studied law; called to the bar, and practised in Ohio till 1847, and at the Supreme Court at Washington, 1858; appointed attorney-general, 1860; secretary of war from Jan. 13, 1862, to June 1, 1868.

STAUNTON, Howard, English author, b. 1810; educated at Oxford. Author of several works on chess, and editor of the 'Illustrated Shakespeare.'

STAWELL, Sir William Foster, English colonial judge, b. 1815; educated at Trinity College, Dublin; called to the Irish bar, 1839; attorney-general, and member of the Executive Council of the colony of Victoria, 1851; appointed chief justice of the Supreme Court of Victoria, and knighted, 1857.

STEANE, Rev. Edward, English dissenting minister, b. March 23, 1798; educated at the University of Edinburgh; pastor of a Baptist congregation at Camberwell since 1823; one of the founders of the Evangelical Alliance. Author of 'Constitutional Principles of the Christian Church;' and other religious works.

STEBBING, Rev. Henry, English author, b. 1800; educated at St. John's College, Cambridge, where he graduated B.A. 1823, M.A. 1826, D.D. 1839; rector of St. Mary Somerset, Upper Thames Street, City, 1857. Author of 'The History of the Church of Christ from 1530 to the Eighteenth Century,' 1839; and other works.

STEIN, Ludwig, German political economist, b. at Eckernförde, Schleswig, Nov. 15, 1813; studied at the University of Kiel, where he graduated in 1840; appointed professor of law at the same University, 1846; suspended, 1852, and appointed professor of political economy at the University of Berlin. Author of 'History of France and of French Law,' 1846–48; 'System of Political Economy,' Leipsic, 1854; and other works.

STEINBRUCH, Eduard, German painter, b. at Magdeburg, May 3, 1802; studied at Berlin. Painted 'Hagar in the Desert,' 1829; 'A Young Girl at Prayer;' and other pictures, chiefly religious.

STEINMANN, Johan, Danish military commander, b. 1812; second lieutenant of artillery, 1830; served in the war of 1849; received the command of the first division charged with the defence of the Isle of Alsen, 1864; appointed general-in-chief of the Danish army, 1864.

STEPHEN, Sir Alfred, English colonial judge, b. 1802; called to the bar of Lincoln's Inn, 1823; solicitor-general and attorney-general of Tasmania, and chief justice of New South Wales, 1841 to 1857; knighted, 1846.

STEPHEN, Sir George, English administrator, b. 1794: practised as a solicitor in the city of London; called to the bar of Gray's Inn, 1849; a deputy-lieutenant of Bucks; knighted, 1838. Author of 'Adventures of an Attorney in Search of Practice,' 1839.

STEPHEN, James Fitzjames, English legal writer, b. March 1829; educated at Trinity College, Cambridge, where he graduated B.A. 1852; called to the bar of the Inner Temple, Jan. 1854; recorder of Newark-on-Trent; legislative member of the Supreme Council of India, July 1869. Author of 'A Treatise on Criminal Law,' 1863; and other works.

STEPHENS, Alexander Hamilton, American politician, b. in Georgia, Feb. 11, 1812; studied law in Franklin College, and called to the bar, 1834; member of the Senate of Georgia, 1842; member of Congress, 1843–59; vice-president of the Confederate States, 1861–65.

STEPHENS, Anne, American authoress, b. in Connecticut, 1810. Author of 'Mary Derwent;' 'Fashion and Famine,' New York, 1854; 'The Old Homestead,' ib. 1856; and other works of fiction.

STEPHENS, Henry, English agriculturist, b. at Keerpoy, Bengal, July 25, 1795. Author of 'The Book of the Farm,' Edinburgh,' 1844; 'The Drainage of Land,' 1846; 'The Yester Deep Land Culture,' 1855.

STEPHENS, Walter, English author, b. in London, Aug. 22, 1832; studied law. Author of 'Blackfriars, or the Monks of Old,' 1844; of 'Vendetta a drama; and other works of fiction and dramas.

STEPHENSON, Sir Rowland Macdonald, English civil engineer, b. 1808; educated at Harrow; civil engineer, and director of the East India Railway Company; knighted, 1857.

STERN, Marie de Flavigny, Comtesse d'Agoult, French authoress, b. at Frankfort on the Maine, 1805; educated at the Convent du Sacré Cœur, Paris; married to the Comte d'Agoult, 1827. Author, under the name of 'Daniel Stern,' of 'Hervé,' 1841; 'Nélida,' 1845; 'Florence et Turin,' 1862; 'Histoire de la Révolution de 1848,' and other works.

STERNBERG, Alexander, Baron von Ungern, German novelist, b. near Revel, Esthonia, April 22, 1806; studied at Dorpat, Russia. Author of 'Novellen.' Stuttgardt, 1832–34; 'Die Gelbe Gräfin,' Berlin, 1848; 'Das Stille Haus,' ib. 1854; and other works of fiction.

STEWART, Sir Houston, English naval commander, b. 1791; served at Flushing, and at the siege of Acre; second in command in the Black Sea, 1855–56; created K.C.B. 1856, G.C.B. 1865; was M.P. for Greenwich, Feb. to July 1852; appointed commander-in-chief at Devonport, 1865.

STIEVENART BETHUNE, Louis, French politician, b. at Valenciennes, Aug. 15, 1817; member of the Corps Législatif for the département du Nord since 1864.

STIRLING, James, English politician, b. 1805; educated at the High School, Edinburgh, and the University of Göttingen; a J.P. and deputy-lieutenant of the county of Dumbarton; M.P. for Dumbartonshire, 1865–68.

STIRLING, Patrick James, English political economist, b. at Dumblane, county of Perth, 1809; studied under Dr. Chalmers. Author of 'Philosophy of Trade,' Edinburgh, 1846; 'The Australian and Californian Gold Discoveries,' ib. 1852; and other works.

STIRLING-MAXWELL, Sir William, English author, b. at Kenmure, near Glasgow, 1818; educated at Trinity College, Cambridge, where he graduated M.A. 1843; J.P. of the county of Perth; M.P. for Perthshire, 1852–68. Author of 'Cloister Life of Charles V.' 1852; 'Velasquez, and his Works,' 1855; and other historical publications.

STOCKER, Rev. Charles William, English author, b. 1793; educated at St. John's College, Oxford, 1812; fellow of St. John's, 1815; principal of Elizabeth College, Guernsey, 1824–29; rector of Draycote-le-Moors, Staffordshire, since 1841. Author of 'Conversations on the Lord's Supper,' 1840; and other educational and religious works.

STOKES, George Gabriel, English mathematician, b. 1820; educated at Pembroke College, Cambridge, where he graduated B.A. 1841; appointed Lucasian professor of mathematics, 1849; elected one of the secretaries of the Royal Society, 1854. Author of various scientific papers contributed to the publications of learned societies.

STOKES, William, Irish physician, b. in Dublin, 1804; graduated M.D. at the University of Edinburgh, 1825; has been regius-professor of physic in the University of Dublin; received the honorary degree of LL.D. from the University of Edinburgh; was president of the College of Physicians in Ireland; physician-in-ordinary to the Queen in Ireland. Author of several medical works.

STONE, Marcus, English painter, b. 1840. Painted 'James Watt's Discovery of the Steam Engine;' and many other pictures.

STONE, William Henry, English politician, b. 1834; educated at Harrow, and Trinity College, Cambridge, where he graduated B.A. 1857, M.A. 1860; a magistrate of Surrey and Hampshire; M.P. for Portsmouth since 1865.

STONEMAN, George, American military commander, b. in New York, 1826; educated at West Point, and graduated in 1846; took part with the North in the civil war, and nominated major of cavalry, 1861; lieutenant-colonel, 1862; major-general, 1863.

STORCH, Ludwig, German author, b. at Ruhla, April 13, 1814; studied at the Universities of Leipsic and Nordhausen. Author of 'Kuntz von Kaufungen,' Leipsic, 1827; 'History of the Emperor Charles the Fifth,' ib. 1854; 'Poems,' ib. 1854; and other, chiefly historical, works.

STORKS, Sir Henry, English military commander, b. 1811; educated at the Charterhouse; assistant adjutant-general in the Kafir war, 1846–47; commanded the British military establishments on the Bosphorus, Dardanelles, and at Smyrna during the Russian war, 1854–55; secretary for military correspondence at the War Office, 1857–59; a major-general in the army; lord high commissioner of the Ionian Islands, 1859–63; governor of Malta, 1864–67; comptroller-in-chief at the War Office, 1868.

STOURM, Auguste Africain, French administrator, b. at Metz, Moselle, July 22, 1797; studied law, and called to the bar, 1819; member of the Constituent Assembly, 1848; councillor of state, 1849; postmaster-general, 1853; created senator, 1861.

STOWE, Harriet Beecher, American authoress, b. at Lichfield, Connecticut, June 15, 1814; married to the Rev. E. B. Stowe, 1835. Author of 'Uncle Tom's Cabin,' Boston, 1852; 'The Minister's Wooing,' 1860; 'The Pearl of Orr's Island,' 1862; and other works of fiction.

STRACK, Johann Heinrich, German architect, b. at Bückeburg, Prussia, 1806. Designed the castle of Fredericksburg for the King of Denmark; the grand ducal residence of Schwerin; the church of St.·Nicholas at Hamburg; and other buildings, chiefly in the Gothic style. Author of 'On the Construction of Theatres in Ancient Greece,' Potsdam, 1843; and other works on architecture.

STRADBROKE, John Edward Cornwallis Rous, Earl of, English administrator, b. Feb. 13, 1794; educated at Westminster; served in the Coldstream Guards, 1810–17; was present with his regiment in all the engagements in Spain and France from June 1812 to the end of the war; lord-lieutenant of the county, and vice-admiral of the coast of Suffolk; succeeded his father, first earl, 1827.

STRAFFORD, George Stevens Byng, Earl of, English administrator, b. 1809; educated at Sandhurst; was a captain in the army; has been comptroller of the Household, a lord of the Treasury, and one of the secretaries of the Board of Control; sat in the House of Commons, 1830–52; summoned to the House of Lords in his father's lifetime as Lord Strafford of Harmondsworth, 1853; succeeded his father, first earl, 1860; deputy-lieutenant of Middlesex, and colonel of the West Middlesex Militia.

STRATFORD DE REDCLIFFE, Stratford Canning, Viscount, English diplomatist, b. in London, 1788; educated at Eton, and King's College, Cambridge; entered the diplomatic service, 1806; was ambassador to the Ottoman Porte, 1841–58; previously ambassador to St. Petersburg and other courts; was M.P. for Stockbridge, 1831, and for Lyme Regis, 1835–41; raised to the peerage, 1852.

STRATHALLAN, William Henry Drummond, Viscount, English administrator, b. 1810; is a deputy-lieutenant of Perthshire; was a lord-in-waiting to the Queen, Feb. 1858 to June 1859.

STRATHEDEN AND CAMPBELL, William Frederick Campbell, Baron, English administrator, b. 1824; educated at Eton, and Trinity College, Cambridge, where he graduated M.A. 1846; was M.P. for Cambridge, 1847–52, and for Harwich, May 1859 to March 1860. Author of 'Letters on the Oath of Abjuration;' and other pamphlets.

STRATHMORE AND KINGHORN, Thomas George Lyon Bowes, Earl of, English administrator, b. 1822; has been in the 1st Life Guards; a deputy-lieutenant of Forfarshire; succeeded his grandfather, eleventh earl, 1846.

STRAUSS, David Friedrich, German theologian, b. at Ludwigsburg, Würtemberg, June 27, 1808; studied at Tübingen; was ordained, 1830; appointed professor of theology and church history at Zurich, 1839; elected member of the Diet of Würtemberg, 1848. Author of 'Life of Jesus,' 1835; 'Life of Schubart,' 1849; 'Life and Writings of the Poet and Philologist, Nicodemus Frischlin,' 1856; and other theological and historical works.

STRICKLAND, Agnes, English authoress, b. at Reydon Hall, Suffolk, 1806. Author of 'The Lives of the Queens of England from the Norman Conquest,' 1840–49; and other historical compilations.

STROGANOW, Alexander, Count, Russian statesman, b. at St. Petersburg, 1805; took part in the wars with Poland and Turkey; was member of the Council for the administration of Poland, and governor of Little Russia; minister of the interior from 1839 to 1841; became adjutant-general to the Emperor, lieutenant-general of artillery, and member of the Council of State; nominated governor-general of New Russia, and of Bessarabia, 1855; charged with the reorganization of the government of the Crimea and the reconstruction of Sebastopol, 1856.

STROGANOW, Sergius, Count, Russian military commander, b. at St. Petersburg, 1803; nominated governor of Riga, 1831; lieutenant-general and adjutant-general to the Emperor, 1835–47; general of cavalry, 1852; president of the Society of Antiquarians of Russia. Author of several archæological works.

STROMEYER, Georg Friedrich Ludwig, German medical writer, b. at Hanover, March 6, 1804; studied medicine at the Universities of Göttingen and Berlin, 1823–26; appointed surgeon to the Hanover School of Surgery, 1828. Author of 'Typhus under the Influence of Methodical Ventilation,' Hanover, 1855; and other medical works.

STRONGE, Sir James Matthew, English politician, b. 1811; a J.P. and deputy-lieutenant of the county of Armagh, and honorary colonel Royal Tyrone Fusiliers; late captain 5th Dragoon Guards; M.P. for the county of Armagh since 1864.

STRUVE, Gustav, German author and politician, b. in Livonia, 1805; studied law, and entered the diplomatic service of the grand duchy of Oldenburg; an advocate at Manheim, 1840–48. Author of 'History of Phrenology,' Heidelberg, 1843; 'System of Political Science,' Frankfort, 1847–48; 'The Public Law of the German Confederation,' Manheim, 1846; and other works.

STRUVE, Otto Wilhelm von, Russian astronomer. b. at Dorpat, May 7, 1819; member of the Academy of Sciences of St. Petersburg ; a counsellor of state. Author of 'Observations of the Comet of Biela in the Year 1852,' St. Petersburg, 1853 ; and other works on astronomy.

STUART, James Frederick Dudley Crichton, English politician, b. 1824; educated at Eton, and Trinity College, Cambridge ; lord-lieutenant of Bute. and J.P. of the counties of Glamorgan and Ayr ; late lieutenant-colonel in the Grenadier Guards ; M.P. for Cardiff since 1857.

STUART, Hon. Sir John, English judge, b. 1793 ; called to the bar of Lincoln's Inn, 1819 ; a vice-chancellor, and bencher of Lincoln's Inn ; was M.P. for Newark, 1847–52 ; and for Bury St. Edmunds, July to Oct. 1852, when he was elevated to the bench.

STUART, William, English politician, b. 1825 ; educated at Eton ; called to the bar of the Inner Temple, 1851 ; a deputy-lieutenant of Beds, and lieutenant-colonel Beds Militia ; M.P. for Bedford, 1854–57, and 1859–68.

STUART DE DECIES, Henry Villiers Stuart, Baron, English administrator, b. 1803 ; sat in the House of Commons as Mr. V. Stuart, 1826–30, and 1831–32 ; lord-lieutenant of the county of Waterford, and colonel of the Waterford Militia.

STUART WORTLEY, Right Hon. James Archibald, English politician, b. 1805 ; educated at Christ Church, Oxford, where he graduated B.A. ; called to the bar, 1830 ; standing counsel to the Bank of England, 1844 ; appointed judge-advocate-general, and sworn in the Privy Council, 1846 ; recorder of London, 1850 ; solicitor-general, 1856–57 ; was M.P. for Halifax, 1835–37, and for Buteshire, 1842–59.

STUCLEY, Sir George Stucley, English administrator, b. 1812 ; educated at Eton, and Christ Church, Oxford ; a J.P. and deputy-lieutenant of Devon and Cornwall ; and lieutenant-colonel Devon Artillery Militia ; was M.P. for Barnstaple, 1856–57, and 1865–68 ; assumed the name Stucley in lieu of Buck, 1858.

STUDER, Bernhard, Swiss geologist, b. at Büren on the Aar, 1794 ; studied mathematics at the College of Berne, and at Göttingen. Author of 'Chart of the Geology of Switzerland,' Winterthur, 1853 ; 'The Geology of Switzerland,' Berne, 1851–53 ; and other works on geology.

STURT, Charles Napier, English politician, b. 1832 ; educated at Harrow ; a lieutenant-colonel in the Grenadier Guards ; M.P. for Dorchester since 1856.

STURT, Henry Gerard, English politician, b. 1825 ; educated at Eton, and Christ Church, Oxford ; a magistrate of Dorset ; M.P. for Dorchester, 1847–56, and for Dorset since 1856.

SUDELEY, Charles George Hanbury Tracy, Baron, English administrator, b. 1837 ; educated at Harrow ; lord-lieutenant of Montgomeryshire ; late captain of the Grenadier Guards ; succeeded his father, second baron, 1863.

SUFFOLK AND BERKSHIRE, Charles John Howard, Earl of, English administrator, b. 1804 ; was M.P. for Malmesbury, 1832 ; is a deputy-lieutenant of Malmesbury ; succeeded his father, sixteenth earl, 1851.

SULLIVAN, Edward, English administrator, b. 1822 ; educated at Trinity College, Dublin, where he graduated B.A. 1844 ; called to the Irish bar, 1848, and Q.C. 1858 ; appointed serjeant-at-law, 1860 ; law-adviser to the Crown, 1861 ; solicitor-general of Ireland, 1865 ; elected M.P. for Mallow, 1865 ; attorney-general of Ireland, Dec. 1868.

SUMNER, Charles, American politician, b. at Boston, Jan. 6, 1811 ; graduated at Harvard College, 1830 ; called to the bar, 1834 ; member of Congress since 1851 ; senator for Massachusetts ; chairman of the Senate's committee on foreign relations since March 1861. Author of 'Orations and Speeches,' Boston, 1850 ; 'White Slavery in the Barbary States,' ib. ; and other political writings.

SURTEES, Charles Freville, English politician, b. 1823 ; educated at Harrow ; was formerly captain in the 10th Royal Hussars ; M.P. for South Durham, 1865–68.

SURTEES, Henry Edward, English politician, b. 1819 ; educated at Harrow ; a magistrate of Herts ; was formerly an officer in the 10th Royal Hussars ; M.P. for Hertfordshire, 1864–68.

SURTEES, Sir Stephenson Villiers, English colonial judge, b. 1803 ; educated at Eton, and University College, Oxford, where he graduated B.C.L. 1831 ; called to the bar of the Inner Temple, 1831 ; appointed justice of the Mauritius, 1840 ; chief justice, and knighted, 1858 ; retired, 1860.

SUTHERLAND, Alexander John, English physician, b. 1810; educated at Christ Church, Oxford, where he graduated B.A., M.B., and M.D. in 1839; fellow of the Royal College of Physicians, 1840; is physician to St. Luke's Hospital, and consulting physician to the South London Dispensary. Author of 'Clinical Lectures on Insanity.'

SUTHERLAND, George Granville William Sutherland Levison Gower, Duke of, English administrator, b. 1828; lord-lieutenant of Sutherland and Cromarty; was M.P. for Sutherland, 1852–61; succeeded his father, second duke, 1861.

SUTHERLAND, John, English physician, b. 1804; educated at the University of Edinburgh, where he graduated M.D. 1831; royal commissioner of sanitary arrangements to the army in the Crimea, 1856; royal commissioner at the International Conference on Quarantine held at Paris in 1851.

SUTTON, Hon. John Henry Thomas Manners, English colonial administrator, b. in London, 1810; educated at Trinity College, Cambridge, and graduated M.A. 1835; under-secretary of state for the Home Department from Sept. 1841 to July 1846; returned M.P. for the borough of Cambridge, Sept. 1839, but unseated on petition; sat for the borough of Cambridge from 1841 to 1847; lieutenant-governor of New Brunswick from June 1854 to Oct. 1861; governor of Trinidad from April 1864 to May 1866; appointed governor-general of Victoria, May 1866.

SWAIN, Charles, English author, b. in Manchester, 1803. Author of 'Metrical Essays,' 1827; 'The Mind, and other Poems,' 1831; 'English Melodies,' 1849; 'The Letters of Laura d'Auverne, and other Poems,' 1853; 'Art and Fashion,' 1863; and other poetical works.

SWAINSON, William, English naturalist, b. 1796. Published 'Zoological Illustrations,' 1820; 'The Naturalist's Guide,' 1822; 'The Birds of Western Africa;' 'The History and Natural Arrangements of Insects;' and other works on natural history.

SWINBURNE, Algernon Charles, English poet, b. 1837; educated at Eton and Oxford. Author of 'Atalanta in Calydon;' 'Chastelard;' 'Poems and Ballads,' 1866; and other works.

SYDNEY, John Robert Townshend, Viscount, English administrator, b. 1804; educated at Eton, and St. John's College, Cambridge, where he graduated M.A.; sat in the House of Commons, 1825–31; lord-lieutenant of Kent, and colonel of Kent Artillery Militia; appointed lord-chamberlain, June 1859.

SYKES, Christopher, English politician, b. 1831; educated at Rugby, and Trinity College, Cambridge; a deputy-lieutenant of the East Riding of Yorkshire; M.P. for Beverley, 1865–68; returned M.P. for the East Riding of York, 1868.

SYKES, William Henry, English politician, b. 1790; entered the Bombay army, 1804; retired with the rank of lieutenant-colonel, 1831; was chairman of the East India Company, 1856–57; lord-rector of Marischal College, Aberdeen, 1854–55; M.P. for Aberdeen since 1857. Author of papers on the 'Statistics and History of India.'

SYME, James, English surgeon, b. at Fife, 1799; admitted a surgeon in London, 1821; appointed professor of clinical surgery at the University of Edinburgh, 1833; appointed professor of surgery in London University, 1834; reappointed to the University of Edinburgh. Author of 'On the Excision of Diseased Joints,' 1831; and other works.

SYNAN, Edward John, English politician, b. 1820; educated at Trinity College, Dublin, where he graduated B.A. 1842; called to the Irish bar, 1843; a magistrate of the county of Limerick; M.P. for the same county since 1865.

SZEMERE, Bartholomew, Hungarian author and statesman, b. at Vatta, province of Bosod, Aug. 24, 1812; studied law and philosophy at the University of Presburg; called to the bar, 1834; appointed judge of the High Court of Justice, 1842; deputy to the Hungarian Diet, 1843–44, and 1847–48; minister of the interior of the Republic of Hungary, 1848; exiled, 1850, and returned to Hungary, 1864. Author of several historical and political treatises on Hungary.

SZIGLIGETI, Joseph Szatmary, Hungarian dramatic writer, b. at Grosswardein, county of Bihar, 1814; studied in his native town and at Pesth. Author of 'Rozza;' 'Korona es Kard;' 'Zsido;' and other dramatic and poetical works.

T.

TAGLIONI, Paul, German musical composer, b. at Vienna, 1808; studied at the Collége Bourbon, and the Conservatoire of Paris. Composed the ballads, 'L'Ondine; 'Don Quichotte,' 'Le Lac des Amazones;' and many other musical pieces.

TAILLANDIER, Rene' Gaspard, French author, b. at Paris, Dec. 16, 1817; studied at Heidelberg; appointed professor of French poetry to the Sorbonne, 1863. Author of 'Béatrix,' a poem, 1840; 'Histoire et Philosophie religieuse,' 1860; 'Maurice de Saxe,' 1865; and other works; contributor to the *Revue des Deux Mondes.*

TAILLEFER, Louis Auguste, French politician, b. at Domme, Dordogne, Dec. 2, 1802; studied medicine, and received the degree of M.D.; deputy of Dordogne in the Constituent Assembly, 1848; member of the Corps Législatif for the department of Dordogne since 1852.

TAILLIAR, Euge'ne François Joseph, French author, b. at Douai, April 7, 1803; studied law at Paris; called to the bar at Douai, and auditor to the court of that town, 1829. Author of 'Essais sur l'Histoire des Institutions,' 1859; 'Notice sur l'Origine' et la Formation des Villages du Nord de la France,' 1863; and other works.

TAINE, Hippolyte Adolphe, French author, b. at Vouzieres, Ardennes, April 21, 1828; studied at the Collége Bourbon, and the École Normale; examiner in literature at the Military School of St. Cyr, 1853–63; appointed professor of history and æsthetic art at the Imperial School of Fine Arts, 1864. Author of 'History of English Literature,' 1864; and other works.

TAIT, Archibald Campbell, Archbishop of Canterbury, b. Dec. 1811; educated at Edinburgh, and at Balliol College, Oxford; head master of Rugby, 1842; dean of Carlisle, 1849; bishop of London, 1856; archbishop of Canterbury, Dec. 1868.

TALABOT, Paulin François, French politician, b. at Limoges, Haute Vienne, 1799; studied at the École Polytechnique, 1819–21; ingénieur des ponts et chaussées, 1824; member of the Corps Législatif for the department of Gaud since 1863.

TALBOT, Christopher Rice Mansel, English politician, b. 1801; educated at Harrow, and at Oriel College, Oxford, where he graduated B.A. 1823; lord-lieutenant of the county of Glamorgan; M.P. for Glamorganshire since 1830.

TALBOT, Euge'ne, French author, b. at Chartres, Aug. 17, 1814; studied at the Colleges Bourbon and Charlemagne at Paris; professor at the Academy of Nantes, 1845–50; professor of rhetoric at the College of Louis le Grand. Author of 'French and Greek Dictionary,' 1858; and other philological works.

TALBOT, William Henry Fox, English author, b. 1800; educated at Harrow, and Trinity College, Cambridge; one of the discoverers of photography. Author of 'Pencil of Nature,' 1844; 'Hermes, or Classical and Antiquarian Researches;' 'Illustrations of the Antiquity of the Book of Genesis;' and other works.

TALBOT DE MALAHIDE, James Talbot, Baron, English administrator, b. 1805; educated at Trinity College, Cambridge, where he graduated M.A.; M.P. for Athlone, 1832–34; a deputy-lieutenant and magistrate of Somersetshire, and a magistrate of the county of Dublin; president of the Board of Superintendence of Public Hospitals; succeeded his father, third baron, 1850.

TALHOUET, Auguste Bonamour, Marquis de, French politician, b. at Paris, Oct. 11, 1819; represented the department of Sarthe in the Legislative Assembly, 1849; member of the Corps Législatif for the department of Sarthe since 1852; secretary to the Corps Législatif during the sessions of 1861–64.

TALLEYRAND PE'RIGORD, Charles Ange'lique, Baron de, French diplomatist, b. Nov. 28, 1821; was successively secretary of legation at Lisbon, Madrid, St. Petersburg, and London, and minister at Weimar, Turin, and Brussels; envoy-extra-ordinary and minister-plenipotentiary to the King of the Belgians, 1861–62; ambassador at Berlin, 1862–63; and at St. Petersburg, 1864–65.

TAMBERLIK, Enrico, Italian singer, b. at Rome, 1820; studied at the Seminary of Montefiascone under Borgua and Guglielmi; made his début at the Theatre del Fonde of Naples, 1841; has since sung in the principal cities of Europe.

TANKERVILLE, Charles Bennet, Earl of, English administrator, b. 1810; educated at Christ Church, Oxford, where he graduated B.A. 1831; a deputy-lieutenant and magistrate of Northumberland, and vice-lieutenant of the county; lieutenant-colonel Northumberland Royal Volunteers; M.P. for Northumberland, 1832–59; succeeded his father, fifth earl, 1859.

TAPPAN, Henry, American author, b. 1810; became president of the University of Michigan, 1852. Author of 'The Doctrine of the Will, applied to Moral Agency,' New York; 'A Sept from the New World,' 1852; and other works.

TARDIEU, Auguste Ambroise, French physician, b. at Paris, March 10, 1818; studied at the Collége Charlemagne and the hospitals of Paris, and graduated M.D. Jan. 1843; appointed dean of the Faculty of Medicine, and consulting physician to the Emperor, 1864. Author of 'Memoir on Poisoning by Strychnine,' 1857; and other medical works.

TARENTE, Alexander Charles Macdonald, Duc de, French politician, b. at Paris, Nov. 11, 1824; appointed chamberlain to the Emperor, 1852; member of the Corps Législatif for the department of Loiret since 1852.

TARVER, Rev. Charles Fe'ral, English divine, b. 1820; educated at Eton, and King's College, Cambridge, where he graduated B.A. 1842, M.A. 1846; curate of the Chapel Royal, Windsor Park, 1852–54; classical tutor to the Prince of Wales, 1855–59; chaplain to the Queen, 1858; appointed vicar of St. Peter's in the Isle of Thanet, 1863.

TASCHEREAU, Jules Antoine, French author, b. at Tours, Dec. 19, 1801; was deputy for the arrondissement of Loches, 1838–42; member of the Constituent Assembly for Indre-et-Loire, 1848; nominated director-general of the Imperial Library, 1858. Author of 'Histoire de la Vie et des Ouvrages de Corneille,' 1829; and other works.

TASMANIA, Right Rev. Charles Henry Bromby, Bishop of, English divine, b. 1812; educated at St. John's College, Cambridge, where he graduated B.A. 1837, M.A. 1840, D.D. 1864; incumbent of St. Paul's, Cheltenham, 1843; principal of the Normal College for Schoolmasters at Cheltenham, 1847–64; consecrated bishop of Tasmania, 1864. Author of 'The Antiquity and Independence of the British Church;' 'History and Grammar of the English Language;' and other works.

TAUNTON, Henry Labouchere, Baron, English statesman, b. 1798; educated at Winchester, and Christ Church, Oxford; was M.P. for St. Michael's, 1826–30, and for Taunton, 1830–59, when he was raised to the peerage; lord of the Admiralty, 1832–34; vice-president of the Board of Trade, 1835–39; president of the Board of Trade, Aug. 1839 to Sept. 1841; chief secretary for Ireland, 1846–47; president of the Board of Trade, 1847–52; secretary of state for the colonies, Nov. 1855 to Feb. 1858; a deputy-lieutenant of Essex, and elder brother of the Trinity House.

TAYLER, Frederick, English painter, b. near Elstree, Herts, April 30, 1804. Exhibited 'Calling out of Cover;' 'Troopers of Two Centuries since;' 'Harvest Carts;' 'Festival of the Popinjay,' 1854; and other paintings in water colours.

TAYLER, John William, English mineralogist, b. 1822; charged with an exploring expedition to Greenland, 1850.

TAYLOR, Alfred Swaine, English physician, b. at Northfleet, Kent, Dec. 1806; studied at Guy's and St. Thomas's Hospitals, and in the medical schools of France, Germany, and Italy; member of the Royal College of Surgeons, 1830; licentiate of the Royal College of Physicians, 1848; professor of medical jurisprudence at Guy's Hospital since 1831, and professor of chemistry in the same since 1832. Author of several works on medical jurisprudence, poisons, and chemistry.

TAYLOR, Bayard, American traveller and author, b. in Pennsylvania, Jan. 1825. Author of 'Views afoot, or Europe seen with Knapsack and Staff,' 1846; 'El Dorado,' 1850; 'Japan, India, and China,' 1855; 'Eastern Poems;' 'Cyclopædia of Modern Travel, comprising Narratives of distinguished Travellers since the Beginning of the present Century;' and other works of travel.

TAYLOR, Henry, English author, b. 1805. Author of 'Philip van Artevelde,' 1834; 'Isaac Comnenus;' 'Edwin the Fair,' 1842; 'Notes from Life,' 1848; 'The Way of the Rich and Great;' and other essays and dramas.

TAYLOR, Isidore Se've'rin Justin, Baron, French traveller and author, b. at Brussels, Aug. 15, 1789; educated at Paris; elected member of the French Academy of Fine Arts, 1847. Author of 'Syria, Egypt, Palestine, and Judea,' 1837; 'Picturesque and Romantic Travels in Ancient France,' 1820–50; and other works of travel.

TAYLOR, Peter Alfred, English politician, b. 1819; a partner in the firm of Messrs. S. Courtauld and Co. crape manufacturers; M.P. for Leicester since 1862.

TAYLOR, Thomas Edward, English politician, b. 1812; a magistrate and deputy-lieutenant of the county of Dublin; formerly captain in the Dragoon Guards; was a lord of the Treasury, 1858-59; M.P. for the county of Dublin since 1841.

TAYLOR, Tom, English dramatic author, b. in Sunderland, 1817; educated at the University of Glasgow, and Trinity College, Cambridge; called to the bar of the Inner Temple, 1845, and went the Northern Circuit; appointed assistant-secretary to the Board of Health, 1850, and secretary, 1854. Author of 'The Contested Election;' 'Our American Cousin;' 'The Ticket of Leave Man;' and many other dramas. Editor of 'The Autobiography of B. R. Haydon,' 1852, and 'Life and Times of Sir Joshua Reynolds,' 1865.

TCHIHATCHEF, Peter, Russian naturalist, b. at Gatchina, near St. Petersburg, 1812; was attaché to the Russian embassy at Constantinople, 1841-44. Author of 'L'Asie Mineure, Description physique, statistique et archéologique de cette Contrée,' Paris, 1853-56; and numerous other works.

TEALE, Rev. William Henry, English author, b. 1810; educated at St. John's College, Cambridge, where he graduated in 1834; appointed vicar of Royston, Yorkshire, 1843; rector of Devizes, Wilts, 1861. Author of 'The Lives of English Laymen;' 'Education in England historically considered;' and other works.

TEICHMANN, Jean François Théodore, Belgian statesman, b. at Venloo, 1788; studied in the École Polytechnique, Paris, 1806-08; was minister of the interior, Aug. to Sept. 1831; member of the Belgian Chamber of Representatives, 1832-35; governor of the province of Antwerp, 1845-62.

TEIGNMOUTH, Charles John Shore, Baron, English administrator, b. 1796; educated at Trinity College, Cambridge, where he graduated M.A. 1816; was M.P. for Marylebone, 1838 to July 1841; succeeded his father, first baron, 1834; deputy-lieutenant and magistrate of the North Riding of Yorkshire.

TEMME, Jodocus, German jurist, b. at Lette, Westphalia, Oct. 22, 1799; studied at the Universities of Göttingen, Heidelberg, Bonn, and Marburg; president of the Superior Court of Munster, 1848-52; appointed professor to the School of Law at Zurich, 1852. Author of 'Treatise on Prussian Civil Law,' Berlin, 1846; and other legal works.

TEMPLE, Rev. Frederick, English divine, b. Nov. 30, 1821; educated at the Grammar School, Tiverton, and Balliol College, Oxford, where he graduated B.A. 1842; ordained, 1846: appointed head-master of Rugby School, 1858; chaplain to the Queen. Author of the first of the seven 'Essays and Reviews,' 1860.

TENERANI, Pietro, Italian sculptor, b. at Carrara, 1800; studied under Thorwaldsen; professor of sculpture in the Academy of St. Luke, Rome. Executed 'Venus Wounded;' 'Descent from the Cross;' 'Cupid extracting a Thorn from Venus's Foot;' a statue of Count Rossi; and numerous groups and statues.

TENNANT, James, English geologist, b. 1802; professor of geology in King's College, London. Author of 'A Catalogue of Fossils found in the British Isles;' 'Art Gems and Precious Stones;' 'Iceland Spars;' and other works on geology.

TENNIEL, John, English artist, b. in London, 1820; educated at Kensington; painted a fresco in the Palace at Westminster; has been a contributor of drawings to *Punch* since 1851; also illustrated 'Lalla Rookh,' 'The Ingoldsby Legends,' and many other works.

TENNYSON, Alfred, English poet, b. at Somerby vicarage, Lincolnshire, 1809; studied at the University of Cambridge; succeeded Wordsworth as poet laureate, 1851; received the honorary degree of D.C.L. from Oxford, 1855. Author of 'Poems, chiefly Lyrical,' 1830; 'Poems,' 1842; 'In Memoriam,' 1850; 'Maud,' 1855; 'The Idylls of the King,' 1858; 'Enoch Arden, and other Poems,' 1864; and other poetical works.

TERME, Jean Marie, French politician, b. at Lyons, May 11, 1828; was mayor of St. Juste d'Avray, and member of the General Council for the canton of Villefranche; member of the Corps Législatif for the département du Rhône since 1863.

TERROTT, Right Rev. Charles, Scottish divine, b. at Cuddalore, in the East Indies, 1790; educated at Trinity College, Cambridge, where he graduated B.A. 1812, and M.A. and D.D.; ordained, 1814; consecrated bishop of Edinburgh, 1841; primus of the Scottish Episcopal Synod. Author of several theological works.

TESNIÈRE, François Pierre, French politician, b. at St. Armand, Charente, July 30, 1827; graduated LL.D. at Paris, 1849; member of the Corps Législatif for the department of the Charente since 1855; one of the secretaries of the Corps Législatif.

TEXIER, Charles Félix Marie, French traveller and archæologist, b. at Versailles, Aug. 29, 1802; studied architecture at the École des Beaux Arts, 1823; elected member of the French Academy, 1855. Author of 'Description of Armenia, Persia, and Mesopotamia; their Geography, Geology, Ancient and Modern Monuments, Manners and Customs,' 1844-45; and numerous other works.

TEXIER, Edmond, French author, b. at Rambouillet, Seine-et-Oise, 1816 ; studied in Paris, at the Colleges Stanislas and Bourbon. Author of 'Journées illustrées de la Révolution,' 1849 ; 'Les Argonautes,' 1856 ; and other works. Editor of *L'Illustration* since 1860.

THALBERG, Sigismund, German pianist, b. in Geneva, Jan. 7, 1812 ; studied under Hummel, 1827 ; first played in public, 1830 ; made his début at Paris, 1835 ; has since played in the principal cities of Europe and America. Composed several fantasias, variations, concertos, and other pieces for the pianoforte.

THIBOUST, Lambert, French dramatic writer, b. 1826 ; entered the Conservatoire, 1848. Author of 'Les Rubans d'Ivonne,' 1850 ; 'La Fille du Diable,' 1860 ; 'Un Mari dans du Coton,' 1862 ; 'Le Supplice d'un Homme,' 1865 ; and other dramas.

THIELE, Just Mathias, Danish author, b. at Copenhagen, Dec. 13, 1795 ; was copyist in the Royal Library, 1820 ; inspector of stamps, 1835 ; secretary and librarian to the Academy of Sciences ; counsellor of state, 1851. Author of 'Breve fra England og Skotland,' 1837 ; 'Thorwaldsen's ungdoms Historie,' Copenhagen, 1851 ; and several novels, dramas, and poems.

THIERRY, Amédée Simon Dominique, French historian, b. at Blois, Aug. 2, 1797 ; appointed prefect of the Haute Sâone after the Revolution of July 1830 ; elected member of the French Academy, 1841 ; nominated senator, 1860. Author of 'Histoire des Gaulois jusqu'à la Domination romaine,' 1828 ; 'Histoire d'Attila,' 1856 ; and other historical works.

THIERRY, Edouard, French author, b. at Paris, Sept. 14, 1813 ; studied at the Collège Charlemagne ; appointed administrator of the Comédie Française, 1859. Author of 'Les Enfants et les Anges,' 1833 ; 'De l'Influence du Théâtre sur les Classes ouvrières,' 1862 ; and other works.

THIERS, Louis Adolphe, French statesman and historian, b. at Marseilles, April 16, 1797 ; studied at the public school of his native town ; called to the bar, 1820 ; appointed under-secretary of state, Nov. 4, 1830 ; minister of the interior, 1832 ; minister of commerce and of public works, 1832 ; president of the Council and minister of foreign affairs, 1836, and from March to October 1840 ; member of the Corps Législatif for the second circonscription of the Seine since 1863. Author of 'History of the French Revolution,' 1823–32 ; and other historical works.

THIRY, Charles Ambroise, French military commander, b. Dec. 9, 1791 ; studied in the École Polytechnique, 1808–10 ; captain, 1813 ; general of brigade, 1848 ; general of division, 1851 ; entered the reserve, 1856.

THIRY, François Augustin, French military commander, b. Feb. 24, 1784, brother of the preceding ; studied in the École Polytechnique, 1810–12 ; captain, 1813 ; general of brigade, 1850 ; general of division, 1854, and commanded in the Crimea ; created senator, 1859.

THISTED, Waldemar Adolf, Danish poet and novelist, b. at Aarhuus, Feb. 28, 1815. Author of 'Oerkenens Hjerte,' Copenhagen, 1850 ; 'Danmark Bestaaer,' 1842 ; 'Hjemme og paa Vandring,' 1854 ; and other works.

THOLUCK, Friedrich August Gottreu, German theologian, b. at Breslau, March 30, 1799 ; studied at the University of his native town and at Berlin ; professor of theology in the University of Berlin, 1824 ; professor at Halle, 1826 ; chaplain to the Prussian embassy at Rome, 1828 ; professor of divinity at Halle, 1829. Author of 'The Doctrine of the Sinner and of the Mediator ;' 'Collection of Flowers from the Eastern Mystics ;' and other theological works.

THOMAS, Charles Louis Ambroise, French musical composer, b. at Metz, Aug. 5, 1811 ; was admitted to the Conservatoire, 1828 ; elected member of the Academie des Beaux Arts, 1851. Composed 'La Double Échelle,' 1837 ; 'Le Caïd,' 1849 ; 'Le Roman d'Elvire,' 1860 ; and many others.

THOMAS, Felix, French architect and traveller, b. at Nantes, Sept. 29, 1815 ; entered the École des Beaux Arts, 1837 ; charged with a scientific and artistic mission to Babylonia, 1851. Exhibited drawings of 'Entrée de la Rivière de Nantes,' 1861 ; 'Bords du Tibre,' 1864 ; and many others.

THOMAS, Frederick William, American novelist, b. at Baltimore in 1810. Author of 'The Emigrant,' 1833 ; 'Clinton Bradshaw,' 1835 ; 'Howard Pinckney,' 1840 ; 'The Beechen Tree ;' and other novels and poems.

THOMAS, George Henry, American military commander, b. in the county of Southampton, Virginia, July 31, 1816 ; studied at West Point ; second lieutenant, July 1, 1840 ; major, 1855 ; brigadier general of Volunteers in the Federal service, 1861 ; major general of Volunteers, 1863 ; commander of the army of the Cumberland, 1863.

THOMPSON, Daniel Pierce, American novelist, b. at Charlestown, Massachusetts, Oct. 1, 1795. Author of 'May Martin, or the Money Diggers,' 1835; 'Locke Amsden, or the Schoolmaster,' 1847; 'The Rangers, or the Tory's Daughter,' 1850; and other works.

THOMPSON, Rev. Henry, English author, b. 1797; educated at St. John's College, Cambridge, where he graduated B.A. 1822, M.A. 1825; appointed vicar of Chard, Somerset, 1853. Author of 'The Life of Hannah More;' 'Pastoralia, a Manual of Helps for the Parochial Clergy;' and other works.

THOMPSON, Rev. Robert Anchor, English theological writer, b. in Durham, 1821; educated at Durham School, at Durham University, and graduated B.A. at Catherine Hall, Cambridge, 1844; appointed incumbent of Binbrooke, 1854; is master of St. Mary's Hospital, Newcastle-upon-Tyne. Author of 'On the Existence and Character of the Supreme Being,' which gained the Burnett Prize in 1855; 'Principles of Natural Theology;' and other works.

THOMPSON, Thomas Perronet, English political writer, b. at Hull, 1783; entered Queen's College, Cambridge, 1798, and graduated B.A. 1802; entered the army as second lieutenant, 1806; captain, 1814; major, 1825; lieutenant-general; M.P. for Hull, 1835–37, for Bradford, 1847–52 and 1857–59. Author of 'Corn-Law Catechism,' 1827; 'Geometry without Axioms,' 1830; 'Audi Alteram Partem,' 1857–61; and other works.

THOMS, William John, English writer, b. in Westminster, Nov. 16, 1803; appointed deputy-librarian to the House of Lords, 1863; founder and editor of 'Notes and Queries.' Author of 'Lays and Legends of Various Nations,' 1834; 'Book of the Court,' 1838; and numerous other works.

THORBECKE, Jan Rudolf, Dutch statesman, b. at Zwolle, 1796; graduated at the University of Leyden, 1820; private lecturer at the Universities of Giessen and Göttingen, 1821–24; professor of political economy at Ghent, 1825–30; professor of jurisprudence at Leyden, 1830–44; elected member of the First Chamber of the States-General, 1840; appointed president of a commission for preparing a new Constitution for the Netherlands, 1848; minister of the interior and chief of the Cabinet, Oct. 30, 1849, to April 19, 1853; professor of jurisprudence at Leyden, 1853–62; again minister of the interior, 1862–66.

THORBURN, Robert, English painter, b. at Dumfries, 1818; studied at Edinburgh, and admitted as a student to the Royal Academy, London, 1836. Painted the portraits of the late Prince Consort, 1845; of the Princess Charlotte of Belgium and the Duke of Brabant, 1847; a group of the Hon. Mrs. Norton's Family; and many other portraits of celebrated persons. Elected A.R.A. 1848.

THORIGNY, Pierre François de, French magistrate, b. at Bessenay, Rhône, July 9, 1798; studied law at Paris, and was called to the bar, 1824; advocate-general at the Royal Court of Paris, 1845; nominated counsellor of state, 1852; first president of the court of Amiens, 1858; senator, March 4, 1853.

THORNBURY, George Walter, English author, b. 1828. Author of 'Lays and Legends of the New World,' 1849; 'History of the Buccaneers;' 'Art and Nature at Home and Abroad;' 'British Artists from Hogarth to Turner,' 1861; 'Every Man his own Trumpeter;' 'Haunted London,' 1865; and other works.

THORNYCROFT, Mary, English sculptor, b. at Thornham, Norfolk, 1814; married to Mr. T. Thornycroft, 1840. Executed 'Penelope;' 'The Flower Girl;' statues of the Princess Alice, Princess Royal, Prince of Wales, Prince Alfred, and a Girl Skipping, at the Paris Exhibition of 1855; and other figures and statues.

THOROLD, John Henry, English politician, b. 1842; educated at Eton; entered the army, and was lieutenant in the 17th Foot; M.P. for Grantham, 1865–68.

THORPE, Benjamin, English author, b. 1808; received a literary pension of £150 per annum. Translated Rask's 'Anglo-Saxon Grammar.' Published 'Ancient Law and Institutes of England,' 1848; 'Northern Mythology,' 1852; and other works.

THOUVENEL, E'douard Antoine, French statesman, b. at Verdun, Nov. 11, 1818; became attaché to the French embassy at Brussels, 1844; secretary of legation at Athens, 1845; chargé d'affaires, 1848, and minister-plenipotentiary at the same court, 1849; appointed minister of foreign affairs after the coup d'état of Dec. 2, 1851; ambassador to Constantinople, 1855; created a senator, May 17, 1859; appointed minister of foreign affairs, Jan. 4, 1860; resigned, Aug. 15, 1862. Author of 'La Hongrie et la Valachie;' 'Souvenirs de Voyages et Notices historiques,' 1840.

THURLOW, Edward Thomas Hovell Thurlow, Baron, English administrator, b. 1837; a deputy-lieutenant and magistrate of Suffolk; succeeded his father, third baron, 1857.

THWAITES, Sir John, English administrator, b. 1815; is a magistrate and deputy-lieutenant of Middlesex; chosen chairman of the Metropolitan Board of Works, 1857; knighted in commemoration of the opening of the great Main Drainage works of London, May 1865.

THYNNE, Lord Henry Frederick, English politician, b. 1832; is a J.P. and deputy-lieutenant of Wilts and Somerset, and cornet of Wilts Yeomanry; M.P. for South Wiltshire since 1859.

TICKNOR, George, American author, b. at Boston, Aug. 1, 1791; studied at Dartmouth College, where he graduated, 1807; called to the bar, 1813; studied philology at the University of Göttingen; appointed professor of modern languages and literature at Harvard University, 1817. Author of 'History of Spanish Literature,' New York and London, 1849; 'Life of Prescott,' 1863; and other works.

TISCHENDORF, Constantin, German philologist, b. at Lengenfeld, Saxony, Jan. 18, 1818; studied philology at the University of Leipsic; received the degree of D.D. from the University of Breslau, 1843; appointed professor of theology and Biblical literature in the University of Leipsic, 1845; discovered the Codex Sinaiticus; ennobled by the Emperor of Russia, 1869. Published editions of the 'New Testament;' several Scriptural 'Codices;' the 'Apocryphal Books of the New Testament;' and other philological works.

TITE, William, English architect, b. 1800; appointed architect of the New Royal Exchange, 1846; erected several railway stations, Gothic churches, and public and private buildings; a J.P. and deputy-lieutenant of Middlesex, and magistrate of Somerset; M.P. for Bath since 1855. Author of 'Descriptive Catalogue of the Antiquities found in the Excavations at the New Royal Exchange,' 1848.

TITIENS, Therese, German operatic singer, b. at Hamburg, 1834; made her first appearance at Hamburg as 'Lucrezia' in Donizetti's opera, 1849, and her début in London as 'Valentine' in 'The Huguenots,' 1858; has performed in the principal cities of Europe.

TODD, Rev. James Henthorne, English author, b. in Dublin, 1805; graduated at Trinity College, Dublin, of which he was elected a fellow, 1831; librarian and regius-professor of Hebrew in the University of Dublin. Author of 'Lectures on Antichrist;' 'Memoir of St. Patrick's Life and Mission;' and other works.

TODHUNTER, Isaac, English mathematician, b. at Rye, 1820; studied at University College, London, and St. John's College, Cambridge, where he graduated B.A. 1848, and M.A.; became fellow, assistant-tutor, and principal mathematical lecturer to his college. Author of 'The Differential Calculus;' 'Plane Co-ordinate Geometry;' 'Spherical Trigonometry;' and other mathematical works.

TODLEBEN, Eduard Ivanovich, Russian military commander, b. at Mitau, Courland, May 25, 1818; studied at the schools of Riga, and at the College of Engineers of St. Petersburg; served in the Circassian campaign, 1848; second captain in the corps of engineers sent to the Crimea, 1855; constructed the fortifications of Sebastopol, and was appointed major-general and adjutant-general, 1854. Author of 'Narrative of the War in the Crimea,' 1864.

TOLDY, Franz Schedel, Hungarian author, b. at Buda, Aug. 10, 1805; entered the University of Pesth, 1819, and graduated M.D. 1829; director of the Kisfaludy Society of Pesth, 1841–44; appointed librarian to the University of Pesth, 1844. Author of 'Handbook of Hungarian Poetry,' Pesth and Vienna, 1828; and numerous other works on Hungarian literature.

TOLLEMACHE, John, English politician, b. 1805; a magistrate and deputy-lieutenant of the county of Chester; M.P. for South and West Cheshire since 1841.

TOMLINE, George, English politician, b. 1807; a magistrate and deputy-lieutenant of Lincolnshire; was high sheriff, 1852; and colonel of Lincoln Militia; M.P. for Sudbury, 1840–41, for Shrewsbury, 1841–47 and 1852–68; returned M.P. for Great Grimsby, 1868.

TOMMASEO, Nicolo, Italian politician and author, b. in Dalmatia, 1803; educated in Italy; became member of the Provisional Government of Venice, and minister of worship and public instruction, 1848. Author of 'Commentary on Dante,' Venice, 1837; 'A Collection of Popular Poetry indigenous to Corsica, Tuscany, Dalmatia, and Greece, with Historical Introductions,' ib. 1849; and other works.

TORCY, Raphael Villedieu, Marquis de, French politician, b. March 18, 1821; formerly an officer in the navy; member of the Corps Législatif for the department of the Orne since 1860.

TORREARSA, Vincenzo Fardella, Marquis di, Italian statesman, b. at Trapini, July 17, 1808 ; took part in the Revolution in Sicily, 1848 ; was deputy from Trapini, and president of the Chamber of Representatives ; president of the Cabinet, and minister of foreign affairs, 1848 ; elected deputy to the National Parliament for Turin, 1860 ; ambassador of Italy to Stockholm and Copenhagen, 1861.

TORRENS, Robert, English politician, b. 1810 ; educated at Haileybury College ; was formerly in the East India Civil Service, Bengal ; retired, 1853 ; M.P. for Carrickfergus, 1859–68 ; returned M.P. for Cambridge, 1868.

TORRENS, William Torrens McCullagh, English author and politician, b. 1813 ; educated at Trinity College, Dublin, where he graduated B.A. 1834, LL.B. 1840 ; called to the Irish bar, 1836 ; formerly an assistant Poor Law commissioner ; M.P. for Dundalk, 1848–52 ; for Great Yarmouth, 1857 ; and for Finsbury since 1865. Author of ' Industrial History of the Nation ;' and other works on political economy.

TORRINGTON, George Byng, Viscount, English administrator, b. 1812 ; studied at the University of Oxford ; governor and commander-in-chief of Ceylon, 1847–50 ; lord-in-waiting to the Queen, 1850 to March 1852 ; reappointed, Dec. 1852 ; a deputy-lieutenant of Kent.

TOTTENHAM, Charles George, English politician, b. 1835 ; captain and lieutenant-colonel Scots Fusilier Guards ; M.P. for New Ross, 1863–68.

TOUCHARD, Philippe Victor, French naval commander, b. July 21, 1810 ; entered the navy, 1826 ; rear-admiral, March 16, 1859 ; charged with the command of the French fleet in the Levant, 1861 ; vice-admiral, 1864 ; appointed member of the Council of Admiralty, 1864.

TOULONGEON, Hippolyte Alexandre, Comte de, French politician, b. at Éclans, Dec. 31, 1820 ; appointed sub-prefect of Dôle, 1851 ; resigned, 1856 ; member of the Corps Législatif for the department of Jura since 1857.

TOURGUENEFF, Ivan, Russian novelist, b. at Orel, Nov. 9, 1818 ; studied at Moscow and St. Petersburg, 1833, and at Berlin, 1838. Author of ' Otzy i Deti,' 1862 ; ' Duim,' 1867 ; and numerous other works.

TOUSSAINT, Anna Louisa, Dutch authoress, b. at Alkmar, Sept. 16, 1812 ; married M. Bosboom, painter, 1851. Author of ' Almagro,' 1827 ; ' De Engelsche in Rom,' 1840 ; ' Leycester in Nederland ;' and other romances.

TOUSSENEL, Alphonse, French historical writer, b. at Montreuil Bellay, 1803. Author of ' Les Juifs Rois de l'Époque, Histoire de la Féodalité financière,' 1844 ; ' Tristia, Histoire des Misères et des Fléaux de la Chasse de France,' 1863 ; and other works.

TOWNSHEND, John Villiers Stuart Townshend, Marquis of, English administrator, b. April 10, 1831 ; educated at Eton ; a magistrate of Norfolk and Herts, and a deputy-lieutenant of Herts ; was M.P. for Tamworth, 1856–63 ; succeeded his father, fourth marquis, 1863.

TRAILL, George, English politician, b. 1796 ; vice-lieutenant of Caithness ; was M.P. for Shetland and Orkney, 1830–34 ; and for Caithness-shire since 1841.

TRAVOT, Victor, Baron, French politician, b. Oct. 7, 1808 ; entered the army and served in Africa as captain ; retired from the service, became mayor of Bouillac ; member of the Corps Législatif for the department of the Gironde, 1852–69.

TREDEGAR, Charles Morgan Robinson Morgan, Baron, English administrator, b. 1793 ; educated at Westminster, and Christ Church, Oxford ; a deputy-lieutenant and magistrate of Monmouthshire and Glamorganshire ; was M.P. for Brecon, 1818–32, and 1835–49 ; appointed major of the Glamorgan Militia, 1849 ; raised to the peerage, 1859.

TREFUSIS, Hon. Charles Henry Rolle, English politician, b. 1834 ; educated at Eton, and Christ Church, Oxford, where he graduated B.A. 1856 ; a magistrate of Devon, and major of the North Devon Mounted Rifles ; M.P. for N. Devon, 1857–68.

TREHERNE, Morgan, English politician, b. 1803 ; educated at Trinity College, Cambridge, where he graduated M.A. 1827 ; called to the bar of the Inner Temple, 1831 ; a magistrate of Sussex, and a deputy-lieutenant of Surrey ; adopted the name of Treherne in lieu of Thomas, 1856 ; M.P. for Coventry, 1863–68.

TRÉHOUART, François Thomas, French naval commander, b. at Vieuville, April 27, 1798 ; entered the navy ; nominated lieutenant after the battle of Navarino, 1829 ; vice-admiral, 1851 ; commanded a fleet in the Mediterranean, 1856–58 ; member of the Council of the Admiralty, 1858–63 ; created a senator, Aug. 13, 1859.

TREILHARD, Achille, Comte, French politician, b. at Toulouse, June 1815 ; magistrate at Rouen, 1848 ; appointed director of the press, 1862, and counsellor of state, 1864.

TRELAWNEY, Sir John Salusbury, English politician, b. 1818; educated at Westminster, and Trinity College, Cambridge; called to the bar of Lincoln's Inn, 1840; a magistrate and deputy-lieutenant of the county of Cornwall; M.P. for Tavistock, 1843–52, and 1857–68; returned M.P. for East Cornwall, 1869.

TREVELYAN, Sir Charles Edward, English colonial administrator, b. 1807; educated at the Charterhouse, and Haileybury College; entered the East India Company's civil service; assistant-secretary to the Treasury in England, 1840–59; appointed governor of Madras, 1859; recalled, 1860; sent to India as minister of finance, 1863; resigned, 1864.

TREVELYAN, George Otto, English politician, b. 1838, son of the preceding; educated at Harrow, and Trinity College, Cambridge, where he graduated B.A. 1861, M.A. 1864; a deputy-lieutenant of Northumberland; M.P. for Tynemouth, 1865–68; returned M.P. for Hawick, 1868.

TRE'VISE, Napole'on Mortier, Duc de, French politician, b. at Paris, Aug. 7, 1804; nominated member of the Imperial Senate, 1853, and chamberlain to the Emperor, 1862; entered the Municipal Council of Paris for the canton of Sceaux, 1864.

TREVOR, Rev. George, English divine, b. 1810; educated at Magdalen Hall, Oxford, where he graduated S.C.L. 1834; and afterwards B.A. and M.A.; chaplain on the Madras Establishment, East Indies, 1836–45; appointed rector of All Saints, York, and honorary canon of York Cathedral, 1847. Author of 'Origin, Constitution, and Form of Proceedings in the Convocations of the two Provinces of Canterbury and York;' and other works.

TRIQUETI, Henri, Baron de, French sculptor, b. at Conflans, Loiret, 1802. Executed 'La Vierge et l'Enfant,' 1838; 'Moïse exposé,' 'Suzanne au Bain,' 1857; and numerous busts, medallions, groups, and bas-reliefs.

TROCHU, Louis Jules, French military commander, b. at Morbihan, March 12, 1815; studied at St. Cyr, and at the École d'Application; lieutenant, 1840; lieutenant-colonel, 1853; general of brigade, 1854; general of division, 1859.

TROLLOPE, Anthony, English novelist, b. 1815; educated at Winchester and Harrow. Author of 'Barchester Towers;' 'Rachel Ray;' 'Can you Forgive her?' 1864; 'Miss Mackenzie,' 1865; and numerous other works of fiction.

TROLLOPE, Rev. Edward, English divine, b. April 15, 1817; educated at Eton, and Christ Church, Oxford, where he graduated in 1839; appointed rector of Leasingham, Lincolnshire, 1843; prebendary of the cathedral church of Lincoln, 1861. Author of 'Illustrations of Ancient Art;' 'Labyrinths, Ancient and Modern;' 'The Use and Abuse of Bricks;' and other works.

TROLLOPE, Right Hon. Sir John, English politician, b. 1800; educated at Eton; a magistrate and deputy-lieutenant of Lincolnshire; chief commissioner of the Poor Law Board, and sworn in the Privy Council, 1852; M.P. for South Lincolnshire, 1841–65.

TROLLOPE, Thomas Adolphus, English author, b. 1810, brother of the preceding; educated at Winchester, and St. Alban Hall, Oxford. Published two volumes on 'Brittany,' 1840; 'The Girlhood of Catherine de' Medici;' 'A Decade of Italian Women;' 'A Life of Filippo Strozzi,' 1860; 'La Beata,' 1861; and other works.

TROPLONG, Raimond The'odore, French judge, b. at St. Gaudens, Haute-Garonne, Oct. 8, 1795; studied law, and was called to the bar; appointed president of the Court of Nancy, 1833; president of the Court of Paris, Dec. 2, 1848; nominated to the Senate, Jan. 25, 1852, of which he became president, 1854; first president of the Court of Cassation, 1852; appointed member of the Privy Council, 1858; elected member of the French Academy, 1840. Author of 'Le Code civil expliqué,' 1833–58; and other legal works.

TROUBRIDGE, Sir Thomas St. Vincent Hope Cochrane, English officer, b. 1817; entered the army, 1834; served in the Crimea, at Alma and Inkermann; lieutenant-colonel, 1854; director-general of the Army Clothing Department.

TROUSSEAU, Armand, French physician, b. at Tours, Oct. 14, 1801; graduated M.D. at Paris, 1825; appointed professor and physician to the Hôtel Dieu, 1850; professor of materia medica to the Faculty, 1864. Author of 'Clinique médicale de l'Hôtel Dieu de Paris,' 1861; and other medical works.

TUCKERMAN, Henry Theodore, American author, b. at Boston, April 20, 1813. Author of 'Italian Sketch-Book,' 1835; 'The Spirit of Poetry,' Boston, 1851; 'A Month in England,' New York, 1853; 'Leaves from the Diary of a Dreamer,' London, 1853; and other works.

TUGNOT DE LANOYE, Ferdinand, French writer, b. near Avignon, 1810. Author of 'Songes et Réveils,' 1838 ; ' Le Niger,' 1858 ; 'Les grandes Scènes de la Nature,' 1862 ; 'Ramesès le Grand, ou l'Égypte il y a 3,300 Ans,' 1865 ; and other works.

TULLOCH, Rev. John, Scottish divine, b. near Tibbermuir, Perthshire, 1822 ; entered the United College of St. Salvador and St. Leonard, St. Andrew's, 1837 ; ordained, 1844 ; appointed principal of St. Mary's College, University of St. Andrew's, 1854. Author of ' Leaders of the Reformation,' 1859 ; 'English Puritanism and its Leaders,' 1861 ; contributor to the *British Quarterly Review*, the *Contemporary Review*, and other periodical publications.

TUPPER, Martin Farquhar, English writer, b. in London, 1810 ; educated at the Charterhouse, and at Christ Church, Oxford, where he graduated B.A., M.A., and D.C.L.; called to the bar of Lincoln's Inn. Author of ' Proverbial Philosophy ;' ' The Crock of Gold ;' ' Paterfamilias' Diary ;' and other works in prose and verse.

TURGOT, Louis Felix Etienne, Marquis de, French diplomatist, b. at Bons, Calvados, Sept. 26, 1796 ; studied at the Military School of St. Cyr ; was an officer in the Royal Guard, but resigned, 1830 ; entered the Chamber of Peers, 1832 ; took part in the ministry, and in the coup d'état of 'Dec. 2, 1851 ; resigned the portfolio of foreign affairs, July 1852, and entered the Senate ; ambassador to the court of Spain, 1853 ; envoy to the United States, 1854.

TURMELIE'RE, Charles Baptiste Joseph Thoinnet de la, French politician, b. at Ancenis, Oct. 26, 1823 ; studied law ; nominated counsellor of the prefecture of Loire Inférieure, 1848 ; resigned, 1857 ; member of the Corps Législatif for the department of Loire Inférieure since June 1857.

TURNER, Charles, English politician, b. 1803 ; a magistrate and deputy-lieutenant of the county of Lancaster ; J.P. of Liverpool, and a merchant in that city ; was M.P. for Liverpool, 1852–53, and for South Lancashire since 1861.

TURNER, Samuel, American theologian, b. at Philadelphia, Jan. 23, 1790 ; studied at the University of Pennsylvania, and graduated, 1807 ; appointed professor of Hebrew in Columbia College, 1831. Author of ' Biographical Notices of Jewish Rabbis, with Translations and Notes ;' ' Thoughts on Scriptural Prophecy,' New York, 1852 ; and other theological works.

TURNER, Rev. Sydney, English writer, b. 1814 ; educated at Trinity College, Cambridge, where he graduated B.A. 1836 ; ordained deacon, 1837, and priest, 1838 ; appointed inspector of reformatories in England and Scotland, 1858. Author of a pamphlet on ' Reformatory Schools,' and other publications on the same subject.

TÜRR, Istvan, Italian military commander, b. at Baja, in Hungary, 1825 ; became a lieutenant in the Austrian army, 1848 ; deserted to Piedmont, and appointed colonel of the Hungarian Legion in the Sardinian service, 1849 ; took part as a volunteer in the campaign in the Crimea ; colonel, and member of Garibaldi's staff, 1859 ; general of division in the army of Italy, 1861 ; resigned, 1864.

TWEEDDALE, George Hay, Marquis of, English administrator, b. 1787 ; succeeded his father, seventh marquis, in the peerage, 1804 ; lieutenant-general in the army ; colonel of the 3d Foot, and lord-lieutenant of the county of Haddington ; was governor and commander-in-chief of Madras, 1842–46 ; aide-de-camp to the late Duke of Wellington during the Peninsular War.

TWISLETON, Hon. Edward Turner Boyd, English administrator, b. 1809 ; educated at Winchester, and at Trinity and Balliol Colleges, Oxford ; called to the bar of the Inner Temple, 1835 ; was assistant Poor Law commissioner in England, 1839 ; commissioner of inquiry into the Scottish Poor Laws, 1843 ; chief commissioner of Poor Laws in Ireland, 1845–49 ; appointed one of the Oxford University commissioners, 1855 ; commissioner of inquiry into English Public Schools, 1861 ; one of the Civil Service commissioners since 1862.

TWISS, Travers, English author, b. at Westminster, 1810 ; educated at University College, Oxford, where he graduated in 1830 ; called to the bar of Lincoln's Inn, 1840 ; admitted an advocate at Doctors' Commons ; regius-professor of civil law in the University of Oxford, 1855 ; chancellor of the diocese of London, 1858. Author of ' The Oregon Question examined with respect to the Law of Facts and Nations,' 1846 ; ' The Law of Nations considered as Independent Political Communities,' 1861 ; and other legal works.

TYNDALL, John, English natural philosopher, b. 1820 ; educated on the Continent ; employed for some years on the Geological Survey of the United Kingdom ; professor of natural science in the Royal Institution of Great Britain, and Sir R. Rede's lecturer at Cambridge. Author of 'The Glaciers of the Alps,' 1860 ; ' Heat considered as a Mode of Motion,' 1863 ; ' Faraday as a Discoverer,' 1868 ; and other works.

U.

UBICINI, Jean Henri Abdolonyme, French political writer, b. at Issoudun, Oct. 20, 1818 ; studied at the Lycée of Versailles, 1836–38. Author of 'Lettres sur la Turquie,' 1847–51 ; 'La Question des Principautés danubiennes devant l'Europe,' 1858 ; and other political and statistical works.

UCHARD, Mario, French dramatic writer, b. at Paris, 1824. Author of 'Le Retour du Mari,' performed March 1, 1858 ; 'La Seconde Jeunesse,' April 27, 1859 ; 'Une Dernière Passion,' 1865 ; and other dramas and romances.

UECHTRITZ, Friedrich von, German dramatic writer, b. at Görlitz, in Prussia, 1800 ; studied law in the University of Leipsic. Author of 'Chrysostomus,' Brandenburg, 1822 ; 'Alexander und Darius,' Berlin, 1827 ; 'Albrecht Holm,' ib. 1851–53 ; and other dramas, poems, and novels.

UHLICH, Lebrecht, German theologian, b. at Köthen, Feb. 27, 1799 ; studied theology at the University of Halle ; professor of the same at Köthen, 1820 ; pastor at Diebzig, near Aix-la-Chapelle, 1824 ; pastor of a 'German Catholic' congregation at Magdeburg. Author of 'Bekenntnisse,' Leipsic, 1845 ; 'Aus der Vernunftreligion,' 1855 ; 'Der Process der freien Gemeinde in Magdeburg,' 1856 ; and other theological works.

UHRICH, Jean Jacques Alexis, French military commander, b. at Phalsbourg, Feb. 15, 1802 ; studied at St. Cyr ; second lieutenant, 1820 ; colonel, 1848 ; general of brigade, 1852 ; general of division, 1855 ; grand officer of the Légion d'honneur, 1862.

ULBACH, Louis, French author, b. at Troyes, March 7, 1822 ; studied in Paris. Author of 'Gloriana,' 1844 ; 'Jacques Souffrant,' 1851 ; 'Mémoires d'un Inconnu,' 1864 ; and other works ; contributor to the *Revue de Paris, Le Temps,* and other French periodical publications.

ULLOA, Girolamo, Italian general, b. at Naples, 1810 ; studied in the Royal Polytechnic School, Naples, and entered the army, 1840 ; colonel and general of brigade, 1848 ; deputy to the Parliament of Naples, 1848 ; commanded troops in the Italian campaign of 1859. Author of 'The Italian War of Independence in 1848 and 1849,' Paris, 1859 ; and other works on Italy and on military tactics.

ULRICH, Titus, German poet, b. at Habelschwerdt, county of Glatz, Prussia, Aug. 22, 1813 ; studied at the Universities of Breslau and Berlin, and graduated Ph.D. 1836. Author of 'Das Hohe Lied,' Berlin, 1845 ; 'Victor,' ib. 1848 ; and other poems.

ULRICI, Hermann, German philosophical writer, b. at Pförten, March 23, 1806 ; studied at Leipsic, Halle, and Berlin ; professor at Berlin, 1833, and at Halle since 1834. Author of 'Charakteristik der antiken Historiographie,' Berlin, 1833 ; 'System der Logik,' Leipsic, 1852 ; and other works.

UNSGAARD, Yves John, Danish statesman, b. at Copenhagen, Sept. 4, 1797 ; nominated grand bailiff of Odense, 1848 ; member of the Second Chamber of the National Assembly, 1850–51 ; minister of the interior, 1854–55, and again 1856–57.

UPHAM, Thomas, American theologian, b. 1801 ; professor of psychology and Hebrew at Boudoin College, Maine, 1824. Author of 'Elements of Mental Philosophy,' New York, 1850 ; 'Life and Religious Opinions of Mme. Guyon,' ib. 1855 ; and numerous philosophical works.

UPPSTROEM, Anders, Swedish author, b. at Hammarby, June 29, 1806 ; professor at the Cathedral School of Upsal, and master of the Academy of the same town. Editor of 'Aivaggeljo Thairh Matthaiu,' Upsal, 1850 ; 'Codex Argenteus, sive Sacrorum Evangeliorum Versionis Gothicæ Fragmenta,' 1854.

URQUHART, David, English author and politician, b. 1805 ; educated at St. John's College, Oxford ; entered the diplomatic service, and was secretary to the British embassy at Constantinople ; M.P. for Stafford, 1847–52. Author of 'Turkey and its Resources,' 1841 ; 'The Pillars of Hercules,' 1850 ; and other geographical and statistical works.

URQUHART, William Pollard, English author, b. 1815 ; educated at Harrow, and Trinity College, Cambridge, where he graduated B.A. 1838 ; a magistrate and deputy-lieutenant for West Meath ; was high sheriff, 1840, and a magistrate of the county of Aberdeen ; M.P. for the county of West Meath, 1852–57. Author of 'Essays on Political Economy ;' and other works.

URQUIZA, Justo Jose de, Argentine statesman, b. in the province of Entre-Rios, 1800 ; nominated governor of his native province, 1842 ; general-in-chief of the Argentine Confederation, 1861 ; governor of the province of Entre-Rios, 1862.

USSING, Johan Louis, Danish philologist, b. at Copenhagen, 1820 ; studied at the University of his native town ; nominated professor of philology and archæology at Copenhagen, 1849. Author of 'Travels in the South,' Copenhagen, 1847 ; and other works.

USSING, Tage Algreen, Danish statesman, b. at Fredericksburg, Oct. 11, 1797 ; studied law at the University of Copenhagen ; appointed professor of law at the same University, 1840 ; member of the Diet, 1840 ; re-elected to the Diet, 1848 ; nominated privy councillor, 1854. Author of 'Handbook of Danish Criminal Law,' 1841 ; and other legal works.

UZE'S, Armand Ge'raud Victurnien, Duc de, French politician, b. 1808 ; served in the army ; was member of the Chamber of Deputies for the arrondissement of Bourbonne, 1844–48 ; elected member of the Corps Législatif for the circonscription of Uzès, 1852 ; retired, 1857.

V.

VACHEROT, E'tienne, French philosophical writer, b. at Langres, July 29, 1809 ; entered the École Normale, 1827 ; graduated Ph. D. 1836. Author of 'Histoire critique de l'École d'Alexandrie,' 1846–51 ; 'Essais de Philosophie critique,' 1864 ; and other philosophical works.

VACQUERIE, Auguste, French author, b. at Paris, 1818. Author of 'L'Enfer de l'Esprit,' a poem, 1840 ; 'Les Funérailles de l'Honneur,' 1862 ; 'Les Miettes de l'His- toire,' 1863 ; and other dramas, poems, and works of fiction ; contributor to the *Globe*, and other French journals.

VAILLANT, Jean Baptiste Philibert, Comte de, French military commander, b. at Dijon, Dec. 6, 1790 ; studied at the École Polytechnique of Paris and Metz, and entered the army as lieutenant, 1809 ; taken prisoner in the Russian campaign, 1813 ; took part in the battle of Waterloo ; captain, 1816 ; colonel, 1833 ; governor of the École Polytechnique, 1839, and director of the fortifications of Paris, 1840 ; lieutenant-general, 1845 ; marshal of France, 1851 ; received the title of count, 1852 ; minister of war, 1854–60 ; governor of the Prince Imperial, 1860 ; minister of the Imperial House, Nov. 14, 1861.

VAISSE, Marc Antoine, French magistrate, b. at Marseilles, Sept. 8, 1805 ; studied law at Aix ; king's counsel at Toulon, 1833 ; vice-president of the Tribunal of Marseilles, 1849 ; president of the Criminal Court of Paris, 1857 ; member of the Council of State, 1856.

VALETTE, Claude Denis, French jurist, b. at Salins, Jura, Aug. 15, 1805 ; licen- tiate of law in Paris, 1827, and LL.D. 1830 ; assistant-professor of civil law at the University of Paris, 1833 ; was member of the Constituent and Legislative Assemblies for the department of Jura. Author of ' Explication sommaire du Livre Ier du Code Napoléon,' 1859 ; and other legal works.

VALLAURI, Tommaso, Italian philologist, b. at Cuneo, Piedmont, Jan. 23, 1805 ; studied at the University of Turin ; professor of Greek and Latin eloquence at the University of Turin, 1838. Author of 'History of Poetry in Piedmont,' Turin, 1841 ; and other works.

VAMBERY, Armin, Hungarian traveller, b. at Duna, Szerdahely, 1832 ; studied at Pesth ; took part in the Revolution of 1848, and was banished by the Austrian autho- rities. Author of 'Travels and Adventures in Central Asia,' London, 1865 ; and other works of travel.

VANDELEUR, Crofton Moore, English politician, b. 1809 ; educated at Harrow, and Trinity College, Cambridge ; a magistrate and deputy-lieutenant of the county of Clare ; was high sheriff, 1832, and colonel of the Clare Militia ; M.P. for the county of Clare since 1859.

VANE, George Henry Robert Charles William Vane Tempest, Earl, English administrator, b. at Vienna, April 26, 1821 ; educated at Eton, and Balliol College, Oxford ; lieutenant 1st Life Guards, 1843 ; retired, 1848 ; was M.P. for North Durham, 1847–54 ; succeeded his father in the earldom, March 6, 1854 ; a magistrate and deputy-lieutenant of the counties of Durham, Montgomery, and Merioneth.

VAPEREAU, Louis Gustave, French author, b. at Orleans, April 4, 1819 ; studied in Orleans, and at the École Normale, Paris ; called to the bar at Paris, 1854.   Author of 'Dictionnaire universel des Contemporains,' 1858 ; third edition, 1865 ; 'L'Année littéraire et dramatique ;' and other works.

VARENNE, Comte Charles de la, French author, b. in Paris, Dec. 2, 1828 ; was a law student, 1848, and took part in the Revolution of February ; officer in the Sardinian army during the campaign of 1848 and 1849.   Author of 'Le Gouvernement provisoire et l'Hôtel de Ville,' 1850 ; 'La Vérité sur les Événements de Turin,' 1865–66 ; and other political works.

VARENNE, Jacques E'douard, French diplomatist, b. at Châlons-sur-Saône, Sept. 21, 1795 ; entered the diplomatic service, and was minister-plenipotentiary to Portugal after 1830 ; member of the Chamber of Deputies for Châlons-sur-Saône, 1842–46 ; ambassador to Berlin, 1852 ; created a senator, 1853.

VASCONCELLOS, Antonio Augusto Teixeira de, Portuguese author, b. at Porto, Nov. 1, 1816 ; studied law, and graduated LL.D. 1844 ; elected member of the Royal Academy of Sciences of Lisbon, 1860.   Author of 'Portugal and the House of Braganza,' 1859 ; 'A Fundaçao da Monarchia portugueza,' Lisbon, 1860 ; and other works.

VAUGHAN, Rev. Charles John, English divine, b. 1817 ; educated at Rugby, and Trinity College, Cambridge, where he graduated B.A. ; elected head master of Harrow School, 1844 ; resigned, 1859 ; was offered, but declined, the bishopric of Rochester, 1860 ; vicar of Doncaster, Yorkshire.   Author of several volumes of sermons.

VAUX, William Sandys Wright, English archæologist, b. 1818 ; educated at Balliol College, Oxford, where he graduated B.A. 1840 ; entered the service of the British Museum in the department of Antiquities, 1841 ; appointed keeper of the department of Coins and Medals, Jan. 1861 ; president of the Numismatic Society.   Author of 'Nineveh and Persepolis ;' 'Handbook to the Antiquities in the British Museum,' London, 1851 ; and other historical and archæological works.

VEHSE, Karl Eduard, German historical writer, b. at Freiberg, Saxony, Dec. 18, 1802 ; studied law at Leipsic and Göttingen ; graduated LL.D. 1826.   Author of 'History of the Emperor Otto the Great,' Zittau, 1828·; 'Geschichte der deutschen Höfe seit der Reformation,' Hamburg, 1851 ; and other historical works.

VELA, Vincenzo, Italian sculptor, b. at Ligurnetto, canton of Tessin, 1822 ; studied sculpture under Cacciatori ; fought as a volunteer in the Italian war of independence, 1848.   Executed 'Spartacus,' 1855 ; a group of 'France and Italy,' and other groups, statues, and bas-reliefs.

VELPEAU, Alfred Armand Louis Marie, French surgeon, b. at Brèche, Indre-et-Loire, May 18, 1795 ; studied at Tours, and in Paris, where he graduated M.D. 1822 ; nominated surgeon to the Hôpital de la Pitié, 1830 ; and professor of clinical surgery to the Hôpital de la Charité, 1835 ; elected member of the Academy of Medicine, 1832, and of the Academy of Sciences, 1842.   Author of 'Traité d'Anatomie chirurgicale,' 1825 ; 'Traitement du Docteur Vriès,' 1859 ; and numerous other medical works.

VENEDEY, Jacob, German author and politician, b. at Cologne, May 24, 1805 ; studied at Bonn and Heidelberg ; member of the German National Parliament, 1848–49 ; exiled from Prussia, 1850 ; appointed professor of history at the University of Zurich, 1853.   Author of 'John Hampden,' 1843 ; 'History of the German People,' Berlin, 1854–58 ; and other historical and political works.

VERDI, Giuseppe, Italian musical composer, b. at Rancola, duchy of Parma, Oct. 9, 1814 ; studied under an organist at Milan, 1833–36, and under Lavinga.   Composed 'Oberto di San Bonifazio,' 1839 ; 'Lombardi,' 1843 ; 'Il Trovatore,' 1853 ; 'La Traviata ;' 'Un Ballo in Maschera,' 1861 ; and numerous other operas.

VERGE', Charles Henri, French author, b. at Paris, July 22, 1810 ; studied law, and graduated LL.D. 1840 ; appointed member and secretary of the High Commission of Law Studies, 1848.   Author of 'Diplomates et Publicistes,' 1856 ; and numerous legal works.

VERNEUIL, Philippe E'douard Poulletier de, French naturalist, b. at Paris, Feb. 3, 1805 ; studied law, and was attached to the Ministry of Justice till 1833 ; elected member of the French Academy, 1854.   Author of 'Mémoire sur les Fossiles des Bords du Rhin,' 1842 ; 'Géologie de la Russie d'Europe,' 1845 ; and other works.

VERNEY, Sir Harry, English politician, b. 1801 ; educated at Harrow and Sandhurst ; a deputy-lieutenant of Bucks ; assumed the name of Verney in lieu of Calvert, formerly lieutenant and captain Grenadier Guards ; was M.P. for Buckingham, 1832; for Bedford, 1847–52 ; M.P. for Buckingham since 1857.

VERNINAC SAINT MAUR, Raymond Jean Baptiste, French naval commander, b. June 11, 1794; entered the navy, 1812; captain, 1842; under-secretary of state in the Ministry of Marine, June 6 to July 17, 1848; appointed rear-admiral, 1848; governor of Réunion, 1849.

VERNON, Augustus Henry Venables, Baron, b. 1829; a deputy-lieutenant of Staffordshire; succeeded his father, fifth baron, 1866.

VERNON, Harry Foley, English politician, b. 1834; educated at Harrow, and Magdalen College, Oxford, where he graduated B.A. 1858, M.A. 1860; a magistrate and deputy-lieutenant of the county of Worcester; M.P. for East Worcestershire, 1861–68.

VERNON HARCOURT, William George, English jurist and journalist, b. 1827; educated at Trinity College, Cambridge, where he graduated in 1851; called to the bar of the Inner Temple, 1854; elected for Oxford, 1868. Author of 'The Letters of *Historicus;*' and several other pamphlets.

VE'RON, Pierre, French author, b. at Paris, 1833; studied at the Universities and the École Normale. Author of 'Les Réalités humaines,' 1854; 'Paris s'amuse,' 1861; 'La Famille Hasard,' 1865; and other works of fiction; contributor to the *Charivari* since 1859.

VERULAM, James Walter Grimston, Earl, English administrator, b. 1809; educated at Oxford; sat in the House of Commons as Viscount Grimston, 1830 to 1845, when he succeeded his father, the first earl; lord-lieutenant of Herts, and lieutenant-colonel of the South Herts Yeomanry.

VEUILLOT, Eugène, French author, b. at Boynes, Loiret, 1818, brother of the following. Author of 'Histoire des Guerres de la Vendée et de la Bretagne, 1790–1832;' 'La Cochinchine et le Tonquin,' 1859; 'Le Piémont dans les États de l'Église,' 1861; and other historical works.

VEUILLOT, Louis, French author, b. at Boyne-en-Gatinais, Loiret, 1813; educated in a school near Paris; editor of the *Univers* from 1843 until its suppression in 1861. Author of 'Mélanges religieux, historiques et littéraires,' 1857–59; 'Biographie de Pie IX.' 1863; 'Satires,' 1863; and other works.

VIARDOT, Louis, French author, b. at Dijon, July 31, 1800; studied law in Paris, and was called to the bar; director of the Italian Opera, Paris, 1838–40. Author of 'Essai sur l'Histoire des Arabes et des Maures d'Espagne,' 1832; 'Comment faut-il encourager les Arts?' 1862; and numerous other works.

VIARDOT, Madame Michelle Pauline Garcia, French operatic singer, b. in Paris, July 18, 1821, wife of the preceding, and daughter of E. Garcia; studied under Liszt; made her début in London as Desdemona, May 1839; married to M. Louis Viardot, 1840; has since sung in the principal cities of Europe.

VICTORIA I., Queen of Great Britain and Ireland, b. at Kensington Palace, London, May 24, 1819, the daughter of Edward, Duke of Kent, fourth son of King George III., and of Princess Victoria of Saxe-Saalfeld-Coburg, widow of Prince Emich of Leiningen; ascended the throne at the death of her uncle, King William IV., June 20, 1837; crowned at Westminster Abbey, June 28, 1838; married, Feb. 10, 1840, to Prince Albert of Saxe-Coburg-Gotha; widow, Dec. 14, 1861.

VIDAL, Francisco Antonio, Uruguayan statesman, b. at Montevideo, 1827; educated at Paris, and obtained the degree of doctor of medicine; minister of the interior of Uruguay, 1865–66; president of the Republic of Uruguay, 1866–68.

VILAIN XIV., Charles Ghislain, Viscount, Belgian statesman, b. at Brussels, May 15, 1803; studied at the Collége Charlemagne, and at the University of Liège; member of the National Congress for the district of Maestricht, 1830; envoy-extraordinary and minister-plenipotentiary to the Holy See, 1832; to the Two Sicilies and other Italian courts till 1839; minister of foreign affairs, 1855–57.

VILCOCQ, Antoine, French politician, b. at Paris, Sept. 14, 1822; sub-prefect of Sancerre, 1848, of Bar-sur-Aube, 1850, and of Vervins, 1852; member of the Corps Législatif for the department of Aisne since 1863.

VILLEMAIN, Abel François, French statesman, b. in Paris, June 11, 1791; studied at the Lycée Impérial; assistant-professor of rhetoric at the Lycée Charlemagne, 1810; member of the Chamber of Deputies for the department of the Eure, 1830; created a peer of France, 1832; minister of public instruction, 1839–44. Author of 'Life of Cromwell,' 1819; 'Studies of Modern History,' 1846; and numerous other, chiefly historical, works.

VILLIERS, Right Hon. Charles Pelham, English statesman, b. 1802 ; educated at Trinity College, Cambridge, where he graduated B.A. 1824, M.A. 1827 ; called to the bar of Lincoln's Inn, 1827 ; a deputy-lieutenant of Herts ; was judge-advocate-general, 1852–58 ; president of the Poor Law Board, 1859–66 ; M.P. for Wolverhampton since 1835.

VINCENT, Alexander Joseph Hidulphe, French mathematician, b. at Hesdin, Pas de Calais, Nov. 20, 1797 ; studied at the College of Douai ; appointed professor of mathematics at the College of St. Louis, 1831 ; elected member of the French Academy, 1850.   Author of ' Origine de nos Chiffres,' 1839 ; and numerous other works.

VINCENT, Louis Charles Marie, Baron de, French statesman, b. at St. Domingo, Sept. 8, 1793 ; studied in the Military School of St. Germain ; was sub-lieutenant in the Russian campaign, and fought at Waterloo ; retired from the army, 1825 ; sub-prefect of Havre, 1848, of the Rhône, 1851 ; created a senator, 1859.

VINCKE, Ernst Georg, Baron von, Prussian statesman, b. at Buch, in Westphalia, 1811 ; studied law at Göttingen and Berlin ; nominated auditor to the Municipal Tribunal of Berlin, 1832 ; was member of the Prussian Diet, 1847 ; of the German National Assembly, 1849 ; and sat in the Parliament of Erfurt from March to May 1850 ; member of the Second Prussian Chamber since 1852.

VIOLLET LEDUC, Euge'ne Emmanuel, French architect, b. at Paris, Jan. 27, 1814 ; studied Gothic architecture under Ach. Leclère ; charged, with M. Lassus, with the restoration of Notre Dame de Paris, 1845 ; of Sainte Chapelle, 1840 ; and of numerous churches and public buildings.   Author of ' Essai sur l'Architecture militaire au Moyen Age,' 1854 ; and other works on architecture.

VIRCHOW, Rudolf, German physiologist and politician, b. at Cœslin, Pomerania, 1821 ; studied under Johann Müller ; and graduated M.D. 1843 ; elected to the German National Assembly, 1848 ; appointed professor of pathology in the University of Berlin, 1856 ; one of the leaders of the 'Progress party' in the Prussian Chamber of Deputies. Author of 'Cellular Pathology, as based upon Physiological and Pathological Histology,' 1860 ; and other medical works.

VIRGIN, Christian Adolf, Swedish navigator, b. at Gothenburg, Sept. 5, 1797 ; lieutenant in the navy, 1814 ; commodore, 1843 ; made voyages to Terra del Fuego, California, India, China, and other parts of the world, 1851–53 ; rear-admiral, 1853 ; Swedish minister to the court of London, 1854.

VISCONTI VENOSTA, Emilio, Italian statesman, b. at Valtelina, 1828 ; nominated, by Count Cavour, royal commissioner to Garibaldi, 1859 ; sent with the Marquis Pepoli on an extraordinary mission to Paris and London, 1860 ; elected member of the Italian Parliament, 1861 ; minister of foreign affairs, 1863–65.

VITET, Louis, French author, b. at Paris, Oct. 18, 1802 ; admitted to the Paris École Normale, 1819 ; appointed secretary-general of commerce, 1834 ; entered the Council of State, 1836 ; one of the vice-presidents of the section of finance, 1846–48 ; elected member of the French Academy, 1845.   Author of ' La Mort de Henri III.' 1829 ; ' Études sur l'Histoire de l'Art,' 1864 ; and other historical works.

VITTORIO EMANUELE II., King of Italy, b. March 14, 1820, eldest son of King Carlo Alberto of Sardinia and Archduchess Theresa of Austria ; succeeded to the throne of Sardinia on the abdication of his father, March 23, 1849 ; proclaimed King of Italy by vote of the Italian Parliament, March 17, 1861 ; married, April 12, 1842, to Archduchess Adelaide of Austria, who died Jan. 20, 1855.

VIVIAN, Charles Crespigny Vivian, Baron, English administrator, b. 1808 ; a major in the army ; appointed lord-lieutenant of Cornwall, 1856 ; sat in the House of Commons as Major Vivian, 1837–41 ; succeeded his father, first baron, 1841.

VIVIAN, Henry Hussey, English politician, b. 1821 ; educated at Eton, and Trinity College, Cambridge ; a magistrate and deputy-lieutenant of Glamorganshire ; M.P. for Truro, 1852–57 ; and for Glamorganshire since 1857.

VIVIAN, Hon. John Cranch Walker, English politician, b. 1818 ; a J.P. and deputy-lieutenant of Cornwall ; formerly captain 11th Hussars ; M.P. for Falmouth, 1841–47 ; for Bodmin, 1857–59 ; and for Truro since 1865 ; appointed a lord of the Treasury, 1868.

VIVIAN, Sir Robert John Hussey, English military commander, b. 1802 ; educated at Gosport, the École Militaire at Beauvais, and at the Royal College, Dresden ; formerly lieutenant-colonel of the 1st Madras Europeans ; adjutant-general, 1848–54 ; major-general in the Madras army ; commanded the Turkish contingent during the Crimean war ; director of the East India Company, 1855–58 ; appointed member of the Council of India, 1858.

VIVIEN DE SAINT MARTIN, Louis, French geographer, b. at Calvados, May 17, 1802. Author of 'Carte électorale et administrative,' 1823 ; ' Études de Géographie ancienne et d'Ethnographie asiatique,' 1850–54 ; 'Le Nord de l'Afrique dans l'Antiquité grecque et romaine,' 1863 ; and numerous other works, chiefly on geography.

VOELCKER, August, English chemist, b. at Frankfort-on-the-Maine, 1823 ; studied at the University of Göttingen ; assistant professor of chemistry at Edinburgh, 1849 ; professor of chemistry at the Royal Agricultural College at Cirencester, 1852 ; resigned, 1862, and appointed professor of chemistry to the Royal Agricultural Society of England. Author of 'Chemistry of Food ;' 'Lectures on Agricultural Chemistry ;' and other works on chemistry.

VOGT, Karl, German naturalist, b. at Giessen, July 5, 1817 ; studied in his native town under Liebig, and at Berne, where he graduated M.D. 1839 ; professor of zoology at the University of Giessen, 1847 ; member of the German National Parliament, 1848 ; appointed professor of natural history in the University of Geneva, 1851. Author of lectures 'On Man, his Place in Creation and in the History of the Earth ;' 'Science and Superstition,' 1855 ; and other works on natural history.

VOIZE, Adolphe de, French politician, b. at Voiron, March 1807 ; member of the Corps Législatif for the second circonscription of the department of Isère since 1851.

VOLK, Wilhelm, German painter, b. at Herdecke, on the Ruhr, June 23, 1815. Painted 'Good Shepherd ;' 'The Murder of Rizzio ;' 'Death of Mary Stuart ;' 'Death of Admiral de Coligny ;' and other works, chiefly historical.

VOLKMANN, Alfred Wilhelm, German physiologist, b. at Leipsic, 1801 ; educated at the University in his native town ; graduated M.D. 1826 ; and studied in the hospitals of Paris and London ; appointed professor of physiology in the University of Dorpat, 1837 ; resigned, 1843, and appointed professor of physiology at Halle. Author of ' The Independence of the System of Sympathetic Nerves,' 1842 ; and other medical works.

VRETOS, Andrew Papadopoulos, Greek author, b. at Ithaca, 1800 ; studied in Italy ; founded *The Greek Mirror*, 1830 ; Hellenic consul at Varna, 1849–51 ; at Venice, 1854–55 ; entered the service of Russia, 1855 ; retired, 1858. Author of ' Bulgaria, Ancient and Modern,' St. Petersburg, 1856 ; and numerous works in French, Italian, and Greek.

VRETOS, Marino, Greek author, b. at Corfu, Sept. 13, 1828, son of the preceding ; studied in Italy, and graduated LL.D. at the University of Pisa. Author of ' Modern Athens,' Paris, 1861. Contributor to the *Moniteur Universel*, and other French journals.

VUILLEFROY, Charles Ame'de'e, French politician, b. at Soissons, Aisne, April 23, 1810 ; studied law in Paris ; auditor to the Council of State, 1832 ; member of the Council of State, 1848, and of the Legislative Assembly ; under-secretary in the Ministry of Public Works, Agriculture, and Commerce, 1852 ; appointed senator, 1863.

VUITRY, Adolphe, French statesman, b. at Sens, 1812 ; studied law in Paris ; appointed chief of department in the Ministry of Justice, 1841 ; maître des requêtes in the Council of State, 1846 ; under-secretary of state in the Ministry of Finance, 1851 ; appointed minister-president of the Council of State, Sept. 29, 1864.

W.

WADDINGTON, Charles, French author, b. June 19, 1819 ; studied at the Lycée of Versailles, and entered the École Normale, 1838 ; graduated Ph.D. 1848 ; appointed professor of philosophy at the Lycée St. Louis at Paris, 1864. Author of 'Essais de Logique,' 1858 ; ' De l'Ame humaine, Etudes de Psychologie,' 1862 ; and other philosophical works.

WADDINGTON, Very Rev. George, English divine, b. 1793 ; educated at the Charterhouse, and at Trinity College, Cambridge, where he graduated B.A. 1815 ; appointed dean of Durham, 1840. Author of 'A Visit to Ethiopia,' 1822 ; 'The Present Condition and Prospects of the Greek or Oriental Church,' 1829 ; 'History of the Reformation on the Continent,' 1841 ; and other works.

WADDINGTON, William Henry, French author, b. in Paris, 1826 ; studied in *England* at the University of Cambridge ; elected member of the French Academy, 1865. *Author of* 'Voyage en Asie Mineure au Point de Vue numismatique,' 1852 ; 'Voyage *archéologique* en Grèce et en Asie Mineure,' 1864 ; and other works.

WADDY, Rev. Samuel Dousland, English dissenting minister, b. at Burton-upon-Trent, Aug. 5, 1804; educated at Woodhouse Grove School, and entered the Wesleyan ministry, 1825; principal of Wesley College, Sheffield, 1830.

WAECHTER, Karl Georg von, German jurist, b. at Marbach on the Neckar, Dec. 24, 1797; studied at the Universities of Tübingen and Heidelberg; professor of law at Tübingen, 1822, and rector of the University of the same town, 1825; professor and chancellor of the same, 1836; president of the Wurtemberg Chamber of Deputies, 1839–51; privy councillor of the King of Saxony, and professor of law at the University of Leipsic, 1852. Author of ' Beurtheilung des Entwurfs eines Civilgesetzbuchs fur das Königreich Sachsen,' Leipsic, 1853; and other legal works.

WAGNER, Moritz, German traveller and author, b. at Bayreuth, Bavaria, 1813; studied in Paris. Author of ' Reisen in der Regentschaft Algier,' Leipsic, 1841; ' Reise nach Kolchis,' ib. 1850; ' Reisen in Nordamerica,' ib. 1854; and other works of travel.

WAGNER, Richard, German musical composer, b. at Leipsic, May 22, 1813; studied at Dresden, and the University of Leipzig; appointed musical director to the Royal Theatre of Dresden, 1843. Composed ' Rienzi;' ' Tannhauser;' ' Lohengrin;' and numerous other operas.

WAHLBERG, Peter Fredrik, Swedish botanist, b. at Gothenburg, June 19, 1800; studied medicine, and graduated M.D. 1827; appointed secretary to the Swedish Academy of Sciences, 1848. Author of ' Flora Gothenburgensis,' 1847; and several treatises on botany in the publications of the Swedish Academy of Sciences.

WAILLY, Joseph Noel, French paleographer, b. at Mézières, May 10, 1805; elected member of the French Academy, 1841; appointed keeper of manuscript department of the Imperial Library, 1854. Author of ' Éléments de Paléographie,' 1838; ' Sur des Fragments de Papyrus écrits en Latin et déposés à la Bibliothèque Royal et au Musée de Leyde,' 1842; and other works.

WAITZ, Georg, German historical writer, b. at Flensburg, Schleswig, Oct. 9, 1813; studied law and history at the Universities of Kiel and Berlin, 1832–36; member of the Provisional Government of Rendsburg, and deputy to the National Assembly at Frankfort, 1848; appointed professor in the University of Göttingen, 1849. Author of ' History of the German Constitution,' Kiel, 1843–47; ' History of Schleswig and of Holstein,' Göttingen, 1851–54; and other historical works.

WALCOTT, John Edward, English politician, b. 1790; educated at Winchester; is a magistrate and deputy-lieutenant of Hants; vice-admiral on the reserved list; M.P. for Christchurch, 1852–68.

WALCOTT, Rev. Mackenzie Edward Charles, English divine, son of the preceding, b. in Bath, 1822; educated at Winchester, and Exeter College, Oxford, where he graduated, 1844; appointed precentor and prebendary of Chichester Cathedral, 1863. Author of ' The History of St. Margaret's Church, Westminster,' and other works.

WALKER, Sir Baldwin Wake, English naval commander, b. 1803; entered the navy, 1812; became lieutenant, 1820; commander, 1834; captain, 1838; appointed surveyor of the navy, 1847, and created a baronet; was rear and vice-admiral in the Turkish service, and made K.C.B. 1841; attained flag rank, 1858; surveyor of the navy, 1847–61; appointed to the command of the South African station, 1861.

WALKER, George Gustavus, English politician, b. 1831; educated at Rugby, and Balliol College, Oxford, where he graduated B.A. 1851, M.A. 1855; a magistrate of the county of Kirkcudbright, and a major in the Scottish Borderers' Militia; M.P. for Dumfriesshire, 1865; re-elected, 1869.

WALLON, Henri Alexandre, French author, b. at Valenciennes, Dec. 23, 1812; studied at the École Normale, 1831–34; member of the Legislative Assembly, 1849; elected member of the French Academy, 1850. Author of ' Géographie politique des Temps modernes,' 1839; ' Du Monothéisme chez les Races sémitiques,' 1859; ' La Vie de Jésus et son nouvel Historien,' 1864; and other works.

WALPOLE, Right Hon. Spencer Horatio, English statesman, b. 1806; educated at Eton, and at Trinity College, Cambridge, where he graduated B.A. 1828; called to the bar of Lincoln's Inn, 1831; a bencher of Lincoln's Inn; a commissioner of ecclesiastical estates; was secretary of state for the Home Department, 1852, 1858–59, and 1866–67; M.P. for Midhurst, 1846–56; and for Cambridge University since 1856.

WALROND, John Walrond, English politician, b. 1818; a magistrate and deputy-lieutenant of Devon, and a magistrate of Somerset; M.P. for Tiverton, 1865–68.

WALSH, Hon. Arthur, English politician, b. 1827; educated at Eton, and Trinity College, Cambridge; a magistrate of Berks and the county of Radnor; was formerly captain 1st Life Guards; M.P. for Radnorshire since 1865.

WALSH, Sir John Benn, English politician, b. 1798; a deputy-lieutenant of Berks, and lord-lieutenant of Radnor; was M.P. for Sudbury, 1830–31, and 1838–40; and for Radnorshire, 1840–65.

WALSIN ESTERHAZY, Jean Louis Marie, French military commander, b. Nov. 12, 1804; entered the Military School of St. Cyr, 1822; lieutenant-colonel, 1842; colonel, 1845; general of brigade, 1850; general of division, 1856; grand officer of the Légion d'honneur, 1859.

WALTER, Ferdinand, German jurist, b. at Wesslar, Bavaria, Nov. 30, 1794; studied law at Heidelberg, 1814–18; elected deputy to the Prussian Chamber, 1848; re-elected, 1849–50. Author of 'Lehrbuch des Kirchenrechts,' Bonn, 1822; 'Deutsche Rechtsgeschichte,' ib. 1853; and other legal works.

WALTER, John, English politician, b. in London, 1818; educated at Eton, and Exeter College, Oxford, where he graduated B.A. 1840, M.A. 1843; called to the bar of Lincoln's Inn, 1847; was M.P. for Nottingham, 1847–59; M.P. for Berks since 1859; chief proprietor of the *Times*.

WARD, Edward Matthew, English painter, b. in Pimlico, 1816; admitted a student of the Royal Academy, 1834. Exhibited 'Napoleon in the Prison at Nice,' 1840; 'The South Sea Bubble,' 1847; 'The Last Sleep of Argyle,' 1857; 'Ante-chamber at White-hall during the Dying Moments of Charles II.' 1861; 'The Night of Rizzio's Murder,' 1865; and numerous other paintings, chiefly historical. Elected A.R.A. 1846; R.A. 1855.

WARNER, Edward, English politician, b. 1818; educated at Wadham College, Oxford, where he graduated B.A. 1840, M.A. 1844; called to the bar of Lincoln's Inn, 1850; a magistrate and deputy-lieutenant of Essex; was M.P. for Norwich, 1852–57, and 1860–68.

WARNER, Susan, American authoress, b. at New York, 1818. Author, under the *nom de plume* of Miss Wetherell, of 'The Wide Wide World,' New York, 1849; 'Queechey;' 'The Hills of the Shatemuc,' ib. 1856; and numerous other novels and tales of American life.

WARNKOENIG, Leopold August, German jurist, b. at Bruchsal, Baden, Aug. 1, 1794; studied at Heidelberg and Göttingen, and graduated LL.D. 1816; appointed professor of ecclesiastical law in the University of Tübingen, 1844. Author of 'History of Flanders and of Flemish Law,' Tübingen, 1834–39; 'History of France and of French Law,' Bâle, 1845–48; and other legal and historical works.

WARREN, Samuel, English author, b. in Denbighshire, 1807; educated at the University of Edinburgh; called to the bar of the Inner Temple, 1837; a Q.C. and recorder of Hull; M.P. for Midhurst, 1856; re-elected, 1857; resigned on being appointed one of the masters in lunacy, Feb. 1859. Author of 'The Diary of a late Physician,' 1830; 'Ten Thousand a Year,' 1839–41; 'The Lily and the Bee,' 1851; and several legal works.

WARTER, Rev. John Wood, English author, b. 1806; educated at Christ Church, Oxford, where he graduated B.A. 1827. Edited Southey's 'Commonplace Book,' and a portion of his correspondence. Author of 'Parochial Fragments;' 'The Last of the Old Squires;' and other works.

WARWICK, George Guy Greville, Earl of, English administrator, b. 1818; graduated at St. John's College, Oxford; sat in the House of Commons as Lord Brooke from Nov. 1848 to Aug. 1853; lieutenant-colonel of the Warwickshire Yeomanry Corps.

WATERFORD, John Henry de la Poer Beresford, Marquis of, b. 1844; succeeded, 1867.

WATERHOUSE, Samuel, English politician, b. 1815; a J.P. and deputy-lieutenant of the West Riding of the county of York, and major of the 2d York Yeomanry Cavalry; M.P. for Pontefract since 1863.

WATERWORTH, Rev. William, English writer, b. 1812; educated at Stony-hurst; entered the order of the Jesuits, and was ordained a priest. Author of 'The Origin and Developments of Anglicanism;' 'England and Rome, or the Religious Connexion between England and the Holy See, from the Year A.D. 179 down to the Reformation.'

WATKIN, Sir Edward William, English politician, b. 1819; chairman of the South-Eastern and other railways; was formerly a merchant in Manchester; M.P. for Great Yarmouth, 1857–58, and for Stockport, 1864–68; knighted, 1867.

WATKINS, Rev. Charles Frederick, English author, b. at Corsley, Wilts, Jan. 16, 1795; educated at Christ's Hospital, and at Christ's College, Cambridge; appointed curate of Windsor, 1820; vicar of Brixworth, 1832. Author of 'An Introduction to Geology and the Rationale of New Discoveries,' 1849; and other works.

WATSON, Rev. John Selby, English author, b. 1815; educated at Trinity College, Dublin, where he graduated B.A. 1838, and M.A.; ordained, 1839; head master of the Proprietary Grammar School at Stockwell, Surrey. Author of 'Sons of Strength, Wisdom, Patience;' 'The Story of Sir William Wallace;' and other works.

WATT, James Henry, English engraver, b. in London, 1799; studied under Mr. C. Heath. Engraved 'The Highland Drovers' Departure,' after Landseer; 'Susannah and the Elders,' after Caracci; 'Christ blessing Little Children,' after Eastlake; and numerous other works of celebrated painters.

WATTS, George Frederick, English painter, b. in London, 1820; studied at the Royal Academy. Exhibited 'Isabella finding Lorenzo dead,' 1840; 'Orlando pursuing the Fata Morgana,' 1848; 'Life's Illusions,' 1849; 'St. George overcomes the Dragon,' 1853; 'Ariadne,' 1863; and numerous other paintings; executed the frescoes in Poets' Hall for the new Houses of Parliament.

WATTS, Thomas, English philologist, b. 1804; appointed assistant in the British Museum, 1838; superintendent of the reading-room of the British Museum, 1857; keeper of the printed books department, 1867. Author of 'Papers contributed to the Transactions of the Philological Society;' contributor to the 'Encyclopædia Britannica.'

WAYLAND, Francis, American political economist, b. at New York, 1796; studied at Union College, Schenectady; entered the Theological Seminary of Andover, 1816; appointed president of Brown University, 1827. Author of 'Elements of Political Economy,' London, 1838; 'The Limitations of Human Responsibility;' and other works.

WEBBER, Charles Wilkins, American author, b. at Russeville, Kentucky, May 29, 1818. Author of 'Old Hicks the Guide;' 'Gold Mines of the Gila,' 1849; 'Wild Scenes and Song Birds,' New York, 1854; 'The Hunter Naturalist,' Philadelphia, 1855; and numerous other works.

WEBER, Wilhelm Eduard, German author, b. at Wittenberg, Oct. 24, 1801; nominated professor of physics at Leipsic, 1845; resigned, 1849; appointed professor of the same at Göttingen, 1849. Author of 'Die Wellentheorie,' Leipsic, 1825; 'Electrodynamische Massbestimmungen,' ib. 1846–52; and other scientific works.

WEBSTER, Benjamin, English comedian, b. at Bath, Sept. 3, 1800; educated for the navy; made his first appearance on the stage at Warwick; and in London, 1825; became manager of the Haymarket Theatre, 1837; built the New Adelphi Theatre, 1858; president of the New Dramatic College.

WEBSTER, Thomas, English painter, b. in London, 1800. Exhibited 'The Soldier's Return;' 'A Village School,' 1833; 'Punch,' 1840; 'A Dame's School,' 1845; 'The Race,' 1855; and numerous other paintings, chiefly of rural and domestic scenes. Elected A.R.A. 1840; R.A. 1846.

WEEKES, Henry, English sculptor, b. at Canterbury, 1807; studied under W. Behnes, and under Chantrey. Executed a bust of the Queen, 1837; the statues of Cranmer, Latimer, and Ridley, for the Martyrs' Memorial at Oxford; the Marquis Wellesley, for the India House; the monument to Shelley in Christ Church Minster; and numerous other statues. Exhibited 'The Suppliant,' 1850; 'A Shepherd,' 1852; and many other works. Elected A.R.A. 1850; R.A. 1863.

WEGENER, Gaspard Fredrik, Danish author, b. at Gudbjerg, Dec. 13, 1802; graduated Ph.D. 1836; director of the National Archives since 1848. Author of 'De Aula Attalica Artium Fautrice,' Copenhagen, 1836; 'Liden Krönike om Kong Frederik,' 1843; 'Actmæssige Bidrag til Danmarks Historie,' 1851; and other historical works.

WEGUELIN, Thomas Matthias, English politician, b. 1809; J.P. of Surrey; a Russia merchant, and late governor of the Bank of England; was M.P. for Southampton, 1857–59; M.P. for Wolverhampton since 1861.

WEIL, Gustave, French philologist, b. at Sultzburg, April 24, 1808; studied at Paris, and in Cairo; received an appointment in the library of Heidelberg, 1836; appointed professor of Oriental languages in the University of the same town, 1845. Author of 'The Poetical Literature of the Arabs,' Stuttgart, 1837; 'Historical and Critical Introduction to the Koran,' 1844; 'History of the Caliphs,' 1846–51; and other works on the East and Oriental literature.

WEILL, Alexandre, French author, b. in Alsace, 1813; studied in Germany; became one of the editors of *La Presse*, 1848. Author of 'Feu et Flamme,' 1845; 'République et Monarchie,' 1848; 'Le Livre des Rois,' 1852; 'Les Livres de Dieu,' 1864; and *numerous other works.*

WEISBACH, Julius, German mathematician, b. at Mittelschmiedeberg, Saxony, Oct. 10, 1806; studied at the Universities of Göttingen and Vienna; appointed professor of mathematics at the Academy of Freiberg, 1833. Author of 'Handbuch der Bergmaschinenmechanik,' Leipsic, 1835–36; 'Treatise on Experimental Hydraulics,' 1855; and other works.

WEISS, Jean Jacques, French journalist, b. at Bayonne, 1827; studied at the College of Louis le Grand, at the École St. Cyr, and the Paris École Normale; professor of French literature to the Faculty of Aix, 1856; and of history to the Faculty of Dijon, 1858; appointed editor of the *Journal des Débats*, 1860. Author of 'Essays on the History of French Literature,' 1865; and other works.

WEISS, Siegfried, German author, b. at Dantzic, May 8, 1822; studied at the University of Berlin, and graduated LL. D. Author of 'Studies,' Berlin, 1845; 'Prussia, Denmark, and the Duchies,' Vienna, 1850; 'Metaphysical Explanation of the Existence of God, and the Immortality of the Soul,' Berlin, 1860; and other works.

WEISSE, Christian Hermann, German philosophical writer, b. at Leipsic, Aug. 10, 1801; studied in the University of his native town; appointed professor of philosophy at Leipsic, 1845; received the degree of D.D. from Jena, 1840. Author of 'Study of Homer, and his Importance in our Epoch,' Leipsic, 1826; 'Luther's Christianity,' 1852; and other philosophical works.

WELBY-GREGORY, William Earle, English politician, b. 1829; educated at Eton, and Christ Church, Oxford, where he graduated B.A. 1851; a magistrate and deputy-lieutenant of Lincolnshire, and lieutenant Leicestershire Yeomanry Cavalry; M.P. for Grantham, 1857–65; M.P. for South Lincolnshire since 1865.

WELCKER, Friedrich Gottlieb, German archæologist, b. at Grünberg, Hesse, 1794; nominated keeper of the library and professor of philology to the University of Bonn, 1819. Edited the *Philological Museum of the Rhine* for more than twenty years. Author of 'Ancient Monuments,' Göttingen, 1849–51; and other philological and archæological works.

WELHAVEN, Johan Sebastian, Norwegian author, b. at Bergen, Dec. 22, 1807; studied at the University of Christiania; appointed professor of philosophy in the same University, 1846. Author of 'Norges Dæmring,' Christiania, 1834; 'Reisebille der og Digte,' ib. 1851; 'Biography of Louis Holberg,' 1854; and other, chiefly poetical, works.

WELLES, Gideon, American statesman, b. in Connecticut, 1805; was postmaster of Hartford till 1840; held an appointment in the Marine Department under President Polk; one of the delegates to the Chicago Convention, 1860; secretary of the navy, 1861–69.

WELLESLEY, Hon. and Very Rev. Gerald, English divine, b. 1809; educated at Eton, and Trinity College, Cambridge, where he graduated M.A. 1830; nominated chaplain to the Queen, 1849; dean of Windsor, 1854.

WELLINGTON, Arthur Richard Wellesley, Duke of, English administrator, b. 1807; educated at Eton and Cambridge, where he graduated D.C.L.; a major-general in the army; elected M.P. for Aldborough, 1829, and for Norwich, 1837; succeeded his father, first duke, Sept. 1852; master of the horse to the Queen from Dec. 1852 to Feb. 1858; a deputy-lieutenant of Hants.

WELLINGTON, Right Rev. Charles John Abraham, Bishop of, English divine, b. 1815; educated at Eton, and King's College, Cambridge; was archdeacon of Waitemate, New Zealand, 1852–57; consecrated first bishop of Wellington, New Zealand, 1857. Author of several theological works.

WELLS, Sir Mordaunt Lawson, English colonial administrator, b. 1817; educated at the Grammar School, Huntingdon; called to the bar of the Middle Temple, 1841; serjeant-at-law, 1855; recorder of Bedford, 1856; judge at Calcutta, and knighted, 1858; member of the Legislative Council of India, 1860–63.

WENDEL, Alexis Charles, Baron de, French politician, b. Dec. 15, 1809; member of the General Council for the canton of Thionville, and director of the Orleans Railway; member of the Legislative Assembly, 1849; and of the Corps Législatif for the department of the Moselle since 1852.

WERLE', Mathieu E'douard, French politician, b. at Rheims, Oct. 3, 1801; president of the Tribunal of Commerce, 1846; mayor of Rheims, 1852; member of the Corps Législatif for the department of the Marne since 1862.

WEST, Auguste Ce'sar, French politician, b. at Soultz, July 13, 1810; secretary-general to the prefecture of Haut-Rhin, 1848; prefect of the same department, 1849; prefect of Bas-Rhin, 1850, and of Haute-Garonne, 1855; member of the Corps Législatif for the department of Bas-Rhin since 1863.

WEST, Lord Charles Richard, English military commander, b. in London, 1815, eldest son of the Earl of Delawarr; entered the army, 1831; took part in the war in the Crimea, 1855; promoted major-general, 1856.

WESTBURY, Richard Bethell, Baron, English statesman, b. 1800; educated at Wadham College, Oxford, where he graduated B.A. 1818; called to the bar of the Middle Temple, 1823; made Q.C. 1840; vice-chancellor of the Duchy of Lancaster, 1850; solicitor-general, 1852; attorney-general, 1856–58 and 1859–61; was M.P for Aylesbury, 1851–59, and for Wolverhampton, 1859–61; appointed lord high chancellor, and raised to the peerage, 1861; resigned the chancellorship, July 1865.

WESTERGAARD, Niels Ludvig, Danish philologist, b. at Copenhagen, Dec. 17, 1815; educated in the University of his native city, and studied Sanscrit at Bonn, 1838; appointed professor of Oriental languages in the University of Copenhagen, 1845. Author of 'Radices Sanscritæ,' 1841; a critical edition of the 'Zendavesta,' Copenhagen, 1852–53; and other works.

WESTERN, Sir Thomas Burch, English politician, b. 1795; educated at Trinity College, Cambridge, where he graduated B.A. 1818, M.A. 1824; a J.P. and deputy-lieutenant of Suffolk and Essex; M.P. for North Essex, 1865–68.

WESTMACOTT, Richard, English sculptor, b. in London, 1797; studied in Italy, 1820–26. Exhibited 'The Cymbal Player,' 1832; 'Paolo and Francesca,' 1838; a bas-relief, 'Go and Sin no more,' 1850; and numerous statues, groups, and bas-reliefs. Elected A.R.A. 1838, R.A. 1849; appointed professor of sculpture to the Royal Academy, 1859. Author of 'Handbook on the Schools of Sculpture;' and other works upon art.

WESTMINSTER, Richard Grosvenor, Marquis of, English administrator, b. 1795; educated at Christ Church, Oxford; was M.P. for the county of Chester, 1818–34; lord steward of the Household, 1850–52; lord-lieutenant of Cheshire.

WESTMORELAND, Francis William Henry Fane, Earl of, English officer, b. 1825; educated at Westminster; entered the army, 1841; captain, 1853; lieutenant-colonel, 1854; served in India; was aide-de-camp to Lord Raglan in the Crimea; succeeded his father, eleventh earl, Oct. 1859.

WESTWOOD, John Obadiah, English entomologist, b. in Sheffield, 1805; educated at Lichfield; appointed professor of zoology at Oxford, 1861. Author of 'Palæographia Sacra Pictoria;' 'The Butterflies of Great Britain;' and other works.

WETHERALL, Sir George Augustus, English military commander, b. 1779; educated at Winchester, and at the Royal Military College, High Wycombe; served at the Cape, and was military secretary to the commander-in-chief at Madras, 1822–25; became a general in the army, 1863.

WEY, François Alphonse, French author, b. at Besançon, Aug. 12, 1812; studied in Paris. Author of 'Enfants du Marquis de Ganges,' 1838; 'Histoire des Révolutions du Langage en France,' 1848; 'La haute Savoie, Récits d'Histoire et de Voyage,' 1865; and numerous other works.

WHALLEY, George Hammond, English politician, b. 1813; educated at University College, London; called to the bar of Gray's Inn, 1839; a magistrate and deputy-lieutenant of the county of Denbigh, and a magistrate of the counties of Montgomery and Carnarvon; M.P. for Peterborough since 1859. Author of 'On the Law of Tithe Commutations;' and other legal works.

WHARNCLIFFE, Edward Montagu Stuart Granville Stuart Wortley, Baron, English administrator, b. 1827; a deputy-lieutenant of the West Riding of Yorkshire; lieutenant-colonel Hallamshire Rifles.

WHATMAN, James, English politician, b. 1813; educated at Eton, and Christ Church, Oxford, where he graduated B.A. 1834, M.A. 1838; deputy-lieutenant of Kent; and a commissioner of lieutenancy of London; M.P. for Maidstone, 1852–57, for West Kent, 1857–59; M.P. for Maidstone since 1865.

WHEATSTONE, Sir Charles, English electrician, b. at Gloucester, 1802; professor of experimental philosophy in King's College, London; inventor of the electric telegraph, in conjunction with Mr. W. F. Cooke.

WHITBREAD, Samuel, English politician, b. 1830; educated at Rugby, and Trinity College, Cambridge; a magistrate and deputy-lieutenant of Beds; M.P. for Bedford since 1852.

WHITE, James, English politician, b. 1809; educated for the mercantile career, and formerly an alderman of the city of London; M.P. for Plymouth, 1857–59, and for Brighton since 1860.

WHITE, Walter, English author, b. 1803; appointed clerk to the Royal Society, 1844; assistant secretary, 1861. Author of ' To Switzerland and Back ;' 'A July Holiday in Saxony, Bohemia, and Silesia ;' 'All Round the Wrekin ;' and other works of travel.

WHITESIDE, Right Hon. James, Irish judge, b. in the county of Wicklow, 1806; educated at Trinity College, Dublin, where he graduated B. A. 1827 ; called to the Irish bar, 1830 ; solicitor-general for Ireland, March to Dec. 1852 ; attorney-general, 1858–59 ; M. P. for Enniskillen, 1851–59, and for Dublin University, 1859–66 ; chief justice of the Court of Queen's Bench, 1866. Author of ' Ancient Rome ;' 'Italy in the Nineteenth Century,' 1849.

WHITTIER, John Greenleaf, American author, b. at Haverhill, Massachusetts, 1808. Author of 'Legends of New England,' 1831 ; 'Voices of Freedom,' Philadelphia, 1836 ; ' Old Portraits and Modern Sketches,' 1850 ; 'The Panorama, and other Poems,' 1856 ; and other poetical works.

WHITWORTH, Benjamin, English politician, b. 1816 ; a magistrate of the county of Lancaster, and a merchant at Manchester ; M.P. for Drogheda, 1865–69.

WIERTZ, Antoine, Belgian painter, b. at Dinant, Feb. 22, 1806 ; studied at the Academy of Antwerp. Painted ' La Révolte des Anges ;' 'Triomphe du Christ ;' 'La Fuite en Égypte ;' and numerous other paintings, chiefly religious or historical.

WIGAN, Alfred, English actor, b. at Blackheath, Kent, March 24, 1818 ; played at the principal London theatres ; manager of the Olympic, London, 1853–57 ; and of the St. James's Theatre, 1860–63.

WIGRAM, George Vicesimus, English author, b. March 1805 ; educated at Queen's College, Oxford ; joined the sect known as the Plymouth Brethren. Author of 'The Englishman's Greek Concordance of the New Testament ;' 'The Englishman's Hebrew and Chaldee Concordance of the Old Testament,' 1843–44 ; and other works.

WIGRAM, Right Hon. Sir James, English judge, b. 1803, brother of the preceding ; educated at Trinity College, Cambridge ; called to the bar of Lincoln's Inn, 1819 ; M.P. for Leominster from July to Oct. 1841 ; knighted, 1841 ; vice-chancellor, 1841–50, when he retired from the bench.

WILBERFORCE, Henry William, English journalist and divine, b. 1809 ; educated at Oriel College, Oxford, where he graduated in 1830 ; appointed vicar of East Farleigh, Kent, 1843 ; resigned, 1850, on joining the Roman Catholic Church ; proprietor and editor of the *Weekly Register*.

WILDE, James Plaisted, Baron Penzance, English judge, b. 1816 ; educated at Winchester, and Trinity College, Cambridge ; called to the bar of the Inner Temple, 1832 ; counsel to the Duchy of Lancaster, 1859 ; made a baron of the Exchequer, and knighted, 1860 ; appointed judge of the Court of Probate and Divorce, 1863 ; raised to the peerage, 1869.

WILHELM I., Duke of Brunswick, b. April 25, 1806, the second son of Duke Friedrich Wilhelm of Brunswick and of Princess Marie of Baden ; undertook provisionally the government of Brunswick in consequence of the insurrection of Sept. 7, 1830, and subsequent flight of his brother, the reigning Duke, Oct. 12, 1830 ; ascended the throne, April 25, 1831.

WILHELM I., King of Prussia, b. March 22, 1797, the second son of King Friedrich Wilhelm III. and of Princess Louise of Mecklenburg-Strelitz; educated for the military career, and took part in the campaigns of 1813 to 1815 against France ; appointed governor of the province of Pomerania, 1840 ; fled from Prussia to England, March 20, 1848 ; elected member of the Constituent Assembly for Wirsitz, Posen, May 15, 1848 ; returned to Berlin and took his seat in the Assembly, June 8, 1848 ; commander-in-chief of the Prussian troops against the revolutionary army of Baden, June 1849 ; appointed military governor of the Rhine Provinces, Oct. 1, 1849 ; appointed regent of the kingdom during the mental illness of his brother, Oct. 9, 1858 ; ascended the throne at the death of his brother, Jan. 2, 1861.

WILKES, Charles, American naval commander, b. 1805 ; entered the navy, 1823 ; appointed by the United States Government to conduct a voyage of exploration in the Southern and Pacific Oceans, 1838 ; commander of the *San Jacinto*, 1861 ; charged with the blockade of the ports of the Confederate States, 1862. Author of 'Narrative of the United States Exploring Expedition,' New York, 1845 ; 'Western America,' 1849.

WILKINSON, James John Garth, English author, b. in London, 1812. Author of 'On the Statute of Limitations ;' 'Swedenborg, a Biography,' 1849 ; 'The Ministry of Health,' 1856 ; and other works.

WILKINSON, Sir John Gardner, English archæologist, b. 1797; educated at Harrow, and Exeter College, Oxford; knighted, 1840. Author of 'Manners and Customs of the Ancient Egyptians, derived from a Comparison of the Painting, Sculpture, and Monuments still existing with the Accounts of Ancient Authors,' 1837–41 ; and other works.

WILKINSON, Rev. Matthew, English divine, b. 1810; graduated at Clare College, Cambridge, 1835; appointed head-master of Marlborough College, Wilts, 1843 ; resigned, and was appointed vicar of West Lavington, Wilts, 1852; one of the select preachers of the University of Cambridge, 1863–64. Author of 'Sermons.'

WILLEM III., King of the Netherlands, b. Feb. 19, 1817, the eldest son of King William II. and of Princess Anna Paulowna, daughter of Czar Paul I. of Russia ; educated by private tutors, and at the University of Leyden; succeeded to the throne at the death of his father, March 17, 1849; married, June 18, 1839, to Sophie, b. June 17, 1818, the second daughter of King William I. of Würtemberg.

WILLES, Sir James Shaw, English judge, b. 1814; educated at Trinity College, Dublin, where he graduated B.A. 1836, LL.D. 1860; called to the bar of the Inner Temple, 1840 ; judge of the Court of Common Pleas, and knighted, 1855. Edited, with Sir H. Keating, 'Smith's Leading Cases,' 1849.

WILLIAMS, Right Hon. Sir Edward Vaughan, English judge. b. in London, 1795 ; called to the bar of Lincoln's Inn, 1823 ; appointed one of the judges of the Court of Common Pleas, and knighted, 1847; resigned, and sworn a member of the Privy Council, 1865.

WILLIAMS, Frederick Martin, English politician, b. 1830 ; educated at Winchester ; a J.P. and deputy-lieutenant of Cornwall ; M.P. for Truro since 1865.

WILLIAMS, Rev. George, English author, b. 1814; educated at Eton, and King's College, Cambridge, where he graduated B.A. 1837, M.A. 1840; chaplain to Bishop Alexander of Jerusalem, 1841–43 ; warden of St. Columba's College, Ireland, 1850–55 ; vice-provost of King's College, 1854–56. Author of 'Holy City, or Historical and Topographical Notices of Jerusalem,' 1845.

WILLIAMS, Monier, English philologist, b. at Bombay, 1819 ; educated at King's College, London, and entered Balliol College, Oxford, 1838, and graduated B.A. at University College, Oxford, 1844 ; was professor of Sanscrit at Haileybury College, 1844–58 ; elected Boden Sanscrit professor at Oxford, Dec. 1860. Author of 'An English and Sanscrit Dictionary,' 1851 ; and other philological works.

WILLIAMS, Rev. Rowland, English author, b. in Flintshire, 1817; educated at Eton, and King's College, Cambridge ; appointed vice-principal and professor of Hebrew at St. David's College, Lampeter, and chaplain to the Bishop of Llandaff, 1850 ; became vicar of Broad Chalke, Wilts, 1859. Author of 'Review of Bunsen,' in the volume of 'Essays and Reviews ;' 'Rational Godliness ;' and other theological works.

WILLIAMS, Thomas Peers, English politician, b. 1795 ; educated at Westminster, and Christ Church, Oxford ; a magistrate and deputy-lieutenant of Berks, Anglesea, and Bucks, and lieutenant-colonel Anglesea Militia ; M.P. for Great Marlow, 1820–68.

WILLIAMS, Sir William Fenwick, English military commander, b. in Nova Scotia, 1800 ; entered the Royal Artillery, 1825 ; first lieutenant, 1827 ; captain, 1840 ; colonel and brigadier-general, 1854 ; defended Kars, 1855 ; lieutenant-general, 1856 ; commander of the troops in Canada, 1859–65.

WILLIAMSON, Sir Hedworth, English politician, b. 1827 ; educated at Eton, and Christ Church, Oxford ; a J.P. and deputy-lieutenant of the county of Durham ; M.P. for North Durham since 1864.

WILLIS, Rev. Robert, English author, b. in London, 1800 ; educated at Caius College, Cambridge, where he graduated in 1826 ; appointed Jacksonian professor of natural and experimental philosophy in the University of Cambridge, 1837. Author of 'Remarks on the Architecture of the Middle Ages and of Italy,' 1840 ; 'Principles of Mechanism,' 1841.

WILLISEN, Wilhelm von, Prussian diplomatist, b. at Strasfurth, 1790 ; entered the Russian service, 1805; colonel, 1840 ; and major-general, 1845; sent on a diplomatic mission to the Emperor of the French, 1861 ; nominated Prussian ambassador at Turin, 1862. Author of 'Théorie des grossen Kriegs,' Berlin, 1840–50; and other military works.

WILSON, Erasmus, English medical writer, b. 1808 ; became a member of the Royal College of Surgeons, 1831 ; consulting surgeon to the St. Pancras Infirmary. Author of 'The Dissector's Manual ;' 'Diseases of the Skin ;' and other medical works.

WILSON, Rev. Henry Bristow, English divine, b. 1803 ; educated at Merchant Taylors' School, and St. John's College, Oxford, where he graduated B.A. 1825 ; Bampton lecturer at Oxford, 1851. Author of 'Schemes of Christian Comprehension,' in the 'Oxford Essays,' 1857 ; 'The National Church' in 'Essays and Reviews ;' and of several pamphlets and sermons.

WILTON, Thomas Egerton, Earl, English politician, b. 1799 ; colonel of the Tower Hamlets Militia ; has been steward of the Household ; succeeded his maternal grandfather, first earl, 1814.

WIMPFFEN, Emmanuel Felix de, French military commander, b. 1807 ; captain in the army, 1840 ; colonel, 1853 ; general of brigade, 1855 ; general of division, 1859.

WIMPFFEN, Franz Emil Lorenz Herman von, Austrian military commander, b. at Prague, April 2, 1797 ; entered the army as second lieutenant, 1813 ; captain, 1822 ; major-general, 1838 ; civil and military governor of Trieste and the coast of the Adriatic, 1849 ; field-marshal and commander of the first corps of the Austrian army, 1854.

WINCHESTER, Right Rev. Charles Richard Sumner, Bishop of, English divine, b. at Kenilworth, 1790 ; educated at Eton, and Trinity College, Cambridge ; prelate of the Order of the Garter ; provincial sub-dean of Canterbury ; and visitor of Magdalen, New Trinity, St. John's, and Corpus Christi Colleges, Oxford ; consecrated bishop of Llandaff, 1826 ; translated to Winchester, 1827.

WINCHILSEA AND NOTTINGHAM, George James Finch Hatton, Earl of, English administrator, b. 1815 ; educated at Christ Church, Oxford ; M.P. for North Northamptonshire, 1837–41 ; succeeded his father, tenth earl, 1858.

WINDHAM, Sir Charles Ashe, English military commander, b. 1810 ; entered the Coldstream Guards, 1826 ; became colonel, June 1854 ; and major-general, 1855 ; appointed to the military command at Lahore, 1865 ; lieutenant-general in the army, and colonel of the 46th regiment.

WINNINGTON, Sir Thomas Edward, English politician, b. 1811 ; educated at Eton, and Christ Church, Oxford, where he graduated B.A. 1833 ; a deputy-lieutenant of Worcestershire ; high sheriff, 1851 ; M.P. for Bewdley, 1837–47, and 1852–68.

WINSLOW, Forbes, English medical writer, b. at Pentonville, Aug. 1810 ; passed at the Royal College of Surgeons, and graduated M.D. at Aberdeen, 1835. Author of 'The Physiology and Pathology of the Human Mind,' 1831 ; 'The Plea of Insanity in Criminal Cases ;' 'On the Obscure Diseases of the Brain and Disorders of the Mind,' 1860 ; and other papers and works on mental diseases.

WINTERHALTER, Frederick, English portrait painter, b. in the grand-duchy of Baden, 1806. Painted a portrait group of the Queen, the late Prince Consort, and the Royal Family ; also of Wellington and Peel, 1850 ; a portrait of the Empress of the French, 1861 ; the Prince Imperial, 1864 ; and of many other royal personages.

WINTHROP, Robert Charles, American statesman, b. at Boston, 1809 ; studied at Harvard College, and law under Daniel Webster ; elected to the State Legislature of Massachusetts, 1834 ; elected to Congress, 1840 ; chairman of Congress during the sessions of 1848–49 ; elected to the Senate, 1850. Author of 'Addresses and Speeches on various Occasions,' 1852.

WISE, Henry Augustus, American author, b. at Brooklyn, New York, May 1819 ; entered the United States navy as midshipman ; became lieutenant during the Mexican war. Author of 'Los Gringos, or an Inside View of Mexico, Peru, Chili, &c.' New York, 1849 ; 'Tales for the Marines,' ib. 1855 ; and other works of fiction.

WISE, Henry Christopher, English politician, b. 1806 ; educated at Rugby, and Oriel College, Oxford, where he graduated B.A. 1827 ; a J.P. and deputy-lieutenant of the county of Warwick ; M.P. for South Warwickshire since 1865.

WODEHOUSE, John, Earl of Kimberley, English statesman, b. 1826 ; studied at Eton, and Christ Church, Oxford, where he graduated B.A. 1847 ; a deputy-lieutenant of Norfolk ; was under-secretary of state for foreign affairs, Dec. 28, 1852, to May 4, 1856 ; envoy-extraordinary and minister-plenipotentiary at St. Petersburg, 1856, to May 20, 1858 ; reappointed under-secretary of state for foreign affairs, June 1859 ; resigned, 1861 ; lord-lieutenant of Ireland, 1864–66 ; created Earl of Kimberley, 1866 ; lord privy seal, Dec. 1868.

WODEHOUSE, Sir Philip Edmund, English colonial administrator, b. 1806 ; entered the Ceylon Civil Service as writer, 1828 ; superintendent of Honduras, 1851 ; governor of British Guiana, 1854 ; special envoy to the Government of Venezuela, 1858 ; appointed governor of the Cape of Good Hope, 1861.

WOHLER, Friedrich, German chemist, b. at Esschenheim, near Frankfort, July 31, 1809 ; studied at Marburg and Heidelberg, and received the degree of M.D. ; appointed professor of medicine and director of the Chemical Institute at Göttingen, 1836. Author of 'Treatise on Organic Chemistry,' Berlin, 1840 ; 'Practical Chemical Analysis,' ib. 1854 ; and other works on chemistry.

WOIRHAYE, Charles François, French magistrate, b. at Metz, May 31, 1798 ; studied law, and was called to the bar, 1818 ; nominated first president of the Imperial Court of Metz, 1856 ; councillor to the Court of Cassation, 1862.

WOLOWSKI, Louis François Michel Raymond, French political economist, b. at Warsaw, Aug. 31, 1810 ; studied in France, and was naturalized,1834 ; founded the *Revue de Législation et de Jurisprudence,* 1833 ; member of the Constituent and Legislative Assemblies, 1848–49 ; elected member of the French Academy, 1855. Author of 'Introduction de l'Économie politique en Italie,' 1859 ; and other works.

WOOD, Rev. John George, English author, b. in London, 1827 ; educated at Merton College, Oxford, where he graduated B.A. 1848, M.A. 1851 ; appointed assistant chaplain to St. Bartholomew's Hospital, London, 1856. Author of 'A Popular Natural History ;' 'My Feathered Friends, or Bird Life ;' 'Our Garden Friends and Foes ;' and other works on natural history.

WOODD, Basil Thomas, English politician, b. 1815 ; educated at Trinity College, Cambridge, where he graduated B.A. 1837, M.A. 1840 ; called to the bar, 1840 ; a magistrate of the North and West Ridings of Yorkshire, and a deputy-lieutenant of the West Riding ; M.P. for Knaresborough, 1852–68.

WOODS, Henry, English politician, b. 1822 ; a deputy-lieutenant of the county of Lancaster ; M.P. for Wigan since 1857.

WOODWARD, Bernard Bolingbroke, English author, b. at Norwich, 1816 ; educated at Norwich, and at London University ; appointed librarian-in-ordinary to the Queen at Windsor, and keeper of the royal collection of prints and drawings, 1860. Author of 'A History of Wales from the Earliest Times to the Final Incorporation of the Principality with England,' 1851 ; and other works.

WORBOISE, Emma Jane, English authoress, b. 1820 ; educated at the School for Clergymen's Daughters at Casterton, near Kirkby Lonsdale. Author of 'Married Life ;' 'Lottie Lonsdale ;' 'Thornycroft Hall ;' and other works of fiction.

WORCESTER, Right Rev. Henry Philpot, Bishop of, English divine, b. Nov. 17, 1807 ; educated at the Cathedral Grammar School, Chichester, and at St. Catherine's College, Cambridge, where he graduated B.A. 1829 ; was master of St. Catherine's College, Cambridge, and three times vice-chancellor of the University ; consecrated bishop of Worcester, 1861.

WORDSWORTH, Right Rev. Charles, English divine, b. 1806 ; educated at Harrow, and Christ Church, Oxford, where he graduated B.A. 1830 ; elected bishop of the united diocese of St. Andrew's, Dunkeld, and Dumblane, 1852. Author of 'Shakespeare's Knowledge and Use of the Bible,' 1854 ; 'A United Church for the United Kingdom ;' and other theological works.

WORNUM, Ralph Nicholson, English author, b. in the county of Durham, 1812 ; educated at the University of London ; appointed keeper and secretary of the National Gallery, 1857. Author of 'History of Ancient and Modern Painting,' 1847 ; 'The Epochs of Painting,' 1864 ; and other works upon art.

WORSAAE, Hans Jakob Asmussen, Danish archæologist, b. at Veile, Jutland, March 14, 1821 ; studied at the College of Horsen, and at Copenhagen, 1836–38. Author of 'Danemark's Oldtid,' Copenhagen, 1843 ; 'Aftbildninger fra de kongelige Museum for nordiske Oldsager,' ib. 1854 ; and other archæological works.

WRANGEL, Ferdinand Petrovich von, Russian navigator, b. in Esthonia, 1795 ; studied at the School for Naval Cadets at St. Petersburg ; sailed in the *Kamschatka* under Captain Golovin round the world, 1817 ; nominated governor of the Russian American colonies, 1827 ; created a vice-admiral, 1847. Author of several works of travel.

WRANGEL, Friedrich, Baron von, Prussian military commander, b. at Stettin, 1784 ; entered the army, 1796 ; commander-in-chief of the allied Prussian and Federal forces in the first Schleswig-Holstein war, 1848–49 ; field-marshal-general, 1856 ; commander-in-chief of allied Prussian and Austrian armies in the second Schleswig-Holstein war, 1864.

WRATISLAW, Rev. Albert Henry, English author, b. 1822 ; educated at Christ College, Cambridge, where he graduated B.A. 1844 ; appointed head-master of Bury School, 1857. Published 'Bohemian Poems, Ancient and Modern,' translated from the *original Sclavonic* ; and is author of several sermons, schoolbooks, and pamphlets.

WRIGHT, Rev. George Newnham, English author, b. 1812 ; educated at Brasenose College, Oxford, where he graduated B.A. 1835 ; appointed master of the Grammar School, Tewkesbury. Author of 'Lancashire in the Nineteenth Century ;' 'The Comprehensive Gazetteer of the World ;' and numerous other works, chiefly topographical.

WRIGHT, Ichabod Charles, English author, b. 1795 ; educated at Eton, and Christ Church, Oxford, where he graduated B.A. 1817, M.A. 1820. Translated Dante and the Iliad into English verse.

WRIGHT, Thomas, English antiquary, b. 1810 ; educated at Ludlow Grammar School, and Trinity College, Cambridge, where he graduated B.A. 1834. Edited Chaucer's 'Canterbury Tales.' Author of 'Wanderings of an Antiquary ;' 'History of Caricature ;' and other works. Translator of the first volume of the Emperor Napoleon's 'Life of Julius Cæsar,' 1865.

WROTTESLEY, John Wrottesley, Baron, English administrator, b. 1798 ; educated at Christ Church, Oxford, where he graduated B.A. 1819, M.A. 1823 ; a deputy-lieutenant and magistrate of Staffordshire ; president of the Royal Society, 1854-57. Author of 'Thoughts on Government and Legislation.'

WUNDERLICH, Karl August, German physician, b. at Sultz, on the Neckar, 1815 ; studied medicine at Stuttgardt and Tübingen ; appointed professor of medicine to the University of Leipsic, 1850. Author of 'On French and German Medicine,' Stuttgardt, 1841 ; 'Essay on the Pathological Physiology of the Blood,' ib. 1844 ; and other medical works

WURZBACH, Constant, German author, b. at Laybach, Illyria, April 11, 1818 ; studied law ; entered the Austrian army as a volunteer, 1836 ; obtained the degree of Ph.D., and retired from the army, 1844 ; appointed keeper of the library of Vienna, and of the archives to the Ministry of the Interior, 1848. Author of 'Mosaik,' 1841 ; 'Volkslieder der Polen,' Leinberg, 1847 ; and other poetical works.

WYATT, Sir Matthew Digby, English architect, b. near Devizes, 1820 ; studied on the Continent. Arranged and restored the Adelphi Theatre, 1848 ; restored the chancel of North Marston Church, Bucks, 1854 ; joint architect with Mr. Scott of the new India Office ; knighted, 1868. Author of 'The Geometrical Mosaics of the Middle Ages,' 1848 ; 'Notices of Sculpture in Ivory ;' and numerous other works on architecture.

WYNDHAM, Hon. Percy Scawen, English politician, b. 1835 ; educated at Eton ; a J.P. of Sussex and Cumberland ; captain 6th Sussex Rifle Volunteers ; formerly lieutenant in the Coldstream Guards ; M.P. for West Cumberland since 1860.

WYNN, Charles Watkin Williams, English politician, b. 1822 ; educated at Westminster, and Christ Church, Oxford, where he graduated B.A. 1843, M.A. 1845 ; a deputy-lieutenant of Montgomery, and captain Montgomeryshire Yeomanry Cavalry ; M.P. for Montgomeryshire since 1862.

WYNN, Sir Watkin Williams, English politician, b. 1820 ; educated at Westminster ; a deputy-lieutenant of Montgomery, Salop, and Merioneth ; lieutenant-colonel Montgomery Yeomanry ; formerly lieutenant 1st Life Guards ; M.P. for Denbighshire since 1841.

WYNNE, William Robert Maurice, English politician, b. 1840 ; educated at Eton ; a J.P. and deputy-lieutenant of the county of Merioneth ; late lieutenant Scots Fusilier Guards ; M.P. for Merionethshire, 1865-68.

WYNTER, Andrew, English physician, b. at Bristol, 1819 ; graduated M.D. 1853 ; and became a member of the College of Physicians, 1861 ; editor of the *British Medical Journal*, 1845-60. Author of 'Sketches of Town and Country Life,' 1855-56 ; 'Subtle Brains and Lissom Fingers,' 1863 ; and other works.

WYVILL, Marmaduke, English politician, b. 1815 ; educated at Trinity College, Cambridge, where he graduated B.A. 1839 ; a deputy-lieutenant of the North Riding of Yorkshire ; M.P for Richmond, 1846-68.

Y.

YARBOROUGH, Charles Anderson Pelham, Earl of, English administrator, b. 1835; educated at Eton; M.P. for Lincolnshire, 1857–61, succeeded his father, second earl, 1862; a deputy-lieutenant of Lincolnshire; lieutenant-colonel Lincolnshire Volunteers.

YATES, Edmund Hodgson, English author, b. July 1831. Author of 'Life and Correspondence of Charles Mathews the Elder,' 1860; 'Broken to Harness,' 1864–65; and numerous other works of fiction.

YATES, William Holt, English author, b. in Yorkshire, 1802; educated at the University of Edinburgh, and at St. John's College, Cambridge, where he graduated M.D. 1826; member of the Royal College of Physicians, London. Author of 'Modern History and Condition of Egypt,' 1843.

YOLLAND, William, English engineer, b. 1810; entered the Royal Military College, Woolwich, and became second lieutenant Royal Engineers, 1828; lieutenant-colonel, 1855; colonel, 1858; appointed one of the inspectors of railways by the Board of Trade, 1854.

YONGE, Charles Duke, English author, b. Nov. 1812; educated at Eton and Oxford, where he graduated B.A. 1835. Author of 'Greek and English Lexicon,' 1849; 'History of England,' 1857; 'History of the British Navy;' 1864; and other works, chiefly historical.

YONGE, Charlotte Mary, English authoress, b. 1823. Author of 'The Heir of Redclyffe;' 'Heartsease;' 'Dynevor Terrace;' 'Landmarks of History, Ancient, Middle Age, and Modern;' and other works. Editor of the *Monthly Packet.*

YORK, Most Rev. William Thomson, Archbishop of, English divine, b. at Whitehaven, 1819; educated at Queen's College, Oxford, where he graduated B.A. 1840, B.D. and D.D. 1856; appointed rector of All Souls, Marylebone, 1855; elected preacher of Lincoln's Inn, 1858; chaplain-in-ordinary to the Queen, 1859; consecrated bishop of Gloucester and Bristol, 1861; translated to York, 1862. Author of 'An Outline of the Laws of Thought;' and other works.

YORKE, Sir Charles, English military commander, b. 1790; educated at Winchester; entered the army; served in the Peninsular campaign, and at Waterloo; military secretary at the Horse Guards, 1856–60; lieutenant-general in the army.

YORKE, John Reginald, English politician, b. 1836; educated at Eton, and Balliol College, Oxford; a deputy-lieutenant of the county of Worcester; and captain 8th Gloucestershire Rifle Volunteers; M.P. for Tewkesbury, 1864–68.

YOUNG, Adolphus William, English politician, b. 1814; a magistrate of Berks; was high sheriff of New South Wales, 1842–49; represented Victoria in the Legislative Council of New South Wales; M.P. for Great Yarmouth, 1857–59; M.P. for Helstone since 1865.

YOUNG, George, English politician, b. 1819; educated at Edinburgh; called to the Scottish bar, 1840; appointed solicitor-general for Scotland, 1852; a magistrate of the county of Dumfries and the city of Edinburgh; formerly sheriff of the county of Inverness, and of the counties of Haddington and Berwick; M.P. for Wigton since 1865.

YOUNG, Sir Henry Edward Fox Knight, English colonial administrator, b. 1810; was lieutenant-governor of South Australia, lieutenant-governor of the Cape of Good Hope, and judge at St. Lucia; governor of Tasmania, 1854–61.

YOUNG, John Radford, English mathematician, b. 1802; was professor of mathematics at Belfast College. Author of 'A Course of Elementary Mathematics;' 'Science Elucidative of Scripture, and not Antagonistic to it,' 1863; 'The Christ of History;' and other works.

YOUNG, Right Hon. Sir John, English statesman, b. 1807; educated at Eton, and Corpus Christi College, Oxford, where he graduated B.A. 1829; called to the bar of Lincoln's Inn, 1834; a lord of the Treasury, 1841–44; secretary to the Treasury, 1844–46; chief secretary to the lord-lieutenant of Ireland, 1852–55; lord high commissioner of the Ionian Islands, 1855–59; governor of New South Wales, 1860–67; appointed *governor-general* of Canada, 1868.

YRIARTE, Charles, French author, b. in Paris, 1833 ; inspector of the Opera. Author of 'La Société espagnole,' 1861 ; 'Les Portraits parisiens,' 1865 ; and other works of fiction. Editor of the *Monde Illustré*.

YVAN, Melchior, French author, b. at Digne, Basses Alpes, 1803; studied medicine at Montpellier, and graduated M.D. 1835 ; member of the Constituent Assembly for Basses Alpes, 1849 ; inspector-general of printing and publishing, 1859. Author of 'La Chine et la presqu'Ile Malaise,' 1850 ; 'Légendes et Récits,' 1861 ; and other works.

YVON, Adolphe, French painter, b. at Eschwiller, Moselle, 1817 ; studied at Paris under Paul Delaroche. Exhibited 'Le Remords de Judas,' 1846; 'Le Premier Consul descendant les Alpes,' 1853 ; 'La Prise de la Tour de Malakoff,' 1859 ; 'Magenta, Évacuation des Blessés,' 1863 ; and other, chiefly historical, paintings.

Z.

ZACCONE, Pierre, French author, b. at Douai, April 2, 1817. Author of 'Histoire des Sociétés secrètes, politiques et religieuses, 1847 ; 'Le Fils du Ciel,' 1857 ; 'Les Deux Robinsons,' 1863 ; and other works.

ZAHN, Johann Carl Wilhelm, German architect and author, b. at Rodenburg, Hesse, Aug. 21, 1800; studied in Paris and Italy. Published 'Neuentdeckte Wandgemälde in Pompeji,' Berlin, 1828 ; 'Ornamente aller classischen Zeiten,' ib. 1852 ; and several works on discoveries in Pompeii and Herculaneum.

ZAMOYSKI, Andreas, Count, Polish statesman, b. April 2, 1800 ; studied at the Imperial Lyceum of Paris, 1812–14 ; and at Geneva and Edinburgh ; sent as representative of the National Government of Poland to the court of Vienna, 1831 ; president of the Agricultural Society of Warsaw, 1861 ; arrested in Warsaw, and sent to St. Petersburg, Sept. 1862 ; exiled, 1863.

ZARNCKE, Friedrich, German author, b. at Bruel, Mecklenburg, July 7, 1825; studied philology at Leipsic and Berlin, 1844–47. Author of 'Die deutschen Universitäten in Mittelalter,' Leipsic, 1857. Founder of the *Literarische Centralblatt für Deutschland.*

ZELLER, Jules Sylvain, French historical writer, b. at Paris, April 23, 1820 ; studied at the Collége Charlemagne ; graduated D.C.L. 1844 ; appointed professor of history at the Faculté des Lettres of Aix, 1854–58 ; and at Sorbonne, 1858–59. Author of 'Histoire de l'Italie depuis l'Invasion des Barbares jusqu'à nos Jours,' 1852 ; 'L'Année historique,' 1860–63 ; and other historical works.

ZETLAND, Thomas Dundas, Earl of, English administrator, b. 1795 ; educated at Harrow, and Trinity College, Cambridge ; M.P. for York and for Richmond, 1818–39 ; lord-lieutenant of the North Riding of Yorkshire.

ZIEBLAND, Georg Friedrich, German architect, b. at Ratisbon, Feb. 7, 1800 ; studied at Munich, and in Italy ; designed the monument of King Otho at Aibling, Munich, 1842 ; the church of St. Boniface, commenced 1835, finished 1848 ; and numerous churches and public and private buildings.

ZINKEISEN, Johann Wilhelm, German historical writer, b. at Altenburg, April 11, 1803 ; studied theology and history at the Universities of Jena, Göttingen, and Dresden. Author of 'History of Greece,' Leipsic, 1832 ; 'History of Parties and Politics in the time of the Revolution,' Berlin, 1852–53 ; and other historical works.

ZOBEL, Thomas Friedrich, Count von, Austrian military commander, b. at Bremen, March 17, 1799 ; entered the Austrian army, 1812 ; colonel, 1848 ; major-general, 1849 ; lieutenant field-marshal, 1855.

ZORRILLA Y MORAL, Jose, Spanish poet, b. at Valladolid, Feb. 21, 1817 ; studied in the Seminary for Nobles at Madrid, and at the University of Toledo. Author of 'Cantos del Trovador, Coleccion de Legendas y Tradiciones historicas,' three vols. Madrid, 1840–41 ; 'Flores Perdidas,' ib. 1843 ; 'Granada, Poema Oriental,' two vols. Paris, 1853–54 ; and other poems and dramas.

ZUNZ, Leopold, German author, b. at Detmold, Aug. 10, 1794, of Jewish parents ; *studied philology* at Berlin, 1815–19 ; one of the editors of the '*Spenersche Zeitung,*' *1824–33.* Author of 'Die Namen der Juden,' Berlin, 1836 ; 'Die synagogale Poesie des *Mittelalters,*' ib. 1855 ; and other works, chiefly relating to the history and literature of the Jews.

APPENDIX.

APPENDIX.

A.

AALI PASHA, Mehemid Emin, Turkish statesman, b. 1815; entered the diplomatic service, 1835; ambassador to Great Britain, 1841–45; minister of foreign affairs, 1846–52, and again 1861; representative of the Ottoman Empire at the Congress of Vienna, 1856; grand vizier, 1852; re-appointed, 1869.

AHLQUIST, August Engelbert, Finnish author, b. Aug. 7, 1826; studied philology at Helsingfors; appointed professor of Finnish language and literature at the University of Helsingfors, 1860. Author of 'A Grammar of the Finnish Language,' St. Petersburg, 1862; and other philological works.

ALISON, Charles, English diplomatist, b. 1810; entered the diplomatic career, and employed on various missions to eastern countries; appointed envoy-extraordinary and minister-plenipotentiary to Persia, April 1860.

ALMONTE, Juan Nepomuceno, Mexican statesman, b. at Valladolid, Mexico, 1804; studied military science, and became aide-de-camp to General Santa Anna, 1836; dictator of Mexico, 1862; field-marshal, and minister of state of the Emperor Maximilian, 1864–67.

AMBROS, August Wilhelm, German author and composer, b. at Mauth, Bohemia, Nov. 17, 1816; studied jurisprudence at the University of Prague, and graduated D.C.L. 1839. Author of 'Geschichte der Musik,' Breslau, 1862.

B.

BAGEHOT, Walter, English political economist, b. 1823. Author of 'Estimates of some Englishmen and Scotchmen,' 1858; 'The English Constitution,' 1867. Editor of the *Economist.*

BAKER, Sir Samuel White, English author and traveller, b. 1821; obtained an honorary M.A. at Cambridge, 1865; knighted for discoveries made in Central Africa, 1866; appointed to the command of an Egyptian expedition for the suppression of the slave trade on the Upper Nile, 1869. Author of 'Eight Years' Wanderings in Ceylon,' 1860; 'The Albert N'Yanza, Great Basin of the Nile, and Exploration of the Nile Sources,' 2 vols. London, 1866; and other works.

BASTIAN, Adolf, German author and traveller, b. at Bremen, June 26, 1826; studied medicine at the University of Berlin, and graduated M.D. 1849; explored the interior of Asia, and parts of Africa, 1851–68. Author of 'Der Mensch in der Geschichte,' 3 vols. Leipzig, 1860; 'Die Völker des östlichen Asiens,' 1869.

BATTLE, Lorenzo, Uruguayan statesman, b. 1812; minister of war under the government of General Flores; provisional president of Uruguay, 1866–68; elected president of the Republic, after the assassination of General Flores, Feb. 28, 1868.

BAXTER, Robert Dudley, English statistician, b. 1827; educated at Trinity College, Cambridge, and graduated B.A. 1849, M.A. 1851; admitted solicitor, 1852. Author of 'Railway Extension and its Results,' London, 1866; 'National Income,' ib. 1868; 'Taxation of the United Kingdom,' ib. 1869; and other works.

BEESLEY, Edward Spencer, English historian, b. at Feckenham, Worcestershire, 1831; educated at Wadham College, Oxford: professor of history in University College, London. Contributor to the *Fortnightly Review*, and other magazines.

BELKNAP, William, American statesman, b. in the State of Iowa, 1831; educated at Princetown Military College, New Jersey; entered the army at the commencement of the civil war, and served as major-general in the campaigns of Tennessee and Georgia; collector of revenue in Iowa, 1866–69; appointed secretary of war of the United States, Oct. 13, 1869.

BESSEMER, Henry, English metallurgist, b. in Herefordshire, 1813; effected various improvements in the manufacture of iron, especially the purification of iron by oxygen, 1856–58.

BLANCHE, August, Swedish poet, b. 1811: studied jurisprudence at the University of Upsala; elected member of the Diet of Sweden, 1858. Author of 'Läkaren,' 1846; 'Berättelser af Klockaren i Danderyd,' 1856; and other works.

BLIND, Karl, German politician, b. at Manheim, Sept. 4, 1820; studied jurisprudence at the University of Heidelberg; envoy of the Provisional Government of Baden to France, 1849; exiled from France, 1849, and from Belgium, 1852. Author of a great number of political works, and contributor to English and German newspapers.

BONALD, Louis Jacques Maurice de, French prelate, b. at Milhaud, Oct. 30, 1787; educated at the seminary of St. Sulpice, Paris, and ordained priest, 1811; bishop of Puy, 1823; archbishop of Lyons, 1839; cardinal, 1841.

BOURBEAU, Louis Olivier, French statesman, b. at Poitiers, March 2, 1811; studied jurisprudence and became advocate at Poitiers, 1834; deputy of Poitiers to the Constituent Assembly, 1848–49; member of the Legislative Body, 1869; appointed minister of public instruction, July 17, 1869.

BOUTWELL, George, American statesman, b. in the State of Massachusetts, 1818; educated for the mercantile career; successively member of the State Legislature and governor of Massachusetts; commissioner of inland revenue, 1861–67; member of Congress since 1863; appointed secretary of the Treasury of the United States, March 11, 1869.

BRETT, John, English painter, b. 1831; educated in London. Painted 'Aosta;' 'The Dead Stonebreaker;' and other landscape and marine pieces.

BRIGHT, Jacob, English politician, b. 1821; manufacturer at Rochdale; M.P. for Manchester since 1867.

BUCHANAN, Robert Williams, English poet, b. at Caverswall, Staffordshire, 1841; educated at the High School and University of Glasgow; went to London as journalist, 1860. Author of 'Poems,' 1860; 'David Gray, and other Essays on Poetry,' 1868. Contributor to the *Spectator*, and other periodicals.

BURDETT-COUTTS, Angelina Georgina, English social reformer, b. in London, April 25, 1814, the daughter of Sir Francis Burdett; assumed the name of her grandfather, James Coutts, banker, on the death of his widow, the Duchess of St. Alban's, 1837.

BUTLER, Rev. Henry Montague, English divine, b. 1833; educated at Harrow and Cambridge; fellow of Trinity College, Cambridge, 1855; appointed head-master of Harrow School, 1859; member of the Royal Commission on Military Education, 1868. Author of two volumes of School Sermons.

C.

CAMPHAUSEN, Otto, German statesman, b. Oct. 21, 1812; studied jurisprudence, and entered the state service of Prussia in 1834; councillor of finance, 1845; member of the second chamber of the Prussian Diet, 1850–52; president of the Seehandlung Company, 1849–69; appointed minister of finance of Prussia, Oct. 26, 1869.

CANDLISH, Robert Smith, English theologian, b. at Glasgow, 1807; educated at Glasgow University, and ordained minister in the Established Church of Scotland, 1831; minister of St. George's, Edinburgh, 1834; co-operated with Dr. Chalmers in the formation of the Free Church, 1843. Author of 'Contributions towards the Exposition of the Book of Genesis,' 1852; and numerous sermons and pamphlets.

CHASLES, Michel, French mathematician, b. Nov. 15, 1793; studied at the École Polytechnique, Paris; professor of geometry at the École Polytechnique, Paris, 1841.; elected member of the Academy of Sciences, 1851. Author of 'Aperçu sur l'Origine et le Développement des Méthodes de Géométrie,' 4to. 1849; 'Traité de Géométrie supérieure, 8vo. Paris, 1852; and numerous other mathematical works.

CHASLES, Victor Philarete, French essayist, b. Oct. 8, 1798; learnt the trade of a printer, and worked for seven years in England; admitted on the literary staff of the *Journal des Débats*, 1830. Author of 'Études de Littérature comparée,' 14 vols. 8vo. Paris, 1847–64. Contributor to the *Revue des Deux-Mondes*, and other periodicals.

COLFAX, Schuyler, American statesman, b. in the City of New York, 1823; learnt the trade of printer, and established himself in the town of South-Bend, Indiana, where he founded the 'South-Bend Register' newspaper; returned member of Congress for the State of Indiana, 1859; chosen Speaker of the Lower House of Congress, 1863; elected vice-president of the United States, Nov. 3, 1868; installed, March 4, 1869.

COOKE, William Fothergill, English electrician, b. at Ealing, near London, 1805; educated at the University of Edinburgh; employed on the staff of the East-Indian army, 1826–31; invented the electric telegraph, in conjunction with Professor Charles Wheatstone, 1836–37; constructed the first telegraph line, from Paddington to West Drayton, 1838.

COUZA, Alexander, Roumanian statesman, b. at Galatz, 1820; educated at Paris, 1834–39; entered the Moldavian army, and promoted colonel, 1845; governor of Galatz, 1850; elected prince-ruler of Moldavia and Wallachia, 1859; deposed, 1866.

COX, Jacob, American statesman, b. at Montreal, Canada, 1828; studied law, and went to the bar in the State of Ohio; entered the army of the United States at the outbreak of the civil war, and rose to the rank of major-general; was governor of Ohio, 1865–69; appointed secretary of the interior, March 5, 1869.

CRESWELL, John, American statesman, b. in the State of Maryland, 1828; studied law, and graduated at Dickinson College, Pennsylvania; admitted to the bar in Maryland, 1850, and elected a member of the State Legislature, 1861; elected member of Congress, 1863, and United States senator, 1865; appointed postmaster-general, March 5, 1869.

CROOKES, William, English chemist, b. in London, June 17, 1832; discovered the new element, Thallium, 1861; elected F.R.S. in 1863. Author of 'Report to Government on the Application of Disinfectants to the Cure of Cattle Plague;' and numerous papers in the Transactions of scientific societies. Editor of the *Chemical News*.

D.

DALE, Rev. Robert William, English author, b. in London, 1829; graduated at the University of London, 1853; minister of the Congregational Church, Carr's Lane, Birmingham, 1856; chairman of the Congregational Union of England and Wales, 1869. Author of numerous sermons and pamphlets.

DAVIES, Rev. John Llewelyn, English author, b. 1826; fellow of Trinity College, Cambridge, 1850–59; rector of Christ Church, Marylebone, London, since 1856. Author of 'St. Paul's Epistles to the Ephesians, Colossians, and Philemon,' 1866; 'The Gospel and Modern Life,' 1869; and several sermons.

DAVIS, Andrew Jackson, American writer, b. 1826. Author of 'The Principles of Nature;' 'The Great Harmonia;' 'The Magic Staff;' and other works on spiritualism and clairvoyance.

DUCKWITZ, Arnold, German statesman, b. at Bremen, Jan. 27, 1802; educated for the commercial career in England; member of the Senate of Bremen, 1841; established steam navigation between Bremen and New York, 1847; minister of commerce of the Germanic government at Frankfort, 1848; burgomaster of Bremen, 1857–63. Author of several works on political economy.

DUVERGIER, Jean Baptiste, French statesman, b. at Bordeaux, Aug. 25, 1792; studied jurisprudence at Paris, and became advocate at the Cour Royale, 1821; elected bâtonnier of the Order of Advocates, 1840; nominated member of the Council of State, 1855; appointed minister of justice and public worship, and keeper of the seals (Garde des Sceaux), July 17, 1869.

E.

EICHTHAL, Gustave d', French ethnologist, b. at Nancy, of Jewish parents, 1804; joined the socialist community of Père Enfantin as editor of the *Globe*, 1832; founder and secretary of the Société d'Ethnologie of Paris. Author of 'Étude sur l'Histoire primitive des Races océaniennes et américaines,' 8vo. Paris, 1845; and other ethnological works.

EULENBURG, Count Friedrich zu, German statesman, b. Jan. 29, 1815; educated for the diplomatic career; consul-general for Prussia at Antwerp, 1849; chief of the Prussian expedition to China and Japan, and ambassador at the court of Pekin, 1860–62; appointed minister of the interior, Dec. 9, 1862.

EVANS, Sebastian, English poet and journalist, b. 1830; educated at Emmanuel College, Cambridge, and graduated B.A. 1854, LL.D. 1868. Author of 'Brother Fabian's Manuscript, and other Poems,' London, 1865. Editor of the *Birmingham Daily Gazette* since 1867.

F.

FARRAR, Frederick William, English author, b. 1831; junior master of Harrow School. Author of 'Eric; or, Little by Little,' London, 1858; 'The Origin of Language,' ib. 1860; and many other works.

FERRARI, Luigi, Italian sculptor, b. at Venice, 1810; studied sculpture under his father, Bartolommeo Ferrari, and Canova. Executed 'Laocoon;' 'David and Goliath;' 'Marco Polo;' and numerous other groups and statues.

FEYDEAU, Ernest, French novelist, b. at Paris, March 16, 1821; educated for a commercial career; engaged on the literary staff of *La Presse*, 1856. Author of 'Fanny,' 12mo. Paris, 1858, which passed through fifteen editions in one year; and many other novels. Founder and editor of the daily journal *L'Epoque*.

FIGUEROLA, Laureano, Spanish statesman, b. at Cala, near Barcelona, July 4, 1816; educated at Barcelona, and appointed master of the Normal School, 1841; professor of political economy at the University of Barcelona, 1847–55; deputy of Barcelona to the Cortes, and leader of the free-trade party, 1854–66; professor of commercial law at the University of Madrid, 1856–68.

FISH, Hamilton, American statesman, b. in the City of New York, 1809; studied for the bar, and graduated at Columbia College; successively member of the State Legislature of New York, member of Congress, governor of the State of New York, and United States senator; appointed secretary of state and of foreign affairs, March 11, 1869.

FOWLER, John, English civil engineer, b. 1817; designed and carried out many railways, docks, and other public works throughout the United Kingdom, and on the Continent; engineer of the Metropolitan Underground Railway, London.

FRANKL, Ludwig August, German poet, b. at Chrast, Bohemia, Feb. 3, 1810; studied medicine at the University of Vienna. Author of 'Habsburglied,' Vienna, 1832; 'Christoforo Colombo,' Stuttgart, 1836; and numerous other poetical works. Translator of some of the poems of Lord Byron.

G.

GARRISON, William Lloyd, American politician, b. at Newbury Port, Massachusetts, 1805; founded the *Liberator*, weekly newspaper, in Boston, 1831; one of the leaders in the Anti-Slavery agitation till the commencement of the civil war.

GRESSIER, Edouard, French statesman, b. Dec. 22, 1815; studied law, and practised as advocate at Paris, 1848–68; elected deputy to the Legislative Body for the département de la Somme, 1863; minister of agriculture, commerce, and public works, Dec. 19, 1868, to July 17, 1869; appointed minister of public works, July 17, 1869.

GUE'ROULT, Adolphe, French political writer, b. Jan. 29, 1810; consul at Mazatlan, 1842–47; deputy manager of the Crédit Foncier, 1852–57; editor of the *Presse*, 1857–59, of the *Opinion Nationale* since 1859. Author of 'Lettres sur l'Espagne;' and other works.

H.

HANKEL, Wilhelm Gottlieb, German electrician, b. May 17, 1814; studied theology at the University of Halle, but devoted himself to experiments in electricity, 1835; professor of chemistry at Halle, 1840, and at the University of Leipzig, 1849. Author of 'Elektrische Untersuchungen,' six parts, Leipzig, 1856–65.

HANNEN, Sir James, English judge, b. 1821; called to the bar, 1848; appointed a justice of the Court of Queen's Bench, and knighted, 1868.

HANSEN, Peter Andreas, German astronomer, b. Dec. 8, 1795; studied astronomy from books, without attendance at school; obtained a post as sub-assistant at the Observatory of Altona, 1821; director of the Gotha Observatory since 1825. Author of 'Theorie der Sonnenfinsternisse,' 8vo. Leipzig, 1858; and other astronomical works.

HARRIS, Thomas Lake, American author, b. 1824; founder of a community of spiritualists at Brocton, Lake Erie, New York. Author of 'Arcana of Christianity;' and several volumes of poetry.

HAUCH, Johan Carsten, Danish poet, b. at Frederickshald, Norway, May 12, 1790; studied philology at the University of Christiania; professor of Scandinavian literature at the University of Kiel, 1846–48, and at Copenhagen, 1851. Author of 'Lyriske Digte,' Copenhagen, 1843; 'Marsk Stig,' ib. 1850; and other poems and dramas.

HAUSSONVILLE, Joseph Bernard, Count d', French historian, b. at Paris, May 27, 1809; entered the diplomatic career, 1828, and successively secretary of embassy at Brussels, Turin, and Naples; retired into private life, 1848. Author of 'Histoire de la Politique extérieure du Gouvernement français de 1830 à 1848,' two vols. 8vo. Paris, 1850; and several other historical works.

HAUTEFEUILLE, Laurent Basile, French jurist, b. at Paris, July 25, 1805; studied jurisprudence at Paris, and called to the bar, 1829; procureur du roi at Algiers, 1830–34; advocate at the Cour de Cassation, 1837–52. Author of 'Code de la Pêche maritime,' 8vo. Paris, 1844; 'Droits et Devoirs des Nations neutres,' four vols. 8vo. ib. 1848–49; and other legal works.

HEYDT, August von der, Baron, German statesman, b. Feb. 15, 1801; deputy to the Prussian Diet, 1842–47; director of the bank of Prussia, 1851–62; minister of finance, March to Sept. 1862; re-appointed minister of finance, June 2, 1866; resigned, Oct. 26, 1869.

HILLER, Ferdinand, German composer, b. at Frankfort-on-the-Main, Oct. 24, 1811; studied music under Hummel, at Weimar; director of the concerts at the Gewandhaus, Leipzig, 1843–44. Author of the operas 'Romilde' and 'Konradin,' the oratorio 'Die Zerstörung Jerusalem's,' and numerous other works.

HINTON, James, English metaphysician, b. at Reading, 1823; aural surgeon to Guy's Hospital, London. Author of 'Man and his Dwelling-place,' 1859; 'Life in Nature,' 1862; 'The Mystery of Pain,' 1866; and other works.

HOAR, Ebenezer Rockwood, American statesman, b. at Concord, Massachusetts, 1817; studied law, and graduated at Harvard College; was for some time judge of the Massachusetts Supreme Court; appointed attorney-general of the United States, March 5, 1869.

HOLE, James, English political economist, b. at Manchester, Jan. 9, 1820; educated for a commercial career; secretary of the Associated Chambers of Commerce of Great Britain, 1867. Author of 'Lectures on the Organisation of Labour,' 1851; 'The Homes of the Working Classes,' London, 1866; and other works.

HOOD, Tom, English author and journalist, b. 1835; educated at University College School, London, and Pembroke College, Oxford; for some years in the Civil Service. Author of several novels, and collections in prose and verse. Editor of *Fun* since 1865.

HUGGINS, William, English astronomer, b. in London, 1826; studied astronomy, and erected an observatory at Tulse Hill in 1855; ascertained, by spectrum analysis, the physical state and chemical nature of some of the stars, 1862; discovered the gaseous state of the nebulæ, 1864; elected F.R.S. 1865, and received the royal medal, 1866; Rede lecturer for 1869. Author of many papers in Transactions of scientific societies.

HYACINTHE, Charles Loyson, called **Pe're Hyacinthe,** French theologian, b. at Orleans in 1827; educated at the Academy of Pau, and at St. Sulpice, and ordained priest, 1849; professor of theology at the seminary of Nantes, 1850–52; curé of St. Sulpice, Paris, 1852–60; entered the convent of the Carmelites, Lyons, 1861, and nominated general of the Order, 1866; resigned, Sept. 1869.

J.

JEVONS, William Stanley, English author, b. at Liverpool, Sept. 1, 1835; educated at University College, London; appointed professor of logic and political economy in Owens College, Manchester, 1866. Author of works on logic, the value of gold, the coal question, and papers in the Journal of the London Statistical Society.

K.

KIMBERLEY, John Wodehouse, Earl of, English statesman, b. 1826, grandson of second Baron Wodehouse; educated at Eton, and at Christ Church, Oxford; succeeded to his grandfather's title, 1846; under-secretary of state for foreign affairs, 1852–56; ambassador to Russia, 1856–58; again under-secretary of state for foreign affairs, 1859–61; lord-lieutenant of Ireland, 1864–66; created Earl of Kimberley, July 1866; appointed lord privy seal, Dec. 9, 1868.

KRUPP, Friedrich, German mechanician, b. 1815; educated by his father, who founded a small ironwork at Essen, on the Rhine, 1827; discovered the mode of manufacturing cast steel in large quantities, 1850; produced twenty-five millions of pounds of cast steel in 1863, and fifty-six millions of pounds in 1865; employed 9,000 workmen, exclusive of colliers, 1865; refused a patent of nobility, 1864.

L.

LEBOEUF, Edmond, French statesman, b. Nov. 5, 1809; studied military science at the École Polytechnique, Paris, and the École d'Artillerie, Metz, and entered the army, 1827; captain, 1837; chef d'escadron, 1846; under-governor of the École Polytechnique, 1848–50; colonel, 1852; general of brigade, 1854; general of division, 1857; commander-in-chief of the artillery in the Italian campaign, 1859; appointed minister of war, Aug. 21, 1869.

LECKY, William Edward Hartpole, English historian, b. 1828; educated at Trinity College, Dublin. Author of 'History of Rationalism in Europe,' 1865; 'History of European Morals, from Augustus to Charlemagne,' 1869.

LECONTE DE LISLE, Charles Marie, French poet, b. in the Isle of Réunion, 1820; studied at the University of Paris. Author of 'Poëmes et Poësies,' Paris, 1855; 'Idylles de Théocrite,' ib. 1861; 'Poësies barbares,' ib. 1862; and other works.

LIDDON, Rev. Henry Parry, English theologian, b. at North Stoneham, Hants, Aug. 20, 1829; educated at King's College, London, and Christ Church, Oxford, where he graduated B.A. 1850, and M.A. 1853; vice-principal of Cuddesdon Theological College, 1854–59; vice-principal of St. Edmund's Hall, Oxford, 1859–62; prebendary of Salisbury, 1864; select preacher at Oxford, 1863–65; Bampton lecturer, 1866. Author of 'The Divinity of our Lord and Saviour Jesus Christ, the Bampton Lectures for 1866;' and various sermons.

LIGHTFOOT, Rev. Joseph Barber, English theologian, b. 1828; educated at Trinity College, Cambridge, where he graduated, 1851; fellow, 1852, and tutor, 1857; Hulsean professor of divinity, 1861. Editor of 'St. Paul's Epistle to the Galatians, with Notes and Dissertations,' 1865; 'Epistle to the Philippians,' 1868; 'St. Clement of Rome,' 1869.

LINTON, Eliza Lynn, English novelist, b. at Keswick, 1822. Authoress of 'Grasp your Nettle,' 'Azesh the Egyptian,' and other works of fiction. Contributor to the *Saturday Review*, and various periodicals.

LINTON, William James, English engraver and author, b. in London, 1812; engaged for some years on the artistic staff of the *Illustrated London News*, and executed numerous engravings for other publications. Author of 'Life of Paine;' 'English Republic;' and many political pamphlets.

LIVERANI, Francesco, Italian theologian, b. at Castel-Bologna, 1823; educated at the Academy of Nobles, Rome; successively domestic chaplain of the Pope, canon of Sta. Maria in Via Lata, and apostolic protonotary of Ravenna; deprived of clerical dignities, 1862. Author of 'La Papauté, l'Empire, et le Royaume d'Italie;' and other works against the temporal power of the Pope.

LOCKYER, Joseph Norman, English astronomer, b. at Rugby, May 17, 1836; elected fellow of the Royal Society, 1869. Author and editor of various works on astronomy, and discoverer of a new method of studying the sun by means of the spectroscope.

LOTZE, Rudolf Hermann, German philosophical writer, b. at Bautzen, May 21, 1817; studied medicine and philosophy at the University of Leipzig, and graduated, 1838; professor of philosophy at Leipzig, 1842, and at Göttingen since 1844. Author of 'Metaphysik,' Leipzig, 1841; 'Mikrokosmus,' 3 vols. ib. 1856–64; and other works.

LOULE', Joan, Duke of, Portuguese statesman, b. 1802, the son of Count Val de Reis, who was nominated Marquis de Loulé 1807, and assassinated March 1, 1824; educated for the diplomatic career; minister of the interior of Portugal, 1860–62; minister of foreign affairs, 1862–65; president of the council of ministers, 1869–70.

LUBBOCK, Sir John, English archæologist, b. in London, April 30, 1834; educated at Eton; a banker in London. Author of 'Prehistoric Times,' 1865; and numerous papers on archæological subjects.

LUSH, Sir Robert, English judge, b. 1807; called to the bar, 1839; appointed one of the judges of the Court of Queen's Bench, 1865.

LUTHER, Robert, German astronomer, b. 1810; established an observatory at Bilk, near Düsseldorf, 1848; discovered seven new planets, April 17, 1852; May 5, 1853; March 2, 1854; April 19 and Oct. 5, 1855; Sept. 15, 1857; and April 4, 1858; elected member of the Institut de France, 1861.

M.

MAC-MAHON, Patrick Maurice de, French statesman and military commander. b. at Sully, department Saône-et-Loire, July 13, 1808; educated at the Military School of St. Cyr, and entered the army, 1828; captain, 1833; colonel, 1845; general of brigade, 1848; general of division, 1852; commander of the second corps of the 'armée des Alpes,' 1859; created field-marshal and Duke of Magenta, June 4, 1859; commander of the third corps d'armée, 1861–64; governor-general of Algeria since 1864.

MAINE, Henry James Sumner, English jurist, b. 1822; educated at Cambridge; legislative member of the Council of Calcutta, 1859–69. Author of 'Ancient Law,' London, 1861.

MANGLES, Ross Donnelly, English administrator, b. 1801; employed in the Indian Civil Service, 1820–40; member of the Council of India since 1857; formerly chairman of the East India Company, and M.P. for Guildford.

MARGGRAFF, Rudolf, German author, b. Feb. 28, 1805; studied at the University of Berlin; professor of art-history at the University of Munich, 1842–55. Author of 'Erinnerungen an Albrecht Dürer;' and many other works, chiefly on art.

MASSON, George Joseph Gustave, English teacher, b. 1819; studied at the Lycée of Tours, and at the Lycée St. Louis, Paris; assistant-master in Harrow School since 1855; French examiner at Christ's Hospital. Author of 'La Lyre Française,' 1861; and other works.

MAUDSLEY, Henry, English physician, b. at Settle, Yorkshire, 1835; studied medicine at University College, London, and graduated M.D. 1857; physician to the Manchester Lunatic Hospital, 1859–62; resident physician to the West London Hospital since 1862; elected fellow of Royal College of Physicians, 1869, and Gulstonian lecturer, 1870. Author of 'The Physiology and Pathology of Mind,' 1867. Editor of the *Journal of Mental Science.*

MICHEL, Sir John, English military commander, b. 1804; entered the army in 1823; served in the Indian mutiny, and commanded a division during the China war; lieutenant-general, 1866.

MIGNE, Jacques Paul, French theologian and journalist, b. Oct. 25, 1800; educated at the Theological Seminary of Orleans, and ordained priest, 1824; curé of Puiseaux, Loiret, 1824–33; founded the journal *L'Univers,* 1833; disposed of the journal, and settled as printer at Petit-Montrouge, near Paris, 1836. Author and editor of numerous theological publications.

MONNIER, Henri Bonaventure, French author and artist, b. at Paris, June 6, 1799; studied painting under Girodet, and illustrated the 'Chansons' of Béranger, and the 'Fables' of La Fontaine. Author of 'Scènes populaires dessinées à la Plume,' Paris, 1830; 'Les Bourgeois de Paris,' ib. 1854; and numerous other works, chiefly on Paris and the Parisians.

MORELL, John Daniel, English philosophical writer, b. 1816; inspector of schools at Manchester. Author of 'History of Speculative Philosophy in the Nineteenth Century;' 'Handbook of Logic;' and other works.

MORTON, William Thomas Green, American physician, b. 1819; discovered the use of ether as an anæsthetic in surgical operations, Sept. 1846.

MOSCHELES, Ignaz, German musical composer, b. at Prague, May 30, 1794; director of the Philharmonic Society's concerts, 1825–46; director of the Conservatory at Leipzig since 1846. Author of numerous musical compositions.

MUDIE, Charles Edward, English librarian, b. at Chelsea, Oct. 18, 1818; founder of 'Mudie's Select Library'—now containing about one million volumes of modern books —in Upper King-street, Bloomsbury, London, 1842; removed the library to New Oxford-street, 1852.

N.

NASMYTH, James, English engineer, b. in Edinburgh, Aug. 19, 1808; served an apprenticeship as practical engineer; established for many years as engineer in Manchester, and invented the steam-hammer; retired from business, 1856.

NE'LATON, Auguste, French physician, b. June 17, 1807; studied medicine at Paris under Dupuytren, and graduated, 1836; professor of clinical surgery at the Paris University, 1851, and of pathology, 1856. Author of 'Traité des Tumeurs de la Mamelle,' 4to. Paris, 1839; 'Éléments de Pathologie chirurgicale,' 5 vols. 8vo. ib. 1844–59; and other medical works.

NIELSEN, Augusta, Danish actress and operatic singer, b. at Copenhagen, Feb. 26, 1823; admitted member of the corps de ballet at the Theatre Royal, Copenhagen, 1830; appeared as actress on the same stage, 1838; studied music and dramatic art at Paris under Prévost and Mazillier; and made her début at the Opéra, 1850.

O.

OERSTED, Anders Sandoe, Danish naturalist, b. June 21, 1816; educated in the house of his paternal uncle, prime-minister of Denmark; appointed professor of natural history at the University of Copenhagen, 1837. Author of 'Planterigets Naturhistorie,' 8vo. Copenhagen, 1839; 'De Regionibus marinis,' 8vo. ib. 1844; and other works.

OPZOOMER, Karel Willem, Dutch theological and philosophical writer, b. at Rotterdam, Sept. 20, 1821; studied at the University of Leyden, and graduated, 1845; professor of philosophy at the University of Utrecht, 1846. Author of 'De Weg der Wetenschapen,' Utrecht, 1851; 'De Philosophiæ Natura,' ib. 1852; 'De Godsdienst,'. Amsterdam, 1864.

P.

PARR, Harriet, English novelist, b. at York, 1828. Authoress of 'Life and Death of Jeanne d'Arc,' and various novels, tales, and essays, under the name of 'Holme Lee.'

PLUMPTRE, Rev. Edward Hayes, English poet and theologian, b. 1821; educated at University College, Oxford, and graduated B.A. 1844; professor of pastoral theology, 1853–63, and professor of New Testament exegesis at King's College, London, since 1863; rector of Pluckley, Kent, 1869. Author of 'Christ and Christendom,' Boyle Lecture for 1866; 'Lazarus, and other Poems,' 1864; 'Master and Scholar, and other Poems,' 1863; a new translation of Sophocles, 1866, and of Æschylus, 1868.

POCCI, Franz, Count, German poet and composer, b. at Munich, March 7, 1807; studied at the Universities of Landshut and Munich; companion of King Ludwig I. in journeys to Italy, 1845–60. Author of 'Soldatenlieder,' Leipzig, 1842; 'Dichtungen,' Schaffhausen, 1843; and other poems. Composer of 'Der Alchymist' opera, performed at Munich, and of numerous songs and musical pieces.

PRICE, Bonamy, English political economist, b. 1807; educated at Worcester College, Oxford, and graduated B.A. 1830, M.A. 1832; professor of political economy at Oxford since 1868.

R.

REVERE, Giuseppe, Italian dramatic author, b. at Trieste, 1812; studied philosophy at the College of Milan; took part in the insurrection against Austria, 1848. Author of 'Sampiero di Bastelica,' Milan, 1836; and numerous other dramas and poems.

ROBESON, George, American statesman, b. in the State of New Jersey, 1824; studied for the bar, and graduated at Princeton College; attorney-general of New Jersey, 1866–69. Appointed secretary of the navy of the United States, June 25, 1869.

RODENBERG, Julius, German author, b. July 6, 1831; studied jurisprudence at Heidelberg and Göttingen, and graduated, 1856. Author of 'König Harald's Todtenfeier,' Marburg, 1853; 'Die Insel der Heiligen,' Berlin, 1860; 'Tag und Nacht in London,' ib. 1862; and numerous poems and works of travel.

ROGERS, James Edwin Thorold, English political economist, b. 1824; educated at Magdalen Hall, Oxford, and graduated B.A. 1846, M.A. 1849; professor of political economy, Oxford, 1862–67. Author of 'Education at Oxford,' 1861; 'Agriculture and Prices, 1269–1793,' 1866; 'A Manual of Political Economy,' 1867.

ROON, Albrecht Theodor, Prussian statesman and military commander, b. April 30, 1803; entered the army, 1821; professor at the Military Academy, Berlin, 1829–32; chief of the staff in the campaign against the Baden insurgents, 1849; appointed minister of war of Prussia, Dec. 5, 1859; and minister of marine, April 16, 1861.

ROSCHER, Wilhelm, German political economist, b. at Hanover, Oct. 21, 1817; studied jurisprudence at the Universities of Göttingen and Berlin, 1835–39; professor of political economy at Leipzig since 1848. Author of 'Geschichte der englischen Volkswirthschaftslehre im 16 und 17 Jahrhundert,' Leipzig, 1851; and other works on political economy.

ROSCOE, Henry Enfield, English chemist, b. in London, Jan. 7, 1833; educated at University College, London, and at Heidelberg; appointed professor of chemistry in Owens College, Manchester, 1857. Author, in conjunction with Professor Bunsen, of 'Memoirs on the Measurement of the Chemical Action of Light;' 'Lessons in Elementary Chemistry,' 1866; 'Lectures on Spectrum Analysis,' 1869; and numerous articles in scientific journals.

S.

SALT, Sir Titus, English manufacturer, b. at Morley, near Leeds; introduced the manufacture of alpaca wool, and erected the factories composing the town of Saltaire; M. P. for Bradford, 1859–61; created baronet, 1869.

SAVIGNY, Karl Friedrich von, German statesman, b. in Berlin, 1813, son of the celebrated jurist; educated under the supervision of Alexander von Humboldt; entered the diplomatic service of Prussia, 1838; Prussian ambassador at Dresden, at Brussels, and at Frankfort-on-the-Main, 1859–66; representative of Prussia in the Council of the North German Confederation, 1866–68.

SEEBOHM, Frederic, English author, b. at Bradford, Yorkshire, 1833; called to the bar of the Middle Temple, 1856; banker at Hitchin, Herts. Author of 'The Oxford Reformers,' 1867. Contributor on historical and economical subjects to the *North British* and *Fortnightly Reviews.*

SILVA, Innocentio Francisco da, Portuguese bibliographer, b. at Lisbon, Sept. 28, 1810; entered the military career, but resigned, 1836. Author of 'Dictionario bibliographico portuguez,' 4 vols. Lisbon, 1858–60; and other bibliographical and historical works.

SINET, Adolphe, Belgian author, b. at Beaumont, 1817; entered the government service, 1836; elected member of the Académie de Belgique, 1855. Author of 'Dictionnaire historique des Peintres des toutes les Ecoles,' 4to. Brussels, 1848; and several dramas and works of fiction.

SKEATS, Herbert Stradling, English author and journalist, b. at Lymington, 1828. Author of 'A History of the Free Churches of England;' 'Popular Education in England;' and several pamphlets on ecclesiastical subjects.

SMITH, Philip, English historian, b. in London, Nov. 12, 1816; educated at University College, London; professor of mathematics and ecclesiastical history in New College, London, 1850–52; head-master of Mill Hill Grammar School, 1853–60. Author of 'The History of the World;' contributor of articles to Dr. William Smith's 'Dictionaries,' and other works.

SMYTH, Charles Piazzi, English astronomer, b. at Naples, Jan. 3, 1819; educated at Bedford; assistant-astronomer at the Royal Observatory, Cape of Good Hope, 1835; astronomer-royal for Scotland, and professor of practical astronomy in the University of Edinburgh since 1845. Author of 'Teneriffe, an Astronomer's Experiment,' 1857; 'Three Cities in Russia,' 1862; 'Our Inheritance in the Great Pyramid,' 1864; 'Life and Work at the Great Pyramid,' 1867; 'The Antiquity of Intellectual Man,' 1868; and many papers in the Transactions of scientific societies.

SNELLAERT, Ferdinand, Flemish author, b. at Courtray, July 21, 1809; entered the Military Academy of Utrecht, and served in the army of the Netherlands till 1830. Author of 'Over de nederlandsche Dichtkunst in Belgie,' Brussels, 1838; and other works in the Flemish language. Editor of the journal *Eendracht* since 1846.

SPENCER, Herbert, English metaphysician, b. at Derby, 1820; educated and practised as civil engineer; contributor to the *Economist* newspaper, 1848–53. Author of 'Principles of Psychology,' 1855; and 'First Principles,' 1860.

T.

TAUCHNITZ, Christian Bernhard, Freiherr von, German publisher, b. Aug. 25, 1816; established a publishing firm, with printing-office, at Leipzig, 1837; originated a 'Collection of British Authors,' 1841; commenced a 'Collection of German Authors,' in English, 1866; obtained a patent of nobility, as Freiherr, from the Duke of Saxe-Coburg, 1860.

TORBERG, Carl Johan, Swedish philologist, b. at Linkoeping, 1807; studied at the University of Upsala, and graduated, 1833; professor of Oriental languages at Upsala, 1835, and at the University of Lund, 1844. Author of numerous philological works, and of papers on the languages and literature of Asia.

V.

VEZIN, Hermann, English actor, b. at Philadelphia, March 2, 1829; educated at the University of Pennsylvania, and graduated, 1847; appeared on the stage at New York, 1850; became manager of the Princess' Theatre, London, and produced the 'Man o' Airlie,' 1867.

VIEUXTEMPS, Henri, Belgian composer and violinist, b. at Verviers, Feb. 20, 1820; studied music under Bériot and Reicha; visited the principal cities of Europe and America after 1837; director of the Imperial concerts at St. Petersburg, 1846–52. Author of numerous compositions for the violin.

VOGEL VON FALKENSTEIN, Ernst Friedrich, Prussian military commander, b. Jan. 5, 1797; entered the army, 1813; colonel, 1848; chief of the staff in the war against Denmark, 1848; commander of the seventh corps d'armée, 1864; commander-in-chief of the 'army on the Main,' 1866; governor-general of Bohemia, July–Sept. 1866; elected member of the Diet of the North German Confederation, 1867.

W.

WOHLER, Friedrich, German chemist, b. July 31, 1800; studied medicine at the Universities of Marburg and Heidelberg, and chemistry under Berzelius, at Stockholm, 1820–24; professor of chemistry at Berlin, 1825–31, and at Cassel, 1831–36; professor at Göttingen since 1836. Author of 'Grundriss der Chemie,' Berlin, 1831; fourteenth edition, Leipzig, 1868; and other works on chemistry.

WULLERSTORF-URBAIR, Bernhard, Freiherr von, Austrian statesman and naval commander, b. at Trieste, Jan. 29, 1816; educated at the University of Padua, and entered the Austrian naval service, 1833; took part as captain in the siege of Ancona, and the capture of Venice, 1849; commander of the 'Novara' expedition in a journey round the world, 1857–59; rear-admiral, 1861; minister of commerce of Austria, 1865–67. Author of numerous contributions to periodicals on astronomical, naval, and commercial subjects.

Z.

ZELLER, Eduard, German theologian, b. at Kleinbottwar, Würtemberg, Jan. 22, 1814; studied theology at Tübingen, under Strauss, and at Berlin, under Neander; professor of theology at the University of Tübingen, 1840–47; at Bonn, 1847–49; at Marburg, 1849–62; and at Heidelberg since 1862. Author of 'Geschichte der christlichen Kirche,' Stuttgart, 1847; 'Die Apostelgeschichte nach ihrem Inhalt und Ursprung,' ib. 1854; and other theological works.

SEVENTH ANNUAL PUBLICATION.

THE

STATESMAN'S YEAR-BOOK,

A STATISTICAL AND HISTORICAL ACCOUNT OF THE STATES OF THE CIVILIZED WORLD.

MANUAL FOR POLITICIANS AND MERCHANTS

FOR THE YEAR

1870.

BY FREDERICK MARTIN.

Crown 8vo. price 10s. 6d.

THE STATESMAN'S YEAR-BOOK is the only work in the English language which furnishes a clear and concise account of the actual condition of all the States of Europe, the civilized countries of America, Asia, and Africa, and the British Colonies and Dependencies in all parts of the world. The new issue of the work—seventh annual publication—has been entirely re-written, revised, and corrected, on the basis of official reports received direct from the heads of the leading Governments of the world, in reply to letters sent to them by the Editor. Through the valuable assistance thus given, it has been possible to collect an amount of information, political, statistical, and commercial, of the latest date, and of unimpeachable trustworthiness, such as no publication of the same kind has ever been able to furnish. The new issue of the *Statesman's Year-Book* has received another improvement in the addition of a Chronological Account of the principal events of the past twelve months, which, continued from year to year, will, it is hoped, make the work still more useful than it has hitherto proved, as a book of reference.